D060043

AMERICA
VERSUS
JAPAN

HD
3616
.U47
A57
1986

AMERICA
VERSUS
JAPAN

Edited by

THOMAS K. McCRAW

WITHDRAWN

*A Comparative Study of Business-Government
Relations Conducted at the
Harvard Business School*

Tennessee Tech. Library
Cookeville, Tenn.

HARVARD BUSINESS SCHOOL PRESS

BOSTON, MASSACHUSETTS

365025

Harvard Business School Press, Boston 02163
© 1986 by the President and Fellows of Harvard College
All rights reserved.

Printed in the United States of America.

90 89 88 87 86   5 4 3 2 1

Library of Congress Cataloging-in-Publication Data

America versus Japan.

  "A comparative study of business-government relations
conducted at the Harvard Business School."
  Bibliography: p.
  Includes index.
  1. Industry and state—United States.
2. Industry and state—Japan.   3. Trade regulation—
United States.   4. Trade regulation—Japan.
I. McCraw, Thomas K.
HD3616.U47A57   1986   338.952   86-19393
ISBN 0-87584-139-2

TABLE OF CONTENTS

PREFACE

This book is meant to shed light on public policymaking for business in America and Japan, by means of nine topical comparisons. As the chapter titles indicate, these comparisons focus on trade, investment, production and distribution, agriculture, energy, the environment, financial institutions, tax, and disinvestment. As a whole, the book deals with the structure, process, and practical outcome of business-government relations as exemplified in these nine areas.

The authors come from diverse backgrounds in economics, political science, history, business administration, and East Asian studies. Various though our training is, we have undertaken here to transcend the boundaries of our separate disciplines, to speak with a coherent voice, and to explain what we see in plain English. While all of us have done extensive research in both Japan and the United States, we are not writing primarily as country specialists. Instead, our book represents a comparative exposition and analysis, addressed to a broad audience, and sharply focused on the single subject of business-government interaction.

As we wrote the book, all of us were tempted to explain our findings in the most monolithic terms of culture or geography. The temptation is natural; for, on the surface, such differences seem to explain everything. But below the surface, they often lead nowhere and end in observations that explain nothing. Thus, a major premise of the book is that no single explanation can adequately account for the different patterns of business-government relations that have emerged in the two countries. Instead, we believe that cultural, geographical, ideological, political, economic, social, and historical forces are all at work simultaneously in determining the patterns found in both Japan and the United States. That conclusion now seems obvious to us, and we hope it will emerge clearly for a majority of readers as well.

Another premise may be less obvious and more controversial: that many of the differences we have observed reflect explicit choices made in America and Japan. Sometimes these choices have been expressed directly, by voters in the two countries. More often, they have been made by professional managers, in both the public and private sectors—the men and women who influence public policy. It is no accident, for example, and no mere reflection of culture or geography, that in recent years the Japanese steel, automobile, and electronics industries have all out-performed the American; or that American agriculture, wholesaling, and retailing can claim to be more efficient than Japanese.

When we began our work, several years ago, we directed attention almost exclusively to this comparative framework, rather than focusing on the *rela-*

tionship between America and Japan. During the period of our research and writing, this relationship has altered, and the two countries have drifted into a zone of conflict. As a recognition of this changed situation, the title of the book, *America versus Japan,* signals our deepening concern about recent difficulties over trade friction and capital movements, plus the general growth of misunderstandings between the two countries. In our title, we intend that readers construe the word "versus" in both of its common meanings: on the one hand, the comparative sense, in which one nation's business-government relationships are measured against the other's; on the other hand, "versus" in the combative sense, in which the two countries' quest for world economic leadership has led them into a sharpening rivalry that may prove difficult to resolve. Some of our chapters, such as those on trade, investment, and agriculture, address this rivalry directly. Others, including those on energy and the environment, are focused on "versus" in its purely comparative sense.

Today, the Japanese-American connection represents, as Ambassador Mike Mansfield puts it, "the most important economic relationship in the world." Here, too, the comparative approach provides a useful first step toward better understanding. Thus, one might compare the dealings between Japan and America with similar connections between other important pairs of countries. Many parallels come to mind: for example, the earlier, long-lived relationship between Britain and France. Those two great powers, which were military and economic rivals from the fourteenth to the nineteenth century, became close allies during the twentieth, mostly out of common cause in the wars against Germany. Over the course of several hundred years, the ups and downs of Anglo-French relations became so broadly significant a theme that the history of the world could hardly be studied without giving close attention to the changing relationship between these two great powers.

So it is with Japan and the United States in the late twentieth century. Yet in their case, very significant changes have occurred in telescoped time—not gradually, over many centuries, but during only fifty years. Of course, the two countries have been engaged with each other for longer than that—ever since 1853, to be exact, when Commodore Matthew Perry's squadron of black ships first sailed into Japanese waters. But the joint relationship did not become vital to either country's interests, or to the history of the world, before the mid-1930s. From then until now represents a shorter period than the lifetime of an average citizen of either country; so the transformations and upheavals in Japanese-American affairs have occurred almost in the twinkling of an eye.

Perhaps the most striking aspect of this brief history has proved to be neither the Pacific War of 1941–1945, nor the American Occupation that followed it from 1945 until 1952. Instead, it has been the economic miracle wrought by Japan in the two decades following the end of the Occupation. During this period, the Japanese recorded the most remarkable economic progress in the history of the world.

Even today, Western scholars have barely begun to reconcile the stark historical facts concerning this miracle with certain long-accepted theories of classical economics, especially those having to do with protectionism and cartelization. Many questions remain unanswered, and certainly this book will not answer them altogether. The book does represent, its authors believe, a further step toward the better understanding of just what has happened in Japan and in America; and even more, of what is likely to happen in the future. In quest of improved understanding, one of our aims is to help explain the Japanese business-government relationship to American readers, and the American one to Japanese readers. At present, this goal seems especially important, because we see, in the late 1980s and early 1990s, the possibility of trouble between the two countries.

In the broadest sense, both the United States and Japan already are caught up in a mix of world economic forces that no single nation can control. Despite the complex and uncertain causes of such problems as bilateral trade imbalances, rising public deficits, and reversals in capital flows, several overarching facts still emerge clearly. For one thing, America and Japan now find themselves to be by far the two most important players in a complex world economy. This contemporary economic world exhibits unmistakable trends that seem to have developed a momentum all their own. The rise of global markets, the unprecedented level of international interdependence among countries, and the mixture of economic forces with domestic politics and foreign policy, all point toward the likelihood of persistent strain on the Japanese-American relationship. The potential for misunderstanding is high, and thus it becomes naive to assume that the existing pattern of friendly relations will continue automatically, without care being taken to preserve it. As the strain increases, a clear mutual understanding will be essential in preventing any deterioration in the Japanese-American friendship—a friendship that itself represents an almost miraculous achievement of the postwar world.

From our perspective in the 1980s, the historical record of the years 1937–1941, during which Japanese-American relations gradually disintegrated, might stand as a reminder to the leadership and the people of both countries that they should take little for granted. This book, among its other purposes, has been written in an effort to reduce that risk: to minimize the chances that vital matters between America and Japan will again be misunderstood.

AMERICA
VERSUS
JAPAN

From Partners to Competitors: An Overview of the Period Since World War II

THOMAS K. McCRAW

This first chapter provides a broad historical survey of Japanese and American policymaking for business. It outlines ways in which the two countries' contrasting goals and different methods of decision making led them gradually from a pattern of cooperation onto what may well be a collision course. The chapter begins with a brief analysis of the Japanese economic miracle, without which any understanding of the remainder of the book, or of the overall Japanese-American relationship, becomes impossible. Next, it provides a sketch of the organization for policymaking in both America and Japan, and how those patterns evolved during the postwar years. It then concludes with an overview of the more recent period of stagflation and gradual recovery in both countries (1971–1986). As we shall see, in both this chapter and in all other parts of the book, the entire economic structure and performance of each country, over the full span of the postwar period, has been directly affected by two very different sets of business-government relationships.

The Economic Miracle

By 1952, when the American Occupation departed, Japan was well on its way to recovery. Compared with the United States, it was then an economic midget—but, as we now know, one that became a giant within the space of a single generation. The story of how all this occurred represents a modern national epic, as well as a challenge to conventional economic theory.

Finding the causes of the miracle will continue to stir controversy, and heated debate will persist over several key elements: the results of such policies as import restrictions, cartelization, and other forms of protectionism; the relative contributions by Japanese business on the one hand, and government on the other; the role of the domestic market as opposed to exports; and

1

the importance of the United States to the entire story. In addition, some difficult questions still remain about the distribution of political power in Japan, and the trade-offs between growth on the one hand and democracy on the other.[1]

In addressing these matters, it is best to start from a wide perspective, lest we later miss the forest for the trees. Let us begin, therefore, with a broad focus on the period 1954–1971. Why those years? For one thing, because the Occupation relinquished its authority in 1952; whatever happened afterward within the Japanese economy derived primarily from the policies of Japanese business and government, and not from the American.[2] Then, too, the year 1954 is late enough for the numbers not to be distorted by either the devastation suffered by Japan during World War II, or American mobilization for the Korean War (1950–1953), which affected the economies of both Japan and the United States in an atypical way.

The concluding year, 1971, proved to be a watershed for both countries. In that year the United States experienced its first overall trade deficit since 1893, a deficit to which Japan largely contributed. Also in 1971, the new economic condition known as "stagflation" started to trouble several countries, including the United States and Japan. In addition, the Bretton Woods system of fixed exchange rates began to collapse in August of 1971, when the Nixon Administration suspended dollar convertibility into gold. At that moment, dollar-yen relationships became much more important than they had been earlier. The American government also imposed a temporary 10 percent surcharge on imports into the United States, a move directed specifically against the Japanese, who commemorated the event, together with President Nixon's unexpected visit to China, by coining a new phrase: "Nixon shock." Just two years later, in 1973, the first oil crisis of the decade hit the American economy hard, and affected the Japanese economy even more severely. Indeed, the impact of the oil shock on Japan was so powerful that it signaled a clear end to the postwar miracle of economic growth.

The numbers presented below for the years 1954–1971 come from the official national income accounts of Japan and the United States. Using these accounts, one can compute several different percentages: in the first two tables, percentages of gross national product in each of the countries that were devoted to the standard categories of Consumption, Investment, Government Expenditure, Exports, and Imports; and in the third table, the compound annual growth rates of each category.[3]

TABLE 1-1
Japan, 1954–1971

	GNP	=	Consumption	+	Investment	+	Government	+	Exports	−	Imports
1954	100%		66.2%		23.5%		11.0%		10.2%		11.0%
1971	100%		53.5%		35.8%		8.0%		11.7%		9.0%

Here, from our satellite photograph of the Japanese economy over this seven-teen-year period, we see some striking changes: an extraordinary increase in the percentage of gross national product devoted to investment, and a substantial decrease in the proportion taken by personal consumption. The 53.5 percent figure for consumption in 1971 is extremely low, indeed one of the lowest in recorded history for any country.[4]

TABLE 1-2
The United States, 1954–1971

	GNP	=	Consumption	+	Investment	+	Government	+	Exports	−	Imports
1954	100%		63.5%		17.3%		18.2%		5.2%		4.2%
1971	100%		62.7%		18.8%		18.5%		5.5%		5.7%

In these American numbers, much less change is evident over the seventeen years. A more stable situation prevails, marked by a slight increase in the percentage of gross national product devoted to both exports and imports. This, in turn, reflects the growing interdependence of the United States with the world economy, and particularly its increased absorption of imports. Note also that when the United States is compared with Japan, a much lower percentage of GNP is devoted to investment, and a higher fraction to consumption. A higher amount went to government expenditures as well, primarily because of America's need to maintain a large defense establishment and Japan's exemption from that need. Overall, however, the most striking thing about the American table is its remarkable stability over the entire seventeen-year period.[5]

This contrast between Japanese change and American stability becomes even more dramatic when measured by the annual growth figures for the same categories of national income accounts in the two countries. The following numbers represent real growth rates, adjusted for inflation:[6]

TABLE 1-3
Real Annual Percentage Increase, 1954–1971

	GNP	Consumption	Investment	Government	Exports	Imports
Japan	10.1%	8.5%	14.5%	5.0%	14.7%	13.8%
USA	3.6%	3.8%	4.4%	2.8%	5.7%	7.3%

The orders of magnitude involved in these growth figures for Japan are exceedingly high. But the most striking thing about the Japanese numbers is their persistence at such rates over a prolonged span of time. We see in Japan's GNP growth over the seventeen-year period first one doubling of the total output of the economy, then another, then a running start toward still another doubling. Put another way, Japan's GNP was about *five times* as large in 1971 as it had been only seventeen years earlier. The growth figures for total investment and for exports, both of which exceeded 14 percent, mean that these categories doubled once, then twice, then a third time, then continued a strong tendency toward still a fourth doubling—all within the brief seventeen-year history.

During those same years, private consumption in Japan doubled only two times; even so, this figure represents more than twice the growth of private consumption in the United States. When one recalls that for the American economy these years represented a period of strong growth, and also that Japan was an advanced industrial nation with a population of about 100 million (and not a tiny underdeveloped country, whose insignificant early production might underlie otherwise astonishing percentage gains), then the dimensions of the Japanese economic achievement come into clear focus. The word "miracle" does not seem inappropriate.

Later in this chapter, these tables will be updated for the years 1971–1985, and we shall see how some things have changed in more recent times. Meanwhile, we might pause to consider some of the hypotheses one might make from the numbers already mentioned. These hypotheses may be explored even in the absence of any additional data about the Japanese or American economy; and they will help us formulate some important questions to ask, once we shorten our perspective and move toward a closer examination.

First, let us assume that the very diverse Japanese growth figures for consumption, investment, government spending, exports, and imports did not just occur randomly, but instead as the result of deliberate actions. Taking note of the remarkable differences between the relatively low rates of growth for consumption and government expenditures as opposed to the much higher ones for investment and exports—so unlike the American numbers for these same categories, which are more uniform—let us assume that the reasons for the differences cannot be wholly accidental. Now let us hypothesize: these differences must be related to the economic policies pursued by business and government in Japan and the United States—actions that were necessarily different. Once we make that important assumption, we can speculate, based on the numbers alone, that Japanese policymakers pursued a certain design, a deliberate strategy calculated to achieve more rapid growth in some areas than in others. In this strategy, judging from the dramatic numbers above, the categories of investment, exports, and perhaps also imports received powerful emphasis through a mixture of measures apparently designed to achieve certain predetermined ends.

We might further distinguish this mixture from the usual monetary and fiscal policies used by all governments to promote aggregate economic growth. In the American case, as can be seen from the numbers, overall progress remained healthy throughout this same seventeen-year period. But the rate of growth of investment did not diverge from that of consumption by a factor of two, as it did in Japan. Nor did exports and imports increase at such extraordinarily high rates. We might speculate, therefore, that the Japanese policymakers did have general economic growth in mind, but also something more specific. Clearly they were aiming at a particular kind of growth.

Why might this be so? Here we can end the speculation and recall the predicament implied by Japan's physical situation: an island chain about the size of the state of California, but with five times the population of California and without that state's rich endowment of natural resources. Only a small portion (less than one-sixth) of Japan's small land mass is even arable. Compared to the United States, Japan has nearly thirty times the density of population per habitable square mile, and about four times that of even the crowded countries of Europe, such as West Germany and Great Britain.[7]

Japan suffers other disadvantages as well. Except for its ancient cultural ties to China, Japan was largely isolated, first by geographic circumstance and second by shogunal edict (which closed the country almost entirely to foreign contact from 1636 to 1853). During the period 1934–1945, anti-Japanese feeling mushroomed almost everywhere, reinforced by the harsh rule imposed by Japan's military forces on much of Asia. Even today, Japan has very few allies upon whom it can depend for help. In the most elemental sense it remains a disadvantaged country, which must import vast quantities of food, oil, and other raw materials in order not only to prosper but even to survive. To earn the foreign currency necessary to pay its inescapably gigantic import bills, it must export at least as much as it imports.

In effect, Japan's circumstances place it about halfway down a deep trap. It has little hope of climbing out of the trap altogether, no matter how hard it might try. The best it can do is maintain its hold on the sides of the trap, and perhaps inch upward bit by bit. By contrast, the United States is more richly endowed with resources than any other country in the world. (The only conceivable rivals would be Brazil and the Soviet Union.) Understandably, most Americans have never felt the visceral insecurity so evident in modern Japanese culture and behavior.

Simply, there is no escape from the logic of Japan's physical setting: a very large population in a small and mostly barren land mass. Thus, whatever other national goals it might conceive for itself—a strong voice in world politics, wide recognition for its artists, honors for its athletes—Japan cannot, even for a moment, forget about its need to export. Further, because it has no major factor endowments comparable to Saudi oil, Brazilian iron ore, or the rich loam of the American breadbasket, Japan's exported goods can only be manufactured items. (In the early years of industrialization, Japan also exported coal and other raw materials, but this is no longer possible.) Its manufactures must be of such high quality and attractive price that they compete successfully in world markets against the products of other advanced industrial countries. If they do not, then Japan might slowly starve. Of all great nations, Japan is therefore the one with the fewest options, the one most vulnerable to balance-of-payments problems, the one most susceptible to catastrophe. It should not be surprising that on the simple evidence of the numbers in its national in-

come accounts, a pattern of deliberate policies based on export and investment is so strikingly evident. The strategy has been designed not only for
growth, but for survival.

Industrial Organization for Export

When, in the early 1950s, the American Occupation forces departed, Japanese bureaucrats and business executives faced several difficult decisions.
Taking it as axiomatic that their strategy must emphasize the promotion of
manufactured exports, they still had to decide exactly what to export, and,
equally important, to whom. In the language of business administration, their
decision was one of "product/market strategy." Because of the high stakes at
issue here, and because the Japanese situation allowed little margin for error,
the decision on products and markets loomed as the most fundamental choice
facing the architects of Japan's recovery.

Unusual though it was, the Japanese seem to have regarded the issue of
where to sell as being quite as important as the decision about what to make.
One thing about the "where" remained clear: this was the vital influence on
the whole strategy of the Japanese home market, a subject discussed later in
this book. As we shall see, tight control over the home market, distinguished
by a rigorous exclusion of manufactured imports, remained indispensable to
the execution of the national plan for growth and development.[8]

In addressing the question of where to export, Japanese business managers
first fixed on Asia, their traditional market, then on the United States. For them,
America represented the most attractive market in the world, on every basis
except proximity. First, the United States had taken a powerful position favoring free trade in the postwar world economy. This meant that its own borders
would likely be open to other countries' imports. At the time, such openness
did not characterize other world markets. China, Eastern Europe, and the
Soviet Union all represented closed economies. The populous nations of Western Europe, though slowly regaining their status as rich countries, remained
committed to a regional plan for postwar recovery, centering on the Common
Market. Many other parts of the world that might have represented important
markets—Africa, Latin America, and much of Asia—were too poor to attract
Japan's primary attention, at least for the moment. In the case of Asia, postwar
ill will toward the Japanese constituted an invisible but sometimes important
barrier to trade. While Australia remained attractive, its population was far too
small to absorb large quantities of Japanese goods.

In America, by contrast, Japan could sell in high volume and without fear of
protectionist retaliation. Since at that time (the 1950s) the U.S. industrial plant
exhibited extraordinary strength, most Americans ignored any threat to domestic industries from foreign competition. In 1960, for example, fifteen years
after the end of World War II, the United States still manufactured 48 percent
of all the motor vehicles produced in the world, compared with about 2
percent for Japan.[9] (Today Japan produces more vehicles than does the United

States.) In the 1950s, this meant that the Japanese would have to struggle to compete with the superior efficiency of American producers, but also that American borders would likely remain open to Japanese goods.

Even more important, the American market was extraordinarily rich. Gross national product within the United States surpassed that of every other nation. In addition to this generalized wealth, the pattern of income growth for the American middle classes suggested that certain types of purchases, such as second and third cars, might constitute a wholly new market for manufacturers. Already, Japanese automakers noted in the 1950s, this segment of the market had enticed Volkswagen of Germany.

A third reason for the attractiveness of the American market to Japan was the direction of U.S. foreign policy. Just as American diplomats wanted to promote European recovery through the Marshall Plan, as a barrier against Soviet expansion in Europe, so too they wished to build up Japan as a bulwark against Soviet and Chinese ambitions in the Pacific Basin. If there had been any doubts in America about the reality of this danger, the triumph of Mao Zedong's revolution in China in 1949 and the onset of the Korean War in 1950 quickly eliminated them. Correctly or not, American policy planners regarded China and the Soviet Union as closely allied enemies of the United States; so these planners interpreted the attack by the North Koreans in 1950 as having been blueprinted in Moscow, and as further justification for Cold War patterns of thinking in the United States.

An important corollary of such thinking held that the Japanese-American alliance must not be allowed to deteriorate for any reason. In the minds of diplomats and defense planners in the United States, Japan stood as the "unsinkable aircraft carrier" in the Northwest Pacific. Of almost equal significance, it represented as well the major hope in East Asia of an exemplar of democratic capitalism. Both militarily and economically, therefore, Japan appeared to be an essential counterweight to Soviet and Chinese influence. This, in turn, meant that the United States was likely to do everything it could to ensure the success of the Japanese recovery—a goal which Japanese business executives and government bureaucrats interpreted as an insurance policy for future trade with America. They did not miscalculate, although some American planners, such as Secretary of State John Foster Dulles, did. Dulles reasoned that the United States must help Japan find other outlets for its exports, because a stable market could never develop in the United States. "The Japanese," Dulles observed in 1954, "don't make the things we want." Of course, Dulles proved wrong, as Japanese business executives and bureaucrats thought through their "product portfolio" with extreme care. Today, we know quite well what they did in fact produce: first, inexpensive toys and textiles, in great volume; later on, higher value-added products such as steel, ships, motorcycles, automobiles, trucks, earth-moving equipment, television receivers, audio and videotape recorders, machine tools, computers, typewriters, word processing printers, cameras, watches, and so on. In many of these industries, the Japanese

gradually attained world dominance, and evidence of that achievement sur-
rounds us today.[10]

Later in this chapter, we will explore in more detail certain elements of the
strategy that led to these successes. For now, let us simply take note of the
breathtaking boldness of the plan as a whole. Perhaps the well-known Japanese
characteristic of pride, bred in isolation, contributed to the national self-
assurance that Japan as a country could succeed with such a strategy. Imagine
the conversations that might have taken place in the 1950s and 1960s as these
products were being discussed by Japanese business and government planners;
the questions asked, the responses to certain pie-in-the-sky proposals being
advanced:

Export steel to the United States, with its rich deposits of iron ore and
coking coal, its immense steel mills around Gary, Pittsburgh, and Birmingham?

Send Japanese-built cars to compete with the world-renowned products of
General Motors, Ford, and Chrysler? (This at a time when Japan had only a tiny
automobile industry, whose products were cursed with a worldwide reputation for shoddiness and cheap engineering.)

Export motorcycles into a world market dominated by long-established and
powerful giants from the United States (Harley-Davidson), Germany (BMW),
and Britain (Triumph)?

Cameras? How could Japan possibly carve out a niche for itself in a world
market dominated at the inexpensive end by Eastman Kodak and Polaroid, and
at the high end by the advanced optics technology of Leica and other German
producers?

Watches? Again, Timex and similar companies already held a tight grip on
the low end of the market. The upper end was occupied even more solidly by
the Swiss, whom all would-be competitors had failed to dislodge over a period
of several centuries.

Export television sets, tape recorders, and VCRs to America, the very nation
whose companies had invented them and which still held proprietary rights to
the necessary technology?

In retrospect, after studying the difficulties involved, we end by admiring the
bold initiatives of the Japanese. They manufactured and marketed all of these
products, both in Japan and abroad. In so doing, they staked the national
economic future on one of the most ambitious efforts—and best calculated
gambles—by any country in world economic history.

Can we doubt that such conversations actually did take place, in painful and
endless detail, at every level of business and government planning? Could the
Japanese possibly have succeeded in the absence of these conversations? Were
not such discussions essential in anticipating all the obstacles that lay in the
path of such an ambitious strategy? Fortunately, we have a great deal of evidence on these points. Abundant primary material is available, and from this

evidence, both Japanese and Western scholars have developed a coherent portrait of an exceptionally purposeful and disciplined economic strategy.

To review the general plan, let us begin with the two key decisions: first, the choice of markets, with emphasis on the home islands and on the huge American market for exports; and, second, the selection of industries to develop. On this second point, from the Japanese perspective as of the early 1950s, it was by no means clear why the nation should not focus permanently on labor-intensive industries such as textiles, where Japan would seem to have a comparative advantage over the United States. Instead, however, the Japanese actually emphasized a timed sequence of products: first textiles, then heavy industries, then knowledge-intensive industries. Here, evidence of the reasons why could hardly be clearer. An official of one of Japan's elite economic ministries, recalling the product/market strategy shaped during the 1950s and elaborated over succeeding decades, put the matter vividly:

> Should Japan have entrusted its future, according to the theory of comparative advantage, to these industries characterized by intensive use of labor? That would perhaps be a rational choice for a country with a small population of 5 or 10 million. But Japan has a large population. If the Japanese economy had adopted the simple doctrine of free trade and had chosen to specialize in this kind of industry, it would almost permanently have been unable to break away from the Asian pattern of stagnation and poverty, and would have remained the weakest link in the free world, thereby becoming a problem area in the Far East.
>
> The Ministry of International Trade and Industry decided to establish in Japan industries which require intensive employment of capital and technology, industries that in consideration of comparative cost of production should be the most inappropriate for Japan, industries such as steel, oil refining, petro-chemicals, automobiles, aircraft, industrial machinery of all sorts, and later electronics, including electronic computers. From a short-run, static viewpoint, encouragement of such industries would seem to conflict with economic rationalism. But, from a long-range point of view, these are precisely the industries where income elasticity of demand is high [that is, as the incomes of consumers in Japan and the United States rose, they would buy proportionally more of such items as second cars or third television sets, as compared with more food or clothing], technological progress is rapid, and labor productivity rises fast. It was clear that without these industries it would be difficult to employ a population of 100 million and raise their standard of living to that of Europe and America with light industries alone; whether right or wrong, Japan had to have these heavy and chemical industries.[11]

In some ways, of course, such planning, however bold its conception, represented the easiest part of the overall strategy. National economic planning of this type has now become commonplace throughout the world. It is not even very difficult, in part because talk is cheap compared with action, and abstract discussion remains far simpler than concrete implementation. What distinguishes the Japanese experience, therefore, is not the act of planning, but its successful implementation.

To underscore this point, consider just two of the many obstacles facing Japan: if the strategy was indeed going to emphasize capital-intensive and high-technology products, then where were the necessary money and technology going to come from?

How They Did It: Accumulating the Capital

In their efforts to generate savings that could be used in capital investment, Japanese bureaucrats and business executives operated on several levels of public and private management. In subsequent chapters of this book, different aspects of the process of capital accumulation will be discussed more thoroughly. Here, a brief overview will suffice, beginning with some plausible alternatives Japan could have chosen but deliberately avoided:

1. The Japanese government rejected the option of heavy foreign borrowing, a strategy later followed by Brazil, Mexico, and other nations attempting in the 1970s the same kind of rapid industrialization Japan achieved during the 1950s and 1960s. Historically, the Japanese sometimes had borrowed abroad—but only reluctantly, because they did not want creditors to have undue influence in shaping Japan's national destiny. They also wanted to avoid the constant pressure that heavy foreign interest expenses would place on Japan's balance of payments.[12]

2. Similarly, Japanese officials rejected a policy, often adopted by other governments, of allowing extensive direct foreign investment by multinational corporations headquartered in the United States and Europe. This new exclusionary policy represented a partial reversal of Japan's own traditional practice. In the decades preceding World War II, the Japanese government had permitted American multinationals some latitude in building factories and marketing goods within the home market. As diplomatic relations between Japan and the United States deteriorated during the late 1930s, most of the American companies were forced to depart.[13]

Many of them never returned. During the postwar period, despite the powerful new friendship between the two countries, most American multinationals were prohibited from building factories in Japan. Sometimes this occurred in clear violation of the basic Japanese-American treaty agreements of 1953. In any case, no Ford Motor Company of Japan has ever developed to match the immense Ford of Europe; no huge foreign plants producing tires, motorcycles, or electrical appliances. Only in the case of absolutely essential items, such as oil (Shell, Esso), and high-technology goods (Texas Instruments, IBM) did the

Japanese government permit important direct foreign investment by multinationals. Even for these, tight controls were imposed on the companies' freedom to manage their affairs. Usually, joint ventures with Japanese firms were required, as in the case of Fuji-Xerox. Often the Japanese government restricted foreign companies' freedom to remit profits to their home countries, their ability to import manufactured capital goods, and any number of other routine business operations.[14]

In comparative worldwide perspective, particularly during the initial years of development (the 1950s and early 1960s), this tight restriction on the freedom of foreign companies represented an unusual phenomenon, for both the United States and Japan. In fact, acquiescence to these restrictions by American companies and by the American government proved to be a condition essential to the overall success of the Japanese economic strategy. Most other industrializing countries, anxious for their economies to grow rapidly, opened their arms to the investments represented by great multinational corporations. Even the recovering European countries welcomed American firms and allowed them such freedom that, by 1967, the French journalist Jean-Jacques Servan-Schreiber was warning that *The American Challenge* threatened to undermine the economic autonomy of European nations. No such best-selling book ever appeared about Japan, where the strategy of inviting unlimited direct foreign investment had been explicitly rejected many years before.[15]

3. A third alternative path to industrial development—a strategy emphasizing state capitalism—was also rejected, even though some precedent existed in Japan's own history. During the late nineteenth century, as the country was beginning to industrialize, the Meiji government had managed several state-owned enterprises as a means of accelerating the development of a Western-style industrial economy. In the post–World War II period, state ownership might once again have been tried. Many European nations were embarking on important experiments in government ownership at just this time, as were an even larger number of developing nations. For Japan, as for these other countries, a strategy based on state-owned enterprises would have had the virtue of forcibly mobilizing capital and giving the government direct and immediate authority over the course of industrial development. The model need not have been anything like a Soviet-style command economy. Instead it might have resembled the Swedish style of democratic socialism; or, if even that seemed too extreme, a pattern of mixed public-private companies such as those later established in France or Brazil.

But the Japanese government dismissed this alternative as well; and to this day, public ownership in Japan remains low in comparison with the pattern in the industrial nations of Europe and in developing countries as well. In fact, in degree of state ownership, Japan came to resemble the United States more than any other country (see *Table 1-4*).[16]

TABLE 1-4
Extent of State Ownership in Seven Countries

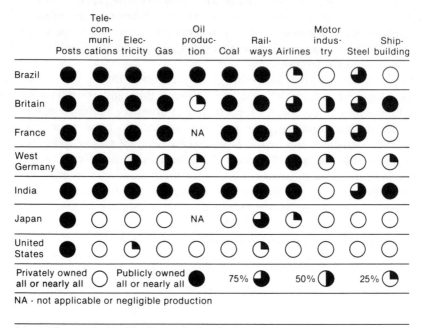

Privately owned ○ all or nearly all
Publicly owned ● all or nearly all　75% ◕　50% ◑　25% ◕

NA - not applicable or negligible production

Adapted from a chart in *The Economist* (London)
December 30, 1978 and reprinted with special permission

4. Having abjured plans based on foreign borrowing, direct foreign investment, and broad state ownership, Japanese policymakers fell back on the only
remaining alternative: a pay-as-you-go strategy. If they were to pursue their
goals of building capital-intensive industries, then they would have to generate
their own capital from within, and employ it through their own privately
owned companies. As remarkable as it seems in retrospect, and as it must have
seemed in prospect during the early 1950s, this is exactly what they did.
Fortunately for the architects of this strategy, the Japanese people had always
showed a relatively high propensity to save their money. Now, to exploit this
national trait, public bureaucrats and private-sector managers throughout Japan instituted a series of devices designed to promote habits of saving and
investment at several levels:[17]

a. The Japanese government penalized consumer borrowing and installment plan purchases through the simple device of taxing interest payments.
Conversely, the government rewarded consumer saving by exempting from
taxation most of the interest income from savings accounts. In both cases, the
policies represented precise reversals of the American system, which encouraged consumer credit purchases and penalized saving. Furthermore, the

Japanese government made it easy for individuals to maintain savings accounts, by placing deposit windows in thousands of post offices throughout Japan. Eventually, this national postal savings system became an extraordinarily effective means of aggregating huge sums of capital from the individual deposits of millions of small-scale savers.

b. The Japanese government indirectly delayed widespread home ownership by allowing mortgage markets to languish and by requiring large cash down payments for housing purchases. Although these policies may not have been as deliberate at the time as they now appear in retrospect, they clearly served the national goal of encouraging savings. First, they forced prospective homeowners to save for long periods, and thus, in the meantime, to accumulate large savings accounts; second, by limiting the total amount of the nation's capital going into housing, they freed up funds for investment in industry. One result of these policies was that, aside from rural homeowners and other families with inherited land, permanent salaried employees of prosperous companies made up the only large group of Japanese people who could realistically aspire to owning a house comparable to those in typical American suburbs. Such houses were financed in part by low-interest loans from the employing Japanese company, in addition to banks.

The overall contrast with American housing policy could hardly be more striking. Ownership of a substantial-sized dwelling place, as an essential component of the American Dream, was vigorously promoted by the federal government's encouragement of savings and loan institutions. These organizations specialized in mortgage loans and were allowed to offer savers interest rates higher than those available from commercial banks. More important, the American government exempted mortgage interest payments from income taxation—including mortgages on extremely large houses and even on second and third vacation homes. This policy, many critics argued, was not only generous, but actually foolish, since it ended by costing the United States Treasury tens of billions of dollars each year in lost tax revenues.

c. Japanese companies, through their payroll practices, made it easier for salaried workers to save a high proportion of their incomes. This was achieved under a compensation system through which bonuses came to constitute a high percentage of total pay: one-fourth to one-third in normal years, even more in exceptionally prosperous ones. Obviously, if a major part of one's income is received in large semiannual bonuses—as compared with smaller weekly or monthly payments throughout the year—it becomes harder to spend it immediately and easier to maintain the habit of saving. Retirement schemes offered by companies followed the same principle: lump-sum payments rather than regular monthly post-retirement pension checks. Again, these payments went into savings accounts, where they became available for industrial investment.

d. The Japanese government, by maintaining a thin and underdeveloped public welfare system, provided powerful incentives for workers of all kinds to save against the contingency of unemployment, death, injury, and especially old age. Until the 1970s, welfare payments in Japan remained extraordinarily low by Western standards. For many years, social security of the European and American variety barely existed, except for civil servants. And, because retirement in Japan came typically around age fifty-five, old age never seemed as far away as it did in most other countries. To this day, many "retirees" in Japan do not in fact cease to work, but instead take part-time jobs in the agricultural, small manufacturing, and service sectors. This in turn minimizes the call they must make on their carefully nurtured savings accounts, which in turn can be borrowed by companies for industrial development.

e. By instituting a rigorous system of capital controls, the government prevented any substantial proportion of Japanese money from leaving the home islands. These funds therefore remained available for investment within Japan. The only important exception to this practice was the furnishing of export financing for Japanese companies selling goods abroad. In such cases, the Ministry of Finance did permit the movement of some capital offshore. But overall, tight controls remained the rule. Such a restrictive policy again contrasts vividly with the American practice of almost unlimited lending abroad. (In recent years, as a subsequent chapter of this book will demonstrate, the loosening of financial markets in Japan has changed this situation, with possibly important consequences for the overall strategy for growth.)

By 1971, the Japanese national habit of saving, encouraged by these systematic incentives set up through public and private policies, had produced an immense pool of funds for industrial growth. Measured by international comparisons, the Japanese had attained an almost unbelievable rate of saving (see *Table 1-5*).[18] A significant proportion of these substantial Japanese savings derived not from households but from businesses. In consequence, the companies began to call on their own retained earnings for financing, in addition to the savings of individuals—even though individuals in Japan continued to out-save their American counterparts by a wide margin.

TABLE 1-5
Total Saving as Percentage of Total National Income, 1971

	Japan	Canada	USA	France	West Germany	Italy	UK
Net Saving	28%	11%	8%	18%	19%	16%	12%
Depreciation (Capital Consumption)	16%	12%	13%	11%	12%	9%	10%
Gross Saving (Total)	44%	24%*	21%	29%	31%	25%	22%

*Figure for Canada does not appear to add correctly, because the numbers for net saving and depreciation were rounded down.

As funds continued to accumulate in banks, Japanese companies placed overwhelming reliance for their capital needs not on the issuance of stocks or bonds, but instead on bank loans. By the 1960s, this practice resulted in extremely high debt-equity ratios in most Japanese firms: about 85:15, versus about 50:50 for the typical American industrial company. In later years, as noted above, an increasing source of capital came from the companies themselves, through the steady plowing back of profits. This flow of retained earnings was augmented by the low dividend payouts characteristic of Japanese firms. In fact, the increased use of retained earnings eventually diminished the degree of influence over investment decisions exercised by the banks and the Japanese government.

Subsequent chapters of this book will examine fiscal policy, capital markets, and the overall financial system of Japan more thoroughly. Here it is necessary only to relate the methods of financing Japanese companies to the broad strategy for economic growth. First, because of the nation's high savings rate, the Japanese banking system came to have vast accumulations of capital at its disposal. Furthermore, in Japan, unlike the United States, these funds were subject to few "crowding out" effects: not from the home mortgage market, nor from large national defense expenditures, nor—at least until the 1970s— from the need to underwrite a welfare state. Thus, most of this highly liquid capital stood ready to finance private enterprise. Equally important, the direction and volume of its movement out of the banks and into the companies was carefully controlled by the Ministry of Finance and the Bank of Japan—much as an experienced firefighting team might control the flow and direction of water from a high-pressure hose. Sometimes powerful gushes of funds in a particular direction might be necessary, to finance major investments within capital-intensive industries. At other times, a light spray toward some other target would suffice—as with short-term financing of trade credits, pending payment by foreign purchasers for exports from Japan.[19]

This overall flexibility benefited from the unusual degree of specialization built into the Japanese banking system through its segmented structure. A few major commercial "city" banks channeled funds to large, well-established Japanese enterprises. Most such banks, like most of their big customers, were members of the distinctive Japanese industrial groups—a subject discussed in later chapters. The city banks maintained important levels of permanent stock ownership in many of the companies they financed, and this practice in turn promoted a thorough interlocking of interests between the banks and their principal customers. In addition to the city banks, several special-purpose organizations such as the Japan Development Bank, the Industrial Bank of Japan, and the Export-Import Bank performed particular tasks such as long-range financing of industries regarded as important to Japan's economic future.

Atop the entire system sat the powerful Ministry of Finance and the Bank of Japan. Both organizations, like the Foreign Ministry and the Ministry of International Trade and Industry, were staffed by a corps of capable bureaucrats.

Within the Ministry of Finance and the Bank of Japan, these officials directed the distinctive Japanese system of "window guidance." Under this system, bank loans were funneled to industries and companies with high-growth potential, while being gradually denied to industries regarded as declining. For many years, one of the most reliable guides for the planners was the direction of the American market—the rise of new products there, the slowdown in sales of others. For one thing, the American market furnished a ready test of the quality, technology, and cost barriers Japanese producers would have to leap over if their export plans were going to work. Then, too, American trends provided glimpses not only of the hot export markets of the future, but also insights into the likely direction of the Japanese home market, which in some important ways followed American tastes. Overall, the multi-tiered, finely coordinated system of Japanese saving, investment, and window guidance channeled a steady stream of investment funds toward the capital-intensive, high-technology industries that lay at the basis of Japan's overall growth strategy.

Acquiring the Expertise for High-Technology Industries

Once the government and business planners had satisfied themselves that the necessary capital would be forthcoming, they then turned to the issue of technology. Where could Japan find it, and how might it be acquired? Here the choices appeared to be four in number. First, Japan could grow its own technology, through intensive educational programs and official sponsorship of organized science and engineering. Alternatively, Japan might import technology through the device of inviting high-tech American companies to build manufacturing plants in Japan, either alone or through joint ventures. Third, Japan could simply buy the necessary technology through licensing arrangements, royalty payments, and management consulting fees. And fourth, Japan could rely on "reverse engineering." That is, Japanese companies could purchase small amounts of high-technology products from other countries, particularly the United States; then proceed to dismantle, analyze, re-engineer, and replicate these products within Japanese factories.

In effect, Japan selected all four alternatives, but strongly emphasized only the last two. For the very long term, the government chose to grow Japan's own technology, and the nation's educational system was charged with ensuring an ample future supply of scientists and engineers. The use of the second alternative, encouragement of direct foreign investment, had to be circumscribed by Japan's desire not to relinquish to foreigners a significant market share of manufactured products within the home islands. In fact, it is a measure of Japan's ardent wish to secure state-of-the-art technology that it lowered some of its barriers here: of all categories of foreign investment, Japan most encouraged those in high technology. Still, many such significant investments were so structured as to be joint ventures with Japanese companies, often with the Japanese firms exercising ultimate control.[20]

During the period of miracle growth, the third and fourth alternatives—buying or reverse engineering the technology—proved more important than the first two. Here, once more, the leading source was the United States. American companies such as AT&T (whose Bell Labs had invented the transistor), RCA (which owned hundreds of patents relating to radio and television), and Ampex (which developed the videotape recorder) provided Japanese firms with their single most valuable source of technology. Starting in the 1950s and continuing down to the present time, the Japanese have paid large sums of money for this technology; but they have received tremendous bargains in return. And in the fourth category—reverse engineering—Japanese companies such as Toyota in the 1960s and Fujitsu in the 1970s reaped even greater bargains by simply adapting the technology they learned while dismantling U.S. products.

Considering the importance of high-technology industries to the Japanese economic miracle, it becomes interesting to explore the underlying nature of both direct purchase and reverse engineering as seen from different perspectives, particularly during the crucial years of the 1950s and 1960s. For all parties concerned, the purchases brought substantial advantages in the short run. The Japanese government received an ingredient indispensable to its overall strategy of economic growth. Similarly, Japanese companies were able to leap-frog generations of intermediate technologies which they otherwise would have had to learn in order to catch up. As for the American government, it too benefited in its ongoing foreign-policy effort to build up the Japanese economy as a beacon of democratic capitalism in the Pacific Basin. This remained true whether purchases or reverse engineering provided the source for Japanese development. Finally, the scores of American companies that sold their technology to Japan received large infusions of cash without any need for additional investment on their part. Thus, everybody won in the short run from Japanese purchases of American technology. In the case of reverse engineering, only the Japanese won. Yet usually there was nothing illegal about it, and in any case little that American producers could do to prevent it.

For the longer term, the principal losers from both purchases and reverse engineering would seem to have been the American companies and the American national industrial interest. Ultimately, manufacturers in the United States lost significant market share to Japanese exporters, who adapted American technology and used it to launch powerful commercial incursions back into the very country from which that technology had originated. In retrospect, therefore, an intriguing question arises of why American companies were so willing to part with so much valuable technology. One answer is simple: they underestimated the Japanese, and overestimated their own future ability to maintain a wide technological lead. This is undoubtedly true, but it hardly constitutes the full story. A second, more important reason lies in other aspects of the Japanese industrial strategy. Because the authorities in Japan kept their home market closed to most of the products of American firms such as RCA, the American companies faced a dilemma: they were compelled to choose between exporting their technology, or exporting nothing to Japan at all. Had they done the latter, then Japanese firms would simply have gone to other sources—namely European high-technology companies such as Siemens, AEG, and Philips—to get what was needed in Japan.

To grasp the peculiar logic of this situation from the American business side, imagine a stockholders' meeting in the late 1950s at RCA. During the meeting, company management announces that it has turned down a Japanese offer to pay $50 million annually for RCA technology. This sum—a *net* inflow of $50 million, since no additional expenditure by the company was required—would therefore be lost. It would not accrue to RCA's income statement, and would not be available for distribution to shareowners as dividends. Such a decision by RCA's management might well have exposed the company to challenges in the form of stockholders' suits.

Nor would RCA's refusal necessarily have hurt the Japanese. They would merely have turned to other American companies or to European sources. As Lenin once remarked, the imperatives of capitalism require that it sell the rope necessary to hang itself. It is in the nature of competitive capitalism that if one source dries up, another stands ready to take its place. And beyond that, it is in the nature of modern industrial life—particularly in the era of the Xerox machine and the high-quality miniature camera—that technology is almost impossible to contain within the walls of a single company, let alone a single nation.

Limiting Imports

Aside from technology, food, and raw materials, the Japanese government permitted the importation of very few items. Determined to maintain tight control of the home market, the government pursued rigorously protectionist policies designed to minimize the entry of manufactured goods from abroad. These policies ranged across the entire portfolio of available measures: tariffs, quotas, deposit requirements, inspections, certifications, administrative delays, and extraordinarily tight control over American and European multinationals operating in Japan. Even for raw materials, the Ministry of International Trade and Industry (MITI) granted import licenses on a selective basis. Here, MITI used its power as a mighty lever to maximize control over Japan's broad-scale industrial policy. For example, as Japan gradually began to relax import restrictions, MITI often announced target dates when foreign competition would again become active. In this way, it encouraged companies to invest frantically in modern facilities, so that they would be able to dominate foreign products once the Japanese market again became open. Meanwhile, the Ministry of Finance instituted severe capital controls and maintained a strict foreign-exchange budget. These measures were designed to conserve Japan's national savings for domestic investment, and also as a means of preventing balance-of-payments problems on the capital account.[21]

All parts of this strategy were supported by a pervasive, well-coordinated management of Japanese economic affairs by the elite bureaucracies. Seldom in the modern world, at least in peacetime, had the government of an advanced democratic country instituted such a thoroughgoing system of business incentives within a national economy; and never had such an effort under such conditions proved so phenomenally successful. Yet Japan never became a "managed economy" in the socialist sense. In fact, because the achievement obviously relied on the distinctive Japanese business-government relationship, it is not easy to say whether business, on the one hand, or government, on the other, deserves most of the credit for Japanese success. Clearly, both parties remained indispensable. In the construction of the edifice called the Japanese economic miracle, the government played the role of architect, but the companies themselves did the actual work. Thus, although the setting in which the companies operated owed its design and management to the government, the miracle itself represented primarily the handiwork and achievement of the private sector—executives and workers within Japanese corporations. Most outside observers, looking back on the miracle, tend to overemphasize the role played by the government, and commensurately to understate the degree to which Japan was, and remains to this day, a company-oriented society characterized by intense inter-corporate rivalry.

For many Americans, the Japanese business-government relationship has proved exceptionally difficult to understand; and this circumstance, in turn, has led to an increasing amount of trouble between the two countries. Within the American business community, a powerful sense that the system constitutes an unfairly advantageous framework for Japanese companies has become pervasive—indeed, a consensus assumption for Americans dealing with Japan in commercial and industrial settings. It therefore becomes useful to review, very briefly, the historical background of the modern Japanese business-government relationship, its partial origins in Occupation-induced policies, and finally the basic elements of the present-day American and Japanese patterns of policymaking.

The Historical Background

The modern relationship between America and Japan dates only from the mid-1930s, when the two countries' geopolitical ambitions began to collide. Within Japan during that decade, the delicate governmental balance of power tipped radically in favor of the militarists, amidst a wave of political assassinations. Meanwhile, the new Japanese government began its fateful drive toward the "Greater East Asia Co-Prosperity Sphere." This undertaking, because it seemed designed to make Japan supreme in the Pacific, struck many American diplomats and military leaders as unacceptable. Japan's activities on the Asian mainland, particularly the steady escalation of its war with China, finally brought American and Japanese interests into direct opposition.

Gradually, between 1937 and 1941, affairs between the two countries deteriorated. The Roosevelt Administration cut off vital exports: iron, steel, petroleum. In turn, the Japanese sought alternate sources in Southeast Asia, where Japan's imperial designs were already bringing it into collision not only with the United States but with even older colonial powers such as Britain, France, and the Netherlands. This rivalry of interests, together with the onset in 1939 of war in Europe, ultimately made armed conflict between the United States and Japan a real possibility. Yet even then, without the emotional shock of Pearl Harbor and the necessity for redeeming the American national honor, such a full-scale and bloody Pacific war as actually occurred would have remained inconceivable to most people in the United States.

During four years of war, and for seven additional years afterward, America and Japan stayed locked in close embrace: first as mortal combatants, then, during the Occupation, in a victor-vanquished relationship. For both countries, this latter period represented a unique historical chapter. The chief of the Occupation forces, General Douglas MacArthur, wielded power on a scale perhaps never before exercised by an individual American, at home or abroad. During the early years, MacArthur's authority in Japan was nearly absolute. But the American dominance did not endure; indeed, by historical comparison, the most remarkable aspects of the Occupation were its brevity and its humaneness. After the American Civil War, for example, the Union army continued to occupy some parts of the southern United States for twelve years, whereas in Japan American forces gave back full control after only seven. (The small southern island of Okinawa constituted a minor exception; it remained under American control until 1972.)

MacArthur's regime, though merciful, did institute pervasive changes, some of which profoundly altered the contours of Japanese society. Among these changes were: a systematic dispossession of many wealthy families, including those involved in *zaibatsu* (financial combines) such as Mitsui and Mitsubishi; a rigorous leveling of social and economic distinctions, marked by universal suffrage, free education for all, and a wide distribution of agricultural lands to millions of peasant families; and the outlawing of war as an instrument of national policy. The Occupation also laid a solid groundwork for the subsequent, thoroughgoing management of the economy by elite Japanese bureaucrats. It did so by delegating many of its powers to such Japanese-run agencies as the Economic Stabilization Headquarters, the forerunner of the present-day Economic Planning Agency. Through this general pattern of delegation, accomplished primarily between 1946 and 1949, MacArthur actually increased the powers of the Japanese government to manage the country's economic affairs beyond what they had been prior to the war.

Of course, not everything the Occupation attempted worked out in just the way its architects intended. In particular, efforts to turn the Japanese business system into a pure imitation of American capitalism produced one frustration after another. Such policies as antitrust, open markets, and industry-wide collective bargaining never fully took root in Japan. In theory, these devices were supposed to instill competition into the Japanese economy and promote the efficient and equitable use of resources—just what the same policies were believed to have accomplished in the United States. While they never succeeded, their failure did not necessarily preclude either competition or efficiency within Japan. In fact, major segments of the Japanese business system became so fiercely competitive as to confound certain tenets of traditional Western economic theory. Such Japanese practices as protectionism, cartelization, credit allocation, and overall top-down planning seemed to fly in the face of Western free-market principles as set forth by Adam Smith, David Ricardo, Alfred Marshall, and other classical economists.

Yet these very policies apparently helped bring about the Japanese economic miracle. Equally important, the way in which they were made and implemented represents still another set of contrasts between America and Japan, and an additional basis of potential confusion and misunderstanding. Thus, it becomes useful to pause here and briefly review the elementary sources of policy in both countries.

Organization for Policymaking: America and Japan Compared

CONGRESS AND DIET

On the surface, the operations of the two national legislatures appear to be very much alike. Both possess sole authority, under a written constitution, to enact national laws. (In Japan, however, the ministries draft most bills, not the Diet.) Both Japan and America have an upper and a lower house, whose members are popularly elected at regular intervals. In both countries, any serious candidacy for a seat in either house quickly becomes an expensive proposition, especially in an age of television advertising. In Japan, campaign expenses are financed overwhelmingly by business contributions. In fact, funds pour into the Liberal Democratic Party's political coffers from Japanese companies and trade associations in ways that would be difficult in America, and perhaps even illegal.[22]

In the Japanese Diet, party discipline on matters affecting the national economic system remains quite strict. In the American Congress, entrepreneurial mavericks in both houses often go their separate ways. They sometimes ignore the organized parties altogether, exploiting their own extensive committee staffs and disrupting the smooth operation of policymaking.[23] Equally important, neither the fundamental federal-state division nor the rigid separation of powers among the branches of American government can be found in Japan. These American traditions, rooted in the Founding Fathers' determination to thwart the growth of absolute power, simply do not apply with equal force elsewhere in the world. Nor does the characteristic and abiding American conviction that the public and private spheres must be kept separate.[24] (This conviction is reflected in stringent American laws concerning conflict of interest and in requirements that public servants make detailed disclosures of their financial holdings.) Such traditions are mostly foreign to Japanese conceptions of the overall role of government.

Japan's parliament—indeed most of its formal political system—is indebted to European rather than American models. It displays no such fearful aversion to government power as can be seen in the American structure. Thus, the Japanese system is more centralized and, in general, more typical of democratic governments worldwide. Japan's prime minister, for example, serves simultaneously as leader of his party, member of the legislature, and head of the executive branch. The familiar American impasse created when the chief executive belongs to one party, while the legislature remains in the control of the opposition, is almost impossible in Japan. No prime minister has confronted this problem. Yet, many postwar American presidents—Harry Truman, Dwight Eisenhower, Richard Nixon, Gerald Ford, and Ronald Reagan—have been forced to contend with it.[25] The relative immunity enjoyed by Japan from a split between the legislature and the executive, or within the two houses of the legislature itself, holds for nearly all parliamentary systems, such as those in Britain, West Germany, and Canada.

One circumstance, however, sets the Japanese experience apart not only from the American but also from that of nearly all other Western governments; and this feature has had decisive results for business-government relations. In Japan, the ruling Liberal Democratic Party has held power continuously ever since its formation in 1955. Among modern democracies, only in Sweden has one party remained in power so long (for over forty years, ending in 1976). The Swedish ruling group represented the political left, a fact reflected in that country's highly developed welfare state. Japan's Liberal Democratic Party, despite its name, has proved to be a deeply conservative party dominated by business interests and supported more enthusiastically by rural voters than by urban ones. It comprises a coalition of factions, somewhat like the Democratic Party in the United States. Most of these, however, are organized not around interest groups, as in America, but around individual leaders who aspire to the prime ministership. The LDP's philosophy, to the extent that it has one, somewhat resembles that of Reagan Republicanism, but without the Reaganites' distaste for bureaucratic government.

Opposition parties are well established in Japan, and some are quite large. But, except for a brief period during the late 1940s, no opposition party has actually run the government since World War II. Thus, compared with the out-of-power party in America, which may retain control of one house or even both houses of Congress, and thus be able to initiate or block important legislation, Japanese opposition parties possess little power in the national government. (They do control a number of important local offices.) While the two American parties have regularly alternated in power, with four Democratic and four Republican administrations since World War II, the LDP has practically never been out of office.[26]

Without question, this LDP control remained essential to the distinctive relationship between business and government that characterized the Japanese economic miracle. Whereas Americans during that postwar period often became preoccupied with the processes of business-government relations, the Japanese government focused its attention sharply on the specific aim of rapid economic growth. It shaped and adapted processes to fit this overall goal, and, in the achievement of the miracle, the Liberal Democratic Party's retention of power was simply indispensable. Had the Socialists (the main opposition) run the government for any considerable period—with their emphasis on equity rather than growth, their opposition to close ties with the United States, and their harsh attitude toward Japanese big business—then the overall economic strategy, and with it the underlying business-government relationship, would surely have evolved in a far different way.

THE BUREAUCRACY IN AMERICA AND JAPAN

In the United States, the same traditions that militated against the growth of a powerful state also tended to minimize bureaucratic influence on policymaking. In fact, prior to the coming of the New Deal in the 1930s, the United States could scarcely be said to possess much of a bureaucracy at all. Moreover, government officials have had to meet no prerequisite for office except American citizenship: no formal training is required for most positions, no education in elite schools, no prior experience in politics or business. In economic policymaking, most of the important decisions are made by "in-and-outers"— talented persons summoned to Washington as Cabinet or sub-cabinet members, on temporary leave from the worlds of business, academia, or law. With the possible exceptions of the State and Treasury Departments, no American tradition of an elite civil service has ever existed, certainly none comparable to long-standing traditions in Britain, France, Germany, and Japan. Even now, in an era of inescapably large government, bureaucratic power is still regarded with deep suspicion by much of the American electorate. Cabinet members come and go regularly, and most of them play little permanent role in party politics or business-government relations. Sub-cabinet officers such as assistant secretaries average only twenty-six months in office. A career government service does exist, fed in part by schools of public administration such as Princeton's Woodrow Wilson School, Tufts's Fletcher School of Law and Diplomacy, and Harvard's Kennedy School of Government. Yet most graduates of these schools do not become career civil servants, but instead attach themselves to promising individual politicians; they ascend the ladder of power by political appointment as much as by meritocratic achievement. In all, the American schools of government exercise no such pervasive influence as do Oxford and Cambridge in Britain, the grandes écoles in France, and Tokyo University in Japan. In fact, Tokyo University was originally established for the specific purpose of educating bureaucrats to run the country.[27]

Among the Japanese, the upper civil service represents a high calling and a most prestigious career. Only a few hundred new recruits are permitted to join the elite ministries each year, and the brightest young people are chosen on the basis of merit, determined by academic performance and scores on standardized examinations. Japanese bureaucrats, in contrast to such American specialists as lawyers and economists, tend to come from the ranks of broadly informed generalists.[28] Once they have entered government service, their pay is not high, but their prestige is. So, emphatically, is their power. The most coveted positions lie in the Ministry of Foreign Affairs, the Ministry of Finance, and the Ministry of International Trade and Industry; but nearly all the economic ministries hold honored places in Japanese society. Year in and year out, the Japanese bureaucracies attract the outstanding talent which, in America, gravitates instead toward law, medicine, consulting, or some other lucrative position in the private sector. In Japan, again in sharp contrast to America, new recruits into the elite bureaucracies and into prestigious private companies tend to stay put. In both government and business, Japanese managers advance by seniority as much as by merit, so that almost no leapfrogging of seniors by brilliant whiz kids ever occurs. Again, in Japan the American style of frequent job-hopping remains rare. To most Japanese, steeped as they are in group loyalty, that practice appears unseemly and unprofessional.[29]

Of the Japanese bureaucracies, the most important for business-government relations have been the Ministry of Finance, the Economic Planning Agency, and MITI. The Ministry of Finance combines in one large organization the functions performed in America by the Treasury Department, the Office of Management and Budget, the Securities and Exchange Commission, and the Federal Reserve Board. Since World War II, the Bank of Japan has been less independent of the Ministry than the Fed has of the Treasury Department. The Economic Planning Agency in Japan has some parallels with the American Council of Economic Advisers. Both function primarily as think-tanks, exercising no line authority over policy. Yet the Japanese agency is larger and far more stable than is the American CEA, which experiences constant turnover of personnel. MITI, about which so much has been written, has no real American counterpart. With its total staff of fewer than 10,000 employees (down from about 14,000 in the 1960s), MITI does in Japan what the much larger Commerce Department, the Special Trade Representative, and the Small Business Administration are supposed to do in America.[30]

Although its influence surpasses the combined powers of those U.S. agencies, MITI is far from omnipotent. Indeed, by the middle 1980s it may have reached the nadir of its post–World War II influence, for reasons detailed later in this book. Americans and other foreign observers have often misunderstood MITI's role and exaggerated its powers. MITI has been portrayed as an organization that steers Japan's development almost like the scientists at Houston's Mission Control guide the flights of American astronauts. In truth, MITI never held such unlimited powers; and it possesses fewer now than it had during the 1950s and 1960s, when it exercised tight control over imports and exports. Today, MITI must operate primarily through persuasion. It must build coalitions to support the policies it identifies as good for the Japanese economy. It has to reconcile its suggestions with those of the much larger Ministry of Finance, with which it often finds itself in bitter disagreement. (Contrary to the world's perceptions, inter-bureaucratic rivalry in Japan remains at least as intense as in the United States, and probably more so.) MITI must listen carefully to what it hears from business associations, particularly Keidanren, the well-staffed federation of the 700 largest Japanese companies. It must consult endlessly with powerful parties in both the public and private sectors. It must cajole, explain, prod. Seldom can it coerce, at least directly. The fact that MITI remains extremely powerful despite all these constraints represents a testament to its skill in negotiations, its extraordinary resources for gathering accurate information, and the proven effectiveness of its policies. Of course, even such an elite bureaucracy as MITI can make big mistakes, such as its misguided effort in the 1960s to reduce the Japanese automobile industry to only a tiny handful of companies. Still, MITI's long-term record of sheer achievement commands extraordinary respect, both within Japan and in economic planning circles throughout the world.[31]

As mentioned earlier, the principle of separation of powers among different parts of government is not taken nearly so seriously in Japan as in the United States. Nor is the deeply held American conviction that business and government must be kept insulated from one another. Thus, relationships among the Diet, the Liberal Democratic Party, the economic ministries, and the community of large businesses are characterized by constant and intimate contact. Far more public-private interaction occurs in Japan than in America, and the overall pattern of interpenetration remains fundamentally different. In Japan, for example, little movement occurs from the private sector into the public, even for temporary duty, at any stage of an individual's career. Shifts from the public to the private sector, on the other hand, have become routine. Upon retirement from government service, which usually takes place at age 55 or younger, a large percentage of Japanese bureaucrats take high-ranking positions with prestigious Japanese companies or trade associations. (This happens in America too, of course, though on a much smaller scale.) Many former bureaucrats run for seats in the Diet, almost always as members of the LDP. Indeed, most of Japan's prime ministers over the last three decades have been ex-bureaucrats. The Diet itself, though not by any means the rubber stamp that some scholars have called it, has sometimes functioned primarily as an instrument of the LDP's ruling faction. The LDP has even wielded influence within the economic ministries, quietly expressing its approval or disapproval of promotions of individual bureaucrats.

Little of this activity fits the image widely held outside Japan of peaceful and happy consensus-building. The brokerage of power in any country cannot be a game for the faint of heart, and Japan provides no exception to this rule. But what *is* different about Japan—especially in contrast to the United States—is its style of political and economic conflict. Whereas in America disagreement proceeds in an open, raucous, and almost joyously confrontational mode, in Japan it usually remains less noisy, more subtle, and often more sophisticated.[32]

PRESIDENT AND PRIME MINISTER

The chief executives of the two countries perform similar roles in the making of policy. They help to set agendas for tax, welfare, and defense programs. They lobby for legislative enactment of their overall economic policies. Yet, in America, the presidential function of serving as a national symbol, directly voted into office by all of the people, can greatly increase the incumbent's power. Such a "bully pulpit," as Theodore Roosevelt called it, can be converted into the exercise of authority far exceeding any limits implied by the United States Constitution. Much depends on the president's own personality and taste for power. The careers of Franklin D. Roosevelt and Ronald Reagan, among other chief executives, attest to the vast potential in the office for shaping the general climate of business-government relations.[33] The Japanese prime minister, by contrast, is a good deal more constrained, and in most instances less powerful as an executive officer.

The president and prime minister are chosen in different ways. Any person aspiring to the American presidency must survive a grueling and seemingly interminable season of state primary elections merely to receive the party's nomination. The candidate then runs for the presidency in a regular quadrennial national canvass. The Japanese prime minister, on the other hand, does not stand for that office directly, but instead is chosen by his party once the party has triumphed in a national election. Such elections must be held at least every four years, but in fact they usually occur more often, on the occasion of a dissolution of the Diet by decision of the prime minister and his cabinet. Custom decrees that no Japanese prime minister serve more than four years in office. An American president, of course, can serve eight, but cannot dissolve Congress and call new elections, even in an economic crisis.[34]

THE PROCESS OF DECISION MAKING: ADVERSARIAL LEGALISM
VERSUS CONSULTATION

Nowhere is the difference between America and Japan more conspicuous than in the roles played by the judiciary and the legal profession in the two countries. Here, as it happens, neither the United States nor Japan provides an example typical of democratic countries, since they occupy opposite ends of the spectrum. America has no fewer than twenty-two times as many lawyers per capita as does Japan. It also has four-and-one-half times as many as West Germany, and three-and-one-half as many as the United Kingdom. While the definition of "lawyer" varies from one country to the next, such figures do provide strong evidence of different styles in conflict resolution. Also implied are other important questions about the trade-offs which different societies have chosen between such values as individual rights versus group welfare, formal versus informal procedures, written versus oral agreements in business, and the level of mutual suspicion versus that of mutual trust among citizens.[35] On all of these matters, as numerous observers have commented, Americans appear to favor the first alternatives—individual rights, formal procedures, written agreements, even mutual suspicion—while the Japanese seem to prefer the second. Here again, underlying values and ideologies remain impossible to measure with much precision; but to discount such contrasts entirely is to preclude, or at least distort, any thorough understanding of the business-government relationship in each country.[36]

Compared with the Japanese, Americans have elevated legal due process into a virtual fetish. Today, few large projects can be undertaken in the United States without endless hearings and appeals in multiple jurisdictions, all conducted under formal proceedings dominated by lawyers and judges. Such legalistic tendencies have always been more pronounced in America than elsewhere—ever since the late eighteenth century, when such lawyers as John Adams, Alexander Hamilton, Thomas Jefferson, John Jay, Patrick Henry, and James Madison actually founded the United States. The American Revolution, unlike practically all others in the world's history, was made primarily by lawyers.

The long-established American tendency toward legalism took a decided upturn during the 1960s, and for the last generation the prevailing style of public discourse in America has been adversarial advocacy. This has been true within politics, business, the press, medical practice, and the overall business-government relationship. Readiness of citizens to accuse, sue, appeal, and in general resort to the judiciary as the final legitimate arbiter, has now become a salient characteristic of the American way. Many Japanese observers regard the American adversarial system as inefficient, obnoxious, and even irrational. They wonder how business ever gets done in America, and they note with amusement that it sometimes doesn't get done at all.[37]

Similarly, many Americans, steeped in a value system that holds individual autonomy supreme, regard Japan's style of decision making as fundamentally alien. To them, the Japanese habit of endless discussions results in postponed and therefore untimely decisions. In the process, individual rights are suppressed, and creativity and entrepreneurship are stifled. Americans are fond of quoting the Japanese proverb, "The nail that sticks up will be hammered down." Some observers even question whether Japan has actually achieved a modern democratic polity. They argue that the Japanese economic miracle was exactly that: an *economic* achievement, quite distinct from any comparable attainment of an open, liberal, advanced democratic society. They point to the practical absence of the one-person-one-vote principle, owing to the Japanese government's perennial refusal to reapportion electoral districts. For some American critics, Japan remains an oligarchical, ethnocentric, and sexist society. Even Japanese homogeneity, they argue, is no accident, but has resulted in part from the systematic exclusion of immigrant groups. Thus, by

American standards, Japan inevitably appears to be a society in which individual rights count for little. Most of the really important economic decisions were, and still are, reached and implemented by a relatively small circle of bureaucrats, politicians, and business executives. Japanese agencies such as the Fair Trade Commission, set up by the Occupation to promote American-style free competition, remain small. They wield little power, at least in comparison with their American counterparts—the Antitrust Division of the Department of Justice and the Federal Trade Commission. In the overall picture, the fabled "consensus" that underlies Japanese business-government relations is no illusion. But that consensus may derive from the forced peace of deliberate public policy as much as from any national satisfaction with things as they are, let alone from some inherent trait of Japanese culture.[38]

Here, however, it is important to keep in mind that the United States may not be the best reference point for judging Japanese democracy. Compared to the United States, Japan, like most other nations, neglects important elements of civil and gender rights, standing to sue, and other privileges reflecting the transcendent American commitment to individualism. But compared with other Asian societies, Japan has achieved spectacular gains in its progress toward democracy: free and open elections with universal suffrage, toleration of opposition parties and of social protest, a free and aggressive press, and a remarkably equitable distribution (more so than in America) of a very high national income.

The same kinds of differences between styles of governmental decision making in the two countries may also be found in the business world: adversarial versus cooperative systems; ad hoc, arm's-length bargaining versus long-term relationships; and so on. Here again, the reference point remains crucial: we must constantly ask the question, "Compared to what?" At a high level of abstraction, all varieties of market capitalism are alike in the sense that they resemble each other more than they resemble command economies. By this standard, the Japanese and American styles have much in common. The central question here, however, takes the next lower level of comparison. Is Japanese market capitalism more like Western variants of the same system, or more unlike them? To put it more precisely, does the Japanese system resemble the American and European systems more than those two resemble each other? Later chapters of this book will address aspects of these questions directly. For now, let us merely update the recent trends in Japanese-American relations, and in the overall world economy.

After the Miracle: 1973 to the Present

Many of the strategies characteristic of Japanese business and government during the era of miracle growth persisted without essential change into the subsequent period. Others were modified considerably. The remaining chapters of this book are devoted to exploring continuities and changes during this

TABLE 1-6
Growth Rates in Real Gross National Products, 1961–1985, Annual Averages

	1961–65	1966–70	1971–75	1976–80	1981	1982	1983	1984	1985
Japan	10.0%	11.3%	4.6%	5.1%	4.2%	3.1%	3.3%	5.8%	5.0%
USA	4.6%	3.0%	2.2%	3.4%	1.9%	−2.5%	3.5%	6.5%	2.3%
EEC Countries	4.7%	4.4%	2.7%	3.0%	−0.2%	0.5%	1.2%	2.1%	2.2%

most recent period. It is appropriate here merely to summarize some of the broad trends characteristic of these years.

In both Japan and the United States, three salient shifts occurred during the period following the oil shock of 1973. Some of the changes were common to nearly all advanced industrial economies, though they differed from one country to the next in degree and timing:

1. A significant slowdown in overall economic growth;
2. A relentless rise in the levels of inflation, unemployment, public expenditures, and government deficits. These trends were compounded by the emergence of an international debt "crisis" that affected numerous countries and threatened to become a permanent aspect of the international economy;
3. A steady growth in trade imbalances, which raised ominous threats to overall relations between Japan and the United States.

The first trend, the slowdown in growth, hit the entire world economy in the wake of the 1973 oil shock and persisted for at least a decade beyond. Whereas Japan had exhibited a spectacular annual GNP growth rate of more than 10 percent during the 1950s and 1960s, it averaged only one-half that during the 1970s, and even less in the early 1980s. The United States experienced the same relative decline, as did other Western industrialized countries, as the numbers in *Table 1-6* show.[39]

Behind these numbers lay a host of unexpected economic events: the shift by most countries to floating exchange rates; the oil shocks of 1973 and 1979; a sharp rise in the prices of many other essential commodities; and the steady increase of inflation and unemployment. For many countries, these events proved to be nothing short of traumatic. Japan, for example, experienced extremely high inflation rates and wage increases during the middle 1970s. And in the early 1980s, the United States and several European countries suffered double-digit unemployment rates, an order of magnitude not witnessed since the Great Depression of the 1930s.

The second salient trend of this period was the emergence of huge public deficits in almost every country, including the United States and Japan (see *Table 1-7*).[40] The reasons behind this dramatic growth of public debt varied

TABLE 1-7

	United States			Japan		
	Federal Deficit	Total Federal Debt	Total Debt as % of GNP	Nat'l Gov't Deficit	Total Debt	Total Debt as % of GNP
	(Billions of Dollars)			(Trillions of Yen)		
1975	53.2	544.1	36.8%	5.3	15.0	9.9%
1980	73.8	914.3	35.5%	14.2	70.5	29.3%
1981	78.9	1003.9	34.8%	12.9	82.3	32.3%
1982	127.9	1147.0	37.7%	14.0	96.4	36.1%
1983	207.8	1381.9	42.9%	13.5	109.7	39.4%
1984	185.3	1576.7	44.0%	12.9	122.0	41.0%
1985	212.3	1827.5	46.4%	11.7	132.9	42.3%

between the two countries, of course. In the United States, the deficit began its rapid climb during the 1960s and 1970s, because of the combination of the Vietnam War and the rise in social welfare entitlements. These, in turn, were followed by the deep Reagan income tax cuts, beginning in 1981, and by an immense growth in American military spending over the next several years. In Japan, where the total debt as a percentage of GNP more than quadrupled between 1975 and 1985, the chief reason can be found in the huge increase in public-sector spending on health and human services. This increase occurred at the very time when overall economic growth in Japan was slowing to half the rate of the pre-1973 miracle period.

Compounding the deficit problem in both countries was the persistent international debt crisis. This problem was worldwide in extent, although the best-publicized situations had to do with Mexico, Brazil, and Argentina. By the middle 1980s, Latin America owed about $500 billion to foreign creditors. Because both Japan and the United States were heavily involved in foreign trade and finance, the international debt crisis had serious consequences for each nation. Circumstances grew especially complicated when the U.S. itself became a net debtor nation in 1985 (for the first time since 1914), and actually began to borrow heavily from Japan. In fact, the overall debt situation threatened to become a permanent Sword of Damocles hanging over the world financial system. Its long-run implications still remain unclear, but they have begun to influence many aspects of public policy in both America and Japan, and to affect the relationship between the two countries in unpredictable ways.

By the 1970s, the most difficult issue between America and Japan lay in trade imbalances: American deficits, Japanese surpluses. Again, subsequent chapters of this book will elaborate on this question in some detail. For now, it will suffice to mark the general outlines of the trade issue as it developed in the years after 1973.

TABLE 1-8
American and Japanese Trade Balances
(With All Nations)

	United States	Japan
1975	$2.2 billion	$ − 2.0 billion
1980	− 36.2 billion	− 10.9 billion
1981	− 39.6 billion	8.6 billion
1982	− 42.6 billion	6.9 billion
1983	− 69.4 billion	20.6 billion
1984	− 123.3 billion	33.5 billion
1985	− 143.8 billion	39.6 billion

The tremendous changes in the overall trading patterns of the United States and Japan are evident in the figures shown in *Table 1-8*.[41] The negative numbers for Japan in the years 1975 and 1980 were atypical, deriving principally from the two oil shocks that preceded those years. The larger point is obvious from the table: Japan characteristically ran large surpluses in its trade balance, and the United States did just the opposite. The Americans, who had run trade surpluses in every single year of the twentieth century prior to 1971, proceeded to set new world records for deficits during each of the four years from 1982 to 1985.

A second revealing dimension of the two countries' trade patterns could be read in the export performances of individual companies. The most pertinent information from each of the top ten exporters of manufactured goods in Japan and the United States is shown in *Table 1-9*.[42]

TABLE 1-9

Japan (1984)			USA (1984)		
Company	Exports ($b)	Exports as % of Total Sales	Company	Exports ($b)	Exports as % of Total Sales
1. Toyota Motor	$10.4b	45%	1. General Motors	$7.3b	9%
2. Nissan	8.9b	58%	2. Ford Motor	6.0b	12%
3. Honda	5.8b	71%	3. GE	3.9b	14%
4. Matsushita	5.1b	37%	4. Boeing	3.6b	35%
5. Hitachi	4.7b	37%	5. IBM	3.1b	7%
6. Nippon Steel	4.1b	34%	6. Chrysler	2.7b	14%
7. Mazda	4.0b	67%	7. Du Pont	2.7b	7%
8. Toshiba	3.1b	29%	8. United Technologies	2.4b	15%
9. NEC	2.7b	34%	9. McDonnell Douglas	2.1b	22%
10. Sony	2.6b	69%	10. Eastman Kodak	1.9b	18%

For the leading ten of each country, we see strikingly different patterns. For the Japanese companies, the average of the third column (that is, exports as a percentage of total sales) is a whopping 48 percent, whereas for the American firms it is only 15 percent. Nor are the overall contrasts confined to the top ten exporters of each country. The number eleven Japanese company, Sanyo, exported 62 percent of its production, the number twelve, Nippon Kokan (steel) 41 percent, and so on.

What should we conclude from these contrasts? First, that in Japan, the leading companies obviously built their production capacities well beyond domestic needs alone, in an effort calculated to serve global markets, and especially the lucrative American market. In fact, quotas on the importation of Japanese goods into many European countries actually increased pressures on the American market to absorb even more Japanese goods. Second, as we review the list of Japanese companies, and speculate on their individual strategies for growth, it seems likely that the general pattern of foreign market penetration proceeded in two distinct steps: first, rigorous price competition at the lower end of the market; then, a gradual "trading up," as the companies marketed goods of higher quality at more expensive prices. This was true of both the automobile firms, which first offered tiny, very cheap cars, followed by slightly larger but more stylish and better engineered ones; and the consumer electronics companies—first radios, then cheap black-and-white television sets, finally color sets as good as or better than those made anywhere else in the world.

By contrast, as we look at the list of companies on the American side, it becomes evident that defense suppliers make up about half the roster. Included are makers of warplanes, helicopters, tanks, munitions, and so on—few of which are manufactured by Japanese companies, and all of which were originally based on investments made to serve America's Defense Department. Thus, in a rather curious respect, we see a similar sort of basic public support system for some of the leading American exporters as for the top Japanese firms: that is, an advantageous position in a captive domestic market. Such a system could be used first to socialize investment costs, then to insure against sudden business downturns, and finally to develop production expertise and experience curve pricing strategies that made the products themselves attractive to buyers overseas. Hypothesizing more broadly, we also see the outlines of a situation in which government policies in both countries positioned the companies to penetrate export markets. In the United States, these policies were based primarily on perceived defense needs, and were only indirectly related to an explicit export strategy. But they nonetheless helped the American companies capture markets abroad.

Finally, *Table 1-9* suggests that the American firms' overall strategy for penetrating foreign markets did not rely primarily on the export of manufactured products from the United States. Rather, as a subsequent chapter of this book will show, it was rooted in a strategy of direct foreign investment: General Electric factories in Mexico and Singapore, Ford plants all over Europe, and so on. Meanwhile, the very attractive Japanese market remained relatively closed to such investments, and this provided still another potential source of friction between the two countries.

As the 1980s wore on, the bilateral trade balances between the two countries yawned progressively wider. Japanese exports to the United States, almost all of which proved to be manufactured goods, increased much more rapidly than did Japanese imports from the United States, which remained mostly food and raw materials (see *Table 1-10*).[43]

TABLE 1-10
American Trade Deficit with Japan

1975	− $1.6 billion
1980	− 10.4 billion
1981	− 15.8 billion
1982	− 17.0 billion
1983	− 21.1 billion
1984	− 37.0 billion
1985	− 40.7 billion

These figures proved extremely galling to many Americans. Business executives from the United States had long believed that the Japanese were exploiting the open American market while excluding them from a fair chance at penetrating the Japanese home market. Now, Japan's immense trade surpluses with the United States actually exceeded its overall surpluses with the world as a whole; and this relationship between the two numbers seemed to form a pattern over the entire decade 1975–1985. In other words, the Japanese often ran trade deficits with much of the rest of the world, excluding the United States; but then offset those deficits through surpluses with the United States alone.[44]

By the middle 1980s, after years of American protest and Japanese procrastination, extremely serious trade friction between the two countries had become a reality. The former partners were well on their way toward becoming commercial and industrial adversaries. A new era of Japan *versus* the United States threatened to undermine a forty-year friendship.

CHAPTER 2

Protecting World Markets

DAVID B. YOFFIE

International trade has gone through turbulent times since the oil shocks of 1973. Growth in world exports and imports has been more uneven than in any comparable period since the 1920s, and a whole series of unusual new trade barriers, ranging from voluntary export restraints to barter requirements, have been erected to protect favored markets.[1] The implications of this trend are potentially ominous for all nations. Should the world retreat into protectionism, there would be no winners.

For the United States and Japan, the first and third largest traders in the world, global protectionism would be especially devastating. By the mid-1980s, one out of every six jobs in the United States relied on exports; almost one-third of all U.S. corporate profits were earned from foreign sales and international business activity; and over 20 percent of U.S. industrial output was shipped overseas (double the level of 1950). For Japan, the story is even more dramatic: over the last thirty years, exports have increased twice as fast as industrial production and have tripled as a percentage of gross national product.[2] In certain manufacturing sectors, such as autos, steel, color televisions, videotape recorders, motorcycles, watches, and machine tools, the Japanese export more than 40 percent of production.[3]

Yet despite common concerns about trade, and despite a shared fear of increasing protectionism, the United States and Japan have pursued very different approaches to the international trading environment. While both countries have spoken out in favor of freer world trade, their governments and firms have employed fundamentally opposite strategies; and they have achieved highly divergent performance results.

Any explanation for these differences in strategy could begin by considering each nation's distinct political and corporate traditions. America's decentralized system of economic and political decision making, for example, contrasts sharply with Japan's highly centralized, government-driven formulation of national strategy. From the beginnings of industrialization in both nations, the United States and Japan have consistently maintained different conceptions of the appropriate interaction between international economics and national politics.

In the specific realm of modern international trade, the peculiar historical circumstances of the Great Depression and World War II led each country to adopt its present trading strategy. As these strategies evolved in the 1940s and 1950s, the governments of both nations created unique organizational systems for implementation; the systems then formulated policies that largely structured the way in which each country's businesses looked at international commerce. The results of these differences have been among the key factors which turned Japan into one of the premier trading nations and contributed to the relative decline of the United States.

Neither nation, however, seems prepared for the world of international trade in the 1980s. Drawing on new empirical research on U.S. and Japanese approaches to countertrade, plus trade in consumer electronics and telecommunications, I will argue that neither Japan nor the United States has made the necessary adjustments. At present, both countries remain unyielding and overly tied to their past strategies, which have now outlived their usefulness. Finally, and perhaps surprisingly, I shall point out why the United States—and not Japan—may well be in the better position to deal with trade challenges of the late 1980s and 1990s.

I: National Trade Policies in Historical Perspective

Japanese and American trade policies seem to have changed dramatically over the past forty years. While the United States has grown more protectionist and less dominant, Japan has reduced its formal trade barriers and little by little become a more "liberal" trading state.[4] Although some analysts view these changes as fundamental, I do not believe that either country has truly altered its basic approach to international trade. Rather, what we have witnessed in the 1970s and 1980s represents nothing greater than an incremental evolution in the trading strategies each adopted after World War II. In sharp contrast to the international monetary or energy arenas, where strategies have undergone revolutionary changes in the last fifteen years, neither the United States nor Japan has altered in any fundamental way its strategic orientation toward international trade.

The American strategy, which started to emerge in the mid-1930s and blossomed in the late 1940s, dictated that American interests would best be served by following two fundamental principles: international trade should be fully liberalized; and domestic economic interests should be secondary to global political considerations. For every president from Franklin Delano Roosevelt through Ronald Reagan, U.S. trade policy has been shaped by this global view of American interests. By contrast, modern Japanese trade policy, from the early 1950s through the 1980s, has been molded around the principle of domestic self-interest. In Japan's trade strategy, external economic expansion has taken precedence over competing domestic and international political concerns.

My first proposition is that the strategic choices made decades ago by the governments of the United States and Japan had profound long-term implications for each country's businesses, and even more broadly for each country's society. Their strategies on international trade were responses to the crises of their time—crises of economic depression and political uncertainty. In each country, the strategies slowly gained legitimacy, ultimately becoming deeply influential in government organizations. The core principles of the strategy created norms for public officials, which in turn were institutionalized in both the structure of government agencies and their standard operating procedures.[5] Once the norms and institutions were in place, they became extraordinarily difficult to alter. As a result, both countries have largely maintained those same basic trade principles of forty years ago. In the absence of another crisis, like World War II or the Great Depression, change in strategic objectives has not been possible. Organizational inertia has persisted in both the United States and Japan, at a time when the original trade strategies of the two countries have become less and less consistent with market and political realities.

THE EMERGENCE OF PAX AMERICANA

During most of the nineteenth and early twentieth centuries, American trade policy was highly protectionist. Like Japanese trade strategy after World War II, the dominant principle was to promote national economic interests by protecting domestic industries and expanding exports. This protectionist-expansionist policy persisted until a severe shock—the collapse of the world economic system in the depression of the early 1930s—forced the United States to reassess its traditional trade philosophy.[6] American leaders found that a 50 percent drop in global exports after 1928 had been surpassed by an even larger decline (66 percent) in U.S. exports. Under these circumstances, most American leaders concluded that the national policy of protecting noncompetitive industries was self-defeating. In 1934 President Franklin D. Roosevelt convinced Congress to grant the executive branch the authority to negotiate tariff reductions by as much as 50 percent on a reciprocal basis.

We now recognize this change as a radical departure in American trade policy; for, from the founding of the Republic until 1934, tariff setting had been the exclusive prerogative of the protectionist-oriented Congress. Henceforth, the executive branch of the U.S. government could legally exercise power over tariffs. While the 1934 Reciprocal Trade Act did not eliminate the influence of special interest groups on trade policy, it significantly reduced the protectionists' power, and allowed the president to take a broader view of America's trade interests.

Yet a truly broad view of American trade strategy did not take hold until after World War II, when the United States emerged as a superpower, militarily strong and economically dominant. During the immediate postwar period,

America accounted for 50 percent of the world's gross national product, more than 30 percent of world trade, and some 70 percent of the world's monetary assets—gold. In its new position of economic leadership, the United States shrugged off all worries about international competition.

Under the spell of these advantages, American leaders formulated their new trading strategy. Operating on the belief that the postwar world had become a "tabula rasa on which can be written the terms of a new democratic order," America's trading strategy was devised as one piece of a larger global plan.[7] Trade was not to be an end in itself. The more important concern was global political and economic stability, not assistance to American firms in maintaining their newly achieved position of dominance. From this larger view, American officials derived two major principles of roughly equal importance: one held that international political interests should dominate purely domestic/national trading interests; the other declared that liberal trade would remain the most desirable long-term outcome for the U.S. market and for the world. To implement these principles, the American government pursued several tactics: (1) using nondiscrimination and the principle of unconditional most favored nation (adopted in 1922) to achieve its goal of freer world trade; (2) sacrificing free trade in specific sectors to appease Congressional pressure while still maintaining momentum for more liberal trade; and (3) continuing the government tradition of refusing to support or promote selected American firms engaged in international trade.[8]

The first principle, that American trade policies be subordinated to broader political goals, has been consistently followed since World War II. During the Cold War, for example, U.S. security objectives led the United States to open its own borders, and allow protectionism in Europe and Japan. Had the United States wished to promote its own exports and maintain American export dominance, it would have used its vast military and economic leverage to lower the tariffs and quotas that plagued world trade in the 1940s and 1950s. Similarly, had the United States blindly followed the prescriptions of classical economics, it would have imposed freer trade as a tool for maximizing global welfare.[9] Instead, the United States waited until Europe and Japan had recovered, and only then did it undertake serious efforts to reduce their formal trade restrictions. By the same token, America's role in the creation of the European Economic Community should be viewed as a service to U.S. political objectives, not American trading interests. The American government supported the EEC, even though the common external tariff would inevitably divert European purchases away from American exports.

The overriding American concern, especially in the 1940s and 1950s, proved to be the spread of American political and military influence—not the expansion of American exports. When the Eisenhower Administration proposed tax incentives to promote overseas investment, it refused to provide similar incentives for export expansion. In principle, American firms manufacturing abroad were good for American foreign policy, but American trade sur-

FIGURE 2-1
Export Licensing Delays for Generally Allowable Technology

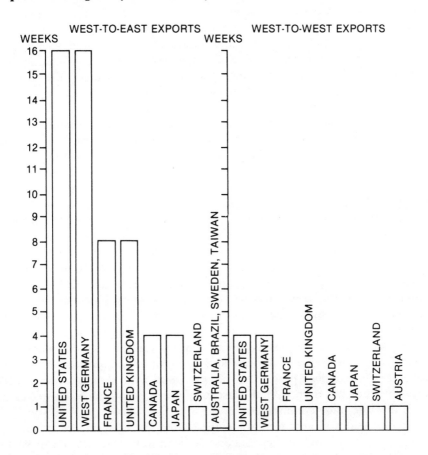

SOURCE: The Report of the President's Commission on Industrial Competitiveness, *Global Competition: The New Reality,* January 1985, Volume 1, p. 43.

pluses were not. Thus, Eisenhower threatened to veto legislation if Congress refused to separate incentives for firms to export capital from incentives to export goods.[10]

A more contemporary example of the dominant role of international politics in American trade policy is U.S. policies toward exports and export controls. The United States (along with West Germany) has maintained tight controls over militarily sensitive exports (see *Figure 2-1*). The precedent for this policy dates from the early years of the Cold War, when American law limited shipments of military-related products to Soviet bloc countries. Over the next thirty-five years, export controls expanded to 100,000 products, without regard for changing economic and business conditions. The American government has adjusted export controls only to accord with current political priorities. Thus, during the period of detente in the early 1970s, controls were loosened; in the tense period of Soviet-American relations in the 1980s, they were tightened. Aside from direct export controls, international politics led the United States to impose numerous other constraints on American exporters. In South America, Africa, and the Middle East, American law has imposed restrictions on U.S. firms in response to allegations concerning unfair boycotts and violations of human rights. In each of these cases, politics have proved to be more important to the United States than trade.

The second building block of America's trading strategy—a preference for freer global trade in the long term—has also shaped the substance of American trade policy since World War II. So long as freer world trade did not conflict with other political objectives, a liberal trading system would be most consistent with America's free market philosophy. Congress, of course, never fully accepted this principle. It refused to consider a powerful International Trade Organization in the 1940s, and for many years it supported protectionist programs such as buy-American provisions for government purchases, peril point laws, and the American Selling Price system. Yet congressional leaders have recognized the potential destructiveness in protectionism. To avoid protectionist pressure from its constituencies, Congress has ceded additional trade authority to the executive branch.[11] Using this authority, successive American presidents have sought freer world trade by committing the United States to lower trade barriers and by providing leadership during the seven rounds of GATT negotiations. The results of these efforts were lower tariffs worldwide and a drop in the average American tariff levels from approximately 20 percent in the 1940s to under 5 percent by the late 1980s. While domestic pressure for protectionism has risen over the last forty years, no president has retreated from this free trade commitment.

Despite its devotion to freer trade, the United States has also been practical in its approach to trade policy. Unconditional most favored nation (MFN), for example, was adopted to implement America's trading strategy because the United States had a negative experience with discriminatory trade policies before World War I. An earlier, conditional MFN worked well enough while the United States was a newcomer in international trade and cared little about political leadership. But as soon as American manufacturers sought to sell in the widest possible markets in the early twentieth century, nondiscrimination was the only sensible policy to avoid retaliation by America's trading partners.[12] In fact, the United States has never been pure in its application of MFN or its pursuit of lower trade barriers. The postwar U.S. policy of unconditional most favored nation, for instance, was never truly "unconditional," because the United States generalized its trade concessions only to signatories of the GATT. Similarly, the executive branch has always been willing to sacrifice free trade in particular sectors, whenever the president was concerned that a politically powerful domestic industry might sabotage his broader political goals. As early as 1956, President Eisenhower departed from his free trade position by negotiating an agreement with Japan to limit exports of textiles to the United States. Eisenhower feared that the textile and apparel industry could threaten the renewal of the Reciprocal Trade Act. And Eisenhower was not alone. Limited sectoral concessions have been made by virtually all subsequent presidents: Kennedy extended protectionism in textiles; Johnson negotiated restrictions in steel; Nixon expanded both textile and steel restraints; Carter added controls on footwear imports; and Reagan protected automobiles.

Yet in each case, the departure from free trade remained industry-specific, and many of the concessions were largely symbolic. When the U.S. government granted import relief, it refused to use traditional tariffs and quotas. Instead, the executive branch employed alternative forms of protectionism, such as voluntary export restraints, orderly marketing agreements, and trigger price systems. Overall, the purpose of these alternatives was political rather than economic; the president moved to satisfy Congress and special domestic interests—not to seal U.S. borders. These "leaky" restrictions allowed the government to maintain its basic strategy without damaging international political relations or severely restricting international trade flows.[13]

A third principle that has guided the implementation of American trade policy has been that the United States should not facilitate special advantages for individual American companies. The general policy decreed that the American government would provide its firms with a relatively even playing field in international trade, but that the government would not give U.S. firms any special aid. Over time, this policy required that U.S. companies learn to fend for themselves in international trade, while the government attempted to keep the playing field of international commerce more or less fair for all nations.

Refusing in principle to assist selected firms has not meant that the U.S. government would abandon American exporters. During the 1970s, for instance, for every $1,000 in American exports, the federal government spent $.56. This assistance included American Export-Import Bank financing and various promotional activities of the Departments of Commerce, State, and the Small Business Administration. The United States also provided limited tax breaks for exporters in the forms of deferred and forgiven taxes on a small percentage of exporting income (i.e., income derived from the Domestic International Sales Corporations of the 1970s and Foreign Sales Corporations of the 1980s). These incentives were not designed to aid particular American firms or to increase American exports; rather they served to offset, at least in part, the much larger advantages enjoyed by America's trade competitors. During the 1970s Japan, for example, spent almost twice as much as the United States on export promotion ($.90), France almost three times ($1.43), and the United Kingdom almost four times ($2.08).[14]

Over time, the strategy and tactics underlying American trade policies slowly made their way into American law and institutions. Once authority for international trade passed from Congress to the executive in 1934, that author-

FIGURE 2-2
Trade Relationships

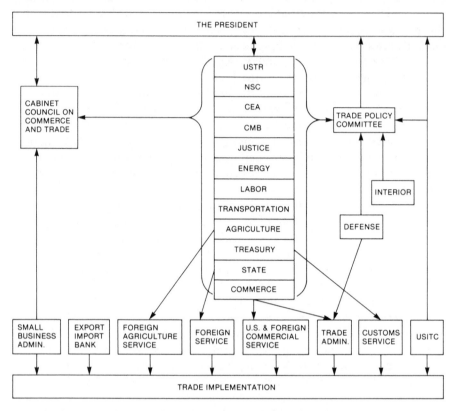

SOURCE: The Report of the President's Commission on Industrial Competitiveness, *Global Competition: The New Reality,* January 1985, Volume 1, p. 40.

ity was soon dispersed throughout the executive branch (see *Figure 2-2*). Since no single entity could determine trade policy (except in agriculture) without wide consultations, protectionist views that might be represented by the Commerce or Labor Departments would always have a free trade counterweight through the representation of the Treasury and State Departments. And even when Congress passed legislation that allowed industries hurt by international competition to petition for protection, the laws generally had an escape clause: the president was empowered to consider the broader "national interest" before he granted any protection. In effect, the practical dispersion of authority weakened the influence of any interest group to challenge the core principles of America's trade strategy.

Once these developments took root, it became extraordinarily difficult to change the substance or direction of America's trade strategy. Bureaucratic inertia has kept the basic trade strategy on course throughout the postwar period. The continuity in strategy, however, has not prevented Congress from altering the process of devising trade policy. Although the executive has acquired greater freedom in implementing American trade policy since World War II, Congress has increasingly demanded that the president become more responsive to industries hurt by international competition. As early as the 1960s, while trade liberalization was moving forward with full force, Congress began insisting on a more balanced trade policy. So, when the Trade Expansion Act of 1962 gave the president unprecedented authority to liberalize trade, it also required that the chief responsibility for international trade policy be shifted from the internationalist-oriented State Department to a new office of the Special Trade Representative (STR). Congress intended STR to be more independent than either the State or Commerce Departments, since STR would answer to no specific domestic or international constituency, but report directly to the president.

The 1974, 1979, and 1984 Trade Acts all reflected Congress's wish for a more balanced trade policy. The 1974 law, for instance, legislated three important changes: it gave the International Trade Commission more independence from the president; it required the president to submit any agreements on reducing nontariff barriers to a majority vote of Congress; and it created an elaborate advisory system to work with the STR in the Multilateral Trade Negotiations. The public purpose of these private sector groups was to give guidance to American negotiators; but Congress also wanted to limit the freedom of the president in reducing tariff and nontariff barriers.[15]

The Trade Act of 1979 and the Trade and Tariff Act of 1984 were probably more significant in their attempts to change the way trade policies were made in the United States. American industries hurt by international competition during the 1970s had complained, with justification, that trade laws were biased against protectionism. Even in cases of illegal dumping or proven subsidies, the trade laws permitted the executive branch to exercise extraordinary discretion and ignore industry pleas. In the late 1960s, for instance, American firms in the color television industry started filing suits against Japanese manufacturers which alleged dumping, illegal subsidies, and injury to American producers. Despite damage to domestic producers and clear evidence that Japanese companies violated American trade laws, the Treasury Department stalled the levying of duties for almost ten years. Concerns over political relations with Japan, ongoing international trade talks (Tokyo Round), and a strong bias in favor of free trade were the major reasons.[16]

The 1979 Trade Act attempted to rectify this bias by transferring authority for dumping and countervailing duty cases from the Treasury to the more protectionist-oriented Commerce Department. Other legal and administrative provisions were also changed to reduce executive branch discretion. Similar alterations in process occurred again in 1984, when Congress gave the president the authority to negotiate "free trade areas" while expanding the president's ability to retaliate against unfair trade practices by America's trading partners. At the same time, Congress directed the International Trade Commission to broaden its criteria for determining whether or not an industry was eligible for import relief.

Together, this broad array of changes in American trade law shifted some of the initiative for American trade policy away from the executive branch and toward American firms and labor organizations. It is now easier for aggrieved parties to appeal for protectionism. Moreover, there is less devotion within the executive branch to the core principles and tactics. Support for free trade areas demonstrates that the United States has become less committed to the MFN concept; and the Commerce Department has imposed a slightly larger number of countervailing duties and anti-dumping duties in recent years. Yet, despite the shift in process and reduced commitments, the substance of trade policy has not significantly changed. While the number of industries filing petitions for import relief climbed from 40 in 1977 to almost 200 in 1984, Presidents Ford, Carter, and Reagan have rejected the same proportion of petitions as their predecessors.[17] Politically powerful industries, such as textiles and steel, continue to receive higher and higher levels of trade barriers, but there is no evidence of any widespread increase in protectionism.

To summarize, the United States' approach to international trade has remained remarkably stable over the last forty years, despite drastic changes in the international and domestic environments, the loss of American hegemony in trade, and substantive alterations in the process of making and implementing trade policy. Since key American leaders have not perceived a crisis in trade, there has been no public consensus in favor of adopting an alternative trade strategy. Of course, American trade policy has not been static: it has protected selected industries and reduced its commitment to nondiscrimination in trade. Yet the United States has continued to sacrifice trading interests for the sake of important political interests. It has not undertaken any serious measures to promote American exports. And, most significantly, the United States has refused to forsake free trade as its overriding goal for its citizens and the world economy.

POSTWAR JAPAN: THE EMERGENCE OF NEO-MERCANTILISM

The most striking feature of America's trade strategy is its contrast with that of Japan. While the United States has focused on international politics and freer world trade since World War II, Japan has been obsessed with the job of building its domestic economy; while the United States dispersed authority for trade throughout its executive branch, Japan concentrated that same power; and while the United States government avoided direct intervention in the affairs of its firms, the Japanese government used its leverage and powers of persuasion to "guide" firms. In short, Japanese and American trade histories could hardly be more different.

Elements of Japanese trade strategy, like parts of the American strategy, can be traced to deep historical roots. While the United States traditionally separated its government's powers and maintained an arm's-length relationship between business and government, Japan in the post–Meiji era (1868 onward) developed a highly concentrated form of national authority and close business-government ties. Yet, these structural and philosophical differences did not in themselves determine the countries' specific trade strategies. For Japan, the nation's extreme political and economic weakness in the late 1940s and early 1950s led its officials to choose a peculiar path. Japan was an occupied nation until 1952, with a per capita GNP below that of Brazil, Malaysia, and Chile; and its weakest sector was international trade.[18] Japan was completely dependent upon importing raw materials, while most industrial nations (excluding the United States) had closed their markets to Japanese manufactured goods. Under these conditions, the Japanese had few choices: to escape from their poverty they would have to gain access to foreign markets. The international political concerns that dominated American trade interests represented a luxury which the Japanese could not afford. Domestic economic considerations had to come first.

The strategy that followed from this extreme situation was simple: the Japanese had to promote manufactured exports. Promotion was to be accomplished by political and economic means, and with macro as well as micro policies. Unlike Japan's prewar trade strategy, military means were now excluded; and unlike U.S. government officials, Japanese officials believed that their firms could not necessarily fend for themselves in international trade. So the Japanese government adopted a second principle of providing guidance for individual firms whenever it seemed necessary.[19] The only major exception to this strategy was the same exception that applied in the United States— agriculture, a subject treated in a subsequent chapter of this book. Domestic political considerations of the ruling Liberal Democratic Party dominated agricultural trade policy, while economic considerations dominated trade in goods and services.

Promoting manufactured exports meant several things to Japanese officials. First, it required that the government achieve and maintain access to foreign markets. Without places to sell their goods, the trading strategy would be worthless. Second, the Japanese needed to improve the competitiveness of their products. This would be done through industrial policy, capital controls, and protectionism. Here, import barriers were not an end in themselves, but instead a form of encouragement for building competitive industries, especially manufacturing industries that could only become competitive with large-scale economies and experience. Third, the government would facilitate export expansion whenever necessary by providing various tax and monetary incentives. As early as the mid-1950s, the Japanese were pursuing all three objectives with great success.

To open foreign markets, Japan's principal tool has been to rely on the United States.[20] Indeed, during the 1950s and early 1960s, the United States was instrumental in opening European markets to Japanese products as well as helping Japan gain admittance to international organizations such as the OECD and the GATT. Overall, then, American policy has not only opened the lucrative United States market, but, in multilateral trade negotiations, has also been critical to expanding Japan's potential markets elsewhere.

Japan has always been practical and largely non-ideological with regard to protectionism in foreign markets. "Managed" trade was no panacea, but the Japanese have long been willing to reduce exports if they were convinced that foreign governments would unilaterally restrict Japanese goods. Since 1955, Japan has been offering voluntary export arrangements to its trading partners in return for continued market access.[21]

The most controversial Japanese trade policies have been import protectionism, industrial policy, and practices toward exchange rates and international investment. All of these policies sought to promote competitive industries: import restrictions sheltered infant industries during their periods of initial growth; capital controls limited foreign direct investment; industrial policies helped to rationalize capacity; and exchange rate policies facilitated favorable export prices. However, as Japanese firms have become more competitive, each of these policies has played a reduced role. Capital controls have continued to restrict certain forms of direct investment, and nontariff trade barriers have continued to be a major impediment to imports. Nonetheless, formal import restrictions have been substantially reduced: in 1982, average tariffs on industrial and mining products entering Japan were lower than American tariffs; at the same time, only five manufactured products were protected by quantitative restrictions.[22] Japan has also reduced import barriers (in products it did not wish to promote) at a faster rate and to lower levels than those typical of most industrial countries.[23]

Industrial policy, which was a critical part of Japanese success in the early postwar years, has proved to be less significant during the 1970s and 1980s.[24] Some key tools of Japan's early industrial policy, such as import licenses and exchange controls, have been entirely phased out. And finally, exchange rate policy (treated elsewhere in this volume) also became less significant. It was much easier for Japan to maintain an undervalued yen during the Bretton Woods regime of the 1950s and 1960s. Under the floating rate regime of the 1970s and early 1980s, it has been more difficult for Japan to manage its exchange rate, and less essential to success in promoting Japanese exports.

A similar pattern of policies can be seen in Japan's use of export promotion measures. During the 1950s and 1960s, Japan spun an impressive web of monetary and fiscal incentives to promote exports: financing by the Export-Import Bank of Japan, export insurance through MITI, below-market export credits from commercial banks, and a wide array of tax advantages that favored exporters over domestic producers.[25] Exports of capital for direct investment also were controlled as a way of preserving Japanese capital for domestic expenditure and insuring that exports of goods would be emphasized over foreign direct investment. Since the mid-1960s, however, Japan has reduced its export benefits and relaxed capital controls. Trade and finance officials felt that both forms of promotion have lost most of their usefulness. The Japanese Ministry of Finance, for example, calculated that one-quarter of the government's special taxation measures for enterprises in 1960 were devoted to promoting exports, which resulted in lost revenues of 11 billion yen. While Japan has continued to employ many export incentives, by 1975 the government had shifted all of its special tax advantages (300 billion yen) to favor domestic projects. Government officials believed that Japanese companies no longer needed extra incentives to ship their products abroad.[26]

Japan's second principle, that of providing guidance to individual firms, played a critical role in organizing the external trading sector. Following the dissolution of Japan's prewar combinations—the *zaibatsu*—Japan's foreign trade sector was highly fragmented. Since most of Japan's export markets were not in East Asia, this fragmentation meant that few Japanese companies would have the necessary scale and expertise to sell effectively abroad. Promoting exports, therefore, required redefining the entire exporting sector. For Japanese officials of the time, the most efficient way to achieve that objective was to concentrate power. First, the government would play a vital role in fostering Japan's general trading companies: providing aid to commercial banks that facilitated the mergers of trading companies; allocating scarce foreign exchange to favored trading firms; and giving large trading companies special tax treatment to expand exports.[27] Second, the Japanese government created export cartels whenever access to foreign markets seemed threatened. As mentioned above, Japan has always been willing to negotiate voluntary export arrangements as a way to maintain market access; but unless either the government or industry could allocate market shares among firms, such export quotas could not function.

Gradually, the two principles of Japanese trade strategy became institutionalized in Japan's trade bureaucracy and law. As in the United States, structure followed strategy; but the Japanese, unlike the Americans, devised a trading strategy which required great centralization of government power. Furthermore, while trade initiatives in the United States grew out of the office of the president, trade policy in Japan usually originated within the professional trade bureaucracy. This meant that bureaucratic decisions, especially the decisions of the Ministry of International Trade and Industry (MITI), assumed the utmost importance. Although MITI did not have exclusive authority in any field (it was obliged to consult with other ministries, such as the Ministry of Finance on tax matters, the Ministry of Foreign Affairs on international trade relations, or the Fair Trade Commission on mergers and cartels), MITI had sweeping legal and political authority to implement the official government trade strategy.[28]

Early in the postwar period, MITI could devise trade policy without a broad consensus from other ministries; after consulting with industry representatives, MITI would set policy and implement it with the substantial tools at its disposal, especially its power to allocate import licenses and foreign exchange under the Foreign Exchange and Foreign Trade Control Law of 1949. As Japan became more successful in international trade, however, MITI's formal authority waned. Since the late 1960s, companies became less dependent on MITI for exporting and importing; and the Japanese Diet and Japanese courts reduced MITI's legal authority. MITI itself dismantled some of its own statutory powers in 1979 by asking the Japanese Diet to revise the Foreign Exchange and Foreign Trade Control Act. The revision, which changed the language on imports from "prohibition in principle" to "freedom in principle," acknowledged that in the world of the 1980s, extensive import protectionism was incompatible with promoting Japanese exports.

While the Japanese Diet has weakened MITI's legal authority over trade policy, MITI has maintained considerable power. Some laws, such as the 1952 Export and Import Trading Act, have continued to give MITI the authority to form export cartels on prices, quantity, quality specifications, and the like.[29] Also, MITI's close working relationship with big business has allowed MITI officials to offer informal guidance on trade matters. The formal weakening of centralized authority, however, has made the formulation of Japanese trade policy more difficult. As more voices are heard, consensus has required longer, more arduous discussions with various ministries and industry representatives. As a result, major decisions on trade issues can be held up for months.[30] As a former vice minister of MITI admitted, the Japanese prime minister may want to reduce Japanese exports or liberalize imports, "but in reality he can move only at a very slow pace. He always has to muddle through the politically murky waters of the Liberal Democratic Party (LDP)."[31] And while the American president is usually surrounded by his national security advisers and free-trade-oriented Secretaries from Treasury and State, the prime minister has had to rely upon "the Liberal Democratic Party's elder politicians, and some of them are very protectionist."[32] Only in periods of clearly perceived crisis—usually externally caused—has the Japanese bureaucracy been willing to move quickly on foreign trade matters.[33]

From time to time, these institutional problems have complicated Japan's trading strategy. While Japanese leaders have explicitly stated their desire to improve the welfare of their citizens and reduce political tensions, it has nonetheless taken years to reduce formal trade barriers.[34] Many old import barriers have remained in place through the early 1980s—despite changes in official trade policies announced in 1977 and supposedly enacted in 1978. Many of these barriers no longer function as vital parts of the trade strategy to promote exports; rather, they have remained as vestiges of bureaucratic power and of the country's industrial organization, especially cartels and enterprise groupings that date from the 1950s.[35] Despite a plethora of official pronouncements declaring liberalization of the Japanese market (see *Table 2-1*) and claims that government policy has deemphasized exports and encouraged more direct investment abroad, Japan has yet to offer strong incentives for an alternative to the original postwar program.[36]

TABLE 2-1
Examples of Japanese Import Liberalization Measures

	Economic Measures for Foreign Trade (December 16, 1981)	Market-opening Measures (May 28, 1982)	Promotion of Urgent Economic Measures for Foreign Trade (January 13, 1983)
1. Reduction or abolition of custom tariffs	Government accelerates by two years all tariff cuts agreed to at the Tokyo Round negotiations.	Tariff reduction on an additional 17 agricultural products and 198 industrial products.	Tariff lowered or abolished on 47 agricultural products and 28 industrial products in addition to tobacco products, chocolate, and biscuits.
2. Easing of import restrictions	Review of residual import-restricted items.	Import quotas raised for herring, pork products, high-test molasses, and canned pineapple.	Import restrictions eased for beans, peas, peanuts, fruit puree, paste, non-citrus fruit juice, tomato juice, tomato ketchup, and sauce.
3. Reform of import inspection procedure	Government reviews import inspection procedures to make inspection procedures more appropriate.	Customs clearance and import formalities made simpler and speedier. Openness and clarity ensured in the formation of standards and criteria.	Liaison and Coordination Headquarters established for discussions on the standards and certification systems.
4. Import promotion measures	Emergency foreign currency lending for import. Stockpiling promoted. Import mission sent overseas to promote additional imports.	Continued implementation of emergency currency lending for import. Promotion of exports of Alaskan oil and other products to Japan.	Distribution of foreign tobacco products further encouraged. Efforts made to expand imports to manufactured goods.

SOURCE: Adapted from Japan External Trade Organization, *White Paper on International Trade*, 1983. p. 60.

In sum, Japan's trading strategy, like America's has remained fundamentally the same since the 1950s. While Japan has abolished several of its obsolete trade policies, it has nonetheless resisted serious change. It has not become a liberal trading state with a truly open market; nor has it become an active leader in international trade relations. Japan has continued to promote exports in high-priority industries via import protection and industrial policy; it has continued to weigh economic objectives more heavily than political consider- ations; and it has continued to employ selective trade measures to assist pre- ferred industries and firms.

II: Comparative Trade Performance

Japan and the United States both devised international trade strategies dur- ing one of the most dynamic periods of world commerce. Not only had the volume of international trade exploded out of the depths of the Depression, but the very structure of international trade had undergone a radical transfor- mation. Throughout the nineteenth century and the first half of the twentieth century, the majority of international trade was in commodities: countries exported raw materials and food to promote the industrial revolution.[37] Manu- factured exports remained secondary, even for the United States, where indus- trial exports did not exceed raw material and food-related shipments until 1936.[38] After World War II, however, manufactured goods quickly assumed a new strategic role in international trade. Whereas in 1938, manufactured ex- ports represented only 46 percent of world exports, by 1948 they had grown to 54 percent. At the time of the first oil crisis of 1973, manufactured goods accounted for 61 percent of international trade.[39] And even though raw mate- rials and agricultural exports have grown faster than manufactures in dollar terms during the past decade, manufactured exports have continued to out- strip all other products in terms of volume.

The performance of the United States and Japan in international trade can be measured, in part, against this background. Both countries have been major players in the world economy, but they have not been equally successful in managing these revolutionary changes in world trade. The American strategy provided U.S. firms with fewer incentives and more disincentives to promote industrial exports, compared to their Japanese counterparts. One result is that Japanese firms have far outperformed most of their American competitors in international trade since the 1950s. America's long-term export strength has been in those few areas that have benefited from government support (aero- space and agriculture) and in industries that had sufficient market power to thrive on their own (certain high-technology sectors and services). In contrast, Japan's export strengths have been far more dynamic. The Japanese first ex- panded in labor-intensive sectors (textiles and consumer goods), then moved into heavy industry (steel and autos) and most recently into higher-technology goods (semiconductors and telecommunications).

One cannot automatically attribute to government policy the sole cause of

Japanese and American trade performance, as the following pages will show. It is possible that companies, for competitive or other reasons, would have achieved the same results in international trade regardless of their governments' strategies. Nonetheless, a compelling argument can be made that companies in both Japan and the United States pursued business strategies that were strongly consistent with the incentives set by their national governments.

THE UNITED STATES IN WORLD TRADE

From a macro perspective, America's trade position in the world has declined dramatically since World War II. In 1950, as we have seen, the United States dominated world markets for goods and services: it supplied 20 percent of total world exports, almost 30 percent of world manufactures, and 50 percent or more of many capital goods and other manufactured products. The unchallenged position of the United States was signified by the $24 billion in international reserves (32 percent of the world total) it had accumulated from its huge surpluses on its current account. By the early 1980s, however, the U.S. position in world trade had deteriorated severely. Even though the United States remained the world's largest exporter, American exports had dropped to between 13 and 15 percent of world trade, America's share of world manufactures had fallen as low as 13 percent (see *Figure 2-3*), and a decade of trade deficits and other current account problems had shrunk America's international reserves to only 6 percent of world reserves. The American trade deficit for 1984 of almost $120 billion was a new record for world trade, amounting to twice the deficit recorded by the United States in 1983 (see *Figure 2-4*). Overall, widespread weakness characterized the American trade position; the United States lost market share to international competitors in every major industrial category, and was in a deficit position with every major trade bloc in the world (see *Figure 2-5*).

Undoubtedly, some of this decline in America's trade position was impossible to avoid and was even desirable: the industrial nations of Europe and Japan would inevitably regain some of the world market share lost to the United States after they recovered from the effects of the Second World War. Some of the decline also can be traced to monetary and fiscal policies which reduced incentives for investment and savings, in turn producing an overvalued dollar and weakening the competitiveness of American goods.[40] A final, and very substantial portion of the overall decline in America's trade performance should be attributed to America's trade strategy.[41]

The most direct impact of U.S. trade strategy on performance has been in the areas of export licensing and export financing. Adherence to the principle that political/strategic concerns are the highest priority has placed American firms at a disadvantage. Between 1978 and 1985, for instance, the Department of State—citing political reasons—rejected export licenses for $520 million in equipment already under contract to Libya. The General Accounting Office

FIGURE 2-3
Export Share, U.S. Share of World Manufacturing Exports

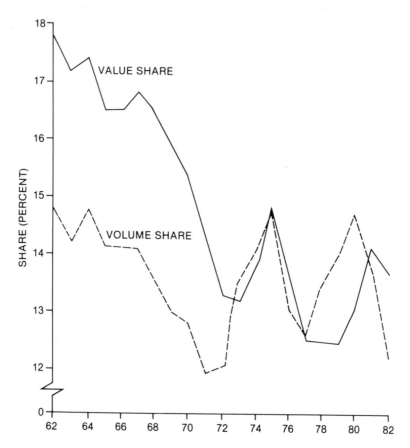

SOURCE: The Report of the President's Commission on Industrial Competitiveness, p. 170.

estimated that a total of $1.2 billion in related contracts were lost to North Africa alone—contracts which the French (among other American allies) proved willing to fulfill.[42] While the measurable impact of these policies is small in relation to total U.S. trade, government denial of export licenses has sometimes severely affected whole American industries. Problems with export licenses seriously injured the sales of American nuclear power reactors, whose share of world trade declined from 100 percent in 1972 to 17 percent in 1977.[43]

Meanwhile, the desire for open borders, the second pillar of U.S. trade strategy, encouraged the rapid growth in imports that provided intense competition for many American industries in their home market. Not since the

FIGURE 2-4
U.S. Balances on Merchandise, Services, and Current Account

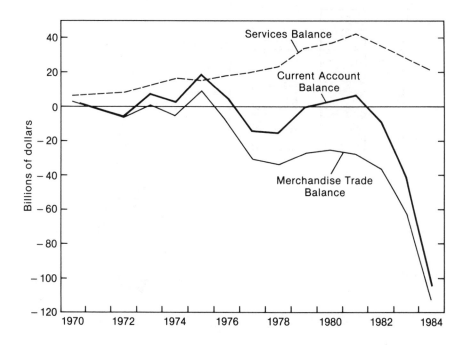

[1] First three quarters at annual rate; seasonally adjusted.
SOURCE: U.S. Department of Commerce.

1920s in fact, has overall American import policy aimed at promoting emerging native industries. Its objective has been to maximize consumer welfare
while providing protection only as a last resort. And even when protectionism
was granted to politically powerful industries, American trade restrictions
have been so "leaky" that they have increased the U.S. trade deficit rather than
reduced it! The largest industrial sectors protected by the U.S. government in
the postwar period have been textiles, steel, and automobiles. When the
United States started restricting textile imports in 1956, total imports
amounted to $156 million (2 percent of the domestic market); after 28 years
of continuous protectionism, textile and apparel imports amounted to $13
billion (almost 40 percent of the market).[44] In steel, restrictions on imports
began in 1968, and, even discounting for short interruptions in protectionism,
imports grew from 16 percent of the market to 26 percent in 1984—
contributing $10 billion to the U.S. trade deficit. Again, in automobiles, the

FIGURE 2-5
U.S. Trade Balances* with Major Trading Blocs

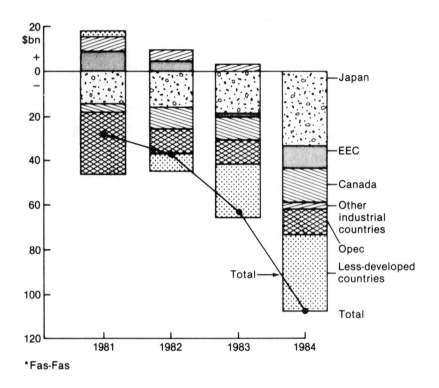

*Fas-Fas

SOURCE: U.S. Department of Commerce.

United States restricted Japanese cars between 1981 and 1985; yet, during those years, Japanese auto exports to the U.S. grew from $8.8 billion to almost $13 billion.

Indirect consequences of America's trading strategy on U.S. firms have also been important. Since part of the American strategy was to provide little special assistance to facilitate American exports, the U.S. government sponsored relatively few official trade missions, provided few tax advantages, gave little preferential export financing, and offered a relatively small number of direct subsidies for nonagricultural, nondefense exports. The U.S. trade promotion budget for all American embassies, trade centers, and agencies was around one-third of the budgets of Japan and France, and one-quarter of the United Kingdom's. As a result, small American firms generally had less incentive to export than did their counterparts overseas. In fact, American companies have generally viewed exports as a means for disposing of excess domestic capacity—not as an important corporate goal, nor as a permanent market.[45] Furthermore, the tax benefits for overseas *investment* (originally proposed by Eisenhower in the 1950s) have become an important factor promoting exports of capital over exports of goods.[46] For large American companies, these tax advantages can be substantial—large enough to alter calculations of after-tax profits, and thus encourage a corporate strategy of foreign lending or direct investment rather than export. In fact, the strong positive balance on the United States service account, which is mostly comprised of repatriated earnings of American corporations overseas and interest on bank loans, is largely a reflection of the American bias against exporting goods.

JAPAN IN WORLD TRADE

America's relative decline in international trade contrasts sharply with Japan's rapid rise. In 1950, Japan had only one percent of world exports, less than 3 percent of world manufactures, and negligible international reserves. Of course, Japan was a "follower" in world trade, which meant that it was less difficult for the Japanese to increase their share of world markets compared to the United States. But even so, by the 1980s Japan had gone far beyond the expected gains of "catch-up": its share of world trade had grown almost eight-fold, its share of manufactures had increased to almost 15 percent; and Japan's stock of international reserves had grown to be ranked among the top five in the world. While the industrial world as a whole experienced widening trade deficits in the wake of OPEC's rise, Japan's trade account (fob) remained in surplus in nearly every year since 1964 (see *Figure 2-6*).[47]

Much of Japan's success has come at the expense of the United States. One look at the growing bilateral trade deficit, which reached $36 billion in 1984 and actually rose to almost $50 billion in 1985 (see *Figure 2-7*) would reveal this trend. Even more telling, however, is that Japanese goods have displaced American products in most third-country markets. One careful study of U.S.-Japanese competition found that almost one-half of the losses in America's share of third markets was directly attributable to Japan; a conclusion which held in almost all industrial sectors.[48]

Japan's success in international trade is the result of many things, such as good business management, sound industrial policy, and Japan's effective trading strategy. When considering the latter, the Japanese government has been very successful in securing market access for its industries, despite the fact that Japan is the target of greater protectionism than any other country in the world. Furthermore, Japanese trade policies succeeded in organizing the country's trading sector and promoting the export of goods over capital. The ten largest general trading companies accounted for over 50 percent of total exports and 75 percent of total imports through the mid-1970s.[49] Finally, prior to the late 1970s, Japanese investment overseas remained low, thus helping to achieve a very high ratio of exports to domestic and foreign production.

When one looks at the import side of Japanese trade, another clear pattern emerges: manufactured imports represent only a small percentage of total

FIGURE 2-6
Changes in the Structure of Japan's Current Account
(Yearly Averages in Billions of Dollars)

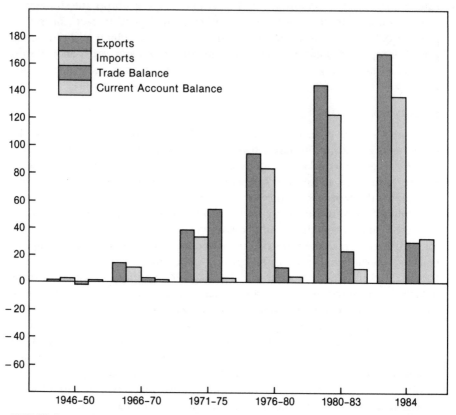

SOURCE: Jetro. *White Paper on International Trade,* 1984; *Economic Report of the President,* 1984.

imports, and that percentage has grown smaller. In fact, compared to any other major industrial country, Japan's share of manufactured imports was consistently between one-half and one-third of the level of its competitors (see *Figure 2-8*). These striking numbers, however, are not necessarily the result of Japanese trade policies alone. Japan's absolute advantage in many industrial product areas and its unique industrial organization could also play an important part in creating this unusual national trade pattern.[50] However, Japan's explicit trade strategy to protect high priority industrial sectors cannot be discounted.

Some of the *weaknesses* in Japan's trade performance may also be traced to its trade strategy. Japan's trade in services, for instance, has persistently been in deficit—a deficit which more than doubled in the last decade, from $4.3

FIGURE 2-7
U.S.–Japan Bilateral Trade, 1980–1985
(in billions of dollars, f.a.s./customs)

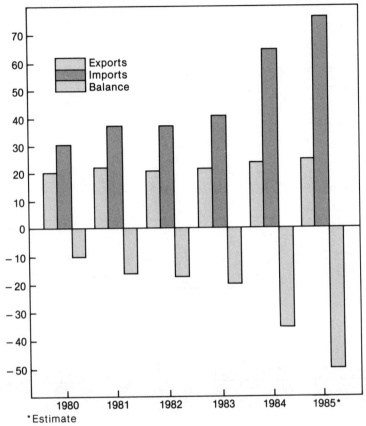

*Estimate

SOURCE: *Business America,* November 12, 1984.

billion in 1973 to $9.3 billion in 1982.[51] The primary reason for this deficit was Japan's one-sided emphasis on expanding exports of goods. In shipping, Japan's payments outweighed its receipts because Japanese ships unloaded far more products in foreign ports (paying foreign port fees) than foreign ships unloaded in Japanese ports. Almost 20 percent of Japan's services deficit was derived from expenses incurred through overseas sales networks that were designed to promote exports of Japanese goods.[52] And Japan's long-standing policy of buying foreign technologies rather than importing foreign goods has led to high royalty payments.

In sum, the trade strategies of both the United States and Japan have significantly influenced their relative trade performances. In a world where manufacturing trade has come to play a more significant role in international

FIGURE 2-8
Share of Manufactured Goods in Total Imports

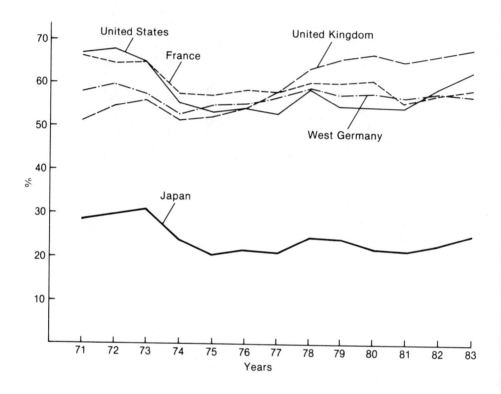

SOURCES: Gary R. Saxonhouse, "Foreign Sales to Japan," in William Cline, ed., *Trade Policy in the 1980s* (Cambridge, Mass.: MIT Press, 1983); *U.N. International Trade Statistics,* 1982; U.S. Department of Commerce, *International Economic Indicators,* September 1984.

competition, Japan has sharply improved its comparative position, while the United States has declined relative to its major competitors. Yet the political and economic efficacy of these trade strategies has increasingly been questioned by both Japan and the United States. Rising protectionism in world markets and changing dynamics of business-government relations in both countries have presented new, special challenges for each nation. The ability of Japan to continue its superlative performance and the ability of the United States to reverse its dismal trade fortunes will depend on how well their governments and firms manage their internal strains as well as the growing external threat. These topics will be explored below.

III: The Trade Environment of the 1980s

As noted earlier, the steady lowering of tariff and quantitative restrictions during the 1950s and 1960s encouraged the overall growth of international trade. Healthy growth in the world economy, combined with technological advances, reduced transportation costs, and improved communications, all helped to create greater confidence in the global trading system. In this climate of reduced uncertainty and newly perceived opportunities, increasing numbers of business executives in many different countries sought to stimulate their foreign sales.[53] However, the supply shocks of the 1970s—the tenfold increase in the price of oil and wide variations in other commodity prices—brought to an end the growing confidence in world markets. After twenty years of virtually uninterrupted expansion, trade suddenly became erratic. During the decade prior to the first oil crisis in 1973, the volume of world exports grew at an average annual rate of 8.5 percent; during the next decade, the volume of international trade swung between a decline of 3.0 percent and growth of 11 percent; the overall average was less than 3.5 percent (see *Figure 2-9*).[54]

The early 1980s proved an especially difficult time for international trade. The deep global recession of 1981 and 1982, surplus capacity in many industries, the frantic restructuring of Third World debt, and problems associated with exchange rate fluctuations all served to stimulate global demands for protection.[55] In addition, the divergent trade performances of individual nations—huge deficits of the United States and some European countries in contrast with the enormous surplus of Japan—brought fresh cries for new trade barriers.

There was an irony behind all this: on the one hand, growing protectionism was an attempt by national governments to regulate international economic activity; but on the other hand, the same governments had begun to deregulate their domestic economic activity. Most industrial countries in recent years have publicly reaffirmed their confidence in the marketplace as the most efficient allocator of resources. The conservative revolutions in the United States, the United Kingdom, Scandinavia, and elsewhere have sharply reversed the interventionist trend of the 1960s and 1970s toward more regulation of business; but protectionism too is ultimately a type of regulation, which attempts to control market competition by regulating the price or quantity of goods entering a nation.[56] Hence, the increasing confidence in domestic markets did not produce a parallel reaction in global markets. On the contrary, declining confidence in the efficiency and equity of global markets, together with the growing conviction that other nations were no longer playing by the same rules of the game, amplified demands for more regulation of international trade flows.

FIGURE 2-9
Growth of World Trade and Output

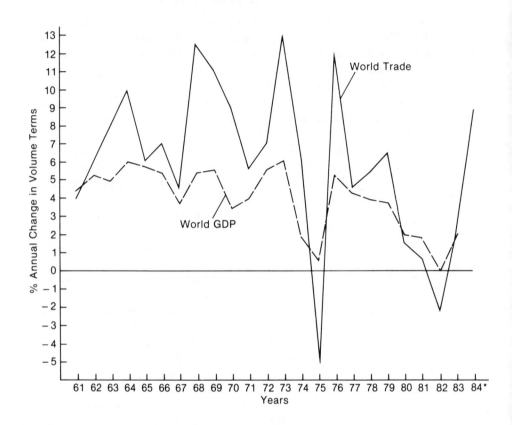

* Estimate

SOURCES: IMF, *Directory of Trade Statistics Yearbook,* 1984.
         IMF, *International Financial Statistics,* 1984.

Although the types of restrictions employed by national governments varied greatly, two generalizations can be made: First, modern protectionism has drifted away from traditional tariff barriers, which have been circumscribed by the GATT, toward nontariff barriers, such as voluntary export restraints, increased domestic subsidies, and more rigorous implementation of anti-dumping laws and countervailing duties. The overall effect of these political and legalistic restrictions has been to heighten uncertainty in trade relations among nations.[57] Second, there have been growing demands for reciprocity in international trade. Governments have been moving beyond previous requests for equal tariff treatment, and have been insisting instead on bilaterally balanced trade. This trend toward reciprocity has been evident in the growing popularity of "countertrade," where buying nations have linked their purchases of a good or service to a seller's willingness to reciprocate. We have also witnessed this phenomenon in the United States, where more than thirty bills were introduced into the 97th U.S. Congress demanding reciprocal access to foreign markets, usually measured by equal bilateral trade flows. In Europe, too, nations have increasingly insisted that markets be shared and that trade become more bilaterally balanced, especially with Japan.[58]

Estimates of the total size and impact of protectionism remain notoriously unreliable, but most scholars, business executives, and policymakers agree that trade restrictions now affect very significant portions of world trade. In the area of nontariff barriers, for instance, one scholar suggested that industrial nations were regulating almost 18 percent of their manufactured imports in 1981 compared to 4 percent in 1974.[59] Others have argued that since 1981 restrictions have expanded even further; in 1985, as much as one-third of all manufactured goods being imported in the United States and Europe were restricted by voluntary export restraints and other quantitative barriers. And while Japan has few overt barriers to trade, it uses numerous covert barriers to serve the same purpose.[60] In the area of countertrade and other reciprocity requirements, the numbers are difficult to ascertain. Yet the popular press has suggested that countertrade may have been as high as 30 percent of world trade in the early 1980s, amounting to $600–$700 billion, and the GATT has estimated that countertrade represented at least 8 percent of world exports, or $160 billion in 1984.

IV: The Japanese and American Trade Challenge

Regardless of the precise extent of global protectionism, it is clear that trade issues have become a serious matter for every nation. During the late 1980s and 1990s, governments and firms alike will be confronted with a set of challenges much different from those of the 1950s, 1960s, and 1970s. For the United States and Japan, this external challenge has special significance. The trade strategies of both nations were premised upon a common goal: the progressive lowering of barriers worldwide, to produce ever freer trade. Japan's great success would not have been possible under any other conditions. To preserve a free trade environment, one might therefore expect the Japanese to provide greater access to their home market and substantively change their established trade policies. Similarly for the United States, the promise of expanding markets abroad was essential to maintaining its domestic political coalition for an open market at home.[61] In addition, while the American people generally supported freer trade in the 1950s and 1960s, public opinion has shifted increasingly in favor of protectionism: a 1985 poll found that 70 percent of Americans supported the idea of limiting imports, and 60 percent continued to believe it was a good idea even if it meant less choice for Americans.[62] Clearly the combination of weakening public support for free trade, the huge trade deficit, and a widespread perception of closed foreign markets should be a powerful incentive for a new American trade strategy.

Still, as we have seen, neither the United States nor Japan has made fundamental changes. In the United States, the trade deficits and the decline of the American position in world markets have not been widely perceived to be problems attributable to an inadequate trade strategy. Instead, the prevailing opinion among both academic economists and government policymakers fixes the blame on exchange rate misalignment or domestic monetary and fiscal policies.[63] Moreover, the re-emergence during the 1980s of a Cold War climate in political relations with the Soviet Union has reinforced the old claim of priority for strategic imperatives over trading interests.

In Japan, it has been equally hard to convince national leaders to alter a winning strategy, despite a general recognition that foreign protectionism may be a real problem. Official Japanese documents have been ringing with proclamations of a new trade approach, but in fact there has been little substantive action.[64] From the perspective of Japanese firms, the traditional practices of sourcing from Japanese suppliers and exporting from the home base has continued to work well in many industries. As long as there is no serious backlash against Japanese exports, as long as Japanese firms remain competitive, and as long as the Japanese government offers relatively few incentives for its firms to increase purchases of foreign goods or invest more heavily abroad, substantial change in corporate or national trade strategy seems unnecessary.

The ability of the Japanese government to successfully manage foreign protectionism has further strengthened resistance to change. Japanese public opinion polls showed strong support for the government on this issue. Most Japanese citizens felt that Japan was being used as a scapegoat in international trade, and that Japanese surpluses resulted from overpriced and poor quality foreign goods, rather than overly aggressive or unfair Japanese trade practices.[65] In fact, external protectionism targeted at Japan has sometimes had the paradoxical effect of increasing bureaucratic incentives to maintain the old strategy of export promotion. When foreign governments or legislative entities in the United States or the European Economic Community have negotiated restrictions on Japanese exports, MITI has invoked the 1952 Export and Import Trading Act to allocate export licenses and form export cartels. At a time when MITI has been losing formal authority, external protectionism has allowed this government agency to regain influence over Japanese firms. In other words, in the absence of trade frictions, MITI's power is reduced; while in the presence of trade frictions which are generated by an export promotion strategy, its powers are often enhanced!

FORCES OF CHANGE: JAPAN

Powerful inertial forces have continued to push the United States and Japan along in continuity with their past strategies. However, other forces have produced changes on the margin of government and corporate strategies. In

Japan, subtle shifts have been underway in the business-government relationship that could have important implications for the future. Historically, Japan relied on a relationship of mutual dependence between business and government. In the early postwar period, that dependence was largely asymmetrical in favor of MITI and the Ministry of Finance (MOF). Firms needed MITI's and MOF's assistance and cooperation if they were to get access to import licenses, technology, and capital. The success of Japan's trade and industrial strategy, however, has reversed much of this dependence. Many large Japanese firms have developed independent sources of capital, either from internally generated funds (e.g., Toyota) or from Eurocurrency markets (e.g., Hitachi, especially since the early 1980s), which have given them greater financial freedom. Specifically in the area of trade, MITI has less formal authority and its advice carries less weight with firms. Especially in high-technology industries, where Japanese firms are at the cutting edge, MITI is itself highly dependent upon Japanese firms for information about industry trends, production, and competitive dynamics.

One important result of this shift in mutual dependence is that firms, especially the largest ones, have become less subservient to MITI guidance. When corporate objectives conflict with MITI's advice on international trade, firms have been more willing to follow an independent course. The following account of Japan's trade conflict with Indonesia in 1982 illustrates this trend.

INDONESIAN COUNTERTRADE

In December 1981, Indonesia issued a new set of regulations that required all foreign companies selling more than $775,000 (U.S.) worth of merchandise to the Indonesian government to facilitate the export of an equivalent amount of Indonesian goods. The original projections made in early 1982 were that three to five billion dollars per year in government purchases would have a countertrade component. Compared to most other countertrade policies, the Indonesian approach seemed especially onerous: foreign sellers were not only subject to a 100 percent counterpurchase requirement; they also faced a 50 percent penalty for noncompliance. In addition, counterpurchased Indonesian goods would have to be "incremental" sales—i.e., shipped to *new* markets or be above historical levels to traditional markets. Finally, oil and natural gas products, Indonesia's largest exports, were excluded from the list of potential counterpurchase products.

From one perspective, Japan appeared to be the country best positioned to manage this new protectionist policy: the Japanese general trading companies (*sōgō shōsha*) were capable of handling a greater variety of goods than most other firms in the world. However, Indonesia was one of the few countries that historically ran a substantial trade surplus with Japan—almost nine billion dollars in 1981. This made incremental purchases from Indonesia to Japan extraordinarily difficult for the *sōgō shōsha*, especially since oil was excluded.

MITI therefore called a meeting of the eleven largest trading companies to formulate a response to Indonesia. All the companies were asked to provide detailed reports of their business dealings in Indonesia as well as an assessment of how they would be affected by the new policy. According to various reports of this meeting and successive ones, there was a great deal of debate and disagreement among the *sōgō shōsha* and between the *sōgō shōsha* and MITI.[66] The trading firms all opposed the Indonesian policy, but the smaller traders, in particular, wanted the government to exert its maximum influence to force Indonesia to back down. Senior management in these smaller firms wanted the Japanese government to threaten a cutback in its foreign aid or reduce Japanese purchases of Indonesian products. This hard line did not appeal to MITI, which proposed a two-tracked strategy: first, it would apply diplomatic pressure; and second, MITI asked the *sōgō shōsha* to form a united front against Indonesian countertrade. No firm was supposed to bid on an Indonesian project that included the 100 percent countertrade requirement. The hope was that if all the Japanese traders refused to do countertrade, the Indonesians might back down.

During the first six months of 1982, the Indonesian government's policy seemed to be failing. Not one contract was signed that met the countertrade terms. But on August 10, 1982, the Indonesians announced that ten companies, including Japan's largest *sōgō shōsha*, Mitsubishi, had agreed to perform 100 percent countertrade as part of a $127 million fertilizer tender.[67] MITI (as well as most of Mitsubishi's competitors) was distressed by Mitsubishi's action. But Mitsubishi defended itself. According to the firm's own account, it did not feel obliged to follow MITI's recommendation: despite the views of some of its competitors, Mitsubishi did not take seriously the united front against countertrade. Instead, Mitsubishi saw an important opportunity in Indonesia, which company managers felt would be "foolish" to give up. MITI, however, remained dissatisfied, and after another series of meetings, it arranged a new unambiguous consensus that no further countertrade tenders would be submitted.

In many ways, Mitsubishi was a uniquely powerful firm in Japan. As a matter of policy, Mitsubishi was virtually the only large Japanese business that did not hire retired bureaucrats; moreover, it had also ignored MITI administrative guidance before, in signing a joint venture agreement with Chrysler in the 1960s.[68] Yet Mitsubishi's independent actions were also symptomatic of the declining dependence upon government felt by many Japanese companies involved in international trade. In several industries, firms have tried to distance themselves from MITI's control by adopting independent business strategies for dealing with growing protectionism. In consumer electronics, for instance, major manufacturers of videotape recorders (VTRs) began setting up European production facilities in anticipation of potential trade barriers and export controls by MITI.[69] Similarly, in telecommunications, companies such as NEC and Fujitsu have set up production in the United States to insure their future presence in the American market. In some cases, of course, direct investments by NEC, Fujitsu, and others were made for largely strategic reasons, such as investments in semiconductors to improve designs of customized chips by being closer to end users. In other instances, however, such as local production of fiber optics, the overriding motivation was concern over the threat of protectionism.

Despite these hints of change, the bottom line on Japan's trade strategy has remained constant: promote exports, do not allow politics to jeopardize those exports, and intervene selectively with firms. In the Indonesian situation described above, for example, the basic thrust of Japan's approach was not to antagonize the Indonesians or do anything that might damage Indonesia as a long-term market. The administrative guidance from the government on not engaging in countertrade lasted only as long as Japanese companies believed their exports were not at risk. But as soon as one company (Sumitomo) lost a sizable contract directly as a result of this anti-countertrade policy, MITI discontinued the embargo and told each company to follow whatever countertrade policy it thought appropriate. The market was to be preserved.

THE SECOND BATTLE OF POITIERS

The continuity in Japan's trade strategy and business-government relationship can be clearly seen in the consumer electronics industry. Despite efforts by these firms to assert some independence, MITI managed to exert extraordinary influence on corporate policies. MITI's ability to use foreign protectionism to enhance its interests was an object lesson in the operation of Japanese trade strategy.

On October 26, 1982, the government of France announced that all imports of videotape recorders could be cleared only through the tiny inland customs post at Poitiers. In addition, the French would now require that all custom clearance documents on VTRs be translated into French, and foreign exporters would have to gain prior approval before they shipped to France. Dissatisfied with EEC efforts to put a halt to the Japanese "invasion," France decided to take matters into its own hands by blocking one of Japan's largest and most profitable exports (about $5.5 billion worldwide in 1982 and growing at about 40 percent per year). Soon, Holland's Philips Corporation and West Germany's Grundig, the only two European producers of VTRs at the time, filed anti-dumping suits against all Japanese VTR exporters—the largest such suit in the history of Japanese-EEC trade.

Again, the initial reaction of Japanese exporters was to demand that MITI take the strongest possible action. As in the Indonesian case, the companies recommended that Japan retaliate. The Japanese manufacturers insisted there was no foundation to the dumping charges (although MITI officials "suspected" that at least a few exporters were selling below home market prices), and that Japan should not submit to such gross violations of GATT rules. But again, as with Indonesia, there were significant differences among the firms.

Newcomers to the European market, such as Sanyo, and firms highly dependent upon European sales, such as JVC, expressed concern that their potential growth would be reduced by any restrictions on exports. On the other hand, Matsushita, which was ready to start local production in the EEC, was willing to accept a voluntary export restraint (VER) in order to end the trade conflict. Export limitations at that time would have also helped Matsushita secure its dominant market share in Europe.[70]

MITI considered retaliation, including a requirement that all imports of French brandy be cleared through an inland custom post, but it ultimately opted to negotiate a VER with Europe in the interest of economic peace. What emerged from the negotiations was no ordinary export restraint agreement: it was probably the most comprehensive and complicated arrangement that Japan had ever negotiated with any nation. First, the Japanese agreed to limit color televisions, TV tubes, cars, light commercial vehicles, forklift trucks, motorcycles, quartz watches, and audio devices; and to set minimum prices on machine tools, in addition to applying the restrictions on VTRs. The extent of these restraints led one European official to wonder if "there [is] a limit to Japanese compromise."[71] Even the specific agreement on videotape recorders went beyond any VER Japan had previously negotiated. Traditionally, VERs covered only export volume of finished products; occasionally, they would include a quota for parts. The arrangement on VTRs, however, limited exports to 4.55 million units including unassembled kits, *and* it set restrictions on price and the overall share of the market available to Japanese producers. Also, MITI imposed floor prices on Japanese VTRs selling in the European market, and it guaranteed that European manufacturers could sell 1.2 million units in 1983, a sharp increase compared to the 80,000 to 90,000 units that Philips and Grundig had sold in 1982. Finally, if market demand proved to be less than 5.7 million units, the Japanese were obligated to reduce their sales even further.

In essence, MITI had negotiated a very sophisticated cartel arrangement with Europe, one that gave MITI tremendous power in allocating export licenses and even overseas production.[72] By guaranteeing the Europeans a set amount of sales, MITI promised to control all Japanese sales, even though the ministry had no formal power over Japanese subsidiaries in Europe or elsewhere. If a firm did not agree to MITI's guidelines on overseas production, then MITI would simply reduce that firm's exports, the most profitable part of the VTR business. Since 1983, MITI had encouraged firms to set up production in Europe, yet it did not encourage them to source all of their components from local manufacturers. If Japanese companies sourced more than 55 percent of their products in Europe, they would be exempted from the quota. Such an arrangement, however, would also reduce Japanese direct exports, reduce profits for the home manufacturers, and limit MITI's ability to control trade and production.

In the end, the trade results of this particular VER were no different from the Japanese trade results in virtually every other case of foreign market protec-

TABLE 2-2
Japanese Exports of VTRs
(Value in 100 Million Yen, Units in 1,000s)

	World		USA	Europe[b]
	Value	Units	Units	Units
1976	310	139	104	23
1980	4,436	3,444	1,090	1,448
1982	10,802	10,661	2,504	5,559
1983	12,608	15,237	5,437	5,716
1984[a]	15,400	20,500		
1985[a]	16,300	22,500		

[a]Projected.
[b]Includes EEC and non-EEC nations.
SOURCE: Japan's Ministry of Finance, 1984.

tionism: total Japanese exports, production, employment, and profits were not seriously damaged. Despite European protectionism, Japanese corporate revenues from the export of VTRs actually increased after 1982 (see *Table 2-2*). While shipments to the EEC dropped, the price floor on Japanese products allowed most exporters to increase their margins, which largely offset the decline in volume.[73] In addition, growing exports to other parts of Europe, the United States and the Middle East more than compensated for the decline in volume to the EEC.

To summarize, deeply entrenched bureaucratic interests in Japan, combined with the momentum generated by success, have made any fundamental change extremely difficult to implement. While the growing independence of some large firms, such as Mitsubishi and NEC, will continue to force changes at the margins, these adjustments seem unlikely to lead to a new strategic approach. So long as Japanese manufacturers can continue to prosper in a protectionist environment, and so long as MITI and other government ministries can enhance their power base by managing that protectionism, there will be powerful incentives for continuity in trade strategy.

This conclusion raises an intriguing question: Under what conditions *is* Japan likely to forge a new trade strategy and develop a new pattern of business-government relations in international trade? Since Japanese firms and Japanese consumers still seem to be content with the status quo, no internal pressure for change is likely to appear in the near future. The only time Japan has demonstrated a willingness to alter its approach has been under *external* pressures. For example, when President Nixon imposed a surcharge on Japanese exports in 1971, Japan subsequently revalued its currency and stimulated imports. This episode suggests that a change in trade strategy is more likely to emerge if other countries can convince Japanese leaders in business and government that their material well-being would be endangered by a continuation of the same Japanese strategy. Then, and not before, will a new consensus on trade be forged. The only place such external pressure could originate is the United States, the subject to which I will now turn.

FORCES OF CHANGE: THE UNITED STATES

Many of the same bureaucratic interests that have impeded change in Japan have similarly slowed it in the United States. The continuing division of trade authority within the executive branch and between the executive and Congress has strongly inhibited the formulation of a new strategy. Yet in America, as in Japan, forces for change inside and outside the country have been pushing the nation toward a new trade approach. Most significant, perhaps, has been the apparent failure of U.S. trade policy to correct the huge and expanding trade deficits. In fact, America's immense trade imbalance has already begun to alter some aspects of business-government relations that influence international trade policy.

Where the relationship between Japanese business and government in trade was historically one of mutual dependence, the interaction between American business and government might be described as an arm's-length transaction. Since American business has traditionally chosen autonomy in international trade, and the American government preferred not to become involved in business affairs, no close dependence, at least in peacetime, ever developed. The American government also does not need as much assistance from business as does the Japanese. MITI, for example, has under 10,000 employees and must rely upon business for information; the U.S. Commerce Department, which is only one repository of trade information, employs 35,000 people. While MITI goes to firms for information, the American government relies upon its own sources or paid consultants.

Yet the American business-government relationship in international trade may be changing. The worsening trade deficit and a general perception of closed foreign markets have helped to drive business and government at least somewhat closer together. The inability of many American firms to penetrate foreign markets—especially the Japanese market—has led businesses and whole industries to reconsider their relationship with Washington. While most firms viewed government as a hindrance in international trade during the 1950s and 1960s, these same companies have begun to see government as a potential ally in the 1980s.

The overall change in perception may be seen in the rapid growth of corporate presence in Washington. As late as 1961, there were only 130 firms represented by registered lobbyists in the nation's capital, of which fifty had their own Washington staffs. By 1979, however, the number had jumped fivefold: 650 companies had their own registered lobbyists and 247 of them had their own staffs; and trade-related issues have been one of the key factors behind the trend.[74] Within the government itself, another consequence of the trade deficit and foreign protectionism has been that some departments have increasingly sought out business advice. The U.S. Special Trade Representative, for example, relied heavily on the industry advisory committees for information and recommendations during the Tokyo Round negotiations, even though these committees were set up, in part, to constrain the government.[75]

TELECOMMUNICATIONS AND MOTOROLA

We can find powerful evidence of this evolution in U.S. trade policy in the telecommunications industry. Here, there is an unmistakable trend toward greater mutual dependence between American firms, like Motorola, and the U.S. government. For many private companies in this high-tech industry, the ability to foster government support has become an essential part of their business. Similar dependence has developed within the government. The Commerce Department and Special Trade Representative, the two agencies principally responsible for trade policy in telecommunications, simply do not have the expertise to handle the trade issues without corporate support.

The beginning of the story in telecommunications is the start of the deregulation of AT&T in the late 1970s. Deregulation created problems for American manufacturers because it suddenly opened the huge American telecommunications market to foreign competition at a time when foreign governments continued to restrict their telecommunications purchases to exclusively domestic firms. By 1979, the United States had a substantial deficit in telecommunications with Japan, even though American firms claimed to have a technological lead in many products and maintained a trade surplus with the rest of the world.[76] Concern over this situation led the telecommunications industry advisory committee to request that the United States negotiate a special agreement with Japan which would open the Japanese telecommunications market to American competition.[77] One of the key members of the industry advisory group was Motorola Corporation, a leading manufacturer of semiconductors and mobile radio equipment.[78] Motorola had held a dominant position in the world market for certain types of telecommunication equipment, such as pagers, yet the company was unable to sell into the Japanese market. Not only did the Ministry of Posts and Telecommunications deny licenses to many Motorola products, but most Japanese companies, including NTT, Japan's monopoly telephone company, refused to buy Motorola pagers and other equipment—equipment that was widely used around the world. Motorola executives believed that, in addition to formal barriers, a legacy of national preferences made the Japanese market difficult to overcome, no matter what the quality or the price of their equipment.

Motorola's strategy for penetrating the Japanese market developed along two tracks: first, the company committed itself to a long-term investment, which included special manufacturing facilities devoted to products for the Japanese market, and increased manufacturing and staff operations in Tokyo; and second, the company sought political assistance by enlisting U.S. government support for opening Japan to Motorola's products. On both fronts, Motorola's strategy bore fruit.

During 1980, the U.S. successfully negotiated a special bilateral agreement with Japan that formally opened NTT procurement to American manufacturers. One of the first test cases of this agreement came in 1981, when Motorola bid for part of Japan's tone pager market. Although the initial contract involved only $9 million, Motorola still required U.S. government assistance before NTT would sign. Initially NTT offered Motorola one-sixth of the NTT pager market, which NTT later reduced to one-seventh. By the end of 1984, total sales of pagers amounted to approximately $10 million, and all additional communications sales amounted to several million dollars more. So some penetration was achieved. Motorola received high marks from U.S. trade officials because they felt the company made an unusually serious effort in Japan, combining a sophisticated technological strategy with aggressive marketing. These American officials, who were willing to intervene on Motorola's behalf, also praised the firm's cooperation, since Motorola kept government officials well informed of its activities and other trends in the Japanese market.

On the one hand, Motorola's success is suggestive of the new, closer ties between American business and government in international trade. Motorola executives stated that the U.S. government was very helpful in providing information to the company and putting diplomatic pressure on the Japanese whenever there were formal or informal barriers to trade. U.S. government bureaucrats also benefited from their closer relationship with companies such as Motorola: by defending the interests of a high technology company against the Japanese, they earned unusual recognition within the executive branch and from Congress.

On the other hand, Motorola's one-seventh market share in pagers and approximately $20 million in communications sales to Japan are indicative of the handicaps faced by large American firms that try to penetrate deeply into high priority markets in Japan. Motorola sold more than $2.0 billion in communications equipment in 1984; if Motorola had a share of the Japanese market comparable to its share worldwide, it would be selling at least $100 million in Japan, and perhaps as much as $750 million. The same is generally true in other areas of the telecommunications market. Japanese imports of telecommunications equipment averaged only 1.4 percent of consumption—the lowest of any industrial country.[79] In fact, despite the much publicized liberalization of NTT procurement after 1980, total U.S. exports to Japan had risen only to $58 million by 1983 (in contrast to $270 million in U.S. exports to the relatively closed European market). Thus, U.S. companies sold only one-fourth as much to Japan as they did to Europe at a time when Japanese consumption of telecommunications equipment was more than half that of the EEC.[80]

Of course, Motorola's struggles did not end the saga of U.S.-Japanese trade tensions in telecommunications. In 1985, the Japanese government partially followed the American and British lead in telecommunications by deregulating its national monopoly. On April 1, 1985, NTT became a private company, left to face competition in the telephone supply market, common carrier service, and in value-added networks.[81] On the surface, many American firms hoped that deregulation in Japan would carry some of the same opportunities that the deregulation of AT&T had already given their Japanese competitors. (In the United States, newly independent local operating companies sought to diversify their sources of equipment and were happy to entertain bids from Japanese firms.) Their hopes were soon dashed, however; like so many other features of trade policy in Japan, the formal change in NTT's status proved to have a relatively small benefit for American access. Deregulation, Japanese-style, has not meant divestiture, nor a significantly smaller role for the government's regulator, the Ministry of Posts and Telecommunications (MPT). The ministry has maintained the authority to license products, much like the Federal Communications Commission did in the United States. However, Japan's MPT has kept a tight rein on foreign competition, while the U.S. FCC has increasingly allowed freer access and competition in the American market. Through mid-1985, American sales of telecommunications equipment inched up only marginally.

Motorola's meager success, combined with the frustrations of other American firms that have attempted to enter the Japanese telecommunications market, symbolizes the conflict and continuity in American and Japanese trade strategies. From the Japanese perspective, this story underscores the national determination to protect high-technology markets in order to promote present and future exports; from the American perspective, the same Motorola story demonstrates Japan's unfair trade practices, and even more, the ongoing reluctance of the U.S. government to exert real pressure to promote American trade interests. The executive branch has continued to emphasize the primacy of political interests over trading interests, and disagreement has persisted over what measures should be taken to open foreign markets. Since the State and Treasury Departments resist the use of overt threats, such as closing the U.S. market, the only tools remaining seem to be jawboning and diplomacy. According to one USTR official, the strongest threat now allowable against the Japanese is to say, "if you don't play right, we'll tell everyone, we'll tell the Congress, we'll tell the president, we'll tell the people in the United States and so on." Under these circumstances, it can be no great surprise that foreign governments—especially Japan—generally refuse to make meaningful compromises in their trading strategies.

Although the executive branch has remained more or less committed to the traditional American trading strategy, many American companies have sought to mandate a change by approaching Congress and sympathetic government agencies. Even Motorola, which has benefited from closer ties to the executive branch and which has traditionally supported free trade, has sought legislation that would force the United States to retaliate against Japan if the Japanese do not alter their trade strategy. Motorola's suggestions have included countervailing duties against those foreign (i.e., Japanese) industries deemed to be subsidized (i.e., protected or provided with other selective assistance); and in 1985, the company urged a 20 percent surcharge on all U.S. imports that would be gradually phased out over a three-year period.[82] Congress and some agencies have become increasingly receptive to such pleas. The Federal Communications Commission, for instance, threatened to tighten telecommunications licensing requirements in order to slow Japanese exports to a "trickle."[83] Similarly, the Congress has seriously considered several bills that would mandate bilateral trade balances and severely penalize "unfair" foreign trade practices. So far, however, no tough administrative action has been implemented nor any punitive legislation passed.

Even when the Reagan Administration announced a new "aggressive" trade policy in the fall of 1985, it did not depart from the traditional American strategy. Using tough words, the president said that "I will not stand by and watch American businesses fail because of unfair trade practices abroad. I will not stand by and watch American workers lose their jobs because other nations do not play by the rules."[84] Mr. Reagan then promised to attack these unfair practices with a variety of measures, including a "war chest" of $300 million for the Export-Import Bank to use against foreign trade subsidies, and an interagency "strike force" that would expedite trade proceedings. The true purpose of the president's program, however, was not to dismantle foreign trade barriers. Since the proposed policies held little promise for changing the behavior of America's trading partners, one can only speculate that the real objective was to contain a protectionist-minded Congress.[85]

In sum, U.S. trade policy has changed very little since World War II, despite the appearance of new patterns in American business-government relations, and despite growing pressures for a new trade approach from U.S. firms, Congress, and a few government agencies. For the future, then, some disturbing questions remain: Will U.S. trade policy change? Can the United States force open the Japanese market in high priority sectors? If the U.S. trade position remains unchanged, what will be the results in the 1990s and beyond?

CAN THE UNITED STATES AND JAPAN PROTECT THEIR POSITIONS IN WORLD MARKETS?

The United States and Japan are caught in a web of political and economic interdependence which is most vividly portrayed in international trade. Both governments rely upon trading strategies that made sense in the 1940s when they were first devised, but have become inconsistent with market and political conditions of the 1980s. Japan's building of trade surpluses year after year, while continuing to protect high priority markets at home, can only exacerbate global trade tensions. Since protectionism is already on the rise, a continuation of Japan's trade strategy might precipitate a serious trade crisis: if not between Japan and the United States, then between Japan and Europe or among an even larger number of nations. That could prove disastrous for Japan, which might once again become a pariah in international trading circles, as it was in the 1930s and late 1940s.

For the United States, other dangers loom, for Americans cannot afford the

FIGURE 2-10
U.S. and Japan: Debtor and Creditor Nations
(Net foreign assets of U.S. and Japan in billions of dollars; negative data indicate debtor status)

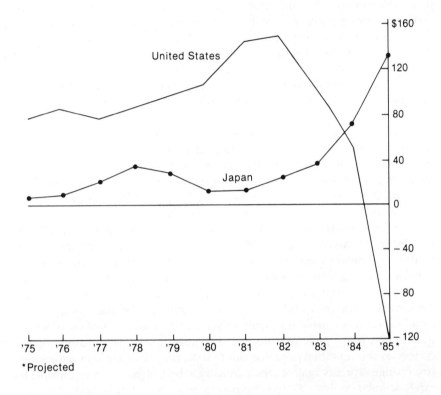

*Projected

SOURCES: U.S. Commerce Department; Japanese Ministry of Finance; projections by Kemper Financial Services; *The New York Times*, September 22, 1985.

luxury of ignoring American trading interests indefinitely. The large and growing deficits on the current account have turned the United States into a debtor nation—for the first time since World War I (see *Figure 2-10*). Should the United States continue to run huge deficits, it will soon outstrip Brazil and Mexico as the largest debtor in the world. No nation, even the United States, can endure such deficits forever.

The dilemma for both the United States and Japan is that each nation's trade strategy is now contingent upon the other's behavior. As I have shown in this chapter, internally generated pressures from business firms, interest groups, bureaucrats, and political institutions have produced only marginal changes in either country. Something greater is required. If business continues as usual in Japan, we can expect Japanese firms to increase their direct investment abroad and assert more independence from their government. But MITI and other important ministries are also likely to continue promoting high priority industries and to retain control over many of the key aspects of international trade policy. Again, if business continues as usual in the United States, the calls for protectionism will become louder and politically more attractive. Congress may grow more receptive to these pleas, which may lead to an increasing number of selective protectionist policies. But so long as decision making in the United States remains diffused, and so long as the president has substantial discretion and the Departments of State and Treasury exert strong influences on trade policy, the thrust of U.S. trade policy will continue to be based on two old principles: the primacy of political interests, and a liberal attitude toward international trade.

Since change will not result from internal causes, it will most likely come from forces outside of each nation. Indeed, in other major policy areas where revolutionary changes have taken place, such as in international monetary affairs and international energy, external crises, such as the huge outflow of gold and the run on the U.S. dollar in 1971, and OPEC's quadrupling of oil prices in 1973, reshaped the strategies of the United States and Japan. In these cases of substantial change, the two national governments suddenly became convinced by external events that they had to act decisively and immediately.

In trade, however, neither nation has yet perceived such a crisis. Key figures in business and government in both Japan and the United States have acknowledged problems, but not crises that demand serious or urgent attention. Japan, for instance, has been under continual pressure to liberalize its markets, restrain exports, and make the Japanese yen a more international currency for at least fifteen years. Japanese business and government have made a series of concessions to external pressure, but to date, they have not opted for substantive change. Threats against Japan, by either the United States or Europe, have rarely seemed credible. Despite myriad threats from every conceivable source, trade actions against Japan by a major power have never materially hurt the Japanese economy. Foreign protectionism aimed at Japanese exports, be they textiles, steel, televisions, autos, or VTRs, have at worst merely slowed the rate of growth of Japanese profits. Indeed, foreign protectionism has at times served to enhance Japan's market position.[86] The only time Japan has been forced into action in international trade was in 1971: President Nixon's 10 percent surcharge coerced Japan to revalue the yen and to restrict its textile exports—two actions that had been bitterly resisted for years. Since the Nixon shocks of 1971, however, the United States has been widely perceived, with justification, as a paper tiger in international trade. It is no wonder that Japanese bureaucrats and business executives have never been convinced that a new trade strategy was necessary or even desirable.

The United States, in contrast to Japan, has the potential strength to rewrite the rules of international trade. Since the U.S. market is the largest in the world and the U.S. economy is less dependent upon trade than those of other industrial nations, virtually all countries need the American market more than the

United States needs any particular foreign market. The great American weakness of the mid-1980s—its huge deficit on the U.S. current account—has actually reinforced the world's dependence on the United States. In 1983, for example, the increase in American imports accounted for one-half of the entire growth in world trade. While Japan's only option in a world of protectionism is to adapt to that protectionism, the United States has the muscle to change the rules of the game. If the United States could issue *credible* threats of protectionism, then foreign nations—and especially Japan—would have few choices but to bend before America's demands.

But what would lead the United States to become such an active player with an ability to make credible threats? Could it selectively threaten protectionism without becoming a truly protectionist nation? The most likely reason that the United States might alter its trade strategy would be if the trade deficits persisted, *and* the value of the U.S. dollar declined, as it did in late 1985 and early 1986. The Reagan Administration clearly stated that the United States did not have a trade problem, but rather a "monetary" problem. *The Economic Report of the President, 1985* detailed the official position that the trade deficits will be reduced as soon as the foreign exchange markets lower the value of the dollar. Should the deficits persist, however, even after a prolonged fall in the dollar (allowing for lags), then policymakers would no longer be able to write off the trade deficits as a reflection of monetary problems. If sizable current account imbalances continue even after the dollar's weakening, then policymakers might be encouraged to reconsider their views on international trade.

A second condition that might generate a change in America's trade strategy would be if Japan pushed exports too heavily in high priority American sectors. So far, when Japanese firms overpowered the American textile and television industries, large American multinational corporations and key American officials did not become overly concerned. Japanese competition was often perceived as a positive stimulus to the American economy and a natural evolution in comparative advantage. Even when Japanese exports of steel and automobiles made strong inroads, American executives and policymakers characterized this loss of market as largely the result of American corporate mistakes, rather than a systematic effort by Japan to dominate American industry.

However, Japanese competition of the 1980s in computers, semiconductors, telecommunications, and the like, is far more serious. This challenge strikes at the heart of American technology and America's own view of its future comparative advantages. Should American multinational firms and American trade officials perceive that an unfair game is being played in this new arena, then conditions for discussing and creating a new consensus on trade policy might emerge. One result might be that the United States would finally move away from a dogmatic free trade position toward a better balance of strategic and economic objectives. If this change occurs, American trade policy can be expected to play a far more aggressive role in trying to reestablish America's commercial leadership in the world.

CHAPTER 3

Production and Distribution: Competition Policy and Industry Structure

THOMAS K. McCRAW AND PATRICIA A. O'BRIEN

Walk into an American discount department store—a K Mart, for example. You see a huge expanse of floor space, but very few clerks. You go from aisle to aisle, marveling at the wide variety of merchandise from all over the world. Some of these goods were manufactured in the United States, some in Japan, some in Korea, Singapore, Hong Kong, West Germany, France, and so on. Most items are offered at very low prices, yet you may have difficulty getting informed advice from a clerk—assuming you can find one at all. Once you have picked out a few items, you may have to wait in a long line for the privilege of paying your money at the check-out counter. Finally, you leave the store with mixed feelings: happy with your bargains, but frustrated and puzzled because no one paid personal attention to you.

Now fly to Japan. Whether you begin your visit in Tokyo or in some small Japanese town, you immediately notice a superabundance of tiny stores lining the street. Each of these Mom-and-Pop establishments offers just a few things for sale, but you are impressed mainly by the enormous number of stores. You soon hypothesize that most Japanese consumers must do much of their daily shopping at these small outlets.

In Japan, you do see a few supermarkets and American-style discount stores, but only a few, in contrast with the many thousands in the United States. Finally, you locate a modern Japanese department store. As you walk in, you see a smaller floor space than was true of the K Mart back in the United States, or even of a comparable American department store. Here, you see a wide variety of goods for sale, a majority of them manufactured in Japan. Items are offered at reasonable prices but, by and large, they do not represent anything like the bargains available at the American K Mart. Even more obvious are the dozens upon dozens of uniformed store employees that you encounter. As you shop, the clerks meet your every inquiry with informed and courteous advice. After you have chosen what to buy, other clerks whisk you through the payment counter. Finally, you leave the store with mixed feelings, just as you did in the United States. But it is the opposite mix: you are not entirely happy with the prices you have had to pay, but you have been treated well as a person.

Now, try a second pair of contrasting visits. Before you leave Japan, go to an industrial district and get permission to walk through a steel mill. If you happen to choose one of Japan's gigantic rolling mills, you will see fully half a mile of floor space stretching out before you, a length equivalent to eight or nine American football fields laid end-to-end. On this floor, the operations are highly automated; very few workers are anywhere in sight. During the tour, you are told, quite accurately, that in Japan steel is produced more efficiently and offered for sale at lower prices than in the United States or any other Western nation.

Considering both experiences, you begin to form a larger impression: in Japan, a curious difference separates the steel mill from the department store. You form the broad hypothesis that, if steel is typical, then Japan's production sector has low cost, lean employment, and high efficiency. The retail sector, however, judging from what you saw in the department store (not to mention the Mom-and-Pop establishments), exhibits the opposite characteristics: overstaffing, high prices, and inefficiency. You begin to wonder why this might be so.

Flying back to the United States, the same kind of question arises in your mind. From the plane, you go to the American Rust Belt for a visit to an American steel plant. There you see a large operation, but not nearly so large as the Japanese rolling mill. The American plant, you notice, is moderately mechanized, but lots of employees still seem to be working on the floor of the mill. Remembering your trip to Japan, adding in your knowledge that American steel is more expensive, you can form a tentative conclusion that the American mill is undersized, undermechanized, and overstaffed. But when you think back again, to your visits to retail stores in both countries, you come to a different conclusion about national opposites: in the American K Mart, low prices and *under*staffing; in the Japanese store, higher prices and *over*staffing.

How do you explain this double contrast between the two countries? The difference is not, you remind yourself, based on some obscure academic theory; instead, it emerges from your own observations. Could geography explain part of it? Is there simply not enough room in Japan for American-style K Marts and supermarkets? Surely geography must mean something, especially if you consider the huge parking lots so essential to the success of American shopping centers. Yet if space is the sole determining factor, then how could Japanese steel mills be so much larger than American ones?

Perhaps the cultures of the two countries help to explain the contrast. On the issue of employment in retail stores, for example, you might speculate that Japanese consumers, given a choice between attentive personal service on the one hand and the lowest possible prices on the other, favor service. Perhaps this is true because Japan's crowded living conditions and homogeneous culture encourage politeness, good manners, and courteous interchange among people. In America, by contrast, with its individualistic culture—every person for him- or herself—the consumer wants low prices above everything else. Of course, American consumers would enjoy being pampered like the Japanese; but if that means higher prices, then no thank you!

Clearly, geography and culture do help explain the remarkable contrasts you have observed. Yet, in the last analysis, a less obvious but ultimately more important factor is also at work: the very different business-government relationships that characterize each country; and specifically, their *dramatically different attitudes and laws relating to competition.*

This chapter addresses those differences in detail. It begins with an overview of the evolution of Japanese and American patterns of business organization and competition policy, showing how the two countries' laws and customs have affected their industrial structures. The chapter next examines the growth of the steel industry in Japan—and the decline of that same industry in America. Having covered steel as an example of the production sector, the chapter moves on to survey the two countries' distribution systems, focusing on the pattern of retailing represented by the contrast between the K Mart and a Japanese department store. Finally, the chapter concludes with a discussion of the broad assumptions behind the very different public policies toward competition that have evolved within Japan and the United States.

Competition Policy and Organizational Relationships

The major structural differences between the American and Japanese business styles lie in the distinctive group orientation of Japanese companies. This overall pattern within Japan, however effective or ineffective it might seem, could never have developed in the United States, for one reason: much of it would have been illegal under the American antitrust laws.[1]

In Japan, powerful inter-firm relationships operate on at least two levels. At the highest level sit the six famous *keiretsu* (groups of affiliated companies), three of which—Mitsubishi, Mitsui, and Sumitomo—originated as *zaibatsu* (family-controlled groups of companies, which together comprised the heart of the Japanese industrial economy before World War II). The other three *keiretsu*—Fuyo, Sanwa, and DKB—developed later on, as clusters of companies organized around major commercial banks. Today, each of the six consists of scores of large firms, most of which remain independent in the legal sense but which coordinate their activities: using the same banks for corporate financing, buying from and selling to each other at favored prices, employing common sales agents for their diverse products, and sharing a mass of information about world market trends. Given the distinctive way in which these transactions are actually carried out in Japan, some of them might be considered illegal in America.[2]

Of the six major *keiretsu,* the largest and best known is Mitsubishi, which encompasses more than 150 companies doing business in a great variety of industries. (No fewer than 126 of these firms are listed separately on the Tokyo Stock Exchange.) Most of the Mitsubishi companies remain legally independent. While there is substantial mutual stock ownership, other forms of cooperation have turned out to be more effective in achieving a joint purpose. Inter-company ties within the group remain powerful, but the most important bonds are informal and have little to do with written contracts and other legal apparatus.

Some of these same practices, of course, can be observed within giant American companies, such as the classic American multidivisional firms like General Electric and Du Pont. In these American companies, the capital budgeting process is closely coordinated, and research, development, and production are decentralized within semiautonomous divisions. But ownership remains entirely in the hands of the parent company, and the divisions have no legal independence whatever.

Nor do the American conglomerates such as Gulf & Western and Textron operate in the manner of Japanese *keiretsu.* Indeed, the financial behavior of such conglomerates, which regularly acquire and divest entire companies, flies in the face of the long-term, carefully nurtured relationships characteristic not only of *keiretsu* but of most other Japanese commercial and industrial enterprises. Overall, Japanese patterns of doing big business differ in some fundamental respects from American: in their methods of administration and promotion of executives; in their reliance on intra-group banks for financing; in their legal status, with heavy cross-ownership of permanently held stock; and in their corporate culture. In fact, a significant part of the Japanese system might be ruled illegal under American securities regulations and antitrust policies.[3]

By way of illustration, consider the operations of Mitsui, the second largest of the Japanese groups. Today, the Mitsui group includes 24 Nimokukai inner-group companies, whose presidents meet together on the second Thursday of each month. In addition, there is a second (Getsuyōkai) group of 62 companies whose executives gather every Monday, and still a third group, Kōhōiinkai (Information Exchange Committee), whose members assemble monthly. If such activities of legally independent companies occurred within the United States, most of them would be suspect under the antitrust laws. Here, at the very core of Japanese group capitalism, we see vivid differences between the laws, customs, and even the underlying premises about the proper role of competition policy as it actually operates in Japan—in contrast to the United States.[4]

The same point holds true at a second level of group relationships in Japan, where we find a complex "family" network of contracting companies, led by

FIGURE 3-1

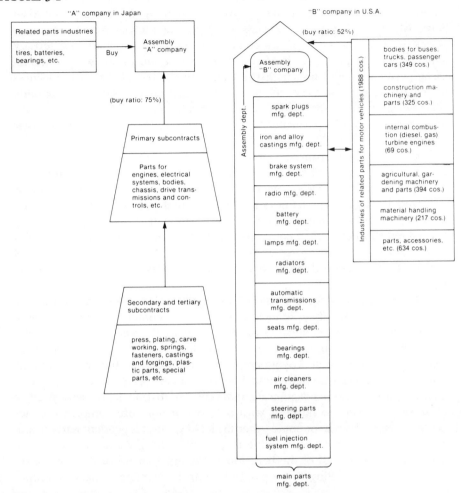

SOURCE: Japanese Ministry of International Trade and Industry 1980.

important new industrial powerhouses such as Toyota and Matsushita. *Figure 3-1* compares such differences between automobile firms in Japan and America: on the left, Toyota ("A" company); on the right, General Motors ("B" company). In the left-hand diagram, the core firm (Toyota) engages primarily in automobile *assembly.* Some of Toyota's contractors (represented in the box at the top left), may be large and independent companies in their own right, such as Bridgestone Tire. A second and very distinct collection of suppliers (represented by the middle box labeled "primary subcontracts"), are all closely related to the core assembly firm. Many primary subcontractors (Toyoda Koki, for example, which manufactures steering assemblies), are part of the core firm's "family of companies." Substantial cross-ownership exists within the family, some of whose members (Toyota Auto Body, for example, or Aisin Seiki, which manufactures transmissions) are themselves very large enterprises. By contrast, most of the companies holding "secondary and tertiary subcontracts" (represented in the bottom box) are small firms, with no necessarily permanent affiliation with the family. In the overall Japanese business system, these companies are the first to lose their contracts during economic recessions. Also in contrast to firms in the family, such smaller companies pay lower wages and offer permanent employment to only a small fraction of their employees.[5]

As the prominent Japanese economist Ken-ichi Imai has described the situation in his country, "There are hierarchical systems of subcontractors that supply many kinds of parts, components, and related goods under continuous contracts to large manufacturers in the automobile, electrical appliance, and related industries." Imai goes on to say: "Although this buying is formally carried out through market contracts, *it is not a pure market transaction and works as if it were an aspect of the firm's internal organization* because of various forms of coordination between the manufacturer and subcontractors."[6]

In General Motors, these divisional and functional units lie *within* the core company. In Toyota, they lie mostly outside, in a complex hierarchy of suppliers. Although both companies produce roughly the same number of vehicles in their home countries each year, GM directly employs several hundred thousand workers, while Toyota employs fewer than one hundred thousand. The other workers who help build Toyota's cars are scattered throughout its family of firms. Another significant difference is that, in Japan, almost all of these smaller firms do business with only one major core company—either Toyota, Nissan, Mazda, or some other firm. No giant independent parts manufacturer exists in Japan comparable to Bendix or Borg-Warner in the United States. Thus, almost all of the bargaining leverage remains in the core firms, with little countervailing power passed into the hands of parts manufacturers.[7]

Horizontal Business Relationships

Both major levels of Japanese group capitalism discussed so far apply primarily to product diversification and "vertical" links among companies buying from and selling to each other. Contrasting the two national styles of business organization, we find the differences between "horizontal" relationships to be just as striking as those between vertical ones. In some industries, the Japanese pattern of horizontal, intra-industry cartels reflects an approach which American competition policy explicitly forbids.

Historically speaking, whether in Japan, the United States, or most other countries, cartels are actually as old as commerce itself. Agreements among producers of similar items or services to limit output, restrict entry into their lines of work, and standardize prices and quality have been made since the

beginning of business history. Medieval weavers, shoemakers, and other arti-
sans routinely organized themselves into "guilds" (cartels) in order to insure
the quality of products and to protect profits. In many countries, cartels long
represented the normal way of managing economic affairs. Prior to the Industrial Revolution, they proved consistent with the general live-and-let-live ethos
of both Japan and the West. In fact, the whole idea of cartels fitted nicely into
the organic conceptions of society typical of medieval life. For many centuries,
although it was universally recognized that they might be subject to abuse by
their members, cartels seemed to bring to society more good than bad, in the
form of quality control and peace among competitors.[8]

Industrialization and the rise of liberal democratic government changed this
pattern, by altering the fundamental context in which cartels operated. The
huge new factories necessary for mass production represented investments of
unprecedentedly high orders of magnitude; their owners and managers felt
compelled to protect such giant investments from the ups and downs of uncontrolled market competition. Hence, the impulse to cartelize acquired a
new urgency, as a form of protection against bankruptcies of giant firms during
periods of economic depression. In its new setting, however, cartelization had
little to do with maintaining quality control. Instead, it came to represent a
convenient way to manage industrial overcapacity—a chronic problem in
Europe and the United States by the late nineteenth century, and in Japan by
the early twentieth.[9]

In nineteenth-century America, however, most tendencies toward cartelization met with increasing resistance, in the specific form of antitrust laws. The
American veneration of individualism, together with the nation's characteristic
abhorrence of centralized power, led to a series of measures culminating in the
Sherman Antitrust Act of 1890, and later in additional legislation such as the
Clayton and Federal Trade Commission Acts of 1914. These laws, though
ineffective in some respects, did prohibit direct horizontal price-fixing and
collusive limitations of output. Perhaps more important, their very existence
conditioned American business executives *not* to think in terms of inter-firm
collusion as their primary response to the overcapacity problem. Instead, such
laws indirectly encouraged them to gather within their own companies all the
means necessary to compete against price-cutting rivals. Thus, instead of setting up horizontal arrangements, American business executives began to build
their companies along vertical lines: to integrate forward into marketing, and
backward into manufacturing and sourcing—and ultimately to build giant,
multidivisional, and diversified firms that were the largest in the world at that
time. Today they remain the largest.[10]

In America, then, legal restrictions against interlocking arrangements discouraged the development of that type of organization depicted on the left
side of *Figure 3-1* (the Toyota "family" of subcontracting firms). Instead, the
antitrust laws promoted, as an alternative, the type of vertical integration
depicted on the right side, for the giant General Motors. Nor was this contrast

limited to the automobile industry alone. It applied to big U.S. business in general. In this sense, antitrust profoundly shaped the American industrial structure—but not the structure in Japan.[11]

Before the 1930s, many Japanese cartels failed, because market pressures forced weak members to disregard the price controls and limitations on output. The 1930s, however, brought a new set of conditions: first, an economic downturn; then, a rapid rise of militarism. Both circumstances pushed the Japanese government into a more activist management of business affairs, as the Diet passed a series of significant laws relating to cartelization. Later on, under the pressures of wartime mobilization, more than 1,500 government-sponsored cartels honeycombed the entire Japanese business system. Not surprisingly, the government's attempt to manage this complicated network ultimately proved a failure; and as a result, the Japanese economy during World War II (somewhat like the American economy during its own brief fling with cartelization under the National Recovery Administration of 1933–1935), did not perform up to expectations. In fact, this was one reason why Japan's military forces suffered chronic shortages of material during World War II.[12]

Even so, the extensive Japanese experience with cartels during the 1930s and 1940s eventually paid high dividends. From the trials and errors of those years, bureaucrats and business executives acquired a clear sense of which techniques would work best in each specific industry. During the postwar years of miracle growth, the Ministry of International Trade and Industry systematically incorporated investment and recession cartels into its general plans for industrial policy.[13] The role played by Japanese cartel policy in the economic miracle—in promoting exports, insulating important industries from the effects of economic downturns, and in making very large capital investments less risky—will be discussed in the next section of this chapter.

In the recent past, cartels and other cooperative activities authorized under various laws have continued to play important roles in Japan's management of its competition policy. Overall, the total number of legalized cartels in Japan reached 595 in 1960, 886 in 1970, and 491 in 1980.[14] Such aggregate numbers should of course be used with caution. The variety of cartels involved represents a mixed bag, to say the least. Even more important, the numbers exclude some significant de facto cartels administered by MITI and other ministries. What the total numbers do make clear is the hospitality of Japanese policy toward cartelization as compared with American policy.

In the next section, we will examine the evolution of the steel industry in Japan and the United States. The story illustrates the two countries' divergent approaches to the issue of both formal and informal cartels—and the dramatically different results that followed.

The American and Japanese Steel Industries Compared

In 1943, at the height of its mobilization for World War II, Japan produced 8.5 million tons of steel, the highest volume in the country's history up to that time.[15] In the same year, the United States produced 89 million tons—more than ten times the output of Japan, and an amount equal to 52 percent of the production of the entire world.

By the mid-1970s, only thirty years later, Japan had actually matched the United States in steel output, with both countries now producing about 115 million tons per year. But, while Japan was exporting about 30 percent of its production, the United States was importing nearly 20 percent of its total domestic usage. In fact, steel imports were flowing into the United States from some thirty different countries. Of these, the largest single supplier was Japan, with about 40 percent of the total.

The dramatic growth of Japan's steel industry, in such sharp contrast to the relative decline of America's, has produced a flood of analytical studies. While the objectives and methods of these studies differed, most researchers reached similar conclusions. By the middle 1970s—as shown in the five different studies summarized in *Table 3-1*—Japanese steel had attained an estimated cost advantage of between $61 and $120 per ton over both American and European producers.[16] Of course, such cost comparisons are difficult to interpret with precision, since different figures are derived from different sets of assumptions about operating rates and costs of capital and raw materials. Moreover, some of the five studies considered only integrated producers, while others included all companies. Every study, however, reached the same overall conclusion: Japanese steel companies had become the world's lowest-cost producers.

How did this happen? Naturally, the answers remain far from simple. For one thing, Japan's steel industry developed within an explosively growing macroeconomy: about 10 percent real GNP growth over the 1950s and 1960s. This meant a constantly increasing demand for steel. The U.S. industry, by

TABLE 3-1
Production Costs Per Net Ton of Finished Steel
1976

	U.S.	Japan	EEC	Difference U.S.–Japan
		(U.S. dollars)		
Barnett (1977)				
Unit Costs	357	291	360	66
Operating Costs	320	236	314	84
Bradford (1977)				
Unit Costs	325	241	NI	84
FTC (1978)				
Basic Input Costs	267	147	NI	120
CWPS (1977)				
Unit Costs	328	267	NI	61
Operating Costs	249	180	242	70
Mueller & Kawahito (1976)	340	233	NI	107

NI: Not included in study.
SOURCE: See Note 16.

contrast, faced a slower growing and, in some years, an actually declining overall demand. In addition, unionized American steelworkers earned substantially higher wages than their Japanese counterparts.

Then, too—and this is the key factor—the managers of American steel companies did not direct their investments where they would do the most good. As one careful report concluded, "The principal strategic error of the American steel industry in the late 1950s involved the failure, given the slow growth in its home market, to target its investments toward performance improvements."[17] Nearly all other studies have agreed. The industry's decline derived in large part from outdated technology and reliance on relatively small-scale plants. Conversely, Japan's cost advantages stemmed primarily from two sources: extremely modern facilities, and companies' full exploitation of scale economies.[18]

The differences in scale seemed particularly striking: by the mid-1970s, the average capacity of an integrated Japanese plant had reached 7.4 million tons, while the average of an American plant was only 2.9 million—less than half as large.[19] Moreover, Japan's five largest plants were capable of producing 62 million tons of steel annually, while America's top five could produce only 35 million tons. Japan's ten largest plants averaged a capacity of 10.6 million tons, America's top ten only 5.9 million. In fact, no less than 71 percent of Japan's entire national capacity was represented by these ten plants, compared with only 37 percent of America's. *Table 3-2* lists the top ten in each country.

Of course, the U.S. steel industry was essentially fully constructed by the early 1950s, when Japan began its own rapid development. Yet, however one might choose to compare the two countries' steel industries, the simple fact remains that Japan's major plants have attained gigantic size—nearly twice that of America's. Similarly, Japan now leads the world in the use of large-capacity furnaces, basic oxygen furnaces, continuous casting, and computer-controlled production processes.[20]

The Economics of Steelmaking

The Japanese superiority in plant and equipment scale is exceedingly important because of one salient fact about steel production: no matter what country steel is produced in, the scale economies are immense. Efficient integrated production requires companies to commit huge amounts of capital, to equip very large facilities.[21] In the 1970s, for example, a "greenfield" American steel plant of 3–4 million tons' annual capacity would have cost no less than $3 billion.[22] Thus, the industry's capital requirements translate into a large fixed-cost component in the final product. This means that it becomes crucial to operate the plant "full and steady"—that is, at or near its full capacity, around the clock, without interruptions. Operating full and steady will, in turn, minimize the unit cost of each ton produced, while operating below capacity will quickly increase the unit cost. Consequently, if any given plant is to attain its maximum efficiency, it *must* be run full and steady. Equally important, nearly

TABLE 3-2
Crude Steel Capacity of Individual Plants
1977–1978

Japan		United States	
	(millions of net tons)		
Fukuyama (NKK)	17.6	Indiana (Inland)	8.5
Mizushima (Kawasaki)	14.0	Gary, IN (USS)	8.0
Chiba (Kawasaki)	10.0	Sparrows Pt, MD (Bethlehem)	7.0
Kimitsu (Nippon Steel)	10.5	Great Lakes, MI (National)	6.6
Wakayama (Sumitomo)	10.2	E. Chicago, IN (Jones & Laughlin)	5.5
Kashima (Sumitomo)	9.9	Burns Harbor, IN (Bethlehem)	5.3
Yawata (Nippon Steel)	9.7	S. Chicago, IL (USS)	5.2
Oita (Nippon Steel)	9.3	Fairless, PA (USS)	4.4
Nagoya (Nippon Steel)	8.3	Cleveland, OH (Republic)	4.4
Kakogawa (Kobe)	7.1	Wierton, WV (National)	4.0
Total (10)	106.5		58.9

SOURCES: Japanese data from IISS, *Steel Industry in Brief: Japan* (1977); U.S. data from IISS Commentary: *Steel Plants USA 1960–1980.*

every stage of the steelmaking process—from the iron furnace to the steel furnace to the rolling mills—is characterized by a series of individual scale economies. As volume of "throughput" increases in each of these phases, overall production costs spiral continuously downward.

During the two decades after World War II, blast furnace technology improved enormously, to make very large-scale furnaces even more efficient. Gradually, the optimal yield of a given furnace increased by a factor of ten: from about 300,000 tons per year to over three million tons. Similarly, a hot strip mill, which is used to roll slabs of steel into sheets, could now produce three or four million tons per year, assuming it ran full and steady. While there remains no precise point of "minimum efficient scale" for an integrated steel plant—because scale economies vary with choices of output and product mix—the optimal plant size during the mid-1970s was widely estimated to be in excess of six million tons. Thus, the scale economies in basic steelmaking had now become immense. Indeed, some experts contended that such economies could actually grow even larger before any upper limit was reached.[23]

Meanwhile, a series of technological innovations provided other cost-cutting methods. The most important of these were, first, the basic oxygen furnace, which requires less time to do its work than the open-hearth furnace, and therefore saves fuel and labor; and, second, continuous casting technology,

which eliminates several intermediate production steps between steel furnaces and rolling mills.

For steel, as for any other industry with enormous economies of scale, the
very efficiency of manufacturing raises serious problems on the demand side. If
steel plants are to be run full and steady, then demand for the product should
be full and steady as well. Yet, overall demand for steel is actually derived from
a host of factors well beyond the control of steel firms: the rate of construction
of capital goods (ships, bridges, steel-frame buildings); the purchase of consumer durables (automobiles, appliances); and, most important of all, the general health of the world economy. Thus, the demand for steel is tightly linked
to overall business cycles; it fluctuates rapidly up or down, making it difficult
for steel managers to run their plants full and steady. As a result, steelmakers—
in all countries and for many generations—have attempted to insulate their
industry from the constant threat of collapsing demand. They have erected all
sorts of cartel arrangements: geographic market divisions, implicit price leadership systems, and organized pools designed to divide up the available demand without the need to cut prices.[24]

It is at precisely this point—the management of demand and supply, and the
explicit use of cartels to hedge investment risks—that the experience of the
Japanese steel industry during the post–World War II period diverged dramatically from that of American steel. While the resulting managerial decisions
could be considered equally "rational" in each country—given their different
industry environments—the two outcomes proved diametrically opposed:
Japanese success versus American failure.

The American Tragedy

In 1945, the United States was the preeminent steel-producing nation. With
only six percent of the world's population, Americans accounted for more than
one-half of all global steel production. This situation did not continue, however, as the postwar industry entered into a long and acrimonious dispute with
the U.S. government over the appropriate level of national steel capacity.[25]
Government planners, aiming for a full-employment economy, sought to stimulate growth in major industrial sectors. Since steel products were central to
the nation's successful economic transition from war to peace (especially the
resumption of new automobile manufacturing, which had been suspended in
1942 in favor of tanks and other military hardware), the U.S. government
anticipated a huge new demand for steel. Public officials were anxious to avoid
a shortage of steel that might restrict the growth of the entire national
economy.

The industry itself, however, remained much less sanguine. Steel executives
believed that existing U.S. capacity could amply provide for all domestic needs.
Industry managers, their memories fixed on the severe economic downturn
that followed World War I, as well as the depression of the 1930s, regarded the
post–World War II spurt in steel demand as only a temporary aberration.

Fearing that the boom would subside, they believed that, in the presence of large new capacity, their plants could never run full and steady. Instead, expansion would lead to overcapacity and very heavy losses. Holding this view, the industry vehemently resisted the government's entreaties to expand.

From 1945 to 1960, this fundamental dispute between American business and government continued to rage within the steel industry. Over these years, each side periodically commissioned "independent" market studies by economists and other scholars. Not surprisingly, each study usually reached the conclusions desired by those who had commissioned it: government-financed studies predicted vigorous growth in demand, while industry-sponsored projections took a gloomier view. When actual demand did in fact climb during the early postwar years, the expansion issue became even more political. Much like the oil crises of the 1970s, the steel capacity question of the 1940s began to revolve around public accusations that the industry was actually conspiring to increase its profits through a policy of "planned scarcity."[26]

Yet for steel executives, the central problem remained that of overcapacity. The president of the American Iron and Steel Institute revealed the nature of the industry's concern when in 1947 he remarked, "[In] all this talk of great shortages and pent-up demand, there is much that recalls the experience of 27 years ago. It was then that the idea of 'accumulated shortages' gained popular acceptance. Then, too, we heard about a steel-starved world. Some prophets of that day saw visions of at least 'ten years of unbroken and unparalleled prosperity' for the steel industry. The very next year your furnaces operated at 35 percent of capacity."[27] Thus, the battle between the steel industry and the government was thoroughly joined. Industry executives, obsessed with the high fixed-cost nature of their business, and the consequent risks to the very solvency of their companies, continued to resist all entreaties to expand overall steel capacity. On its side, the government—now substantially supported by public opinion—continued to urge expansion while insinuating that the industry kept resisting in order to protect high prices and high profits.

At this juncture in the dispute, geopolitical considerations intervened. As the Cold War and the Korean War imposed new burdens on the Department of Defense, the American government decided to change its tactics. Rather than continue trying to persuade steel companies to assume privately the immense risk of investing their own capital in new capacity, the government instituted a series of subsidy programs designed to reduce the risk. First, Congress passed an accelerated-depreciation tax provision for defense-related plants, including steel mills. Under this program, the Defense Department would provide "certificates of necessity" to approved projects, allowing them to be depreciated over five years (rather than the usual twenty). In a related program, the Reconstruction Finance Corporation, a government agency, could offer low-cost loans to holders of such certificates.[28] In response to these incentives, the steel industry embarked on its largest growth program in the twentieth century. Established producers and new entrepreneurs alike flocked to the government with proposals for new steel plants. From 1951 to 1960, the industry's frenzied construction programs raised overall national steel capacity from 100 million tons to 148 million—a 48 percent leap in only ten years. At last, the government had found a way to achieve its original goals for steel.

Despite the optimism that underlay this enormous construction program, the industry had now worked itself into an exceedingly vulnerable position. While overall demand remained as cyclical as ever, new technologies in competing industries had brought a host of substitute materials to the market: prestressed concrete for buildings and bridges, plastic pipes for water mains and plumbing fixtures, aluminum for automobiles and metal containers. Each of these new products cut into the overall demand for basic steel. In fact, national steel production actually declined for three consecutive years after its peak year of 1955, and that peak was not again matched until 1964. Then, too, bitter hostilities between management and organized labor produced major strikes in 1949, 1952, and 1956. Of course, these strikes wrought havoc with the "full and steady" prerequisite for low-cost production at individual plants.[29]

As if these events of the 1950s were not bad enough, the worst still lay ahead. During the fifteen years after World War II, foreign steel manufacturers gradually rebuilt their own plants; and in that process, they were often able to leap-frog a generation (or more) of steel technology. By the late 1950s, therefore, many foreigners were well positioned to compete with the American producers. Thus, in 1959, when a disastrous 116-day strike paralyzed the American steel industry, imports suddenly surged into the domestic market. That year, in fact, turned out to be a watershed: from 1959 onward, the United States became a net importer of steel.

With fierce competition from imports mounting, American steelmakers realized that the only solution was to modernize their aging plants and equipment.[30] Once again, however, the producers' strategy, like the one they had favored a decade earlier, ended in a bitter dispute between government and industry. This time, the issue was pricing policy. Major steelmakers, convinced that price increases would be required to underwrite modernizations, tried through covert "signalling" to raise domestic steel prices across the board. The government, now preoccupied with the growing problem of inflation, resolutely opposed any steel price increase. The most common forum for this business-government dispute was "jawboning" of the industry by the government, and the most conspicuous result was the famous confrontation between President John F. Kennedy and Chairman Roger Blough of U.S. Steel—a confrontation which Kennedy, perhaps inevitably, won, thereby forcing the industry to rescind its price hikes. More to the point, successive U.S. presidents now threatened the industry with antitrust prosecutions if its pricing policies appeared to the government as collusive or "noncompetitive."[31]

Forced by these circumstances to accept lower prices and to make uncoordinated investment decisions—within a market where few plants operated full and steady—American executives could launch only modest modernization programs. Companies retrofitted new technology onto often antiquated facilities. In some cases, open-hearth furnaces were replaced with more efficient basic oxygen technology, as a few American companies, motivated by price competition from imports, tried to rationalize the flow of materials and manufacturing processes within their plants.

Unfortunately for the American industry as a whole, these investments came too late to head off the invasion by foreign imports. Despite some modernizations, most American companies still remained saddled with old, unrefurbished capacity in too many small-scale plants. By the 1970s, only four of the industry's 44 integrated plants had an annual capacity of six million tons—the figure generally regarded as optimal efficient scale. According to some analysts, even these four big American plants could not benefit fully from scale economies, because they were poorly laid out and cursed with obsolete technology. As imports took larger and larger market shares, capacity utilization in the American plants steadily declined. In fact, during the period 1958–1977, overall American steel capacity remained underutilized during all but three years.[32] As early as 1970, it seemed evident to many steel managers that their industry was caught in a deadly trap: a vicious cycle of rising imports, falling volume, high labor and manufacturing costs, and low profits. Concluding that in such a market no individual company could cope effectively, U.S. steel managers reached desperately for a political solution: protection against foreign imports.

In the brief period from the early 1950s to the middle 1970s, the American steel industry had fallen from the largest and most technologically advanced in the world, to the condition of a lagging competitor that could not even maintain its domestic market share. Steel imports into the United States increased from one percent of domestic consumption in 1950 to 14 percent in 1976, and to 22 percent by 1982. Indeed, without the protectionist political measures that the industry had been able to wheedle from the American government during the intervening years, the 22 percent figure in 1982 would likely have been much larger. By the late 1970s, the U.S. steel crisis had reached drastic proportions, as the industry's net income actually fell to zero. More than 50 percent of capacity stood idle; almost half of all American steelworkers had been laid off. Finally, with losses relentlessly accumulating year after year, America's major steel companies began to diversify—that is, to invest their remaining assets in other industries, such as oil, chemicals, and fabricated metal products. As the chairman of U.S. Steel, David M. Roderick, commented, the entire process amounted to a "state of accelerating self-liquidation."[33]

How had all this happened? Naturally, the reasons are complex, but there can be no doubt that industry management had failed to make the required capital investments. As one recent study has noted, "What is not understandable is the lack of initiative on the part of steelmakers to invest aggressively for expansion, productivity improvements and export. . . ."[34] Yet, is it really so difficult to understand their behavior? For the fact remains that under the customary ways of doing business in the United States—with intra-industry coordination being against the antitrust laws, with investment decisions by each company becoming necessarily independent—an aggressive pattern of capital investment by any individual company might well have proved irrational. Given the underlying economics of the industry, together with the uncertainty of demand and price in the unprotected U.S. market, steel executives lived with an almost morbid fear of excess capacity.

Of course, other factors—in addition to excess capacity and uncertain demand—also influenced managers' investment decisions. For example, as capital and labor costs continued to rise, rates of return fell and alternative investments looked more attractive to steel companies. But these very cost-benefit calculations which led the companies to retreat, and eventually to diversify into other industries, were themselves affected by the uncertainty of demand and the inevitability of price-cutting. Consequently, in steel, as in other high fixed-cost industries, managers became preoccupied with trying to stabilize price and volume. Since cartels remained illegal, the industry could only attempt to coordinate its activities through implicit price leadership schemes. Although it did this with some success, steel could never escape the risk of heavy losses from overcapacity—brought on not only by industry leaders but at the urging of the United States government. So long as explicit inter-firm negotiations over investment capacity remained illegal *per se,* there was simply no way out. Losses and eventual bankruptcies now seemed almost inevitable. In such a situation, company managers shifted their attention from technological modernizations to the difficult task of minimizing losses. To do this, they tried to avoid price-cutting—thereby making themselves vulnerable to even more import competition—and they assiduously shunned large capital investments.

Thus, the attention of American steel executives, quite rationally under the circumstances, became fixed on the minimizing of losses. Under the American system, no countervailing force existed that would have motivated a rational manager, in possession of adequately functioning equipment, voluntarily to raise short-run fixed costs by scrapping old plants and investing heavily in new technology. Such a strategy would have seemed suicidal. And yet, as we shall see, in Japan this very strategy provided the fundamental basis for the Japanese miracle in steel.

The Japanese Achievement

In 1945, when the Pacific War ended, five companies accounted for about two-thirds of Japan's total steel output. In 1975, the same five firms still dominated the industry. During the intervening thirty years, Japan's national capacity had risen from less than two million tons to 150 million, yet little change had occurred in the industry's structure. At first glance, the industry appears to have grown through aggressive company strategies that centered on continuous investments in large, modern manufacturing equipment and facilities. No overall government action compelled these successful business policies. Japanese steel managers appear to have allocated resources so as to maximize the profits and the long-run viability of their firms—more or less in the same manner as business executives elsewhere in the world.

On closer examination, however, we can see that the particular pattern of investment decisions pursued by Japanese steel executives was *not* followed in any other major market economy. In the first place, the expansion strategies of the Japanese steel companies reflected an enormous gamble, based on a pronounced optimism concerning the continued stability and growth of the world steel market. Year after year, Japanese companies increased their production capacity, despite the persistence of cyclical recessions. Second, Japanese steel firms did invest in plant rationalizations that required a sacrifice of short-term profits in favor of uncertain gains in long-term productivity. Both of these decision patterns—which differed radically from those followed by American steel companies during the same period—made sense only within the new system of industrial organization fashioned by Japan's government.

During the immediate postwar years, the government's primary objective was simply to rebuild the country's devastated economy. Because Japan had few natural endowments, it depended on external sources for necessities such as food and raw materials. Reindustrialization also required the importation of expensive technology and heavy machinery. In order to earn the foreign currency to pay these large import bills, Japan needed a correspondingly large volume of exports, preferably of the high-value-added variety. Thus, MITI targeted several industries for potential export growth: steel was one of these. MITI targeted steel for two quite different reasons. First, world steel demand was already strong during the postwar period, and it was expected to become even stronger as national economies recovered and reconverted to peacetime production. Steel exports, because of their high value added, would contribute more to Japan's foreign currency earnings than would other manufactured items—such as low-value-added textiles, which remained Japan's primary export item until 1951. Second, as a basic material, steel was used in such key industries as shipbuilding, automobiles, and machinery, and thus would prove essential for Japan's own domestic economic development. Once these other industries had reestablished themselves within Japan, they could become important exports on their own, thereby earning Japan still more precious foreign exchange. For any of these ambitious plans to materialize, however, a significant level of steel production represented an absolute prerequisite. So the chief question for government was not *whether* to develop the Japanese steel industry, but rather *how.*

As MITI bureaucrats grappled with this question, one aspect of their strategy began to emerge clearly. For the eventual export strategy to work, the Japanese domestic market must play a vital function: it must become a greenhouse where the essential factors of competition—supply, demand, and price—could be carefully controlled. Like sunlight, temperature, and humidity, they might be adjusted up or down, in order to nurture the development of Japanese steel companies. Through this strategy, MITI would alter the economic environment in which Japanese steel managers made investment decisions.

Overall, the new environment was built on three central elements. First, most foreign imports had to be excluded, since they might underprice domestic steel and prevent full and steady utilization of Japanese plants. Second, even within Japan, MITI worked out a system designed to protect domestic steel companies from the dangers of overcapacity and competitive price-cutting. Thus sheltered from the risk of low utilization rates and resulting price wars, Japanese companies could undertake ambitious expansion and modernization programs. Third, and most unusual of all, MITI helped the industry to coordinate a system of new capacity allocation rights, based on each company's demonstrated efficiency (as defined by its record of productivity). Here, MITI's central premise was that the best route to minimizing long-run costs and securing world market share was to *invest continually in more efficient means of production.*[35]

This last element of the strategy, which became known by the term *sangyō no gōrika* (industrial rationalization), established high productivity as a prerequisite for growth. In response to the challenge of productivity, steel companies now began to compete fiercely: they upgraded existing facilities to become more productive, in order to earn the right to build new capacity. MITI's program thereby kept constant pressure on the industry and forced its standard of productivity farther and farther out into new frontiers of efficiency.

This unusual and seemingly paradoxical combination of administrative guidance with market forces worked to yield the combined benefits of stability and market rivalry. In a truly extraordinary way, MITI succeeded in circumventing the classic risks inherent in steelmaking. As the new goal became ever-increasing productivity, Japanese steel companies entered a competitive race to outrationalize each other. In the process, they transformed Japan's collection of small and backward plants into the most productive and technologically sophisticated steel industry the world had ever seen.

The Japanese Domestic Steel Market and Government Policies

By 1951, Japan's economic environment had become propitious for reindustrialization. The war in Korea, domestic reconstruction, and a tight world steel market all had stimulated demand for Japanese steel. As a result, in 1952 the industry's output almost regained its World War II level.[36] Despite rapidly growing demand, MITI continued to focus attention on potential problems, especially those that might arise from "excess competition."[37] Here, the first threat came from imports. With small plants and obsolete equipment, the Japanese steel industry exhibited manufacturing costs approximately twice those of U.S. firms—which left Japanese companies with no hope of entering world markets except during periods of extreme global shortages. Moreover, if

Japan's domestic market were open to imports, then low-cost steel would flood in and prevent the Japanese steel industry from developing at all.[38]

A second source of instability, MITI reasoned, lay within the free market system itself: if Japanese steel companies responded freely to burgeoning demand, then the industry as a whole would experience an explosion of new capacity, spread across a number of companies. This would prevent any companies from operating full and steady and in turn deprive them of scale economies. Moreover, as Japan's postwar monetary policies continued to cause cyclical fluctuations in domestic demand, the steel market often swung from booms (in which steel remained in short supply while prices soared) to recessions (in which overcapacity threatened some firms with actual bankruptcy). MITI feared that within any pure free market system, the steel industry would enter a vicious circle of overcapacity, price-cutting, low margins, and large losses.[39]

Thus, the Japanese government stood face to face with the central dilemma of managing competition: should public policy—in Japan or any other market economy—attempt explicitly to equilibrate supply and demand? In the case of a market downturn, for example, how could the government insulate companies from the price-cutting that so often accompanied oversupply? How could companies' decisions on investment in new capacity be coordinated, especially in periods of economic downturn? How would such decisions affect Japan's future export potential? Finally, if government intervention did prove to be necessary, what specific policies might reduce market instability without simultaneously stifling the entrepreneurial rivalry that fostered innovation? Considering the American government's policy for the same industry at the same time, it seems remarkable that the Japanese government asked such questions at all. The most striking aspect of the Japanese steel market was not the economics of steelmaking—for those are universal—but rather MITI's *fundamental decision to intervene so systematically in routine business affairs.*

Once MITI reached that decision, however, its pattern of intervention became clear. First, because rapid economic development remained Japan's top priority, and because steel appeared to be central to that goal, the problems and risks of steelmaking became national concerns. Here, Japan's competition policy sharply diverged from conventional American thinking. For the United States, as noted earlier, excess supply, price-cutting, and the risk of losses were considered inevitable, and even beneficial—to steel as well as to other industries. Price wars were viewed as boons to consumers. To Japanese bureaucrats working within MITI, however, the disorder that accompanied such normal market operations, when applied to the Japanese steel situation, would produce investment choices that were deleterious to the entire steel industry—and, by extension, to the Japanese economy. Thus, MITI saw no alternative except to alter the free market system.

The first, easiest step was simply to protect Japanese companies from foreign competition. Until the mid-1960s, therefore, imports were generally prohibited. Then, with MITI's guidance, the industry began systematically to coordinate its investments in new capacity, thereby attempting to keep supply in balance with domestic and export demand. Until the late 1950s, MITI exercised enormous influence over each firm's investment decisions, by allocating its capital. In a decision obviously calculated to build up strong companies at the expense of weaker ones, MITI concentrated the flow of government funds toward a tiny handful of large steelmakers. From 1951 to 1956, for example, 72 percent of the steel industry's entire funding went to only four of Japan's forty-four steel companies—under conditions essentially dictated by MITI.[40] In fact, one of these four, Kawasaki Steel, received its allotment only after a notorious fight with MITI.[41]

By the late 1960s, MITI's power to direct company investment decisions had diminished, and the steel industry was left to manage supply and demand itself. Acting with MITI's assistance, Japanese companies developed a practice known as *jishu chōsei* (voluntary self-regulation), under which managers of leading steel companies met regularly to coordinate new capacity investment plans. While no written records exist of precisely what transpired at these industry-wide meetings, it now appears that the companies attempted to maintain an orderly, stable rate of capacity growth that matched the changes in domestic and export demand for steel. For example, in late 1964, when steel demand declined, Japanese managers agreed to limit investments to those projects already under construction. Then, as the economy worsened in 1965, the industry announced an actual moratorium on *all* new steel capacity. Only investments for modernization were permitted.[42]

Meanwhile, MITI discovered that balancing supply with demand did not by itself ensure the steel industry's success. Business cycles in the global and domestic markets continued to cause volume and price fluctuations, and thereby threaten the short-term solvency of individual companies. Even with the existing government protection from overcapacity and price-cutting, there still remained little motivation for companies to sacrifice profits in favor of upgraded equipment. Thus, in response to the problem of price fluctuations, MITI helped the industry to stabilize prices during market downturns. Through organized price announcements (called "open sales systems"), together with outright recession cartels, the industry was able to maintain high prices for domestic steel.[43]

Again, on the issue of forced modernization, MITI began to advocate a remarkable "scrap and build" strategy for the entire industry. Overall, the government's successive exhortations finally came to be instituted within the industry's own *jishu chōsei* system. Steel company executives themselves would negotiate capacity expansions, guided by a combination of MITI-sponsored criteria: past market share, proven efficiency of existing capacity, and expected future world demand. Thus, for any company to win the right to build new plants (or later, even to maintain its existing capacity), it must demonstrate that it had invested in the most modern and efficient equipment available. This process of allocating national capacity according to demonstrated productivity drove managers decisively away from the marginal-cost analyses typical of most business planning; instead, they entered a frenzied race for the right to construct giant modern facilities. In place of short-run profitability, their goal now became improved long-run productivity.

At several critical junctures, MITI acted directly to compel particular companies to make a certain decision. Sometimes MITI succeeded in such efforts, sometimes not. Overall, however, MITI's role was mostly hortatory, as final investment decisions remained in the hands of steel executives. Yet the obvious political and economic consequences of those decisions actually left managers with few realistic alternatives. Within such a controlled environment, rational business behavior for a steel executive came to mean investing single-mindedly in successive modernizations, in order to maintain the company's honorable standing within the Japanese steel industry—and to ensure its right to add new capacity.

Investment Decisions

Throughout the postwar decades, Japanese steel companies' investments reflected two distinct but continuous patterns. First, supported by MITI's formidable efforts to prevent overcapacity and price-cutting, Japanese managers invested with an eye toward unlimited growth. The major companies emerged from each recession bullish on investment.[44] In 1960, for example, during a time of tremendous economic uncertainty, when many Japanese anticipated an end to their country's rapid growth, the steel industry ignored all signs of slowdown. Instead, it cooperated with the government's overall "income-doubling" plan by raising its own projections to the government's new growth targets. In fact, rather than merely agreeing to double capacity in ten years (the government's plan), the steel industry publicly announced that it would triple Japanese capacity. Every major company then accelerated its construction schedule, to prevent any loss of market share under the new forecasts.[45]

Such relentless optimism—in an industry noted for its high fixed costs and uneven levels of output—can be understood only in the context of Japan's protected economic environment: since overall capacity and price levels could be coordinated through *jishu chōsei,* companies could invest for booms, confident that they would not suffer unduly during troughs. Sheltered in this way from the risks endured by steelmakers in other countries, the major Japanese companies adopted go-for-broke strategies. In the process, they built capacity not only for domestic consumption, but for a growing export market as well.

By the 1960s, Japanese managers inevitably found themselves in the classic entrepreneurial dilemma brought on by rapid technological change: the industry as a whole had invested huge sums of capital in plants that were becoming obsolete. Japanese firms, like American ones, had invested in conventional plants and equipment while, at the same time, production technology was improving and the optimal plant size was growing ever larger. At this point, Japanese business decisions again diverged fundamentally from traditional American practice. This happened because, in order to win the right to build new capacity, Japanese companies were engaged in a fierce domestic race to outrationalize each other. Thus, they were actually willing to scrap still useful equipment and replace it with even more modern facilities.

In 1960, the Japanese steel industry operated 150 open-hearth furnaces, more than half of which were almost new, having been constructed since 1950. Others had been fully renovated. By 1980, however, *all* open-hearth furnaces in Japan had been replaced with the more efficient basic oxygen furnaces.[46] For Kawasaki Steel, this change required that the company dismantle six huge open-hearth furnaces built between 1952 and 1961. Starting in 1964, Kawasaki did exactly that, replacing each furnace with a new basic oxygen facility. In America, such a "scrap and build" philosophy would have been unthinkable.

Yet many Japanese companies went to astounding lengths to rationalize. In the mid-1970s, Nippon Kokan (NKK), Japan's second largest steel company, actually razed a fully operational 5.5 million ton facility at Keihin and replaced it with a new 6 million ton, ultramodern plant.[47] With this single step, NKK scrapped over twenty years of accumulated investment at Keihin to build a greenfield facility that added almost no new capacity to the company. To accomplish its goal of modernization, NKK built a new land mass onto a small island situated off the coast of its own Keihin Works. The company then proceeded to construct a large, modern plant on the new site. To do all this, NKK literally moved a mountain from Futtsu City, near Chiba, to the coast off Yokohama, then carried it—millions of cubic meters of earth and rock— across the bay in barges, to dump on Ogishima Island. After building a land mass comprising 7.3 million square meters, NKK then installed an entirely new plant with the most modern equipment available. When the new Ogishima complex began operations, NKK closed all of the blast furnaces, basic oxygen furnaces, and rolling mills at Keihin, even though 80 percent of this equipment had been installed as recently as the 1960s. The whole episode epitomizes the almost incredible lengths to which Japanese companies were willing to go in their fundamental "scrap and build" strategy.[48]

Such decisions, which formed a persistent pattern in the Japanese steel industry, are impossible to comprehend on the basis of standard business practice in the United States. Most American managers will not routinely abandon useful equipment the moment some new technology becomes more efficient. Orthodox logic dictates instead that, so long as the marginal cost of production on the old, depreciated equipment remains less than the full cost of producing with new equipment, the company will stay with existing facilities. Japanese steel executives, operating within a protected yet still fiercely competitive environment, chose to forgo short-run profits for the sake of greater long-run productivity.

Of course, no industry can grow from two million tons of capacity to 150 million without significant greenfield construction. But the unusual way in which this growth occurred, involving a number of separate "scrap and build" episodes, remains critical to any real understanding of the ultimate success of Japan's steel industry. With MITI's prodding, Japanese managers cooperated systematically on volume and price decisions. But managers also competed, and with feverish intensity, to make their firms the leaders in productivity: to achieve the biggest, best laid-out, and most technologically sophisticated plants in Japan. The final results of this entire system proved exceptionally satisfying. By 1976, Japan had nineteen integrated plants, which together could produce well over 100 million tons of steel per year. Of these, eleven possessed over six million tons of capacity. Thus, with a few modern and extremely large-scale plants, the Japanese industry surpassed all competitors and grew into the world's leading producer and exporter of steel.

The Japanese government's measures in steel constituted a tight system of interdependent regulations which, taken together, amounted to a partial cartel. Yet instead of promoting inefficiency, as economic theory might predict, Japan's coordination of *some* of the elements of competition actually pushed technology toward new frontiers of efficiency. Throughout the period of major growth, the key devices remained the management of supply and the allocation of capacity rights according to productivity. These unusual practices lowered the risk of investment and compelled firms to compete on the basis of productivity.

Of course, no economic problems are solved permanently. By the mid-1980s, Japanese steel companies were operating at less than 70 percent of capacity. New entrants from Korea, Brazil, and Taiwan had emerged as serious rivals. In one year, 1983, Japan actually imported 6 percent of its domestic steel consumption, while continuing to export about 30 percent of its production. While it remains impossible to foresee precisely how Japan will deal with such changes in the global steel market, it does seem clear that the United States and Japan had—and still have—diametrically opposed attitudes and laws regarding competition. In the postwar decades, American steel companies were forced to cope individually with the risks of cyclical demand, price-cutting, and heavy losses. Competition policy in America, as expressed in antitrust laws, explicitly forbade cooperation among firms. This drove companies toward their only rational solutions: to minimize losses by avoiding new costs. Japan, by contrast, restrained competition in the sense that it coordinated prices and capacity; but it promoted innovation in such a way that it attained the most modern steel industry in the world.

Today, these Japanese policies continue largely unchanged. Here, for example, is a recent newspaper account of how Japanese steel policy is coordinated:[49]

[The setting]: The Iron-Steel Building in Nihonbashi, Tokyo. Around noon every Monday, elderly gentlemen arrive in black cars. . . . They go to Room 704, on the entrance of which is a sign reading, "The Regular Monday Club Meeting." The members consist of the senior executives of eight major steel producers. They sit at a rectangular table around the section chief of the Ministry of International Trade and Industry, who is seated at the head of the table.

Ogawa, who heads the Iron and Steel Section of the Basic Industries Bureau of MITI, presides over the meeting. On his left is Vice President Ohashi of [Nippon Steel] and on his right is Senior Director Yamaguchi of [NKK]. . . . During the lunch, few speak. . . . After coffee, the members listen to Ogawa's presentation. The meeting ends after about an hour. The official name of the Monday Club is the General Session of the Market Policies Committee. It was organized in 1958 and since then has served as a point of contact between MITI and the industry. . . . Among the ranks of the senior directors of the major steel firms are former MITI officers who "descended" to those firms. [NKK's] Counselor Matsuo (former MITI vice-minister); Sumitomo Metal's President Kumagai (former MITI vice-minister); Kobe Steel's Vice President Komatsu (former MITI vice-minister).

Of course, the mere fact of regular meetings among steel executives and government bureaucrats proves little about any overall pattern of economic policy. In the steel industry, however, we have seen that the strategy of Japanese business and government during the postwar decades is exceptionally clear. A handful of large companies, their number strictly limited by MITI, availed themselves of the world's most advanced technology and proceeded to build gigantic, state-of-the-art plants. Then, insulated by government policies from the shocks of imports and from periodic domestic downturns, the companies rode the powerful wave of rising demand that prevailed throughout most of the period of miracle growth. Today, the habits ingrained during those glory years continue; and, with only minor exceptions, so do the successes of the Japanese steel industry in world markets.

Distribution

So far, this chapter has been mostly concerned with *big* business in America and Japan. Left out have been the tens of thousands of small craft shops, restaurants, and retail establishments—which together form the backbone of small business in both countries, and which employ far more of the total labor force than do all big businesses combined. As the American economy continues to become more one of entrepreneurial enterprise, characterized by services rather than dominated by large industrial companies, this difference between big and small business looms ever more important. In the case of Japan, small establishments are so extraordinarily distinct from the giant industrial enterprises such as Mitsui, Mitsubishi, Toyota, and Nippon Steel that in the overall sense Japan represents a clear instance of a modern "dual economy." In fact, dualisms within Japan are numerous, but none of them is more striking than the double levels of the Japanese economy, divided between the production sector and the distribution sector.

The postwar Japanese economic achievement represented primarily a miracle of production, supplemented by the very efficient external and overseas networks of distribution and raw materials sourcing. Together, Japan's nine great *sōgō shōsha* (general trading companies) purchased and sold about half of the entire nation's imports and exports.[50] Yet, within the Japanese home market, distribution as a whole remained less efficient than in the import-export sector, and seemed far less efficient than the overall Japanese production sector. Here, in fact, recent Japanese triumphs and American failures become almost precisely reversed.

Today, the Japanese distribution network as a whole, in contrast with the American one, remains extraordinarily complex—weighted with multiple layers of middlemen who not only seem unnecessary, but who may represent actual hindrances to the efficient distribution of goods. Nor does this cumbersome Japanese system contrast with the United States alone (see *Table 3-3*).[51]

TABLE 3-3
International Comparisons of Wholesalers and Retailers

	Japan	Britain	France	W. Germany	United States
Number of wholesalers	369,000	57,000	97,000	113,600	383,000
Employees per wholesaler	10	14.8	6.4	9.9	9.4
Population per wholesaler	315	1,095	542	540	565
Number of retailers	1,673,000	351,000	533,000	340,500	1,855,000
Employees per retailer	3.6	6.9	2.6	6.1	8.1
Population per retailer	69	160	99	180	117

Thus, with only about half the population of the United States, and three-fourths the per-capita GNP, Japan has almost as many wholesalers and retailers. Even more indicative are the key numbers for population per wholesaler and population per retailer (the third line and the bottom line of *Table 3-3*). In both cases, Japan exhibits a very different pattern from all four of the other countries.[52]

Many Japanese scholars, bureaucrats, and business executives openly acknowledge the multilayered complexity of their country's distribution system. *Figure 3-2,* for example, is one very revealing figure contrasting the

FIGURE 3-2

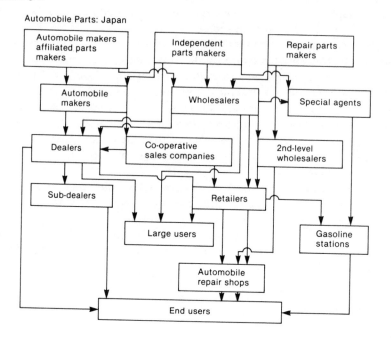

Automobile Parts: Japan

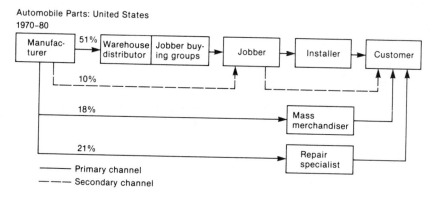

Automobile Parts: United States
1970–80

distribution patterns for automobile parts in Japan with those in America: Figures such as these commonly appear in books and articles about distribution systems in Japan. In every case, the point remains the same: the Japanese system, compared with either the American or with those of European countries, appears to have a host of superfluous middlemen.[53]

Within Japan, several notable exceptions to this pattern do exist. Matsushita, the appliance and electronics giant, has integrated forward into retailing, with an effective network of franchise stores. So have other major appliance com-

TABLE 3-4
Department Stores/General Merchandisers

	Japan			USA		
Company	Annual Sales	Number of Stores	Company	Annual Sales	Number of Stores
1. Daiei*	$5.1 billion	166	1. Sears*	$35.9 billion	831
2. Ito-Yokado*	3.6b	116	2. K Mart**	18.6b	2,370
3. Seiyu*	2.9b	164	3. Safeway¶	18.6b	2,454
4. Jusco*	2.9b	148	4. Kroger¶	15.2b	1,262
5. Nichii*	2.3b	160	5. Penney*	12.1b	1,984
6. Mitsukoshi§	2.2b	14	6. Southland§§	8.8b	7,722
7. Takashimaya§	2.0b	6	7. Federated§	8.7b	508
8. Daimaru§	2.0b	8	8. Lucky¶	8.4b	1,590
9. Seibu§	1.9b	10	9. American¶	8.0b	1,027
10. Uny*	1.6b	104	10. Winn-Dixie¶	7.0b	1,222
Average	$2.65b	89	Average	$14.1b	1,994
			Average without Southland:		1,472

KEY: * = General Merchandise Stores, which in Japan usually include food sales. ¶ = Supermarkets, which in each country sell food plus other items as well. § = Department Store Chains. ** = Discount Houses. §§ = Convenience Stores. (Southland in America operates 7-Eleven stores, of which there are now nearly 8,000. Under a contractual agreement with Southland, Ito-Yokado operates about 1,400 7-Elevens in Japan, which are not included in Ito-Yokado's totals above.)

panies. Then, too, since the mid-1960s, the Daiei chain has opened dozens of outlets that resemble American mass retailers, such as Safeway and Sears. Other prominent Japanese innovators include Ito-Yokado, Seibu, and Tōkyū. Yet each of these exceptions remains exactly that. Despite endless discussions within Japan during the last twenty years of a "distribution revolution," the historic pattern of thousands of small retail shops, served by layer upon layer of wholesalers, remains the overall Japanese style of domestic distribution.[54]

For the retail sector, perhaps the clearest way to illustrate the differences between Japan and the United States is simply to list the leading companies in retailing, and then to note the different sizes of those companies in the two countries as shown in *Table 3-4*. (The year in question is 1983.)[55] Thus, U.S. chain retailers are far larger than their Japanese counterparts. *Precise* cross-national comparisons are impossible, however, because stores in the two countries do not sell exactly the same kinds of goods.[56] Many Japanese general merchandisers, for example, and even some department stores, sell food as well as other items. A typical Daiei or Ito-Yokado in Japan will be multistoried, with groceries available on the ground floor, clothing on the second, and so on. Yet, even with the pattern of comparison distorted in this way, the overall point remains clear: Japanese stores do not possess anything like the size or economies of scale that U.S. retailers do.[57]

Reasons for the Differences

As we consider the contrasting Japanese and American styles of wholesaling and retailing, it is difficult to say exactly what is causing what. Obviously, a host of factors are involved. In retailing, severe limits on available land make it impractical for the Japanese to emulate American-style shopping centers, with their huge malls and prodigal parking lots. Over the last thirty years, urban land prices in Japan have skyrocketed.[58] Then, too, in the case of food purchases, Japanese consumers (like French ones) are said to prefer small specialty shops offering highly perishable goods, and characterized by personalized service.

Even though overall prices for many consumer items in Japan remain noticeably higher than those in the U.S., it may well be that Japanese and American consumers are still not buying *exactly* the same thing. Thus, it may be slightly inaccurate to assert simply that American distribution is more "efficient" than Japanese, when different things are being bought. Japanese consumers may be paying, quite willingly, for superior information and service; or they may be purchasing time, through the device of buying at the nearest store rather than at the least expensive one. They may be engaged in the cementing of long-time family and neighborhood relationships with local merchants, in addition to paying for the goods themselves. Furthermore, some of the Mom-and-Pop stores can charge prices only a little higher than those available at supermarkets, because the owners often live on the premises, work long hours, and pay no rent. It is difficult, therefore, to draw a sharp line between the effects of consumer preference, on the one hand, and public policy, on the other.

Even so, the history of regulatory measures in both countries reveals very different patterns of government intervention; and such interventions, beyond any doubt, have played a significant and perhaps a decisive role in shaping different patterns of distribution in the two countries. Only by starting with a careful historical analysis of the evolution of such regulatory policies can we hope to understand the reasons for the different configurations of American and Japanese wholesaling and retailing.[59]

In nearly all market economies, including both Japan and the United States, fierce political battles between big and small retailers have been fought throughout the twentieth century.[60] In many countries, the coming of chain stores and supermarkets wrought havoc on the livelihoods of small local merchants. And almost everywhere, these merchants battled long and hard to protect their interests. In nearly all countries, for example, "fair trade" laws (resale price maintenance, or price fixing) represented a favorite device for protecting small local grocers, druggists, and other shopkeepers. Today, resale price maintenance is still commonly used in Europe and, for a few items (books, cosmetics, and drugs) in Japan. In the United States, by contrast, the practice was first ruled illegal three generations ago—in 1911, by the Supreme Court, under the authority of the Sherman Antitrust Act.[61]

In the years after 1911, tireless lobbying in America by associations of small merchants continued without interruption. New bills to legalize price fixing were introduced into every session of Congress, and many state legislatures passed laws restoring price fixing to legality. Finally, during the deflationary years of the Great Depression, the United States Congress followed suit.[62] This action came too late, however, because consumers and chain retailers had developed ways to circumvent "fair trade," which never again regained its original potency in suppressing price competition. In fact, during the inflationary years of the middle 1970s, Congress acted once again to outlaw it, through legislation significantly entitled the Consumer Goods Pricing Act.[63]

As for chain stores, small merchants in America fought them with extraordinary tenacity throughout the 1920s and 1930s. The whole issue became a perennial hot potato in state and local politics. Many state legislatures, responding to the pressures of local merchants, passed laws imposing heavy discriminatory taxes on retail chains, which continued to proliferate despite these laws. Always, the chains protested that such laws were unfair; and indeed, the United States Supreme Court stepped in from time to time, ruling certain kinds of discriminatory taxation unconstitutional. But the most decisive blow in favor of the chains was struck in 1936, when a popular referendum in the State of California rejected, by a two-to-one margin, a proposed tax on chain stores. This decisive result derived in large part from energetic lobbying by the chains, including newspaper advertisements pointing out their low prices and identifying their high-volume, cut-rate goals with the consumer's own interest.[64]

This pattern of lobbying by the chains quickly spread to other states, laying the groundwork for eventual victory almost everywhere. But always, the local battles remained intense and bitter. Passion and extravagant rhetoric usually prevailed—naturally enough, since the very livelihood of thousands of small merchants was at stake. Even the Supreme Court often found itself sharply split over the proper course for public policy to take. Should the interests of consumers be emphasized, or those of local merchants? Should economic considerations take precedence, or social ones?

One brief example of the many cases that shaped American policy will illustrate the intense feeling characteristic of this issue. In the 1920s, the State of Florida passed a law designed to suppress the growth of drug and grocery chains. That law laid a discriminatory tax on chains, a tax that did not apply at all to local merchants. It thereby placed a heavy additional expense on the chains, and put them at a disadvantage in their effort to offer cut-rate prices. In response to this action by the Florida legislature, the Liggett drug chain challenged the law as a violation of the U.S. Constitution. Liggett's attorneys argued that the equal protection clause of the Fourteenth Amendment specifically forbade discriminatory action of this type. When, in 1933, the case of *Liggett v. Lee* finally reached the Supreme Court, it proved troubling for the Justices, precisely because it seemed to represent a clear clash between economic and social values. Six of the nine Justices, after giving the matter thorough consideration, ruled that the Florida law did indeed violate the Constitution and was therefore invalid.

Three other Justices disagreed, however. Their spokesman in this case, the great Louis D. Brandeis, argued passionately that state governments *should* have the right to protect their small business people, as a means of preserving the glue that held communities together. In a ringing dissent, Brandeis wrote that the Florida legislature "may have believed that the chain store, by furthering the concentration of wealth and of power and by promoting absentee ownership, is thwarting American ideals . . . it is sapping the resources, the vigor and the hope of the smaller cities and towns."[65] Brandeis's analysis, heavily footnoted to studies of social unrest, went on in this vein for page after page—providing an unusually long and powerful argument.

So, even in the United States, the war between large cut-rate national chains and small local merchants was protracted and bitter. During the campaign, the chains lost a few important battles, as in the passage of the Robinson-Patman Act of 1936 (which limited the wholesale discounts that chain stores could command because of their tremendous buying power). Yet, in the most significant decisions concerning American public policy, low prices have almost always been accorded far greater importance than the preservation of small enterprise. In the United States, the consumer has been made king.[66]

In Japan, the overall policy has tended toward the opposite direction. The consumer has sometimes paid higher prices so that small retailers and wholesalers might prosper. Moreover, the choice of Japanese policy has been taken with open-eyed awareness at every step. Both government bureaucrats and private business executives remain acutely conscious of the deliberateness of Japan's choice. They well know, for example, the turbulent history of American retailing and its regulation. *Figure 3-3*, for example, is a reproduction of a chart prepared by a Japanese consulting firm and widely distributed in retailing circles. The diagram summarizes in remarkably concise detail the history of American retailing.[67] Some of the characterizations in this chart are open to question, in part because its designers attempted to squeeze too much complex information into too small a space. Even so, a number of relevant points emerge clearly: First, American chain stores go back a very long way, well into the nineteenth century. The first chain, The Great Atlantic & Pacific Tea Company—A&P, as it came to be called—actually began operations in 1858. Later in the nineteenth century, the large urban department stores (Macy's, Filene's, Wanamaker's) as well as the great mail-order houses (Sears, Ward's) entered their own periods of rapid growth. Then, early in the twentieth century, the era of the chain store arrived, as chains of drugstores, groceries, and apparel houses began to spring up all over the United States. Beginning in the 1930s, the great self-service supermarket chains spread very rapidly, spurred by the rise of the automobile culture. Sometimes the supermarkets grew directly out

FIGURE 3-3
History of Development and Diversification in U.S. Retail Industry

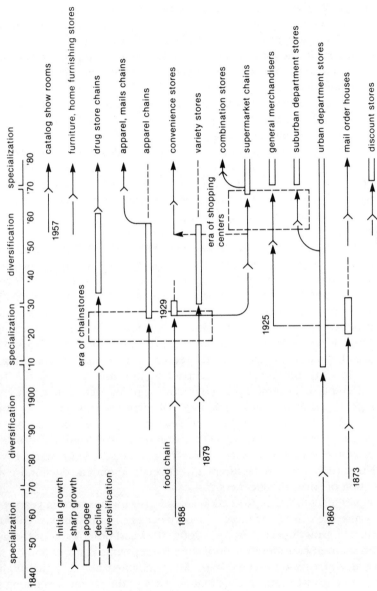

SOURCE: NRI.

of companies that had been more specialized chains—tea, for example, in the case of A&P, which was the most successful of the early grocery chains.[68]

As one looks at the entire diagram, it is useful to bear in mind that the story it tells may appear to be simply a routine evolution in business history. Yet the reality was quite the opposite: nearly every episode in the rise of national retailers was accompanied by a fierce political battle which ended in victory for consumers, in the form of low prices. This result often derived not primarily from legislative or executive action, but rather from the rulings of the American judiciary. In fact, it remains today an open question whether the outcome might have been somewhat different had the American political system not accorded such extraordinary power to the courts, and such unusual emphasis to the whole institution of judicial review.

To this American history, of course, Japan provides a distinct contrast. As in many other aspects of Japanese business-government relations, the administration of policy concerning retail and wholesale trade does not lie primarily in the hands of judges. Instead, policy is implemented by government bureaucrats, acting under general legislative guidelines.

In Japan, the regulation of retail competition began in earnest in 1937, with the passage by the Diet of the Department Store Act. As in America, powerful department stores had long existed in major Japanese cities, but they had refrained from extensive branching. That idea, adopted from the American experience of Sears and Penney's , was tried out in Japan during the 1930s. The legislation of 1937 was designed to slow the spread of chain branches of department stores, and thereby to protect small-scale retailers.[69] Over the next decade, in Japan as in the United States, preoccupations with other national priorities (especially World War II) reduced concerns about retailing. After the war, in 1947, the American Occupation authorities, as part of their broadscale attempt to prompt open competition in the Japanese economy, encouraged the Diet to revoke the 1937 Department Store Act, and the Diet complied. In 1956, however, just four years after the Occupation's departure, the old law was restored in virtually its original form. Two decades later, an additional measure, the Special Act for the Adjustment of Retailing, extended regulation to cover manufacturers' direct retailing outlets, once more for the protection of small shopkeepers.[70]

The pressures for such protection abated over the next dozen years, primarily because the overall Japanese economy became so prosperous. Throughout the miracle growth period of the 1960s, MITI and other parts of the government permitted considerable innovation by department stores and by rapidly emerging supermarket chains. Here, MITI reasoned not only that high macroeconomic growth rates meant that all parts of the Japanese retailing sector could prosper together, but also that, with inflation becoming a problem, large-scale, cut-rate operators could help to put downward pressure on prices, and thereby perform a service to the Japanese economy. So MITI permitted existing department stores such as Seibu to open numerous branches, and allowed major new chains such as Daiei to spread. In an effort to protect small retailers from future pressures, MITI also encouraged the establishment of voluntary chains, in the form of federations of small independent operators who might pool their purchases from wholesalers, for the purpose of achieving scale economies. This policy has enjoyed little success, but even today, MITI continues to encourage voluntary rationalization by groups of small and medium-sized retailers, and of wholesalers as well.[71]

In the early 1970s, when overall Japanese economic growth slowed and the specter of stagflation first appeared, small retailers began to be squeezed hard by competition from the giants. These small operators, always strongly represented in the Diet, then lobbied intensely for new protection, using buzzwords such as "competition with order" and "co-existence, co-prosperity." Any precise meaning for these appealing terms, however, depended on the particular interest group that was uttering them. But in every case, regardless of rhetoric, the goal of the small operators remained straightforward and simple: government protection from the cut-rate prices of mass retailers. Pressures for government action grew intense.[72]

In 1973, the Diet responded by passing the Large Scale Retail Store Act. This powerful measure marked the real beginning of a modern period of restrictive regulation. Its provisions applied to any store whose floor space exceeded 1,500 square meters—a size approximately that of a medium-scale American food supermarket. (For ten major Japanese cities, the figure was raised to 3,000 square meters.) Under this new law, when any retail firm proposed to establish or expand such a store, it must first receive the permission of MITI, which in turn is advised by a local Council for Regulating Commercial Activities. These local boards, dating back to the 1956 Department Store Law, are active in communities throughout Japan. Sponsored by local chambers of commerce and industry, they are composed of twelve to twenty-one persons appointed from the ranks of local merchants, consumers, and scholars—but seldom having any representation from chain store interests. After passage of the 1973 Act, chain executives naturally began to experience greater difficulty in expanding their operations. Although the local boards possess no legal authority, MITI did pay attention to their recommendations. Consequently, chain stores now came under increased pressure on a variety of matters: the size of their stores, the hours during which they could be open for business, their days of operation. Usually, the chains sought to maximize everything—area, hours, days—while small local interests strove to minimize each item. The whole process soon became excruciating and seemingly endless—a series of negotiations more analogous to the diplomatic sparring between unfriendly countries than to any simple commercial operation. Months, then years, began to elapse between original applications and final approval, and often the approval never came. When it did appear, invariably it permitted much less than had been requested.[73]

During the negotiations themselves, the large-store interests, in their effort to win approval, would sometimes sugarcoat their proposals by offering to set up entire shopping centers, with low-cost rentals to local merchants. Such centers might also contain "culture clubs," where citizens could gather for discussions of various topics. Some centers even offered tennis courts and swimming pools for the young people of the community. As a result of all these efforts, some Japanese market malls today, though still nowhere near so numerous or so large as their American counterparts, resemble an unusual combination of shopping center and country club. Large-store interests also tried other tactics: to stay within the area limitations on floor space, they constructed stores just under 1,500 square meters.[74]

In response to such innovative tactics, local merchants continued to lobby in both the Diet and their own prefectural governments for still more protection. The Diet responded again, in 1978, by extending the provisions of the 1973 law to all stores of more than 500 square meters; and once more the law was slightly adjusted for the ten designated cities. Under this new act (which took effect in mid-1979), prefectural governments received a voice in the final decision, and new arbitration mechanisms were set up.

The combined effects of the powerful 1978 amendments to the 1973 law can be read in the number of applications to MITI asking for permission to open new stores. For Class I (1,500 square meters and up) establishments, the pattern of new filings ran as follows:[75]

TABLE 3-5
Number of Class I Applications Per Year

1974	1975	1976	1977	1978	1979	1980	1981	1982	1983	1984
399	281	264	318	243	576	371	194	132	125	156

From these numbers, it becomes plain that the 1978 law severely dampened the growth of large stores. Note that the table represents not permissions granted, but rather new applications made. As mentioned earlier, the total elapsed time before MITI—plus the local boards, plus the prefectural governments—could complete action on any given application might range from one to six years. Here, the compelling point documented in the table is that even *applications* declined by approximately 50 percent. Notice also the very high number for the year 1979. This reflects the frantic effort by executives of large stores to submit their applications before the stringent new regulations went into effect.

The same frenzied rush to submit new applications can be seen even more clearly in the totals for Class II stores—those with areas between 500 and 1,500 square meters. The 1978 law represented the Japanese government's first thoroughgoing attempt to regulate stores of such small size:[76]

TABLE 3-6
Applications to MITI for New Stores of 500–1,500 Square Meters (Class II)

1979	1980	1981	1982	1983	1984
1,029	424	306	270	276	288

From MITI's viewpoint, this second class represented less of an administrative headache than the first class, because most regulatory details could be worked out by local governments and councils, which did not feel as threatened by the smaller stores, and were therefore less dependent on MITI's powerful helping hand. Yet some results of the 1979 law remain clear: first, a sudden flood of applications, just before the new legislation takes effect; then a gradual stabilization at numbers slightly below 300 per year.

When one recalls that Japan has a population of about 120 million persons, this 300 figure comes into appropriate perspective: only one new store of this small size even *applied for,* per every 400,000 Japanese consumers. Putting the issue into American terms, it would be as if, for an entire city the size of Milwaukee or Cincinnati, applications to open only two new stores of 500–1,500 square meters' floor space would be filed in any given year. Thus, in comparison with the United States, with its many thousands of stores of both Class I and Class II size, the Japanese system reflects the actions of a much heavier regulatory hand.

From the viewpoint of Japanese chain retailing executives, the present regulatory system is much too restrictive and cumbersome. For them, its effect on entrepreneurship can only be stifling. Like their American counterparts in the 1920s and 1930s, Japanese chain store managers in the 1980s argue that such a thoroughgoing system of concessions to small merchants works serious economic injury not only to the chains but to millions of consumers as well. This argument has become more conspicuous since 1982, when MITI, in response to political pressures, began to provide administrative guidance to chain retail companies, asking them to curb plans for opening large new stores. Some chain store executives, looking back over the years since 1973, believe that in the absence of legislation and administrative guidance, approximately twice as many supermarkets and other large stores would have opened in Japan, simply because their low prices and other conveniences would have attracted droves of consumers.[77]

From the perspective of the MITI, the picture looks a good deal more complicated. In the first place, MITI takes careful note that Japan's hundreds of thousands of small retailers exert their powerful political influence with great energy, and in every conceivable direction: toward local governments, prefectural diets, the national Diet, and even toward the big retail companies. Circumstantial evidence suggests that, in MITI's considered judgment, such political pressure cannot be ignored. Second, in many particular instances of new applications, the prospective new retailer has been opposed not only by small merchants but also by large chains which already operate near the site of the proposed new store. Thus, the theoretically simple issue of small versus large becomes, in reality, one of small plus *established* large against a *new* large applicant. Third, MITI itself may find it difficult to speak with a single voice. Although the Industrial Policy Bureau might want to rationalize the Japanese distribution system as quickly as possible, other parts of MITI—those charged with promoting the interests of small and medium-sized businesses—express an altogether different point of view.[78]

Civil servants working within MITI's Industrial Policy Bureau therefore conceive of their own role as the strategic management of a delicate balancing act: on the one hand, to rationalize retailing, for the benefit of the Japanese consumer; on the other, to pacify the huge electoral bloc represented by hordes of small and medium-sized merchants. MITI bureaucrats readily acknowledge that if market forces had been allowed to work unencumbered over the last twenty years, then the share of overall retail sales attained by large chains in Japan would have grown very much faster. So in that way, the Japanese government has retarded rationalization of the distribution sector.

Yet if MITI had remained completely out of the picture—that is, if it had provided *no* administrative guidance at all—then powerful political pressures from small merchants might have retarded rationalization even more. With this possibility in view, MITI bureaucrats reason that, cumbersome though the existing system is, some significant introduction of big, self-service stores into Japan has occurred. An overall summary of what has happened in Japanese retailing over the last two decades provides some support for this view (see *Figure 3-4*).[79] Note that the market share enjoyed by "Other retail stores" (principally the hundreds of thousands of very small shops) shrank significantly between 1966 and 1979; but it stabilized after 1979, as we have seen, in response to the stringent new law. Note also that even during the period of declining market share, no actual shrinkage of the small operators' revenues necessarily occurred—because the Japanese economy was growing fast enough to permit the simultaneous growth of chains, supermarkets, and superstores without damaging the small merchants. (See the lines labeled "Retail sales trends" at the bottom of the chart.) Thus, while big stores captured much of the new business available in a booming economy, they did not displace existing small interests. Under these advantageous circumstances, partial rationalization did occur; and, from MITI's viewpoint, this half a loaf was economically and politically better than nothing.

Conclusion: Competition Policy and National Economic Strategy

By taking into account the larger themes of this chapter—the different patterns of development characteristic of the Japanese production and distribution sectors, and the gulf separating both from their American counterparts—we can now suggest a few broad generalizations about competition

FIGURE 3-4
Market Shares in Japan's Retail Sector, by Category

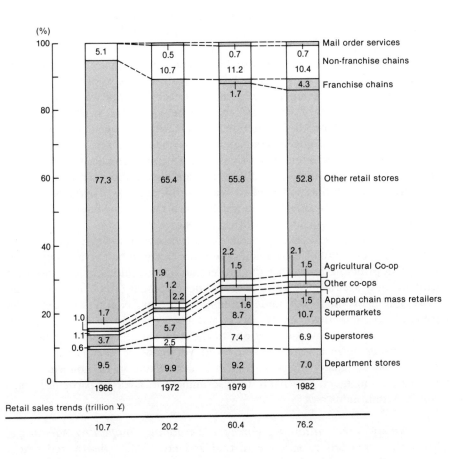

NOTE: Excluding restaurant, automobile and gasoline sales.
SOURCE: Japan Census of Commerce.

policy in the two countries. Here, three underlying differences can be identified; and in each of these categories, Japanese and American premises and policies appear to be fundamentally at odds.[80]

1. *Different Policies for Different Industries.* In the Japanese view, the economic and social functions of individual industries differ markedly from one to another. Steelmaking, for example, has little in common with retail distribution—or even with other manufacturing enterprises such as electronics and semiconductors. Public policies that make good sense for one sector, when applied in exactly the same way to another, might cause severe economic or social damage. Therefore, the objectives and regulatory methods of the Japanese government differ from one industry to the next. In steel, for example, the government sought technological supremacy in the world market; while in retailing, social and political objectives took priority. Because of such differences, governmental regulation of each industry was tailored specifically to that industry. Thus, the contrast between MITI's management of distribution, as opposed to production, could hardly have been more different, even though the same government agency remained in charge. Whereas in the production sector, as exemplified by the steel story, rationalization went forward at a pell-mell pace—with all sorts of innovative and even breathtaking measures—distribution was handled in a very different way. There, rationalization could not go forward nearly so fast, in part for economic reasons, but even more so because of social and political pressures.

In the American view, as expressed in classical economic theory as well as in antitrust policies, uniform principles are more likely to be applied. One such prevailing principle holds that the protection of most industries, without regard to their specific nature or stage of development (steel or small retail stores), remains inherently undesirable—because protection is by definition usually anti-competitive in its effects and likely to lead to inefficiency. In practice, of course, many exceptions to the rule can be cited: aid to agriculture, housing, defense industries, and so on. Yet the point remains valid that, in comparison to Japan, American policy is more likely to be uniform across industries, and much less likely to discriminate in favor of particular companies within industries.

2. *Timely Coordination as a Force for Developing Competitive Advantage.* Through protracted experience of trial and error, MITI discovered that a group of firms could effectively coordinate supply, demand, and price—all without unduly harming long-run investment decisions. The lessons of just how a government bureaucracy should undertake such a thoroughgoing management of competition did not come easily. In fact, the learning process stretched over several decades—from the 1920s to the 1960s—a period dominated by seismic shifts from a peacetime economy to a war footing, then back again. But, once MITI learned how to frame incentive structures properly for

particular industries, the behavior of business firms often followed according to the details of the Japanese government's plan.

Under this system, a specific group of firms—represented in this chapter by the steel companies—could almost cease to worry about the risk and uncertainty that would have been present in an uncoordinated market. The resulting stability proved to be an enormous advantage to participating firms, and a corresponding disadvantage to companies in other countries, which were forced to make autonomous, ad hoc, high-risk decisions in a less stable situation. The U.S. domestic market, of course, was just such an unstable one. Managers in the American steel industry, fearing overcapacity and price-cutting, yet prohibited by the antitrust laws from coordinating their capital investments, were powerfully inclined to defend their short-run positions. Thus, they assiduously shunned large investments, and inevitably fell behind in the international race for technological efficiency.

3. *Rivalry as a Force for Business Dynamism.* The competition policies of both countries took this assumption to be a central organizing principle. What made the Japanese system different was the remarkable feat of preserving inter-company rivalry even within a coordinated group of firms. Here, the steel industry again provides an apt illustration: the incentive structure designed by MITI encouraged each Japanese company to coordinate capacity and pricing decisions, while competing on technological efficiency. Only by proving themselves efficient could they earn MITI's permission to expand capacity. Thus, Japanese competition policy focused on motivating companies to minimize long-run production costs. The assumption was that, over time, prices would decrease in accord with declining costs. MITI's thinking was much less concerned with minimizing short-run consumer prices, for it presumed that consumers, in their other roles as employees and citizens, would benefit from the entire country's economic development. In this way, the costs—and especially the risks—of a focused industrial development were borne jointly by private industry and by Japanese society in general.

In America, on the other hand, government policy regulated companies' behavior in precisely the opposite direction. U.S. antitrust enforcement attempted to prevent inter-company cooperation, with the expectation that more competitive rivalry would result. Yet, what actually ensued was neither fierce competition nor purely independent behavior. Rather, steel companies tried, with erratic success, to coordinate their activities clandestinely. At the same time, as noted above, they minimized their capital investments as a means of protecting themselves from losses.

This stark difference in the official policies of the Japanese and American governments, together with the results—Japanese success and American decline—suggests that in certain high-fixed-cost industries, the abiding American shibboleth of unlimited inter-firm rivalry may not always serve the long-run interests of either producers or consumers. To the extent that the Japanese system can be any useful guide, then cartels and other forms of cooperation—when administered by able bureaucrats, and as part of a coordinated overall plan for certain types of capital-intensive industries—may actually prove more conducive to industrial growth and efficiency than the American style of autonomous investment decisions and unbridled price competition.

As for which national system was "better," such a question becomes meaningless without further specification of the standards being applied. What is clear, as the title of this chapter implies, is that competition policy in both countries often had a decisive role in shaping industry structures. Beyond that, perhaps the most useful generalization is simply that in America, competition policy since World War II has clearly reflected a preoccupation with the welfare of domestic consumers—an approach doubly at odds with the Japanese approach, which was focused on producers and international markets. Although several exceptions to this generalization about the United States could be cited—investment tax credits, concessions to aerospace and agriculture—the overall record shows an unmistakable favoritism toward consumers.

Japan's policies, on the other hand, remained consistently producer-oriented and, in many product sectors, decidedly geared toward world markets. In addition, Japan's *external* distribution sector, dominated by the great general trading companies, proved extraordinarily efficient in facilitating exports of manufactured goods and imports of food and raw materials. The internal distribution sector, by contrast, remained multilayered and, by American standards, primitive—a handicap to Japanese consumers. In effect, the government's protective policies toward both the steel industry and the internal distribution sector forced Japanese consumers to pay an implicit short-term tax to underwrite the overall economic strategy of the country.

CHAPTER 4

Cross-Investment:
A Second Front of Economic Rivalry

DENNIS J. ENCARNATION

Everyone knows that Japan has profited for more than a decade from a continuous trade surplus with the United States. During 1984, manufactured exports from Japan, bolstered by a strong dollar, jumped 39 percent from the previous year, to claim some $57 billion in the American market. This meant that in 1984 every American spent an average of $243 on Japanese imports—a sum that was likely to increase during 1985 as auto imports alone grew by at least $5 billion. No such growth was likely for American exports to Japan, however, as the trade gap between the two countries continued to widen, even in the face of a declining dollar.

For much of the previous decade, this trade balance with America was barely sufficient to cover Japan's imports of oil and other raw materials, and its payments for services. But by 1984, Japan's current account balance had enjoyed its fourth straight year of surplus, reaching an unprecedented $35 billion that year alone. This infusion of foreign exchange, supplemented by a level of domestic savings that exceeded the capital demanded by local investors, allowed Japan to become a large capital exporter—with America, previously a major capital exporter, now being a principal recipient.

Japanese investments in America and elsewhere take many forms: bonds, loans, stock portfolios, as well as direct investments. While bonds now account for the largest flow of funds, direct investments attract the greatest attention, since they mix equity ownership with managerial control; and they have been growing rapidly[1] (see *Table 4-1*). Between 1979 and 1984, Japanese direct investments in the United States rose over 33 percent annually, a rate of increase that easily outpaced investments by every other foreign nation.[2] Over those four years, in fact, Japan moved ahead of Canada, Germany, and Switzerland to become America's third largest foreign investor, behind Britain and the Netherlands. From the new Japanese factories, assembly plants, and ware-

TABLE 4-1
American-Japanese Cross-Investment (FDI), 1974–1984[a]

Year-End	U.S. FDI to Japan	Japanese FDI to U.S.
1974	$3.3 billion	$0.3 billion
1979	6.2 billion	3.5 billion
1984	8.4 billion	14.8 billion

[a]According to the definition employed by the U.S. Commerce Department direct investment position abroad (FDI) is equal to parent companies' equity (all stock, additional paid-in capital, and parents' shares of undistributed earnings) in, and net outstanding loans (long-term debt, trade credits, and other current liabilities owed to parents) to, foreign affiliates.

SOURCES: United States Department of Commerce, Bureau of Economic Analysis, *Survey of Current Business,* various issues; U.S. Department of Commerce, Bureau of Economic Analysis, *Selected Data on U.S. Direct Investment Abroad, 1950–76,* February 1982, pp. 20–27.

houses that have begun to dot the American landscape, McKinsey and Company estimates that each American in 1984 purchased an additional $44 of "Japanese" goods—the value added by these investments over and above components imported directly from Japan.[3] Looking ahead, such sales will undoubtedly grow as new projects, typically wholly owned by the Japanese, proliferate. So, like the original trade competition, this second front of economic rivalry represents an increasingly formidable Japanese challenge to U.S. business—now mounted on America's home grounds.

Simultaneously, although with less publicity, American business has also been encroaching on the Japanese home market. Here again, traditional trade represents the more obvious American thrust: in 1984, for example, each Japanese spent an average $215 on imports, largely commodities, from the United States—some $30 less than his or her American counterpart paid for manufactured imports from Japan. But these trade data tell only part of the full story, since they measure nothing more than the flow of goods across national frontiers. A more complete measure would also take into account the sale of goods assembled or manufactured by overseas subsidiaries of U.S. multinationals—America's own second front of economic competition.

For nearly thirty years after World War II, Japan was an unlikely host for American investors; but by 1983, only Canada and Switzerland surpassed Japan as the target for new U.S. direct investment abroad.[4] And by 1984, again according to McKinsey, the largest 150 affiliates of these American multinationals, typically through minority-U.S. or equal-partnership joint ventures, sold to each Japanese an additional $266 of locally produced goods—this being the value added by American-affiliated plants, over and above components imported from the States. Such sales seem likely to increase with the continued expansion of American investments in Japanese manufacturing—already growing 10 percent annually during the decade ending in 1984—thereby retaining for America its title as Japan's largest foreign investor.[5]

When the accounts of multinationals operating in both countries are fully acknowledged, Japan and the United States appear to have expanded their once-simple trade rivalry into a modern economic contest that must be fought simultaneously on several fronts. One new front—American-Japanese cross-investment—is the subject of this chapter. At one level, such investment may be understood as a natural outgrowth of macroeconomic forces, including the capital surpluses existing at various times in the two countries.[6] But the full story of cross-investment involves a larger tale, that of growing similarities and persistent differences in the government policies, industrial structures, and corporate strategies operating in two modern economic superpowers. These interdependent forces will ultimately determine subsequent trends in cross-investment.

Cross-Investment: A Brief History

Cross-investment between Japan and the United States is not a recent development. Even before World War II, IBM, General Motors, and other American multinationals operated in Japan; just as Mitsui, Mitsubishi, and other Japanese trading and financial organizations invested directly in the United States. In financial terms, such cross-investment in 1936–37 was roughly equal: $47 billion in Japan, $41 billion in the United States.[7]

After World War II, this rough symmetry disappeared, as American investment in Japan quickly spurted, growing nearly 25 percent annually between 1950 and 1970—a period of large capital exports from the United States to the rest of the world. Still, Japan remained a relatively insignificant recipient of American direct investment. Before World War II, such investment accounted for less than 1 percent of annual American outflows; and it did not exceed 6 percent for over 20 years after the war.[8]

During the same postwar years, Japanese investments in the United States grew by less than one-half as much (indeed, there were years when investment actually declined), and the U.S. Commerce Department data did not even show a separate entry for Japan until 1959. Much of this period was marked by continued trade deficits and industrial reconstruction, so Japan could ill afford investments abroad that employed scarce foreign exchange. Yet subsequent trade surpluses did little to alter Japan's foreign investment picture, especially in the face of vast investments at home. To the extent that the Japanese invested overseas at all, most of their attention focused on the developing countries of Southeast Asia.[9] As a result, as late as 1974, American direct investments in Japan remained ten times larger than the total value of all Japanese investments in the United States; while the Japanese total for that year stood at the same level as American investments in Japan in 1957—seventeen years earlier.

For American investors, manufacturing has long been the principal concern, as investments have favored machinery (broadly defined), followed by chemicals (see *Table 4-2*). The Japanese, by contrast, have historically concentrated

TABLE 4-2
Sectoral Distribution of American-Japanese Cross-Investments (FDI)[a]

Sector[b]	Distribution at Year End			Compound Annual Growth Rates	
	1974	1979	1984	1974–1979	1979–1984
A. American FDI in Japan					
Manufacturing	45.5%	45.2%	48.8%	13.3%	7.9%
Trade[c]	9.1	16.1	16.7	27.2	7.1
Finance[d]	2.9	3.2	4.8	15.6	15.3
Petroleum	42.2	30.6	25.0	6.4	2.1
Other	0.3	4.9	4.7	151.9	5.4
Total Position[a] ($ billion)	$3.3	$6.2	$8.4	13.4%	6.3%
B. Japanese FDI in the U.S.					
Manufacturing	95.7%	19.9%	15.5%	19.4%	26.9%
Wholesale Trade[e]	− 128.1	50.6	65.5	110.4	40.5
Finance[f]	95.1	18.3	10.1	17.6	18.5
Other	37.4	11.2	8.9	28.5	27.4
Total Position[a] ($ billion)	$0.3	$3.5	$14.8	63.5%	33.4%

[a] Direct investment position abroad, as defined in Table 4-1, note a.

[b] Each foreign affiliate was classified in the major industry group that accounted for the largest percentage of its sales at year end.

[c] Includes retail and wholesale trade.

[d] Includes insurance.

[e] During 1974, affiliate receivables from their Japanese parents (e.g., trade credits for exports from America to Japan) exceeded affiliate payables to their Japanese parents. As a result, the net Japanese position in the U.S. wholesale sector was negative that year. Because the column as a whole must net arithmetically to 100%, this distortion also makes the numbers for manufacturing, finance, and other Japanese investments appear to be overstated.

[f] Includes banking.

SOURCES: United States Department of Commerce, Bureau of Economic Analysis, *Survey of Current Business*, various issues; U.S. Department of Commerce, Bureau of Economic Analysis, *Selected Data on U.S. Direct Investment Abroad, 1950–76*, February 1982, pp. 20–27.

in the U.S. service sector, where in the 1970s, wholesale trade surpassed finance as the largest target of Japanese investment. Aside from this shift, the pattern of Japanese-American cross-investment remained remarkably stable over 40 years, and the following description of the cross-investment pattern in 1934 remained accurate for 1974 and beyond:

> While American companies in Japan were in the technologically advanced sectors and preeminently in manufacturing, Japanese business in America aimed at aiding Japanese commerce by providing needed financial, insurance, trading, and shipping intermediaries.[10]

The American Pattern Explained

Concentration of American multinational investment in the Japanese manufacturing sector was not unique; it imitated the general pattern that U.S. multinationals established everywhere in the world.[11] Generally, multinationals were among the first to invest in innovative products or in manufacturing processes which, as they matured, satisfied growing demand in countries less industrialized than the United States. At first, such innovations were usually diffused through trade, as Japanese demand increased for higher priced products or for processes that saved labor or material. Only after that trade became threatened did foreign investment emerge as a more viable option for Americans.

Here, the principal threat to continued trade was local competition. Japanese competitors were aided by high transportation costs across the Pacific, cheaper Japanese labor and capital, and the protective policies of Japanese government—especially the last factor. Historically, tariffs and other government restrictions on import competition have proved to be powerful determinants of those foreign investments designed to service a local, as opposed to an export, market.[12]

American investment in Japan proved no exception, as the case of American automakers clearly demonstrates.[13] When Ford and General Motors began exporting to Japan (where they hoped to exploit the same innovations that had made them dominant in the U.S. market) both companies seemed positioned to satisfy growing Japanese demand by trade alone. In 1930, for example, only 458 automobiles were fully manufactured in Japan, all by Japanese producers. This amounted to 2.5 percent of the Japanese market. GM and Ford supplied the remainder through imports, which consisted of complete "knocked-down" kits shipped from the United States and assembled in Japan. Next, the Japanese government imposed restrictions on the number of kits that could be imported, and during the 1930s those restrictions tightened. Thus, to maintain their sales in an increasingly protected market, the American automakers had to consider direct investment in Japan. Trade no longer could work.

Capital Controls by the Japanese

Foreign trade restrictions do not always spur foreign investment, however, as the early moves of American automakers again illustrate. Other kinds of host government policies may actually limit foreign investment in a newly protected local market. Soon after Ford and General Motors first invested in Japan, for example, Japanese buyers of Fords and Chevrolets demanded replacement parts, and many small and medium-sized Japanese companies quickly moved to fill the void with the government's encouragement. Nissan Motor, as one of these, initially supplied parts for Ford; while the Japanese suppliers emerged altogether as a visible nucleus of a fledgling automobile industry. Yet their growth remained slow. In 1935, Ford alone sold in Japan two-and-a-half times the number of cars and trucks produced by all Japanese-owned automakers combined.

In the following year, however, this pattern changed as a result of government regulations, which required greater local production of automobiles. So Ford responded by applying for a license to begin manufacturing automobiles in Japan. Subsequent legislation (still in 1936) restricted such licenses to companies with at least 50 percent Japanese ownership. As a result, both Ford and GM then sought joint venture partners, initially with little success, since the Japanese could easily copy American products and mimic the technology of mass production. In fact, only Nissan and Toyota received licenses during 1936. The next year, the Japanese government blocked remittances by Ford, following a year of good profits; and then after 1938, the Japanese took a final step by limiting the import permits of Ford and GM, thus curtailing severely the sale of knocked-down kits.

During the war these American investments were nationalized, but immediately afterward, Ford and GM expressed interest in reentering Japan, despite Japanese regulations that blocked foreign investors for the next two decades.[14] First, the Occupation government proscribed American firms from buying "undervalued" Japanese enterprises, and before the Occupation ended, these restrictions were extended and codified in the 1950 Law Concerning Foreign Investment. Reflecting the Japanese government's continuing shortage of foreign exchange as well as deep fears of losing managerial control over industrial development, the 1950 legislation established a system of prohibitions on all external transactions, including capital transactions. Yen-denominated profits, for example, were usually not convertible into other currencies; and even when IBM and a few other foreign firms were granted convertibility, additional restrictions controlled the means and timing of such transactions. Most important, all transactions involving foreign capital outflows and inflows required time-consuming administrative approval.

So the 1950 legislation actually marked a resumption of traditional Japanese policy. Government regulations kept foreign multinationals at bay by insisting that technology licensing be decoupled from foreign equity; or, failing to secure the requisite technology, by insisting on joint ventures rather than wholly owned foreign subsidiaries. These regulations became tighter in 1964, when Japan, as a new member of the OECD, was forced to make the yen convertible. To protect existing foreign reserves in the face of narrow surpluses on the current account, the Ministry of International Trade and Industry (MITI) and the Ministry of Finance (MOF) approved fewer foreign investment applications, and narrowed the acceptable range of technology remittances.

Three years later, in the midst of growing current account surpluses, the Japanese government again reversed policy by decontrolling foreign capital remittances, in the first of what later would be called the "five liberalizations." At this first hint of liberalization, in 1967, Ford and GM returned to Japan (along with Chrysler) to find partners for joint ventures. Their search was complicated, however, by MITI's forced merger of Japan's smaller automakers with either Toyota or Nissan.[15] Luckily for the Americans, Mitsubishi refused to merge, and instead—to the dismay of MITI—sought a partnership with Chrysler. Isuzu and Toyo Kogyo (renamed Mazda) also violated MITI's directives soon thereafter. Isuzu sought out General Motors as a partner, and Mazda pursued Ford. By this process, American automakers indirectly entered the Japanese market. Even more important, the number four, five, and six Japanese automakers broke the stranglehold exercised by MITI and the industry's two Japanese giants.

American investors in other industries, although faced with constraints on foreign trade and investment comparable to those imposed by the Japanese government on the auto industry, sometimes managed to turn adversity into opportunity. During the late 1960s, this typically was achieved by American companies that were also technological leaders, such as Texas Instruments (TI), which entered the Japanese semiconductor market.[16] Like U.S. automakers, TI viewed high Japanese tariff barriers to trade as an incentive to invest in Japan, because Sony and other Japanese electronics companies, especially those producing calculators, made Japan the second largest and the fastest growing semiconductor market. Moreover, even TI's potential Japanese competitors viewed TI's technology as key to their own development of integrated circuits; and those competitors had barely entered semiconductors in 1964, when TI asked for a government license to establish a wholly owned subsidiary. NEC, for example, was the first Japanese company to enter the semiconductor industry (1963)—using less advanced technology licensed from Fairchild—followed by Hitachi (1965), Toshiba, and others in 1966. As for TI's foreign, principally American, competitors—tariff barriers would hold them at bay, at least in the short term, while Japan's foreign equity controls would force less technologically advanced competitors to settle for licensing agreements or, at best, joint ventures.

From TI's perspective, the same proprietary technology that had made TI the market leader in the world semiconductor industry would also force MITI to grant it an exception from foreign capital controls. Such dispensation, however, did not come easily. As noted above, the Japanese had just agreed to make the yen convertible in 1964, and they intended to protect existing foreign reserves through more stringent capital controls. Negotiations dragged on for four years, a period designed by MITI to compensate for Japan's late entry into the semiconductor race. By the time MITI and TI reached an agreement in 1968, during the first full year of "phased liberalization," Japan's domestic production of semiconductors amounted to less than 10 percent of TI's total world production.[17]

The Price of Agreements

TI won its demand for a wholly owned subsidiary in Japan, but not without allowing MITI two important concessions.[18] First, TI had to establish a 50–50 joint venture with Sony, one of the major Japanese buyers of semiconductors. Although few knew it at the time, this joint venture was scheduled to last only three years; so by 1971, Sony sold its equity holdings to TI at a prearranged price. TI also acceded to MITI's second demand: that TI make its proprietary technology available to Japanese companies for a 3.5 percent licensing fee— for TI, a unique arrangement and clearly a major concession.

MITI raised numerous objections to market entry by foreign-owned semiconductor producers who were not at that time technological leaders.[19] Fairchild, for example (the first American producer to license semiconductor technology with a Japanese firm—NEC, in 1959), repeatedly failed to secure MITI approval for a wholly owned transistor and diode assembly plant on the Japanese mainland. As a substitute, Fairchild established a wholly owned subsidiary in Okinawa, a U.S. territory in 1969, with preferential access to the Japanese market, which it lost when Okinawa reverted to Japanese control in May 1972. At that point, MITI forced Fairchild into a joint venture with TDK, which lasted only until 1977. National Semiconductor, after failing to enter the Japanese mainland, also set up a wholly owned facility on Okinawa, but unlike Fairchild, National refused to reorganize as a joint venture after 1972. Finally, TI's principal global competitor—number two-ranked Motorola—recognized these government-imposed entry barriers, and settled in 1968 for the right to open a Japanese sales office to boost exports as well as monitor TI's moves.

In contrast, MITI raised relatively few objections to IBM's plan for building a plant whose production would be completely consumed by other IBM operations in Japan.[20] Aside from TI, however, IBM was the only other foreign semiconductor manufacturer to establish a wholly owned subsidiary before the near-elimination of foreign equity controls in 1973.

The difficulties experienced by American semiconductor producers were repeated again and again in other industries. By 1974, only one out of every ten foreign manufacturers operating in Japan was fully foreign-owned.[21] Most of the remainder were equal partnership joint ventures, each with a single Japanese company. Nowhere in these statistics, of course, are the multitude of prospective investors who stayed away from Japan altogether because of foreign equity controls, or who left Japan after a disappointing experience with a joint venture partner. Indeed, by 1974 Japan was host to only 2 percent of all new American direct investments entering manufacturing industries overseas. As a result, the growth rate of American investments, as well as the total position of U.S. investors, was lower in Japan than in Brazil and Mexico, not to mention the six largest EEC countries.[22] Yet Japan by then ranked among the world's four largest economies. Again, it should be clear that Japanese equity restrictions left an indelible mark on foreign investment long after the original restrictions had disappeared.

Japanese Controls and the Invasion of America

The same postwar Japanese legislation that tightly regulated foreign investment at home also specified that every Japanese investment located in the

United States and elsewhere abroad had to be approved by the Ministry of Finance and the Bank of Japan.[23] Here, Japanese government policies encouraged—to the extent that they encouraged foreign investments at all—natural resource projects upstream and trade-related services downstream. Such policies were often consistent with Japanese corporate strategies, meaning in the United States that Japanese companies increasingly concentrated their investments in the wholesale sector. Within that sector, affiliated wholesalers bought American raw materials for export to Japan, or channeled Japanese consumer exports to the United States.

No Japanese investor in the United States faced foreign capital controls like those imposed on American investors in Japan, however; and as a result, investments in the United States were typically owned exclusively by Japanese parents. Outside of America, Japanese joint ventures with local companies became far more prevalent, especially in developing countries where Japanese investments concentrated in the extractive sector and manufacturing rather than wholesale trade.[24]

The early concentration in the American wholesale sector, moreover, remained largely unaffected by shifts in Japanese government policy, even after 1969, when a series of liberalizations began (parallel to those affecting U.S. investment in Japan). Even with such policy changes, however, Japanese investment in the United States grew only slowly—at least through 1974, when the Japanese government reimposed restrictions on overseas investment in response to both the first oil price shock and Japan's immediate (and first postwar) recession.

By 1974, Japanese direct investments in the U.S. wholesale sector were already integral to overall trade strategy. That year, Japanese-affiliated wholesalers exported (principally to Japan) $8.5 billion of American raw materials, and distributed in America $9.3 billion of finished goods imported largely from Japan.[25] These Japanese investments in wholesaling thus contributed to the growing trade surplus with the United States. Of course, the prospect of additional trade has long provided an important incentive to increase foreign investment, as the growth of Japanese affiliates in the U.S. wholesale sector itself testifies.

At the same time, these investments were also an integral element in Japan's response to U.S. protests over the trade imbalance. To offset receipts from large trade surpluses, the Ministry of Finance (MOF) sought to stimulate the outflow of long-term loans and equity investments. Foreign direct investment provided one mechanism for achieving this objective; in the name of "balancing the basic balance," MOF in 1975 removed the last remaining capital controls. In fact, MOF quickly changed from being a cautious regulator of Japanese investment overseas to being an enthusiastic promoter. It initiated, for example, a loan program through the Export-Import Bank of Japan to help Japanese investors going abroad. When internationalization of Japanese companies became a central plank of national foreign economic policy, Japanese direct investment in the United States shot up.[26]

The Great Turnaround

In fact, during the 1970s, earlier asymmetries in American-Japanese cross-investment dramatically reversed, until by 1978, annual Japanese investments in the United States had exceeded comparable flows of American direct investments to Japan. By 1981, the direct investment position of Japanese companies in America had surpassed the position of all U.S. investors in Japan; and only three years later, such Japanese investments in America stood at nearly twice the value of U.S. investments in Japan. American-Japanese cross-investment had created a new asymmetry—this one dominated by Japan. Such phenomenal growth, moreover, testified to the increased importance of the U.S. market for Japanese investors. In fact, during the 1980s, over two-fifths of all annual investment outflows from Japan were destined for America, which had replaced Southeast Asia as the principal target for new direct investments.[27]

Within the United States, the wholesale sector continued to attract Japanese interest: by 1984, it accounted for nearly two-thirds of their new investment in the United States, having grown 40 percent annually since 1979 (see *Table 4-2*). In that year, Japan accounted for nearly 40 percent of all direct investments by foreigners in U.S. wholesale trade, meaning that Japanese companies controlled nearly 5 percent of the total stockholders' equity invested in the entire U.S. wholesale sector.[28] As before, limited investments paid off in the wholesale trade of metals, minerals and farm products (see *Table 4-3*), where in

TABLE 4-3
Japanese Direct Investments and Trade by Japanese Subsidiaries in the United States, 1983

	Position in U.S.[a] ($ billion)	Total Exports from U.S. ($ billion)	Total Imports to U.S. ($ billion)	Imports (% from Japanese Parent)
Wholesale Trade	$7.6	$21.8	$34.9	77.1%
Of which:				
Motor vehicles/parts	1.7[b]	[c]	15.8	72 + [c]
Metals and minerals	0.9[b]	8.9	6.5	62.8
Other durable goods	4.2[b]	0.7	9.0	98.0
Farm products	0.3[b]	9.3	3.2	75 + [c]
Other nondurables	0.5[b]	[c]	0.6	74.7
Manufacturing	$1.7	$1.0	$1.1	77.6%
Other	$1.8	$0.1	$0.2	94.0%
Total	$11.1	$22.9	$36.2	77.2%

[a] Direct investment position abroad, as defined in Table 4-1, note a.

[b] Estimated.

[c] Specific details of intra-company trade suppressed by the U.S. Department of Commerce to avoid disclosing the operations of a few large companies; estimates here are mathematically derived, if possible using other data provided.

SOURCES: United States Department of Commerce, Bureau of Economic Analysis, *Survey of Current Business* 65 (October 1985) p. 26; data for estimating investments within the wholesale trade sector, and all trade data, were supplied separately by the International Investment Division, Bureau of Economic Analysis, U.S. Department of Commerce.

1983 they channeled—largely to Japan—some $18 billion of U.S. commodity exports (up from $11 billion in 1980).[29]

But the vast bulk of new Japanese investments went into automobiles and other durable goods—mostly to provide American distribution channels for products exported from Japan (see *Table 4-3*). By 1983 (the most recent year for which detailed data are currently available) over two-fifths of all imports by Japanese affiliates in the United States belonged to the wholesale auto sector; and nearly three-quarters of these auto imports were shipped by Japanese parents (not trading company intermediaries). In other words, Japanese auto-makers used their formally affiliated wholesalers downstream in America as conduits for the export of motor vehicles, subassemblies, and spare parts to the United States. The same relationship also holds for other Japanese export-ers, especially of durable goods: their investments provided conduits for ex-ports, principally from the Japanese homeland.[30]

Between 1974 and 1983, exports by Japanese manufacturers to their U.S. wholesalers grew nearly 16 percent annually.[31] In 1983, such intra-company trade represented over three-fifths of all Japanese exports to the United States.[32] In other words, the main, initial objective of Japanese investment in America was to promote international trade, principally through exports from Japan.[33] But by the 1980s, continued Japanese exports were being threatened by American trade policies, and those restrictions soon emerged as the most powerful determinants of investment strategies upstream from distribution.

The Japanese Respond to Protectionism

The relationship between foreign trade and investment showed itself clearly in automobiles, where American restrictions on imports prompted new Japa-nese spending, this time moving beyond wholesale trade into the assembly of autos. Between 1981 and 1985, "voluntary export restraints" limited Japanese imports to a fixed quota of fully assembled cars and trucks (which did not cover parts or knocked-down kits, an obvious omission soon to be exploited). Within that quota, the market shares of Japanese producers remained fixed at the annual average level prevailing during the last three years of free competi-tion. For each of the largest Japanese exporters—Toyota, Honda, and Nissan—this meant a virtual guarantee of a 4–6 percent share of the U.S. market, to which could be added all sales from American assembly plants. Thus, by di-rectly investing in such a plant, Japanese producers could circumvent trade barriers on finished autos by exporting parts and knocked-down kits for final assembly in the United States. Such a foreign investment strategy was reminis-cent of the earlier American automakers' program in Japan.

Faced with indefinite constraints on exports, Nissan and Honda quickly established wholly owned assembly operations in the United States.[34] Next, their largest competitor in Japan—Toyota—came on stream during 1985 in a Japanese-managed joint venture with General Motors. A fourth firm—Mazda—announced that in 1986 it would acquire an existing American facility from its largest shareholder, the Ford Motor Company. Finally, Mitsubishi announced that it would invest directly in the United States during 1986, selling most of its production there through its shareholder, Chrysler. Meanwhile, analysts awaited news of a wholly owned Toyota assembly plant to be completed by 1987–1988. Collectively, by 1988, these Japanese automakers would be assembling in the United States no fewer than one million cars annually, or slightly more than the total production of Chrysler scheduled for that year. Indeed, the number of Japanese automakers operating in the United States will soon exceed that of American-owned automakers in their home market.

To protect an existing market in the face of restrictive American policies, therefore, these Japanese corporations relied on additional foreign investment. Americans, in turn, called for local content legislation, and the specter of further trade restrictions in the auto industry grew menacing. So all the proposals from Japanese automakers for new assembly plants in the United States had to include detailed timetables for the phasing-in of local purchases in the United States to replace imports from traditional suppliers in Japan. Indeed, in 1985, Honda became the first Japanese automaker to claim 50 percent American content—parts and labor—in its Ohio cars.[35]

Honda's expansion in the United States had to be ambitious largely because that company, among Japanese automakers, stood to lose most from foreign trade restrictions, since expansion at home had long been blocked by Toyota and Nissan. When access to Honda's largest and fastest growing overseas market was threatened, management responded quickly and decisively: Honda became the first Japanese automaker to produce cars in America. In contrast, Toyota responded cautiously, entering into a joint venture with General Motors (1985) that provided for 200,000 cars a year by 1988. Honda, on the other hand, expected to produce 300,000 cars by 1986. Indeed, in 1984, Honda replaced Toyota as the Japanese leader in the U.S. market; and the following year, Honda became America's fourth largest automaker, having exceeded the production of American Motors.[36]

The NEC Story

Aside from Honda, Japanese producers in other industries have also undertaken "preemptive expansion" before the Americans restrict market access. The history of NEC's operations in the United States, for example, shows both the close linkage among Japanese industries and the effect on foreign investment. By 1983, nearly one-quarter of NEC's total revenues came from semiconductors; in the open market for semiconductors, it was the third largest manufacturer in the world, after Texas Instruments and Motorola.[37] By 1985 NEC even surpassed them.

As the first semiconductor manufacturer to invest in America, NEC moved rapidly to increase its operations by both acquisition and new construction. Here, at least three factors accounted for the unusual speed of NEC's expansion.[38] First was the sheer size of the U.S. market. Even before NEC began to invest substantially in the United States, one-third of its semiconductor sales came from exports, and one-third of those exports were destined for the U.S. market. These export sales were valued at several billion dollars in 1976, and they made the future in America attractive (especially as NEC's Japanese buyers also moved to America). But in 1978, increased export sales were threatened by yen-to-dollar appreciation, a second factor that accelerated NEC investment. Such appreciation also reduced the yen cost of that investment, at least temporarily, so NEC opted first for the speedy acquisition of a U.S. company already trading with NEC.

Finally, the specter of new U.S. trade restrictions (modeled on those in consumer electronics) invited rapid action, beginning in 1975, when American semiconductor manufacturers charged NEC and other Japanese producers with selling capacitors in violation of U.S. antitrust provisions.[39] Although the United States Tariff Commission dismissed these charges, competition grew intense in 1976, when several U.S. manufacturers—Fairchild, Intel, National Semiconductor, and Motorola (but *not* Texas Instruments, the only American company with major investments in Japan at that time)—formed the Semiconductor Industry Association (SIA). In that year Japanese semiconductors accounted for almost 7 percent of total U.S. sales, while U.S. producers supplied just over 12 percent of total Japanese sales. But SIA anticipated a rapid growth of Japanese imports to fill growing IBM orders for 16K RAMS. American companies could not fill these orders because they had failed to expand capacity after the 1974–1975 recession—in sharp contrast to the Japanese. SIA's fears were justified as the balance of trade in semiconductors shifted to favor the Japanese after 1977; and by 1979, the Japanese had captured 43 percent of the U.S. market for 16K chips.[40] SIA had already begun to consider appropriate political responses to the Japanese invasion.

In such a politically charged atmosphere, the acquisition of an existing company often seems preferable to building a new plant, in part because it can be accomplished quickly. In 1978, as SIA began to muster political support, NEC acquired its first American company, Electronic Arrays (EA), a financially troubled firm with which NEC had previously dealt. More generally, acquisitions have played a small role in the rapid growth of Japanese direct investment in the United States, in contrast to America's European investors.[41] At home, Japanese acquisitions also are more frequent—especially of financially distressed suppliers and other affiliated companies.[42]

New Ventures

New ventures have provided Japanese multinationals with a common form of entry to markets, not only in the United States but elsewhere in the world. NEC demonstrated this broader tendency when it constructed a new American manufacturing plant in 1982 and made plans for other new facilities. In the same year, the U.S. Justice Department responded to SIA pressure by initiating antitrust investigations of NEC. By 1984, the Justice Department had dropped all charges, and in that year, NEC's two American plants supplied nearly one-fifth of all NEC semiconductor sales in the United States—thus encouraging the company to plan further expansion in U.S. production. New investments in the United States actually began to exceed the value of new investments in Japan, not only for NEC but for Fujitsu and other Japanese electronics companies as well. Until 1984, in fact, electronics producers accounted for the greatest share of Japanese investment in American manufacturing, surpassed that year only by Japanese auto assemblers.[43]

Japanese Gaming Strategies

U.S. trade restrictions, both existing and proposed, represent the most important determinants of Japanese direct investment in U.S. assembly and manufacturing. But trade barriers are not the only determinants. In addition, various competitive forces in an industry may dictate foreign direct investment, among which the gaming strategies of oligopolistic competitors figure prominently.[44] Under this pattern, companies make foreign investment decisions by following the industry leader and other rivals, or by punishing a rival for an aggressive move made elsewhere. Thus, a risk-averse manager will often match a competitor's moves so as to reduce the probability that the competitor will later jeopardize the future of that manager's own company. According to this reasoning, it is better for both companies to move sequentially—even at the risk that both will suffer losses—than for a single company not to move and thereby risk a competitor's net gain.

Such logic also applies to industries in which the initial foreign investment was largely a response to trade restrictions. Japanese semiconductor manufacturers, for example, have seemed especially prone to imitative, "follow-the-leader" behavior in their U.S. investments. After NEC, the Japanese industry leader, initiated the first move in 1978, its Japanese competitors followed in rapid succession: Hitachi and Fujitsu moved in 1979; Toshiba, in 1980; Hitachi again, in 1981; Mitsubishi, in 1983. This sequence of investments is typical of imitative behavior among oligopolistic rivals.

Now, contrast the timing of Japanese investment with the behavior of U.S. producers in Japan. After IBM's entry in 1971, no other American semiconductor producer established manufacturing operations in Japan until the 1980s, when Motorola and Fairchild reentered Japan. In other words, the liberalization of foreign equity controls by the Japanese government in 1974 had little impact on the strategies of foreign companies. Nor did the simultaneous liberalization of import controls.

Undoubtedly, several factors accounted for the different patterns of American and Japanese investment in semiconductors. From the American point of view, with U.S. demand booming and competition in the Japanese market ever more formidable, there were simply few incentives to invest in Japan. After all, in 1974, even though the Japanese market was growing rapidly, it was still only one-third the size of America's domestic market.[45] Then, too, the frustrating experiences of most early investors also discouraged would-be American producers from trying to enter Japan.

Moreover, differences in the organization of the American and Japanese industries meant that imitative strategies could be pursued far more effectively by the Japanese. In economic theory, such strategies appear most frequently in moderately concentrated industries—not in less concentrated ones, where interdependence is not recognized by rivals; nor in very concentrated industries, where rivals often collude.[46] In 1978 the top four companies—NEC, Hitachi, Fujitsu, and Toshiba—collectively controlled 63 percent of the open market for integrated circuits. NEC alone held 18 percent of the market.

The comparable figure in the United States for the top four companies was 49 percent. The U.S. industry was less concentrated in part because of U.S. antitrust policies: IBM and AT&T, for example, were both proscribed from entering the open market. Japanese government policies, by contrast, promoted concentration. MITI prohibited specialized manufacturers of integrated circuits from entering the industry, thus promoting instead the entry of large, diversified electronics companies that had more in common with each other than did their American rivals.[47]

Common industry structures have often bred common corporate strategies. For example, the largest Japanese semiconductor manufacturers were themselves horizontally diversified electronics companies of roughly comparable size. The average ratio of semiconductor sales to total sales for the top six Japanese companies was 7 percent in 1979, compared to 70 percent for the top nine U.S. semiconductor companies.[48] In other words, Japanese companies, unlike most of their American counterparts, competed in other consumer and industrial product areas as well as in semiconductors. Such diversification heightened pressures for imitative behavior at home and abroad. Sequential foreign investment was one response.

Again, since Japanese production has concentrated in a few diversified conglomerates which consumed a small-to-moderate proportion of their own production, cross-purchasing strategies were common among large Japanese companies. In 1979, for example, the top six companies (which produced over one-half of all semiconductors) consumed at least 60 percent of noncaptive domestic production. Cross-purchasing, like vertical and horizontal integration, contributes to an imitative, follow-the-leader behavior that characterizes Japanese semiconductor producers—and other oligopolies in Japan as well. In the U.S. semiconductor industry, by contrast, a large proportion of noncaptive sales flowed from National Semiconductor, Intel, and other full-line semiconductor companies, which themselves consumed little of the production of their competitors. With a few captive makers, several full-line companies, and many smaller specialized producers, competitors in the United States remain far more numerous than those in Japan. As a result, such competitors exert little of the buyer power that shaped Japanese investment.

As in the semiconductor industry, initial investments in the United States by Japanese automakers were made largely in response to trade pressures; but the timing of subsequent moves also at times reflected a pattern of imitative behavior common to oligopolistic rivals.[49] Toyota, for example, accelerated its planned entry into the United States after Nissan had announced that auto production would be added to Nissan's existing truck assembly operations in Tennessee. A Toyota joint venture with GM soon followed; next would come plans for a wholly owned assembly plant. For the Japanese, follow-the-leader strategies held a strong appeal.

The Imitative Suppliers

Oligopolistic competitors in the automobile industry can exert considerable pressure on their existing suppliers to follow their trail overseas. That is, they can exert buyer power—another competitive force that stimulates increased foreign investment flows—even in the absence of government restrictions on trade. Japanese parts suppliers, for example, have been increasingly persuaded to set up American production facilities as a convenience to onshore buyers engaged in manufacturing.[50] When Honda invested in Ohio, its Japanese-based suppliers of headlights, auto fuel tanks, exhaust pipes, steering wheels, and auto engine parts also established plants within that state. Honda found parts from nearby plants, including American-owned plants, to be cheaper than imports. And having suppliers nearby facilitated Honda's adoption of the same just-in-time delivery system that it used in Japan. Finally, by utilizing suppliers at hand, whether Japanese- or American-owned, Honda also satisfied its political agenda; such purchases could be classified as "local content" should Congress impose content requirements.

For transplanted Japanese suppliers, new sales in America represented one of the few possibilities for growth, given a stagnant home market and U.S. restrictions. Since the proximity of buyers in this industry mattered, foreign investment was a logical step—even for small-to-medium-sized companies not otherwise known for their rapid movement overseas.[51]

When buyers were not geographically concentrated and markets were more robust, pressures to move became especially intense if suppliers sold only commodity-like products with ready substitutes. For example, vendors of commodity-like semiconductors found that they had to follow existing buyers overseas if they wished to maintain the relationship.[52] So, when Sharp, Matsushita, and other Japanese consumer electronics firms moved to Southeast Asia, NEC and other Japanese suppliers moved with them. Then, when those same consumer electronics companies moved to the United States, just as an orderly marketing agreement went into effect in 1977, their Japanese suppliers followed in 1978. Here, the fear of new trade restrictions on commodity-like semiconductors combined with the exercise of buyer power to stimulate foreign investment.

In addition, customization of parts also encouraged suppliers to locate in close geographic proximity to those buyers who required it—a common condition in industrial and communications electronics. Both IBM and AT&T, major buyers in that semiconductor segment, demanded customization for their computers and telecommunications equipment. The growing need for repetitive and close interaction among engineers from semiconductor suppliers and their buyers—IBM or AT&T—added pressure on NEC, as one of those suppliers, to invest in the United States.

Competition Among the States

Aside from trade restrictions imposed by the American *federal* government, other governments in the United States actively influenced Japanese investments. In particular, fiscal incentives, infrastructure expenditures, and marketing practices of state and local governments also shaped Japanese decisions, even when such state and local policies did not play a role in the initial decision to invest in America.[53] They especially helped to determine the Japanese company's final choice of plant location. Here, competition among American states and localities often proved intense, especially since Ohio and other industrialized states of the Midwest and Northeast looked to foreign investment as one way to defeat economic stagnation. Finally, almost every community wanted more jobs, so competition became heated.[54]

Ohio, for example, beat out several contenders by offering Honda an incentive package which included: a $2.5 million grant to develop the site; a $90 thousand annual reduction in property taxes; designation of the site as a foreign trade subzone with reduced import duties; a guarantee that the federal government would make railroad improvements valued at $300 thousand; and free English tutoring for Japanese expatriates and their children at a nearby state university.[55] At roughly the same time, Ohio's competitor, Tennessee, proposed a comparable incentive package to Honda's rival, Nissan. Among many inducements, Tennessee spent $12 million for new roads to the Nissan plant, and $7 million to help train plant employees. The county government reduced property taxes by $1 million over the first ten years of the project.

In all, Ohio and Tennessee, like other governments, tailored a package of incentives to the needs of each investor.[56] Usually, among comparably sized firms, the first Japanese entrant in each industry received the most lucrative package. Across industries, those that offered the greatest employment potential typically received the greatest assistance. Aggressive bidding strategies were adopted by most states, but California, by far the favorite site for Japanese investors, remained a notable exception. Indeed, that state's unitary tax, a subject of vitriolic debate, was often cited as a disincentive for Japanese investment there.

Bidding with incentives has not been the only competitive strategy used by state and local governments. They have also sought investors by creating images of attractive business climates, a strategy that parallels efforts used by private firms to differentiate their products from those of competitors. For example, governments in the United States have introduced industrial parks and foreign trade zones, which appeal to only a narrow segment of Japanese investors. Governments also market possible location sites through media advertisements, promotional and sales offices, and overseas missions sent in search of new investors. These efforts at differentiation complement aggressive bidding and occasionally even substitute for that bidding. State governments, in particular, have placed great emphasis on differentiating their jurisdictions among possible investment sites. Again, Ohio stands out: the Ohio Development Board represents the "marketing arm" of the state government, which not only grants incentives but also conducts complete marketing operations, with offices in Japan and Europe as well as at home.[57]

The Stakes of the Game

As the stakes rose in value, aggressive marketing in Japan and in other capital-exporting countries became increasingly important. By 1981, foreign direct investment contributed 5 percent to the gross fixed capital formation of the United States—the highest level in modern American history.[58] The comparable figure in 1971 was one percent. During the intervening decade, only Britain and the Netherlands (and occasionally Canada) among industrialized host countries could boast such a large contribution by foreign investors.

Japan's contribution to U.S. capital formation grew throughout the 1970s. By 1981, as we have seen, the direct investment position of Japanese companies in America first exceeded the value of all comparable U.S. investment in Japan, and three years later, Japan emerged as America's fastest growing and third largest foreign investor, behind Britain and the Netherlands. More recently, to the delight of many American states and localities, employment-generating manufacturing and assembly operations have become increasingly attractive to Japanese investors. In fact, such investments have rapidly approached the size of American investments in the Japanese manufacturing sector. For example, the ratio of American to Japanese cross-investment in manufacturing was 5 to 1 in 1974, 4 to 1 in 1979, and less than 2 to 1 in 1984 (see *Table 4-4*).

Despite impressive growth, Japanese investments in U.S. manufacturing still pale in contrast with Japanese investments in U.S. wholesale trade. By 1984, these Japanese investments alone exceeded the value of all U.S. investments in Japan. Even more importantly, they supported Japan's overall trade strategy by forming an effective second front of economic competition with American interests.

Liberalization and the American Counterattack

In contrast to the American situation, foreign investors have played no important role in generating Japan's national income. Throughout the 1960s and 1970s, foreign direct investment contributed just one-tenth of one percent to the gross fixed capital formation of Japan—the lowest figure among all industrialized countries.[59] As a result, during this period Japan never represented an important target for American investment overseas, accounting for less than six percent of annual American outflows for over twenty years after the war.[60] Better opportunities in other foreign markets, Japanese government policies, and the emergence of strong Japanese competitors—three sets of

TABLE 4-4
American-Japanese Cross-Investments in Manufacturing[a]

Industry[b]	1974	1979	1984
Machinery[c]			
In Japan[d]	59.4%	53.8%	43.6%
In USA[e]	f	18.0	23.8
Chemicals			
In Japan[d]	21.5	24.3	20.5
In USA[e]	12.7	29.0	11.8
Food			
In Japan[d]	5.9	6.2	4.7
In USA[e]	f	4.2	8.7
Metals			
In Japan[d]	1.2	2.4	f
In USA[e]	f	32.0	23.7
Other			
In Japan[d]	12.0	13.3	20.2
In USA[e]	34.5	16.8	32.0
Total Cross-Investment in Manufacturing ($ billion)			
In Japan[d]	$1.5	$2.8	$4.1
In USA[e]	$0.3	$0.7	$2.3

[a] Distribution of direct investment position at year end in each country's manufacturing sector.

[b] Listed in the order of importance to U.S. investors.

[c] Includes electrical and nonelectrical machinery, and transport equipment.

[d] American direct investments in Japan, as defined in Table 4-1, note a.

[e] Japanese direct investments in America, as defined in Table 4-1, note a.

[f] Data suppressed by the U.S. Department of Commerce to avoid the disclosure of individual company operations.

SOURCES: United States Department of Commerce, Bureau of Economic Analysis, *Survey of Current Business,* various issues; U.S. Department of Commerce, Bureau of Economic Analysis, *Selected Data on U.S. Direct Investment Abroad, 1950–76,* February 1982, pp. 20–27.

conditions that were all tightly interrelated—serve to explain the continued paucity of American investment into the 1970s.

Even so, by the 1970s, an unheralded U.S. counterattack on the Japanese home market was well underway, stimulated by a further relaxation of Japanese capital controls. In 1973, for example, the government removed a key restriction on foreign entry: the 10 percent ceiling on foreign shareholdings in existing Japanese companies. Even then, the foreigner, by law, had to secure the firm's approval before purchasing larger shares of its equity; and the government continued to restrict foreign investment in certain companies and sectors, to regulate the value and timing of selected foreign transactions, and to insist on formal government approval of many transactions. These restrictions were largely eradicated in 1980, when a new era of foreign investment promotion began in Japan. Subsequently, the typical foreign investor simply notified the Bank of Japan about upcoming foreign financial transactions, and then proceeded without further government approval.[61]

In this more liberal climate, American investments grew: 13 percent annually between 1974 and 1979, then 6 percent annually over the next five years (see *Table 4-1*). While such growth was still much slower than the rise of Japanese direct investments in America, annual U.S. outflows to Japan (especially those in manufacturing) began to exceed comparable American direct investments to any other country.[62] By 1983, fully one-fifth of all new U.S. investment overseas went to Japan. Aside from large American *dis*investments in the petroleum industry—a peculiar, one-time result of the energy situation and a misleading indicator in our context—the trend toward increasing American investment in Japan continued during 1984.

Manufacturing long remained the principal domain of these American investors, accounting in 1984 for nearly one-half of all investments (see *Table 4-2*). Within manufacturing, however, there was some deviation from earlier patterns (see *Table 4-4*). Still, through 1984, American machinery and equipment manufacturers continued to account for at least two-fifths of all U.S. investment in Japan, with chemicals contributing an additional one-fifth. This pattern differed markedly from the recent influx of Japanese manufacturers into America, who were more widely diversified and who entered industries (e.g., metal fabrication) largely unknown to American investors operating in Japan.

While nearly all of these Japanese investments in America were wholly owned by their foreign parents, given the absence of U.S. capital controls, minority foreign-owned and equal-partnership joint ventures were more common in Japanese manufacturing, even after liberalization. By 1978, for example, U.S. multinationals able to exploit marketing and technological advantages (in pharmaceuticals, for example) held a majority interest in nearly one-half (45 percent) of their manufacturing subsidiaries in Japan.[63] In a few industries where U.S. firms enjoyed marketing and supplier advantages (food or paper products, for example), they held majority shares in roughly one-third of their manufacturing affiliates. And where such advantages were not generally available, majority-U.S. ownership was far less prevalent, as in transport equipment (where U.S. parents owned majority shares in less than one-tenth of all American affiliates) and in nonelectrical machinery (where such majority shares were owned in less than one-quarter). Even by 1981, foreign multinationals owned, on average, a majority of the equity in only about one-third of their Japanese manufacturing affiliates, up from one-sixth in 1974.[64]

To account for the continued high incidence of minority American-owned joint ventures in Japan, even after liberalization, we must consider the timing of these investments: nearly two-fifths of all American investments in 1984 actually flowed into Japan before the 1974 abolition of foreign equity controls (see *Table 4-1*). In the few years following liberalization, American investments doubled, as did the proportion of majority-owned, foreign manufacturing subsidiaries in Japan. So liberalization of government policies was important, even though such rapid growth cannot be attributed solely to a relaxation of capital controls. Other changes in government policy also contributed, especially in certain targeted sectors.

Industry Deregulation and Investment

Consider, for example, pharmaceuticals.[65] By 1983, over 300 foreign pharmaceutical companies had direct investments in Japan, the number having doubled in less than eight years. Eight companies controlled assets in excess of ¥5 billion each; for two of these, Merck (U.S.) and Ciba-Geigy (Swiss), assets exceeded ¥20 billion. Merck alone ranked among the three largest pharmaceutical producers in Japan, following its acquisition of Banyu and Torii in the early 1980s—a situation that would have been unthinkable and perhaps illegal before the liberalization of foreign equity controls. Much of the growth in foreign investment in this industry came on the heels of dramatic changes in Japanese health insurance policies. During the 1980s, deregulation here and in other industries such as telecommunications opened up new opportunities for foreigners.

In the Japanese pharmaceutical industry, the relationship between government policies and foreign investment remained complicated. Japanese national health insurance reimbursed patients for 90 percent of their medical costs, including drugs (which collectively accounted for two-fifths of these costs, versus one-fifth in the United States). The Ministry of Health and Welfare regularly updates an official list of prices at which it will reimburse patients for prescriptions. The doctors themselves filled prescriptions at the regulated price, using drugs that they purchase at a discount from pharmaceutical companies, and pocketing the difference. Here, a pharmaceutical company's profits depend to a considerable extent on keeping discounts to a minimum while maintaining a high official price. But between 1980 and 1984, the government sought to reduce health care costs by cutting official prices by 40 percent. (To make matters worse for the companies, new user fees for repeated visits to physicians reduced the number of prescriptions.)

Not all pharmaceutical companies were equally affected by these changes, however. Banyu and other Japanese manufacturers of product lines for which there were numerous substitutes felt the most pain, while Merck and other makers of drugs with more limited substitutes fared better, since the government had spared from price controls products new to the Japanese market. Often such products were directed at Japan's rapidly aging population—a market segment that also appealed to foreign companies. Merck was especially responsive to this confluence of demographic changes and government policies; its earlier licensee and subsequent acquisition target, Banyu, was not.

Merck preferred to acquire an existing company rather than to exercise other expansion options, for reasons that also appealed to other American investors. In particular, dollar-to-yen appreciation in 1983–1984 had diminished the profitability of U.S. exports, while reducing the dollar cost of investments in Japan. Given the volatility of exchange rates, Merck preferred a speedy acquisition to a long-term investment program. Other reasons that favored acquisition were largely peculiar to pharmaceuticals. The speed of the transaction, for example, was enhanced by Merck's already extensive business relations with Banyu. Like other American pharmaceutical companies, Merck principally had exported technology to Japan prior to 1982. In fact, between 1978 and 1982, over one-half of all drugs officially approved by the Japanese government were manufactured using foreign technology.[66] Finally, several reasons favoring an acquisition over a new investment were peculiar to this specific deal. For example, Banyu already relied heavily on Merck for technology. Moreover, Banyu's large marketing network made the company an attractive takeover target, as did its large cash balances. For all of these reasons, Merck quickly implemented its decision soon after the Japanese government liberalized the pharmaceutical industry.

Yet, while liberalization provided a necessary precondition to acquisition, few other foreign companies joined Merck in executing this entry strategy. Generally speaking, acquisitions have played a minuscule role in the growth of American investment in Japan, as opposed to their larger place in the comparable growth of U.S. multinationals elsewhere.[67] For industrialized countries outside of Japan, market entry through acquisition often rates as the most common investment strategy pursued by American multinationals; but entry into Japan was different.

Simply, differences in capital markets have accounted for Japan's exception to the general rule of multinational behavior. By itself, the dearth of Japanese acquisitions in America testifies to the fact that standard business practice in Japan continues to favor new investment over acquisition. Of course, corporate preferences were supported for many years by Japanese government policies that expressly denied foreign investors any opportunity to enter Japan through merger and acquisition. But even the formal dissolution of these policies left standard business practices unchanged. Only the internationalization of Japanese business promises any real change.

Japanese Buyers and American Investment

The liberalization of Japanese markets, including financial markets, and of the foreign role in those markets opened up new opportunities for American investors. They were now in a better position, according to one long-time observer, to respond to the intense pressures of "Japanese buyers, especially of capital goods, [who] tend to think local producers are more reliable than importers."[68] Under these conditions, it should come as no surprise that at least two-fifths of all U.S. investments in Japan have always been concentrated in machinery and equipment, where buyer power constitutes an important determinant of foreign investment.

Buyers of capital goods in Japan and elsewhere have typically required machinery and equipment to be customized to meet local needs. Pressures for customization were especially pronounced on U.S. manufacturers of the expensive machinery and equipment used to produce and test the semiconductors sold by NEC and other Japanese producers.[69] Of particular concern was the modification of U.S.-designed equipment to the specific requirements of Japanese chip-makers. In response to these pressures, Thermco became the first American semiconductor equipment company to establish a manufacturing plant in Japan, a 50–50 joint venture with TEL in 1968, before the liberalization of foreign equity controls. With an investment in 1984 valued at ¥2 billion and over 50 percent market share in its product lines, TEL-Thermco planned to establish a second manufacturing plant. By then, thirteen American semiconductor equipment companies operated manufacturing facilities in Japan—three times the number of American semiconductor (end-product) vendors operating there. Seven of these equipment manufacturers became operational during 1983–1984; they included the wholly owned subsidiaries of such industry giants as American Machine Tools (¥1.9 billion invested in Japan) and Shipley (¥1.2 billion invested). For all of these manufacturers, having a large and visible local presence demonstrated a market commitment sought by Japanese buyers generally, and especially by purchasers of expensive capital goods such as the $5+ million items used in the manufacture and assembly of semiconductors.

Building a Japanese presence often required very extensive efforts: to quote Peter Drucker, "in service, in market research, in market development and in promotion—given the behavior of Japanese buyers."[70] Certainly this has been true in the Japanese pharmaceutical industry. The decentralized distribution of drugs through the government-financed health insurance program encouraged foreign companies to establish their own distribution channels and sales forces. Thousands of detail men were required to visit the tens of thousands of doctors and hundreds of hospitals, which together served as the principal purchasers of prescription drugs in the absence of retail pharmacies. The typical foreign pharmaceutical company initially responded to Japan's national health scheme by licensing local distributors to sell their exports to Japan or, increasingly, to sell products manufactured locally, usually in joint ventures, using the foreign company's technology.

A notable exception to this trend began with Pfizer in the late 1950s, when it embarked on a long-term plan designed to establish its own independent channels and sales force. Other companies followed Pfizer's lead, but in the case of Merck, management preferred the acquisition of Banyu's 1,600 veteran detail men and elaborate marketing network. Merck's acquisition of Banyu (including its aging plant and equipment) therefore represented primarily an investment in wholesale trade rather than in manufacturing—but because many of Merck-Banyu's capsules and tablets were finally processed in Japan, official statistics labeled the acquisition as an investment in manufacturing.

Japanese Imports and U.S. Multinationals

Before processing those capsules and tablets, however, Banyu had to import pharmaceutical formulations and bulk chemicals, with increasing reliance on Merck's global operations. Indeed, by 1978 imports accounted for nearly three-fifths of the materials used by U.S.-affiliated pharmaceutical manufacturers in Japan.[71] Such import dependence was also characteristic of other American affiliates in food processing, paper products, electrical machinery, and electronics. Typically these imports were shipped directly by U.S. parents who, in these industries, owned a controlling stake in over one-third of their Japanese affiliates. By contrast, in most other Japanese industries, where minority-U.S. or equal partnership joint ventures were more prevalent (transport equipment and parts, for example) the sourcing of material inputs outside of Japan was virtually nonexistent.

Such outside sourcing by American affiliates, when it did occur, was not limited to imports for a U.S. parent. In addition, third-country suppliers played an important role in at least a few industries; and again, much of that trade was intra-company—between two subsidiaries of the same U.S. parent.[72] In the semiconductor industry, for example, U.S. subsidiaries in Southeast Asia became important vendors for American-owned manufacturing plants in Japan. Beginning in the 1960s, U.S. semiconductor companies began to move their most labor-intensive assembly operations to Asia; by the 1980s, fully 80 percent of their assemblies were conducted there or in Latin America. On the other hand, Japanese subsidiaries in America relied far less on third-country sourcing.

Again in semiconductors, Japanese companies did not move their labor-intensive operations overseas (in fact, overseas production amounted to less than 4 percent of total production). Instead, the Japanese invested in automatic wire bonding machines and other special machinery that dramatically improved Japanese domestic productivity. As a result, the Japanese parent companies—and not third-country subsidiaries—supplied most of the outsourcing requirements of their American affiliates.

While these and other Japanese investments in America remained integral to Japan's export strategy, the same could not be said for U.S. manufacturers in Japan. To put it simply, American multinationals have been far less successful in using their Japanese investments as a beachhead for exports of finished products, subassemblies, and manufacturing inputs from the United States. In 1983, total exports from the United States to the Japanese affiliates of American companies barely exceeded $2.5 billion of which 95 percent was shipped by the U.S. parent[73] (see *Table 4-5*). This contrasts with the $28 billion exported by Japanese parents to their U.S. affiliates the same year (see *Table 4-3*). In other words, intra-company trade involving Japanese parents was about ten times larger than comparable exports by American parents—even though cross-investments between the two countries were only twice as large for the

TABLE 4-5
American Direct Investments and U.S. Trade, 1983
($ billion)

	U.S. Exports to U.S. Affiliates Operating in Japan	U.S. Imports from U.S. Affiliates Operating in Japan
Manufacturing	$1.1	$3.1
Of which:		
Motor vehicles and parts	$0	$2.6
Chemicals[a]	$0.3	$0.1[b]
Wholesale Trade	$1.3	$0.5
Other	$0.1	$0
Total	$2.5	$3.6

[a] Especially industrial chemicals and pharmaceuticals, the largest sources of U.S. exports to American affiliates operating in Japan.

[b] Specific details of intra-company trade suppressed by the U.S. Department of Commerce to avoid disclosing the operations of a few large companies; estimates here are mathematically derived using other data provided.

SOURCE: U.S. Department of Commerce, Bureau of Economic Analysis, *Annual Survey of U.S. Direct Investment Abroad, 1983* (Washington, D.C.: U.S. Government Printing Office, forthcoming, 1986).

Japanese. When contrasted with the Japanese invasion of America, the U.S. counterattack appears less integral to America's export strategy.

Japan as an Export Platform

American investment in Japan was, however, integral to the strategy of global sourcing pursued by several U.S. multinationals.[74] When Merck acquired Banyu, for example, the American company announced that it would begin to market in the United States certain antibiotics and dermatological products manufactured by its recently acquired subsidiaries in Japan. By using Japan as an export platform for the United States, Merck followed the lead of a few other majority-owned American companies. By 1982, for example, Texas Instruments-Japan exported, principally to its parent, one-half of the estimated $300 million worth of memory chips it produced. And IBM-Japan, the only IBM subsidiary in the world making XT disk drives, exported 100 percent of its production to its U.S. parent. But these examples still must be regarded as idiosyncratic. The vast majority of American subsidiaries in pharmaceuticals, electronics, and elsewhere still have sold very little overseas (see *Table 4-5*). Most entered Japan to supply the domestic Japanese market, and were encouraged initially to do so by Japanese barriers to trade and the demands of Japanese buyers.

So far, the paucity of these American exports from Japan contrasts with the export activity of Japanese affiliates operating in America. By 1983, the Americans exported $3.6 billion of manufactured goods from Japan to the United States (see *Table 4-5*), in contrast to $18.2 billion of metals, minerals, and farm products exported by the Japanese from America that same year (calculated from *Table 4-3* above). Again, the source of American exports from Japan was different: nearly three-quarters of the total were shipped largely to the parents of U.S. affiliates in just one industry—motor vehicles and parts.

American automakers increasingly integrated Japanese production into their larger global strategies. For example, auto exports by Isuzu and Suzuki to their largest shareholder, General Motors, as well as Mitsubishi sales to Chrysler, swelled in 1985 when the Japanese government revised its "voluntary restraints" on car shipments, and allotted much of the increased quota to these captive producers. In fact, to ensure better coordination of these imports with domestic American production, Chrysler increased its minority equity holdings in Mitsubishi, following a strategy charted earlier by GM and Isuzu. By contrast, Ford had no captive imports, but that American multinational held large, albeit minority equity investments in Mazda and several other Japanese parts suppliers, which have been increasingly integrated into Ford's global operations. Similarly, GM relied on several original equipment manufacturers, who in 1985 established a formal supplier association to discuss issues of mutual concern. Exports from these suppliers were not limited to the United States. According to a 1978 study, more than one-fourth of the total sales of American affiliates operating in the Japanese transport equipment industry were exported to third-country markets, largely those in East Asia.[75] Whether for export to the United States or to subsidiaries in third countries, the use of Japan as an export platform for parts, subassemblies, and finished products meant expanded investments by American multinationals.

The Role of Japanese Local Government

In the United States, the possibility of increased foreign investment in the automobile sector prompted intense competition among American states for the right to serve as a new plant site. Not so in Japan, where new American investment went into existing automakers and parts suppliers which, like much of Japanese industry, were already concentrated in a 300-mile corridor from Tokyo to Osaka. There, Japanese industry could minimize transportation costs in a country with limited flatlands. And there, Japanese industry could achieve economies of scale and scope conducive to mass production and mass marketing. In short, Japan's strategy of industrial development—constrained by geography—narrowed the opportunity for industrial investment in rural Japan.

Nevertheless, in the late 1960s, the central government tried to lure Japanese and foreign companies out of the congested Tokyo-Osaka corridor and into new, rural, industrial parks. Less expensive real estate was their principal incentive; to this, the central government added infrastructure expenditures, tax breaks, and subsidized loans. Among other objectives, the central government sought to stem the tide of out-migration that had depopulated much of the countryside. Oita Prefecture, for example, on the southernmost island of Kyushu, was among the hardest hit. By the early 1970s, its economy was "on the verge of collapse," according to both public and private accounts.[76]

In addition, the central government sought to reduce the dependence of rural areas on government subsidies.[77] As urban Japan grew and prospered, jobs in outlying regions were generated in part by infusions of central government expenditures, notably for public works, funded largely by urban tax revenues. The redistribution of revenues from urban to rural populations was a central plank of successive Liberal Democratic governments, which depended on continued rural support for their political survival. But the oil price shock of 1973 changed all this: a reduction in receipts during the ensuing recession generated a series of budgetary deficits that prompted the central government to curtail spending on public works and other regional development programs. With few other options in the midst of these "fiscal crises," *prefectural* governments intensified their efforts to attract private investment.

The prefectures first turned to Japanese business, but met with little success. By the time recession hit in 1974, Japanese companies were often more interested in cutting back capacity than in spreading out geographically. Even those who thought to invest in rural areas soon discovered that managers and skilled workers "refused to move" and give up their urban lifestyles, to quote one consultant involved in the process. As a result, few Japanese companies moved to the countryside, and the new industrial parks scattered around Japan's 47 prefectures began to look "like industrial wilderness areas."[78] Another option involved the mobilization of local resources, but these were limited in quantity and scope.[79] The final option was to attract foreign direct investment. Here, prefectures became more active.

In contrast to the aggressive behavior of American states, Japanese prefectures adopted strategies that were simpler and more predictable.[80] For example, the investment incentives that made up a typical Japanese package—while large in value—were few in number, and their mechanics were well understood. Prefectures usually offered newcomers tax holidays and subsidies for such things as recreation centers. They also helped foreigners to get loans from local banks and to secure land. Even special loans to foreigners available from the Japan Development Bank (as well as other incentives whose levels were negotiated rather than automatic), were largely based on simple and known criteria. As a result, bidding wars among Japanese prefectures remained almost nonexistent, in sharp contrast to the American scene.

While the U.S. federal government typically stayed out of the fray, the Japanese central government did not. MITI considered competitive bidding among prefectures to be counterproductive, and negotiated an implicit understanding with potentially competing prefectural governments to refrain from competition for foreign investors.[81] To promote accord, MITI exercised further control over the incentive packages assembled by the prefectures. Within each of the regional development authorities, MITI dispatched personnel on two-year assignments, ostensibly to aid the investment promotion process. A supplementary goal was the curtailment of competition and the coordination of nationwide policy.

Until recently Japanese prefectures, unlike American states, engaged in little direct "marketing" of investment sites. Much of that marketing, in fact, was carried out by agencies of the central government: the Japan External Trade Organization (JETRO) and the Industrial Guidance Division of MITI. JETRO, for example, provided potential foreign investors with consulting and translation services through its overseas offices. Similarly, MITI established a computerized English-language service to match project proposals with possible investment sites, and to report on available incentives. While MITI and JETRO tried to promote investment impartially, central government policies inevitably encouraged some differentiation among rural prefectures. The "Technopolis" program, for example, allowed certain regional governments to target investment in high-technology industries while at the same time drawing attention to that region's special advantages.

Some individual prefectures also spotlighted the advantages they could offer foreign investors. For example, Governor Hiramatsu in Oita Prefecture of Kyushu became famous for the services he provided to prospective investors.[82] As a former MITI official, Hiramatsu proved adept at moving foreign investment proposals through the bureaucratic labyrinth that still existed during most of the 1970s. Texas Instruments was among several foreign companies he placed in Oita during that period, helping to transform Kyushu into "Silicon Island." In fact, this new image subsequently bolstered the efforts of additional prefectures in Kyushu to attract Fairchild and other American producers of high-technology electronics. In 1982, TI and fourteen other majority foreign-owned enterprises established manufacturing plants in Japan. Thirteen of these plants were located in Oita and other economically underdeveloped regions; only two were located in the Tokyo-Osaka corridor.[83]

Certainly regional incentives contributed in some measure to this geographic dispersal of foreign investment in Japan, just as they did in America. Such incentives, however, had far less impact on the initial decision to invest in Japan or in the United States. In both countries, trade policies and prospects, along with the competitive structure of industries, proved to be far more important. Yet we should not forget that, in Japan, regional incentives take on added significance because of what they represent: a fundamental change in the attitudes of government at all levels toward foreign investment.

Here, the career of Governor Hiramatsu of Oita conveniently symbolizes an historic change: as a MITI official in the early 1960s, he was actively involved in the decision to deny Texas Instruments a license to establish a wholly owned subsidiary in Japan, insisting instead that TI establish an equal-partnership joint venture.[84] Then, years later, after Japanese semiconductor suppliers had become fully competitive, relations between Governor Hiramatsu and TI became quite different when TI offered employment to residents of Oita Prefecture in exchange for the governor's promotion of the proposed investment. Hiramatsu's slow evolution from regulator to promoter of foreign investment can be measured in a single lifetime, but the change also represents the shift in Japan's foreign economic policy and its new regional development objectives. At present, with U.S. critics decrying limited foreign access to the Japanese market, active promotion was essential to overcome the lingering specter of strict regulation, fostered by decades of policy pronouncements by the central government after World War II.

Conclusions

Government policymakers and business managers have long recognized that foreign direct investment is a formidable weapon in commercial competition. Indeed, early fears of American industrial prowess prompted Japan's erection of foreign trade barriers to encourage fledgling competitors. By themselves, these barriers were insufficient to reduce American competition, since tariffs and quotas in several industries actually served as strong inducements for American companies to invest in Japan. Recognizing this, the Japanese government also instituted capital controls to limit the expansion of foreign investors in the protected Japanese market. Not only was the volume of American investment diminished by these regulations, but the restrictions also minimized American managerial control over the occasional joint ventures permitted by the Japanese government. In such a hostile environment, few American multinationals invested in Japan—fewer, in fact, than in any other major overseas market. Those companies that did invest were able to exploit, in a newly industrializing Japan, the same marketing and technological innovations that earlier had given them formidable competitive advantages in U.S. manufacturing—especially in machinery and in chemicals.

Early Japanese investors in America pursued a far different strategy. Rather than diversify horizontally, as the Americans in Japan were doing with their assembly and manufacturing plants, the Japanese integrated vertically—unencumbered by any American version of foreign equity controls. Early investments upstream in the wholesale trade and finance of food products, metals, and minerals satisfied Japan's growing demand for America's natural resources. Later investments downstream in the wholesale trade of motor vehicles and other durables complemented Japan's export strategy. With few marketing and technological advantages to exploit early on, with few impediments to continued trade with America, and finally, with Japanese capital controls limiting large outflows of still-scarce foreign exchange, Japan's direct investments in the United States remained minuscule for nearly thirty years after World War II. Even by 1974, those investments were one-tenth the size of otherwise small American investments in Japan.

But during the late 1970s, all of this changed, as Japan's current account surpluses grew—all, that is, except for the concentration of Japanese direct investment in downstream wholesale trade. In fact, by 1984, the position of Japanese investors in the U.S. wholesale sector alone—mainly in selling autos and other durables—exceeded the entire value of all American investments in Japan. Those Japanese-affiliated wholesalers distributed at least 70 percent of all Japanese exports to America, and gave Japanese manufacturers an unusual degree of control over the marketing of their exports to America. From the perspective of Japanese foreign economic policy, these direct investments also provided a mechanism for recycling ever-growing export receipts, in an effort to quiet U.S. critics of Japanese trade policies. But, somewhat paradoxically, new Japanese investments, most of which entered the U.S. wholesale sector, stimulated even more Japanese exports.

The composition of those Japanese exports gradually changed, however, as subassemblies and knocked-down kits began to be shipped to new Japanese assembly and manufacturing plants in America. While the book value of these new plants paled in contrast to the total value of Japanese investments in U.S. wholesaling, Japanese investments in U.S. manufacturing nevertheless experienced rapid growth following America's erection of new barriers to Japanese exports. Japanese manufacturers, like their earlier American counterparts, sidestepped these barriers by investing within the protected market. But unlike the Americans, several Japanese investors now were able to exploit their earlier beachhead in U.S. wholesaling by integrating backward into assembly and manufacture. Japanese manufacturers often moved sequentially to America, following their industry leaders; and when Japanese manufacturers moved, they tended to bring their suppliers along. Once both buyer and supplier had decided to invest in the United States, their subsequent plant-location decisions were sometimes shaped by the proposals of American state and local governments, competing with one another for employment-generating investment. Given this constellation of forces between 1974 and 1984, Japanese investments in U.S. manufacturing grew rapidly—in fact, twice as fast as U.S. manufacturing investments in Japan.

Still, American direct investments in Japan, most of which remained in manufacturing, did increase substantially during the ten years following Japan's 1974 liberalization of capital controls. Similarly, the proportion of wholly owned foreign subsidiaries in Japan doubled after this liberalization; and in high-technology industries, these proportions were even greater. Japanese buyers of American goods, and especially capital goods, often demanded an increased American presence. Like many Japanese investors in America, some U.S. manufacturers in pharmaceuticals and other industries discovered that increased sales were possible only when they controlled their own distribution channels downstream. But unlike the Japanese, few U.S. multinationals used their Japanese investments to expand their exports from America. To the extent that they traded at all, these U.S. subsidiaries, and especially those in the automobile sector, supplied their American parents and third-country affiliates with parts and equipment manufactured in Japan. Whether they were built for export or not, the location of U.S. manufacturing plants inside Japan was increasingly influenced by the pleas of Japanese prefectures in those economically backward regions that actively sought employment-generating investment.

Indeed, the strategies of local governments competing for foreign investment in both Japan and the United States illustrate a larger theme that emerges from this chapter: the growing similarity in the patterns of American-Japanese cross-investments. These patterns are reflected in the corporate strategies of Japanese and American investors; they can be explained in part by declining variation, not only in government policies, but also in product markets and in the competitive structures of industries. Even the widely touted reluctance of Japanese enterprise to invest in manufacturing and assembly plants overseas— a reluctance typically explained in terms of cultural and organizational factors—began to diminish when Japanese exporters came face to face with many of the same conditions that once sent American multinationals to Japan: ever-larger capital surpluses at home, government-induced barriers to trade overseas, and, to a lesser extent, the demands of local buyers and the competitive pressures of concentrated industries.

In explaining the growing "multinationalization" of Japanese enterprise (to use a phrase popular in Japan today) one other consideration should also be added—the increasing comparability of Japanese and American policies toward investment outflows and inflows: policies of benign neglect or active promotion, but no longer of simple regulation. In the coming years, these and other similarities of corporate strategy and government policy should become even more prominent, as American-Japanese cross-investments continue to grow. Indeed, such growth represents for both countries an increasingly potent weapon in the arsenal of business managers and government policymakers—a weapon that barely existed for the Japanese until the mid-1970s.

Because of its newness, this investment weapon will undoubtedly be exploited in many different ways by business and government in both countries, as one nation maneuvers to counter the other. The persistence of important differences in the government policies and corporate strategies adopted in America and Japan provides a second theme of this chapter. Many of these differences are legacies of the past. For example, to account for the higher incidence of minority American-owned joint ventures (compared to the preponderance of wholly owned Japanese subsidiaries in America), one must take into consideration the timing of these investments: nearly two-fifths of all American-owned stocks flowed into Japan before the 1974 abolition of foreign equity controls. Those controls had no counterparts in America. Moreover, American regulators did not inhibit foreign companies from entering the U.S. wholesale sector, in contrast to the stringent actions of Japanese policymakers prior to liberalization.

After liberalization, of course, American investors might have expanded rapidly in manufacturing and wholesale trade if they had actively acquired existing Japanese companies—an investment strategy common to the rapid expansion of American multinationals in other foreign markets. But standard business practices in Japan (and for a long while, Japanese government policies as well) simply denied foreign investors any opportunity to enter Japan through mergers and acquisitions. These business practices also shaped Japanese investments in America; in fact, until recently, the dearth of American acquisitions in Japan has been matched by the relative infrequence of Japanese acquisitions in the United States. The divergence in the functioning of Japanese and American capital markets illustrates the continued variation of corporate strategies in the two countries even after government-induced barriers to change have diminished.

The persistence of important differences in corporate strategies and government policies also shows itself in recent developments. Over time, pressures for change in the two countries have actually pushed them in opposite directions, thus increasing their differences. Japanese manufacturers, for example, have become even more concerned about controlling the marketing of their autos and other durable exports to America—and, correspondingly, they have increased the proportion of their total investments going into U.S. wholesaling, from one-half of all Japanese investments in 1979 to two-thirds in 1984. With fewer manufacturing exports to Japan to worry about, American investors, by contrast, either have viewed Japan as an export platform (in auto parts, for example) or, more generally, have sought to establish a visible presence in industries (such as electrical machinery and customized semiconductors) where close interaction with a limited number of buyers has been important. Pressures for changing government policies in the two countries have also pushed in opposite directions. In trade policy, the threat of greater U.S. protectionism increased just as Japan's long-existing import restrictions began to wane. In foreign investment policy, the slow decline in Japanese resistance to foreign investors was paralleled by a growing concern in the United States that Japan might someday control America's most productive assets and thus become victorious in the ongoing economic rivalry between the two countries.

At the present juncture in the history of American-Japanese cross-investment, the greatest threat to bilateral relations is that the growing asymmetry already evident in 1984—with Japanese investments in the United States almost two times larger than American investments in Japan—would become another source of tension. That new "investment gap," like the already present "trade gap," added further credence to the claim that Japan has moved much too slowly in opening its markets to Americans. Fearing this criticism, Japanese attempts to promote the inflow of American investments have been carefully orchestrated by their national government—in contrast to the indifference still manifested by U.S. federal agencies. While Japanese promotional efforts have so far met with limited success in attracting American investors, they have partially stymied for the moment those U.S. critics who earlier pointed to Japanese constraints on market entry through foreign direct investment.

Still other American critics, pointing to the flood of Japanese investment into U.S. industry, claim that Japanese companies are financing their expansion at America's expense: using profits from exports to the States, the Japanese can build new state-of-the-art plants, which will generate new profits to be wholly repatriated to Japan. Others complain that their new Japanese rivals are misrepresenting themselves by putting the "Made in America" label on products merely assembled here, after most of the work was done in Japan with lower labor costs and with the benefit (up until late 1985) of favorable foreign exchange rates. In defense of Japanese investments, several American states have argued that Japanese companies contribute jobs, tax revenues, and even dividends to their American stockholders—all benefits to the society from which they are reaping profits. Perhaps the most unlikely defenders of Japanese investments in America can be found in the U.S. auto industry, where both labor and management have long wanted to bring the Japanese to America's shores. In a 1980 speech, Chrysler Corporation Chairman Lee A. Iacocca succinctly explained: "That way, we draw from the same pool, pay the same taxes, meet the same regulations and contribute to the health of the economy we all compete in."[85] His may be the best argument yet for continuing unimpeded cross-investments between America and Japan.

CHAPTER 5

Agriculture: The Political Economy of Structural Change

MICHAEL R. REICH, YASUO ENDO, AND
C. PETER TIMMER

Introduction

Japan and the United States are both undergoing a fundamental structural change in the role of agriculture in the national economy. Although the two countries are at significantly different points on this general path of structural change, each confronts a similar issue: the declining share of agriculture in overall economic output, and the political difficulties of moving resources out of agriculture. Agricultural policies in both countries are designed to cushion the pressures on farm incomes caused by this basic and chronic problem. But in doing so, the domestic policies in Japan and the United States also produce conflict in the two countries' agricultural trade relationship.

These bilateral tensions are symbolized by the recent conflict over beef and oranges, trivial items in the actual trade accounts between the United States and Japan, but the focal point of heated talks on agricultural trade. This recent trade dispute reflects fundamentally different national approaches to structural adjustment in agriculture. The Japanese approach has restricted imports of agricultural products of high value, including beef and oranges, and has protected basic commodity producers, especially rice farmers. The American approach has required access to foreign markets for agricultural exports, with a recent emphasis on products of higher value than such traditional bulk commodities as corn, wheat, and soybeans. When the growing bilateral trade deficit and the difficulties of selling American manufactured products in Japan were added to the equation in the early 1980s, the level of discord over agricultural trade reached a fevered pitch.

This chapter examines the political economy of structural change, through an analysis of Japanese and United States agricultural policies and the tensions between those policies expressed in the trade conflict over beef and oranges.

151

The first section of the chapter briefly explains the problems that structural change created for agriculture in both economies. The term structural change is used throughout to mean not simply farm size, but also the overall evolution of agriculture in the economy, including agriculture's contribution to national output and to total employment. The section reviews the patterns of structural change in the economies of the two countries and then compares and contrasts the approaches of general agricultural policy. The contrasting approaches have produced a trade relationship characterized by both interdependence and conflict.

The second section of the chapter analyzes the strategic choices of Japanese and U.S. agricultural policy in confronting the issues of structural adjustment over the past two decades. The section presents the range of policy choices generally available for coping with such problems. Choices made by the Japanese contrast with those made by Americans, for reasons of resource endowment, political structure and strategy, and sheer pace of change. The analysis explains why certain choices of policy unleashed a chain of related events in agricultural output, costs, and prices—with major consequences for the government's budget, particularly in Japan.

Conflicts between Japan and the United States over agricultural trade resulted in large part from choices of national policy. Japanese policy used higher degrees of protection, but also developed some sectors that could compete internationally. United States policy became increasingly export-oriented, but still maintained protection for certain agricultural sectors. The two countries developed highly interdependent ties in agricultural trade, with each nation vulnerable to policy changes in the other. When Japan's refusal of market access for certain American agricultural goods that had a clear cost advantage became symbolically linked to trade problems with manufactured products, the stakes of agricultural trade negotiations became even higher.

The third section of the chapter discusses the politics of agricultural policy development in both countries, as revealed by the trade dispute over beef and oranges. The recent negotiations are summarized, beginning with the Multilateral Trade Negotiations in 1978 and ending with the conclusion of the latest round in spring 1984. The connection of beef and oranges to basic problems of structural adjustment and to national strategies of agricultural development significantly complicated the politics of both countries. Politically active groups seized on beef and oranges and transformed the negotiations into a major political issue, reflecting far more than the economic questions at stake.

The chapter's conclusion sets forth lessons for future agricultural trade relationships between the United States and Japan.

The Problems of Structural Change

Based on both the historical record and theoretical models, agriculture becomes a declining sector during the process of economic growth. Factors of production must leave the agricultural sector as a country industrializes, be-

TABLE 5-1
Comparative Indicators of the Role of Food and Agriculture in Economic Structure

	United States	Japan	Market Economies Industrial	Market Economies Middle Income	Market Economies Low Income	European Centrally Planned Economies
GNP per capita ($, 1980)	11,360	9,890	10,320	1,400	260	4,640
Percentage of Gross Domestic Product (GDP) from agriculture (1980)	3.0	4	4	15	36	15
Percentage of labor force in agriculture (1980)	3.2	12	6	44	71	16
Gross Domestic Product share as a percentage of labor force share	94	33	67	34	51	94
Percentage of consumers' expenditures on food, beverages & tobacco (1977)	16[1]	35[2]	28	47	62	46[3]
Percentage of exports from agricultural raw materials (1979)	25	2	15	15	42	11
Percentage of imports from food (1979)	9	15	12	11	17	na

[1] 1978.
[2] 1975; food only.
[3] Based on data for Hungary, Poland, and Yugoslavia.
SOURCE: Partially drawn from Alan J. Webb, "Protection in Agricultural Markets," ERS Staff Report No. AGES840524, U.S. Department of Agriculture, Washington, D.C., September 1984.

cause technical change raises agricultural productivity faster than the capacity of the human stomach to absorb the potential expansion of farm output. Capital and labor must leave agriculture, but both of these factors are relatively immobile in the short run. Countries that have succeeded in modernizing their economies and in reaching high standards of living have faced severe problems of relatively low incomes to agricultural workers during the process of adjustment to structural change. The United States is farthest down this path of structural change, as *Table 5-1* shows.

The data presented in *Table 5-1* must be understood against a historical background of at least 150 years. In the first half of the nineteenth century, the U.S. agricultural labor force dropped from 79 to 55 percent of the total labor force, with small relative declines continuing in the latter half of the century. By 1910, agriculture had reached 31 percent of the total labor force, and from then on, the farm labor force actually declined in absolute numbers (from 11.8 million in 1910, to 9.6 million in 1940, to 3.6 million in 1969).[1] Agriculture became increasingly commercial in the nineteenth century, and agricultural exports served as the major source of U.S. foreign exchange earnings throughout the 1800s. Expanding exports and a growing domestic market provided a basis for the vast enlargement of farmland, contributing to increased agricultural output.

After the Second World War, large numbers of people in the United States continued to move out of agriculture, while consolidating many landholdings into larger size farms and raising the yields and total production of agriculture. Even though total production continued to rise at a steep rate, the relative *share* of agriculture in the overall economy continued to decline, with agriculture's portion of gross domestic product in 1980 about half the figure it had been in 1950. Despite these dramatic changes, however, problems of adjustment remain. The heated debate over the 1985 farm bill and the current plight of American farmers demonstrate that many issues of adjustment are still important in the United States in both economic and political terms.[2]

Japan is also well along in this structural change, as illustrated in *Table 5-1,* but it lags behind the United States and other industrial economies in key aspects. Although the current structure of Japan's economic output is very similar to that of its industrial partners, its labor force remains relatively out of balance. Japan's agricultural labor force (in proportion to total labor force) resembles that of "middle income" countries such as Brazil and South Korea more than the figure for industrialized countries such as the United States and West Germany. It should be noted, however, that the figure of 12 percent for Japan's labor force in agriculture overstates the ratio by using all persons engaged in farming, both part-time and full-time (6.97 million in 1980), rather than only full-time farmers plus some fraction of part-time farmers. U.S. statistics similarly overstate the agricultural labor force, although not to the same extent as Japanese figures.

This feature of Japan's agricultural labor force represents a key problem of structural change confronting that nation. Again, the historical background is important to any understanding of the present situation. In 1880, Japan's farm labor force was about 75 percent of the total labor force. That percentage declined slightly over the next several decades, reflecting the growth of non-farm employment. In the 1920s and 1930s, the decline in agricultural labor force leveled off at about 50 percent, reflecting a slowdown in the increase of nonfarm jobs. In the immediate post–World War II period, the farm labor force increased temporarily from returning soldiers, and then large amounts of labor moved out of agriculture as the Japanese economy grew. Indeed, the flow from agriculture to industry and services has been remarkably rapid: the total farm labor force declined from 16.0 million in 1955 to 6.97 in 1980. *Table 5-2* shows that the rate of decline in farm employment in Japan was similar to the rates for the European Community and the United States in the late 1950s and

TABLE 5-2
Annual Rates of Decline in Farm Employment, 1955–1979
(Percent per year)

	1955–1960	1960–1970	1970–1979
European Community	−3.2	−4.6	−3.4
United Kingdom	−2.5	−3.8	−1.0
Canada	−3.6	−2.7	−0.7
Japan	−2.6	−4.0	−4.1
United States	−3.3	−4.5	−0.5

SOURCE: D. Gale Johnson, "World Commodity Market Situation and Outlook," *U.S. Agricultural Policy: The 1985 Farm Legislation,* Bruce L. Gardner, ed. (Washington, D.C.: American Enterprise Institute for Public Policy Research, 1985), p. 47.

1960s, and was significantly faster during the 1970s. But even rapid movement of labor from agriculture to industry has not been fast enough for Japan to avoid an acute case of structural lag, with more workers than needed still in agriculture. The persistent problem of adjustment for the agricultural sector derives in part from the extraordinarily fast pace of economic growth.

Comparison of General Agricultural Policies

Agricultural policies in Japan and the United States have faced similar problems and stated similar goals, but have used strikingly different means to achieve the objectives. Japanese policy has relied on a highly interventionist approach, guided by a long-range strategy which seeks to target specific commodities for development by Japanese farmers. That approach in agriculture resembles Japanese policy in various industrial sectors. United States policy, on the other hand, has relied much more on a market orientation, especially since the late 1960s. But U.S. government programs have also invested heavily in extensive research on new agricultural technologies along with promotional efforts (including significant subsidies) for exports of agricultural products, as well as commodity price support programs. This approach is more interventionist than is U.S. policy in most industrial sectors, and it represents what some see as a more desirable model for government-business relations in the United States.[3]

U.S. government intervention in the agricultural sector has a long history, beginning in 1862 when President Lincoln signed the Land Grant College Act (or first Morrill Act) to establish a college or university in each state, which became the basis for applied agricultural research and education. Later in the nineteenth century, the county-agent system was inaugurated, to provide expert advice to farmers everywhere. Overall farm productivity continued to climb, indeed so much that it actually became a problem for public policy. In the 1930s, faced with excess supplies, the federal government instituted production restraint programs (under the Agricultural Adjustment Act of 1933) to reduce agricultural surpluses and increase farm prices and incomes. Then, following the enactment of Public Law 480 in 1954, the United States actively sought to export its growing agricultural surpluses, by using concessionary sales to help develop overseas markets. The 1960s saw low prices for grain and the expansion of a livestock sector, despite the government's price supports and land diversion payments under the Emergency Feed Grain Act of 1961. Subsequent agricultural laws maintained similar patterns of governmental intervention.[4]

Meanwhile, change was also occurring rapidly in Japan, though not in exactly the same direction. Changes in Japanese agricultural policies reflect the evolving shape of Japan's food system and the shifting nature of the government's priorities. In the immediate postwar period, the principal objectives of agricultural policy were to provide staple food supplies and alleviate hunger, to carry out national land reform, and to create employment opportunities, as well as to democratize rural society. Government intervention was direct and extensive, first during the war, then under the U.S. Occupation, and later under Japan's own postwar policies. The main laws were the Food Control Act of 1942, to control prices, purchasing, and distribution of major food items during the war; the Agricultural Cooperative Union Law of 1947, to establish farmer organizations outside governmental control; and the Agricultural Land Law of 1952, to protect the redistribution that occurred under land reform (described in more detail later in the chapter). These three laws had lasting influence on Japan's agricultural system,[5] just as the supply-management policies (aimed at limiting supply and maintaining price parity for farm outputs relative to inputs) initiated during the Depression in the United States continued to influence the design of U.S. agricultural policies for at least two decades after the Second World War.

The Basic Agricultural Law of 1961 marked the start of a second period of agricultural policy in Japan, with a new set of objectives. This law directly recognized the problems of structural change and specifically set out to support the development of agriculture relative to manufacturing and to maintain the income of farmers relative to the wages of urban workers. The production of livestock, fruits, and vegetables was promoted and introduced into Japan's traditional agricultural system under the "selective expansion policy," as an effort to meet changing demand. The aggregate share of such products in gross agricultural output increased significantly throughout the 1960s and 1970s. These sectors came to be considered strategic commodities in Japanese agricultural policy—as high value-added products and as appropriate for full-time farmers. But the use of rice price policy to support the income of farm households—with the government's purchase price rising to over *four times* the world price between 1960 and 1980—had very important consequences for the structure of agriculture in Japan, as discussed below.

Food consumption also changed dramatically during the 1960s and 1970s, with a considerable increase in food calorie intake per person and a diversification of food consumption patterns. The Japanese people moved from a starchy staple diet oriented around rice and other grains (used in noodles) to much more variety, leading to an increase in the consumption of protein and fat. With rising per capita incomes, Japan's diet gradually shifted toward the pattern of consumption found in the United States and Europe, although the Japanese pattern remains much lower for total caloric intake and consumption of red meat. Annual per capita consumption of rice dropped steadily over the twenty years following 1960, going from 115 kilograms in 1960 to 79 kilograms in 1980, and for nonagricultural households from 98 to 46 kilograms. Roughly one-fifth of the protein in an average person's diet still comes from fish, although per capita fish consumption has recently declined, in part owing to rising fish prices. These dietary changes resulted in higher consumption expenditures for meat at the same time that the share of food expenses in the total household budget was declining rapidly. The ratio of food expenditures to total expenditures dropped from 84.5 percent in 1946–1950, to 35.9 percent in 1970 and then to about 30 percent in the early 1980s.[6] Japan's dietary changes reflect the rapid growth of the postwar economy, and also broader social transformations common to all industrial countries: the increasing number of nuclear families, the participation of women in the labor force, the rapid urbanization of Japanese life, and the growing tendency to eat out.

Much of the transformation of the food system has been accomplished using imported raw food and feedstuffs, and Japan is now highly dependent on foreign supplies for domestic food processing. The United States is the principal supplier. The final consumer products are manufactured domestically, but the raw materials come from abroad as feed grains for livestock (poultry, pork, and beef), wheat for bread and noodles, and soybeans for soy meal and cooking oil. From 1960 to 1979, Japan's self-sufficiency ratio for agricultural products used as food decreased dramatically, from 90 percent to 72 percent (*Table 5-3*). During the same time, total agricultural exports from the United States *increased* dramatically, reaching roughly 30 percent of the dollar value of U.S. agricultural output by 1980. The mirror image is nearly perfect—Japan imports about 30 percent of its foodstuffs by value while the United States exports the same share.

On a commodity-by-commodity basis, however, Japan's self-sufficiency ratios for agriculture show a two-tier structure. In dry field crops such as wheat, feed grains, and beans, the self-sufficiency ratio is very low, while in livestock products, fruits, and vegetables, the ratio has been maintained at more than 80 percent. The ratio for rice sometimes has actually exceeded 100 percent, representing troublesome surpluses. The structure of production indicates a basic strategy of Japan's current food policy: to support a high self-sufficiency in consumer-ready food, and to rely heavily on foreign sources for raw-material types of agricultural products. This approach resembles Japan's industrial strategy of importing raw materials and then processing them, while blocking higher value-added imports to protect domestic manufacturers, especially in early stages of development. For a variety of reasons, however, the

TABLE 5-3
Self-Sufficiency of Food and Agricultural Products in Japan

	1960	1970	1980
Rice	102	106	87
Wheat	39	9	10
Barley	107	34	15
Beans	44	13	7
Soybeans	28	4	4
Vegetables	100	99	97
Fruits	100	84	81
Eggs	101	97	98
Milk and Dairy Products	89	89	86
Meat	91	89	91
Beef	96	90	81
Pork	96	98	87
Sugar	18	23	29
SSR of Agricultural foods[a] and[b]	90	78	72
SSR of Food Grains[c]	89	74	69
SSR of all Grains[b]	82	45	33
SSR of Feed Grains[d]	63	38	28

[a] SSR = Self-Sufficiency Ratio = (domestic production value/domestic consumption value) × 100. Both domestic production values and domestic consumption values are in 1975 wholesale values, and double counting is avoided by exempting feeds. "Agricultural Foods" (*Shokuyō nōsanbutsu*) means agricultural products used for food.

[b] The SSR of agricultural food and food grains are estimated, presupposing the equilibrium of rice supply and demand.

[c] SSR of each commodity, of food grains and of all grains = (domestic production/domestic consumption) × 100 (in quantum terms); however, SSR of food grains is that of rice, wheat, and barley except for feed.

[d] SSR of feed = (feed supply by domestic production/feed supply). Based on total amount of Total Digestible Nutrients.

SOURCE: Ministry of Agriculture, Forestry and Fisheries, Japan: *Shokuryō jukyū hyō* and *Shiryō jukyū hyō*.

objectives of the 1961 law in achieving high productivity and diversified agriculture were not achieved, and subsequent policies have had to cope with these persistent problems.

United States policy for agriculture, on the other hand, in the 1960s and 1970s emphasized the export of basic commodities, and achieved remarkable success with that strategy when world markets suddenly expanded. Exports became an increasing share of U.S. agricultural output, making the agricultural economy more susceptible to fluctuations in world market prices and volumes. When market conditions changed in the late 1970s and early 1980s, U.S. policy adapted rather poorly. The United States confronted increased competition in the international market for many agricultural products: grains, citrus, rice—without a clear strategic response from U.S. policymakers. This new competition resulted in part from the international debt crisis, which pushed Third World countries to earn foreign exchange through agricultural exports.

Brazil's exports of citrus and soybeans and China's exports of corn are revealing examples, for in both cases, Japan has become a major buyer, fitting with Japan's desire to diversify its sources of supplies. The principal U.S. response has been to criticize subsidized agricultural exports as unfair trade and to call for more free trade, while watching U.S. market share shrink.

United States policy currently concentrates on protecting threatened but politically powerful producers of a few commodities such as sugar and dairy products, while leaving other products more or less on their own to compete for export markets. Efforts to cushion the farm-income consequences of such competition when world prices are low, either through government storage of surplus commodities or paid acreage reduction schemes, have proven very expensive to the U.S. public treasury or to consumers. In 1985, for example, the United States continued to pay domestic sugar producers 20 cents a pound (consumers paid 35 cents a pound), while the world price of sugar fell to 4 cents a pound. Whereas the Japanese strategy protects its infant industries in agriculture (higher value-added commodities) and seeks to move farmers out of declining sectors that are protected (rice), the American strategy provides protection for noncompetitive sectors (such as sugar and dairy) without seeking to move those farmers into other crops or out of agriculture.

Interdependence and Conflict

Agricultural trade between Japan and the United States increased rapidly from 1960 to 1980, in many ways representing a highly successful trade relationship. In nominal terms, Japan's agricultural imports from the United States rose nearly twenty-five times, from $262 million in 1960 to $6.5 billion in 1980 (Japan CIF basis)—compared to an increase of about sixteen times in Japan's total agricultural imports. In 1980, agricultural products made up about one-quarter of Japan's total imports from the United States (27 percent), and U.S. supplies provided about 40 percent of Japan's overall agricultural imports. From the U.S. side, agricultural exports to Japan reached $6.1 billion in 1980 (U.S. FAS basis). The United States shipped 15 percent of its total agricultural exports to Japan, more than it shipped to any other country. In short, the United States is the largest food supplier for Japan, and Japan is the largest export market for U.S. agricultural products. In fact, more land in the United States is devoted to growing food and fiber for Japan than is cultivated in Japan itself.

The high flow of U.S. agricultural products to Japan has brought benefits to the agricultural and food economies of both countries. American agriculture has gained a stable and sizable export market in Japan. That export market has contributed to maintaining the livelihood of American farmers and to helping the trade balance for the United States. The Japanese people have improved the nutritional quality of their diet and increased the diversity of foods in the average diet, in both cases at much lower cost than could have been achieved through domestic production only. In addition, the availability of low-cost U.S. agricultural raw materials has encouraged the development of new agricultural sectors in Japan, especially a livestock industry in what was traditionally rice-centered farming.

But conflict also accompanied interdependence. Agricultural trade between Japan and the United States has erupted in sharp disputes, especially during the past decade. The major point of contention is the degree of protection that Japan provides for agricultural producers, in the face of recent large U.S. balance-of-payments deficits with Japan—at the same time that Japan enjoys relatively open markets for manufactured products in the United States. The United States has demanded a continuing liberalization of trade and greater access to Japan's agricultural market, while Japan has continued to insist on protection of its farmers and greater security through higher self-sufficiency for its food supply.

These conflicts and demands result directly from the structural changes in the two countries' economies and from the choice of policies to meet those changes. Agricultural interests in the United States, on the basis of past trends in Japanese food consumption, expect an expansion of the Japanese food market and want a larger share of it, especially for the more lucrative consumer-ready food and value-added products. They therefore have demanded changes in agricultural import quotas and other measures that protect Japan's farm sector. The Japanese have become increasingly sensitive about the drop in self-sufficiency of food production and the dangers of depending on a single country—even so close an ally as the United States—for such a large proportion of its food imports.

The security of stable and reliable food supplies has thus become a politically salient issue in Japan. Food security is connected to the perceived vulnerability of a resource-poor island society. Particular events reinforce these perceptions, especially the "Soybean Embargo" in 1973, when President Nixon briefly banned soybean exports in an ill-considered effort to prevent a predicted shortage from fueling domestic inflation.[7] The self-image of Japan as resource-poor is also linked to deeply rooted social fears: Japan's older generation can still remember widespread hunger after the Second World War. In addition, Japan's political leaders are concerned about maintaining the incomes of rural residents relative to that of factory workers, for reasons of social policy and political stability.

The conflicts in agricultural trade thus connect to broader issues of social transformation, including changes in industrial structure and demographic patterns. The demands for stability on the one hand, and change on the other, raise basic questions about who bears the costs of social and economic transformation—both within and between nations.

Policies for Adjustment

Only a limited number of policy instruments exist to deal with the problem of low incomes in agriculture during the process of structural change. Over the long run, agricultural incomes are determined less by government farm policy than by the income levels attainable in nonagricultural jobs.[8] Short-run imbalances, however, can be quite severe, because of the difficulties in moving resources out of agriculture. Much of agricultural policy in developed countries is designed to cope with these short-run imbalances. All industrialized countries use some combination of seven basic interventions to protect their farmers' incomes from the rapid decline that would otherwise occur relative to urban incomes as economies grow. The seven categories of government instruments that can be used to increase farm incomes are:

1. Investments in technological research to raise yields;
2. Investments in rural infrastructure (such as irrigation), which contribute to higher yields as well as increased cropped acreage;
3. Policies that affect average farm size by encouraging land consolidation, off-farm employment, and rural-to-urban migration;
4. Investments in development of mechanized implements to reduce the number of hours per acre cultivated;
5. Price policy designed to raise domestic farm commodity prices above international prices;
6. Subsidies on purchased inputs such as fertilizer, pesticides, and fuel; and
7. Direct income supplements to make up any shortfall between average farm incomes and average urban incomes.

The United States and Japan have chosen fundamentally different combinations of these policies, and their historical paths of productivity growth in agriculture show an extremely sharp divergence (*Figure 5-1*). From the late nineteenth century until the 1960s, Japanese agricultural researchers and farmers focused on creating a labor-intensive agriculture that incorporated biological technology to give very high yields per hectare. During the same period, the United States was rapidly expanding the total area of cultivated land and increasing farm size through mechanization.[9] Although the United States has been coping with the problems of structural change ever since the 1880s, such problems became acute for Japan only after the Second World War, with changes in the land ownership system and the rapid rise of real wages outside of agriculture.

With the onset of the "economic miracle" (1950s to 1970s), Japanese policymakers confronted potentially severe consequences of structural change for income distribution between urban and rural areas. One might expect that all of the available instruments would have been used fairly intensively to deal with the problems; but policymakers in the 1960s and early 1970s relied increasingly on rice prices as the vehicle to maintain farm incomes at levels commensurate with urban incomes. *Table 5-4* shows that the objective has been largely achieved: in the early 1980s, farm household expenditures (a proxy for expected income) were somewhat above urban household expenditures—but only for part-time farm households with a permanent wage earner and in which the agricultural income is less than nonagricultural income. Full-

FIGURE 5-1

Historical Growth Paths of Agricultural Productivity of France, Japan, and the United States for 1880–1980

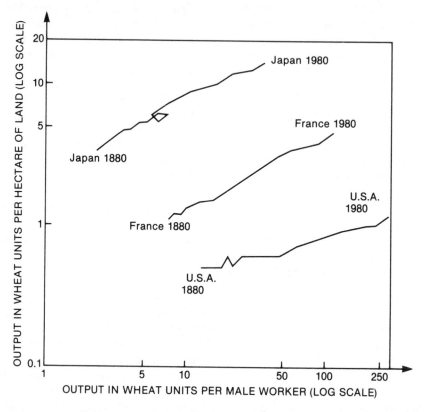

SOURCE: Adapted from Yujiro Hayami and Vernon W. Ruttan, *Agricultural Development: An International Perspective* (Baltimore: Johns Hopkins University Press, 1971, 1985), p. 131.

time farm households had somewhat lower expenditure levels than urban households. In short, rural prosperity has been achieved through a combination of part-time farming (especially of rice) and nonfarm work (in local industries and seasonal work in urban areas).

The reliance on rice price policy to support farm incomes in Japan has produced unintended consequences for both domestic and international agricultural relations. An analysis of agricultural policies in Japan illustrates the central role of rice price policy and commodity targeting in the adjustment process, and indicates how that strategy helped produce the dispute over beef and oranges as a source of intense friction in U.S.-Japanese trade relations.

TABLE 5-4
Per Capita Household Expenditures: Comparison Between Farm Households and Wage-Earning Households in Japan
(Wage-Earning Households = 100)

			Nationwide
	Average of	1960	75.9
	all farm	1970	95.3
	households	1980	110.6
1983	Full-time households		90.3
	Class I part-time farm households		93.5
	Class II farm households		115.2

NOTE: *Full-time farm households:* No family member is engaged in an occupation other than agriculture. *Class I part-time farm households:* One or more family members is engaged in nonfarm job but agricultural income of family is more than nonagricultural income. *Class II part-time farm households:* One or more family members is engaged in nonfarm job but agricultural income is less than nonagricultural income.
SOURCE: Ministry of Agriculture, Forestry and Fisheries.

Agricultural Policy Instruments in Japan

An examination of the seven policy instruments described above shows Japan's main strategy for dealing with the problems of structural change. This analysis also indicates the scope and limits of the various approaches.

Agricultural *technology* in Japan is among the most advanced in the world in terms of yield per acre of rice, as shown in *Figure 5-1*. Agricultural research during the postwar era, which concentrated on rice farming, raised these yields from their already high base. But the higher yields also required sharply increased use of purchased inputs—fertilizer applications increased from 237 kilograms per hectare of paddy in 1950 to 760 kilograms in 1980, mechanical power increased from 0.03 horsepower per hectare to 13.93 horsepower in the same period, while rice yields increased from 3.27 tons per hectare to 4.61 tons. Fertilizer use per hectare increased threefold, mechanized power 460-fold, but yields increased only two-fifths, so the resulting higher yields could contribute only modestly to higher farm incomes.[10]

Further investments in *rural infrastructure* similarly held little potential for improving agricultural productivity after 1960. To the extent that improved farm roads and farmlands allowed some consolidation and greater mechanization, such investments contributed to increased labor productivity, which released family members for nonfarm work. By the time the Japanese economic miracle gained momentum in the 1960s, however, relatively little scope existed for raising farm incomes through investments in physical infrastructure in rural areas, without major changes in farm size. But such investments, especially in roads and communication, did contribute to increases in the nonfarm incomes of part-time farmers, by providing better access to industrial and service jobs. In the United States, by contrast, broad-based investments by private farmers in irrigation began only in the early 1970s, with rising prices for grain. (The large-scale public water projects in the arid West were largely an outgrowth of Federal spending in the 1930s.)

Substantial scope still exists in Japan for raising farm income per household if average *farm size* could be increased and mechanization could reduce the number of hours required per hectare, along the lines of the United States experience. Output per worker would rise, and total hectares per worker would also increase, resulting in a significant gain in total income per household. Yet the operational size of farms has been limited by government policy. Japan's postwar land reform, directed by the U.S. Occupation, achieved a radical redistribution of property: from 54 percent owner-cultivated land in 1945 to 90 percent in 1950, and from 46 percent tenant-cultivated land in 1945 to only 10 percent in 1950.[11] That reform increased the number of small plots, contributing to the relatively equal distribution of incomes and wealth. The many small farms are widely believed to have been critical in establishing a popular political base for the Liberal Democratic Party (LDP), a base that remains important to the LDP's continued success in winning elections.[12]

Subsequent laws preserved both the redistribution and the fragmentation. In 1952, the Agricultural Land Law (no. 229) was enacted to prevent the reemergence of the landlord system. This law limited the farm size of resident landowners to three hectares, prohibited nonresident landowning, and strengthened the contract rights of tenants who continued to farm rented land— thereby maintaining the reallocation of land. Indeed, the law effectively restricted Japan's agriculture to small plots (averaging about one hectare), by making agricultural land very difficult to accumulate and to rent.

Average farm size in Japan, therefore, has been effectively frozen by public policy. Factors that have inhibited consolidation include the land laws, rising land prices, and only a token tax on agricultural land. The average rice paddy land per farm increased from 0.5 hectares in 1960 to only 0.6 hectares in 1980. Average total farm size is still only 1.1 hectares per household: a radically low figure that compares with 14 hectares in West Germany, 24 hectares in France, 64 hectares in the United Kingdom, and 157 hectares in the United States. In these other countries, average farm size is increasing steadily as part of the adjustment to structural change; but Japan has not chosen this route. The restrictions on farm size have created a distinct problem of viability for Japan's full-time farmers.[13]

In the early 1960s, as productivity in Japanese manufacturing rose much faster than productivity in agriculture, the small scale of agricultural plots became recognized as a problem. The Agricultural Land Law was amended in 1962 and 1970 to encourage land rental to full-time farmers, who could increase the scale and improve the efficiency of production. These changes in policy, however, had little effect on average farm size, which actually decreased 0.3 percent between 1970 and 1975. In 1975, the Agricultural Land Planning Law was revised to shift the focus of legal protection from tenant's rights to landowner's rights, especially regarding conditions when leased land reverted to the landowner. Further revisions in 1980 were designed to expand the lagging rental market by promoting short-term leases and involving municipal governments. These recent changes have contributed to some increases in land mobility and farm size.

The emphasis on rental derives from persistent difficulties with the sale of agricultural land in Japan. Between 1960 and 1980, the average price of rice paddy land increased 19.3 times, while the producer price of rice increased only 4.25 times. This situation made it extremely difficult for farmers to expand their farm units. In 1982, agricultural land on average sold at ¥1.4 million ($56,000) per hectare, about 3.4 times the price in West Germany, 8.5 times that in England, and 16 times that in France.[14] The high price of land, in turn, was significantly influenced by the government's policy of setting a high price for rice, especially in the early 1960s, as well as by expectations about development, a point examined later in this chapter. In addition, part-time farmers make a good total income, with only a small percentage from agriculture. They want to keep their land as an investment, as a hedge against inflation, as security for retirement, and as part of their family heritage.

Japan's low tax on agricultural land has also contributed to the small average farm size, by allowing people to hold onto low productivity farmland at relatively low cost. At one point, the Liberal Democratic Party considered a higher agricultural land tax, but then abandoned the idea for fear of losing rural votes to opposition parties.

The extremely low rate of sales and slow pace of rental of agricultural land have encouraged Japan's Ministry of Agriculture, Forestry and Fisheries (MAFF) to consider policies that consolidate farm operations without affecting land ownership or tenure. Owing to the difficulty of pushing part-time farmers out of agriculture, the Ministry is now encouraging custom subcontractors for specific operations and supporting the formation of cooperative units for common use of machinery. The cooperative units are designed to create larger operational units and more efficient use of machinery and to avoid overinvestment within a given community. This approach could reduce the operations of part-time farmers, while still allowing them to take back their land, when they want, for sale or operations.

Mechanization as a vehicle to raise average productivity per worker in Japan has also been constrained by the structure of landholdings, for the machines must "fit" on tiny plots. The response has been the development of a unique set of tiny farm implements, from tillers to combines, which are very labor-intensive by American or European standards but which dramatically reduced the average number of hours needed to cultivate a hectare of rice, from 141 hours in 1965 to 69 hours in 1979. Labor productivity in agriculture

TABLE 5-5
Full-Time and Part-Time Farm Households in Japan

		Farm Households and Farming Population (unit: 1,000)				
Year	Farm Households	Agricultural Population (A)	Population Engaged in Farming (B)	Total Population (C)	A/C %	B/C %
1960	6,056	34,083	14,542	94,301	36.4	15.4
1970	5,342	26,282	9,826	103,720	25.3	7.9
1980	4,661	21,366	6,973	116,133	18.4	6.0

			Number of Part-Time and Full-Time Farm Households (unit: 1,000)	Part-Time Households	
Year	Total No. of Farm Households	Full-Time Farm Households	Total	Class I Part-Time	Class II Part-Time
1960	6,056	2,078	3,978	2,036	1,942
1970	5,342	832	4,510	1,801	2,709
1980	4,661	623	4,038	1,002	3,036
1984	4,473	605	3,868	689	3,179

NOTE: *Full-time farm households:* No family member is engaged in an occupation other than agriculture. *Class I part-time farm households:* One or more family members is engaged in nonfarm job but agricultural income of family is more than nonagricultural income. *Class II part-time farm households:* One or more family members is engaged in nonfarm job but agricultural income is less than nonagricultural income.

SOURCE: Ministry of Agriculture, Forestry and Fisheries.

per workday rose only 0.4 percent annually between 1930 and 1955, but rose 6.8 percent per year between 1955 and 1970.[15] Perhaps more importantly, the machines have greatly reduced the physical effort required in growing rice, thus permitting women and the elderly to be the primary cultivators. The "able-bodied male," meanwhile, becomes a full-time wage earner off the farm and a part-time weekend farmer. Without such an employment pattern, rice cultivation could not continue to exist at anything near its present level.

Such a part-time employment pattern for the primary agricultural commodity has advantages and disadvantages. The advantages are that most rural households are not totally dependent on agricultural earnings. In 1980, part-time farmers lived in the vast majority of Japan's farm households, with only 13.4 percent of households full-time or dependent solely on agriculture (*Table 5-5*). Only one-fifth of Japanese farm households had a full-time male working on the farm, and these farmers concentrated on non-rice commodities. In total, approximately 70 percent of the income of farm households was earned from nonfarm sources, somewhat higher than the 57 percent earned from similar sources by American farm households in the 1976–1980 period. Mechanization thus provided Japanese farm households a technical ability to pursue part-time farming, which increased the off-farm earning potential of farm households and alleviated some of the economic stresses from structural change and rapid industrialization.

On the negative side, the nation's food supply is increasingly in the hands of its elderly population, who tend to be more traditional and less efficient farmers. In 1984, nearly 70 percent of the total agricultural labor force was at least fifty years old, a much higher proportion than in nonfarm industries.[16] Most older farmers work part-time, and thereby contribute to the growing gap in the cost of production between part-time and full-time farmers. The large population of elderly farmers thus helps maintain Japan's small-plot agriculture and serves as an obstacle to increases in labor productivity.

The lack of consolidation of Japan's agricultural land has prevented mechanization from achieving greater increases in labor productivity, which in turn would allow adequate incomes, perhaps even from rice cultivation, without substantial governmental intervention. Larger farms in Japan show increasing rates of labor productivity and decreasing costs of production for rice, demonstrating the economies of scale that could be gained through greater consolidation.[17]

Japanese policymakers hope that if younger, full-time farmers purchase the lands of retired elderly farmers, the possibility of larger, consolidated holdings could then be realized. Special interest focuses on farms with the head of household over sixty years old and no inheritor to continue farming. But that approach may depend on changes in land laws and in cultural attitudes about land, as well as a change in the retirement pattern of corporate workers who leave their companies at the mandatory retirement age and take up farming as a second career (perhaps encouraged by inadequate pensions, especially at small companies). Since 1981, the number of people abandoning other occupations to enter agriculture as the main job has actually exceeded the number leaving agriculture for other occupations. In 1983, moreover, 96 percent of males going into farming as the main job were over fifty, and most of them had worked previously as part-time farmers.[18] Innovative mechanization that facilitates small-scale part-time farming makes this trend possible, and may thereby serve as an obstacle to the consolidation of farmland and the formation of cooperative units.

Two potential policy instruments for alleviating low farm incomes have played only small roles in the development of postwar agriculture in Japan. *Input subsidies* (for example, for fertilizer) cannot effectively transfer much income. *Direct income payments* to farmers, on the other hand, could effectively improve farm incomes, with a relatively low level of distortion to the agricultural economy; but direct payments have high administrative costs and would place farmers in the politically vulnerable position of requiring a direct budget outlay for income supports each year. A shift from price supports to income supports could also jeopardize the asset structure of farmers. The problems with all of the above approaches have promoted a focus on price policy.

Most industrialized countries have used *price interventions* to support farm incomes in the short run. At the same time, they have encouraged consolidation of farms and movement of labor out of agriculture in the long run to complete the process of structural change. Nearly constant farm size has constrained Japan in this process. Moreover, much of its labor flow out of agriculture has been only in sector of occupation, not location of household. All of this, in turn, has placed increased emphasis on price intervention.

Japan has a long history of such intervention, especially for rice. In the early twentieth century, the Japanese government began to consider the purchase, sale, and storage of rice. It recognized the importance of inexpensive rice in the early stages of industrial development as a means of keeping the living costs and wages of industrial workers low and thereby of promoting the export of manufactured goods.[19] A rice control policy was initiated in 1920, and in 1939, the government took legal control of rice distribution. In 1942, the Food Control Act gave the government authority over almost all food items. During the postwar period, those controls were slowly lifted, except for rice, wheat, and barley. From the end of the Korean War until 1960, rice prices remained relatively stable, somewhat above the level of world prices. These stable prices for rice significantly contributed to Japan's industrial development without causing major problems of foreign exchange or budget subsidies.[20] Yet even as late as 1955, *rice alone* still required one-eighth of the average urban worker's entire budget, with overall food expenditures nearly half of total expenditures. In the United States at the same time food expenditures required only a quarter of total expenditures.

In the 1960s, however, Japan enacted a series of price increases for rice, far above world prices, in order to boost farmers' income to the level of urban workers—that is, to help compensate for structural change. The objective of food control in Japan thus shifted radically from protecting consumers in times of crisis to protecting farmers in times of growth. All industrializing countries seem to go through this same shift, but in Japan the change occurred over a very brief time.[21]

Rice Price Policy and Its Consequences

Since the early 1960s, the Japanese government has responded to the problems of structural change with an extraordinarily heavy reliance on rice price policy to support Japanese farm incomes. In 1960, Japan adopted a new formula for setting rice prices called the Production Cost and Income Compensation Formula. This mechanism established a direct link between hourly incomes earned from rice farming, and average urban wages. The Basic Agricultural Law of 1961 similarly stressed rural and urban income parity as a central objective. The policy reflected the political power of Japanese farmers, but also the government's desire to create a rural market for Japan's manufactured goods. According to the formula, any shortfall in rice earnings was made up by a subsequent increase in the government's purchase price for rice. This policy created the engine for rapid increases in rice prices.[22] In 1960 the producer price was only slightly over the import price; by the late 1970s the producer price was three to four times above the world price.[23] In effect, Japan had raised the domestic price of rice as a substitute for expanding farm size, and as a way to deal with the decline in income per acre relative to nonagricultural incomes.

Two factors accounted for the steep rise in rice prices, only one of which was foreseen by the lawmakers. Land costs were included in the formula in addition to labor costs, which were linked directly to industrial wages. As rice prices rose, it became more profitable to grow rice, and land prices were bid up accordingly. The increases in land prices showed up as higher costs of production, which reduced apparent farm income for a given level of gross revenue, thus requiring a yet higher rice price in the next round. The consequence was a mutual spiral in the prices of both rice and land, particularly in the early period of rice price increases. As noted earlier, the average price of farmland in Japan by the early 1980s was very much higher than that in European countries.

Other factors in addition to rising rice prices contributed to increases in farmland prices in Japan. Extensive development plans contributed to land speculation in rural areas. Expanding cities also created an urban sprawl that consumed farmland—and increased rural land prices. These two factors are most commonly cited in Japan as responsible for the high price of farmland (and for farmer expectations of high prices). The role of government price policy for rice has not been carefully examined, and therefore deserves particular attention here—especially because it helps provide an understanding of links to other commodities in Japan's food system.

The rice price policy implemented since 1960 has had two main effects: to raise domestic rice prices above import costs, and to contribute to higher land prices and hence shift the contribution of land prices to the cost of production. Rising labor costs also helped boost the costs of production at this time. The increased values of farmland contributed importantly to a redistribution of wealth toward rural areas in Japan, especially the small farm households, continuing the efforts of the postwar land reform to improve equity. The likely outcome was that farmers developed a strong interest in protecting their new land assets, which in part meant maintaining high prices for rice.

The steep increase in rice prices dramatically affected both supply and demand. Rice production increased, but at high cost, as farmers applied inputs intensively and managed their rice fields with care. Per capita rice consumption fell, as other carbohydrates, especially wheat products, became relatively cheaper sources of energy, particularly in the 1960s. Although Japan's consumer price for rice did not rise as rapidly as the producer price in the 1960s and early 1970s, consumer prices for rice increased much more rapidly than did those for wheat, thus encouraging the shift from rice to wheat products.

In the late 1970s and early 1980s, however, the Japanese government worked to contain increases in the producer price for rice and to continue increases in the consumer wholesale price (the government's resale price). By 1985, such actions had narrowed the difference to under 2 percent and reduced the strain of subsidies from the government's Food Control Account for rice.[24] In fact, the producer price of rice was not raised at all in 1985, marking the first time since 1969 that the government did not increase the price even a little. The government has thus sought to shift the burden of rice supports from taxpayers to consumers. That policy, however, has encountered some difficulties, since the rising consumer price has contributed to declines in rice consumption and to problems of surplus supplies.

As the price of rice increased through the 1960s and 1970s in Japan, creating a strong incentive for more production, imports were gradually displaced and a rice surplus developed. By the late 1960s, Japan's Food Agency faced a serious management problem: huge financial deficits in the rice control program and enormous surpluses of government-stored rice stocks.[25] From 1967 to 1970, Japan produced a rice surplus of 7.2 million metric tons, which required one trillion yen (about $2.7 billion) to liquidate, with funds transferred from the general account to the Food Control Account from 1971 to 1979 to cover the deficit. Then, from 1975 to 1978, Japan produced a stockpile of 6.5 million metric tons, creating a deficit in the Food Control Account of two trillion yen (over $8 billion), with transfers from the general account beginning in 1979 and expected to continue to 1989.[26] While the first surplus occurred in Japan's period of rapid economic growth, the second came in the recent slow growth period, increasing the budgetary pressures of the rice crop deficits and diversions, which accounted for 30 to 40 percent of MAFF's budget in the 1970s.

Rice is expensive to store for long periods of time, and exporting the surplus creates two additional problems: an export subsidy is required because of high domestic prices relative to world market prices; and such subsidies, which clearly constitute dumping, cause severe trade friction with traditional rice exporters, especially Thailand and the United States.

In 1979, for example, the Japanese government decided to reduce the 4.8 million metric tons of surplus rice through subsidized exports (along with increased industrial usage and usage in formula feed production). When export sales of rice reached 600,000 metric tons instead of the Japanese government's projection of 200,000 metric tons, the U.S. Rice Millers' Association in early April 1980 filed a complaint about subsidized exports. An agreement was reached between the two countries to restrict Japanese rice exports to a total of 1.6 million tons over a four-year period, with additional restrictions on exports to countries that are traditional markets for U.S. rice producers. Controversy over Japanese rice exports erupted again in 1980, when Japanese exports reached 720,000 tons, or 5 percent of world trade, because of emergency shipments to South Korea. Those exports reduced U.S. rice export prices by 1.7 percent, for a total loss of export revenues to U.S. farmers of about $20 million.[27]

In the late 1970s, Japanese rice policy began to recognize budget pressures and complaints from trading partners, and policymakers initiated three major programs to divert production from rice. The goal was to encourage Japanese farmers to shift out of rice cultivation and into commodities where growth in demand was more promising and where Japan remained a net importer. These programs followed the objective of the selective expansion policy of the 1961 Basic Agricultural Law to meet domestic demand through greater domestic production. The list of commodities was long: wheat, soybeans, barley, fruits, vegetables, hay, poultry, pork, and beef. All received some encouragement from the Ministry of Agriculture, Forestry and Fisheries; but a major problem with the programs has been their extraordinary expense: ¥303 billion ($1.4 billion) in 1980, or about 8 percent of the MAFF budget.[28] With rising government deficits, the pressures of a tight budget have become increasingly intense in the 1980s, making it more difficult to allocate funds for agricultural crop subsidies. For example, the government did not increase its purchase price for wheat or barley in 1984, or, as noted earlier, for rice in 1985.

To solve the problems of both the rice surplus and the budget subsidy, Japanese agricultural policymakers have emphasized the middle ground, including beef and citrus, as a central adjustment vehicle for the nation's full-time commercial farmers. These commodities can be produced on relatively small farms, they offer high returns to careful and intensive management, and beef in particular faces rapidly growing domestic demand, some of which has been supplied from imports.

To avoid subsidies, however, production of beef must be able to compete with imports. But land-based costs cause problems for even these intermediate commodities. Beef operations require roughage and some pasture if possible. The secondary effects of high land prices, including the connection with rice prices, thus have influenced the cost structure of nearly all of Japanese agriculture, including its key commodity, for the transition to more full-time commercial agriculture.

The apparent solution to the potential problem of government subsidies for beef and citrus producers was to control imports tightly and keep domestic prices well above international prices—effectively shifting the burden of adjustment to domestic consumers and foreign producers. Such an import policy was essential if Japanese policymakers were to achieve both of their objectives: reduced rice surplus and smaller budget subsidies. To open the Japanese market suddenly to imported beef and oranges was seen as jeopardizing a critical component of the long-run agricultural adjustment strategy.

Of course, the current strategy remains a roundabout way of dealing with the core problem of rice price policy. The economically efficient answer, as opposed to the politically feasible answer, would be to drop domestic rice prices to world levels, and let the structure of Japanese agricultural costs, production, and imports adjust. Although there has been much academic debate in Japan over what this adjustment might look like, such a solution is not seriously considered in government debates over policy.[29]

The reasons for this reluctance are clear. They are fundamentally political, and they have direct parallels in the debate over the 1985 farm bill in the United States. Lower rice prices in Japan would directly affect the incomes of the approximately 3.8 million households that produce rice. They would also reduce land values and hence the assets of all farm households (about 4.5 million). Although the average farm household relies on rice for only 6 percent of its household income, its farmland may well represent three-quarters of its net assets. The impact, however, is likely to be more significant for farmers in rural areas than for those near large cities. It is no wonder that Japanese farmers fight hard every year to increase rice prices,[30] and that the trade negotiations on beef and citrus seemed to farmers to be only a prelude to such discussions on rice.

The problem of high-value agricultural land has its parallel in the United States, but for rather different reasons. The price of agricultural land in the United States rose sharply in the 1970s, not because of governmental intervention in price policy, but because of the boom prices generated during the "world food crisis" of 1972 to 1974. Those prices were capitalized into land values, as in Japan.[31] The higher land values, reflected in the financial carrying costs of mortgages incurred as farmers expanded their operations, significantly raised the costs of production, especially when interest rates were deregulated. Unlike Japanese farmers, however, most American farmers do not have the strong guarantee of a high and stable output price. As real interest rates rose sharply, as the exchange rate of the dollar rose, and as world market prices declined, American farmers faced in the mid-1980s their lowest relative real incomes since the Great Depression, plus a very significant erosion of their assets. Average farm prices declined 12 percent in 1984, following declines of 1 percent in 1983 and 6 percent in 1982. After inflation, the value of farmland by 1985 was roughly 30 percent less than it had been just three years earlier, the sharpest drop since the 1930s.

For policymakers in all countries, avoiding such painful adjustments is certainly a desirable goal, but preventing the adjustments can become very costly. Japanese policy was designed to foster the structural adjustments of agriculture gradually and to use beef and oranges as important commodities in the transition phase to full-time, commercial farming that would more closely match domestic production with consumption. The objective was to relieve the national budget of heavy subsidies and reduce the worst manifestations of rice price policy—the surpluses and direct rice subsidies.

But broader concerns entered the story. The large and growing trade surplus that Japan runs with the United States produced a vehement backlash among potential American exporters to Japanese markets. Access for United

States producers to beef and orange markets in Japan suddenly acquired a symbolic significance far beyond the dollar value of the trade. In Japan as well, the controversy over beef and oranges gained both material and symbolic importance through its connection to national agricultural policy. The negotiations over beef and oranges consequently became more difficult and certainly far more important than they would have been otherwise. With an understanding of this background on structural change and agricultural policy, we can proceed to an analysis of the negotiations themselves, which provides a vivid case study in international political economy.

Beef and Oranges

Ever since the mid-1970s, one of the most provocative issues in trade relations between Japan and the United States was Japanese restrictions on imports of beef and citrus (primarily oranges). In 1978, after two years of debate in the Tokyo Round of the Multilateral Trade Negotiations (MTN), the two countries reached an agreement that established two new concepts—"high-quality beef" and "seasonal citrus." The agreement temporarily eased American pressures for improved access for beef and citrus to Japan's home market, but it also defined the terms of future conflicts concerning agricultural trade in those categories.

The concept of high-quality beef, defined as grain-fed beef, was primarily designed to increase imports from the U.S. (the only exporter with a large lot-feeding industry) to meet expanding demand in Japan's restaurant and hotel trade. The concept did so without disrupting the Japanese system of production and distribution or opening the Japanese market to the grass-fed beef products from Australia or New Zealand. The 1978 agreement obliged Japan to import 16,800 tons of high-quality beef in the first year, with annual increases culminating in a total of 30,800 tons in fiscal year 1983. The idea of seasonal citrus allowed a blending of different production and growing schedules between Japan and the United States, to balance interests between the two countries and within each country. The total import quota for oranges was increased from 45,000 tons in 1978 to 82,000 tons in fiscal year 1983, with seasonal citrus (June, July, and August—the off-season months for Japanese mikan producers) going from 22,500 tons to 45,000 tons. By providing for imports outside the seasonal quota, the agreement assured Florida shippers a share and prevented California growers from shipping the entire quota.[32]

In announcing the agreement on 5 December 1978, Japan's Minister of Agriculture, Ichirō Nakagawa, made clear that its terms had merely postponed a painful dilemma. Japanese agricultural interests, with their strong political pressures against import liberalization, had been temporarily reconciled with conflicting United States governmental demands, especially with the powerful American desire to pry open the Japanese market. But the tension persisted. In 1978, Nakagawa argued that expanded American imports would not displace domestic production, especially for beef, because Japanese domestic demand would continue to grow—in effect, that the agreement was not a zero-sum game. At about the same time, Alan Wolff, the U.S. Deputy Trade Representative who concluded the details of the Tokyo agreement of 1978, characterized the expanded quotas for beef and citrus as a success for the U.S. side. Yet he also noted that the United States had not obtained complete liberalization for these products, nor had it changed the system for allocating Japanese licenses to import citrus products.[33] Thus, in December 1978, these contrasting explanations signaled that more conflict over beef and citrus lay ahead.

The next round of negotiations over beef and citrus became even more provocative. Contrasting interpretations of a clause in the 1978 agreement on renewed consultations on beef and citrus imports guaranteed that the debate over liberalization would persist. In addition, the United States trade deficit with Japan shot up after 1978, and American demands for improved access for manufactured goods as well as agricultural products became louder and more insistent. Moreover, troubles in the U.S. agricultural economy focused attention on exports. These economic changes affected the politics of interest groups, political parties, and bureaucratic agencies in both countries, transforming the negotiations over beef and citrus into a hot political issue.

Renewed Japanese-American negotiations can be considered in four stages of development. The first stage, which we shall call "warmup," began in December 1980, with U.S. negotiators informally preparing the Japanese for the next round and with internal governmental consultations about the problem. The second stage, "breakdown," started with official talks in which both sides put forth hard-line positions, as negotiations in Washington and Honolulu ended in stalemate. The third stage, "hard bargaining," lasted from late 1982 to early 1984, while each side softened its demands and explored possible paths to resolution. The final stage, "last-minute talks," occurred under pressure of a deadline, as the 1978 agreement expired, allowing government negotiators to push agricultural interest groups to agree to a resolution.

Warmup: At the annual U.S.-Japan consultation on agricultural trade in December 1980, the American side insisted on discussing beef and citrus, and the Japanese side resisted. The result was an agreement to speak informally about the issues but not put them on the formal agenda—what was called the "Zebra approach" (you see white stripes, we see black stripes). This preliminary sparring reflected a pattern of U.S. insistence and Japanese resistance that would continue, and served notice that the next round of debate over beef and citrus would soon begin in earnest.

The Ezaki Mission in January 1982, brought to Washington important members of the LDP's Special Committee on International Trade Problems, headed by Diet member Masumi Ezaki, who had just served as minister for MITI. This committee had been formed to have LDP politicians rather than government bureaucrats create Japan's new trade policies. Ezaki presented two market-opening "gifts" to the United States, neither of which dealt with beef and oranges.

The Ezaki Mission intended to explain concrete efforts by Japan to open its home market, and thus hoped to calm rising American criticism, especially demands for increased protectionism as a part of United States policy. Meeting in Washington with high-level bureaucrats, ranking members of Congress, and key industry representatives, the Ezaki Mission found a severely critical attitude toward Japanese positions and a consistent demand for measures that would open Japan's domestic market to U.S. products—especially agricultural products. The threat of protectionist legislation in the U.S. Congress, just what the Japanese hoped to avoid, seemed imminent.

On the American side, this consensus position could be traced to an unusually successful degree of governmental interagency coordination. In December 1981, agricultural trade officials in the U.S. Department of Agriculture (USDA) and the Office of the U.S. Trade Representative (USTR) drafted a document on the beef and citrus issues and circulated it for comment to all trade-related agencies. A staff-level interagency group headed by USTR worked to coordinate revision and then to inform all agencies and individuals whom the Ezaki Mission would see. This action helped tie beef and citrus into broader concerns about market access for industrial products. As one U.S. official explained, interagency coordination "seemed like the sensible thing to do, since in the past the Japanese have exploited the weakness of having different positions from different agencies."[34]

When the Ezaki Mission returned to Japan, the country's attitude toward trade problems with the United States began to show some changes. In late March 1982, for example, Prime Minister Zenko Suzuki tested the political taboo of agricultural liberalization by requesting officials in MAFF to examine new possibilities of liberalization for certain agricultural products, especially marine goods.[35] Also in March, at the third meeting of the U.S.-Japan Trade Subcommittee, Japan agreed to resume talks on agricultural trade, especially on beef and citrus, and to begin new discussions of market-opening measures in October 1982.

BREAKDOWN

In mid-April 1982, negotiations collapsed in Washington at the U.S.-Japan Working Group on Agricultural Products Import Restrictions. The United States argued for a total and immediate liberalization, and Japan proposed no increases in import quotas for beef and citrus. While this failure received little public attention in the United States, in Japan the consequences were enormous; the American position was faulted in all major news media and in public opinion, as well as by powerful agricultural interests. Thousands of farmers protested in Tokyo against the intransigent stand of the United States. The Japanese response expanded the trade negotiations into a major domestic political issue.

During these failed consultations, negotiators in both countries pursued a common short-term objective: to find some path toward progress in agricultural negotiations prior to the Versailles Summit meeting in June, 1982. Such progress might reduce American criticism of Japanese trade policy and also limit the movement toward American protectionism. But despite a shared goal, the gap between the negotiating strategies of the two countries proved to be too wide, and the talks ended in confusion. While the Japanese wanted a policy of gradually expanding import quotas, the United States demanded total liberalization in 1984, arguing that the beef and citrus restrictions violated the General Agreement on Tariffs and Trade (GATT), in particular Article 11, which prohibits the use of quotas (with certain exceptions). This American position reflected domestic political pressures, including those resulting from a depressed agricultural economy. Squeezed by high debt and low prices, and faced with a surge of bankruptcies, farmers pressed for relief from the U.S. government. Thus, Japan-U.S. trade talks were set against a background of increasing crisis on the farm as well as against industrial appeals for protectionist legislation from Congress, notably local content bills for automobiles.

While most Japanese negotiators felt that the American application of free trade principles to agricultural trade would be difficult to achieve, Japanese agricultural groups considered the situation a crisis and responded by hardening their political opposition to all liberalization. Japan's industrial interests, on the other hand, especially Keidanren (Federation of Economic Organizations), began to promote changes in policy that would encourage agricultural liberalization, and perhaps help reduce bilateral trade friction on industrial goods.[36]

Meanwhile, such hard-line Japanese reactions as the demonstrations by farm organizations in April 1982 were gaining public attention in the United States, where the issue of beef and citrus trade became a media favorite. Americans began to view agricultural trade conflicts between Japan and the United States as another example of the closed Japanese market. U.S. trade negotiators, however, somewhat moderated the demands for total liberalization at an informal meeting (Geneva, 5 May 1982). The United States thus followed a zigzag course in negotiations, because of conflicting political pressures. While the USTR focused on general aspects of international trade policy, the USDA stressed the domestic interests of international agricultural policy, leading to different negotiating objectives and strategies. And Congressmen from both the Democratic and Republican parties (with the support of various interest groups) sought to use agricultural trade as a bargaining weapon in political battles.

By May 1982, when discussions resumed on agricultural trade issues, both countries sought to repair damaged relations by achieving some agreement on restrictions other than beef and citrus. Japan agreed to expand its import quotas on three agricultural items (prepared and preserved pork, high-test molasses, and canned pineapples) and to reduce or eliminate tariffs on seventeen agricultural products. A written assessment by USTR of this trade package, however, downplayed the economic significance to the United States of Japan's concessions on import quotas and tariffs and noted that the package "has produced no major opening of the Japanese market, nor completely resolved any major problem," referring obliquely to beef and citrus issues. The USTR report also mentioned rapidly increasing protectionist sentiment in Congress, as demonstrated by "widespread support" for the local content bill.[37]

Beginning in late September of 1982, a series of consultations opened in Washington. These talks focused on wheat, feedstuffs, and soybeans, but also included preparatory discussions on liberalization, scheduled to begin in Honolulu during late October. In Washington, each side reiterated its position: the United States repeated the link between agricultural trade and industrial protection, and Japan repeated the difficult political situation surrounding liberalization. Overall, these meetings reflected an effort by Japan to discuss restrictions on agricultural items other than beef and oranges with the hope of moderating U.S. pressures on those two commodities, which represented extremely difficult concessions for the Japanese.

In Honolulu, Japanese and American negotiators did discuss beef and citrus, but the talks ended in stalemate. Once again, the United States contended that the Japanese import quota system was illegal under GATT, and that Japan must eliminate its import restrictions on beef and citrus without replacing that system with any substitute border mechanism. The Japanese responded by citing specific efforts to expand imports and alleging that the United States had hardened its earlier position. Finally the Japanese representatives declared that the nation had no intention of dismantling its beef and citrus import restrictions after 31 March 1984, when the 1978 agreement expired. In all, the Honolulu meeting closed on a harsh note. The United States ended the talks a day early by walking out when the Japanese offered nothing on beef and citrus.[38]

HARD BARGAINING

After this second breakdown, U.S.-Japan relations began to mend late in 1982 and early in 1983, after the inauguration of Japan's new Prime Minister, Yasuhiro Nakasone. In early December, when the U.S.-Japan Trade Subcommittee met in Tokyo, beef and citrus took center stage, and both sides agreed that it would be desirable to begin serious negotiations as soon as possible. As a sign of good faith, the United States indicated that it would postpone its appeal to a GATT panel for review of Japan's residual import restrictions on agricultural items. In discussions that began 17 December 1982, and continued over the next several weeks, Japan prepared yet another package of agricultural trade concessions to the United States that again did not include beef and citrus. As a result, those issues emerged at the summit meeting in mid-January between Prime Minister Nakasone and President Reagan in Washington. Secretary of Agriculture John Block, who attended the session, requested significantly more market access for American beef and citrus. Nakasone responded that although Japan could not agree on immediate liberalization, he did expect to settle the problem by March 1984, through calm discussions between agricultural experts representing the two governments.[39] American pressure on beef and citrus questions abated.

U.S. and Japanese negotiators met again, in late April 1983, to prepare for another meeting of Reagan and Nakasone in late May, prior to the OECD summit meeting in Williamsburg. Now the Japanese proposed specific increases in quotas for beef and citrus, while the American representatives demanded a clear statement on the date for full liberalization. When no agreement was reached, the United States threatened an appeal to the GATT on thirteen categories (not including beef and citrus) of agricultural import restrictions. On 1 July 1983, just after Japan's Upper House elections in June (which produced marginal gains for Nakasone and the LDP), the United States carried out its threat on the thirteen items and went to the GATT for consultations. This move signaled to Japan that the American hard line was more than a bluff, and that the United States was willing to go to the GATT on beef and citrus if necessary.

LAST-MINUTE TALKS

In the fall of 1983, the U.S. negotiators presented the Japanese with a specific schedule for "eventual" liberalization. The Japanese responded informally with much smaller quota expansions, and by October, formal proposals were on the table. On 20–21 January 1984, in Tokyo, U.S. Deputy Trade Representative Michael Smith proposed an annual increase of 10,000 metric tons for high-quality beef, with the same increase in the total global beef quota (in part to avoid complaints from the Australians) for four to five years, and a 15,000 metric tons per year increase for oranges. Japan's chief negotiator, Hiroya Sano, responded that any deal would require the approval of the "Gang of Eight" (key LDP parliamentarians concerned with agriculture) and the Diet, but he still suggested specific numbers: 4,200 tons for high-quality beef, and perhaps an equivalent increase in the total quota, and 8,200 tons a year for four years on oranges. This stage marked real progress, even though many questions remained to be worked out.

By early February, a final agreement appeared within reach. The Japanese were anxious to avoid going to the GATT, and they welcomed a statement of accommodation from Smith: "In the face of this stiff opposition [from Japan's farm organizations], we have recognized that Japan's entire quota system cannot be dismantled overnight, and we are therefore willing to negotiate a schedule for removal of some of these barriers over time." But U.S. officials wondered whether anyone on the Japanese side had enough power to take the risks and responsibilities for a new agreement, reflecting the political vacuum created by the death of former MAFF Minister Nakagawa, who had negotiated the 1978 deal with Robert Strauss. The bargaining had clearly shifted from the administrative to the political sphere. Meetings in February and March cleared up a few points but left key numbers far apart—and 31 March passed without any agreement.

In early April 1984, MAFF Minister Yamamura arrived in Washington at the head of a large delegation from Japan to negotiate with USTR William Brock. The first two days of talks, on 4 and 5 April, ended in disagreement, especially on the size of expansion for high-quality beef. The negotiations were extended one day to Friday, but Yamamura and Brock still failed to reach an agreement. The Japanese team seemed on its way home, with a delegation expected to return later in April. Brock instructed his staff to prepare the GATT case and he went home early. U.S. press reports declared that the negotiations had failed and the United States was on its way to the GATT.

Later on Friday, Brock received a telephone call from Japanese Ambassador Okawara, requesting another meeting. Yamamura reportedly had telephoned Nakasone, who agreed to increase the beef quota by 6,900 tons annually, in order to settle the dispute and protect overall relations between the two countries. Brock then consulted Agriculture Secretary Block, who called the National Cattlemen's Association. Under pressure, the Cattlemen agreed to settle. (They were perhaps also concerned about going to the GATT and the risk to their own legislation, the U.S. Meat Import Act, which allows for import restrictions and promotes voluntary restrictions.) On Saturday, the negotiations concluded with an overall settlement, although without a joint agreement. Instead, each side issued its own press release, with some differences remaining.

Once back home, Minister Yamamura reassured Japanese farmers and promised financial assistance where necessary, as offered after the 1978 agreement. Also, he warned that U.S. pressure for liberalization of agricultural trade would continue. Japanese agricultural organizations denounced the agreement as "most regrettable," and Iwao Yamaguchi, Executive Director of Zenchū (Central Union of Agricultural Cooperative Associations), summarized their reservations: "We were able to prevent liberalization of beef and oranges . . . but we were not able to apply a brake on the increasing of import quotas."[40] In the United States, meanwhile, Brock expressed satisfaction because the agreement would provide an estimated annual increase of $300 million in livestock exports for four years. If, by the end of that time, the Japanese government had not made its trade programs consistent with GATT rules, Brock warned, American pressure would be renewed. The U.S. beef industry, on the other hand, recognized some advances in the agreement but announced its strong dissatisfaction at the continued lack of free access to the Japanese market.

The final agreement appeared in mid-August 1984, after a summer spent haggling over details, including the language for the period after 1988. In the end, over a four-year period, orange imports were increased 11,000 tons each year, orange juice was increased 500 tons each year, high-quality beef by 6,900 tons each year (with an additional increase in the hotel quota by 1,000 tons), and grapefruit juice would be liberalized by 1 April 1986. Some aspects of the agreement remained private, in confidential documents, apparently to shield the governments from unpleasant political questions at home. The Japanese government also agreed to start consultations on fresh oranges, orange juice, and beef "at a mutually convenient time" during Japanese fiscal year 1987— for the next round of talks.

The Negotiations and Agricultural Politics

The negotiations over beef and citrus illustrate the political processes of agricultural policy in the United States and Japan, and also reflect the political consequences of structural adjustment in both countries. The negotiations directly affected important economic interests in the beef and citrus industries. But broader political groups also mobilized substantial resources out of concern for long-term issues and for organizational or ideological reasons.

In both countries, the economic changes of structural adjustment, with the decline of agriculture, have posed a basic challenge to various social organizations, but especially to farm interest groups, government bureaucracies, and political parties. The negotiations over beef and citrus illustrated that challenge and showed that political influence is not simply a reflection of the direct economic interests at stake. Organizations will mobilize symbolic and material resources to maintain their power, seeking to postpone the decline in political influence that generally follows the decrease in economic importance. These general political forces provide clues about why the specific talks over beef and citrus became so important, and why the dispute was so difficult to resolve.

Negotiations between nations are highly political processes as well as technical ones, especially when the issue at hand requires trade-offs and concessions among domestic interests. Politics constrains government positions in negotiations and shapes acceptable limits. The negotiations over beef and citrus illustrate the rocky path cut by political pressures. Not all interests involved were equally represented in the talks, and not all issues raised could be resolved in the negotiations. Some broad issues were raised as tactical bargaining; some issues remained implicitly stated as part of grandstanding for constituents; and some core issues showed economic interests that ran counter to political ideologies. While negotiators sought to increase their leverage by expanding the issue into public debate, the political consequences of that approach had counterproductive consequences for broader bilateral relations.

INTEREST GROUPS

A striking difference between Japan and the United States is the structure of farm organizations. Japan has a national association of farmer cooperatives, which includes 95 percent of all farmers, organized on national, prefectural, and local levels, with 5.64 million members and 2.18 million associate members in 1980. The peak organization, Zenchū, provides a national focus for influence on policy.[41] The United States, on the other hand, has a diversity of general farm organizations, the three most important being the American Farm Bureau Federation, the National Farmers Organization, and the Farmers Union. These three groups represent different economic cross sections of farmers and different political perspectives on policy. The single organization in Japan contrasts with the multiple organizations in the United States and provides the potential in Japan for more sharply focused and persuasive influence on politicians and bureaucrats.

The beef and citrus negotiations provided farm groups in both countries with the opportunity to demonstrate their organizational effectiveness to members. In Japan, Zenchū sought to show that the cooperative association's activities had persuaded the government to keep the growth in quotas to a minimum, an important point to make to 340,000 families involved in cattle raising and feeding, and 300,000 families in citrus growing. Moreover, Zenchū strove to connect beef and citrus to rice, since about 85 percent of Japan's farm households produce rice, making that group the major constituency for the organization and making rice a powerful symbol for mobilizing the members. The farm cooperatives have a strong interest in maintaining the current structure of rice farming, since a more efficient structure would reduce the number of rice farmers and consequently the number of organization members. A more efficient structure could also encourage producers to find low-cost supplies, which would cut into the cooperatives' profitable sale of inputs.

Japan's agricultural cooperatives have recently confronted a number of problems related to structural change. In addition to the inability of cooperatives to meet grassroots members' demands to increase the government purchase price of rice, the organizations have faced pressures from the livestock and citrus cooperative groups to oppose liberalization, and problems of new interests created by fewer full-time farmers and more part-time farmers. In the midst of these problems, outside pressure for beef and citrus liberalization provided Zenchū with the opportunity to mobilize the national and regional capacities of farm cooperatives. In that sense, the cooperatives as well as Zenchū used public conflict over beef and citrus to help justify their existence.

The farm cooperatives seek to protect their own organizational interests, which differ from the interests of individual farmers.[42] The cooperatives have sought to maintain their strength by encouraging nonfarming rural residents to belong as associate members and by providing various economic services that extend beyond farm activities, including large-scale life insurance and banking services. In these ways, Japan's agricultural cooperatives are fighting to retain their economic and political viability in the face of continuing structural change in the economic role of agriculture. Zenchū's leadership claimed that the beef and citrus agreement of 1984 demonstrated the organization's continuing influence, but the quota expansions seemed more to reflect the continuing decline.

In contrast to Zenchū's basic strategy of seeking to maintain control over the domestic market, some U.S. farm organizations have emphasized a basic strategy of seeking to expand access to foreign markets. While Zenchū proclaims a protectionist stance, the American Farm Bureau argues for free trade.

In the beef and citrus controversy, U.S. commodity organizations played more important roles than the general farm groups. The National Cattlemen's Association became the industry representative on beef, and Florida Citrus Mutual, the California-Arizona Citrus League and Sunkist on citrus. On both commodities, the government's initial negotiating position of total and immediate liberalization did not represent the real economic interests of certain groups. Meat packers had an interest in maintaining Japan's guaranteed purchases of high-quality beef, rather than full liberalization, as a means for reducing uncertainty in the business and for restricting the competition from other countries. But the packers had limited influence in the Cattlemen's Association, a powerful interest group composed mainly of cattle producers, with relatively little experience in selling meat in Japan. The group tended to stress the ideological principle of full liberalization (except, of course, for meat imports into the United States) more than the economic interests of meat packers. For citrus, some tension persisted between California and Florida producers, although increases in the total quota for oranges helped reduce conflict among U.S. orange growers. Some California producers sought to maintain the seasonal quota at the last minute of negotiations, as a means of assuring that a large share of increased exports to Japan would not be taken by Florida producers. Despite the strong rhetoric of liberalization, some U.S. agricultural interests saw an advantage in maintaining quotas to protect preferential treatment and competition (between nations on beef and within the United States on citrus).

Agricultural interests are not monolithic, and the potential for conflict exists, especially among different commodities. Tension arose, for example, between U.S. beef exporters and U.S. feed grain exporters, since increased beef sent to Japan might displace some domestic production that depends on U.S. feed. Outside the negotiations, some Japanese informally sought to exploit this tension by suggesting that Japan would diversify its sources of commodities, and thereby reduce imports from the United States, if forced to increase purchases of beef and citrus.

The Japanese strategy of seeking to use the powerful U.S. grain interests to restrain the demands of U.S. beef and citrus interests strikingly resembled the American strategy of seeking to use the powerful Japanese industrial interests to restrain the demands of Japan's agricultural interests. Both strategies sought to use divided interests in the other country to further one's own interests. Both strategies included an explicit threat: the U.S. threat of protectionism against Japanese manufactured products, and the Japanese threat of reduced purchases of U.S. grains and soybeans.

But an important difference existed. The U.S. strategy was probably more effective in the short run. Japanese industrial organizations were publicly and privately opposed to agricultural subsidies and protectionism; such policies have increased budget deficits and strained international relations, thereby threatening access to overseas markets for Japanese manufactured goods. Keidanren, for example, proposed specific changes in policy to improve the productivity and efficiency of Japanese agriculture.[43] Similar positions were taken by academic researchers: the Forum on Policy Innovation proposed measures to liberalize beef and reviewed broader issues of agricultural protection;[44] another research group suggested changes in agricultural structure that could transform some sectors into export industries.[45] U.S. grain interests, on the other hand, were more ambivalent. They announced that they could sell feed grains to the U.S. beef industry if Japan were compelled to increase its beef imports and decided therefore to reduce its feed imports. Moreover, U.S. grain dealers, like Japanese big business leaders, fundamentally believe in and depend on free trade and access to foreign markets.

In contrast to the sharp tension between agricultural groups and Keidanren in Japan, there emerged an ad hoc alliance between agricultural and industrial interests in the United States. In discussions between U.S. and Japanese business representatives (in the Advisory Council on Japan-U.S. Economic Relations), when Japanese industrial representatives proposed that questions of agriculture be set aside, the Americans unanimously refused, insisting that the problems of market access and business practice for beef and citrus were the same problems as for industrial goods and services. Because of the clear U.S. cost advantage for beef and oranges, barriers to exporting these commodities to Japan served as powerful political symbols in the United States for industrial sectors that sought more protection from Japan as well as for high-technology sectors that sought more access to Japan.

The positions of Japanese consumers were mixed. Major consumer groups opposed liberalization, to protect domestic food production and improve food self-sufficiency rates, to prevent importation of food products with potentially harmful additives or chemicals, and to support the activities of the agricultural cooperatives.[46] Individual Japanese consumers, on the other hand, tended to support gradual liberalization. According to a public opinion poll conducted in 1983, 53 percent of the respondents supported increasing beef imports to reduce domestic beef prices and 50 percent supported the liberalization of oranges and orange juice imports from April 1984.[47]

BUREAUCRATIC AGENCIES

In both countries, diverging interests existed among government agencies. The U.S. State Department and Japan's Ministry of Foreign Affairs tended to be strongly concerned about the consequences of continued conflict for the overall bilateral relationship, while MAFF and the USDA focused on meeting the demands of agricultural constituents. MITI and the Departments of Commerce and Treasury sought increased exports to the other country. Japan's Ministry of Finance maintained a neutral position, in part because of uncertainty about the financial consequences of liberalization and in part because of concern that an agreement on beef and citrus would put pressure on tobacco restrictions which are under MOF's control. The rising trade deficits in America increased the pressure from Commerce and Treasury to obtain trade concessions from Japan, which made it more difficult for State to maintain a pro-Japan position. The 1979 reorganization of trade responsibilities in the U.S. government also significantly weakened the State Department's influence on these matters and strengthened the USTR's role and its hard-line position on Japan. The efforts by USTR and USDA officials to create a governmental consensus on beef and citrus, combined with the relative decline of the pro-Japan State Department, greatly contributed to the emergence of these commodities as important political issues. The image of beef as an all-American symbol also assisted efforts to organize various agencies behind the USDA position.

In situations of conflicting bureaucratic interests, which agency takes the lead in particular negotiations becomes an important question. In the United States, for most agricultural trade issues, the views of the USDA tend to dominate interagency consultations, either directly from the Foreign Agriculture Service in USDA or indirectly through former USDA officials in USTR. In Japan, MAFF's position usually dominates on agricultural questions in the various interagency committees, although some tensions exist between MITI and the Ministry of Foreign Affairs, reflecting a deep-rooted competition over control of international trade talks. On beef and oranges, the export-oriented views of USDA dominated the American bureaucracy, and the protectionist position of MAFF dominated the Japanese bureaucracy, despite different opinions within the governments of both countries.

The agricultural agencies also sought to balance long-term policy goals with short-term constituency demands. For MAFF, a sudden liberalization would have threatened the long-run policy of gradual adjustment for Japanese agriculture as well as the immediate interests of beef and citrus producers. On the other hand, MAFF officials realized that Japan needed to increase imports of beef and citrus to meet growing domestic demand. Indeed, as USTR officials pointed out, the expanded quotas in the final agreement fit with MAFF's projected demands (although without the negotiations, the proportion of grain-fed beef in total beef imports would undoubtedly be much smaller). Moreover, a full liberalization could significantly reduce MAFF's direct influence on the economy. If governmental intervention were replaced by market mechanisms, that change could diminish MAFF's ability to distribute economic or political resources, something no bureaucratic agency easily decides to give up. Thus, MAFF agreed to expand the import quotas to meet long-term policy goals; but the agency also established assistance programs for the producers affected, as a concession to important constituencies.

U.S. negotiators focused on the principle of free trade as a long-term goal, but in the end recognized the importance of an assured market as a short-term demand of constituencies. The U.S. objective was to increase agricultural exports, especially of higher value-added products. Reflecting the ideology of the Reagan Administration and important farm organizations, the negotiators demanded liberalization, even if it benefited the producers of other nations more than U.S. producers (as it might with orange juice). The negotiators argued that U.S. producers would take their chances with fair competition, that removal of import quotas would result in a substantial expansion of the market, and that the benefits of an expanded market would exceed those of preferential treatment. But in the end, the negotiators settled for expanded quotas that restrained competition and met the interests of some U.S. meat packers for guaranteed purchases by the Japanese.

The agricultural negotiators in both countries played a risky game in negotiating tactics, by encouraging interest groups and politicians to become involved in the beef and citrus issues. Negotiators referred to the activities of farm groups and politicians in arguing for concessions from the other side (including the public protests of Japanese farmers and local content bills of the U.S. Congress). Negotiators generally understood these arguments as tactics to increase one's leverage and as masks in political theater, even referring to the talks as a form of kabuki; but some participants outside the negotiations viewed their own actions as real rather than as theater. Negotiators then needed the public drama of the deadline to get concessions from interest groups and politicians. The bureaucrats thus used outside groups to affect the negotiating process, and finally used the negotiating process to control the outside groups. Such an approach, however, can produce uncontrollable and undesirable effects. In the end, the friction generated by the beef and citrus controversy led to rising anti-Japanese sentiments in the United States, and to anti-American sentiments in Japan.

POLITICAL PARTIES

The attention a political party gives to agricultural issues depends largely on the electoral influence of the farm vote. Here again a major difference emerges between Japan and the United States. While the United States has adjusted electoral districts after each national census to account for the population shift from rural to urban areas,[48] Japan has resisted reapportionment and redistricting. As a result, the direct influence of farmers in the U.S. House of Representatives has declined markedly in the postwar period, while the influence of urban consumers has increased. In Japan, on the other hand, the principle of one-person-one-vote has not been implemented, owing largely to LDP resistance. Two efforts at reapportionment of the Lower House in 1964 and 1975 simply increased the total number of seats and added new districts in highly urban prefectures. The unequal weight of rural and urban votes (reaching a four to one difference in some cases) has remained a point of controversy in postwar politics, and has been the focus of numerous court cases. Moreover, a high correlation exists between the LDP popular vote and the rural population ratio, with the LDP much more successful in rural areas. That pattern makes rural voters doubly important to the LDP: because of their greater likelihood to vote LDP and because of the greater weight of their vote in parliamentary representation. Thus, a critical difference in the aggregate importance of rural voters in the two nations persists.

In each country, however, substantial similarities also exist. Interest groups representing particular commodities exert pressure on political parties. These groups have explicitly organized many LDP Diet members, on livestock (138 members), citrus (190 members), and rice (300 members), which combined into the Liaison Committee on the Liberalization of Agricultural, Fishing and Farming Products in December 1982, to fight U.S. advances on beef and citrus. To emphasize this influence, prior to Nakasone's visit to Washington in January 1983, a map of Japan was prepared in English to show the economic production of beef and citrus in each prefecture, with the number of political representatives.

In the United States, the production areas for beef and oranges cover a broad range of electoral districts for Congress, with six main states for beef production and a total of twenty states involved in the beef industry (nearly every state west of the Mississippi), and with four Sun Belt states involved in orange production. These states constitute important political constituencies for President Reagan, giving beef and citrus interests considerable political influence, especially before elections.

But the influence of agricultural interests should not be exaggerated in either country, since the major political parties must balance diverse demands, as "catch-all" parties. Despite the LDP's dependence on rural voters, the party also needs to satisfy nonagricultural interests (including rural residents who are increasingly dependent on industry and exports), but especially the interests of business. Similarly, although conservative farm groups are important to Reagan's Republican party, they are only one element of his political foundation.

The ideological side of political parties played a more important role in the United States than in Japan. The free-trade ideology of Reagan's Republican party promoted a focus on Japan's beef and citrus restrictions, and fit with the market-oriented farm policies initiated under the Nixon Administration, which expanded production and exports.[49] The Democratic party, on the other hand, had supported a more interventionist farm policy from the early 1930s to the late 1960s, which restricted output to boost farm prices and thereby support farm incomes.[50] Both parties, however, maintain the image of the American family farm as a symbolic basis of policy.

In Japan, the image of the farmer remains a key national symbol that is primarily associated with the LDP, although the Socialist party also gets a majority of its votes from rural areas. The urban-based opposition parties (Communist, Social Democrat, and Clean Government) also seek to be identified as friends of the farmer, and all parties play a game of parliamentary one-upmanship for the interests of farmers. In hopes of attracting rural voters, to overcome the LDP's margin in the Diet, opposition parties have insisted on raising agricultural price supports and increasing self-sufficiency for food— even above the levels of government policy.[51] They similarly opposed agricultural trade liberalization and helped push the LDP into a protectionist position. But the LDP makes most decisions on agricultural policy considering the economic and political interests of specific farm groups as well as the interests of national policy. The LDP has been able to maintain the ideological support of farmers while very slowly opening the agricultural economy.

Another critical difference between political parties in the two countries is the ability to coordinate diverse interests. In Japan, the LDP mobilized agricultural subcommittees of the party's Policy Affairs Research Council, including one faction of Diet members who represented the narrow interests of farm groups and another faction of LDP politicians (the Gang of Eight) who stressed the interests of farmers within the broader contexts of foreign policy, budgetary issues and overall economic growth. These two factions split in their responses to U.S. demands for beef and citrus liberalization. But the party was able to coordinate these groups in the final negotiations, and to achieve consensus on the proposed agreement—in part through the activities of an agricultural specialist in the LDP's organization who has developed relations of trust within the bureaucracy, the party, and the farm groups. In the United States, a similar power on agricultural issues was once exercised by Representative Jamie Whitten as Chairman of the House Agricultural Committee, but that power was formal and institutional, and not based on widespread trust and respect. Currently, the U.S. Trade Representative seeks to coordinate diverse interests, but that office lacks the informal power that has been institutionalized within the LDP through its many years in control. Consequently, on beef and citrus, the interests were less well organized in the United States, with a more peripheral role exercised by the Republican party. This pattern reflects the general decline of the U.S. party system, with a greater influence of constituency politics than party politics.[52]

In both countries, beef and citrus constituted important political interests for the particular party faction in power. Both the Reagan Administration and the Nakasone Cabinet sought to meet the demands of these single-interest pressure groups, but also to exert control and influence over the groups. Reagan and Nakasone faced potential losses to opposition parties if the interest groups were not partially satisfied. Nakasone especially felt vulnerable to pressure from these commodity groups, since his faction of the LDP is only the third largest in the party and depends on the support of other factions to stay in power. If Nakasone had mismanaged the trade talks, the opposition of farm groups could have upset the balance of power among factions and jeopardized his premiership. Both leaders sought to use the agricultural negotiations for domestic political purposes but to avoid substantially damaging bilateral relations.

Conclusion

Conflicts between Japan and the United States over agricultural trade represent common problems in international relations. No country really likes to negotiate agricultural policies with another country. Those policies are often based on historically constructed domestic agreements that have developed strong constituencies. Moves toward more liberal international trade can affect those domestic agreements, with adverse economic and political consequences. Agricultural policy therefore represents an important realm of national sovereignty that political leaders seek to protect from outside interference.[53]

This chapter has shown how conflicts in agricultural trade between Japan and the United States are based in both economic and political structures and strategies. Resolving the conflicts over beef and citrus in the 1977 and 1978 negotiations was no simple matter. Concessions were required on both sides. The resolution was reached in 1978 through the creation of two new concepts—high-quality beef and seasonal citrus; the negotiations completed in spring 1984 were messier and less creative.

A strategy to deal with conflicts in U.S.-Japanese agricultural relations must take into account the connections and tensions between the recent U.S. emphasis on increasing value-added exports (such as beef and oranges) and the traditional Japanese stress on restricting farm imports to avoid disrupting the expansion of value-added agricultural production. The U.S. export strategy has sought to use the growth of Japan's domestic market as a means to relieve U.S. producers of beef and oranges faced with excess supplies—in effect, as part of U.S. domestic adjustment policies. The Japanese import strategy has sought to use selective imports in combination with efforts to shift agriculture from its small-plot, rice-centered approach to a mixed-farming, larger scale approach, while seeking to provide more food security by improving levels of self-sufficiency. Both the U.S. export expansion policy and the Japanese import restriction policy were designed to deal with the domestic issues of structural adjustment, and the resulting conflict in trade relations may have been inevitable.

But the beef and citrus case demonstrates that it is possible, through concessions on each side, to help resolve agricultural production and income issues in the United States and to help improve consumer benefits and agricultural adjustment policies in Japan at the same time. The objective of negotiations should be to achieve those goals through mutual concessions and with minimal frictional costs. Given the deep interdependence of the two economies, the pursuit of mutual interests in the agricultural economies of both countries should be a top priority.

The Reagan Administration sought to place conflicts over agricultural trade within the larger context of relations between Japan and the United States, sometimes exacerbating and sometimes downplaying bilateral tensions over agricultural issues. The Administration used the threat of congressional action to protect manufactured goods as a way to gain negotiating leverage over Japan, and thus tended to raise the importance of agricultural issues. Similarly, the linkage of agricultural and industrial conflicts in congressional debates and in the U.S. Trade Representative's statements enhanced the importance of agricultural trade conflicts. On the other hand, after the appointment of George Shultz as Secretary, the State Department worked to keep agricultural conflicts from disturbing the overall relations between the United States and Japan. These American strategies were not always coherent, in part because the U.S. government sought agricultural concessions from Japan both as an end in itself and as a means to other policy and political goals.

Agricultural trade conflicts between Japan and the United States are thus both created and constrained by domestic politics in each country. The conflicts also arise, as this chapter has stressed, from the evolving structures of agriculture in Japan and the United States. As a result, solutions for short-term conflicts (often related to political pressures and government policies) often fail to meet the long-term conflicts related to the structural adjustments in the agricultural economies of both countries.

The agreement in 1984 for an expansion of the import quotas for beef and citrus may briefly reduce tensions in agricultural trade between Japan and the United States; but (as occurred after the settlement in 1978 for the Tokyo Round of the Multilateral Trade Negotiations) U.S. interest groups and producers are unlikely to be satisfied with anything less than total liberalization. Even if beef and citrus were fully liberalized, tension could still continue in bilateral agricultural trade relations. While beef and citrus are important issues for the specific interest groups and became strong symbols for industrial interests that want market access to Japan, they are symptoms and not causes of the major problems of agricultural adjustment in Japan. It is those adjustments in Japanese agriculture that have the largest potential consequences for bilateral trade.

The central issue for the long-term adjustment of Japanese agriculture is deeply related to rice production and especially rice price policy. Through the government's general support system for the producer price of rice, Japan's farmers receive about four times the world price of rice. That policy is one of the major factors that skew the allocation of resources in Japan's domestic agriculture toward rice production and away from other crops. It is also a factor in the high cost of land, and thereby plays a role in making Japanese agriculture high cost, small scale, and uncompetitive. That policy, in effect, requires protection for many Japanese crops and agricultural products to assure survival. Such protection, in turn, puts Japanese agricultural policy in conflict with the policies of other countries, including the United States, that seek export markets for agricultural crops to resolve their own domestic issues of structural adjustment.

Japan's price policy for rice is widely debated each year in domestic agricultural and political circles. However, the price of rice appears not to be a central issue for consumers, partly because of the decline in the percentage of household budget spent for rice, partly because of the decline in the consumption of rice, and partly because large government subsidies historically have kept prices to consumers somewhat below prices paid to farmers. Consequently, rice prices are not so much a consumer issue as they are a tax and budget issue; and the very large budget deficits in Japan make rice price policy an important political and economic issue.

On the other hand, it is important to note the declining influence of rice policy in Japan's overall agricultural economy. The value of rice production to total agricultural production has declined from 47 percent in 1960 to 31 percent in 1980. For both full-time farmers engaged in mixed agriculture and part-time farmers specializing in rice growing, the percentage of income derived from rice production has sharply declined. Rice price policy is only one of several factors influencing the actions of these farmers, in relation to the allocation of agricultural labor and land resources, and the distribution of production between rice and other activities (such as beef and citrus).

Policies designed to foster the long-term adjustment of Japanese agriculture need to incorporate a broader set of issues than just rice production and price policy. How will production, price and trade policies influence the income potential from increasingly strategic agricultural products such as beef and citrus? How will the development of the overall economy affect the demand for labor from agricultural areas? How will the price of agricultural land be affected by continuing urbanization and the demand for nonagricultural uses? Can agriculture continue as a favored way of life in the context of an industrialized Japan?

In addressing these broader issues, Japan's aging agricultural labor force and stagnant small farm size are two critical problems of structural adjustment that have been left unresolved by the recent settlement. These two issues, in turn, are related to Japan's policy on rice prices. By holding the producer price so far above the world market price, Japan makes it possible for marginal workers and marginal farms to continue to produce rice. The two problems are also related to employment and social welfare policies for the elderly, and to high agricultural land prices and the relationship between urban development and agricultural development policies.

Despite the domestic debate, Japan's price policy for rice is a taboo in the agricultural negotiations between the United States and Japan. In some ways, the two countries debated beef and citrus as a surrogate for dealing with the much more difficult and important issue of rice. Japanese agricultural and industrial interests have insisted that Japan must produce its own rice, to protect the nation's food security. California rice growers, on the other hand, have expressed a strong interest in being able to ship rice to Japan. U.S. rice growers also objected strenuously when Japan subsidized rice exports to other countries that have bought U.S. rice in the past. Even in 1984, when Japan experienced a temporary shortage in rice supplies (because of several below-average harvests, the success of acreage diversion programs, and the discovery of residues of the fumigant bromine in the government's rice stockpiles), the United States did not seek to initiate trade talks on rice. In the past, U.S. government representatives have acknowledged that rice remained "sacred territory" for Japan. Whether that policy is maintained in the future may well depend on world rice market conditions and the U.S.-Japanese trade balance.

While U.S. and Japanese negotiators have been able to resolve the immediate conflicts over import restrictions on beef and citrus, they still need a forum to discuss the long-term issues of adjustment for both the United States and Japanese agriculture and the consequences for bilateral agricultural trade. How can the United States help provide adequate food security and a strong agriculture for Japan? What would a lower cost, more efficient structure of Japanese agriculture look like? What form should U.S.-Japanese agricultural trade take in the future?

Agricultural issues remain fundamental problems for any nation's political economy. Because of the large share of the population engaged directly and indirectly in a country's food system, policies aimed at maintaining the health of that system are viewed by all governments as inherently national concerns; and yet one country's domestic agricultural policy often infringes on the welfare of other countries' farmers and consumers. Short of starting a retaliatory trade war, the recourse in such situations is to enter bilateral trade negotiations, as the United States and Japan did over beef and citrus. But it must be recognized that enormous stakes are on the table, stakes not even hinted at by the small value of trade in these two particular commodities.

Japanese negotiators were being asked to bargain over basic elements in their *domestic* agricultural policy, elements which have powerful political and income distribution consequences for Japanese society. No country willingly puts such issues on the bargaining table. As the above analysis indicates, they arrived there only because of intense political and economic pressures from the United States. The very intensity of these pressures is seen in Japan as a threat to national sovereignty; and certainly the United States would respond similarly if, for example, New Zealand or Denmark insisted that all U.S. restrictions to dairy imports be lifted.

Without the domestic political pressure from industry and labor on U.S. negotiators to "open Japan's markets," the agricultural trade talks would have been much less pressured and emotional. From a historical perspective, the development of U.S. agricultural exports to Japan has been an enormous success, and working out additional access for beef and citrus should in no way jeopardize this larger farm trade. But the broader domestic pressures do exist, insisting on "fair access" for all U.S. products in Japan, starting with those that are obviously competitive in existing markets. Once the Japanese negotiators realized that the talks could not be restricted to the narrow venue of beef and oranges, but carried critical symbolic meaning as well, the task became one of finding a suitable process by which to make the painful decisions acceptable to their own political constituency.

Neither the process nor the outcome are what trade economists would design if they had a blank sheet as a starting point, but that is precisely the point of this chapter. Even on issues so fundamental as the structure of an economy and how it copes with changing sectoral competition during the course of development, political choices influence, even determine, the path. These choices in turn alter the vested interests along the path and hence feed back to the choices themselves. Structural change is therefore at least as much a matter of politics as it is of economics.

CHAPTER 6

Energy Markets and Policy

RICHARD H. K. VIETOR

Since World War II, the energy strategies of both Japan and the United States have changed course four times. These changes corresponded to shifts in the worldwide supply, demand, and price of petroleum. In the first period, during the 1950s, energy strategy was shaped by the emergence of an oil glut in the Middle East. The second period began around 1960, when the oil surplus stopped deepening and the governments of both countries adopted policies to stabilize prices and the distribution of market share in their domestic energy markets. This second period lasted until the early 1970s, when long lines at American gas stations and hoarding by Japanese consumers dramatically signalled a new time of shortages and rising prices. Finally, an oil glut reemerged in 1981, and it was accompanied by yet another major shift in public policies.

In Japan and the United States, energy companies are privately owned by investors, yet regulated closely by government. In most other countries, government owns the energy companies. For this reason, the national energy strategies of Japan and the United States—despite obvious differences between their indigenous resources—have been shaped by imbalances in the world oil market. In both countries, actual implementation of policy has depended largely on the structure of industry and government, and on the institutional means for managing business-government relations. These are the two key themes of this chapter: that in Japan and the United States, markets define energy strategies while institutional structure shapes implementation.

I have divided the chapter into three parts. Part one contrasts energy resources and the structure of industry and government in Japan and the United States. In part two, I describe the conduct of energy policy over time, as the international oil market fluctuated from glut to shortage, and back again. Here, I focus on the domestic petroleum industries and the importation of liquefied natural gas (LNG). These two sectors illustrate a range of policy tools and business-government relations, from active day-to-day control to passive, long-term guidance. I have not considered nuclear power at length, although it is an important energy source, since even a brief analysis of its peculiar fuel cycle, separate regulatory system, and unique security problems would overwhelm an already complex story. In conclusion, the third part of the chapter offers my own observations about the nature and effectiveness of business-government relations in the two countries.

Energy Supply and Demand

Japan is now all but barren of fossil fuels. In fact, by the mid-1950s, its domestic energy capacity from coal and hydroelectric power had already peaked. Even with government subsidies, domestic coal output fell steadily during the next two decades. Since the early 1950s, then, Japanese industrial growth has depended almost entirely on imported petroleum, and, more recently, on imported natural gas and coal. As miracle economic growth drove energy demand ever higher, Japan came to depend on foreign oil for 75 percent of its energy supply by 1973. Since then, development of imported coal, LNG, and nuclear power has gradually reduced this dependence to about 60 percent.[1]

The United States, by contrast, is so richly endowed with energy resources that it supports a far larger economy than Japan's without importing more than a quarter of its fuel (see *Table 6-1*). The United States has also been less dependent than Japan on any single fuel; in 1982, petroleum contributed only 40 percent of total supply, while coal and natural gas each contributed about 25 percent.

TABLE 6-1
Fossil Fuel Supplies of Japan and the United States*

	Reserves		Production		Imports	
	1973	1982	1973	1982	1973	1982
Petroleum (bil. barrels)						
United States	35.3	27.9	3.45	3.16	2.28	1.86
Japan	0	0	0**	0**	1.83	1.31
Natural Gas (tril. cu. ft.)						
United States	250	201	21.7	17.8	1.03	0.93
Japan	0	0	.116#	.082	.125	.926
Coal (mil. tons)						
United States	483,000		598	838	0.1	0.7
Japan	1,000		15	19	58	76

*The United States also has uranium reserves (at $50/lb.) of 576 thousand tons.

**Negligible Domestic Production.

#Although Japan has no reserves of natural gas, it manufactures town gas domestically from coal and oil. It also imports liquefied natural gas (LNG).

SOURCES: U.S. Department of Energy, Energy Information Administration, *Annual Energy Review 1983* (DOE/EIA-0384), April 1984; Ministry of International Trade and Industry, *Energy in Japan, Facts and Figures,* April 1984.

CHART 6-1
Energy Consumption Patterns (1982)
(millions of tons oil equivalent)

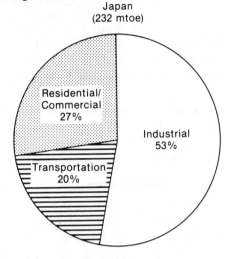

Japan
(232 mtoe)

Residential/
Commercial
27%

Industrial
53%

Transportation
20%

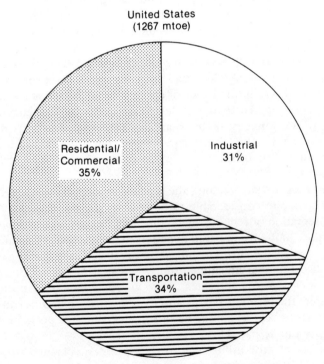

United States
(1267 mtoe)

Residential/
Commercial
35%

Industrial
31%

Transportation
34%

SOURCE: Adapted from Ministry of International Trade and Industry, *Energy in Japan, Facts and Figures* (Tokyo: April, 1984), p. 8.

In the two decades before the oil shock of 1973, Japan's total energy demand grew by 12 percent annually, or somewhat faster than its GNP. During the nine years 1973–1982, consumption in Japan actually declined 1.7 percent annually, primarily owing to conservation and modernization of industrial plant. During this entire period in the United States, energy consumption grew by 3.5 percent a year (slightly less than GNP) until 1973, slowed to a growth rate of .2 percent until 1979, then turned slightly negative through 1982. By 1985, energy demand was growing again in both countries, but at a slower rate than GNP. Even so, the *patterns* of energy consumption in Japan and the United States differ markedly. Japanese industry accounts for more than one-half of total demand; transportation, about one-fifth. In the United States, by contrast, industry, transportation, and residential/commercial each account for about one-third of energy demand (see *Chart 6-1*).

Industry Structure

Although Japan's energy industry is privately owned, its structure, like its energy-product markets, does not resemble that of the United States. Japanese companies are fewer and relatively larger: two dozen petroleum refiners, nine electric utilities, a few urban gas companies, and some of the giant trading companies constitute the principals of the energy business.

Japan's oil industry is dominated by about a dozen refiners/wholesalers. During the postwar reconstruction, would-be Japanese refiners lacked capital, technology, and access to crude oil. To expand rapidly, most Japanese refiners formed partnerships with American multinational oil companies, such as Exxon, Mobil, and Standard Oil of California. By 1955, three-fourths of Japan's refining capacity was in the hands of companies financially affiliated with foreign firms. This dominance, which developed under the influence of capacity licensing by the Ministry of International Trade and Industry, declined to about 50 percent by 1972, but the percentage has drifted upward again since then. Also, only four of the eight largest companies are now affiliated with foreign interests.

Relative market shares among the leading refiners have scarcely changed since 1972, despite considerable turbulence in the oil markets (*Table 6-2*). Vertical integration of refining, marketing, and foreign production operations has been quite limited, compared to patterns characteristic of the major American firms. Instead, the Japanese industry is organized in "groups," consisting of sales and distributional affiliations, joint ventures, and interlocking ownership of equity. As *Table 6-3* indicates, these group tie-ups have been relatively stable, despite the recent wave of capacity reductions, mergers, and consolidations.[2] The retail sector, consisting of some 60,000 independent outlets, remains largely unintegrated.

In Japan, the electric utility sector evolved under a planned rationalization. During World War II, thirty-nine generating companies and seventy distribution companies were reorganized into nine regional distributors. This struc-

TABLE 6-2
Structure of the Japanese Petroleum Refining Industry, 1972–1983

1972 Rank by Capacity	Company	Percent	1983 Rank	Percent
1	Idemitsu	12.4	1	12.8
2	Nippon Petroleum*	10.2	2	11.1
3	Toa Nenryo*	9.0	3	8.3
4	Mitsubishi Oil*	6.5	5	6.1
5	Maruzen Oil	5.8	4	6.8
6	Koa Oil*	5.4	8	4.3
7	Nippon Mining	5.0	6	5.8
8	Daikyo Oil	4.6	10	3.6
9	Showa Oil*	4.5	9	3.7
10	Showa Yokkaichi*	4.2	7	4.8
11	Kashima Oil	4.2	14	2.9
12	General Sekiyu Seisei*	4.1	12	3.4
13	Fuji Oil	3.3	11	3.5
14	Kansai Oil	2.6	[13 Seibu Sekiyu*]	3.1
15	Kyushu Oil	2.3	15	2.7

Concentration (Share of Total Markets)
Top Four Firms		38%		39%
Top Eight Firms		59		60
Top Fifteen Firms		85		83

* Affiliation with foreign companies.

SOURCE: The Japanese National Committee of the World Petroleum Congresses, *The Petroleum Industry in Japan,* 1972 and 1983, pp. 22, 55 respectively.

TABLE 6-3
Refining-Marketing Groups in the Japanese Oil Industry

Groups	1974 Market Share	Groups	1983 Market Share
Nippon Oil-Caltex	16.2%	Nippon Oil-Mitsubishi	27.3%
Exxon-Mobil	14.9	Idemitsu Kosan	14.7
Idemitsu Kosan	14.3	Maruzen-Daikyo	13.4
Kyodo Oil	12.9	Kyodo Oil	13.2
Shell-Showa	11.8	Shell-Showa	11.5
Mitsubishi-Getty	8.9	Esso-General	9.2
Maruzen	8.2	Mobil-Kygnus	7.7
Daikyo	5.2		
Total for groups	92.4%		90.0%

SOURCES: 1974 data from Robert G. Burke, "Japanese Oil Policy, 1945–1974: The Influence of the Ministry of International Trade and Industry on the Structure and Development of the Japanese Oil Industry" (Ph.D. diss. The Fletcher School, 1979), pp. 46, 203; 1983 data from Richard J. Samuels, "MITI and the Market: The Japanese Oil Industry in Transition" (MIT Energy Laboratory, working paper E1 84-016), p. 41.

ture remains intact today. Two quasi-public entities also play minor roles in power generation: the Electric Power Development Company and the Japan Atomic Power Company. Both are affiliated with MITI. During the 1960s, imported oil replaced coal and hydropower as the principal power-plant fuel. LNG and nuclear-generating capacity have developed steadily throughout the 1970s, as cleaner, more diversified sources of electric power.[3]

Tokyo Electric Power (TEPCO), with seventeen million customers and 30 percent of Japan's total generating capacity, is the country's largest fuel purchaser and power supplier. Because of TEPCO's unique economic importance, its senior executives are prominent among the *zaikai* (elite business leadership) that helps shape economic policy in Japan.[4] Japan's gas industry, on the other hand, consists of more than 200 utilities, which manufacture and distribute "town gas" (methane from coal and oil) and imported LNG (liquefied natural gas). Three companies—Tokyo Gas, Osaka Gas, and Toho Gas— account for 70 percent of sales. These companies, as well as the electric utilities, receive LNG from the three big trading companies—Mitsubishi, Mitsui, and Nissho Iwai—that developed and operate several international LNG projects. By the mid-1980s, LNG contributed 9 percent of Japan's total energy supply.

In the United States, the petroleum, natural gas, coal, and electric power sectors *produce* fuel domestically, as well as refine and distribute it. That fact, together with America's size and system of state-by-state utility regulation, has resulted in a far more diverse industry structure than in Japan. The American petroleum industry is made up of five distinct types of firms: (1) vertically integrated international companies; (2) vertically integrated domestic companies; (3) independent crude oil producers; (4) nonintegrated refiners; and (5) independent distributors and retailers. Only the last two groups have analogues in Japan. *Table 6-4* summarizes the market shares and level of concentration among the fifteen largest American companies. The relative positions of these market leaders have remained stable, albeit less so than those in Japan.

Large American oil firms have not influenced public policy as much as their size and market power would suggest because of the often contrary political influence of nonintegrated refiners and crude oil producers. With their significant contributions to local tax revenues, their effective political organization, and the credibility they derived from America's small-business ethos, these smaller firms could command attention from Congress. It was their interests that were so well represented over the years by such powerful producer-state politicians as Sam Rayburn, Robert Kerr, and Lyndon Johnson.

Natural gas, with huge domestic reserves, is a major industry in the United States. (Only four percent of U.S. supply is imported, mostly from Canada.) The gas industry consists of three relatively nonintegrated sectors: production, transmission, and distribution. Gas production, which has been federally regulated since 1954, is not markedly concentrated; the fifteen largest producers

TABLE 6-4
Share of Refining Capacity and Domestic Crude Oil Production of Largest Fifteen U.S. Oil Companies, 1951/55 and 1979

1951 Rank	Company	Refining (1951)		Production (1955)	1979 Rank	Company	Refining (1979)		Production (1979)
1	Exxon	11.1%		6.1%	1	Exxon	9.0		9.4
2	Mobil	7.9		3.4	2	St. Calif.	8.4		4.0
3	Texaco	7.3		4.9	3	St. Indiana	7.1		6.0
4	St. Indiana	7.2		3.4	4	Shell	6.5		5.8
5	Gulf	6.6		3.4	5	Texaco	6.0		5.4
6	St. Calif	5.6		3.6	6	Gulf	5.4		3.8
7	Shell	5.5		4.1	7	Mobil	5.2		3.7
8	Sinclair	5.2		1.8	8	Arco	4.7		6.2
9	Cities Service	3.1		1.5	9	Marathon	3.4		1.9
10	Sun Oil	2.9		1.7	10	Union Oil	2.8		1.9
11	Tidewater	2.8	Getty	2.5	11	Sun Oil	2.7		2.0
12	Phillips	2.6		1.8	12	Phillips	2.7		1.4
13	Atlantic	2.4		1.3	13	Ashland	2.7		3.1
14	Union Oil	2.2		1.5	14	St. Ohio	2.6	Getty	6.8
15	St. Ohio	1.7	Conoco	2.0	15	Conoco	2.2		1.7

Concentration (Share of Total Market)			Concentration (Share of Total Market)	
Top Four Firms	33%	19%	Top Four Firms	28%	31%
Top Eight Firms	56	31	Top Eight Firms	47	52
Top Fifteen Firms	74	43	Top Fifteen Firms	63	71

SOURCES: Compiled from U.S. Department of Treasury, *Implications of Divestiture*, June 1976, pp. 24, 32; also, U.S. Congress, House, Commerce Committee, Subcommittee on Energy and Power, *The Energy Factbook* (96th Cong, 2nd Sess.), 1980, pp. 110, 111, 407.

(all oil companies) account for half of total output. Interstate transmission, which is also federally regulated, is dominated by thirteen companies with three-fourths of all interstate sales. In the distribution sector, about sixty companies operate regional franchises, regulated by state public utility commissions.[5]

Investor-owned electric utilities in the United States are generally organized to operate on a regional, state, or local basis. The Public Utility Holding Company Act of 1935, together with the pattern of state regulation, largely prevented interstate consolidation (as it did in the gas sector). No electric power companies in America exercise anything like the national political influence wielded by Tokyo Electric Power.

The American coal industry is similarly fragmented, although for entirely different reasons. It includes several hundred companies, of which the fifteen largest have 40 percent of market share. Except with regard to environmental issues, this sector has historically exerted little influence in Washington.[6]

These differences in industry structure between Japan and the United States have several important implications for energy policy and its implementation. The oil industry in Japan, which lacks the assets and revenue stream involved in production and is affiliated with foreign interests, has exercised relatively little influence politically. Fuel-*user* groups, on the other hand, including the electric and gas utilities and strategic heavy industries, have exerted far greater influence on energy policy. Thus, Japanese energy policy has tended to be user-oriented, although a little less so since the first oil shock of 1973.

In America, the economic and political interests of the companies in these industries are extraordinarily fragmented, compared with the Japanese situation. Before 1973, the various producer interests in oil and gas did exercise significant influence on energy policy, but with little coherent design. Industrial-user groups, including the utilities, were too geographically and politically dispersed to have much of an impact. Since 1973, residential and consumer-interest groups have played a larger role, but this has merely aggravated the overall incoherence of the policy process in America.

Government Structure

The structure of government, no less than of industry, is obviously an important factor in energy policy. In Japan, MITI's Natural Resources and Energy Agency (Shigen Enerugī Chō) employs about 500 people to regulate and administer all petroleum, gas, coal, electric, and alternate-energy commerce in Japan. In the United States, the same responsibilities are shared by 21,000 employees of the Department of Energy and nearly 12,000 in the public utility commissions of fifty states. By American standards, Japan's centralization of energy regulation in a single administrative agency—the Ministry of International Trade and Industry—is remarkable. Yet it derived from clear historical foundations.

Over time, MITI's responsibilities in the energy sector grew by accretion.

When its predecessor, the Ministry of Commerce and Industry, was established in 1925, coal mining was one of the new agency's three functional divisions (along with industry and commerce). In 1934, under the rising influence of militarism, the Diet enacted a Petroleum Industry Law which gave government broad authority over imports, refining, stockpiles, and price. To administer this system, the Ministry of Commerce and Industry established a Fuel Bureau—its first industry-specific bureau and the model for MITI's postwar organization. In 1943, when the Ministry of Munitions superseded the Ministry of Commerce and Industry, it acquired responsibility for electric utilities as well. The MITI Establishment Law of 1949 reorganized these energy functions into a separate, external bureau—the Resources Agency. Although abolished after the Occupation, the Agency was reinstated by Yasuhiro Nakasone, then Minister of MITI, in July 1973, just three months before the first oil shock.[7]

Within Japan, MITI's authority over energy matters is not geographically limited. Unlike interstate commerce in the United States, intra-regional commerce has no jurisdictional significance in Japan's prefectural organization. Thus, MITI's Resources and Energy Agency regulates such local matters as electric rates and power-plant siting, as well as nationwide policies for petroleum pricing, tariffs, and taxation. This comprehensiveness helps MITI implement its policies with a minimum of friction among regions, producers, and users. Internally, however, there remains a degree of bureaucratic conflict, since MITI's other bureaus make and administer industrial policy for Japan's energy-intensive heavy industries.

In the United States, before the oil shock of 1973, the national government was not well-organized to administer energy policy. Responsibility was dispersed among nearly all of the congressional committees, and among some eighty-five bureau-level organizations within the executive branch.[8] For example, six different agencies within the Interior Department administered the government's major programs for fossil fuels. The oldest was the Bureau of Mines, which conducted research in coal mining and safety. The Office of Coal Research funded contract research and pilot-plant development of synthetic fuels. The Bureau of Land Management was responsible for leasing minerals on federal lands. The Geological Survey measured domestic energy resources. The Office of Oil and Gas provided staff functions as liaison to the National Petroleum Council (a business advisory group). Finally, the Oil Import Administration regulated imports.

Outside the Department of Interior, the Federal Power Commission, a five-member, independent regulatory agency created in 1920, regulated interstate transmission of electric power and, beginning in 1938, interstate gas pipelines as well. After 1954, this commission also set field prices for natural gas. Meanwhile, the Atomic Energy Commission was established in 1946 to promote and regulate nuclear power.

Periodic suggestions for consolidation and reorganization of policymaking went unheeded until the early 1970s, by which time even industry executives were advocating a more coordinated approach. In 1973, at the same time that MITI was reorganized, President Richard Nixon unsuccessfully proposed a Department of Energy and Natural Resources. Instead of this new department, however, the oil shock and ensuing panic inspired Congress to create a new Federal Energy Administration to allocate petroleum products and regulate their price. In the following year, Congress consolidated energy research in a new Energy Research and Development Administration (ERDA) and established an independent Nuclear Regulatory Commission.

Partly because of the chaos that prevailed in federal energy policy, President Jimmy Carter finally achieved a major reorganization of energy functions, early in his administration. In 1977, Congress approved legislation to establish a Department of Energy, combining the energy responsibilities of the Interior Department, the Federal Energy Administration, the Federal Power Commission (renamed the Federal Energy Regulatory Commission), and the ERDA. Only nuclear regulation remained entirely separate.[9] Despite this consolidation, energy policy continued to be fragmented under the influence of congressional overseers, state regulators, and the federal courts.

One other aspect of government organization is worth noting; *legislative* influence on energy policy has been completely different in the United States as compared to Japan. The Japanese Diet has almost always played a relatively passive role in the formulation of energy policy, and has exercised even less influence on its implementation. By contrast, several committees of the U.S. Congress, and their chairmen in particular, tended to dominate the formulation of energy policy, and then to intervene continuously in policy implementation through their "oversight" responsibilities. Thus, while the reorganization of MITI was designed by its own ministers, the Department of Energy represented the will of Congress. This difference in origin was reflected in subsequent policy. For example, while MITI chose to discontinue emergency price controls on petroleum products in 1974, the Congress prevented the Federal Energy Administration from doing so.

These institutional contrasts had many other important implications for the quality and effectiveness of energy policy. Bureaucracies, although not immune to political pressure, are at least organized to perform coherent administrative tasks. Legislatures are not. The U.S. Congress wrote energy legislation too narrowly for effective administration; and then it politicized implementation. In Japan, on the other hand, the bureaucracy used its authority so extensively that it tended to foster dependence of the private sector on the public, and sometimes to stifle the evolution of a more efficient industry structure.

Business-Government Relations

In the United States and Japan, the channels for interaction between business managers and government officials are not at all similar. Differences in the organization of industry and government, and even geography, account for this. Greater concentration in Japan's energy industries and in its government means that there are fewer important participants in the policy process. Most of them, moreover, work in the same city—Tokyo. Whenever issues arose over refinery capacity during the last thirty years, for example, spokesmen for fifteen or twenty firms and their trade association, a couple of academic "experts," and a handful of MITI-men would be directly involved. These people, most of whom know each other, would discuss the issue formally in meetings of an advisory committee, circulate drafts of a policy proposal, and talk it over further by telephone or at dinner. Usually, after MITI had made minor concessions, a "consensus" (or at least, silent consent) would emerge.

In the United States, the situation could hardly have been more different. For example, when technical problems arose in the Entitlements Program (a complicated crude oil allocation scheme developed during the 1970s), the Federal Energy Administration would solicit comments and hold hearings in various cities for scores of refiners, crude oil producers and importers, bulk distributors and retailers, user groups, and mayors. All the while, the diverse interests vigorously lobbied their congressmen and any other officials who would listen. After clearing a decision with the White House, the Office of Management and Budget, and other interested agencies, the FEA would eventually publish a formal ruling in the *Federal Register;* then the appellate process would begin, as injured parties used the federal courts to defend the status quo.

In both Japan and the United States, trade associations have played an important role in the policy process. In Japan, they have proved useful in consensus-gathering; in the United States, their primary role has been simple lobbying. About a dozen Japanese trade organizations represent commercial interests in energy; and of these, the Petroleum Association and the Federation of Electric Power Companies have been the most important. Since their memberships are relatively homogeneous, these associations can speak with one voice on most issues of policy.[10] Nor have the activities of such groups been especially constrained by antitrust considerations. Prior to 1974, the Petroleum Association acted as coordinator for MITI's "administrative guidance." On broader issues of energy policy, user groups such as Keidanren (Federation of Economic Organizations) have been even more influential. These energy-user organizations had superior resources and more influential members among the *zaikai.*

In America, at least eight national trade associations and a score of regional and specialty groups have been involved in energy issues. The most important are the American Petroleum Institute, the American Gas Association, and the Edison Electric Institute, which command substantial resources and broad bases of political support. Yet more often than not, they have failed to take strong, effective positions on major issues, because the interests of their memberships are so diverse. Thus, for example, the pipeline and distribution companies which belonged to the American Gas Association could not agree on gas-price regulations. Similarly, the American Petroleum Institute could never achieve a meaningful consensus on the issue of oil-import restrictions.[11]

Advisory councils represent another traditional means of facilitating interaction between government officials and business managers. In Japan, such councils usually serve as prominent forums for policy formulation, deliberation, and consensus. Of the thirty-one councils attached to MITI, two have been particularly important in energy policy: Sōgō Enerugī Chōsakai (Overall Energy Council) and Sekiyu Shingikai (Petroleum Deliberative Council).[12] In the United States, advisory councils from all industries have long been subject to antitrust scrutiny and to congressional criticism. Until 1973, when Congress enacted legislation to curb their activities, more than a thousand such councils advised federal agencies on a variety of policy issues. The oldest and most influential was the National Petroleum Council.[13]

The contrast in the makeup and activities of these advisory councils illustrates some of the fundamental differences in the political processes of the two countries. In Japan, the Overall Energy Council was established by MITI in 1961 to deliberate over energy policy proposals for adjusting to liberalization of foreign exchange restrictions. The original eight-member group included prominent academics and newsmen, a Keidanren staff director, and the Vice Minister of MITI. It was subsequently expanded to include representatives of the major energy trade groups. The Energy Council now deals with broad issues of strategic purpose, energy mix, and the preparation of forecasts for energy supply and demand. The Petroleum Council, mandated by the Petroleum Law, has twenty members representing refiners, dealers, a variety of user groups, academics, and the media. This Council provides a vehicle for implementation, review and discussion of MITI's capacity licensing, standard prices, and five-year oil supply plans.[14]

These two groups, with extraordinary continuity of membership, have provided a two-tiered forum for consensus-building, in which MITI's energy initiatives were aired, discussed, circulated, occasionally revised, and finally sanctioned. Neither council made policy, but they did make it legitimate.

The National Petroleum Council in America, set up by President Truman in 1946, was a different sort of institution. Its eighty members were corporate chief executives, representing all sectors of the oil industry. The council's purpose was to provide expert advice to the Secretary of the Interior, alleviating the need for an energy bureaucracy that could exercise significant power. Operating procedures were intentionally made formal, to prevent allegations of political impropriety. In the American political context, the Petroleum Council was no real counterpart to the advisory councils of Japan. For most American observers and some participants, it represented a necessary evil.[15]

In Japan and the United States, energy policy has been formulated and then carried out by all of these public and private institutions. To understand how the issues of policy were framed and how the organizations interacted, we need to look at imbalances in the market, starting with the emergence of a worldwide glut of petroleum in the mid-1950s.

ENERGY STRATEGIES

The Oil Glut (1949–1959)

Shortly after the Korean War, crude oil prices in the Middle East first stabilized at about $2 per barrel, and then began to fall. A burst of successful exploration and development had created more oil production capacity than peacetime economies could absorb. To increase their revenues, Middle East sovereigns urged multinational contractors to pump more and more oil. In Japan and the United States, imported oil first supplemented, then supplanted, domestic fuels. This posed two policy problems: protection of domestic energy producers, and import dependency. The governments of both countries were drawn into heavy-handed allocation schemes.

In the early 1950s, the Japanese government vacillated over the competitive struggle between domestic coal and imported oil. Revitalization of the coal industry to an annual production level of 50 million tons had been a critical strategic objective in Japan's recovery. But it was no sooner accomplished than oil importers began making inroads into coal's industrial markets. In less than four years during the 1950s, the entire Kyushu area, where the coal industry was concentrated, faced the prospect of imminent decline.

In 1955, following extensive *kondankai* (informal discussion meetings), Keidanren recommended that coal should remain at the center of Japan's energy strategy. The government issued a "Comprehensive Fuels Policy," calling for subsidies to the coal industry and import restrictions on heavy oil. The Diet promptly enacted two bills. MITI sponsored one that called for a "scrap and build" program of rationalization in the coal industry. The other imposed a tariff on imported oil and a tax on oil-fired power plants. The revenues from these two measures funded the rationalization of coal.[16]

Such policies helped ease the transition, but hardly stemmed the tide. Japan's oil consumption grew at an annual rate of 23 percent for the next six years. MITI, meanwhile, used its foreign-exchange authority to limit importation of refined products and thus nurture a domestic refining industry. By 1961, Japan's trading partners were urging liberalization of such import restrictions. Japan's trade position was nearly balanced, and its reserves of foreign exchange approached $2 billion. Yet liberalization of imports would severely threaten domestic refiners and would certainly ruin domestic coal. This situation elicited a new round of *kondankai.*

In the United States, domestic oil and coal producers first complained about foreign oil in 1949, when the U.S. became a net oil importer. As East Coast refiners expanded to process more oil from the Middle East, regulatory authorities in the oil-producing states reduced domestic output pro rata, to keep it from exceeding estimated market demand. Domestic oil producers complained to their congressmen, to the White House, and to their multinational competitors, whom they pressed for voluntary curtailment of imports. Invoking two of America's favorite shibboleths—national security and competition—these independent producers warned that "Middle East oil could not be defended in time of war, these fields were only six hours bombing time from Russia, and that the companies who owned these fields were in effect a monopoly."[17] For the coal industry, imported oil was just the most visible part of a massive decline in coal's competitiveness versus natural gas, diesel fuel, and heavy oil. In 1954, domestic coal production hit its postwar low of 392 million tons, down from 630 million in 1947. More than 150,000 miners lost their jobs.[18]

Neither the Eisenhower Administration nor the oil-industry leadership wanted to engage in formal protection (although the coal industry was ready to do so). The Administration was trying to promote trade liberalization generally, and the oilmen framed their rejection of government intervention in ideological terms. What they really wanted was for the eight or ten international oil companies to refrain voluntarily from increasing oil imports faster than the growth of domestic demand. This was called "industrial statesmanship." But with the price of foreign oil already 40 percent below the domestic price, it did not work.

As oil imports steadily gained market share between 1954 and 1959, political pressure from domestic producers intensified. Over this period, three successive cabinet committees reported a worsening threat to the national security. With support from the National Petroleum Council, the Interior Department then began coordinating a program of "voluntary" quotas, prorated semiannually among major importers and enforced by publication of noncompliance. This, too, failed. By the end of 1958, seventy potential new importers were clamoring for "voluntary allocations." Yet the older importers would sacrifice no more, and domestic producers remained adamantly opposed to imports.[19]

By February 1959, the Eisenhower Administration deliberated over an oil-import dilemma not dissimilar to that which MITI would face two years later: stabilization and a semblance of self-sufficiency on the one hand, versus cheap oil imports and market-clearing prices on the other. The strategy of balance between imported oil and domestic fuels proved unsustainable in both countries. The glut of oil simply swamped all attempts at voluntarism in the U.S. and cross-subsidy in Japan.

Stabilization of Oil Markets (1959–1972)

On March 10, 1959, President Eisenhower used his executive authority to impose mandatory quotas on imported crude oil and petroleum products. As stated, the objective was to preserve a "vigorous, healthy petroleum industry in the United States" in order to insure the national security. The overall quota was fixed at 12 percent of domestic production, approximately the level of import penetration reached in 1957. Tariffs on refined products were maintained at levels sufficient to protect all domestic refiners.[20]

The Secretary of the Interior created an Oil Import Administration to allocate the quota among all refiners in proportion to their average throughput. But since the majority of refiners were located inland, without access to foreign oil, it became necessary to sanction trading of quota "tickets" (a ticket represented the right to import one barrel per day). Coastal plants, with more refinery capacity than their import allocation, could acquire tickets from inland refiners in exchange for domestic oil. The value of a ticket (about $1.20) reflected the lower price of foreign oil. This aspect of the program was obviously redistributive: as one importer put it, "nothing more than industry subsidizing industry by government sanction."[21]

The implicit objective of this strategy was to insure a stable, relatively secure supply, at above-market cost. Domestic refiners could not have competed unless the government somehow neutralized the multinational companies' crude oil cost advantage. Likewise, domestic producers would not have survived unless the government had stabilized the price of their high-cost oil, well above the world level.

Japan made a different choice. In 1961, MITI drafted legislation for an Oil Industry Law and circulated it among interested parties. MITI also appointed a deliberative council of so-called *gakushiki keikensha* (learned men of experience). In December 1961, this council unanimously endorsed two objectives: a "cheap and stable supply" of oil, and a fixed proportion of market share for Japanese-owned companies.

But on the issue of implementation, there was no consensus. The majority recommended adoption of MITI's bill, but two council members opposed it. Within the business community, the debate divided among several views. Small independent refiners advocated an elaborate system of regulation, to encourage a Japanese "national capital" presence in the oil industry of at least 30 percent of capacity. They also suggested a "national-policy company" to buy crude oil and sell it at a pooled price. Most of Japan's larger refiners, as represented by the Petroleum Association, supported a limited or temporary role for government, to prevent "excess competition." But Japan's largest independent refiner, Idemitsu Kosan, was an outspoken opponent of any regulation, on the grounds it would hurt consumers. The energy-user interests, represented by Keidanren, also opposed regulation that might raise fuel prices and give MITI too much authority. So did the international oil companies, although they wisely remained quiet.[22]

After months of ex-parte debate and several revisions, the Petroleum Industry Law was approved by the Diet in 1962. It contained five significant provisions:

1. Each year, MITI would prepare a five-year plan for petroleum supply and demand, forecasting the volume of crude oil imports and refinery output;
2. Guided by the plan, MITI would license refining capacity, new installations of equipment, transfers of refining capacity, and mergers;

3. Petroleum refiners (as well as importers and distributors) would be required to submit annual production plans; MITI could "recommend" that plans be changed, if its overall supply plan would otherwise be "inconvenienced";
4. MITI could fix "standard prices" for petroleum products if they were anticipated to "rise or fall unreasonably";
5. A Petroleum Council would be established, to "make investigations and deliberations" in response to an inquiry by MITI.[23]

Throughout the 1960s and into the early 1970s, the Petroleum Law in Japan and Mandatory Import Quotas in the United States succeeded in stabilizing their respective domestic markets. As we have noted, industry structure and concentration in both countries changed little, except that in Japan the market share of foreign-affiliated oil companies declined. The price of kerosene in Japan did not change between 1962 and 1972; gasoline prices rose, but the price of heavy oil fell. In the United States, crude oil prices remained about 30 percent above the world market price until 1973.

In both countries, therefore, stabilization was achieved at considerable cost: inefficient industry structure, product-market distortions, and preemption of gradual adjustment to changes in the world petroleum market.

MITI used the Petroleum Law to establish its control over petroleum supply. In an effort to curb "excess competition," MITI set "standard prices" for more than three years. Standard price was usually a minimum price, in practice more than a guideline but less than a mandatory requirement. MITI also recommended levels of capacity utilization for refineries. This none-too-subtle form of administrative guidance was generally accepted, since MITI also licensed refinery capacity. In fact, the Petroleum Association eventually assumed the role of coordinator for these controls, making standard prices unnecessary.

Acquiescence to administrative guidance was not, however, unanimous. In a now famous incident, Sazo Idemitsu, the founder of Japan's largest independent oil company, took issue with MITI late in 1963. Idemitsu had recently completed the expansion of one of his refineries, nearly doubling its capacity to 242,000 barrels per day. Yet the Petroleum Association, reflecting MITI's guidance, recommended that the company limit throughput to 117,000 barrels. Idemitsu refused, and withdrew from the Association. After two months of informal negotiations, a face-saving compromise was reached. MITI revised the company's recommended throughput to 131,000, and the company agreed to comply (Mr. Idemitsu stubbornly refused, however, to rejoin the Petroleum Association).[24] Although exceptional, this incident and its quick resolution reveal the nature of MITI's so-called "power of life and death" over the petroleum industry.[25]

Between 1962 and 1972, MITI also used its authority to shape industry structure. For example, it used capacity licensing and reduced import duties to facilitate construction of *konbināto* (combination project) refineries. These large-scale plants, adjacent to steel mills, power plants, and petrochemical complexes, were designed to produce low-cost fuel oil or naphtha. They worked well, at least until the first oil shock. MITI also helped Japanese-owned refiners grow faster than foreign affiliates, increasing their share of total capacity from 43 percent to 53 percent. On the other hand, MITI's efforts to foster vertical integration and more efficient distribution channels met with little success. Its only accomplishment here was the creation of Kyodo Oil in 1965, through a merger of the sales operations of three small oil companies. And even with preferential treatment thereafter, Kyodo Oil remained a relatively weak performer.

MITI's implementation of a strategy for "cheap and stable supply" looks better, however, when compared to the administrative nightmare of America's oil-import program. Here, the contrast with Japan is sharpest. During the first five years of the American quota program (1959–1964), business and government struggled with the competitive distortions caused by quotas. For "historic" importers (the multinational companies with holdings in the Middle East) the program represented a disaster. They were forced to concede their share of imports, and eventually to make absolute reductions, so that domestic refiners and new importers could compete "fairly." Coastal refineries, as a result, were underutilized or forced to process high-cost domestic oil. Inland refiners were subsidized by exchanging their import "tickets." Preferences for small refiners, "hemispheric imports" (Canada and Mexico), and residual oil from Venezuela, caused wild distortions that multiplied the overall economic inefficiency of the plan.

In the quota program's second five years, exemptions proliferated on a firm-by-firm basis to the point where all political credibility was finally lost. Lyndon Johnson's Administration, for example, allowed exemptions for a motley list of causes: economic development in Puerto Rico, regional and local hardships, asphalt production, air-pollution control, petrochemicals, heating oil, and foreign-trade zones. The strategies of major corporations came to depend on the political logic of quota exemptions. "These favors," as one oil executive complained to the president, "have come close to emasculating the program." A White House aide put it even more bluntly in May 1968: "the oil import program is a mess."[26]

But it was worse than a mere mess. By prohibiting price from clearing the market, the quota program actually weakened American multinational oil companies and facilitated the depletion of spare capacity in the United States. Both of these consequences made the ensuing period of shortage far worse than it otherwise might have been.

The tightening of world oil markets was evident as early as 1969. Years of strong economic growth, topped off by environmentalist resistance to coal-fired power plants, helped absorb excess oil-production capacity in the United States and the Middle East. Although the real price of oil had continued to fall, drilling costs in the United States had risen sharply, thereby squeezing oil-industry profitability and slowing the rate of discovery. For the first time ever, the American Petroleum Institute reported in 1968 that net additions to proved reserves had turned negative. Oil production actually peaked in 1970, and in April of 1972, regulators in Texas and Louisiana allowed oil producers to operate at 100 percent of capacity. The inevitable result was that market power had now shifted decisively to OPEC. Over the next twenty months, OPEC proceeded to raise its price from $1.75 to $11.65 a barrel.

Reactions to Crisis (1973–1974)

In Japan and the United States, the immediate effects of this upheaval were similar—panic buying, price controls and product allocation, emergency legislation, and recrimination. The process of effecting a change of policy, however, was different.

In Japan, kerosene shortages first appeared during the winter of 1972–1973. The Japanese use kerosene primarily for home heating, much like fuel oil on the U.S. East Coast. Retail prices of kerosene rose as much as 40 percent during 1973, and consumer groups in northern Japan pressured the government for price controls. As localized shortages spread, "kerosene demonstrations" developed in Iwate prefecture. A run on toilet paper in Osaka evolved into a generalized commodities panic that spread to soy sauce, sugar, and kerosene. As winter deepened, farmers, fishermen, taxi drivers, and other small business persons complained of shortages of diesel oil and LPG (liquid petroleum gas). Allegations of corporate greed and conspiracy appeared in the press.[27]

In this setting, it was the energy industry, not MITI, that moved first to constrain consumption. The oil refiners jointly agreed to allocate product shipments, while the electric utilities asked industrial users to cut consumption by 10 percent. Talks between MITI officials and industry leaders succeeded in converting these voluntary measures into a temporary emergency program.[28] Next, MITI circulated a draft of emergency energy legislation that provided a focus for discussion among business leaders, bureaucrats, and politicians. At issue was the degree to which government should intervene in energy markets, as well as the form of intervention. Leaders of big business, speaking through Keidanren, urged reliance on administrative guidance and "stabilization cartels," rather than formal, statutory controls over product allocation and pricing. This approach, endorsed by MITI Minister Nakasone, was viewed by its advocates as the embodiment of business-government *kyōdō kōi* (cooperation). The Fair Trade Commission, however, was opposed to such measures as likely violations of the Anti-Monopoly Law. Consumer activists and opposition groups supported the FTC.[29] In the midst of the debate, MITI froze the retail price of kerosene, and MITI Vice Minister Eimei Yamashita remarked, evidently for political effect, that "the oil industry is the root of all evils."[30]

These less-than-consensual deliberations resulted in a pair of compromise measures introduced into the Diet on December 7, 1973, and passed two weeks later. The Petroleum Supply and Demand Adjustment Law authorized

MITI to order changes in the level and mix of refinery outputs, and to allocate all kinds of petroleum products among the various user categories. The specifics of the program were left to administrative discretion. The issue of price controls was resolved in a more general statute for controlling inflation—the Law on Emergency Measures for National Life Stabilization. This Act established a cabinet-level headquarters that could set prices for the duration of the emergency.[31]

In January 1974 the Cabinet designated standard prices for kerosene and LPG that allowed refiners to pass through only a portion of OPEC's crude-oil price increases. MITI, meanwhile, established an allocation system and informal controls over wholesale fuel prices. The resulting gap between feedstock costs and product prices was too large for oil refiners or electric utilities to tolerate for long. Both groups now agitated for higher prices. In mid–March, the Cabinet approved a "new price system," raising average wholesale prices by 62 percent. Two months later, MITI also raised average electric rates by 57 percent. Industrial users and motorists bore the brunt of these increases, which neither the refiners nor utilities felt were large enough.[32]

This discretionary legislation, meanwhile, did not deter the Japanese Fair Trade Commission from attacking administrative guidance. Widespread distrust of the oil industry's motives gave the FTC an unusual degree of political leverage. In February 1974, FTC Chairman Takahashi declared that twelve oil companies and the Petroleum Association of Japan were violating the Anti-Monopoly Law. Two weeks later, the FTC issued criminal charges. It accused officers of the Petroleum Association of illegally restricting production in 1972 and 1973, and officers of the twelve companies of fixing prices from 1971 to 1973.[33]

The production case was based on the method by which MITI's administrative guidance had come to be implemented. As the refining industry expanded, MITI relied on the Petroleum Association, through the concerted action of its membership, to implement its guidance on capacity utilization. It was this practice of *gyōsei shidō ni yoru jishu chōsei* (self-regulation under administrative guidance) that the court eventually found objectionable. The price-fixing case seemed even more blatant. As crude oil acquisition costs rose, members of the Petroleum Association met informally and agreed to a range of product-price increases. Afterward, a spokesman would share this information with responsible MITI officials, who then *ryōshō* (acknowledged) it. To those involved, this passive extension of administrative guidance seemed natural enough.[34]

Litigation aside, the period of crisis and emergency policy in Japan ended just nine months after it began. From an American perspective, this is the most extraordinary part of the story. By August 1974, recession and conservation had so reduced energy demand that product prices actually softened. With that, the Cabinet abolished allocation and standard prices (except on kerosene, which continued until March 1975), and declared an end to the emergency. Of course, MITI's administrative guidance continued, although more circumspectly than before.

In America, the crisis started out much as it had in Japan. Before long, however, energy policy turned into a matter of distributive equity that lasted for nearly a decade. As spare oil-production capacity in the United States had dissipated in the early 1970s, prices began to rise. Until March 1973, President Nixon relied on the overall wage-and-price controls that he had inaugurated in August 1971, in an effort to arrest overall inflation. But those mandatory controls caused several ill effects for domestic oil markets. Since the imposition of controls occurred in midsummer, when the demand for heating oil was seasonally low, heating oil prices were fixed at a low point, and gasoline rather high. Refiners accordingly maximized output of gasoline, and failed to build up their normal inventories of heating oil. This, together with unusually cold weather, resulted in heating oil shortages in the winter of 1972–1973. But since heating oil prices (like kerosene prices in Japan) were politically sensitive, the U.S. Cost-of-Living Council, which enforced these measures, made it difficult for the oil companies to raise heating oil prices. Instead, they were encouraged to recover these losses on other products, such as gasoline. Meanwhile, attempts to restock heating oil caused *gasoline* shortages and price increases the following June. Combined with the lines at service stations, these price hikes gave rise to the view that the crisis was contrived.

In 1973, when the Cost-of-Living Council relaxed its authority over most industries, it retained mandatory price control on the twenty-four largest oil companies, and soon extended control to include the entire petroleum industry. To prevent "windfall profits" (margins in excess of "normal profits"), the Council adopted a two-tier pricing system; "old oil" (in production before May 1972) was priced at $4.25 per barrel, while "new oil" became free of controls.

Among other things, the creation of a two-tier price structure meant that, for refiners, there would be a two-tier cost structure. This would obviously hurt firms without access to "old oil." Until 1973, most independent refiners (and, indirectly, the thousands of independent retailers they supplied) had depended on cheap foreign oil (or their allotment of import-quota "tickets") to remain competitive. When OPEC raised its prices late in 1973, the delivered price of imported oil surpassed the regulated price of domestic oil, most of which was controlled by the major companies. Not surprisingly, a clamor for protection went up from the independent refiners and marketers, who now invoked the time-honored goal of "preventing monopoly."[35]

Richard Nixon addressed the nation on November 7, 1973 just a week before the Japanese cabinet announced its first emergency program. He called for voluntary conservation and urged Congress to grant him authority to allocate crude oil and petroleum products.[36] In a rare display of bipartisanship, Congress enacted the Emergency Petroleum Allocation Act in less than three weeks. The Act authorized a temporary Federal Energy Agency (FEA) to implement allocation and take over enforcement of price controls, which were extended for another year. To protect "independents," the Act specified that relative market shares should be restored to 1972 conditions. Oversight by the Federal Trade Commission would insure "the competitive viability of independent refiners, small refiners, non-branded independent marketers, and branded independent marketers."

Questions about the nature of the energy crisis, meanwhile, had arisen with the heating-oil shortages and natural gas curtailments of the previous two winters. Monopoly power was a leading suspect. In May of 1973, Senator Henry Jackson asked the Federal Trade Commission to report on "the relationship between the structure of the petroleum industry and related industries and the current and prospective shortages of petroleum products."[37] Six weeks later, under continuing pressure from Senator Jackson, the FTC issued a preliminary complaint against the eight largest American oil companies.

The Commission charged that since 1950 the eight companies had individually, jointly, and through a "common course of action," maintained a "noncompetitive market structure at every level of the petroleum industry." Price leadership, competitive forbearance, exchange of pricing and production data, and self-imposed restrictions had all contributed. Most importantly, the FTC alleged that they had taken a "common course of vertical integration" that suggested "interdependent conduct"—a sort of shared monopoly. To remedy this the Commission sought vertical divestiture of all eight firms.[38]

Public suspicion of the oil industry intensified throughout 1973, as it had in Japan. When the problem became a crisis after the OPEC boycott, confusion and general suspicion turned to blunt accusations of corporate ill will. Congressional spokespersons led the attack. Representative John Dingell, a Democrat from Michigan, wanted to know why big oil companies, and not government, had the facts. "Whether or not there is an energy crisis," said Dingell, "there most certainly is a crisis of confidence."[39] In the Senate, Henry Jackson, chairman of the Interior Committee, called the chief executives of major oil companies onto the carpet to answer the "public's questions":

> The American people want to know if there is an oil shortage; The American people want to know why oil companies are making soaring profits; The American people want to know if this so-called energy crisis is only a pretext, a cover to eliminate the major source of price competition—the independents, to raise prices, to repeal environmental laws, and to force adoption of new tax subsidies.[40]

This was the environment in which the newly organized Federal Energy Agency tried to implement an emergency allocation system and price controls for the hundreds of diverse firms in the American oil industry. The FEA, which recruited 3,200 people by 1976, was discouraged from hiring people with experience in the industry; the few that it did hire were continually investigated by Congress. So were senior officials. William Simon, the first FEA Administrator, was required to appear before Congress 102 times during his first 9 months in office.[41]

The FEA moved quickly to freeze supplier-purchaser relationships, from wellhead to gas pump. Refiners with access to old oil were effectively vested with property rights. A program was established to equalize capacity utilization among refiners with varying degrees of dependence on purchased crude oil. In June 1974, although the embargo had ended, the FEA restructured this program to require the fifteen largest integrated companies to sell crude oil to small and independent refiners, based on each firm's refinery capacity. To alleviate cost differences, the FEA also instituted the Entitlements Program, a system of cross-subsidies from low-cost to high-cost refiners, designed to bridge the gap that regulation itself had created. It was the import "ticket" system in reverse.

This system of allocation and price controls continued to metastasize, despite the passing of the supply crisis which OPEC's boycott had triggered. Certainly within the Ford Administration, and on the minority (Republican) side of Congress, there was sentiment favoring decontrol. But for several reasons no such action occurred.

In the United States, there were no institutional alternatives to formal, legalistic regulation, dictated by recent statutes and by the Administrative Procedure Act. In Japan, by contrast, MITI continued to manage energy markets through administrative guidance. In the United States, a strong Congress, preoccupied with issues of equity, fairness, and domestic competition, dominated the policy process. The Diet in Japan did not. In the United States, there were domestic oil producers and vertically integrated companies for which the oil shock had proved a windfall. At the same time, the competitiveness of independent refiners and marketers still depended on a now-defunct regulatory regime. In Japan, American-style diversity of interest within the industry, and between the domestic refiners and the citizenry, simply did not exist. And finally, in the United States, many politicians disregarded the interdependence of market forces: supply, demand, and price were often treated as separate policy issues. In Japan, MITI bureaucrats restored market-clearing prices as soon as the crisis passed.

This entire episode, which was critical for longer-term adjustment policies in both countries, underscores the major differences between Japan and the United States. With distributive issues easily resolved, the Japanese government could focus on demand management and security of supply. In the United States, distributive issues continued to predominate for years to come.

National Energy Planning

MITI had already gained considerable experience with energy planning, even before the first oil shock. The Petroleum Law of 1962 required the

Petroleum Council to prepare a rolling five-year plan for petroleum supply and demand. This was coordinated with a similar plan by the Overall Energy Council, for supply and demand of energy. As early as 1971, the Energy Council had noted a shift in "power relationships" between the international oil companies and OPEC. It suggested then that Japan's energy-intensive industry structure "should be switched over to that of the minimum-energy-consumption type by promoting knowledge-intensive industries." The Council recommended that sources of fuel supply should be diversified, that vertical integration in the oil industry be encouraged, that a Petroleum Special Account (funded from import duties on petroleum) be established, and that the Japan Petroleum Development Corporation be expanded.[42]

Between 1971 and 1975, as the oil crisis unfolded and as MITI crafted the necessary political "consensus," a series of white papers and council reports reflected the evolution of a new energy policy for Japan. The focus on cheap oil, as a critical input to Japan's strategic industries, was abandoned. Security of supply, through planning and diversification of sources, became the new national goal. In MITI's 1975 plan, petroleum's share of the energy market would decrease from 77 percent to 63 percent, by 1985; coal's share would also decline, to 13 percent. Nuclear power and imported LNG would be the principal substitutes; the contribution of each was projected to grow from less than 1 percent to about 8 percent.[43]

Japan's national energy plan represented a de facto consensus among the political and economic leadership—*zaikai,* MITI, and the Liberal Democratic Party. It was reached through a protracted process of *kondankai,* orchestrated by MITI with its industry councils as instruments. Even the oil industry, faced with the sure prospect of smaller market share and marginal profitability, acquiesced. With the plan as a political charter, MITI then used a combination of administrative guidance, concessionary credit, tax incentives, utility-rate structures, and its special accounts to implement the new strategy.

The first step, to reduce petroleum consumption, was accomplished by allowing prices to rise to market-clearing levels. "From the perspective of guaranteeing a stable supply of oil which is a typical international commodity," the Council declared, "it is necessary to pay full attention to balancing domestic oil market prices with international price levels."[44] MITI used administrative guidance of refining capacity, as before, to restrict excess competition, to buffer kerosene prices, and, where possible, to encourage vertical integration.

MITI's use of special accounts meant that it need not depend on the Diet or the Ministry of Finance for annual appropriations to support its energy policy agenda. In 1975, for example, the Petroleum Special Account provided ¥48 billion, four-fifths of which was used by the Japan Petroleum Development Corporation to subsidize exploration. In 1978, the Diet approved a special Petroleum Tax of 3.5 percent on crude oil, earmarked for implementation of oil and alternate-energy development. By 1983, this tax yielded ¥429 billion in addition to ¥129 billion from duties. Similarly, the electric power account, funded by a user tax of ¥.44 per kilowatt-hour, provided about ¥200 billion to subsidize research, uranium enrichment, and power plant construction.[45]

In the United States, similar long-term energy strategies were proposed by three successive administrations. Only the third—President Carter's National Energy Plan—was adopted; and even the Carter package was enacted only in part, and then was cut short by the second oil shock. In all three cases, the political process, and especially the strained relations between business and government, undermined chances for consensus. Incoherence and indefinite extension of emergency measures prevailed.

President Nixon had proposed the first "comprehensive integrated national energy policy" in April 1973. Relying primarily on recommendations from the National Petroleum Council, Nixon called for deregulation of natural gas prices, a larger budget for energy R&D, accelerated leasing of mineral resources, and an easing of environmental regulations. This initiative, however, was swamped by the political tide of Watergate.[46]

President Gerald Ford did no better. In 1975, he proposed "Project Independence." This plan called for a strategic petroleum reserve and price decontrol of petroleum and new natural gas. It would levy a tariff on imported oil and a "windfall profits tax" on domestic oil producers. These would fund an array of fiscal incentives designed to promote conservation, coal utilization, and energy research. But Democrats in the Congress flatly rejected the plan. Consumer groups adamantly opposed price decontrol, while the various interests in the oil and natural gas industries failed to reach internal agreement. The Federal Energy Administration, mired as it was in red tape and political criticism, offered little by way of effective support.[47]

If there were any sense of national direction, it was obscured by the rhetoric of distributive equity. Ford's program was "cruel and unfair," as one congressman put it, "designed to sock the poor, the workingman and the middle-income people by leaving allocation of hardship entirely to the marketplace." Instead, Congress passed the Energy Policy and Conservation Act. Among its other accomplishments, this law imposed mandatory fuel-efficiency standards on the domestic automobile industry, allowed the entitlements program to continue, and extended two-tier price controls on crude oil for forty months more.[48]

In April of 1977, Jimmy Carter unveiled his National Energy Plan, calling it the "moral equivalent of war." Carter's goals were to reduce the growth rate of energy demand to below 2 percent and to cut oil imports to six million barrels daily, from a projected potential level of sixteen million by 1985. The Plan for supply would replace oil with coal, nuclear power, and unconventional sources such as solar energy and synthetic fuels. In all, the Plan entailed more than a hundred legislative proposals, including mandatory measures for conservation and fuel substitution, tax incentives and fiscal subsidies, and new price regulations for natural gas and petroleum.[49]

The Plan was comprehensive, but extraordinarily complicated. It was prepared under wraps by a team of policy analysts, supervised by James Schlesinger, the President's energy advisor. The Administration held no advance briefings, and only a few informal discussions with legislators and industry representatives. At the time, this seemed like the best way to get a coherent plan together.[50]

Congress debated the Plan for eighteen months before finally passing the National Energy Act. In the intervening period, one of the many sticking points proved to be the Crude Oil Equalization Tax. This oil-pricing scheme was designed to compromise the interests of equity and efficiency. The Administration recognized a need for higher prices to induce exploration and conservation. But Carter and most of his advisors were unwilling to concede "windfall" profits to domestic oil companies by allowing them to charge OPEC-level prices. To do so, at any rate, was infeasible politically. So the Administration proposed increasing the price of "old oil" at the rate of inflation, but still keeping it under control. The price of "new oil" would be allowed to increase to the world price level over three years. Meanwhile, a tax would be levied on all domestic oil, in order to "equalize" the difference between its price and OPEC's.

Since consumer groups and the oil industry alike rejected this Crude Oil Equalization Plan, and were unwilling to compromise, the Energy Act was passed without its centerpiece. Thus, the oil policy of the United States continued, until the second oil shock, to encourage consumption, to subsidize imports, and to discourage domestic exploration.

Alternative Fuels: The Case of LNG

During this period of energy shortages, private companies in both Japan and the United States tried to develop alternate sources of energy. The two most immediate and feasible options were imported liquefied natural gas (LNG) and nuclear electric power. In Japan, MITI's energy policies, unhampered by litigation, helped to shape a business environment conducive to the timely development of five large LNG systems and more than twenty nuclear power plants. Together, these systems replaced nearly one-third of Japan's oil-fired electric generating capacity. In the United States, by contrast, opposition from users and environmental interest groups, constant litigation, and fragmented regulations by government posed insurmountable obstacles to large-scale power projects. None of America's LNG systems have succeeded, and no fewer than seventy-five nuclear power plants have been cancelled, including twenty-eight already under construction.[51]

The case of LNG provides an especially good illustration of how implementation of energy strategy differed so dramatically between the two countries. Japan's first LNG project was initiated in the late 1950s by an entrepreneur named Hiroshi Anzai, who subsequently became chairman of Tokyo Gas. He was looking for a way to alleviate the air pollution caused by the manufacture of town gas from coal and petroleum. In the face of rapid growth, it was becoming difficult to find sites for new plants that were acceptable to local residents. In fact, when plans to build a new thermal power plant in Yokohama were blocked by a determined socialist mayor, Tokyo Electric itself also began considering importation of LNG.

Phillips Petroleum and Marathon Oil had first offered to sell the Japanese LNG from Alaska in 1960. Discussions with Tokyo Gas, Tokyo Electric, and Mitsubishi Corporation as facilitator, dragged on for several years. At issue was a delivered price about thirty percent higher than the energy-equivalent price of petroleum. In 1966, after Hiroshi Anzai convinced MITI to waive the prevailing customs duty of 20 percent, a twenty-year fixed-price contract of 52 cents per million Btu was negotiated. The first delivery arrived in Japan in November 1969.[52]

Negotiations for a second and much larger project were concluded just as this first one came on-stream (*Table 6-5*). The second project, involving LNG from Brunei, was a joint venture between Mitsubishi, Shell, and the Brunei government. Once again, Tokyo Electric and Tokyo Gas were the principal buyers. Because Mitsubishi, a Japanese firm, was directly involved, the government-owned Export-Import Bank provided one-fourth of the $250 million financing for the liquefaction plant; thirteen Japanese city banks provided an equal amount. Deliveries began in December 1972.

Although the government's involvement in these projects suggested "silent support," MITI had not yet embraced LNG as part of its overall energy policy. At a meeting of the Energy Council in 1969, according to Hiroshi Anzai, a MITI official omitted LNG from the draft forecast of supply and demand. Anzai, a member of the council, asked why. "Since the total cost is higher than those of crude oil and heavy oil," answered the official, "no such high price of energy will be used in the future." After the first oil shock, that same official, who had since become director-general of MITI's Public Utility Department, walked into Anzai's office at Tokyo Gas, apologized for being wrong, and promised, "now MITI will try to support LNG."[53]

In September 1973, in its White Paper on Energy, MITI adopted LNG publicly as part of a new strategy for energy security. Noting that gas usage remained low in Japan relative to other industrial countries, MITI announced that "it is above all necessary to actively promote independent development of LNG overseas to guarantee its secure supply to cope with the growing demand." MITI also suggested promotion of tanker construction and distribution systems, to be integrated with overseas production.[54] Diversification of supply had become the keynote of Japanese energy policy; price was relatively less important.

This LNG initiative was immediately reinforced by political support from the highest levels. When Prime Minister Tanaka visited Indonesia in January 1974, he helped finalize, on a bilateral basis, the world's biggest LNG project up to that time. Next, the Energy Council weighed in with an optimistic forecast. It projected LNG imports to reach forty-eight to eighty-two million tons by 1985, contributing as much as 9 percent of Japan's total energy supply. In December 1975, MITI again urged that government "grant positive assistance for prospecting and exploiting natural gas, constructing liquefaction plants abroad, and building LNG tankers and receiving bases in Japan." According to MITI, "it would also be necessary to organize in each place latent demand for LNG." With this sort of targeting for growth in the national interest, LNG's risks were reduced and its profitability reassured.[55]

The new LNG projects all involved one or more trading companies, several electric and gas utilities, and the Japanese government. In the Indonesia projects, the Japan Development Bank provided concessionary financing for LNG tankers, regasification facilities, and new gas-fired power plants. The Export-Import Bank, working jointly with Japanese city banks, financed a significant part of the foreign liquefaction plants (53 percent for Abu Dhabi and 73 percent for the first Indonesian project). MITI, meanwhile, allowed special low rates for new industrial users, and introduced a "third sector program" in order to encourage small towns and rural users to develop LNG distribution systems. And "most important" was the exercise of administrative guidance by MITI.[56]

In such an environment, the LNG business thrived. Occasional problems with plant siting or price renegotiations with supplier governments did not delay the projects. All five of them, as shown in *Table 6-5,* were completed in five years or less. The Abu Dhabi and Indonesian projects became operational in 1977; the Malaysian project and the Indonesian expansion projects were completed by 1985. Cost overruns were relatively minor, and the wholesale price has proved comparable to that of crude oil, since 1973.[57]

Entirely different economic and political circumstances surrounded the importation of LNG to the United States. With abundant domestic reserves, the natural-gas industry in the United States was well developed by the 1970s, providing about a third of America's gross energy supply. But with price controls based on historic costs in effect since the mid-1950s, gas had become significantly underpriced, and demand had gradually outstripped available domestic supply. A shortage had developed in 1970, and it lasted until 1979. Demand for LNG was a result of this temporarily imbalanced market.[58]

The first large-scale project for baseload demand was undertaken by El Paso Natural Gas, a pipeline company serving the Southwest. In the early sixties, the company had done exploratory work for Sonatrach, the Algerian national oil company. El Paso's top management held a long-standing conviction that depletion of gas resources in America was inevitable. In 1969, El Paso agreed to buy 1 billion cubic feet of LNG per day from Sonatrach, at a price of 30 cents per thousand. El Paso planned to operate nine tankers to deliver the gas to three East Coast gas utilities for about 80 cents per thousand cubic feet.

The Federal Power Commission approved the deal, with some reservations, in 1972. By 1978, however, Algeria's liquefaction plant and El Paso's tankers

TABLE 6-5
Japan's LNG Projects

Project	Imports Started	Volume Billions M^3	Importers	Other Participants
I. Clean energy projects, in operation				
Alaska	1969	1.3	Tokyo Gas Tokyo Electric	Phillips/Marathon Mitsubishi
Brunei	1972	7.0	Tokyo Gas Osaka Gas Tokyo Electric	Shell/Brunei Gov't Mitsubishi
II. Energy security projects, in operation				
Abu Dhabi	1977	2.8	Tokyo Electric	BP/CFP Mitsui
Indonesia (Badak, Arun)	1977	10.3	Kansai Electric Chubu Electric Kyushu Electric Osaka Gas Nippon Steel	Pertamina/Mobil Huffington JILCO (Nissho Iwai et al.)
Malaysia	1983	8.2	Tokyo Electric Tokyo Gas	Shell Mitsubishi

(cont.)

Table 6-5 (cont.)

Indonesia (Badak)	1983	4.5	Kansai Electric Chubu Electric Toho Gas Osaka Gas	Pertamina/Huffington Nissho Iwai
Indonesia (Arun)	1984	4.6	Tokyo Electric Tohoku Electric	Pertamina/Mobil Mitsubishi
III. Energy diversity projects, planned				
Australia	1988	8.2	Electric (Tokyo, Kansai, Chubu, Chugoku, Kyushu) Gas (Tokyo, Osaka, Toho)	Shell/BP Mitsui Mitsubishi BHP/Woodside
Canada	Late 1980s	4.0	Electric (Chubu, Chugoku, Kyushu) Gas (Osaka, Toho)	undetermined
IV. Energy diversity projects, under discussion				
USSR	1990s	4.1	undetermined	Sakhalin Petroleum Development
Alaska II	1990s	10.3	undetermined	ARCO, Sohio
Thailand	1990s	3.9	undetermined	undetermined

SOURCES: Shigen enerugicho sekiyubu (MITI, Petroleum Dept.), *Sekiyu sangyō no genjō* (Conditions in the Petroleum Industry) (Tokyo: Sekiyu Tsushinsha, 1980), pp. 282–283; also, MITI, *Energy in Japan, Facts and Figures*, April 1984, p. 25; also, J. D. Davis, *Blue Gold: The Political Economy of Natural Gas* (London: Allen & Unwin, 1984), pp. 210–211.

had experienced dramatic cost overruns, pushing combined costs to nearly $3 billion. The consortium petitioned for a rate hike, which pushed the wholesale price to $1.94, even before the project reached operating capacity in mid-1979. User groups tried to block this increase, since it would result in a retail price of $3.45.[59]

None of the other American LNG projects, meanwhile, had fared any better; there were just too many hurdles. The Trunkline/Algeria project won FPC approval, but even today it remains indefinitely delayed. Environmentalists blocked the Pacific Indonesia project until 1982, when its sponsors finally gave up. And the Secretary of Energy, James Schlesinger, blocked several other projects (see *Table 6-6*). Schlesinger did not view LNG as a secure or economically viable long-term substitute for domestic natural gas. LNG, he thought, created new foreign dependencies, and, in order to be sold at all, would require the benefit of undesirable price-averaging with cheap domestic gas.[60]

When the second oil-price shock struck in 1979, Algeria's new government demanded that El Paso now pay $6.11 for LNG, reflecting the energy-equivalent value of OPEC oil. The U.S. Department of Energy was unwilling to approve anything higher than the import price already negotiated bilaterally with Canada and Mexico ($4.47 per thousand cubic feet at the U.S. border). In April 1980, after several rounds of unsuccessful negotiations, Algeria cut off the flow of gas. Six months later, El Paso gave up and wrote off its share of the investment.[61] Collapse of this project marked the end of large-scale LNG development in the United States, to the considerable benefit of energy consumers. The shortage was all but over.

Reversing Course: The Second Shock

Energy policy in both Japan and the United States responded more rationally to the second oil-price shock than to the first. The second shock, precipitated in 1979 by the Iranian revolution, allowed OPEC to raise the price of crude oil from about $14 to $32 per barrel by March of 1980. The threat of shortage, however, proved fleeting. With conservation from the first shock already taking hold, this newest price hike flattened demand and tended to promote future excess capacity. The worldwide glut that ensued undermined and discredited the energy policies of the United States and Japan.

The United States was first to react. For a few months, at least, the shut off of Iranian oil exports (four million barrels per day) caused some panic in Congress. Secretary Schlesinger recognized a "window of opportunity" for deregulating oil prices before OPEC price hikes made that step politically infeasible. He convinced President Carter to decontrol oil prices gradually, as soon as mandatory controls expired, over the next thirty months. With this process in motion, Carter asked Congress to enact a windfall profits tax. The tax was designed to capture half the additional gross revenues that domestic producers would receive as oil prices rose. (The anticipated tax revenues were to be channelled to an energy trust fund, for developing synthetic fuels and subsidizing energy prices for the poor.)

TABLE 6-6
United States LNG Projects

Project/ Participants	Date Imports Started/Status	Volume Billion M^3	Importers	FPC Filing Date	Approval/ Denial Date
Distrigas/Algeria (I)	1973	1.4	Boston Gas	1970	1972(A)
Distrigas/Algeria (II)	cancelled	4.2	Boston Gas Brooklyn Union Gas	1977	
El Paso/Algeria (I)	1979/ suspended 1980	10.0	Southern Energy Co. Consolidated Natural Gas Columbia Gas Systems	1970	1972(A)
El Paso/Algeria (II)	cancelled	10.0	Transco Energy Consolidated Natural Gas Columbia Gas Systems	1973	1978(D)
El Paso Alaska	cancelled	20.0	various companies	1974	1977(D)
Pacific Indonesia [Pacific Gas & Electric, Pacific Lighting, and Pertamina]	cancelled	5.5	Pacific Gas & Electric Pacific Lighting	1973	1979(A)
Tenneco Atlantic [Sonatrach, Tenneco]	cancelled	10.0	Tennessee Gas Pipeline	1976	1978(D)
Trunkline [Sonatrach, Panhandle Eastern Pipeline]	suspended/ 1983	4.5	Panhandle Eastern Pipeline	1973	1977(A)

SOURCES: El Paso Natural Gas Co., "LNG Import Dockets"; also, J. D. Davis, *Blue Gold: The Political Economy of Natural Gas* (London: Allen & Unwin, 1984), pp. 210–211.

Typically, the tax proposal and trust fund now became legislative controversies that occupied Congress for nearly a year. The issues were all the more difficult because OPEC price hikes had inflated the estimated windfall profits to an estimated $227 billion. Producer and user groups alike fought desperately over the distributive effects of the program. But for once, the Carter Administration held the cards. Price controls were phased out gradually through February 1981, when the incoming Reagan Administration eliminated them altogether.

The upheaval in natural gas markets was even more dramatic. The Natural Gas Policy Act of 1978, part of the National Energy Act, provided for deregulating the price of new natural gas over five years. This, together with conservation and the permanent loss of some industrial users to alternate fuels, promptly restored equilibrium to gas markets. By 1981, a considerable surplus, or "gas bubble," had developed. This left high-cost gas, including imports from Canada and LNG, no longer competitive. In fact, pipeline companies that had scrambled to buy up high-priced, deregulated gas, subsequently had to back out of those fixed, long-term purchase contracts.

As domestic oil and gas markets were restored to surplus, political support for oil-company divestiture waned. In 1981, the Federal Trade Commission dropped its shared-monopoly case against the eight largest oil companies. As if by signal, a merger movement then swept the petroleum industry, revaluing assets and restructuring capacity. Several of the major firms, including Gulf Oil, and dozens of nonintegrated producers were bought outright by competitors. By 1984, the wave of mergers had spread to the gas pipeline sector as well. For the first time in more than a century, the United States had a free domestic market for primary fuels. This was indeed a new strategy.

In Japan during the early 1980s, when refiners raised prices to pass through the crude oil costs of the second shock, MITI did not interfere. This time around, the industry was too weak to absorb those increases, even temporarily. Demand for most petroleum products—especially naphtha, kerosene, and fuel oil—declined sharply between 1979 and 1982. As capacity utilization among domestic refiners fell from an already low 72 percent to 50 percent, the entire industry recorded losses in 1981, and the barest of earnings in other years.[62]

Given this new situation, the Petroleum Council completed a study of excess capacity in December 1981—a harbinger of changing strategy. As it turned out, the oil industry's troubles were even worse than suspected. As in the United States, the problem was not monopoly, but lack of concentration.[63] Then, too, a substantial shift had occurred in the pattern of demand, from the heavy fuel oils consumed by industry to the lighter distillates used by households and motorists. Ironically, this left the refiners that had cooperated most with MITI's industry policy in a very weak condition. Firms that pursued more independent strategies of refining and marketing gasoline were less enfeebled. Excess capacity and emphasis on heavy fuels had also discouraged technological modernization. And, although MITI never made it explicit, the agency's own stabilization policies had alleviated the need for either horizontal mergers or vertical integration. Thus, economies of scale remained suboptimal, and distribution channels relatively inefficient.[64]

Under these conditions, the Petroleum Council now recommended a restructuring of the industry by disposal of surplus refining capacity, modernization of remaining capacity, integration among refiners, distributors and wholesalers, and rationalization of the retail sector. These suggestions were disseminated by MITI and discussed in its councils and less formal channels in the months that followed. By May of 1982, consensus, based on desperation, was reached. A specific capacity reduction target of one million barrels per day was announced, and a Working Group for Upgrading Facilities was established.[65]

By the end of 1984, 970,000 B/D of the capacity reduction had reportedly been accomplished. The process of upgrading had begun, and several mergers and "business tie-ups" were either underway or already consummated. The process began in September 1983, with a merger of refining operations between Daikyo Oil and Maruzen Oil; then, in rapid succession, came the merger of Shell Oil and Showa, a tie-up for sales between Nippon Oil and Mitsubishi Oil, and tentative sales tie-ups between Esso Sekiyu and General Sekiyu and between Mobil Oil and Kygnus Sekiyu. MITI's overall goal was the formation of eight groups—none with less than 10 percent market share, and industry leaders (to provide stabilization) with 25 percent market share (refer back to *Table 6-3*). The tools MITI used to achieve its objectives included control of capacity expansion and modification, and low interest (5 percent) financing from the Japan Development Bank.[66]

The oil glut had implications for LNG as well. By 1981, Japan already depended on LNG systems for 4 percent of its energy supply. Projects under construction or in planning stages would eventually raise this figure to 8 percent (and to 18 percent of electric generating capacity). Liquefied natural gas had helped achieve a more diversified, clean, and secure source of supply. But it was a relatively expensive and inflexible alternative. At least since 1973, the twenty-year contracts contained not only price escalators tied to oil, but also take-or-pay clauses. With the second oil shock, LNG prices therefore increased dramatically; and by 1983, residential gas rates in Japan were three times as high as those in the United States. For electricity generation, LNG was no longer competitive with coal or nuclear power. But because of the take-or-pay terms, Japanese utilities were prevented from reducing their consumption of LNG in the face of slowing demand.

MITI now urged Japan's utilities to exercise their considerable market power, in what had become a buyer's market, to force fuel suppliers to renegotiate pricing formulas and take-or-pay clauses. This was exactly what was happening in the United States. At the same time, MITI began working with the utilities to improve the load factor of LNG-fired capacity by developing more commercial and industrial customers.[67]

These developments in domestic oil and LNG were part of the broader challenge that the second oil shock posed for Japan. After evolving its new strategy during two years of deliberation, MITI made the strategy explicit in September 1983:

> We must first work to guarantee security (of supply) and secondly to minimize cost. Thirdly, we must pursue the realization of an optimum energy supply-demand structure. . . . With the government's supplemental energy measures, the price mechanism is expected to prove the basic, efficient road to such an optimum supply-demand structure.[68]

In the new forecast, petroleum would continue to decline in importance, and the role of LNG would be curtailed. Nuclear power and alternative energy sources would take center stage in the 1990s. MITI would still provide guidance, but price would become a more important criterion.

Conclusion: Market-Conforming Energy Strategies

Imbalances in the world oil market over the past thirty-five years broadly shaped the energy strategies of both Japan and the United States. The patterns of policy were similar because market capitalism prevailed in the energy sectors of both countries (see *Table 6-7*).

Market structure was nearly as important a factor in shaping energy strategies, but with different effects in the two countries. In Japan, industrial users dominated the political process, at least prior to 1973. Oil refiners, although lacking influence, were sufficiently homogeneous so that policy was at least coherent. Electric and gas utilities were concentrated and influential, which no doubt facilitated policies to promote nuclear power and LNG. In the United States, the petroleum, natural gas, and electric utility sectors were exceedingly

TABLE 6-7
Market-Defined Energy Strategies

Japan	World Oil Market	United States
1. 1949–1961 Balanced coal & foreign oil	1949–1959 Emerging oil glut falling real price	1949–1958 Voluntary oil import controls
2. 1962–1973 Petroleum Law: cheap oil & stable industry	1960–1972 OPEC stabilized glut stable real price	1959–1972 Mandatory quotas high-priced oil & stable industry
3. 1974–1980 Secure & diverse supply	1973–1980 Shortages & rising prices	1973–1980 Secure supply & distributive equity
4. 1981–present Balance secure & low-cost supply	1981–present Glut and falling prices	1981–present Restoration of market equilibrium

fragmented and diverse. This meant that virtually any issue of energy policy had differential competitive impacts on particular companies. And, since producer interests were rarely coordinated, the policy process was generally chaotic. Industrial users were far less important than in Japan, so policy, in times of surplus, tended to be producer-oriented; in times of shortage, it favored motorists and residential fuel-users.

Implementation of energy policy was somewhat more effective—but not necessarily more efficient in the narrow economic sense—in Japan than in the United States. MITI simply had more control over the authorship of policy, and the Diet less, than their counterparts in America. MITI's policy tools, especially administrative guidance and the use of advisory councils to facilitate consensus, have no match in America.

MITI probably deserves credit for its oversight of a domestic refining industry capable of fulfilling the demands of miracle growth; for its relatively quick restoration of market-clearing prices after the first oil shock; and for its effective promotion of non-oil energy sources since 1973. On the other hand, MITI-men have tended to underutilize competition and entrepreneurship, and to excessively promote inefficient fuels. As a result, Japan's oil industry remains structurally inefficient, and gas and electric prices very high. In addition, some very inflexible long-term commitments have been made to foreign natural gas suppliers and to nuclear power.

In the United States, the Carter Administration deserves credit for decontrolling oil prices and phasing out the controls on natural gas. But for the most part, energy policy in America has weakened the structure and reduced the efficiency of its otherwise impressive energy industries. The Congress, as well as all the administrations since Franklin D. Roosevelt's, have repeatedly succumbed to interest-group pressures by creating (or tolerating) jerry-built and sometimes even absurd distributive schemes: natural gas price controls, oil import quotas, power-plant conversions, entitlements, and windfall profits taxes, among others. The ill effects of programs contrived in the name of "fairness" or "national security" have been legion.

From the comparison of energy policies in Japan and the United States, we can draw three important conclusions. First, the goals of national strategy have both substantive and procedural content, but in dramatically different proportions. As *Table 6-7* suggests, Japanese energy policy has been oriented primarily toward concrete performance objectives, while American policy has been preoccupied with process: competitive balance, distributive equity, and regulatory procedure.[69] Professor Chalmers Johnson has noted some recent signs of realignment between these perspectives in both countries. Perhaps so, but the United States still seems mired in procedural concerns that swamp attempts to set economic objectives. This is a luxury which, by the late 1980s, the United States may no longer be able to afford.

Similarly, the implementation of economic policy requires at least a minimum of administrative discretion and some institutional channels for meaningful deliberation. Japan has had these, the United States has not. In retrospect, the role of Congress in energy policy during the 1970s seems nothing less than a national embarrassment. The legislation Congress enacted was detailed far beyond its technical skills, making effective implementation by administrative agencies all but impossible. This situation was aggravated by constant and intensely politicized oversight, and by the virtual absence of legitimate channels of communication between business managers and bureaucrats. Problems of implementation could only be addressed at arm's-length, and be resolved only by adjudication. Certainly in areas of microeconomic policy, the imbalance between policy formation and administrative implementation is sorely in need of organizational reform with appropriate safeguards.

Finally, strategies and policy tools are effective when they conform reasonably well to the broad dimensions of the market. Guiding or adjusting domestic markets, to better serve the public interest, can work; simply bludgeoning them cannot. Bureaucrats in Japan and politicians in America underestimated or misunderstood the power of dynamic markets. Although MITI-men tried not to diverge too far from market-clearing prices, they seemed preoccupied with stabilization of industry structure. Accordingly, the petroleum industry did not begin to adjust seriously to changing patterns of demand or supply until the 1980s; meanwhile, inefficiency and excess capacity resulted.

In the United States, most congressmen treated energy policy as if supply, demand, and price were unrelated phenomena. Thus, conservation would be achieved by legislative mandate, and production would somehow be increased by quashing conspiracy. What might have been a more effective policy— selective use of financial incentives to nudge producers and consumers toward a more efficient relationship—was for the most part politically infeasible. And the price mechanism itself was deemed socially illegitimate by large numbers of policymakers.

Fortunately, competitive markets are usually powerful enough to resist long-run distortion. This is the great strength and basic commonality of the market economies of Japan and the United States. The greater the gap between supply and demand, or cost and price, the more intense becomes the economic and political pressure toward equilibrium. Eventually, pressures from producers and consumers force politicians to adjust. Thanks to the second oil shock, and to the more recent glut of oil, genuine adjustment has at last begun in the energy sectors of both countries.

CHAPTER 7

Coping With Crisis: Environmental Regulation

SUSAN J. PHARR AND JOSEPH L. BADARACCO, JR.

In January 1974, the B.F. Goodrich Company announced that within the past two years, three workers in its vinyl chloride (VC) plants had died of a rare and deadly cancer of the liver, angiosarcoma.[1] Virtually overnight, a prosperous worldwide industry that transformed the colorless gas VC into polyvinyl chloride (PVC), a ubiquitous plastic used for making flooring, upholstery, food wrapping, phonograph records, and even baby pacifiers, was thrown into disarray. In 1974, worldwide investment in VC and PVC equipment exceeded $8 billion. Shell, Conoco, Dow, Union Carbide, and B.F. Goodrich were among the major U.S. firms producing VC or PVC; most of the Japanese manufacturers were also large firms, many of them members of powerful *keiretsu* (enterprise groups) such as Mitsubishi, Mitsui, and Sumitomo. In both countries, thousands of people worked at VC and PVC plants, and hundreds of thousands fabricated PVC into final products.

Workers could be exposed to VC in several different ways: in plants that manufactured VC gas, in plants that converted VC into PVC, and in plants that fabricated PVC into final products. The urgent question confronting manufacturers of VC and PVC around the world, therefore, was how to reduce the exposure of all workers to this deadly gas.

In the United States, the B.F. Goodrich announcement set in motion a bitter, emotional struggle among officials of the Occupational Safety and Health Administration (OSHA), major chemical companies, and labor unions. Within six months, OSHA had begun to hold public hearings in Washington, D.C., at which hundreds of individuals testified on the health problems caused by VC exposure, and the likely costs and technological requirements for reducing VC exposure levels. The lines of the conflict were soon drawn. Union officials argued that VC was clearly a human carcinogen, and that any level of worker exposure was unsafe. Industry remained divided: although the major U.S. companies producing VC and PVC had begun efforts to reduce exposure levels before the hearings began, they could not agree on what standard constituted a danger. Some companies argued that OSHA's then-current VC standard of 500 parts per million (ppm) should remain in effect, while others advocated an interim "working level" of 50 ppm.

By May 1974, OSHA had taken a position. After deliberations lasting only a few weeks, OSHA officials announced a proposed VC "safe" standard at the "no detectable level," and set a date in late June for further public hearings.

From an industry perspective, the announcement was a bombshell. In public statements, industry officials called the proposed standard "impractical," "un-achievable," and "a disaster for the country." A spokesman for Firestone said that the standard "would literally cripple the industry." The Society of the Plastics Industry, an association representing most of the major plastics pro-ducers, released a study by Arthur D. Little, Inc., which concluded that a shutdown of VC-PVC production would cost 1.6 million jobs and reduce the gross national product by at least $65 billion. As the date set for hearings approached, one OSHA official predicted that they would be "the biggest show we've ever had."

When the June hearings opened, the rancor and acrimony of the previous months reached new levels. Public hearings lasted eight days, and the official record was held open until August, so that parties could submit further infor-mation. In the end, the VC record exceeded 4,000 pages and included over 800 oral and written submissions. The Department of Labor, industry and labor representatives, OSHA, other government agencies, public interest groups, independent experts, physicians, and specialists of all kinds presented tes-timony and cross-examined each other before an administrative law judge. Media coverage became intense.

In October 1974, OSHA published its final VC standard of 1 ppm, which would go into effect in January 1975. In effect, the standard represented little change from the "zero acceptable" ppm level proposed by OSHA earlier, sug-gesting to business that its arguments had fallen on deaf ears. Within *two minutes* of the announcement, B.F. Goodrich, Firestone, Union Carbide, and other major producers filed suit in various circuit courts in an attempt to overturn OSHA's ruling. All the industry petitions were then consolidated for review by the Second Circuit Court of Appeals in New York in a case called *Society of the Plastics Industry v. OSHA.* With both sides preparing to do battle, the AFL-CIO intervened on behalf of OSHA.

The court case itself produced a virtual reenactment of the earlier hearings, with attorneys for industry, OSHA, and labor presenting the same data and arguments of the previous summer. Industry attorneys cited the virtually un-animous testimony of company officials who agreed that the proposed stan-dard could not be met with existing technology. As at the hearings, they argued that a standard as low as 1 ppm could be supported by no proven medical justification. In January 1975, however, the court ruled in OSHA's favor, closing its remarks with this acid comment: "The examination of the 4,000 page record in this case has been a prodigious task aggravated by duplications of testimony, irrelevant exhibits and letters . . . and a generally blunderbuss approach in the petitioner's briefs." When industry appealed still again, the U.S. Supreme Court refused to hear the case. So, one year after the B. F. Goodrich announcement, with all legal channels exhausted, industry announced that it would "concentrate its resources on compliance."

By April 1976, tests administered by OSHA established that 90 percent of samples taken in VC and PVC industries were in compliance with the standards. The total cost of such compliance has been estimated at $200–280 million—a substantial sum, but a far cry from the staggering projections of Firestone and of many other industry studies. Three companies did close rather than operate under the new regulation, and 375 jobs were lost. Once again, however, this figure seems minuscule alongside the dire predictions of the industry-sponsored study by Arthur D. Little, which had predicted a loss of 1.6 million jobs. Industry had fought hard, but in the end, it complied—and with far fewer disruptions and lower costs than had been predicted.

In the U.S. response to the VC threat can be seen typical features of the American approach to the larger issue of environmental protection. That approach has been overwhelmingly adversarial: government and industry have tried to face each other down, and typically the victor has been decided in the courts. In general, the level of confusion has remained high, as a wide range of actors, including public interest lobbies, play a significant role after entering the fray. Yet the actual decision-making process remains quite formal. OSHA hearings, for example, are court-like proceedings at which parties testify and then are subject to cross-examination. Much attention focuses on the written record—on the wording of standards and the amassing of published testimony. On all sides of the battle, key roles are played by the lawyers who represent various participants and the judge who decides the outcome of the conflict. Though certain of these features vary with the particular environmental issue in question, the basic character of the American response must be regarded as adversarial in nature.

The United States versus Japan: Two Divergent Approaches

In Japan, the response to the growth of environmental regulation contrasts with the U.S. approach in almost every important respect. By extending this review of the VC case to include developments in Japan, we can study the two nations' methods directly, almost as a controlled experiment: both countries confronted the identical problem at precisely the same historical moment.

In Japan, B.F. Goodrich's first announcement reached a far smaller group of listeners, and the VC problem finally was resolved through cooperative rather than adversarial efforts. The Ministry of Labor, the Japan PVC Association, and, to a far lesser extent, trade unions representing workers in VC and PVC plants all played a role. The decision-making process consisted almost entirely of private, generally informal meetings among government officials and industry representatives—of which no public record was kept. Even labor, the sole "outsider" group whose views were solicited, entered this process only at the end, when some final regulations had to be specified. Again, the Ministry of Labor held no public hearings, and none of the parties went to court to challenge the standard that ultimately was set. Everywhere in this process, bureaucrats played key roles. Japanese companies stood as one (unlike chemical producers in the United States, who pulled and hauled in opposite directions at many points in the VC struggle). Throughout the discussions, virtually no lawyers intruded into the proceedings, except for legally trained Ministry of Labor officials, who gave the VC standard a routine check to insure that it complied with relevant statutes.

After the B.F. Goodrich announcement in January 1974, the Japanese response took shape quickly. Within two weeks, representatives of all Japan's VC and PVC producers had met in Tokyo and had received an official request from the Ministry of Labor for cooperation in solving the problem. The executive director of the Japan PVC Association was a former official of the Ministry of International Trade and Industry (MITI). He had stepped into his post by virtue of *amakudari* (literally, "descent from heaven"—the common Japanese practice of leaving bureaucratic posts for positions in industry), and he played a key role. He represented the Association, but kept in continuous communication with bureaucrats in the Ministry of Labor. By April of 1974, the Association had organized the Industrial Hygiene Committee to deal with the VC problem. The committee, and the Association itself, became the centerpiece of an informal network linking government officials, industry, and labor representatives through meetings, telephone conversations, and by the exchange of studies, documents, and memos. By May 1974, the Industrial Hygiene Committee of the PVC Association had developed a temporary emergency standard for VC of 50 ppm. Less than a month later, the Ministry of Labor issued emergency technical guidelines that were virtually identical to those recommended by the PVC Association.

In the months that followed, VC and PVC companies continued their efforts to lower VC exposure levels, step by step. In September, the PVC Association issued a second set of voluntary guidelines reducing VC exposure levels, this time to 25 ppm. A third set of guidelines came from the Association in November, recommending a drop to the level of 10 ppm or below. Each new set of standards had been agreed to by all of the Association's twenty-two member companies before any public announcement was made.

In developing its guidelines, the Japanese PVC Association did the type of work that, in the United States, was undertaken by OSHA. It reviewed information about the efforts in other countries to control VC exposure and dispatched two study missions, one to the U.S. and one to Europe, to review each situation firsthand. Present during American deliberations, but absent from the Japanese, were representatives of public interest groups; indeed, in Japan, even labor unions did not formally join the deliberations at this early stage.

While industry efforts were underway in late 1974, officials of Japan's Ministry of Labor conducted their own information gathering, and held internal discussions and bilateral meetings with labor representatives. By the end of 1974, at the request of the unions, the ministry convened more formal tripartite discussions among labor unions, ministry officials, and representatives of the PVC Association. In February 1975, after numerous additional formal and informal consultations among delegations from all three groups, and a joint industry-labor research mission to Europe, the Ministry of Labor issued a fourth set of technical guidelines. These had been circulated in advance both to industry and labor, so neither group was surprised at the new VC exposure level of 2 ppm. Already, discussions had clearly indicated that Japanese companies were prepared to comply both technically and financially with these standards. In fact, measurements of workplace exposure to VC made between December 1974 and February 1975 had shown that roughly 85 percent of the companies had already achieved exposure levels of 2 ppm; while 97 percent had levels below 3 ppm. In explaining the new standard, officials of the ministry and the PVC Association emphasized that the "spirit" of the guidelines encouraged the companies to try to reduce VC concentrations to the lowest possible levels, and that companies did not intend to rest once they had achieved the 2 ppm standard.

Two years after the B.F. Goodrich announcement—by the end of 1975—most Japanese companies were attaining levels of VC exposure under 1 ppm. The total cost of this compliance was approximately 22 billion yen ($100 million). Thus, Japan's cost of controlling VC exposure appears to have been roughly 20 percent less than that in the United States, as measured in cost per ton of VC and PVC production capacity. A small portion of this cost was defrayed by a subsidized loan from the Japan Development Bank. No Japanese plants were closed because of inability to meet the VC standard, and no jobs were lost. Moreover, no litigation occurred at any stage of the process. When company officials were asked why they had not taken legal action, they cited an "everlasting relationship" with government officials, which might be impaired by judicial action. Even more important, the consensual process that preceded the setting of a specific standard had left them with little or no reason to turn away from negotiations, to the courts.

Ironically, the U.S. regulations for VC exposure—for all the conflict and acrimony that surrounded them were finalized almost a year before Japan's; yet the resulting standards were virtually the same in both countries. What emerges from these two national experiences is important nevertheless: the processes of decision making illustrated in these two cases (rather than the results) reveal profound differences in American and Japanese approaches to regulatory issues concerned with the environment.

Cooperation versus Adversarialism

On its surface, the "cooperative" approach adopted by the Japanese in the VC case has much to recommend it over the adversarial approach that characterized the United States' response to the VC issue. Japanese industry officials were heavily involved in setting the standard for VC exposure; they gave labor a hearing in the process. In fact, informal consensual decision making in Japan, even when it severely limits the formal participation of outside groups, can, from one vantage point at least, be regarded as more "participatory" than the American rule-setting process, in which OSHA officials and judges reach their decisions in virtual secrecy. Furthermore, in the United States, OSHA officials seem to be cast as "regulatory czars" while industry leaders constantly "cry wolf;" unnecessary and burdensome disruptions block all parties from taking the more harmonious route followed by the Japanese to the same regulatory outcome.

In general, the Japanese approach to the vinyl chloride case fits comfortably with the widely held view that in Japan, business-government relations, government policymaking, and even decision making generally are cooperative and harmonious.[2] Most studies that have provided the basis for this modal view of Japanese policymaking and implementation, however, come within the domain of economic policymaking. Given the strong commitment to economic growth as a goal of the state in Japan, and a long tradition of close cooperation between government officials and the business community—going back to the symbiotic relation between samurai and merchants in feudal times—it should be no surprise to see non-adversarial decision making on economic issues. But to find government-business cooperation in the very different area of environmental regulation is another matter—especially when the inherent trade-offs between profitability and expenditures on pollution control are part of the decision.

Questions Raised by the VC Case

As we consider the cooperative response to environmental regulation in Japan alongside the far more adversarial U.S. approach to the same VC problem, two larger questions emerge. The first centers on the Japanese approach itself: to what extent is the cooperative pattern of policymaking found in the VC case to be regarded as typical of Japan's approach to environmental regulation in general? Here, to anticipate a bit, much of this chapter will provide an answer that details the special nature of the VC case in the area of environmental policymaking and regulation. As a victory of cooperation in Japan, it has been hard-won and based on changing historical circumstances. For the VC challenge, which arose in 1974, appeared just at a point in national history when Japan was emerging from its own adversarial period in handling environmental issues. In many ways, then, the VC issue must be regarded as a "best case" of Japanese government-business cooperation in environmental matters. For many reasons (to be discussed below) the VC case exhibits a level of government-business cooperation that has seldom been achieved anywhere in the world in the handling of pollution issues. With this said, however, the fact still remains that Japan's current pattern of government-business relations seems extraordinarily cooperative, as compared with the U.S.'s uniformly adversarial approach to environmental regulation.

This recognition brings us to a second question: what are the advantages and disadvantages of the two distinct approaches to environmental policymaking and regulation that are now in place in these two countries? Before beginning to answer, we first must understand how the Japanese regulatory response of the mid-1970s and 1980s came into being.

Three Eras of Environmental Regulation

In the post–World War II history of environmental regulation in Japan, government-business relations have been characterized by three distinct phases. In the first, which extended into the mid-1960s, that relationship can be characterized retrospectively as *tacitly collusive.* Government and business cooperated, but in order to avoid environmental regulation. This is not to say that the relationship was *consciously* collusive. Rather, government officials throughout the ministries, with only rare exceptions, were in general agreement that high levels of national growth were critical for Japan, and that such a goal necessarily took precedence over all others. A general consensus in government held that the state should devote its efforts toward sponsoring, rather than regulating, economic growth. Thus, when severe pollution problems began to emerge in Japan during the 1950s and early 1960s, governmental officials and the ruling Liberal Democratic Party stood back from taking regulatory action or, in other cases, from enforcing regulatory measures already in effect.

In effect, they took the side of business in pollution disputes, as the following review of one of Japan's earliest and most tragic pollution cases, which arose in the town of Minamata over the issue of mercury poisoning, illustrates. Before we turn to that example, however, it is important to note that in all industrial countries, the relationship between government and business on environmental issues initially was collusive. In that sense, developments in Japan were no different, at least in kind, from those in the United States and in other countries on the issue of pollution control. Even so, Japanese government officials themselves have admitted in retrospect that the lack of a regulatory effort in Japan prior to the mid-1960s made the country a "polluters' paradise."[3] So the Japanese situation must be regarded as extreme.

When significant changes did occur, government-business relations entered a second and dramatically different phase, dating from the mid-1960s. Here, we find relations characterized by an *adversarial* posture on both sides— during a stage that lasted for almost a decade. The struggle between government and business over the issue of auto emissions control, for example, vividly illustrates the combative nature of relations in this second phase. Then a new setting for policy emerged in the mid-1970s; and Japan entered a third, or *cooperative* stage, which we saw illustrated in the case of vinyl chloride and which has continued more or less to the present.

Of course, all Japanese pollution cases have not been handled in ways that allow each to be fitted neatly into one of the three phases. Even in an era characterized, in an overall sense, by tacit government-business "collusion," there were some cases of adversarial confrontation, when a minority of bureaucrats pressed business to comply with existing regulations. Similarly, in the "cooperative era" of the present, there are cases that reveal collusion or combat more than cooperation. By distinguishing the three eras, however, we gain a critical foundation for understanding how regulatory patterns in Japan have developed, and for examining in some detail how government-business relations in the area of pollution control have been evolving.

Tacit Collusion in the Early Years: The Minamata Case

If vinyl chloride constitutes a best case of Japanese government-business cooperation to control an environmental threat, mercury poisoning outbreaks in the form of Minamata disease could be considered a "worst case." The origins of this tragic episode can be traced to April 1956, when six or seven people—several of them children—living in the city of Minamata in southwestern Japan came down with a mysterious malady.[4] They and subsequent victims, of whom there were to be a total of over 1,000, with almost 5,000 others whose claims are still pending, displayed symptoms that later came to be identified as signs of organic mercury poisoning: difficulty with speech and walking, loss of peripheral vision, loss of feeling around the mouth and extremities, hearing impairment, stiffening of the muscles, and mental incapacitation.[5]

The disease had spread inexorably from contaminated fish to humans who consumed them, unaware of the danger. One of the first books on Japan's pollution problems to appear in English provides a vivid description.

> By the early 1950s, a number of Minamata fishermen and their families were experiencing the disquieting symptoms of a previously unknown physical disorder. Robust men and women who had formerly enjoyed good health suddenly found their hands trembling so violently they could no longer strike a match. They soon had difficulty thinking clearly, and it became increasingly difficult for them to operate their boats. Numbness that began in the lips and limbs was followed by disturbances in vision, movement, and speech. As the disease progressed, control over all bodily functions diminished. The victims became bedridden, then fell into unconsciousness. Wild fits of thrashing and senseless shouting comprised a later stage, during which many victims' families, to keep the afflicted from injuring themselves or others, resorted to securing them with heavy rope.[6]

The earliest victims had been brought to a hospital attached to the Minamata factory of the Chisso Corporation, a large chemical company headquartered in Tokyo. Chisso was the major local industry in Minamata City. Within a few weeks, the director of the hospital, Dr. Hajime Hosokawa, who became a key figure in the story, officially reported the unidentified disease to the Minamata City Health Center which, soon after, set up a "committee on the strange disease." The prefectural government became involved by asking Kumamoto University, the major university in the prefecture, to study the disease, with support from the national Ministry of Education. By November 1956, the Ministry of Health and Welfare had set up a special subcommittee on the disease under its Research Committee on Food Hygiene, one of the *shingikai* (advisory councils) made up of ex-bureaucrats, representatives of business groups, university professors and other professionals, that play key decision-making roles in Japan.

At that point, little more than a few months after the initial outbreak, city, prefectural, and national officials in two government ministries had already taken preliminary action in responding to a potential health crisis. Industry was not yet involved, since no one had suggested a link between the disease outbreak and any industry source. In fact, only after research had begun to point at Chisso Corporation did a pattern of what might be termed tacit collusion begin to emerge. Results that indicated some type of pollution as the cause of the outbreak came from the Kumamoto University study group as early as November 1956, when they reported that the strange disease was caused by eating fish that had been contaminated by a heavy metal, which they could not yet identify. By September 1958, this group had linked the disease to organic mercury, and by 1959, they were prepared to specify organic mercury as the cause of the outbreak. Tracing the problem to Chisso itself came as the result of the work of Dr. Hosokawa, director of Chisso's own hospital, who discovered in October 1959 that cats which were given drainage water discharged by Chisso showed precisely the same symptoms as those of "Minamata disease," as the malady had come to be called. Meanwhile the number of Minamata patients continued to grow and the Ministry of Health and Welfare authorized the modest sum ¥6 million ($16,667) to help subsidize a special hospital for them.[7]

The Business Response

Despite the increasing horror of the problem and the growing protest movement led by the victims, their supporters, and fishermen whose livelihood was threatened by the contamination of fish in Minamata Bay, it was almost a decade before either government or industry acted decisively to bring the mercury pollution of Minamata Bay under control. Chisso adopted the position that the causal link between organic mercury poisoning of the victims and its plant's discharges remained unsubstantiated. In the single act that later was to prove most damaging, the company ordered its hospital director, Dr. Hosokawa, to stop his experimental work at the point when his results had established that consumption of food mixed with the plant's discharges caused mercury poisoning in cats, and to keep his findings secret.[8] Also, Chisso worked out a settlement with a key victims' group whereby it paid ¥300,000 ($833) to families of victims who had died, ¥100,000 ($278) to adult patients, and ¥30,000 ($83) for patients under 20. These disbursements were explicitly marked as "sympathy payments" rather than compensation, and were made only on the condition that the recipients waive their right to future amounts even if it was later proved definitively that Chisso drainage had caused the disease.[9] Chisso enjoyed strong backing, especially in the early years, from the Japan Chemical Industry Association. A study group led by the Association—of the very kind that almost a decade and a half later would prove so effective in addressing the VC problem—consistently provided evidence to challenge the mounting body of findings linking mercury poisoning to plant discharges.

The Governmental Response

Government officials held back from regulatory action. The key decision that was to shape the nature of the government's response over the period ahead finally was made in November 1959, when the Ministry of Health and Welfare's special subcommittee on the Minamata problem prepared a draft report stating definitively that Minamata disease was caused by consuming contaminated fish. On the critical issue of causation, however, the subcommittee stated that it could only "be inferred" that the contamination was caused by Chisso. The subcommittee was unable to go further, it claimed, because Chisso had refused to submit a drainage sample to the Ministry of Health and Welfare. According to ministry officials, questions involving factory drainage fell within MITI's jurisdiction; thus, the Ministry of Health and Welfare had been unable to force Chisso to submit the sample.

There is no evidence to suggest that MITI ever had attempted to pursue the matter. When the subcommittee offered its draft report to the Ministry of Health and Welfare, ministry officials took the position that, in the absence of definitive scientific proof, it was unwise to say anything about causality. So the subcommittee's final report dropped all reference to Chisso and to the "inferred" possibility that the company might be responsible for the disease. Having submitted its report, the subcommittee was dissolved, and a four-ministry liaison conference on the Minamata problem, established by the Health and Welfare Ministry, MITI, the Economic Planning Agency, and the Ministry of Agriculture, Forestry and Fisheries, took up its task. But the group met only four times, and died out in March 1961 without producing any report. In fact, no further official action to address the Minamata problem with regulatory or other measures occurred for a number of years. Not until September 1968, twelve years after the outbreak of the disease, did the Minister of Health and Welfare finally acknowledge officially, in a statement that was de-

scribed as "the government's unanimous view," that Minamata disease had
been caused by discharges from the Chisso factory.[10]

Tacit Collusion as a Policy Response

To hold that the Japanese government-business relationship in these early
years was "tacitly collusive" is, of course, a simple statement that masks a
complex reality. The main intent is to suggest that—in contrast to the cooperative pattern that had emerged by the mid-1970s, in which government and
business worked together to address pollution issues—the two key parties in
this first era both held back from dealing with a horrible problem. In effect,
each cooperated with the other to evade the issue. Thus, in dealing with
Minamata victims in the early 1960s, Chisso was able to argue that no official
body had linked mercury poisoning to Chisso, while government officials
could profess to be powerless in the face of Chisso's refusal to submit drainage
samples for government testing. Here, a crucial issue emerges: whether regulatory measures then in force did, in fact, empower government officials to act,
had they chosen to do so.

On this question, many knowledgeable observers are unequivocal, pointing
to the regulatory powers provided to government (both the Economic Planning Agency and MITI) under two key laws passed in 1958—the Public Water
Zone Conservation Law and the Law on Industrial Effluents. The long period of
government inaction on the first outbreak almost certainly contributed to a
second outbreak of the disease, which occurred in Niigata prefecture during
the mid-1960s.[11] According to one bureaucrat who played a key role in spur-
ring the government to act in the Minamata case, the Japanese government
became culpable in 1960, when Chisso failed to do more than change its
drainage site,[12] with the result that signs of fish contamination soon appeared
again. "At that point," he states, "the government should have taken action."[13]

It is hardly a coincidence that these troublesome developments took place
in a period when Japan was experiencing phenomenal economic growth.
Prime Minister Ikeda's national income-doubling plan, announced in 1960,
united government and business efforts in a common pursuit of growth. Until
the late 1960s, legislative measures that occasionally were enacted to address
Japan's growing pollution problems were either defeated on the grounds that
they would retard economic recovery and growth, or, when passed, were
seldom enforced. In 1958, for example, the Ministry of Health and Welfare
drafted an Environmental Pollution Prevention Standard Act, but the legislation was opposed by virtually every other ministry as well as by business
interests, all claiming that it would impede economic growth. Even the federation representing local governments throughout Japan opposed the measure.[14]
In a larger sense, then, the government-business relationship that took shape in
this earliest period can most favorably be described as cooperation to achieve

a national goal, rather than collusion to avoid regulatory action on pollution issues. The net effect, however, was identical.

The Policy Environment Shifts: Onset of the "Stormy Period"

By the mid-1960s, new forces were gathering that were to transform the nature of the government-industry response to pollution problems in Japan. Although no single episode stands out, a convergence of several factors dramatically altered the way in which government officials and the public came to perceive environmental issues. As pressure for action mounted on many sides, officials were forced into the role of adversaries vis-à-vis industries which, in the normal course of their activities, were contributing to pollution. Today, many participants refer to this era as "the stormy period."

Factors Transforming the Policy Environment

At least three sets of factors helped to create the change: first, a variety of domestic forces that came to press in on government; second, dramatic events that called attention to a mounting environmental crisis; and third, pressures from abroad.

DOMESTIC FORCES

Initially, a wide range of domestic forces created a loose coalition to bring changes in Japan's response to pollution issues. Here, victims' groups played a key role. Minamata disease was not the only pollution disease that had left many Japanese with highly visible deformities and impairments. *Itai-itai* disease due to cadmium poisoning, Yokkaichi asthma caused by severe air pollution, and serious ailments resulting from PCB poisoning had all appeared in Japan by the early 1960s. Each outbreak brought forth new victims' groups seeking care, compensation, and redress for suffering. In this important respect the Japanese environmental struggle—in which human life appeared to hang in the balance—was quite different from the American struggle, in which threats to wildlife and wilderness motivated the early environmental movement and in which the health effects of pollution took less dramatic forms.

By supporting the humane appeals of victims' groups, and then taking on pollution issues at the local level, Japanese citizens' movements provided strong reinforcement. By 1973, it is estimated that 10,000 local disputes over pollution had sprung up throughout Japan.[15] They remained highly localized and never converged to form a truly national organization or a permanent public interest lobby of the American type. Still, these local groups kept attention focused on pollution problems, and thus they created a groundswell of pressure on politicians at all levels of government to address them.

The media also played a dominant role in developments, serving as a powerful and ever-present watchdog of the public interest.[16] Certainly, no major social issue in postwar Japan received more media coverage than did the pollution problem during the mid-1960s. Each of the national dailies assembled teams of reporters—science writers, political reporters, local news reporters, editors, and others—to cover the pollution story. Of course, as a part of the press club system widely used by the Japanese media, each government ministry also had its own team of reporters on more or less permanent assignment there. During the "stormy era," however, the teams swelled dramatically, as the public clamored for stories about the government's response to the latest pollution issue.

As Japanese media coverage mounted, public opinion began to shift toward the view that pollution control had become essential, even if control meant some slowdown in economic growth. This perspective, however, proved surprisingly slow to take shape in Japan. In communities where pollution disease appeared, the public often shunned the victims, many of whom were poor or of the working class. Initially, their maladies were attributed to their own bad hygiene or inferior lifestyle; and, once protest movements began to form, the patients and their supporters frequently were seen as troublemakers who were putting their own interests before the economic and social well-being of the community. Demands for compensation were regarded by many Japanese as manifestations of greed. Such attitudes reflected Japan's cultural emphases on self-denial, aversion to conflict, and the primacy of the welfare of the group or community over that of the individual.[17] Media attention thus challenged basic cultural assumptions, aiding a process of social change in which Japanese public opinion shifted, especially in large cities, toward support for pollution control.

In addition to victims' groups, citizens' movements, the media, and public opinion, two other domestic forces were important in altering the climate of feeling about pollution in Japan: the activities of progressive local governments, and court rulings (resulting from litigation brought by victims' groups). Although the Liberal Democratic Party (LDP) has kept a firm hold on national power in Japan since 1955, a growing number of local administrations, particularly in large metropolitan areas, came into the hands of opposition parties, notably the Japan Socialist Party. By the mid-1960s, progressive local governments began to use pollution issues as a way of challenging national authority. National politicians and officials in turn felt increasing pressure to act and recapture the initiative. Notably, the popular socialist administrations of Tokyo and Yokohama challenged national government officials in their own backyard. By the early 1970s, key court rulings favoring victims of Minamata disease, *itai-itai* disease, and Yokkaichi asthma also gave legitimacy to the growing movement, both inside and outside government, to control pollution. In particular, these rulings provided vital support for the embryonic Japanese Environment Agency (formed in 1971), when it began to take regulatory action that challenged business interests.

POLLUTION EVENTS

Meanwhile, pollution in Japan seemed to have become a full-fledged crisis, as environmental conditions continued to deteriorate. Japanese high-growth policies of the 1960s—while they did bring prosperity to many communities—produced unmistakable evidence of pollution in rural areas that had been targeted for rapid development. Every pollution outbreak brought its own political reaction. Air pollution at Yokkaichi and the asthma victims it produced, for example, encouraged a citizens' group in Mishima City, in Shizuoka prefecture—another region slated for "special industrial development"—to organize under the slogan, "No More Yokkaichi Cities." They actually managed to force an abandonment of the local plan for industrial development.

Continuing appearances of environmental deterioration during the late 1960s and early 1970s kept public attention fixed on pollution problems. Typical incidents occurred in 1970: in May, a physician's group testing the blood of residents in one of Tokyo's most densely populated and heavily trafficked areas reported startlingly high levels of lead content, thus encouraging a public reaction of panic.[18] Two months later, in another part of Tokyo, some forty high school students fainted, overcome by what was diagnosed as photochemical smog. These events, so near at hand, made it impossible for government and business decision makers to ignore pollution.

THE FOREIGN FACTOR

As a final factor, developments abroad had major impact on the growing campaign for pollution control in Japan. As the vinyl chloride case indicates, and as numerous studies of Japanese decision making have shown, not only are Japanese decision makers responsive to *gaiatsu* (external pressure) per se; they are also remarkably sensitive to international developments in a general sense, and take them into account in shaping Japan's policies.[19] During the late 1960s, the message Japan was picking up from both Europe and the United States was that the world was declaring war on pollution. In addition, there was a growing fear that Japan was gaining an international reputation for being a do-little nation in regard to pollution. Government officials attending environmental symposia abroad were shocked to hear Japan referred to as the most polluted country in the world.

Later in the "stormy period," well after Japan had enacted a dramatic series of regulatory measures to control pollution, media coverage of the 1972 world conference on environmental issues in Stockholm rekindled Japanese urgency. Here, the shocking physical condition of a delegation of Minamata victims drew world attention. As the media portrayed Japan as the ultimate example of environmental neglect, the reaction at home was national shame. There was also considerable anger at the victims, who, after receiving compensation and seeing numerous anti-pollution measures passed, continued to characterize

Japan as a land of uncontrolled pollution. In several complex ways, then, developments abroad helped to alter domestic attitudes.

The convergence of so many influences inside and outside Japan naturally placed enormous burdens on government officials and politicians alike. They were under pressure from many sides to control pollution through legislation and regulatory action. Together, domestic and international influences were forcing government into a position that was essentially adversarial vis-à-vis business interests—or at least more adversarial than at any other time in the postwar period. To illustrate how government-business relations took this new shape, we shall concentrate on a case study from that era, and look closely at the story of emissions standards in Japan.

Adversarialism in the "Stormy Period": The Struggle Over Auto Emissions Control

Auto pollution poses an extraordinary problem for Japan. Within a land area less than the size of California, the Japanese people operate some 45 million autos.[20] Traffic congestion is such that even in many "rural" areas it is far faster to take public transportation than to drive, and many Japanese in large cities seldom drive their cars out of fear of relinquishing a hard-won parking space. Yet the prosperity of the 1960s, directly rooted in Japan's national plan for income-doubling, spurred a countrywide desire for car ownership. By 1970, outbreaks of photochemical smog, caused in part by auto pollution, were becoming common in urban areas. Japanese autos did not pollute more than American cars did; indeed, since their average size was smaller, Japanese engines polluted less. Yet the rapidly growing concentration of autos in Japan after 1960, combined with an absence of strict auto emissions standards, made Japanese people increasingly aware of auto pollution.

EARLY DEVELOPMENTS

This Japanese awareness may be dated from the tempestuous period leading up to the passage of the 1967 Basic Law for Environmental Pollution Control. The act represented the first attempt in Japan to formulate a comprehensive framework for dealing with pollution. The major focus of the law was pollution from industrial plant discharges, but the widespread coverage of the problem in Yokkaichi had focused national attention on air quality. Already, a special advisory group under the Prime Minister's office had—over objections from the auto industry—set a requirement that cars produced after 1966 must have engines that kept carbon monoxide (CO) low. The *gaiatsu* factor was also at work, since Japanese cars destined for the California market were required after 1968 to meet strict hydrocarbon (HC) emissions standards. Inevitably, the Japanese auto industry soon came under criticism for resisting domestic standards that it had already met in cars designed for export. During the late 1960s the Ministry of Health and Welfare began to spar with the Ministry of Transport over tightening the standards for both CO and HC emissions.

1970 as a Watershed Year

In the epic year 1970, fourteen major environmental laws swept through what came to be known as the "Pollution Diet." Among the new measures was a fundamental revision of the Basic Law for Environmental Pollution Control which had been passed in 1967. The old version included a clause, controversial at the time, that "Preservation of the living environment must always be in harmony with economic prosperity." This phrase had provided a mainstay to industry in its resistance to pollution control measures. Now, the revised 1970 version simply omitted the "harmony clause" leaving the old arguments behind. Also of immediate relevance to the auto emissions question was another passage, this one in a revised Air Pollution Control Law, which provided that auto exhaust control standards henceforth were to be set by administrative ordinance. So, after the work of the "Pollution Diet," the stage was set for combat between government officials and leaders of the auto industry over the standards.

Government Takes the Initiative

In 1971, the bureaucratic challenge was to implement the pollution laws that had been passed the previous year, or, in effect, to generate the political energy to get things done. Implementation involved three interrelated tasks: first, by keeping public opinion directed at pollution questions, to generate pressure on bureaucrats, politicians, and business alike; second, to create and then maintain a united front within bureaucracy and thus support the entire implementation effort; and third, to keep the politicians at bay. Given the longstanding close ties between Japan's ruling party and the business community, LDP politicians naturally were under strong pressure from industry to side with business on regulatory issues. Overall, then, the key to implementation was to keep a steady pressure—exerted by the media, the opposition parties, and public opinion—on the politicians. This steady pressure made political intervention into regulatory issues a very risky game.

In July 1971, the Japanese Environment Agency was established and given the task of coordinating governmental initiatives on pollution control. As it carried out the work of generating political energy on all three fronts, no issue appeared to demand more attention than did the question of auto emissions standards, since the lead poisoning scare and the photochemical smog incident in Tokyo (both in 1970) had increased Japanese concern over auto exhausts. Buichi Oishi, a physician-turned-politician-turned-agency-head, set the conflict in motion with a single cannon shot. After little more than two months in office as the first head of the agency, he requested that the agency's newly formed advisory council study how to control auto emissions, specifically CO, HC, and nitrogen oxide (NOx); and he made known his own preference that the council adopt the U.S. "Muskie Law" as Japan's national standard.

No move could have angered the Japanese auto industry more. The "Muskie

Law," actually designated the amended Clean Air Act, had been approved by the U.S. Congress in 1970. Introduced by Senator Edmund Muskie, the bill imposed uniform auto emission standards that were the strictest in the world. The law required that U.S. automakers (and foreign producers who wanted to sell in the American market) reduce their CO and HC levels 90 percent by 1975, and their NOx level similarly by 1976.

In the United States, this law had been met with hostility from the auto industry, especially on two counts. First, the law "forced technology;" that is, it set regulatory standards that could not be met with existing technology, on the premise that doing so would spur innovation. Second, the American auto emissions standards (and the deadlines for achieving them) were, in the final analysis, arbitrary. No defensible, firm scientific basis existed for calculating how much of a reduction in auto emissions would be necessary to achieve any desired health effect; the 90 percent American reduction figure represented little more than a political judgment by Congress.[21] Thus, for Oishi to have pointed his advisory committee in the direction of the "Muskie Law" seemed a radical step. Even today, Japanese auto industry executives, and those bureaucrats sympathetic to the industry position, react with anger when reminded of the Environment Agency's early initiatives on auto pollution. Said one former MITI bureaucrat who, in the climate of the times, had been forced to help implement the "Japanese Muskie Law": "The Environment Agency officials were like clowns on the stage. They had no ideas of their own, so they just borrowed whole a bad U.S. law that had no scientific basis to begin with."

How the standards set out in the U.S. Clean Air Act won favor with Oishi and the newly formed agency is a story in itself. Before the Japanese Environment Agency was created, a special office on pollution control existed as a part of the Prime Minister's office. In June 1971, as the Environment Agency was about to be announced, the deputy director of this special office attended a U.S.-Japan conference on environmental pollution problems in Washington, where the Clean Air Act dominated discussion. By the time this deputy director returned to Tokyo, he was convinced that Japanese standards should match those set out in the American law. (No other example better shows how the "foreign" factor works.) When the deputy director publicly supported the U.S. law as Japan's standard, Prime Minister Sato, reflecting the mood of the day, quickly endorsed this view. Oishi, in turn, picked up the cue when he came in as the Liberal Democratic Party's choice for Environment Agency head a month later.

According to Oishi, however, he consulted no one in his party before pressing for Japan's adoption of American standards. Even though Sato was supportive, Oishi knew that most members of the LDP would oppose these standards—especially representatives of the auto industry, who claimed that the American standards would be impossible to meet in Japan. They urged him to change his mind, "but I said no to all."[22] Based on his discussions with scholars, and with bureaucrats who had just been assigned to the new agency, Oishi felt convinced that the U.S. law was the strictest and therefore best law on auto emissions standards. "This was a case," he said, "in which *nemawashi* [preparatory "root-binding" activity or preliminary discussions—in this instance, within the ruling party] would have been useless. The opposition parties completely supported the Agency's position on autos. The public favored it, too. If I had consulted with others in the party, I know what they would have said."[23] Oishi thus acted on his own, and in the climate of the times, no one in the party was in a position to challenge him.

On receiving its instructions from Oishi in the fall of 1971, the newly formed advisory council of the Environment Agency established an Experts Subcommittee on Automobile Pollution to look into the question of what standards were most appropriate for Japan. Less than a year later, the Experts Subcommittee had completed its interim report, which proposed regulatory standards. These were adopted officially by the Environment Agency in October 1972; and so closely did they parallel the standards of the U.S. Clean Air Act of 1970 that they soon came to be called the Nipponban Masukīhō (Japanese Muskie Law).

The Business Response

What the agency actually announced was a "regulatory outline": it set a general standard for auto emissions, in average grams per kilometer, but did not establish maximum permissible limits nor define the measurement (or "mode") to be used in determining compliance with the regulation. In recent years, environmental issues have often been dealt with in Japan according to the "cooperative" pattern of decision making described at the outset of the chapter, which works through informal meetings between the regulating agency and industry representatives. During the highly charged "stormy period," however, informal meetings alone could not resolve all the differences. Resistance from the auto industry was too great, and in addition, disunity among auto companies made any single industry position impossible to articulate. Led by the large manufacturers, the Japanese auto industry mounted sporadic opposition that reached its climax in April 1973. At that time, the United States itself postponed for one year any implementation of the very standards that the Japanese industry was being asked to meet, leaving many Japanese industry leaders angry at the seemingly unyielding pressure from the bureaucracy. With government-industry relations testy, Japan's Environment Agency, in May and June of 1973, resorted to holding closed hearings with each of the automakers, one by one, to discuss technological problems and to determine both the maximum permissible limits and the method of measurement.

At these hearings, the larger automakers (notably Toyota and Nissan) testified that technologically they could meet the standards, but that numerous problems remained. They held that time was too short to ask that the standards on CO and HC be applied to all models, and they argued that the 1975 standards should apply only to a portion of the models being produced. Pointing to the recent U.S. decision to postpone enforcement of the Muskie Law standards, they held this delay to be wholly rational and appropriate. Their arguments gained further backing when, late in 1973, OPEC triggered a world oil crisis. Now, Japan's automakers argued that stricter emissions standards would mean higher energy costs.

That same fall, American automakers gained a swift reprieve from emissions standards with the same argument. In November 1973, Senator Muskie himself—father of Japan's "Muskie Law"—introduced into the U.S. Congress a bill that would allow a temporary relaxation of environmental standards in the face of the oil crisis.[24] In Japan, however, objections by the auto industry attracted far less sympathy from the media and the public. So in January 1974, the Environment Agency proclaimed the world's strictest standards for carbon monoxide and hydrocarbon emissions from autos, and upheld the 1975 deadline for meeting them. The Japanese "Muskie Law" had been put into operation.

Adversarialism as a Policy Response

The developments described so far, from the early discussions of emissions standards in the late 1960s to the struggle over CO and HC levels that came to a close in 1974, show some degree of adversarialism in relations between government and business in Japan. Emissions standards themselves were recommended by the Japanese Environment Agency's advisory council without any consultation with business; and they were pushed forward as Japan's proposed standards despite protests from the country's leading automakers. In all this, the traditions of consensus and accord, and of finding a middle ground, that have characterized government-business relations in so many domains of policy—including their joint response to the later vinyl chloride case—were sorely lacking.

From its beginning, the Japanese adversarial pattern (in which the government emerged as victor in early regulatory battles) displayed two significant characteristics. First was the unified front presented by government bureaucrats. Though some ministries (such as MITI and Transport) were only reluctantly swept along, they had little recourse, given the prevailing climate of feeling, but to join in a struggle against the auto industry. Such cooperation seems all the more remarkable when we consider that the fledgling Environment Agency, with a key role to play, had little prestige in the hierarchy of ministries and agencies. So its success during the stormy period must be accounted for in terms of the other forces discussed earlier: the media, public opinion, citizens' movements, victims' groups, progressive local administrations, and court rulings. All these proved instrumental in keeping domestic pressure on decision makers. Other pressures from abroad, particularly the influence of the U.S. Clean Air Act as a usable model for Japan, also played a role, as did the march of successive pollution scandals. From this unlikely mixture of elements grew the Agency's success in harnessing political energy in Japan and then putting into practice the strict auto emissions standards.

A second characteristic of the Japanese situation also proved important: the industrial disunity that split the ranks of the auto companies. The division began to appear in the early fall of 1972, when two of the smaller companies, Honda and Toyo Kogyo (Mazda), refused to join with large car-makers in opposing a "Muskie Law" for Japan. Then in February 1973, the same two companies startled the world by announcing that they already had produced engines capable of meeting the proposed CO and HC standards. They reaffirmed that position in hearings at the Japan Environment Agency the following summer. These claims, however, did not prevent the larger companies from attacking the standards. The giants shifted their arguments to place more emphasis on the "foreign factor," by pointing out that the United States had already postponed enforcement. Thus, during this era, the auto industry's bargaining position in discussions with government officials was seriously impaired by disunity in the ranks.

The Emergence of the Cooperative Pattern

It is difficult to distinguish a precise dividing line between the Japanese era of adversarialism in government-business relations and a more recent one of cooperation. As we noted earlier, in any given period of history a number of cases simply do not fit our classification. Yet, without fixing an exact date, we begin to find increasing evidence of a critical shift toward greater cooperation between government and business in the events of 1974 and after.

Certain profound changes in the Japanese policy environment have paved the way for a more cooperative approach. First has come a decline in public concern with environmental pollution as an issue. This does not mean that the public has ceased to support pollution control. On the contrary, public opinion surveys suggest that the Japanese continue to see environmental issues as of national importance. What has declined is what sociologists call "issue salience"—the public's sense of immediate personal interest in environmental issues.[25] Since the mid-1970s, a feeling has been growing that the environmental crisis is no longer a crisis.

In Japan, this change has resulted from a decline in virtually all the forces that earlier had pressured public officials on pollution questions. The citizens' movements born in the mid-1960s for example, were already disappearing by the mid-1970s. By that time, too, many pollution victims had received compensation in court or out-of-court settlements. Indeed, by the late 1970s and early 1980s there was growing suspicion that many still-pending claims were weak or even spurious.[26] Again, media attention began to flag by the mid-1970s, as local governments shifted their concern to other issues, and many progressive administrations were voted out of power. All together, the various domestic forces that had gathered behind environmental issues to change Japan during the era from 1967 to 1974 gradually began to erode. At the same time, developments abroad ("the foreign factor") shifted direction, thereby pushing the Japanese to move, not toward vigorous pollution control measures, but away from them. In the post-oil crisis era, industrial countries favored a cautious approach to any measures that might hinder fuel savings. Indeed postponements in the United States in applying the legal standards of the Clean Air Act dramatically altered the U.S. image in Japan in the environmental field: America, the former leader, now became a backslider in environmental regulation. In Japan, among automakers and their allies within government, who had already pledged early compliance with the world's strictest CO and HC standards, considerable bitterness appeared as the Americans deserted the cause. Some Japanese went so far as to argue that Japan had been duped.[27] Yet the march of "pollution episodes" that characterized the stormy era had also slowed by the mid-1970s, and some notable improvements in urban air quality worked to soothe what remained of public unrest.

These changes in the broader policy environment had a net effect of relieving pressure on public officials to address the issue of pollution control. The strong, unified front with which public officials had pursued environmental issues during the stormy era, and that had set them at loggerheads with industry, now simply broke down. Ministries such as MITI and the Ministry of Transport, earlier forced to toe the government's line against business, now began first to pull away, and then gradually to ally with business in moderating future pollution control measures. This shift to cooperation can be clearly shown in the auto emissions case. During the stormy era, the Environment Agency held the lead role in orchestrating the government's position on emissions standards; but gradually other agencies began to assert greater influence. In June 1976, for example, MITI set up a new Subcommittee on NOx Pollution Prevention, under its powerful Advisory Council on Industrial Structure. This move was widely regarded as a victory for automakers.[28] By wresting a portion of bureaucratic initiative on NOx regulation from the hands of the Environment Agency and pressing to see it transferred to MITI, business interests strengthened their own position in future decision making on pollution.

Meanwhile, a change on the business side of the equation also helped to move that relationship toward greater cooperation. Just as unity diminished on the side of government, so it increased among existing business interests, which kept locating more common ground. Again, the auto emissions case vividly illustrates this change: whereas the early years of struggle were marked by disunity and conflict among automakers, by 1974 the entire industry stood together in calling for a two-year postponement of the NOx standard, which originally had been scheduled to go into effect in 1976. Their unified position helped automakers gain a sympathetic hearing from the Environment Agency's chief advisory council in the fall of 1974; and later they gained the formal postponement.

In effect, then, a decline in unity on the government side combined with a growth of unity among business to force government into a pattern of greater cooperation with industry over pollution issues. Yet this analysis remains incomplete, for it ignores the vital element of a profound change in consciousness that occurred in Japan over the issue of environmental protection, and that came to encompass businessmen, bureaucrats, and the public alike. In Japan, all parties shifted over time toward the mutual recognition that pollution control had become a necessity. In contrast to the early era of tacit collusion, when government and business had, in effect, cooperated to *avoid* pollution control, these same parties have more recently cooperated in full recognition that some degree of pollution control is unavoidable and perhaps even desirable.

All the basic elements of the cooperative approach to decision making were illustrated in Japan's response to the vinyl chloride crisis described at the outset of this chapter. In that episode, a small number of primary actors worked together to set regulations. Since that time, the number of parties whose views actually get aired has often been reduced still further, thus making cooperation easier.

The cooperative relationships here may be illustrated by reference to the corners of a triangle. At one corner sit government officials; at a second, the representatives from the industry affected; and at the third corner, the advisory council to the appropriate ministry or agency, where bureaucrats and businessmen, along with representatives of other groups, meet. Of course, the power relations among the corners will vary, depending on the ministry concerned and the specific issue. In the VC case, for example, the industry association proved so effective in responding to the crisis that both government officials and their advisory council found little to do except approve industrial efforts at self-regulation. Yet in similar cases, such advisory councils often have played the dominant role. For example, as decision making on auto emissions issues shifted, after 1975, from adversarial to cooperative, the advisory council of the Japanese Environment Agency took on an increasingly important role.[29]

In other cases, government bureaucrats themselves exercised a dominant influence. But all the recent patterns of decision making display one common thread—the growth of consensual and cooperative relations, rather than adversarial ones, between government and business. This pattern sharply contrasts with the earlier stormy era in Japanese history.

Even with that trend noted, however, the vinyl chloride affair exhibits an unusually high degree of cooperation, for several reasons. First, the *gaiatsu* factor was powerfully at work, especially after B.F. Goodrich announced its intention to address the problem. Japanese decision makers in government and industry immediately felt involved. Second, the announcement acknowledged a link between pollution and human health, thus helping to settle a question of scientific causality that has made the settlement of numerous pollution cases —including both the Minamata and the auto emission problems in Japan— difficult. Third, given the pattern of familism in Japanese employment, industry officials tend to be more supportive of regulations that protect company workers than regulations aimed at those outside the company family. Finally— and crucial to our understanding of why business later responded cooperatively—nearly two-thirds of the VC and PVC companies in Japan had been involved, directly or indirectly, in the controversy surrounding the Minamata case. The Chisso company, which ultimately was held responsible for dumping organic mercury into Minamata Bay, belonged to the Japan PVC Association. Member companies found their production methods under scrutiny as a result of the conflict, and were criticized for standing behind Chisso in the early years. Working and living in the shadow of one of Japan's worst pollution outbreaks, VC and PVC officials were understandably anxious to avoid further notoriety.[30]

Japan's Environmental Record

Aside from the "best case" example, the achievement represented by Japanese government-business cooperation in environmental protection is no small matter—particularly when we contrast it with American adversarialism between government and business in dealing with the environment. But at the same time, it is not easy to determine just how successful the cooperative approach has been in resolving environmental issues. Considering the period from 1974 to the present as the era of cooperation, Japan's environmental record emerges as mixed at best. In the Environment Agency's report for 1979, for example, no overall improvement in air or water quality was claimed. In 1984, despite the strict regulation on passenger car emissions already in place, NOx levels were not diminishing.[31] Again, particulate matter as a source of air pollution was reported as increasing in Japan during 1984.[32] Also, after a dramatic reduction in photochemical smog during the decade of the 1970s, the absolute number of Japanese smog alerts nearly doubled between 1982 and 1983.[33]

Meanwhile, pollution in small- and middle-sized rivers and lakes, especially in urban areas, continues to constitute a serious problem, and cases of marine pollution in coastal ocean waters are on the rise. A 1982 survey conducted in fifteen Japanese cities revealed extensive groundwater contamination; yet corrective action has so far been very limited. Noise pollution has emerged as a key issue of the present and future—concerning which little has yet been done. Critics of Japanese environmental policy are quick to point out, in addition, that the major anti-pollution initiative of post-1974 Japanese legislative history—the Environmental Assessment bill—has (as of early 1986) failed to pass in the Diet.[34] Almost alone among industrial nations, Japan does not require a nationally mandated environmental impact assessment for government projects. In all, then, a variety of problems remain to confound any claims for complete success based on the cooperative approach.[35]

Before we can fairly judge the success of the Japanese record on pollution control since 1974, however, other considerations deserve attention. One such factor is the large concentration of pollutants in relation to the tiny Japanese land area. The pollution challenge thus looms greater in Japan than in any other major industrial nation. For example, the most convincing explanation for the failure to improve NOx pollution levels in Japan—despite the strictest auto emission standards in the world—is found in the sheer number and concentration of automobiles.[36] Another factor requires our recognition: many types of pollution can be traced to nonindustrial sources, and these sources are harder to control by any means of government-business cooperation, including regulation. Policymakers thus have faced formidable problems for which there were no easy solutions. It is difficult to regard the Japanese post-1974 era of cooperation as an unqualified success, however, even when we grant special dispensation given the seriousness of the problems confronting Japan.[37]

Our own review of a longer, twenty-year record, in fact, leads to a quite contrary conclusion. In pollution control, Japan's greatest gains came *not* in the recent decade of cooperation, but rather during the earlier period of adversarialism between government and business. This conclusion is especially noteworthy because it challenges so much recent opinion—which places Japan's government-business cooperation at the center of national success. Even though important environmental gains also occurred during the cooperative era in Japan, as the VC case has clearly illustrated, the fact remains that, during the adversarial period, Japan's achievements in environmental policy and regulation were so extraordinary that they pose a serious challenge to the conventional wisdom. The 1967 Basic Law for Environmental Pollution Control, the battery of laws passed by the "Pollution Diet" in 1970, and the outcome of numerous regulatory struggles of the early 1970s represent such achievements. By implication, of course, this challenge also extends to another popular view—that in both Japan and the United States, adversarialism per se represents a barrier to effective protection of the environment.

Clearly, there are advantages and disadvantages both to the cooperative and the adversarial approaches in environmental matters. Each one requires careful assessment, so that the trade-offs become clear. So far, we have presented the record of each approach with special attention to Japan. Now we shall concentrate briefly on the problem of environmental regulation in the United States, to see how adversarialism has differed in the two countries and how various stages of the pollution struggle may be compared and contrasted.

Environmental Regulation in the United States: An Overview

In the United States, the response to the vinyl chloride problem took shape as a pattern of policymaking and regulation-setting based on confrontation between government and business. Government officials and representatives of VC companies remained at loggerheads from the moment of the B.F. Goodrich announcement which admitted a risk of cancer in the workplace, through all the rounds of hearings and litigation that followed. Only a final court decision put this particular government-business conflict to rest. Nothing resembling the Japanese shift from adversarialism toward greater cooperation in environmental regulation-setting seems to have appeared anywhere in the American record, where consistent adversarialism still reigns.

Much earlier in U.S. history, Americans did share the attitude of tacit collusion that we have described among the Japanese. In both countries, such relationships between government and business predated any popular consciousness of environmental dangers. Environmental issues, when they did appear in the United States (as later in Japan) were regarded as local, to be handled by incremental regulation that employed an almost silent partnership of federal and state governments.[38] Of this arrangement, the Federal Pollution Control Act of 1948, with its 1956 amendments, provides a good example. That legislation established federal authority to regulate interstate water pollution, but federal enforcement powers remained weak. Primary responsibility remained with the states. In practice, the result was an abrogation of regulatory responsibility, for few states had any effective laws for pollution control. Until the late 1960s, then, the federal government stood back from assuming broad authority for the environment.[39]

Local governments, intent upon maintaining good relations with industries whose activities seemed vital to the economic health of the community, also refrained from vigorous regulation. Air pollution emergencies (smog alerts, for example) were accepted as a way of life in many cities of the United States for decades prior to the protests of the 1970s; during that earlier time, local officials frequently did little to challenge business interests or to confront the problem openly.[40] As a result, until the 1970s, there was a pattern of tacit collusion on environmental issues not unlike the one we found in Japan. Only when that wall of tacit collusion in America fell before the legislative wave of the 1970s did the federal government undertake an enlarged role in environmental pollution controls, one that replaced collusion with adversarial action.

That such a shift was required for any remedies to ensue may be illustrated by one vivid example. In the late 1960s and early 1970s, Kepone poisoning made its presence felt in Hopewell, Virginia, near an Allied Chemical plant. From 1966 until 1973, Allied produced Kepone—a highly toxic chemical pesticide similar to DDT. The dangers of Kepone, developed by Allied during the late 1940s and 1950s, were already well known. Studies by Allied during the early 1960s found strong evidence that the compound induced "DDT-like tremors."[41] Tests on rats, quail, and mice revealed a range of severe problems, including "whole-body" tremors, liver enlargement, atrophy of the testes in males, impaired reproductive performance in females, and possible cancer links.[42]

Despite these results, commercial production of Kepone persisted at Hopewell, where Allied also continued to discharge Kepone wastes—without treatment of any kind—into the James River. Only in 1970, after the federal government had resurrected the Refuse Act Permit Program (which required all industries seeking to discharge wastes into navigable waters to obtain permits from the U.S. Army Corps of Engineers) could the federal government claim a sound legal basis for regulating the problem. In its application for a permit, Allied managed to bypass any inherent threat to its operations by listing its discharges as merely a temporary phenomenon, to be discontinued within two years.[43] The permit was granted, and by the time it expired in 1972, an entirely new permit program had been put into place, under the Federal Water Pollution Control Act Amendments (1972), now administered by a newly created federal Environmental Protection Agency. At this time, Allied once again sidestepped waste regulation without challenge, as the Hopewell discharges were now described as "unmetered, unsampled, temporary outfalls."[44] American tacit collusion between government and industry had prevented the government from effectively implementing its own regulatory (permit) system.

After 1973, when Allied turned Kepone production over to Life Sciences Products Company through a "tolling" agreement, tacit collusion took on a more ominous definition.[45] To keep Allied supplied with Kepone, Life Sciences—operating out of an abandoned gas station—doubled its output by using teams of employees working three shifts per day, seven days a week. Now, the safety guidelines previously followed by Allied were largely ignored by Life Sciences, even though it was being run by former Allied managers. In fact, conditions at the makeshift Life Sciences plant, to quote one account, "would have shocked Dickens." According to one Life Sciences employee, Kepone dust was so thick in the atmosphere that "he couldn't comb his hair after an eight-hour shift."[46] Clouds of Kepone dust coated the equipment and the floor, and tended to obscure vision in the vicinity of the plant. When the loading chute failed, workers—unaware of the danger of absorbing Kepone through the skin—actually packed barrels with their bare hands. Over some sixteen months of operations at the factory, two dozen workers visited doctors or hospital emergency rooms, complaining of work-related health problems. One employee filed a complaint at the Richmond field office of the U.S. Occupational Safety and Health Administration. Yet no regulatory action was taken until a young Taiwanese physician became suspicious that Kepone poisoning was occurring. His protests ultimately triggered both state and federal actions, which promptly resulted in the plant's closing in 1975.[47]

The lack of any effective government response to countless irregularities at the Kepone factory over a long period reveals the dangers of tacit collusion. For example, OSHA officials, confronted by a worker's complaints concerning the plant (and later, his dismissal for having filed them), responded by sending a letter of inquiry to the Kepone manufacturer and accepting their reply without further investigation.[48] When Life Sciences requested permission to discharge wastes into the Hopewell sewer system (and thus into the city treatment plant), permission was granted by the city manager—who did not set guidelines or requirements other than that such discharges not interfere with the normal treatment process. Hopewell's Director of Public Works, formerly an

Allied manager who was well acquainted with the dangers of Kepone and the safety precautions in force earlier at Allied, fully supported Life Sciences' application to the city.[49]

The Kepone poisoning at Hopewell—which left dozens of workers and nearby residents with serious health damage, and which resulted in contamination of the James River that would require some $2 billion in dredging operations to clean up—appeared rather late in the American pollution struggle. Hopewell made news well after the EPA had been established and after government officials had begun to deal effectively with numerous other environmental ills. But, as in the early Japanese pollution cases, effective regulation was delayed by the predisposition of both local and national governments to overlook mounting evidence of corporate culpability.

In the United States, the transition from a pattern of tacit collusion to one of adversarialism occurred as a result of many of the same forces that operated in Japan: media attention to pollution issues, rising public consciousness of environmental problems, and the worldwide surge of pollution events. Once Rachel Carson's *Silent Spring* had moved the debate over pollution from the domain of technical specialists and opened it to discussion by the general public, citizen activism grew throughout the 1960s and peaked in a public celebration of Earth Day in 1970. Popular American consciousness of the environment had become active; and, as in Japan, one result of the emergence of new forces was an outpouring of environmental laws during the late 1960s and early 1970s. These laws set the stage for a confrontation between government and business.

In fact, the adversarial pattern that emerged in the United States in the late 1960s closely resembled the one in Japan, at least initially. In both countries, outside pressure—from citizens' groups, media attention, and the public— forced government officials and politicians to stand together in addressing environmental problems. For a period of time during the late 1960s and early 1970s, it became politically and bureaucratically unacceptable, once a pollution issue became public, to side with business. This created a standoff between industry and the public. How such adversarialism worked in the United States was well illustrated by the vinyl chloride case, in which OSHA and the courts were able—over a period of less than a year—to regulate workplace exposure to VC, through a procedure that ultimately led to compliance by industry.

Again, in both Japan and the United States, environmental issues also began to lose their potency at roughly the same time, in the mid-1970s. For the Japanese, as we noted earlier, the result was a gradual shift to greater cooperation between business and government; rancor declined as both sides sought a middle ground. For Americans, however, adversarialism continued as the characteristic regulatory approach. Indeed, adversarialism in the United States has sometimes taken extreme forms. In the case of auto emissions control, the standoff between the EPA and the American auto industry over the implementation of standards for hydrocarbons, carbon monoxide, and nitrogen oxide has resulted in repeated frustration: extensions of government deadlines for enforcement, costly litigation, and, in the end, a delay of more than a decade in enforcing standards set in the Clean Air Act of 1970.

Overall, by any measure, the total amount of litigation concerned with environmental issues has been remarkable. In the Kepone case, for example, once the issue became the focus of widespread public attention, and tacit collusion between government and business turned to adversarialism, litigation on every front became the primary result: former Life Sciences employees, the Commonwealth of Virginia, and commercial fishermen all sued Allied or Life Sciences; the federal government sued the City of Hopewell; and the Commonwealth of Virginia even attempted to sue its own city, Hopewell. By 1980, as many as 30,000 persons—affected workers, local residents, seafood wholesalers, retailers, processors, distributors, restaurateurs, owners of charter boats, marinas, and tackle shops—all had come forward to press claims totalling hundreds of millions of dollars.[50] But as of June 1985, a decade after Kepone dumping ended, the only settlement Allied had been required to pay was $5.25 million; while as much as 42,000 pounds of the chemical may still remain on the bottom of the James River, with no clean-up program in sight.[51] In the Kepone case, the effectiveness of American adversarialism remains difficult to demonstrate.

Conclusions

Yet it would be a mistake to conclude that adversarialism in the United States over the past decade has failed to lead to improvements in the environment, just as it would be wrong to conclude that the cooperative approach in Japan over the same period has failed to produce positive gains. In both countries, there is a broad consensus that an environmental crisis has been averted. The body of environmental law that was developed in both countries during late 1960s and early 1970s remains on the books in the middle 1980s. In both countries by a number of measures air and water quality have improved significantly. Environmental protection agencies were firmly entrenched as part of the bureaucracy in both Japan and the United States. Even dedicated environmental activists of the 1970s were ready to acknowledge by 1985 that very significant gains had been made—although much still remained to be done.[52]

Looking closely at the past decade, however, it cannot be said that *either* American adversarialism or Japanese cooperation produced clear advantages as overall approaches to resolving environmental problems. Despite the claims of numerous recent writers that Japan's cooperative approach to environmental regulation offers a better and more successful path than the more adversarial route that has been followed in the United States, the evidence remains quite mixed. Our own study of the past twenty years of environmental developments in Japan suggests the arresting conclusion set out in this chapter: that the Japanese actually achieved far more in the domain of environmental regulation during their own era of adversarialism than in their more recent decade of cooperation. Thus, both adversarialism and cooperation should be studied with a view to the trade-offs that each involves—before either is heralded as an ideal pattern.

Cooperation in government-business relations, at least in the Japanese pattern, can claim numerous advantages. The number of decision makers remains throughout relatively small; this then allows those participants most knowledgeable of the technical issues involved to make the key decisions. In addition, the decision-making process, although it is closed to most outside groups, stays remarkably informal, leading participants toward frank expression of their views and helping them to locate middle ground. But some disadvantages of the Japanese pattern remain evident. Outside groups—victims of pollution, other interest groups, and the public at large—generally have no ready access to the decision-making process. In Japan, the advisory councils attached to governmental ministries and agencies, where much regulatory activity takes place, only rarely include representatives of such outside groups. Since members are chosen by the ministry or agency involved, persons likely to mount fundamental challenges to the decision process are seldom selected.

In the United States, where the types of hearings provided under the adversarial approach to regulation are formalistic, and the decisions that result are made by judges or public officials—some channel of influence in decision making is always available to interested parties. This access is usually missing in comparable Japanese regulatory decision making. In addition, because of the absence (for now) of a nationally prescribed environmental assessment law in Japan, there is no uniform provision for public participation in environmental decision making at the crucial initial stages in economic development projects. This, of course, is precisely the point at which public and private interests are most likely to clash, and where fundamental choices have to be made.

As this chapter has suggested, the basic regulatory arrangements now in place in Japan have worked relatively well—as they did during Japan's adversarial era, from the late 1960s to about 1974. Through informal meetings between government and business, and relying on the more specialized activities of advisory councils, government was able to pressure and even override business interests, forcing them to accept measures that served the public interest. In that sense, the public's position was taken fully into account by bureaucrats during Japan's stormy era. But the main reason lay in the complex and volatile pressures on decision makers—pressures created by the many separate factors discussed earlier: the numerous domestic forces at work, developments abroad, and the march of pollution events themselves, during an era when public opinion was riveted on pollution issues. Once these forces began to weaken, as they did after 1974, the public lacked any formal means for guaranteeing that their interests would be represented. Given the reality of virtually continuous conservative party rule in Japan, as well as a long-standing national commitment to economic growth, it is a remarkable commentary on Japanese democracy that government bureaucrats and business interests have proved as responsive as they have to the need for pollution control. This has remained true even since the end of the stormy era, and in the absence of formal guarantees for public participation in decision making.[53] Yet after 1974, the shift to a cooperative relation between government and business served to vitiate the far bolder approach of the earlier period. This shift may have left Japan less well prepared to confront environmental challenges that today remain among the most serious in the world.

The adversarial approach naturally imposes its own trade-offs, as our study of the United States has shown. There, adversarialism between government and business over pollution regulation has produced a battery of legal guarantees and avenues of legal evasion, not only for business but for public interests as well. Critics of the U.S. approach are, of course, quick to point out that the economic and organizational resources available to groups representing the public are scant alongside those available to business interests. But the presence of a broad spectrum of American environmental groups, functioning nationally and participating routinely in environmental regulatory activity, provides a stark testimony—not merely to a long-standing tradition of effective voluntarism in the United States, but also to the use of avenues of access that ensure participation. In Japan, the almost total absence of just this type of highly organized, national, professionalized environmental interest group, with thousands of dues-paying members, indicates profound differences between the two countries.

Some disadvantages of the U.S. approach are only too real. Legal guarantees for participation of all groups are now so firmly in place and mutual suspicion is so high, that compromise becomes extremely difficult. Regulatory hearings, of necessity, are formalistic and, in many cases, ritualistic. Litigation, by its very nature, is costly, may cause long delays in compliance, and leads contestants—whether they are business interests resisting regulation, public interest lobbies, or individuals affected adversely by pollution—to exaggerate their own case or claims, and to deny all merit to the opposing view. Perhaps even more serious, a battery of legal guarantees made available to each of the many groups affected by environmental regulation, from business to victims, offers little encouragement for developing a sense of social responsibility. Victims seek as much as they can get, often without concern for those who will have to pay the costs, whether it is a company, the taxpayer, or the general public through higher insurance rates. In a system based on adversarialism, American business has few incentives for adopting costly pollution control measures until legal avenues have been explored.

The situation often produces striking ironies. During the 1970s, for example, the U.S. auto industry elected to resist virtually every major type of regulation, from auto emissions standards to mandatory safety devices. Many critics of the industry—and, indeed, many Japanese auto industry officials—hold that the

American industry's opposition damaged its image and actually made it less competitive in the international marketplace, including the United States itself.

Finally, the availability to various groups of institutionalized means for participation in the regulatory process removes from public officials some of the onus of safeguarding the public interest, or acting on behalf of disadvantaged groups. Public officials may feel such a responsibility, of course, and obviously many do. But the onus is not always there. It is all too easy for public officials to fall prey to the assumption that groups adversely affected by a decision or a regulation will resort to legal remedies to register their opposition.

In that sense, the approach of Japanese decision makers, which involves an effort to identify a middle ground and to take all interests into account, could be considered more socially responsible and even more "democratic" than the U.S. approach. Certainly in Japan, the significant gains in environmental protection over the past decade—which have been worked out by government and business in the absence of strong external pressures from the public or of active participation from outside groups—could not have been achieved without such a sense of social responsibility. Both approaches, then, have advantages as well as costs, and both will continue to be tested as they are brought to bear on the environmental challenges that still lie ahead.

CHAPTER **8**

From Relationship to Price Banking:
The Loss of Regulatory Control

M. COLYER CRUM AND DAVID M. MEERSCHWAM

Introduction

This chapter describes and compares the financial systems of the United States and Japan during the middle and latter parts of the twentieth century. In these decades of transition, both countries have moved from tightly regulated national systems, through a period of erosion in regulatory authority, toward an international financial system. In this new system, regulatory authority is diminished and participants gain flexibility to choose assets or liabilities based largely on price.

In both nations, the traditional financial system (for our purposes, the system in the United States after 1933, and in Japan after 1952) reflected a unique national context. In the United States, a traditional fear of centralized power remained manifest in the variety of specialized financial institutions—commercial banks, investment banks, savings banks, savings and loan associations, and consumer finance companies; in the very large number of these institutions (more than 15,000 banks, for example); in the extraordinary fragmentation of regulatory power among state and multiple federal authorities; and in a national preference for equity finance and consumer and mortgage lending.

In Japan, a traditional national consensus emphasizing economic progress can be seen in the strong authority granted to the Ministry of Finance and to the Bank of Japan, and in the central importance of the thirteen city banks, with their emphasis on financing industry through loans. A limited Japanese reliance on common stock financing, a sluggish development of consumer and mortgage finance, and the primitive condition of short-term Japanese money markets all served to channel funds to banks, which became instruments in an emphasis on industrial growth.

In short, the Japanese and American systems appear to have been very different in major ways. Nevertheless, we believe that both systems shared one important characteristic: Regulators in both nations acted to create specialized banking institutions that enjoyed little or no freedom to modify their products. Moreover, regulators subjected these institutions to a blizzard of specific restrictions covering almost every aspect of operations—pricing, geographic service area, customers, and product design.

Under banking regulations, innovation was neither rewarded nor permitted. Instead, prices and procedures were set to protect the less efficient. Amazingly, despite wide variations in their activities, almost every one of the 15,000 U.S. commercial banks showed a profit every year. It was almost as if a marathon race ended in a 15,000-way tie, as the best runners were slowed down and the weakest were assisted to the finish line. In Japan, the city banks' behavior was compared to a "convoy system," as a way of describing the overall similarity of strategies and results. For many years, each city bank paid the identical dividend, ¥2.5 per year per share of common stock; and bank shares sold at almost identical prices, symbolizing parity among all of them.

In a sense, financial institutions in both countries were given specialized local monopolies, based on products, customers, or geographical location. Customers' (that is, depositors' and borrowers') prices were set to assure a bank profit, yet these customers were prevented from obtaining the same or similar products outside the banking system.

Financial affairs in every country, by their fundamental nature, tend to be sensitive and confidential. They are based on intangible factors such as confidence and character, because every lender knows how fragile his claim to repayment is—even with collateral and a strong legal system. Therefore, it is not surprising that in both America and Japan financial institutions and customers worked to develop *special relationships* with each other as a primary means of competition. Such relationships permitted lenders to develop knowledge and confidence in borrowers; while, in turn, borrowers, through continued good repayment, earned the right to further credit. Since these advantages could not, because of regulation, be overcome by competitors who offered better features or prices, relationship-building became paramount. Of course, such ongoing relationships encouraged each partner to behave responsibly and to overlook temporary problems. In this sense, relationships represented a healthy long-term development. In Japan, such relationships became important especially in the form of *keiretsu* groups—banks and corporations with special business connections reinforced by cross-stock ownership and regular management meetings.

Here, our point is simply that in Japan *and* in America the financial regulatory structure brought forth similar forms of national banking. We call these systems, both of which developed under a traditional regulatory regime, "relationship banking." In each nation, such a form of banking represented a stable, effective financial system, and one that developed as a common response to two unique national cultures and strategies. For many decades in each nation's history, relationship banking held sway.

But gradually, this once stable structure began to decay, in both countries. As institutions aspired to do better than the norm permitted by the regulators, they sought to innovate in products, prices, or services—all in an attempt to increase their profits and market share. Customers as well sought freedom from restricted products and regulated prices. "Nonbanks," without regulatory burdens or responsibilities, began to encroach on the product domain of the regulated institutions. Finally, the segmented financial institutions increasingly began to compete with each other.

Many innovations arose during the larger process of change, especially on the American side. The development of the Euromarket permitted the avoidance of U.S. and other national restrictions on interest rates. The introduction of the negotiable certificate of deposit (CD) by Citibank in 1961 permitted banks to pay market rates on large deposits while giving the large investor liquidity, because the CD could be sold—or negotiated—to another investor independent of the bank. The rise of such technological devices as credit cards, wire transfer, computers and satellite communications facilitated rapid, low-cost funds transfers. Simplified regulations (such as SEC Rule 415 on "shelf registrations") permitted corporations to raise very large sums through public underwritings simply and quickly. The development of money market funds extended market rates to individuals.

Money market funds, essentially a by-product of the low interest rates for deposits regulated by Federal Reserve Regulation Q, attracted small amounts from many investors, and then were invested in large amounts at deregulated higher market rates. Because money funds managers invested their large sums in a small number of large banks, the large banks, in effect, attracted deposits from throughout the nation, thus avoiding geographic restrictions.

In Japan, traditional central regulation remained stronger, the national objectives more focused, and the financial industry more concentrated and less internationalized. Deregulation therefore came later and slower, but for the same reasons. Japanese corporate customers and securities firms took the lead here, rather than the more powerful but much more severely regulated Japanese banks. In fact, some companies sought to use equity finance as an escape from domination by banks and government. Others wanted to borrow without collateral or by issuing commercial paper. Japanese firms were sometimes able to do their financing in other nations in ways that were prohibited at home. Later, they sought similar services from Japanese financial institutions. Again, as Japanese industrial and trading firms increasingly made sales (and, later, direct investments) overseas, Japanese banks naturally tried to follow them abroad and to provide services and products that would be competitive in a new market. Finally, as corporate demand for funds slowed and government debt grew after the first oil shock, the bargaining power and operating needs of corporations, banks, and government all changed. Innovations, ideas, and products entered the financial markets at a more rapid pace. Soon, the surge in the Japanese trade surplus created a need to recycle funds outside Japan. As Japan's goals became more complex and contradictory, the financial system encouraged more and more innovators to challenge the old regulatory order. Regulators too had conflicting goals, and therefore less impact.

In both America and Japan, government regulators observed all these changes without being certain about just how to respond. At first, corporate innovators were punished. But gradually, novel situations developed in which the regulators determined not to risk their traditional authority. Many regulators did not challenge private-sector initiative, either because they themselves might lack jurisdiction (more likely in the United States than Japan); or because they were confounded by alternatives that threatened to erode regulatory control even while promising other benefits (such as reduction of Japanese-American frictions or increased support for the internationalization of Japanese industry).

In all, the new environment developed more and more opportunities for all participants to be financially creative—flexible on products and prices. So the cultivation of established, ongoing relationships in banking began to give way to impersonal, price-oriented, and largely ad hoc financial transactions. We call this "price banking," and it represents a sharp contrast to the older and far more stable system of "relationship banking" that preceded it in both Japan and the United States. The collapse of Continental Illinois Bank in Chicago—which had purchased both loans and deposits from others who had *no* ongoing relationship with the bank—may be the most significant evidence to date of the dangerous potential for financial instability in the new system.

In historical summary, the small, mostly isolated examples of breakdowns in the regulatory structure during the 1950s and 1960s were magnified by the collapse during the 1970s of the Bretton Woods system of fixed exchange rates. Among the most serious results, we find: wide fluctuations in foreign exchange rates, worldwide inflation, commodity price instability, especially in oil; large and seemingly permanent fiscal deficits in most industrialized nations; and, most recently, a great trade imbalance between the United States and Japan. At present, both the American and Japanese governments face complicated sets of interconnected problems. Both financial systems are now required to serve several goals at the same time. Here a truism applies: the more dynamic and complex the problem faced, the less able any planned or regulated economy has been to achieve superior performance. The collision of free market forces and a tightly regulated economy now poses questions of enormous importance, especially for Japan.

As the regulators lose control, what will happen to the remaining stability of financial institutions and of the world financial system? Will interest rates and foreign exchange rates move outside of all control by national governments? Will impending changes make it difficult or even impossible for any one nation—even the United States or Japan—to manage its own economy? Already, corporations and banks routinely move enormous amounts of money from one account to another, with very little attention paid to relationships, but with the utmost concern for price. In fact, multinational corporations increasingly seek to spread their operations across national boundaries as a method of escaping from all sovereign governments' efforts to impose tax, social, monetary, protectionist, or other restrictions.

Americans have been especially quick to take advantage of the higher returns from money market funds outside the bank regulators' authority. Will Japan follow the American patterns in venture capital, takeover bids, restructuring and disinvestment, performance investing of pension funds, high financial rewards for share ownership, and other aspects of a less regulated environment?

As greater freedom to move funds at low cost becomes more available, then mobility of ideas, technology, and people must follow. The implications for national economies—especially previously sheltered economies such as Japan's—are staggering. Perhaps Japan will seek the benefits and assume the responsibilities inherent in making the yen a reserve currency, and then impose its influence on the free world's financial system. Or, Japan might attempt to retreat once again into isolation, reducing its trade and financial involvement with other nations.

From what we can see now, the next important international competition between the United States and Japan could well occur in the financial arena. What appears unlikely, however, is that the present trends toward deregulation and price banking can be reversed. Both countries will continue to be affected by a loss of regulatory control. Each nation's future success or failure will depend on how successfully its system can learn to cope with the freedom, rapid change, price orientation, and diminution of the old emphasis on relationships. The complexities of each system—their similarities and differences, as well as prospects for their convergence in the supranational financial system of the future—provide the substantive foundation for the analysis that follows in this chapter.

We begin with an explanation of how banking relationships developed, first in Japan, then in the United States. Next, our discussion evaluates the important changes that have occurred in both countries. Finally, we end the analysis with a comparison of the Japanese and American systems as they are today, and as they may develop in the near future.

The Japanese Relationship System

Japan's financial institutions have antecedents that go back to the Meiji Restoration of 1868, when note issuance, which is central to any financial system, lay in the hands of several banks.[1] Rapid inflation (which reached 20 percent in 1879) forced some change, and Japan's rulers imposed a system that largely depended on a central bank. Shortly after its creation in 1882, the new

Bank of Japan held a monopoly on the issuance of notes; and as the bank grew, the skeleton of a modern banking system began to emerge.[2]

The system that developed in Japan before 1900 was comparable to those of many European countries—similar in that the Japanese system developed around a powerful central bank, but different because the large demand for credit created by industrialization could be partly satisfied by various specialized banks. These banks serviced particular products according to maturity (long-term/short-term) and purpose of financing (international trade, agriculture). Some of the specialized banks were owned, and most were directly influenced, by the Japanese government. For example, the Yokohama Specie Bank (currently the Bank of Tokyo), founded in 1880 at the urging of private citizens, was soon supported by the government as an instrument for financing international trade.

By 1901, the number of private banks in Japan had grown to more than 1,800 institutions. After that date (and unlike the period following World War II), many banks were simply allowed to fail; while, during the same years, many small banks merged, often after official encouragement and legislation.[3] As a result, between 1932 and 1945, the number of "ordinary" banks fell from 538 to 61. Of greater importance than this reduction in the number of banks, however, was another fact: segmentation in commercial banking had also taken place. Those banks located in the cities largely dealt with a rapidly industrializing Japan, while smaller local banks still concentrated their activities on the financial needs of rural areas.[4]

In addition to urban and rural banks, there also were other specialized financial institutions. Life insurance companies, trust companies (especially after 1922, when the Trust Law and the Trust Business Law were introduced), and agricultural and industrial banks all developed to meet particular needs. Stock exchanges also opened, but they played only a modest role in Japan's system (much less than did stock exchanges in the United States), because equity financing through public offerings was not popular among key members of the *zaibatsu* (prewar industrial conglomerates). Instead, *zaibatsu* banks stood at the center of the groups—precisely because they could provide funds efficiently to group members on good terms and through difficult times without reliance on less certain equity or bond markets.[5]

Equity financing in Japan came to be seen as a way to cement a long-term relationship, not as a purely financial transaction or as a way to exercise corporate control. To strengthen that relationship, companies sold new equity at par value (often far below market value), and gave to existing shareholders the right to purchase at the bargain price. As a result, existing owners participated pro rata in new stock issues—resulting almost in a "permanent shareholder" relationship with the company. Entrepreneurial ownership, financially unable to participate in successive rounds of financing, of course, would have preferred to sell shares at higher market value even if this interfered with the ongoing relationships between stockholder and company. Thus, loans obtained from banks became the preferred form of new capital, while most stocks ended up in the hands of the banks and other corporations that belonged to the same *zaibatsu;* or, in the post-Occupation period, in the hands of long-term holders such as corporations or financial institutions, rather than in the pockets of small shareholders among the Japanese public.

MARKET SEGMENTATION

The outstanding feature of Japan's financial system has been its division into particular market segments, in each of which a different type of financial institution could operate.[6] Although recently the entire system has undergone great change, moving toward liberalization, the fact remains that before the mid-1970s most funds were obtained from a small group of lenders, acting through a well-defined segment of the financial system—and then allocated to a specific group of borrowers.[7]

To channel funds to specific markets along a predetermined path, no nation could rely on market mechanisms alone. Instead, careful product segmentation and constant price regulation had to be maintained—as in Japan they were. Yet this does not mean that *no* competition existed within the Japanese financial sector. In fact, many banks that participated in the market have described it as highly competitive.[8] What remains unsaid, however, is that financial institutions could only compete within their product area; and, since interest rates remained strictly regulated, the real competition existed in levels of service and in the strength of special relationships.

PRICES AND AVAILABILITY OF FUNDS

In Japan, government authorities not only set the discount rate—as in many other countries—but they also controlled most other rates of interest as well.[9] Here, the Temporary Interest Rate Adjustment Law of 1947 (currently still in effect) provided justification by enforcing strict relationships between various rates at which banks could attract funds, and by granting the power of adjusting interest rates to the Minister of Finance (see *Chart 8-1*).[10] A "bank cartel" organized by the Bank of Japan determined lending rates.

Just as private banking institutions in Japan have been heavily regulated, so official public institutions of finance (such as the Postal Savings System) have been even more tightly controlled by the authorities.[11] The Postal Savings System is a most important feature of the overall Japanese arrangement. Using 22,000 convenient branch locations (compared to 2,500 city bank branches and 4,600 regional bank offices) the system offers absolute safety, an interest rate usually higher than the banks' savings rates, and useful tax advantages for citizens. By 1982, the Postal System had attracted 31 percent of personal savings in Japan.[12] It is a significant competitive force against the banks, with interest rates set by the Cabinet. The funds are used increasingly for politically popular programs and are allocated by the Trust Fund Bureau within the

CHART 8-1
Procedure to Change Interest Rates

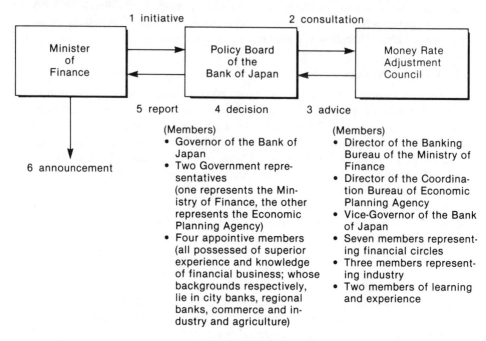

1 initiative   2 consultation

| Minister of Finance | → | Policy Board of the Bank of Japan | → | Money Rate Adjustment Council |

5 report   4 decision   3 advice

6 announcement

(Members)
- Governor of the Bank of Japan
- Two Government representatives (one represents the Ministry of Finance, the other represents the Economic Planning Agency)
- Four appointive members (all possessed of superior experience and knowledge of financial business; whose backgrounds respectively, lie in city banks, regional banks, commerce and industry and agriculture)

(Members)
- Director of the Banking Bureau of the Ministry of Finance
- Director of the Coordination Bureau of Economic Planning Agency
- Vice-Governor of the Bank of Japan
- Seven members representing financial circles
- Three members representing industry
- Two members of learning and experience

SOURCE: Federation of Bankers Associations of Japan, *Banking System in Japan* (Tokyo: The Federation, 1984), p. 89.

Ministry of Finance. Clearly government controls both the price and allocation of these funds.

But even in the private sector, aside from control of interest rates, public authority also influences the availability of funds. Convenient examples can be found in the operation of "city banks" and in the interaction between these banks and the Bank of Japan.

"City banks" are the thirteen major banks that hold a special position in Japan's financial system, particularly in dealing with the shorter maturity end of the financial spectrum. The largest city banks are Dai-Ichi Kangyo, Fuji, Sumitomo, Mitsubishi, and Sanwa. As *Table 8-1* shows, for the period before 1975, most funding for these banks came from deposits, the call money market, and direct borrowings from the Bank of Japan. Moreover, the city banks obtained their deposits through an extensive branching network. While there were only thirteen city banks in 1975, the total number of their offices exceeded 2,000.[13] The second source of funds, the call market, is a short-term interbank market; money is lent by banks that have excess liquidity (often rural ones), to those in need of funds (often city banks). Surplus funds are thus moved to point of need.

TABLE 8-1
City Bank Data
(Trillion Yen)

	A	B	C	D
	Total Deposits	Loans from BoJ	Call Money	Total Liabilities*
1955	2.4	0.03	0.07	2.9
1960	5.6	0.4	0.2	6.9
1965	12.5	1.1	0.9	16.3
1970	24.3	2.1	2.0	32.6
1975	52.9	1.5	2.4	71.7
1980	85.4	1.8	4.5	110.4
1981	94.0	1.1	5.9	118.0
1982	99.0	1.7	6.8	127.6
1983	107.9	3.2	7.1	139.9

*A + B + C equals approximately 85% of Total Liabilities.
SOURCE: Bank of Japan, Research and Statistics Department, *Economic Statistics Annual, 1983*.

Loans from the Bank of Japan reflected a special aspect of the Japanese system. During the period of rapid growth in Japan, before the first oil shock, the need for funds was especially high among large corporations. Since new equity financing was rare, city and other banks found ample opportunities for lending funds to the industrial sector for short periods. These "short-term" loans often remained outstanding for long periods. Article four of the Standard Bank Loan Agreement gave banks retroactive access to collateral at the banks' option and thus encouraged "short-term unsecured" lending by the banks.

Meanwhile, lending at longer maturities was carried out by institutions such as the Long Term Credit Bank. Unlike the city banks, this institution was authorized to obtain funds through the sale of long-term debentures.[14] Thus, long-term sources funded long-term loans. In past practice, as the industrial sector borrowed more heavily, the city banks "overlent." In fact, the term "overlending" became the standard way of referring to the behavior of the large city banks during the period 1950–1975. The banks wanted to lend to rapidly growing large corporations, both to make profits and to strengthen their relationships with their corporate customers; but, since government regulations prevented the banks from paying high interest rates or inventing new instruments to attract funds, the banks were forced to seek funds from the Bank of Japan.[15]

Table 8-1 makes it clear that such borrowing from the Bank of Japan remained a small part of overall activity by the city banks. What matters here is more subtle: even *limited* borrowing indicates that city banks were "loaned up," and thus that the steering power of the central bank was exercised to a degree far out of proportion to the amount of its funds involved in the actions of the city banks.

When we consider other private Japanese financial institutions such as the several long-term credit banks, *sōgo ginkō* (mutual banks), trust banks, security houses, insurance companies, and other specialized financial institutions, it becomes clear that they have served differentiated product markets. Moreover, the government maintained strict regulation of virtually all aspects of their activities. To these institutions might also be added a group of official financial intermediaries (such as the Postal Life Insurance System, the previously mentioned Postal Savings System, the Industrial Investment Special Account, the Japan Development Bank, and the Export-Import Bank), which have served to strengthen the grip of government authorities on both price structures and distribution mechanisms for funds of all kinds.[16]

THE BANK OF JAPAN AND THE MINISTRY OF FINANCE

In general, the Bank of Japan acts as banker to the government, as lender of last resort to commercial banks, and as Japan's monetary policy authority.[17] Within the Bank itself, the Policy Board, operating very closely with the Bank's management, defines strategy and objectives. Its seven members (the Governor of the Bank, one representative each from the Ministry of Finance and the Economic Planning Agency, and four members selected by the Cabinet and the Diet) oversee Bank policy. In addition, the Bank supervises the behavior of private banks, and effectively "guides" their lending and funding activities, as we have seen above. Just how to describe this guidance, whether to call it "window guidance" or "moral suasion," remains merely a semantic issue.[18]

In terms of authority, however, the Bank of Japan is not the ultimate power in the Japanese system. Its dependence on the Ministry of Finance, which is based on the Bank of Japan Law, makes the Bank legally responsive to Ministry efforts to steer Bank policy. The Ministry of Finance is the most prestigious of Japan's bureaucracies and the most influential in the national economy. The Minister of Finance relies on career bureaucrats who are considered the most capable and knowledgeable experts in their fields. The Ministry is, through formal and informal relationships, in close contact with almost all actors in the Japanese economy. The relationships are developed through the various bureaus of the Ministry. Separate bureaus are led by civil servants who ultimately report to the politically appointed Minister or to the career Vice Minister. As noted earlier, the Ministry of Finance sets interest rates and is involved in policies affecting many aspects of Japanese economic life such as securities, taxes, tariffs, and banking. However, the influence of the Ministry extends far beyond its "official" channels. The method of influencing the private sector often relies on formal authority only as a last resort. Long-term relationships between the bureaucracy and private sector exist and are enhanced by the fact that many officials join private corporations after a career at the Ministry. In view of the ambiguity in the relationship between the Bank of Japan and the Ministry of Finance, one can safely argue that Japanese monetary policy is jointly determined by the Bank and the Ministry.[19]

INTERDEPENDENCE IN THE SYSTEM

Special relationships and interdependence are central features of the Japanese financial system. To demonstrate their importance, let us turn once more to the city banks, which have long maintained a special relationship with the central bank.[20] Since part of their funding came directly through loans from the Bank of Japan, city banks could not easily disregard any "advice" sent to them from the Bank. Moreover, the Bank functioned as a kind of overseer. Frequent examinations by the Bank of Japan were made of the city banks, and individual credits had to stand up to such inspection. In the early post-Occupation years, quarterly limits on loan growth were set by Bank of Japan and applied equally to all the city banks—yet another example of regulation which inhibited innovation. Under these circumstances, it is not surprising that the lending behavior of the city banks reflected the interests and desires of the Bank of Japan.[21]

Thus, the special relationship between city banks and the central bank affected both the liabilities and the assets of the balance sheets of city banks. When high growth rates in the Japanese economy created heavy loan demands by corporations, for example—since banks could not compete on price to gain additional funds (because the prime lending rates were effectively controlled)—the banker and his client depended on relationships to influence the allocation of scarce funds. Relationships rather than price competition therefore became a dominant pattern between city banks and large corporations.

Again, it is worth noting that both the city banks and the corporations with which they maintained special relationships usually profited from this system. For banks, the relationship created a fairly simple environment in which to do business. Funding became a well-defined and largely routine business, free from innovations. Similarly, lending relied more on carefully evaluating and maintaining long-term relationships with well-known partners than on looking at applications from unknown potential new customers willing to pay rates which reflected both riskiness and reward in an uncertain investment project. Under the traditional Japanese system, the task of banks and of their customers remained to define, control, and maintain an existing relationship. Credit analysis and independent rating agencies played little part in evaluating specific individual lending opportunities.

For those companies with access to needed funds—at regulated prices—the relationship system was profit-stable. For those who did not enjoy such access, the alternative was to seek out other institutions willing to finance them—albeit at higher rates and a sharp reduction in the borrower's overall business profits. Since established firms, which had already entered into strong relationships, acted as engines for the growth of the Japanese economy as a whole, and since newer firms lacked any such relationships, they simply did not represent any credible threat to the system. In this stable framework, the services of Japan's financial institutions obviously did not depend on price competition. Rather, an institutional ability to cooperate and deal effectively with long-established partners provided the key to success. Only in the call market did what we call "price banking" really matter.[22]

Given the lack of alternatives, interdependence became a crucial feature of the Japanese financial system. This placed a high premium on prudent behavior, not only in the present but also as a way of promising compliance in the future. Each party had a great interest in continuing to use the system, so long as it remained profitable to all participants. Thus, after World War II, a stable banking system—based on established relationships—grew without any apparent threat of new bank failures such as those that had occurred before the war.

MONETARY POLICY TOOLS IN JAPAN

Relationships long provided a key to banking success; they also determined the tools of monetary policy that could be used in Japan. Of the three traditional policy tools—open market operations, reserve requirement ratios, and discount rate policies—open market operations simply were not a feasible policy alternative in the Japanese context. For such operations to be effective, government securities have to be bought and sold in an open market. To engage in open market operations at all, government authorities must be willing to let the market determine the price of (that is, the rate of interest on) government securities. Thus, the Bank of Japan—being unwilling to allow a freely determined interest rate—in effect rendered open market operations out of order.[23]

As *Chart 8-2* shows, prior to the first oil shock, the Japanese government did issue public debt—though the amounts were small, following the Dodge Line policy of balanced budgets imposed in 1950.[24] Typically, such debt was offered at a rate of interest which, by itself, would not have attracted sufficient demand to sell the offerings. Instead, the Japanese city banks were forced to absorb these long-term bonds through a system of quota subscription, made proportional to the assets of each bank.[25] For their part, the banks were willing to accept this arrangement for a number of reasons: First, the size of each issue was small; second and more important, the bankers realized that bargaining power lay with the government authorities rather than with the banks—which were already overlent. The city banks, while losing money on their government dealings, also knew that they could easily absorb these losses, since the spreads granted to them on other activities remained generous. In effect, the fund providers to the banks received lower than market returns, while borrowers (other than government) paid more, thereby providing a public subsidy in the form of below-market borrowing by government.

Of the other policy weapons, changing the ratio of required reserve assets to total deposits has proved to be unimportant in most countries, including Japan and the United States. Its effect is hard to predict in the short run, since the willingness to hold excess reserves can easily change. Furthermore, when compared to increasing or decreasing the level of reserves, a change in reserve

CHART 8-2
Government Securities and Borrowing*
(Trillion Yen)

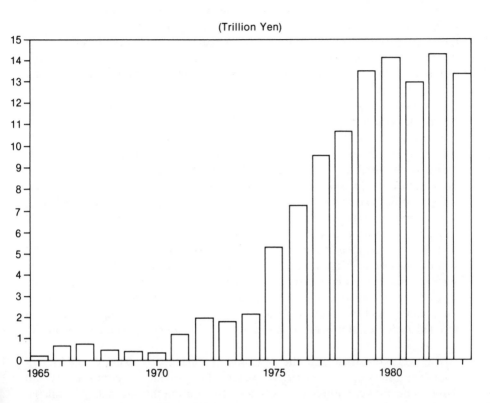

(Trillion Yen)

*Securities Issue and Borrowing per fiscal year.
SOURCE: Bank of Japan, Research and Statistics Department, *Economic Statistics Annual, 1983.*

ratio requirement will generally take a much longer time to work its way through the system.

Discount rate policy, on the other hand, has played a large regulatory role in Japan. Both the quantities discounted and the rates charged have been significant—because banks were overlent, and because of the tight linkages between the various rates that were enforced through the Temporary Interest Rate Adjustment Law of 1947. Finally, the discount rate proved to be effective because it served as an indicator of the desires of the Bank of Japan.

POLICY OBJECTIVES IN JAPAN

Using this picture of Japanese finance as background, we can now evaluate the policy objectives of the national banking system from the end of World

War II until the changes beginning in the mid-1970s.[26] Already, it is clear that one objective was to keep interest rates low. In fact, a case is frequently made that, in order to stimulate investments, Japanese monetary authorities kept interest rates well below market rates (at least for some classes of borrowers).[27] In Japan, the real effect of interest rate policy was to maximize the distributive power of the authorities—a pattern made possible because of dependencies in the system that resulted from a clear lack of alternatives in the rationed market. This is the relationship system in full operation—a salient fact of modern Japanese history.

Of course, it can be argued that the negative result of this policy may be that savings are discouraged. Yet, given the large existing Japanese savings pool—which was not interest-elastic—and given that capital accounts were mostly balanced during this period, the national income identity indicates that investments, both public and private, were also large.[28] Again, the size of this savings pool can be explained by the limited number of alternatives. The underdeveloped mortgage market, the bonus system for employees in corporations, the modest retirement plans, various tax provisions, and the memories of wartime deprivation all encouraged savings. The high savings and the absence of a government deficit almost guaranteed that sufficient private investment would take place.[29] In a regulated environment, where interest rates in some sectors remained so low that rationing had to be imposed, window guidance by a central authority could have a maximum effect; and in the Japanese case, the policy objective of the government was not so much to keep interest rates low (in order to stimulate investment) as to influence particular credit decisions.

The Bank of Japan and the Ministry of Finance, working together, encouraged a national financial environment that provided overall stability and fostered desired economic development. By limiting the alternatives available to suppliers and demanders of funds, and through skillful use of a regulated environment that nurtured strong interdependencies and existing relationships, the Bank and the Ministry succeeded in both shaping Japanese industrial policy and in maintaining their own power.

The U.S. Relationship System

Like the consideration of Japanese finance above, our description of the traditional U.S. financial system also begins in the period just after the Second World War. Yet we should recall some earlier historical developments which helped to define that traditional American system.[30] To understand these antecedents, we must acknowledge a deep-rooted suspicion of all powerful and centralized financial institutions that has characterized American history since the beginning. In fact, many of the developments in the American financial system must be viewed in the light of a continuing national struggle between those seeking fragmentation and diversity (to minimize centralized power) and those seeking financial stability even if large centralized institutions were created.

In the early years of the republic, bank charters were granted primarily by the various states. No federally chartered banks existed, except for the first Bank of the United States (1791–1811) and the second Bank of the United States (1816–1836), both of which fell victim to the fear of central authority.[31] The National Currency Act of 1863 provided for federally chartered national banks that could issue national notes. It also created the Office of the Comptroller of the Currency, as a means of assuring compliance with federal charters.

By the time of the American Civil War (1861–1865), the national financial system had become complex, but also highly unstable. The federal government had no control over the state banks, and many such banks were regarded as unsafe, even though state authorities attempted to regulate them. A variety of other financial institutions existed—insurance companies, savings banks, building and loan associations, investment banks, and stock exchanges. Again, these were only lightly regulated, if at all, by state governments.

In such an environment, various financial institutions arose and grew, competing against each other without the benefit of any central regulator either to control their activities or to act as a lender of last resort. Yet state banks remained responsive to state legislatures, which naturally imposed diverse regulations. Confusing as it seems, this situation remained basically unchanged until passage of the Federal Reserve Act in 1913. This landmark legislation reorganized American banking, vesting broad powers in an unusual institution, the Board of Governors of the Federal Reserve System. Of course, the old distrust of centralized power had not disappeared, and so the new "Central Bank" was actually created as twelve separate regional Reserve Banks, with specified directorships representing various constituencies, including borrowers. The new Federal Reserve exercised narrower authority than did central banks in most other countries.[32] Moreover, under Federal Reserve supervision, the financial system continued to show instability. Bank failure remained an all too common phenomenon: from 1920 to 1933 more than 15,000 banking companies failed.[33]

Today, the financial system of the United States owes many of its distinguishing features to legislation that followed the financial crisis of 1933, especially to the Glass-Steagall Banking Act of 1933, which separated commercial banking from the distribution of securities (underwriting). The Banking Act of 1933 created the Federal Deposit Insurance Corporation,[34] and provided additional regulation and deposit insurance to reassure depositors and reduce bank failures.[35] The Securities Act of 1933 provided pervasive regulation of public issues of securities, with emphasis on disclosure to protect investors. Finally, the Securities Exchange Act of 1934 created the Securities and Exchange Commission (SEC), which regulates stock exchanges and investment companies (mutual funds). Between 1945 and 1970, the U.S. financial system in general operated effectively, without major problems. Through these years, many different types of financial intermediaries grew up to service the needs of corporations, individuals, and the U.S. Government.

SEGMENTATION IN THE MARKET

In its mature form, the U.S. financial system has been segmented along both geographical and product lines. A census during the mid-1970s showed close to 15,000 commercial banks, 4,000 savings and loan associations, and 5,000 insurance companies.[36] In addition, other types of institutions, such as investment and finance corporations, leasing and brokerage businesses, and credit card companies enhanced the diversity and number of financial entities on the American scene.[37] Only by keeping this complexity in mind can we appreciate the inherent pressure on financial institutions to differentiate among themselves.

During the nation's early years, geographical segmentation was inevitable, given the rudimentary state of communications, information, and management. The segmentation was maintained, however, through a system of state regulations, long after technological progress arrived. In some states, branches were permitted statewide; in others, only in selected regions of the state; and in still others, no branches at all were permitted. The state branching laws also controlled nationally chartered banks after the McFadden Act of 1927 and the Douglas Amendment of 1956 in effect prohibited interstate banking altogether.

But, as we have seen, geographical segmentation was not the only regulatory influence at work in American banking. Product segmentation also limited the alternatives available to customers. Traditionally, commercial banks in the United States covered only a narrow spectrum of the product market: checking, savings, and time deposits were offered; while for their assets, these banks relied on short- and medium-term business loans, mortgage loans, consumer installment loans, and other forms of credit. Trust business (and in more recent years, leasing business) also played a role. However, not all areas of financial intermediation were open to commercial banks—securities underwriting, brokerage, and insurance were proscribed by various regulations.

For commercial banks, the most direct competition for deposits came from the so-called "thrift institutions" (savings and loan associations, mutual savings banks, and credit unions). These institutions concentrated their lending on home mortgages and mortgage-backed securities—as regulations directed them to do. At the end of 1973, for example, almost 85 percent of the total assets of all savings and loans were in mortgage holdings, along with 70 percent of the total assets of mutual savings banks.[38]

Again, while many financing needs in the United States were handled through the various types of financial intermediaries, others were satisfied through direct placements. Here, bond and stock issues held special importance, since they took place at negotiated (rather than regulated) prices. Still, new equity financing never became a major source of funds in America, though equity provided from profits retained in the business remained very significant. In bond placements, underwriters made active use of their relationships with buyers. As in Japan, severe price regulations also allowed American authorities to influence the allocation of available capital, the best example being the higher rate allowed for thrift institutions as a deliberate incentive to the housing industry.

RELATIONSHIPS IN THE UNITED STATES

When we study the comparative importance of price and relationship banking in the United States, however, we must conclude that the price at which funds could be obtained and placed mattered more to participants in the American market than to their counterparts in Japan. But it becomes equally clear that the price of a banking product represented something besides the interest rate charged. In the American financial system, relationships between particular businesses and particular banks were enhanced by the geographic and product segmentation of the entire financial industry. Segmentation restricted alternatives; therefore, repeated transactions between individual banks and individual corporations often took place. Continued access to funding and a long-lasting relationship between the borrower and the bank became common goals. This meant that the value of relationships in banking remained high, particularly since deposit accounts, which provide most banks with their largest and most stable source of funds, were not priced competitively. Deposits were accessible only to banks located in a particular region, so restrictions on branching acted to enhance the value of established relationships.

IMPACT OF THE FEDERAL RESERVE SYSTEM

The authority for monetary policy in the United States held by the Federal Reserve is exercised in a very unusual way. Since there is no single central bank, the Federal Reserve System and its Board of Governors perform the role of central monetary authority.[39] We have noted that the Federal Reserve System came into existence in 1913, when twelve Federal Reserve Banks and a Board of Governors were set up by federal law. Since that time, the Board has coordinated the actions of the twelve Banks, operating to assure that the primary objective of the entire system remains fulfilled: to maintain a supply of currency sufficient for the needs of the national economy.

In reality, the banking crises of the late 1920s and the Great Depression served to shift the focus of the Federal Reserve's attention: maintaining the stability of the entire financial system became the top priority. To accomplish this, the powers of the governors were increased relative to those of the individual Reserve Banks, and a Federal Open Market Committee (FOMC) was established to help determine monetary policy, especially through the use of open market operations and the discount rate.[40]

In pursuing its policy objectives, the Federal Reserve Board acts independently of other public organizations. The seven Governors of the Board are appointed for a term of fourteen years by the president of the United States; and once appointed, they cannot be forced to resign. One of the governors is asked by the president to serve as Chairman of the Board, filling a four-year term. As these arrangements suggest, the traditional American fear of central-ized power has led to a very strange form of "central bank," and it is difficult to evaluate the precise degree of independence being shown by the Federal Reserve Board at any particular time—but it can be considerable.

Apart from determining monetary policy, the Federal Reserve Board also acts significantly (although not alone) in regulating the financial system. Yet even in this regulation, some diversity remains. Each individual state exercises its own responsibilities, and federal regulatory power remains fragmented: the Federal Reserve, the Comptroller of the Currency, and the Federal Deposit Insurance Corporation (FDIC) all have their separate interests. Here, we shall briefly examine some of the most significant.

FINANCIAL REGULATION IN THE UNITED STATES

The U.S. financial system is now regulated at both the state and federal levels, with varying degrees of effectiveness.[41] Membership in the Federal Reserve System implies federal examination of the books for each commercial bank. Members also have to honor reserve requirements and to join the FDIC, which sets the insurance premium level for deposit insurance.[42] Again, the clear objective of these regulations is to ensure maximum stability of the system— by enforcing "prudent" banking behavior and mandatory deposit insurance.

State regulation pursues more diverse objectives, the most important of which are prescribed in policies imposed by the fifty state legislatures. The legislatures are diverse in their natures and interests, and their policies may regulate any aspect of banking that takes place within a state. For the purposes of this brief review, we will note the diversity of state activities but return to the larger matter of federal action.

In interest regulation, for example, the federal burden historically fell heavily on time and savings deposit rates. Maximum rates were set as early as 1933, when Regulation Q was announced. It applied to all members of the Federal Reserve System, and, one year later, was extended to cover all other banks as well.[43] Thrift institutions, which specialized in home mortgages, were regulated by a separate body—the Federal Home Loan Bank Board—and al-lowed to offer slightly higher deposit rates. Thus, in channeling these funds to the housing market, the U.S. Congress and the several regulatory authorities assumed a role in distributing funds not unlike the role played by their counterpart regulators in Japan, but distributed those funds in a different direction: toward housing rather than industrial development.

By now, it should be clear that regulation played an important part in the operation of U.S. financial markets. Detailed regulation of banks included re-strictions on amounts of capital, dividends paid, maximum loans to borrowers, number of directors, certain characteristics of directors, dates and hours of operations, types of names used, and reporting requirements—as well as the more obvious controls on interest rates, reserves, and geographic location.

Various federal and state laws separated the financial markets product by product, and state legislation superimposed geographical compartmentalization on this segmented system. Regulation of many rates (such as those for deposits) proved extremely important, because it strengthened relationship banking by limiting price competition. Yet, even after all this, some interest rates were still left free.

TOOLS OF MONETARY POLICY IN THE UNITED STATES

In the American system, in contrast to the Japanese, the most effective single tool for monetary policy remains open market operations. Here, the sale or purchase of government securities directly affects interest rates in the bond markets, and either action also changes the amount of reserve assets held within the system. Reserves, in turn, affect both the money supply and credit availability throughout the economy. When these and other effects have worked their way through the entire system, interest rates for the other financial instruments are certain to respond as well, owing to a generalized willingness to substitute one financial instrument for another. Thus, open market operations will effectively steer interest rates. We should notice, however, that this method of control does not rely on direct regulation, but instead on varying the amount of credit available in the economy: open market sales will reduce the amount of credit creation and raise interest rates, while open market purchases will increase credit and lower interest rates.[44]

In the past, discount rate policies also have been used by the authorities, although it is still not clear how effective they were as a tool for policy. Some observers have argued, for example, that discount rates simply follow other rate changes in the short-term overnight, interbank, federal funds markets; and that they can function only as signalling devices to indicate the wishes of the Federal Reserve. As in Japan, reserve requirement ratio changes have been unattractive to American authorities as a policy tool.

Unlike the Japanese situation, however, it is clear that the particular American framework of financial institutions did not develop extensive use of moral suasion. In fact, any implicit threat that the monetary authority would take action against individual banks (if voluntary cooperation was not forthcoming) appeared impotent, since American banks generally did not depend on the Federal Reserve for funding. Thus, the blunter instrument of open market operations has proved more central to the implementation of monetary policy in the United States.

AMERICAN POLICY OBJECTIVES

In effect, the central objective of past American policy has been the creation of a stable financial system that would encourage growth—but without relying on any single set of centralized, powerful private financial institutions.[45] The emphasis on stability and the concern with high growth objectives by monetary authorities grew out of various theories. In this chapter neither the American flirtation with Keynes nor the more recent influence of monetarist beliefs will receive specific consideration. We merely note here that the United States does not isolate financial policy from economic theory.[46]

The development of macroeconomic thought, starting in the late thirties, placed additional emphasis on interest rates and money supply—on occasion, interest rate policies were expected to create either deflationary or stimulatory effects. At other times, money stock policies were considered more important as a way of controlling inflation. And, while the Federal Reserve Board did influence interest rates in the economy, fiscal policies (with their effects on the government budget and on the prices of government bonds) also played a major role.[47] Here, it is useful to recall again how traditional American suspicions of powerful financial institutions worked to fragment financial markets and to create much diversity, while limiting the alternatives in each individual transaction. American financial institutions relied on severely restricted funding sources, because of both geographical and product limitations. On the other hand, similar geographical and price restrictions also limited the alternatives available to individuals who wished to enter American financial markets. As a result, special relationships developed and increased in value as they helped, over many years, to maintain a stable yet diverse system in the United States.

The Two Traditional Systems Compared

In comparing the traditional financial systems of Japan and the United States, one can choose to stress either similarities or dissimilarities. The Japanese developed a highly centralized system, which offered only a limited number of alternatives. Tight regulation, both along product and price dimensions, systematically reduced the opportunities and benefits for substituting partners in financial transactions. As a result, long-lived relationships flourished. In the United States the exact opposite development took place with respect to centralization. From the historical American distrust of powerful financial institutions, an alternative system of highly fragmented parts was bred, its diversity guaranteed by product and geographical regulation. Yet one important effect of this fragmentation brought the United States close to the example of Japan, in that alternatives in financial transactions were reduced, and relationships made more important. This common thread—the greater importance of relationships over price banking—constituted a fundamental similarity between the two systems. In each system, there was some suppression of the latitude to transact—at freely determined prices, and between any two factors. The fact of such restriction provides a useful key to understanding both systems.

This is not to say, of course, that the two systems were ever identical. In Japan, price regulation always remained stricter. As a result, the channeling of funds in Japan remained far more specific than in America. Again, the equity market became far less important as a secondary market in Japan than in the

United States. Also in Japan, but not in the United States, the primary tool of monetary policy was moral suasion rather than open market operations. At the same time, in both systems, we note a separation between the banking and underwriting businesses and systematic regulation of interest rates. In both countries also, the sheer number of financial institutions varied dramatically before the present systems became stable.

Thus, even as we argue that these two national systems were fundamentally similar in limiting alternatives and in nurturing relationships, we do not suggest that the objectives of the policymakers were the same. While it is clear that the authorities in both Japan and the United States remained deeply concerned about the stability of each financial system, clearly the practical influence of Japanese central authorities outweighed anything exhibited by the Americans. The precise contribution of the financial sector is hard to quantify but, in both the United States and Japan, there can be no doubt that financial regulation has been used to affect the allocation of funds. Yet this fact can also lead to exaggeration, as Japan's industrial policy now resembles a cliché, while the influence of institutions such as MITI in Japanese life has frequently been overstated.[48]

In Japan, the relationship structure guaranteed that certain firms could gain access to the capital market at attractive regulated rates. Although we will not consider the broader implications for international competition, we should observe that, so long as these rates remained below the rates that would have cleared the markets, those Japanese companies or individuals with such access stood to profit from this financial environment. At the same time, of course, those companies or individuals that were denied access must have suffered. In all, the effectiveness of the traditional Japanese policy depends on the relative efficiency of a rationed market—when compared to a price-competitive market and the ability to formulate consistent goals. When we recall that both traditional systems functioned without major problems during the first quarter-century following the Second World War, the entire system of relationship banking appears in historical retrospect to have been a major achievement in both countries.

Once this common achievement has been acknowledged, we may consider whether, in their totality, the Japanese and American systems were actually more similar than different, or vice versa. After carefully evaluating both, it seems to us that the similarities outweigh differences, because of the importance of market restrictions and special relationships. Note that our view contrasts with the conventional wisdom, which associates the Japanese environment with a controlled system and defines the American environment as a purely price-driven system. In fact, nonprice competition played a key role in both systems, since both restricted the freedom to transact at purely negotiated prices.

As a way of exemplifying such similarities, we selected two traditional phases of development and showed that relationships were fundamental to financial operations. Both phases were characterized by stability and both preceded periods during which the financial system showed fundamental change, as partner substitution in financial transactions became much more common. Now, we are ready to move away from these traditional phases in both nations, and concentrate on changes. Here, we argue that relationship banking became less important relative to price banking in both the United States and Japan.

The U.S. Move Toward "Price Banking"

We shall illustrate the move toward price banking by giving a number of examples which, while differing in timing and orientation, show how new, price-oriented instruments were increasingly developed. Financial instruments were offered that no longer relied on established relationships. Instead, the ability to take advantage of market opportunities became much more important.

From 1945 to the present, the financial history of the United States can be seen as a secular trend from low to high interest rates (long-term government bonds yielded 2.3 percent in 1950 and 13.7 percent in 1981); from simple financial instruments and structures to complex ones; and from conservatism, even pessimism, to optimism and aggressive financial policies. The early period reflected the overwhelming impact of the stock market crash of 1929, the Great Depression of the 1930s, and World War II. The pattern for prevailing attitudes and behaviors in the financial markets was set by the Great Crash— the Dow Jones Industrial Average declined by 90 percent from 1929 to 1933; the severity and duration of the Depression—unemployment stood at 25 percent in 1933, and little significant improvement took place before preparations for war began in 1940; and by a lack of consumer spending, owing first to the Depression and later to war shortages. Meanwhile, government deficit financing dramatically expanded the assets of the banks (in 1950, 37 percent of bank assets were invested in U.S. Treasury Securities, yet by 1984 this number had fallen to 13 percent as commercial lending increased).

More important, participants who remembered the traumas of the 1930s dominated the financial scene. There were few new jobs and almost no innovation in finance, where the collective human experience emphasized safety and simplicity. Du Pont, America's largest chemical company, was widely admired as a paragon of financial wisdom and virtue because it had no long-term debt on its balance sheet in 1945. Institutional financial advisors, such as bank trust departments, concentrated on safe, bond-type investments rather than risky common stocks. Reputations and salaries of financial experts were low. After all, when money is cheap and operations simple, there is no need for expensive expertise. In 1945, the U.S. financial system was stable, fragmented, tightly regulated, cautious, and awash in money.

In one way, the postwar financial development of the United States can be regarded as a continuous process of absorbing this money glut. With money cheap and the economy remaining free from the predicted postwar depression, confidence returned, slowly and gradually. Individuals, companies, and governments all spent liberally until the money glut became a money shortage. Over the years, meanwhile, the price of money (the nominal interest rate) increased, finally reaching postwar peak levels in 1981. Waves of innovation occurred as newer participants—those with little or no memory of the Crash and Depression—became attracted by potential rewards and began to attack the entrenched conservative order. The regulators were outflanked, compromised, or simply overwhelmed.

There are many strands to this story, and here we can treat only a few. But the larger pattern is important—the movement from conservative and simple practice to more venturesome and complex behavior has been constant.

Postwar economic growth was impressive, fueled in part by government programs such as the G.I. Bill, to provide housing and education for veterans; the Marshall Plan, to stimulate European economies; preparations for war in Korea, with resulting military and aid expenditures in Japan; and also by massive catchup spending in the civilian economy, after fifteen years of depression and war. Still, the conventional wisdom in finance continued to reflect the trauma of the Crash and Depression. It seemed to ignore the high prices for bonds and low prices for stocks.

Over time, however, those who financed their capital needs with very cheap debt capital (i.e., low interest cost and high prices for bonds) prospered. At the same time, investors who placed their savings in common stocks made gains, while investors in bonds lost money. In short, stocks went up and bonds went down. Yet orthodox professional experts continued to remember the lessons of 1929.

By the early 1950s, some young investment managers began to challenge conventional thinking. An entrepreneur named Jack Dreyfus, for example, promoted a mutual fund which invested only in common stocks. As equities rose and bonds declined, Dreyfus (and other young Turks) won, while traditional wisdom lost. Soon, the concept of "performance investing"—selecting equities for capital gains as opposed to dividend income—began to flourish, thus shifting the emphasis from a relationship to a price orientation. The development of sophisticated historical analyses of long-term investment performance suggested the superiority of equity returns versus bonds, and short-term performance measurement services began to calculate quarterly or even weekly measures of performance. Traditional managers, heavily committed to bonds, lost money as interest rates continued to rise. Then, even more aggressive managers organized unregulated partnerships, called hedge funds, and began to seek unrealistic goals (outperforming the market averages by fifteen or twenty percentage points per year).

Corporate entrepreneurs, such as James Ling of LTV Corporation, soon appeared, to create high-growth securities based on financially oriented mergers, new organizational forms, and accounting aberrations. In fact, Ling himself pioneered many nontraditional concepts. He acquired companies by purchasing their common shares in return for a variety of complex securities, usually bonds, to take advantage of the tax deductibility of interest payments. He frequently reorganized or recapitalized his companies, in deals of great complexity, while taking full advantage of accounting conventions to produce dramatic changes in earnings per share. In short, Ling brought complexity, constant change, and a tolerance for financial risk-taking unknown in American finance since the 1920s. Securities firms, rather than commercial banks, were his primary allies in these early efforts at financial engineering. Here too, Ling was widely emulated.

Meanwhile, in the early postwar years, the banks gradually converted bond investments to loans; and, when interest rates rose to then-historic highs, banks increased the maturities of their loans, to lock in the high interest rates. As rates continued to increase, the banks began to charge floating rates on these "term" loans. At the same time, depositors became disenchanted with the low interest rates paid on bank deposits; so they sought more attractive places to invest. By 1961, Citibank had invented the negotiable CD, which allowed it to pay high rates of interest and thus retain and attract funds which then could be loaned at even higher rates.[49] The CD was an important innovation because it permitted investors to obtain a high rate of interest for a fixed maturity while also obtaining liquidity if needed by selling the CD to another investor. The bank which issued the CD was in turn assured of retaining the funds to the maturity of the CD. Rather than relationships, only price (return) now mattered. Similarly, corporations with excess funds loaned directly— without going through banks—to corporations or others seeking higher short-term returns (the so-called commercial paper market).

In life insurance, companies had traditionally obtained funds by selling "ordinary life," a combination of pure life insurance and savings. The insurance companies normally invested their long-term funds in publicly traded bonds, or, increasingly, negotiated directly with corporations needing funds. The life insurance companies originally were cautious, lending only part of their funds and maintaining excess cash in bank deposits; but slowly they too began to reduce holdings in this low return cash, and to expand their long-term, high-yield investments. Relying on their predictable sale of insurance to generate future cash flows, the insurance companies soon further reduced their excess cash in banks. By the late 1960s, they were even making forward commitments of loans before receiving the cash. More recently, in the 1980s, the low interest rate implicit in traditional ordinary life policies became uncompetitive with other investments, and ordinary life rapidly began to be replaced by "universal life," which promised higher market-oriented rates of return.

Beginning in the late 1950s, each time that market rates increased (owing to Federal Reserve efforts to tighten money and deter inflation), the regulated rates paid by the banks became increasingly unsatisfactory to depositors with access to other types of funds. Soon, large banks and large corporations sought to escape regulatory controls by using the unregulated Eurodollar market in London.[50] In effect, both customer and banker did business at market rates outside the reach of U.S. regulators.

Following the lead of James Ling, a number of corporations (first in regulated industries such as banks, railroad, and airlines—but later in others as well) began to explore holding company structures. These were specifically designed to isolate the regulated activities and permit activities prevented by regulation. For banks, this meant greater flexibility in raising funds; for example, the holding companies could sell commercial paper, whereas regulated banks could not. Also, it meant an extension of business activity through subsidiaries which were not banks and therefore not restricted by bank regulation.

Banks also sought to retain their trust business by managing the rapidly growing pension funds of large corporations, in competition with performance-oriented nonbank investment managers. By 1974, the largest, most respected banks were competing on the basis of performance investing. The traditional notions of prudent investing had focused on avoiding loss of capital, and on maintaining interest or dividend income. In contrast, the new approach focused on "total return"—the sum of interest or dividends plus the change in price of the investment. Capital gain possibilities soon overwhelmed notions of traditional income, and the so-called two-tier market developed. This market peaked in 1974, when pension managers (including the banks) emphasized a small number of corporate stocks—often selling at high price/earnings ratios of fifty times or more—while ignoring the stock of large heavy-industry companies, which sold at low price/earnings ratios of five times or less. The irony was that the largest pension funds often came from employees of these same heavy industry companies. As with other developments, improved performance *promised* benefits to corporations (reduced pension costs) and also to banks (larger assets under management earning a fee).

As memories of the Depression continued to fade, more entrepreneurs pressed the limits of traditional risk-taking. In 1968, for example, DLJ, an energy securities firm, developed a program for selling call options on listed common stocks. Speculators, often managers of hedge funds, could buy the option, hoping for extraordinary rates of gain in return for the risk of total loss of the premium paid—usually only a minuscule percentage of the value of the stock. These options, in turn, were sold by conservative investors who owned the stock and hoped to get a small return for small risk.

Again, entrepreneurs extended the idea and soon, in 1973, an organized exchange, the Chicago Board of Options Exchange (CBOE), provided a central market for trading options. The volume of trading in such options sometimes exceeded the volume of share trading on the New York Stock Exchange. The success of options soon led to organized trading in bond futures, stock index futures, foreign exchange futures, and even options on futures. Viewed by some as purely speculative activities, these new markets were defended as providing opportunities for banks, corporations, or investment organizations to limit (or hedge) their risks owing to the growing volatility of interest levels, foreign exchange, or share prices.

Other innovations arose as well. Entrepreneurs, noting that small bank deposits (under Regulation Q of the Federal Reserve) earned low interest rates, while large deposits were free to earn higher market rates, invented the money market fund. The funds are not "banks" under law, and are regulated by the SEC as mutual funds. They proved to be a close substitute for bank deposits, however; and when market rates rose in the late 1970s, the funds attracted more than $200 billion—providing yet another money market alternative to bank deposits. They also served as nationwide vehicles for collecting savings for big banks, since the funds attracted money from everywhere, but tended to invest mostly in the very largest money center banks. With low costs of operations, such funds (like commercial paper) proved to be a very efficient form of intermediation.

In response to the increasing volatility of interest rates—especially their steady rise—a variety of attempts were made to convert long-term fixed rate assets (such as home mortgages) to a security which could be sold on a market to an investor willing and able to accept price risk. A lender could arrange a mortgage and then sell it—charging fees for services but avoiding the chance of loss if the security declined in price as interest rates rose. Currently, there are many other such efforts to convert illiquid assets to tradeable securities. Securities underwriting has also adapted to market volatility, a notable example being SEC Rule 415, which permits large corporations to notify the SEC of a possible intention to issue securities at some future date. The corporation can then decide on very short notice to issue a specific quantity and type of security. The previous time-consuming registration with the SEC and the development of a complex syndicate of underwriters was thereby transformed to a quick, efficient transaction—almost as if the corporation sold the entire issue to an underwriter as a normal securities trade.

As a final example, both banks and nonbanks began to trade foreign currencies in enormous volumes. Thus, both speculators and others trying to minimize risk could respond to the fluctuations in exchange rates.

Clearly, the simplicity and stability of 1945 have been transformed to the complexity and innovation of the middle 1980s. In the process, a tightly regulated financial environment has become freer. First the Euromarket and now very large segments of U.S. financial markets have led the way. Enormous sums, dwarfing the resources of all government entities, flow here and there as events and attitudes change. There have been casualties, of course. Among American banks, the second largest in Chicago, Continental Illinois Bank, has almost been nationalized; the largest in the Pacific Northwest, Sea First Bank, has failed; and in 1985 alone, more than 100 smaller banks closed. In addition, large numbers of savings banks and savings and loans have failed or been merged, and many hundreds of banks—especially savings banks and agricultural banks—are in trouble. So, part of the freedom achieved in the American system has been a freedom to fail.

Why did the regulators permit such freedom? The short answer is that they had no sensible alternative. Originally banks were regulated for several reasons—to guard savings, to facilitate the payment mechanisms, and to manage the level of economic activity through monetary policy. Thus, interest rates sometimes were driven up for monetary reasons, while Regulation Q held bank deposit rates down because bank earning power was too low. Yet, with an unregulated Eurodollar market available in London, U.S. corporate depositors could escape from Regulation Q—that is, unless capital outflows were restricted. But the overall policy of the United States was to encourage free trade and free flow of capital. Unwilling, therefore, to stop the capital outflow, the only choice for the regulators was to force the funds outside the U.S. banks or to permit at least some exceptions to Regulation Q. They chose the latter.

Often particular innovations raised questions of regulatory jurisdiction, as in the case of money market funds. The funds were regulated by the SEC, which saw no reason to protect banks, which were not its responsibility. The sharp division in U.S. law between banks and securities firms encouraged a lack of coordination among regulators. Meanwhile, the commercial banks—once the beneficiaries of a government-granted monopoly of the deposit-taking function, and regulated in such a way as to assure profitability and stability—have seen their monopoly erode, as near substitutes for deposits have evolved through new technology. The old bank monopoly, based in part on legal restrictions on branch locations, has been overwhelmed by credit cards, loan officers using jet airplanes, and efficient electronic communications.

Banks have responded in many ways to the emerging environment. Citibank, now the largest bank in the world, has moved aggressively to try to serve all customers in all markets with all products. Bankers Trust has moved closer to offering many of the services of a securities firm or investment bank. Bank of America, the leading example of a traditional commercial bank and once the largest in the United States, has faced great difficulties trying to adjust to the new environment.

Without question, the skill of American bankers, corporate treasurers, and others has increased enormously, and they have developed policies, techniques, and institutions that will survive and flourish in the new environment.[51] In effect, the barriers are now down, and market participants find themselves free to seek their own unique opportunities. The U.S. capital market appears close to a totally free and efficient market.

The Japanese Move Toward Price Banking

In our study of Japan, we should begin by noting four fundamental forces which have tended to erode the traditional relationship-oriented financial system and to promote a movement toward price banking: first, the collapse of the Bretton Woods monetary system in 1971; second, the oil shock of 1973;

third, an increasing international thrust of Japanese manufacturing and financial organizations, culminating in the enormous Japanese trade surpluses of the 1980s; and fourth, the multitude of innovations by particular individuals and organizations seeking to achieve their own distinct goals—in spite of apparent restriction by regulatory authorities. Together, these forces have brought about considerable change in Japanese practice; and today scholars, government officials, and managers agree that deregulation will continue at an accelerating rate in Japan. Here, we will emphasize the multiple forces behind deregulation and the considerable staying power of the process now underway.

JAPAN AND SLOWER GROWTH

The historic breakdown of the Bretton Woods system and the associated Nixon shock of August 15, 1971 were followed quickly by the first oil crisis in 1973—when Japan's economic miracle came to a sudden stop. As we remarked earlier, such growth actually represented a fundamental component in the stability of Japan's traditional financial system. Rapid growth and a variety of mechanisms for sharing the benefits of that growth, on the one hand, had compensated Japanese savers for their regulated low interest earnings; while, on the other hand, growth had created the dependency of corporations on city banks and, in turn, of city banks on the Bank of Japan for new funds to satisfy credit demands. In brief, the oil shock of 1973 marked an end to traditional stability: Japan's dependency on imported energy caused the current account for that year to move into deficit, while explosive energy prices brought with them rapid inflation and the most significant slowdown in Japan's economic growth since the Second World War. For 1974, real GNP declined by more than 1 percent, in contrast to real growth rates of 9 percent for each of the two preceding years.[52] This slowdown naturally dampened the credit appetites of Japanese corporations. Yet it also caused the government to choose expansionary fiscal policies as a way of partially offsetting the contractionary effect of the huge increase in the cost of imported oil. The resulting large new issues of government bonds put heavy stress on the carefully balanced financial system, which had always relied on delicate interdependencies.[53]

Government debt, suddenly issued in significant amounts, soon proved inconsistent with the traditional regulated, administered system. From the end of the Occupation in 1952 to 1965, no major government debt issues had been made; but in 1965, the actual financing need of the Japanese government (debt issues minus General Account surplus) was ¥147 billion, or 3.9 percent of total revenues. From 1965 to 1974, the financing need rose to 5.5 percent of revenues. In 1975, however, issues of government debt suddenly jumped to 21.7 percent. In subsequent years, the financing need has grown to an average of 28.2 percent (1976–1983).[54] *Chart 8-3* plots the actual debt issues as a percentage of the total revenues, as well as the actual *ex post* financing needs.

As our description of the traditional Japanese financial system suggests, this

CHART 8-3
Issue & Financing Need as Percentage of Revenue

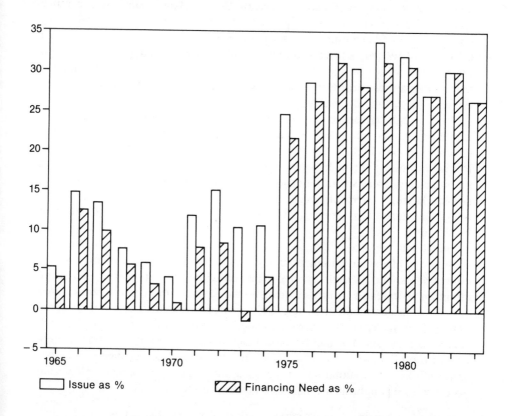

SOURCE: Bank of Japan, Research and Statistics Department, *Economic Statistics Annual, 1983*.

sudden appearance of slower growth and increased debt issues *had* to produce a severe dislocation. Corporations previously dependent on banks for funds to support growth now began to finance their much slower growth from internal funds, or even moved to reduce their debt. The banks, now with diminished demand for loans, were no longer so dependent on the Bank of Japan; they also needed to seek other areas of profit.[55] Indeed, as the government deficit surged, the bargaining power of government and banks reversed; and the most difficult task shifted from financing business to financing government. In essence, the banks' profitability in lending to corporations had declined, weakening their ability and willingness to absorb government bonds at a loss, at just the moment when the quantity of such government bonds increased dramatically.

Their plight turned Japanese banks into advocates of change. They began modestly, seeking new customers and products to replace corporate borrowers. Japan's earlier success had set the stage for overseas expansion and movement into markets previously ignored by the city banks, such as consumer lending, and into other new areas such as the reselling and later trading of government bonds to others. This second trend tested the legal separation of banking and securities firms mandated by the Occupation-imposed version of the American Glass-Steagall Act. Consumer lending, previously of little importance in Japan, would increase as the nation as a whole sought to stimulate domestic growth and raise the standard of living of the Japanese people.

On their part, corporations also began to seek change, largely because they had excess funds but fewer attractive investment opportunities. The Japanese government had limited the growth of the short-term money market, so as to channel funds through banks, but corporations found low bank interest rates unacceptable; so they began to explore more attractive opportunities outside Japan. As a result, corporate funds were placed in the Euromarket, which, because of its competitive threat, in turn encouraged liberalization inside Japan.

Individuals in Japan—like those in America—enjoyed fewer options and therefore held less bargaining power. But as they became aware of interest rate comparisons, and as their savings grew, individual investors paid increasing attention to rates of return on investment. Overall, then, the unanticipated slowdown in economic growth quickly changed Japan from a rationed capital market to a market with a national capital surplus. As the trade surplus continued to grow and as Japan became a capital exporter (with the brief exception of the oil shock period of 1979) the shift from once profitable relationships of the old regulatory order to a more flexible market orientation accelerated throughout the Japanese financial system.

INTERNATIONALIZATION OF JAPANESE BUSINESS AND TRADE SURPLUS

Since the Meiji Restoration, Japan had struggled constantly to export enough to pay for imported food, raw materials, and technology. Usually an unfavorable trade balance and inadequate foreign exchange provided serious problems, as they did during the early years after World War II. For the Japanese, however, such conditions served to stimulate a fierce renewal of the prewar search for exports, and this impressive effort has since produced a series of enormous annual trade surpluses, especially with the United States. Here, Japan's phenomenally successful national campaign to export is of particular interest because it worked to alter the Japanese financial system, as so many managers, businesses, and banks were put in contact with the far less rigid financial systems operating outside Japan. In fact, Japanese corporations and banks could also participate in the unregulated Eurodollar market—when Japanese authorities approved. As in America, these government regulators did not wish to create alternatives to Japan's regulated domestic market. Sometimes, however, they had no choice. In 1971–1972, when Japan achieved its first significant trade surpluses, authorities wished to facilitate offsetting capital outflows, so the Japanese banks placed funds aggressively abroad until ordered abruptly to reverse these flows after the oil shock.

As corporations developed exports from Japan, Japanese banks naturally increased their overseas contacts. When a Japanese company found American bankers or practices (e.g., efficient and flexible short-term capital markets) with relatively less stringent regulation, it could be expected that the company would seek to use the U.S. system; so Japanese bankers had to attempt to offer the same services overseas and later, at home. As a result, both corporations and banks, once having seen the possibilities in the Euro- or U.S. markets, then began to press for changes at home in Japan. Briefly, this meant that government regulators, anxious to preserve the home system, found themselves opposed by a growing number of well-informed and increasingly restive Japanese participants, who pointed out that traditional controls might conflict with the goal of encouraging a trade surplus.

Japanese business managers and bankers argued that the need for competitiveness and for managing their foreign exchange risk (increasingly critical as both interest rates and foreign exchange rates fluctuated more widely after 1971) forced them to increase their overseas presence. With the rise in foreign direct investment by Japanese firms, the desire for acceptance abroad has resulted in closer ties with local bankers, lawyers, governments, and suppliers—thus, in many entangling interrelationships. Again, for our purposes here, the point remains simply that a more complex set of goals, relationships, and opportunities developed. To some extent, any firm becomes less Japanese or American or German—and therefore less controllable—as it becomes involved outside its home nation.

One possible (and extreme) form of this tension would be demands by outside governments to change the nature of a domestic financial system—or else to face some form of trade restriction. An example of such pressure has been widely characterized in recent actions by the American government, which has encouraged Japan to open its financial system.[56] While outside political pressure may have some effect, we believe that it represents only a minor cause of the evolution in the Japanese financial system, compared with the large variety of internal forces operating on all Japanese participants in the markets.

INNOVATIVE APPROACHES

Japanese executives themselves often describe with great vigor the inability of government agencies to enforce their policies. Perhaps the failure of MITI to reduce the number of automobile manufacturers is the most discussed example. Of course, our effort to describe financial regulators' policies must also acknowledge this phenomenon—and in particular, the attempts of many Japanese companies to circumvent the official relationships fostered by regulations. To illustrate the point, we offer a brief story—of the growth of a Japanese retailing company, Ito-Yokado, from one small store to a very large and profitable multi-line retailer.

Ito-Yokado is a good example of a company outside the relationship system, forced to innovate beyond the traditional banking system. The company began as a small clothing store, which by 1961 had become one of Japan's first supermarkets. Although in most countries supermarkets are not generally capital intensive, in Japan, because of very high land prices, taxes, and societal attitudes that affect land, the financing of stores represents a critical issue for supermarket companies. With little cash, no collateral for bank loans, and no important financial relationships, Ito-Yokado necessarily took a distinctive approach to obtaining sufficient financing for continued growth.

Ito-Yokado's management began by emphasizing profitability—each store had to be profitable each year—as a source of cash flow for maximum growth. Next, it developed a creative and complex form of leaseback arrangement designed to accommodate landlords. Still unable to grow quickly enough to seize a window of opportunity before competitors or government restrictions intervened, Ito-Yokado next sold its common stock at market value, rather than at par value. Because of the company's unusual emphasis on profitability and its bright prospects for rapid growth, these shares jumped from ¥880 to ¥1,600 during the first day of trading, a phenomenon that naturally generated immense investor interest in additional Ito-Yokado shares. Also, Ito-Yokado sold shares in Europe as well as Japan, thus tapping new markets that added still more funds needed for rapid growth.

Next, this Japanese domestic retailer ventured to New York, sought a bond rating there, and borrowed American dollars through both convertible debentures (without collateral) and straight debentures (without bank guarantee). Then, to avoid foreign exchange exposure, Ito-Yokado took the unprecedented step of selling yen-denominated debentures to the government of Kuwait. Soon, Ito-Yokado sold yen-dollar-linked bonds in New York and effectively transferred the foreign exchange risk from the company to the investors. Later, at home, in anticipation of slower growth in supermarkets, Ito-Yokado diversified into convenience stores and fast-food restaurants. Separate companies were formed and listed on the stock exchanges. In nearly all of its operations, this domestic Japanese company, working outside the traditional financial system and innovating at every turn, achieved enormous success. The Ito-Yokado group's shares were worth more than $3 billion by 1984.

These events began a quarter of a century ago—financial deregulation takes a long time—and to most observers of the financial system, the individual steps appeared unimportant. A small Japanese company, in an industry unrelated to government priorities, insignificant to the financial system as a whole, did manage to produce a series of related financial and managerial innovations. By means of these innovations, the company solved its original problems—but far more important, Ito-Yokado created important precedents as a role model for others. For each step—while seeming to be a mere technicality—involved a new alternative to traditional methods of finance. When the overall system began to change, Japanese banks and regulators often either ignored or overlooked most of the small increments. Indeed, sometimes Ito-Yokado's own initiatives were positioned in line with government policy, as in the yen financing with Kuwait, when the Japanese government desired such financing in the wake of the oil crisis. In a larger way, the Ito-Yokado experience represents the myriad pressures on the established system—less visible or powerful than the slowdown in national growth or the internationalization of Japanese business, but which collectively contributed to a significant movement toward price, rather than relationship, banking.

THE NEW NONREGULATED MARKETS

Our earlier discussion of the Japanese financial system stressed the importance of regulating interest rates in individual, segmented markets. Yet within the traditional system, one rate remained unregulated: the call money market rate. It fluctuated in response to the demand and supply for short-term financing. This freely determined rate did not threaten the stability and regulation of the system, especially since banks made use of this market only when subsequent transactions in the regulated markets would allow for profits.

Gradually, another financial market developed that was only partially controlled by Japanese authorities—the *gensaki* market.[57] A *gensaki* transaction is a sale and an agreement to repurchase at a fixed price at a fixed time. The difference between the sale and repurchase price constitutes the effective interest on a loan. In Japan, this market dates from about 1949,[58] when securities firms financed their investment inventory with repos (as these instruments are called in America). Gradually, despite various restrictions imposed on these *gensaki* transactions, the securities firms (prevented from using the call money market) began using repos as a way to place and obtain funds. After 1975, the *gensaki* market grew rapidly, and regulation (early ceilings had been set for the size of, and return on, transactions) became less and less stringent, so as to facilitate the sale of government debt.[59] As the *gensaki* market developed, city banks argued that they needed new instruments to compete, and a CD market with free rates was approved in 1979 (see *Table 8-2*).[60] Further, the government began to issue Treasury bills in 1986, and a market will quickly develop in this instrument as well. Notice that these developments appear recent, but the pattern actually began to take shape almost forty years ago, with seemingly unimportant attempts to escape the system.[61]

The government's monetary policy tools have evolved also, of course. As moral suasion has become less effective, new instruments such as *gensaki,* CDs and bills permit more reliance on open market operations as interest rates are increasingly determined by market forces. Earlier, we argued that Japan's main policy objective during the traditional phase was to maintain a stable system with maximum influence on fund allocation by the central authorities. In the recent environment, the stability of the system remains a primary objective,

TABLE 8-2
Growth of the CD and *Gensaki* Market
(Billion Yen)

Year	City Bank CDs	Direct *Gensaki*
1969–1974	—	271
1975	—	452
1976	—	846
1977	—	2,181
1978	—	2,755
1979	925	1,784
1980	1,061	2,496
1981	1,855	2,816
1982	2,085	2,762
1983	2,750	2,717

SOURCES: Bank of Japan, Research and Statistics Department, *Economic Statistics Annual, 1983*; Nomura Research Institute.

but now it has to be attained in a different way. Whereas the old relationship system provided stable profits through market segmentation and price regulation, price competition now must increasingly play a more important role.

The old system of simple, broadly accepted goals, few alternatives, and a variety of institutional arrangements augmented the power of the very skilled and sophisticated Ministry of Finance. Earlier, the emphasis on selling shares at par, the systematic attenuation of motivation to innovate, as in the pervasive idea of the convoy system of banking, and tremendous statutory and informal powers of the Ministry of Finance and the Bank of Japan: these worked together to produce an effective and very workable system.

But slower growth, overall internationalization of capital markets, and the creativity of many participants have combined to produce an enormous variety of innovations in finance. Here are some examples:

• The Tokyo Stock Exchange, on November 29, 1985, admitted six non-Japanese firms (three American and three British) to membership; undoubtedly, other non-Japanese firms will be admitted in the future. At present, Tokyo promises to become one of three main centers (with London and New York) for "round the clock" trading markets. Thus, the international flow of capital will be even more efficient and even harder for regulators to control.

• Large Japanese firms with excess funds (Toyota Motor and Matsushita, for example, are often referred to as "banks" because of their hoard of cash and lack of debt) have created pools of capital to invest for profit in securities. The reports of their trading have become increasingly important as a sign of diversification from manufacturing and as a symbol of increased emphasis by established organizations in skillful trading for profit.

- The Tokyo Stock Exchange began trading a government bond futures contract in November 1985. Ironically, within a week an unusually sharp fall in bond prices occurred and caused very large losses and gains. Nevertheless, the Tokyo Exchange announced a study of stock index futures in January 1986, with prospects for trading them.
- A Nomura Securities subsidiary applied for commercial banking authority in the United Kingdom. A boomerang effect of non-Japanese banks seeking greater access to Japan is inevitable, and Article 65 ("Glass-Steagall") is under attack both in Japan and overseas. Some form of universal banking now seems inevitable.
- In 1983, Mitsubishi Bank offered a form of money market fund called the Mitsubishi Money Capsule, comprising a mixture of a bank term deposit and government bonds. The yield appeared extraordinarily high to consumers, and the product sold very well, suggesting a new way to sell government debt and demonstrating the potential for intensified competition for savings between securities firms and banks.
- Toa Nenryo, a Japanese petroleum refiner (with Exxon and Mobil each owning 25 percent) internally developed very sophisticated funding and foreign exchange skills to minimize the interest cost and foreign exchange risk during the 270-day period between purchase of crude oil and receipt of cash by the Japanese refiner. Among Japanese refiners, this financial skill played a significant role in Toa Nenryo's achieving unusually high profitability.
- Marui, a moderate size retail chain, has extended its unique system for selling merchandise on credit into a broad program of financial services, including easy credit card-based installment sales and cash loans. As an example of a "nonbank," Marui provides more convenient service and longer hours than banks.
- In 1983 Fuji Bank succeeded in a contested takeover bid for two subsidiaries of Walter E. Heller, and in 1984 Mitsubishi Bank won a contested takeover bid for the Bank of California. Earlier, Japanese firms had resolutely sought to avoid such contests.
- In 1982 Nissan announced a new American factory in Tennessee costing more than $600 million. Financing involved tax-free industrial revenue bonds purchased by an American subsidiary of Nissan, but with ultimate funding from the parent company, Japanese commercial banks, and the Japanese Export-Import Bank.
- Nomura Securities and Morgan Guaranty announced in 1983 their intention to form a joint venture to manage security portfolios for pension funds and others. This arrangement promises the beginning of comparative performance investing of the rapidly growing pools of Japanese funds.
- In 1981 Hitachi, Ltd. became the first Japanese firm to receive a Triple A bond rating from Standard & Poor. Hitachi thereby obtained visibility in world capital markets, demonstrating its financing alternatives to Japanese banks and government officials.

In the Japanese financial system, regulators are extraordinarily well trained and have studied deregulation in the United States very carefully. Furthermore, significant cultural, institutional, and other differences obviously remain between Japan and the United States. Thus there are powerful reasons to wonder whether Japan will follow the U.S. pattern. But, as the saying goes, "money-is-money-is-money," and regulatory barriers in Japan are clearly being overcome. Price competition in open markets is overtaking the once stable, relationship-oriented, traditional financial system. We believe that, as the pace and size of international capital flows increase, this trend will continue.

Conclusion

Both the United States and Japan have attempted to regulate their national financial systems; each country has sought to achieve its goals within a unique national context. Government regulators in both nations have emphasized segmented markets and specialized institutions, as well as detailed regulation of prices, products, and procedures.

In the United States, while individual institutions and customers were severely limited in their alternatives, and therefore vulnerable to government regulations, the plurality of national goals, the diversity of financial instruments and markets, the fragmented regulatory authority, and the geopolitical responsibilities of the United States—all acted to weaken large-scale regulatory management of the financial system. Tightly regulated it was, but as time passed the potential for breakdown appeared ever more clearly. In Japan, early control seemed more complete. Until very recently, the Japanese economic system has been kept isolated from world affairs. Financial flows were channeled largely to banks, and the banks were regulated by a very strong central regulatory authority comprising the Ministry of Finance and Bank of Japan.

We have described the two traditional systems in some detail, and have illustrated through examples a common erosion of regulatory control. In the United States, the process has already gone very far indeed. The array of markets and financial instruments available to citizens and institutions alike is now enormous, and is still expanding—stocks, bonds, options, futures, indexes, and many more. Today, we can only sympathize with the overworked and overwhelmed regulators. To a large extent, American regulators have lost meaningful control.

Japan, we suggest, although less far along the road to deregulation, has gone farther than is generally supposed. This has happened for reasons mostly unrelated to the widely publicized threats of trading partners, who claim that the Japanese financial system must be opened to outside forces. Rather, we argue that the process in Japan has gradually begun to imitate changes in America. In Japan, the initial pressures came from individual companies and institutions seeking competitive advantage by escaping in some way from the restrictive traditional system. The slowdown in growth after the oil shock carried the process further by shifting the bargaining power away from the authorities, while internationalization allowed external influences to affect the domestic environment. As a result, the external variations in interest rates, foreign exchange rates, and trade balances have inhibited the regulators and provided even more incentives, to ever more Japanese participants, to challenge the traditional system.

The Japanese system did begin as the more regulated; but we have shown numerous examples of an erosion of that traditional regime. Japanese companies and, increasingly, Japanese financial institutions are experimenting at home and overseas. With these new alternatives has come a degree of freedom previously unknown, as regulatory erosion accelerates. We believe that, in Japan as much as in America, the regulators—even disciplined and powerful experts and managers at the Ministry of Finance and Bank of Japan—will finally be overwhelmed by the market forces that have now been unleashed.

Of course, the specific cultural and institutional context of Japan has many distinctive features. It would be inappropriate and even foolish to suggest that Japan will follow the American pattern in all respects. In fact, there are many reasons to predict that regulatory power will remain in place longer, and relationships will be more persistent, in Japan than in America. Also, it is very important that Japanese regulators have been able to study thoroughly the American experience.

But while the pace of this movement toward deregulation is uncertain, we are confident that only one of two results is possible: either Japan will attempt to isolate itself from effective participation in the world economy—and we believe that Japan will find this alternative both unattractive and extremely difficult—or (much more likely) the Japanese financial system will move toward extensive deregulation—to a degree now almost unimaginable to many Japanese.

In any case, the financial system remains an essential part of every modern industrial economy; and everywhere, dramatic changes are apparent. If, as we believe, the future competition between Japan and America will take place in a deregulated financial environment, it becomes fascinating to consider whether America—with its traditional belief in the freedom of the individual—or Japan—with its emphasis on group behavior and individual acceptance of authority—will prevail. That contest should hold interest for everyone.

CHAPTER 9

Fiscal Policy and
Business-Government Relations

MICHAEL G. RUKSTAD

At both the macroeconomic and microeconomic levels the exercise of fiscal policy constitutes the largest governmental intervention into the economic affairs of the private sector. By taxing, borrowing, and spending, the governments of the United States and Japan annually reallocate almost two trillion dollars in resources, redirecting them from private to public objectives. Yet, among the seven largest industrial countries, the United States and Japan remain the two with the smallest public sectors relative to their total economies.[1] In 1985 Japan and the United States had general government expenditures on goods, services, transfers, and interest payments amounting to 33 percent and 37 percent of gross domestic product (GDP) respectively. The other five major industrial countries supported substantially larger public shares of GDP: 46 percent for the United Kingdom, 49 percent for Canada, 49 percent for Germany, 52 percent for France, and 55 percent for Italy[2] (see *Table 9-1* for a comparison of all seven, 1965–1985).

In the study of business-government relations, however, the differential microeconomic impact of fiscal policy on private firms and their competitors is as important as the size of the public sector and its macroeconomic consequences. In varying degrees, governments attempt to influence the microeconomic behavior of the private sector with selective tax and expenditure measures, while businesses in all countries seek to gain preferential treatment. Of course, political institutions and processes set the constraints within which these decisions are made. Therefore, the two general questions addressed in this chapter are, How do the institutions and processes of decision making lead to particular fiscal policies? and, How do these policies affect business?

The chapter will assess these two questions comparatively within the context of fiscal policy and business in Japan and the United States. Even when dealing with the same economic and fiscal problems, such as worldwide stag-

TABLE 9-1
Major Industrial Countries: General Government Expenditures
(Percent of Gross Domestic Product)

	1965	1970	1975	1979	1985
Japan	18.5	18.2	25.9	30.2	32.6
United States	28.1	32.8	36.0	33.0	36.7
United Kingdom	33.8	36.6	44.5	41.4	46.0
Canada	29.9	36.4	41.3	40.2	48.5
West Germany	33.8	39.1	49.5	48.0	48.5
France	37.5	38.2	42.5	45.4	52.4
Italy	32.8	32.5	41.0	42.9	54.6

NOTE: Between 1965 and 1979, 60 percent of the increase in the ratio of government expenditures to Gross Domestic Product (GDP) was attributable, on average, to increases in transfer payments. If the period from 1979 to 1985 is examined, one finds that interest payments and transfer payments each account for about 40 percent of the increase in the ratio, on average, while purchases of goods and services account for the remaining 20 percent.

SOURCE: International Monetary Fund, *World Economic Outlook,* April 1985, p. 109.

flation after the early 1970s, fiscal policy response in the two countries and its effect on business have differed. The dominant theme in this chapter is that increased deficits have plagued both countries since the mid-seventies; but the impact of these deficits on business in the two countries has been sharply different in important ways. A related theme is that policymakers have been forced by political realities to trade off a continuation of selective fiscal measures for deficit reduction—a trade-off that U.S. policymakers have been less willing to make in comparison with their Japanese counterparts.

Deficits appear to have played a much larger role in affecting the economic performance of the United States than that of Japan, even though the magnitudes of both deficits represent a comparable percentage of the gross national products (GNP). In fact, high real interest rates aggravated by the deficit contributed to a more than 50 percent appreciation of the real effective exchange rate for the American dollar during the period 1981–1985. This appreciation of the dollar, in turn, forced U.S. firms to cut their costs and prices by 50 percent if they wanted to maintain prices at levels comparable with those of five years ago! Since such drastic price cuts are virtually impossible, American firms became significantly less price-competitive in the world markets, and, in frustration, turned to protectionist legislation. The sharp depreciation of the dollar against the yen, which began in late 1985, may help American exporters regain some lost market share; but severe damage still remains, and at least several years will pass before all the damage is undone, if in fact it ever is.

In Japan, although the macroeconomic effect of deficits on the economy has been less than in the United States, institutional pressures to reduce the deficit have actually been greater. In particular, the Japanese Ministry of Finance, attempting to maintain its bureaucratic power and to promote internal harmony among its many bureaus, was compelled to reduce its microeconomic fiscal intervention in selective sectors, as a way of responding to the macroeconomic deficit problem. Here, two of the main targets for reductions have been the annual corporate tax cuts and the selective corporate tax incentives—measures designed to encourage business during the "economic miracle" of 1952–1971, when the Japanese economy achieved an average 10 percent annual growth in real GNP. Although these fiscal incentives have virtually disappeared, the Japanese have not abandoned all methods of channelling resources. The form of intervention has changed, however: an increased reliance on subsidized credit of government agencies financed through the Fiscal Investment and Loan Program (FILP) has replaced tax measures as the favored method of government control of private sector behavior in Japan.

From about 1962–1986, the U.S. trend had been toward larger selective tax incentives, despite both the Japanese example and the traditional U.S. refusal to embrace policies that subsidize particular industries or firms.[3] Yet this trend does not result from any conscious economic strategy built on national policy; rather, it must be viewed as an ad hoc conglomeration of measures granted to special interests through the tax code instead of by direct government expenditures. Also, in opposition to the trend in Japan, U.S. federal direct and guaranteed credit has been reduced since 1980.

These different responses in Japan and the United States can be explained in part by differences in their institutional decision making. In general, Japan has responded to every fiscal problem by introducing incremental changes; this practice maintains the power of the Ministry of Finance over the budgeting process, although at the cost of inertia in decision making. The American fiscal system, on the other hand, has characteristically responded to leadership, most often presidential initiatives, to overcome interest group pressures. Post–World War II presidents have so greatly altered American fiscal priorities that we label the programs of their administrations with their names: Johnson's "Great Society," Nixon's "Revenue Sharing," and Reagan's "Supply-Side Economics." Elective leadership plays a lesser role in Japan; and, overall, this chapter shows how the institutional decision-making processes in each country have led it to a distinctive fiscal outcome with important consequences for business.

Fiscal Policy as a Concern of Business-Government Relations

At the macroeconomic level, fiscal policy is a tool of aggregate demand management which serves the objective of stabilizing prices and production. For example, think of a broad-based personal income tax reduction designed to stimulate private spending. It could offset an economic recession without igniting inflation so long as it did not strain the productive capacity of industries. At the microeconomic level, fiscal tools are targeted to promote specific sectors of the economy, such as export industries or high-technology industries.

A business may be affected by fiscal policy either through its market or through its costs. In the market, the demand for products may be influenced by fiscal policy directly, as in the case of government purchases; or indirectly, as in the case of increased disposable income resulting from a tax cut, which allows private customers to undertake additional purchases. Moreover, to the extent that a firm's sales are sensitive to interest rates, a fiscal deficit may also indirectly affect sales by increasing customers' financing costs associated with a major purchase.

The other channel for fiscal policy to affect business is through a firm's costs. Income and sales taxes levied on corporations represent a business expense, which will either reduce profits and internal cash flow or increase prices to customers. Even personal taxes paid by savers and workers will affect a firm's costs (although indirectly) to the extent that they increase the before-tax compensation that firms must pay to get savers and workers to supply the necessary capital and labor resources. This is the rationale behind proposals to reduce capital gains taxes and social security contributions in order to reduce business costs. Of course, fiscal subsidies have the opposite effect on corporate and personal taxes. Similarly, a fiscal deficit will have both direct and indirect costs to the extent that the cost of capital increases and the firm's competitive position erodes.

Through these channels fiscal policy exerts a significant influence on competitiveness—which is the ability of a firm to deliver to the customer a product with comparable quality at a lower price. The international competitiveness of both Japanese and American companies is influenced, among other factors, by differences in the two nations' fiscal policies.

The Institutional Processes

Major differences in the institutional processes for conducting fiscal policy in Japan and the United States are shown in *Table 9-2*. Here, the processes are compared along two broad dimensions—the rules used to formulate policy and the role of participants in the process. The rules guiding the process include: the time allocated for the decision; the formal authority granted by national constitutions to propose, appropriate, and authorize budget legislation; the informal procedures ("rules of thumb") that facilitate decision making, such as the numerous budget conventions, guidelines, and automatic expenditures and revenues; and the nature of control over the flow of information among participants. Again, such participants are divided into two groups: those directly involved in the decision making, and those (such as interest groups) merely proximate to it.

The Japanese fiscal policymaking process is relatively short, centralized in and largely controlled by the Ministry of Finance (MOF), procedurally limited by informal rules that prescribe fiscal outcomes, and characterized by incremental changes. The American process, on the other hand, is longer, largely decentralized among various executive agencies and congressional commit-

TABLE 9-2
Comparison of the Institutional Processes of Fiscal Policy

	Japan	United States
Rules:		
Decision Period	Short, Inflexible	Long, Flexible
Authority	Centralized in MOF[1]	Decentralized in Congress
Propose	MOF	President and OMB[2]
Appropriate	MOF	Congressional Committees
Authorize	Diet	Congressional Committees
	No Independent Appeals	Many Opportunities to Appeal
Procedures	Institutionalized Rules on Budget Outcomes (Balanced Budget Rule, Bond Dependency Ratio)	Institutionalized Rules on Budget Process (Entitlements; Reconciliation)
Information	Closed Proceedings	Open Proceedings
	Estimates Controlled by MOF	Independent Estimates by OMB and CBO[3]
	Overlapping Budgets	Unified Budgets with Separate Credit and Tax Expenditure Budgets
Participants:		
Decision Makers	Internal Conflict Among "Cooperating Administrators"	External Conflict Among "Competing Advocates"
	Permanent Bureaucracy	Transitory Personnel
Interest Groups	Indirect Involvement Through LDP[4]	Extensive Involvement at Many Junctures in Process

[1] Ministry of Finance.
[2] Office of Management and Budget.
[3] Congressional Budget Office.
[4] Liberal Democratic Party.

tees, subject to extensive interest group pressures, governed by procedures specifying fiscal process, and more open to new budgetary initiatives, particularly from the executive branch. These differences in processes play an important role in helping to explain differences in national policies, as we shall see in the next section.

BUDGET TIMETABLES

Table 9-3 gives an overview of the national budget-making timetables for Japan and the United States.[4] On the basis of this comparison, we can understand (since the American process is substantially longer and more diffused) why a participant in the U.S. budget process would find it more difficult to implement a countercyclical fiscal policy.[5] The annual Japanese budget cycle begins less than a year before the start of the Japanese fiscal year, on April 1;

TABLE 9-3
The Budget Cycle in the United States and Japan

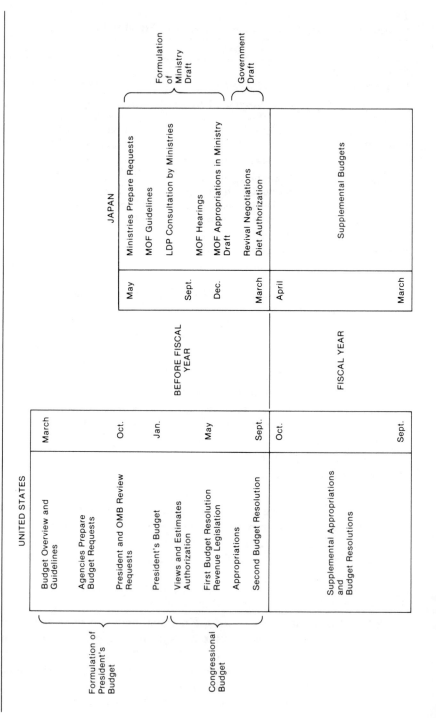

whereas the U.S. budget cycle begins about a year and a half before the U.S. fiscal year starts on October 1. In addition, the Japanese budget proceedings are almost entirely closed to the public until the release of the Ministry draft of the budget, three months before the start of the fiscal year. By contrast, once the U.S. president announces his budget in January, all proceedings are open during the following nine months. The short timetable and less public expo- sure give MOF a greater ability to adjust the budget to fit current macroeco- nomic conditions.

DELEGATION OF FISCAL AUTHORITY

The Japanese Constitution gives the National Diet authority to approve or reject the budget hammered out by MOF;[6] but, in effect, real budgetary power remains with MOF, which initiates and appropriates budget funding and tax proposals. While the locus of effective power has rested predominantly with MOF, especially in the 1950s and 1960s, the trend since the 1970s has been toward a greater involvement of LDP politicians in the formulation of fiscal policy.[7] The consolidated organization of MOF contributes to the con- centration of power over a broad array of economic affairs within one bureaucracy. As *Figure 9-1* shows, seven powerful bureaus compose the muscle of MOF:

FIGURE 9-1

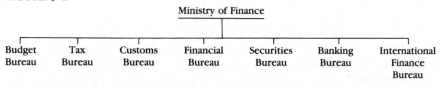

Ministry of Finance

| Budget Bureau | Tax Bureau | Customs Bureau | Financial Bureau | Securities Bureau | Banking Bureau | International Finance Bureau |

Once prepared by MOF, virtually all budgets are accepted without major modification by the Japanese Diet, usually after a short, stylistic debate.[8]

In the United States, however, the process is less orderly, since authority has been spread among various agencies of the executive branch (which typically initiates budget and tax proposals) and the two houses of Congress (which authorize fiscal proposals and appropriate funds). In the executive branch the major actors are the president, the Treasury, the Office of Management and Budget (OMB), the Council of Economic Advisers (CEA), and the government agencies requesting the funding. In Congress, power is distributed among the Authorization Committees, the Appropriations Committees, the Budget Com- mittees, the Senate Finance Committee, the House Ways and Means Commit- tee, and the Congressional Budget Office (CBO). Legally, substantial changes may be incorporated by these participants at any of the numerous junctures during the long formal budget process.

INFORMAL PROCEDURES

Rules play an important role in the fiscal decisions for both the size and distribution of the budget and tax proposals. A formal or informal rule that requires a balanced budget actually guides fiscal *outcomes;* a rule that defines eligible participants for entitlements benefits merely guides fiscal *processes.* (Entitlements, it should be noted, do not guide outcomes, since entitlements do not set levels of funding or tie funding to performance.) All countries have both types of rules, but not in equal measure.

In Japan, the rules of fiscal policy have generally guided fiscal outcomes; in the United States, rules have guided the fiscal process. Since World War II, Japan has adopted numerous outcome rules at various times, such as the balanced budget rule to which policymakers adhered until 1965.[9] These rules give MOF power over the ministries (and other interest groups) by helping to hold the line on spending requests. They also contribute to balance and stability of fiscal policy outcomes.

For the Japanese, *baransu* (balance) is also achieved by the informal procedure of "incrementalism," whereby a given percentage increase over the preceding year's base is evenly applied to virtually all requests. During the MOF hearings each October and November, budget examiners start with the preceding year's expenditures as the base, which allows MOF to achieve real spending cuts whenever necessary.[10] For spending ministries that are dissatisfied, resolution of any remaining differences takes place at the more senior level in November. Such petitioners must be clear on their priorities, since no appeals to a third party are allowed; instead, senior MOF bureaucrats simply determine the validity of all claims made on the government.[11]

The rules of U.S. fiscal policy generally prescribe the process by which policy should be formulated (despite occasional flirtations with rules that specify outcomes, such as the proposed balanced budget amendment or the recent Gramm-Rudman bill). The Congressional Budget Act of 1974 formalized the rules of the budget process, such as the resolution and reconciliation procedures. The first budget resolution, due before the May 15 deadline, sets nonbinding targets for the aggregate spending and functional allocations, such as national defense, income security, and transportation; but it does not specify allocations for programs. Later, between May and September, specific legislation is considered, and the culmination of this process occurs in September, with passage of the binding second budget resolution, made powerful by the reconciliation process. Under reconciliation, Congress instructs committees to report on any differences between the second resolution and their allocations. These figures are then voted on by the House or Senate in one or more reconciliation bills, until differences are finally resolved.

CONTROL OVER INFORMATION

Almost as important as process and rules, the Japanese Ministry of Finance exercises more control over the flow of information to other Japanese participants than does any one of the U.S. budget participants.[12] Here, the closed Japanese proceedings are a significant factor, but so are MOF's ability to impose strict spending ceilings and to supply the revenue estimates used in budget debates. Because of MOF control over fiscal information, other participants tend to follow MOF's lead in fiscal policy.[13]

First, MOF releases its ceilings for the percentage increases of the new requests from the spending ministries; this happens well before the end of August, when the ministries must submit their expenditure requests to the Budget Bureau of MOF.[14] The spending ceilings force the ministries to limit new programs, which can be added only at the expense of existing ones. More importantly, ceilings help the budget examiners to achieve *baransu,* whereby relative shares in total expenditures can be maintained among competing interests.[15] In the United States, the degree of control over agency requests largely depends on the budget management system used by the president. President Reagan and his first budget director at OMB, David Stockman, instituted a "top-down" budget process which gave them more effective control over expenditures.[16] Earlier presidents such as Ford and Carter were not able to exert such control.

In Japan, at the same time that the spending ministries are preparing their requests for the Budget Bureau of MOF, decisions on the overall size of the proposed budget are made by senior MOF bureaucrats, after discussing expenditures, revenues, and deficit financing with the Budget, Tax, and Financial Bureaus. The Tax Bureau of MOF prepares preliminary (sometimes political) estimates of expected revenues for the coming fiscal year, based on their own economic forecasts and those of the Economic Planning Agency (EPA). Again, MOF's monopoly over revenue estimates represents an important source of power, since it allows MOF to argue that funds will not be available to support new programs. In the United States, a system of checks and balances provides the decentralized decision makers with their own sources of information on the budget. Since 1974, with the establishment of the nonpartisan Congressional Budget Office, Congress has gained an important counterbalance to the presidential Office of Management and Budget.

MOF power would be further enhanced if that ministry could institute *sōgō yosan shugi* (comprehensive budgeting), in which all expenditures and revenues were consolidated into a single account.[17] So far, however, inertia and continued interest group pressure have resulted in three types of budgets which are presented to the Japanese Diet each year: (1) the general account budget, (2) the special accounts budget, and (3) the budget for government-affiliated enterprises. The relationship among these budgets is illustrated schematically in *Table 9-4,* where the height of the boxes indicates the approximate level of funds. These three budgets should not be considered as mutually exclusive accounts for managerial control over a fiscal function, in the way that a company's current and capital budgets usually are. Instead, they are viewed by spending ministries and interest groups as alternative avenues for channelling funds to specific purposes.

TABLE 9-4
Sources and Uses of Funds for the Japanese Government Budgets

SOURCES

USES

Special Accounts (SA)	General Account (GA)		General Account (GA)		Special Accounts (SA)	Government Enterprises Account (GEA)	Fiscal Investment & Loan Program (FILP)
	Personal Income Tax		Social Security				
			Public Works				
	Corporate Income Tax		Education				
	Indirect Taxes		Defense				
	Non-Tax Revenues		Others				
	Construction Bonds		Local Government Transfers				
	Deficit Bonds		Debt Service				
Postal Savings Deposits					Special Accounts for 1. Government Enterprises 2. Insurances 3. Public Management 4. Public Investment and Loans 5. Consolidated Funds		
Welfare and National Annuity Funds							
Postal Life Insurance and Annuity Funds						Japanese National Railway Japan Development Bank Ex-Im Bank etc.	
Government Guaranteed Bonds							

When we speak of "the budget" in Japan, we are usually referring to the general account budget. The general account (GA) includes all expenditures for major government programs and all tax revenues; any deficit is financed by national bond issues. The special accounts budget records the expenditures of the thirty-eight accounts (as of 1985) established by the government in order to manage specific funds or to finance specific projects. Each one has its own source of revenue (including borrowed funds).[18] On net, the special accounts comprise roughly the same amount of expenditures as the general account.[19] Finally, there is the budget for government-affiliated enterprises (GAEs).[20] In recent years total expenditures for all of the GAEs have amounted to approximately one-tenth of the general account expenditures.

The Japanese budgetary process also includes a unique summary document, the Fiscal Investment and Loan Program (FILP), which is not a budget (although it is as important). The FILP provides a complete statement for the coming fiscal year of investment and loan activity by government-affiliated enterprises and public financial institutions, often at subsidized interest rates.[21] It is prepared by MOF around December to be used as a reference by the Cabinet and the Diet; but during the course of any fiscal year, FILP can be adjusted by MOF to respond to the current economic situation without Diet approval (though the Diet has stipulated ceilings). It does not include any new accounts—all items on FILP may be found in the general account, the special accounts, or the government-affiliated enterprise accounts. The total of FILP funds has grown relative to GNP from 3.4 percent in 1955 to 7.1 percent in 1984.

The U.S. unified budget document has provided, since 1968, a consolidated presentation of federal funds (general funds) and trust funds (earmarked funds, such as Social Security and unemployment trust funds) with interfund transfers eliminated.[22] Federal tax revenues provide most of the funding for the unified budget, but any shortfall is made up by borrowing from the public. As in the case of the Japanese central government, the U.S. federal government also extends credit to the private sector by direct loans and guaranteed loans.[23] Since 1980, the total amount of direct and guaranteed loans has been recorded on a credit budget, which allows Congress some limited ability to control the government's lending activities.[24]

DECISION MAKERS IN FISCAL POLICY

Conflict is an inevitable part of budgeting. Given that the key budgetary decision makers in Japan are predominantly MOF bureaucrats, the organizational structure guarantees that the major conflicts will occur within the Ministry of Finance itself. Such dissension among bureaucrats can lead to inertia in decision making, resulting in low-risk outcomes—reinforcing the already prevalent norm of incrementalism.[25] Since the problems of MOF are closely interconnected, failure by the Budget Bureau to hold the line on expenditures, for example, creates problems for the Financial Bureau, which must then

finance an additional deficit. Again, banking deregulations in 1983–1984 allowing banks to deal in government bonds, which were granted by the Banking Bureau, were prompted by the need to market the huge quantities of
government bonds necessitated by the deficit. This move, however, upset the
competitive balance with the securities industry represented in MOF by the
Securities Bureau. Moreover, liberalizations of the yen since 1979 by the International Finance Bureau have helped to force the Financial Bureau to pay
market rates of interest on government debt.[26]

In Japan, the existence of a permanent cadre of elite bureaucrats in the key
ministries has tended to reinforce the "sectionalism" or "departmentalism"
that exists in government, particularly since there is no movement of personnel between ministries, limited communication among them, and little control
over the ministries by the Cabinet. In addition, sectionalism is reinforced by
the budget process itself, because the ministries exercise responsibility for the
initial drafting of legislation and budgets. As a result, conflicts between interest
groups or political parties often are reflected in ministerial conflicts, as the
groups and parties align themselves with various advocates within the ministry.[27]

INTEREST GROUPS AND FISCAL POLICY

Among the Japanese, pressure from interest groups can be brought to bear
only indirectly on MOF, through the ruling Liberal Democratic Party (LDP)
petitioners in the Diet. There, Seichōkai (the Policy Affairs Research Council)
of the LDP consults with the ministerial representatives before the ministries
submit their budgets to the LDP at the end of August of each year. Then, in
December, just a few days before the release of the Ministry draft, the LDP
Policy Research Council announces its annual Budget Compilation Program—
a political document that sketches the LDP position in rather vague terms,
without taking a stand on priorities. Serious debate begins only after release of
the Ministry draft, during a week of intensive "revival negotiations," which
includes final appropriations.[28] At the conclusion of the revival negotiations,
the Cabinet ratifies the budget, and it becomes the "government draft," which
is then sent in January to the National Diet for approval by March. There is
little opportunity for interest groups to influence fiscal policy in the Diet,
except for supplementary budgets discussed during the summer.

History of Fiscal Policy in Japan and the United States

This section will briefly survey the history of fiscal policy in Japan and the
United States, explaining how the institutional process of decision making led
to the fiscal policies adopted in each country. The side-by-side comparison
considers, first, whether the objective of the fiscal policy was national or
sectoral; and second, whether policy predominantly affected demand or costs.

The discussion will be divided into three periods: (1) the origins of modern
fiscal policy, before the early 1960s, (2) the rise of fiscal activism in the late

1960s and early 1970s, and (3) the era of large deficits since the mid-1970s. In general, Japan's fiscal policies were broadly similar to those of the United States for many of the postwar years because of a conscious effort to avoid countercyclical fiscal activism. Yet, since the second oil shock of 1979, Japanese and American policies have diverged dramatically. Japan had long used fiscal policy as a means of reducing business costs for selected sectors, whereas the United States historically had refused to follow that path. In recent years the United States has promoted microeconomic supply-side fiscal stimulus without regard for the macroeconomic consequences of the deficit; the Japanese, on the other hand, have focused on the macroeconomic consequences of the deficit while all but abandoning microeconomic sectoral policies.

THE ORIGINS OF FISCAL POLICY

The origins of modern Japanese fiscal policy coincided with the development of the modern state as outlined in the Imperial Constitution of 1890. In 1889, Japan enacted a sophisticated Law of Government Accounting—the primary law regulating fiscal activity until World War II. One unique feature of this law (still in effect) was the division of the government budget into a general account handling routine collections and disbursements, and various special accounts covering the government's industrial and entrepreneurial activities. During the Meiji years, special accounts included: ironworks, shipyards, railroads, mines and silk mills.[29] Thus, from its origins, the modern Japanese state has used fiscal instruments to promote sectoral objectives.

The chief legacy of Japanese public finance before World War II was an increasingly large public sector fueled by the growth in military expenditures;[30] while the United States supported a small decentralized public sector. The rate of growth of Japanese government expenditures led that of GNP during the entire prewar period. *Table 9-5* shows the upward trend in the share of central government expenditures to GNP.

In comparison, until the mid-sixties the size of the U.S. federal government was smaller, its objectives were applied more evenly among sectors, and its effects on aggregate demand seemed generally contractionary. The share of government expenditures out of national income in the United States

TABLE 9-5
Central Government Expenditures (percentage of GNP for selected years)

	1880	1900	1920	1940	1960	1980
Japan	7.2	15.9	23.5	40.0	28.7	30.2
United States	3.0	2.4	8.5	9.6	18.3	33.0

NOTE: General government expenditures for Japan include all general account and special account expenditures less duplications between accounts.
SOURCES: Koichi Emi, *Government Fiscal Activity and Economic Growth in Japan, 1868–1960.* (Tokyo: Kenkyusha, 1963); Appendix A-1. U.S. Dept. of Commerce, *Historical Statistics of the United States, 1975,* Series F. IMF; *World Economic Outlook,* April 1985, p. 109.

amounted to less than half that of the Japanese share, although since the turn of the century, government expenditures in both countries have generally increased faster than has GNP.

Of course, the American federal system results in more decentralized allocation of total resources among the state and local governments. During the years before World War II, the federal government accounted for about a third of total government expenditures in the United States; in Japan, the comparable figure was three-quarters. In America, the federal government's share of national income increased with each major war; but, unlike the experience in Japan, it declined substantially afterward.

After the Second World War, the American Occupation forces imposed a reformation of the fiscal system, along with the other political, economic, and social institutions in Japan. A special commission, headed by the American banker Joseph Dodge, was charged with the task of designing fiscal policies consistent with noninflationary economic growth. In addition, Columbia Professor Carl Shoup led a special tax mission that in 1950 implemented a comprehensive set of basic revenue measures. Among the Shoup reforms was the elimination of preferential treatment for specific industries and for certain classes of income such as capital gains. This practice has not survived, however.

As with other Occupation-induced regulations, the Japanese succeeded in transforming their postwar tax system to meet native demands for control over industrial sectors. As a whole, the Japanese claimed that the Shoup reforms were "somewhat too idealistic to fit with the reality of the Japanese economy."[31] So during the 1950s, some taxes, such as the capital gains tax on securities transactions, were eliminated, while special tax incentives were reestablished for particular industries—as a way of stimulating investment and exports.

Yet rules guiding fiscal outcomes were often continued from the American Occupation. Such rules limited the extent to which the Japanese government could use fiscal policy to implement macroeconomic, but not microeconomic, objectives. After the war, the primary fiscal principle became a balanced budget, a practice institutionalized in the Finance Act of 1947 and further strengthened by the Dodge Mission in 1949; that principle was followed quite faithfully by the central government until 1965. A second principle was the "20 Percent Rule," followed during most of the postwar years, which kept total tax revenues at or near 20 percent of national income. The annual tax cuts, made possible by very rapid economic growth that pushed incomes into higher tax brackets, played an integral part in the implementation of this rule.[32]

Together, these rules tended to contain the growth in government expenditures that had been prevalent before the war. The net contribution of these fiscal principles to overall economic growth during the period between the Occupation and 1965 was to restrain aggregate demand, because budgets were kept in surplus during most of this period, and the size of government expenditures grew less rapidly than did GNP. Moreover, there was relatively little reliance on fiscal policy for countercyclical objectives, since monetary policy fulfilled that purpose.[33] Institutionally, these rules strengthened MOF's influence over the ministries on macroeconomic policy, by providing a rationale that "the funds do not exist" while maintaining an appearance of fairness. And allocations for special purposes could still be made through the annual tax cuts, the special accounts, or selective credit subsidies.

Unlike Japan, the United States did not have a legacy of a rapidly expanding government sector and hyperinflation to cope with after World War II. In fact, memories of high unemployment during the 1930s had a far greater impact on American postwar fiscal policy. With a legacy of economic depression in mind, Americans feared that their country might relapse into stagnation; so in 1946, Congress passed an Employment Act that affirmed the federal government's commitment to high employment. Behind this legislation, however, lay a history of confusion, compromise, and ambivalence. American lawmakers did not agree, either on the use of fiscal policy as a tool for employment, or on the usefulness of government planning, a long tradition in Japan. Nor were these disagreements matters of economic theory alone.

The ambivalence toward countercyclical fiscal policy displayed in the Employment Act of 1946, for example, showed itself clearly in the practices of the American government. There, the primary responsibility for initiating fiscal policies consistent with the objective of high employment rested with the president. Long before, the Budget and Accounting Act of 1921 had significantly increased executive leadership in the budget process. Yet rhetoric of both Presidents Truman and Eisenhower endorsed the virtue of balanced budgets and left activist fiscal management aside. Even though countercyclical fiscal policy was generally shunned by policymakers, however, automatic fiscal stabilizers—legacies of Depression-era and World War II legislation—continued to operate in the United States.

Overall, the net impact of fiscal policy from 1947 to the early 1960s proved to be as contractionary in the United States as in Japan. Neither country showed enough political nerve to risk an experiment with countercyclical fiscal policies in a time of relative growth and prosperity. Japan was limited by its fiscal rules—rules that aided MOF's dominance of other ministries and that allowed continued microeconomic uses of fiscal policy. American presidents were limited by their fiscal ideology; and even the three American recessions of 1947, 1954, and 1958 did not provide sufficient catalysts for a change in basic American attitudes toward fiscal policy.

THE RISE OF FISCAL ACTIVISM

In Japan, the turning point in the use of fiscal policy came during the recession of 1965, with the near bankruptcy of Yamaichi Securities, the nation's second largest securities firm. The downturn had been induced by tight monetary policy during 1964, and then aggravated by a reduction in the supplementary budget at the end of that year.[34] As one consequence of this near panic, the Finance Act was amended to allow the issuance of national public debt for financing general expenditures. This, in turn, would give the government the ability to stimulate the economy by deficit spending.

In effect, the standing balanced-budget rule was now replaced by two other rules: bonds should be used only to finance construction expenditures, and bond issues should meet the "test of market acceptance" by not being sold directly to the Bank of Japan.[35] These new ad hoc rules could be easily followed during a period of high and stable real growth (which actually exceeded 11 percent annually between 1966 and 1971). In these years, the Ministry of Finance also agreed on a rule limiting national government bond issues as a percentage of government expenditures (the "bond dependency ratio") to 15 percent. For the years 1965–1966 and 1971–1972, therefore, fiscal policy in Japan was expansionary.[36] During the other years, it ranged from neutral to mildly contractionary. When compared to the real growth in GNP and the growth in the money supply, fiscal policy was more countercyclical and more consistent with monetary policy after 1965, unlike the practices of the preceding two decades.

By 1973, a noticeable change had occurred in Japanese economic and social attitudes. Eventually, this new thinking would affect the conduct of fiscal policy and produce the rise of a welfare state in Japan. Up to that time, the goals of economic planning had consistently emphasized rapid growth, to the exclusion of other social objectives.[37] For each of six previous formal plans, the Japanese had exceeded their growth targets. But the Basic Economic and Social Plan enacted in February 1973 abruptly shifted emphasis to an "active welfare society," even though it included a goal for real GNP growth of 9.4 percent per year for the next four years.[38] This shift in emphasis can be partly explained by domestic demands for an improved quality of life (including an improved environment) and for increased social security by a more affluent population. In addition, international pressures on Japan to reduce its trade surplus had intensified, and the Japanese were advised to stimulate their domestic economy and thus to reduce their huge current account surpluses.[39]

The situation in the United States from the mid-1960s to the first oil shock in 1973 foreshadowed this Japanese fiscal activism; fiscal policy was used to solve an economic problem, but it also provided its share of mistakes. In general, recession and slow growth prompted the adoption of an activist fiscal policy in the United States; yet presidential leadership was required to make it a reality. American changes did not occur as rapidly as in Japan because there was no economic crisis comparable to the stock market crash and the imminent bankruptcies in Japan during 1965.

Yet things did happen: President John F. Kennedy publicly announced his intention to seek large personal and corporate tax cuts, after carefully studying the contents and timing of such a proposal during his first two years in office. In 1962, a "first stage" tax incentive package, including a 7 percent investment tax credit, was passed; but the macroeconomic impact remained muted, since its effect on revenues was essentially neutralized by offsetting tax increases. During the later and much larger "second stage" reduction in income taxes, the Kennedy Administration met charges of "fiscal irresponsibility" with arguments about the potential for additional growth, and by stressing the "reform" features of the new proposal. After Kennedy's assassination, President Lyndon B. Johnson finally cleared the way for passage of the Revenue Act of 1964 by promising to hold the line on expenditures during the 1965 fiscal year.

The healthy growth generated by the tax cut of 1964 soon became dwarfed by the enormous expenditures authorized for the Vietnam War. Defense expenditures increased by 12 percent in 1966 and then by an additional 20 percent in 1967, at a time when unemployment reached a postwar low. On top of this stimulus, annual expenditures for President Johnson's Great Society programs almost doubled in the three years from 1965 to 1968. All measures of fiscal stimulus clearly show an expansionary fiscal policy. Then, a temporary 10 percent income tax surcharge announced by President Johnson in 1968 proved to be too little, too late—at least for halting a persistent inflation that had increased for seven consecutive years. President Richard M. Nixon's major new fiscal initiative was the introduction of revenue sharing, which would prove to be very important in succeeding years. In all, transfers to state and local government rose from 0.2 percent of the budget in 1965 to 4.3 percent in 1975; transfers thus came to represent one of the fastest growing budget components of that decade.

We can see that both Japan and the United States turned toward activist fiscal policies in the mid-1960s, as a way of solving either an acute crisis (imminent collapse of securities markets in Japan) or a chronic problem (a decade of relatively slow growth in the United States). Japanese bureaucrats responded to the crisis in 1965 not by abandoning the old fiscal rules, but by making minor modifications. American presidential leadership brought even more volatile fiscal policies to the United States. In both countries, some increased spending seemed unavoidable given the changing attitudes of the two populations. Prosperity in the late 1960s clearly led to much greater demands for social security programs, as citizens sought to protect their gains, first in the United States and then later in Japan. Finally, the United States extended itself even beyond this point, by running fiscal deficits in order to finance the Vietnam War. By 1973, poor fiscal management in each nation had resulted in a domestically generated inflation. Neither national system proved very effective in implementing a well-timed contractionary policy.

THE MODERN ERA OF LARGE FISCAL DEFICITS

A quadrupling of crude oil prices in late 1973 marked the beginnings of an economic crisis in all industrial countries, but especially for Japan, which imports all of its petroleum. In 1974, real economic growth turned negative for the first time in Japan's postwar history. Since economic policy had already allowed inflation to reach double-digit levels before the oil shock, no further accommodation of inflation could be tolerated. Yet monetary policy had already turned contractionary during the previous year, as part of the government's attempt to combat inflation. Fiscal policy, on the other hand, continued on the same course as before the shock, to become even more expansionary during 1974 and 1975.

In 1975, confusion beset the Ministry of Finance, as a result of conflicting pressures to both stimulate growth and avoid further inflation. Deficit financing seemed inevitable, as slow economic growth brought minimal increases in revenues at the same time that social spending was increasing. Despite some cutbacks in public works outlays, it was still necessary to issue government bonds in large amounts. During 1975, Japanese bond issues jumped to 25 percent of total expenditures—a sharp increase from 11 percent in the previous year.

For MOF, placing these securities proved to be more difficult than it would have been for treasuries in countries with less rigid capital markets. The Bank of Japan, for example, refused to accept a large volume of government bonds because such action would increase the money supply growth beyond its target rates. Since these bonds were issued at very low (nonmarket) interest rates, and because they had to be placed largely with securities firms and banks, deficit financing meant that MOF had to force financial institutions to purchase and hold large portfolios of unprofitable assets.

Figure 9-2 shows the difference between issue rates and secondary market rates for those securities, over a ten-year period. During this decade, the secondary market interest rate and the issue rate for government bonds converged, while larger proportions of the bonds were placed with private financial and nonfinancial institutions. In general, the increased need to finance a deficit resulted in greater pressure to liberalize the domestic capital markets.

Japan recovered only gradually from the 1973 oil shock, and slowed growth contributed to the government's inability to manage the increase in its expenditures for social programs. Pressure for annual tax cuts also continued, and some personal cuts were granted on a temporary basis. But these were partly or wholly offset by increases in corporate and indirect taxes. All together, such pressures led to a rapidly increasing deficit. Then, in 1977 and 1978, as the dollar plummeted, new pressures were applied to MOF, which was expected to increase fiscal expenditures and thus to stimulate, once again, the Japanese economy.

As 1979 began, fiscal policy in Japan had become expansionary. Once it became clear that the second oil shock would be quite sizable, however, this policy was reversed, and some expenditures were postponed until 1980. Fiscal policy for 1980 and the subsequent years has been increasingly contractionary, as successive prime ministers have tried to reduce deficits. Prime Minister Ohira attempted to introduce a value-added tax (VAT) in order to broaden the revenue base; but this proposal was soundly rejected, contributing to his

FIGURE 9-2
The Issuing Term of Government Bonds and Secondary Market Rates in Japan

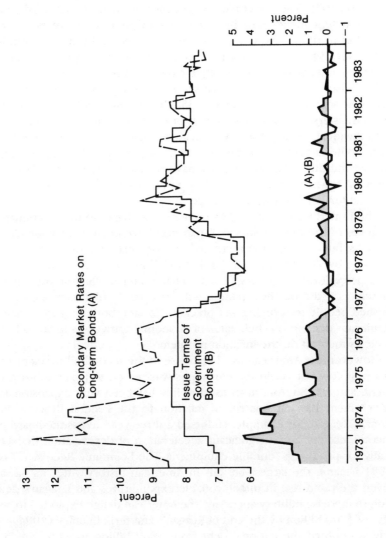

departure from office in June of 1980. Japan's contractionary macroeconomic stance did succeed in reducing the severity of the inflation accompanying the second oil shock, but at the cost of significantly lower growth.

In fact, the budget for fiscal year 1980 marked another turning point in the conduct of Japanese fiscal policy. Nominal government spending had grown at an annual rate of only 4 percent, compared to the 12.3 percent rate between 1974 and 1979. The growth in tax revenues also had slowed considerably, but the bond dependency ratio had continued to fall in recent years—evidence of the effort to reduce expenditures. Attempts at administrative reform between 1981 and 1983 increased public awareness of the need for both reduced subsidies and smaller administrative expenditures.

The austere 1984 budget increased expenditures only 0.5 percent on average—the smallest increase since 1955. The only items allowed larger increases were transfers to local governments, interest payments, and defense. Tax cuts for individuals were offset by increases in the corporate income tax and in some indirect taxes.[40] Despite all the fiscal churning that has occurred since the second oil shock, the changes have remained incremental, balanced, and directed toward maintaining MOF's power. As a package, they have actually delayed further institutional change.

The United States was no less immune than Japan to the inflationary consequences of the two oil shocks. Japan may have been more dependent on oil imports, but U.S. inflation increased proportionately more. Energy prices, increasing by 29 percent in 1974, led the Consumer Price Index upward at a 12.2 percent rate. Of course, inflation had a similar effect on the American tax system as it did on the Japanese—the real tax burden increased as inflation pushed people into higher tax brackets. In fact, both countries experienced significant declines in their rates of economic growth, as fiscal and monetary policies focused on the inflation problem.

However, the American fiscal response to the second oil shock provides the sharpest contrast yet in the entire postwar period to Japanese fiscal management. Since 1980, American fiscal policy has been very expansionary, while government has left control of inflation to the Federal Reserve. President Ronald Reagan, for example, endorsed a three-year across-the-board personal income tax cut and a significant acceleration of depreciation benefits, especially for producers' durable equipment. The Economic Recovery Tax Act of 1981 became the largest tax cut in American history. After its passage, and given the rapid rise in uncontrollable expenditures and Reagan's determination to increase military spending, the American deficit exploded to an annual rate of $200 billion by the end of Reagan's first term in office (1984)—a trend which doubled the national debt from $800 billion to $1.5 trillion in four years.

On balance, the shares of budget expenditures have been far more stable in Japan than in the United States, particularly since President Reagan entered office. Most programs in Japan held approximately the same share of the budget in 1984 as they did in 1975[41] (see *Table 9-6*). This may also be said of

TABLE 9-6
Changes in the Percentage Share of the Budget

	Japan			United States		
	1965–1975	1975–1980	1980–1984	1965–1975	1975–1980	1980–1984
Social Programs	3.2	0.4	-0.3	16.7	3.2	-0.2
Defense Programs	-2.0	-1.0	0.6	-12.8	-6.4	4.0
Transfers to Governments	2.3	-2.9	0	4.1	-2.1	-0.5
Interest Payments	4.3	7.7	5.5	1.7	-1.6	4.2
Public Works	-6.3	1.9	-2.7	-1.4	2.0	-3.4
Other Programs	-0.4	-6.1	-3.1	-8.3	5.5	-4.7
Magnitude of All Changes	17.4	17.1	12.2	45.0	20.8	17.0

NOTE: Changes in the percentage share of the budget are calculated by subtracting the percentage share in the terminal year of the period from that of the initial year. For example, in the United States in 1984, defense programs amounted to 26.7 percent of the total budget; in 1980 they were 22.7 percent. The change in the percentage share of the budget was 4.0 percent, as indicated under column "1980–1984" for the United States.

SOURCES: Nomura Research Institute, *Japanese Bond Market*, No. 5, "Public Finance in Japan," April 1984, pp. 16–17; Ministry of Finance, *Financial Statistics of Japan*, September 1983, p. 14; *Economic Report of the President*, January 1985, pp. 316–317.

TABLE 9-7
Relative Magnitudes of Total Tax Changes in Japan and U.S.
(All tax changes are compared to the largest tax change in Japanese postwar history, the 1974 tax cut, which was 0.9 percent of GNP. Index base is (1974 Tax Cut/GNP) = 100.)

	Japan (no tax change has ever exceeded ± 100)	
1954–1974	Annual tax cuts (on average)	− 45
1975–1984	Annual tax increases	22
	Average Magnitude (all changes since 1954)	− 33
	United States (selected tax changes)	
1964	Kennedy-Johnson Tax Cut	−190
1968	Johnson Tax Surcharge	122
1975	Ford Tax Cut	−155
1978	Carter Tax Reforms	− 90
1981	Economic Recovery Tax Act	−490
1982	Tax Equity and Fiscal Responsibility Act	222
	Average Magnitude (all changes since 1954)	− 45

SOURCES: Joseph Pechman, *Federal Tax Policy* (Washington, D.C.: Brookings Institution, 1983), p. 40; *The Economist,* Sept. 1, 8, 1962; Bank of Japan, *Economic Statistics Annual,* 1969; and Research Division, Tax Committee, House of Councillors of the National Diet, *Databook on Public Finance,* 1984, Table I-19, p. 40.

tax changes in recent years. Japan has had a tax increase in each of the past eight years, but the magnitude of the change has been small. The United States, on the other hand, has enacted tax changes that are five times as large as even the enormous Japanese tax cut of 1974 (see *Table 9-7*). Here, the Japanese incremental approach has been more effective in reducing the national deficit than has the American policy of neglect—which seems to respond only if the pain of the deficit reaches crisis proportions, or if the president provides effective leadership on the deficit issue. In the meantime, the two different national approaches have broad implications for business costs and market demand, a topic to which we now turn.

The Effects of Fiscal Policy on Business

As mentioned at the beginning of this chapter, fiscal policy may affect business through changes in market demand and business costs. Except for those businesses that are largely dependent on government contracts for their sales, most businesspeople would probably claim that it is through costs, and not sales, that companies feel the hand of fiscal policy in the marketplace. This section will estimate and compare the magnitudes of these effects for both countries.

FISCAL POLICY AND MARKET DEMAND

By contributing to the total spending and income in a country, fiscal policy directly and indirectly affects business sales. The difficult questions are how much and who benefits in each country. Estimates of the *direct* contributions to GNP growth resulting from the current year's fiscal policy are averaged over three periods between 1965 and 1985 in *Table 9-8* below:[42]

TABLE 9-8
Average Annual Contribution of Fiscal Policy to Real GNP Growth, 1965–1985 (in percentage points)

	Fiscal Activism	First Oil Shock	Second Oil Shock
	(1965–1973)	(1974–1978)	(1979–1985)
Japan	0.2	1.3	−0.5
U.S.	0.3	0	0.7

SOURCES: OECD, *Economic Outlook*, Occasional Studies, July 1978, p. 31, and IMF, *World Economic Outlook*, April 1985, p. 221.

As the numbers suggest, during the period 1965–1973, both countries were starting to use fiscal instruments as an integral component of their economic strategies, as described in the previous section. On average, the contribution during this period to real GNP in Japan and the United States was a moderate expansion of 0.2 to 0.3 percentage points respectively. The significant differences occurred during the next two periods, in response to the oil shocks. The average effect on demand for the first shock and its aftermath was very expansionary in Japan and neutral in the United States. Since the second shock in 1979, Japan has maintained a contractionary fiscal policy while the United States has been expansionary.

These trends are particularly important for firms in certain industries, such as construction, consumer durables, and capital equipment, where sales are sensitive to changes in the levels of domestic income. To the extent that fiscal expansion or contraction is caused by government expenditures, there will also be significant repercussions on the defense industries in the United States and the construction industries in Japan.[43]

Thus, fiscal policy can produce complex changes in the nation's portfolio of industrial output depending on how it is implemented. The preceding data indicate the direction and magnitude of the effects for the vast majority of businesses whose sales are made directly to the government or to other domestic customers. But an expansionary fiscal policy in the United States will, in theory, contribute significantly to the growth of the export-oriented businesses in Japan, and vice versa. In practice, U.S. exports to Japan contribute less than one percent of the U.S. GNP, whereas Japanese exports to the United States contribute about 4 percent of the Japanese GNP.[44] The primary U.S. beneficiaries of an expansionary fiscal policy in Japan will be U.S. agricultural and raw material producers; the primary Japanese beneficiaries of an expansionary fiscal policy in the United States will be the Japanese machinery, automobile, and metal industries.[45]

FISCAL POLICY AND BUSINESS COSTS

No single measure captures the direct and indirect effects of fiscal policy on the costs that a firm faces when making its business decisions. Business costs are more than accounting expenses; they are the costs of capital and labor, which include all opportunity costs associated with the acquisition and use of those resources. Business decisions, such as a decision to export, to invest, or to develop a new product, are influenced by these expenses.

In the following sections, I will isolate, first, the financial effects of deficits on a component of business costs—the real interest rate—and subsequently, on investment and trade decisions. Then I will compare the relative tax burdens of firms in both America and Japan. Finally, I will examine those business decisions that are exempted from full tax burdens in order to identify government priorities.

THE EFFECTS OF DEFICITS ON BUSINESS

Fiscal deficits increase business costs by pushing up real interest rates.[46] The ultimate damage from high real interest rates is not the short-run additions to the financing costs for business, but the long-run consequences in terms of slower capital formation and diminished trade competitiveness. Real interest rates for both Japan and the United States since 1980 have been significantly higher than the average level of approximately 2 to 3 percent that existed in the 1950s and 1960s (see *Figure 9-3*). The coincidence of large fiscal deficits during the same period as the high rates raises the question of the extent to which the deficits are responsible.

The first step in determining the contribution of the deficits to higher real interest rates in each country is to assess the relative size of the deficits. Because of the complexity of the interactions, the relationship between the size of deficits and high interest rates has been very controversial in recent years, particularly in the United States. *Figure 9-4* shows the deficits as a percentage of GNP for Japan and the United States for the period 1975–1984. The relative magnitudes of the deficits have been generally larger in Japan, but the projections for each country show the United States with substantially larger deficits in the late 1980s.

A major reason for muddled public debates over the consequences of the deficits is that most participants do not consider all of the determinants of interest rates. Interest rates are not determined only by deficits; if they were, then we would always observe increased deficits leading to increased interest rates. Rather, interest rates are determined by the complex interactions of those who are demanding credit (government and business) and those who are supplying it (the central bank, the private sector, and foreign savers).

As economic growth decreases, the demand for credit by the private sector decreases, and vice versa. Consequently, real interest rates rise and fall with business recoveries and recessions. It is not surprising, then, that during the

FIGURE 9-3
Real Short-Term Interest Rates

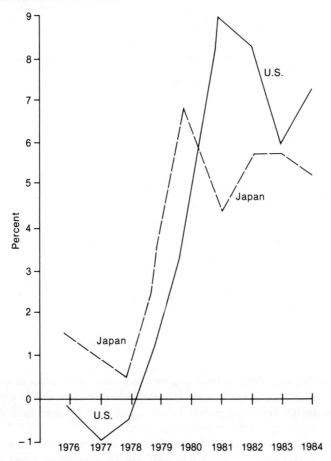

SOURCE: IMF, *World Economic Outlook*, April 1985.

severe recession of 1981–1982 in the United States, the reduced demand for corporate and personal borrowing led to lower real interest rates, as shown in *Figure 9-3*. At the same time, however, the deficit was rising, in large part on account of the falling tax revenues attributable to the recession. Nonetheless, real interest rates were necessarily higher than in the absence of the deficit because investors would only accept large new issues of government securities in their portfolios if they would receive higher real returns.

The supply of credit provided by both domestic and foreign savers, and controlled by the central bank, also affects interest rates; such rates rise and fall as the supply falls and rises. In fact, that is exactly the principle that the Federal Reserve or the Bank of Japan uses when it attempts to control the economy by

FIGURE 9-4

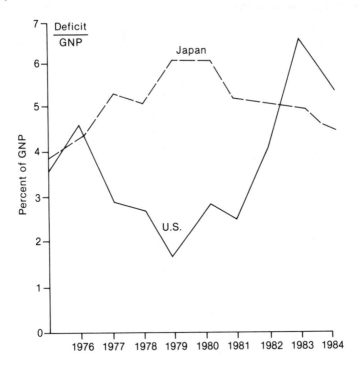

changing the supply of money and credit it provides to the public. The rate of growth of the money supply in each country is shown below in *Figure 9-5*. Notice that the fall in money growth is associated with a rise in the real interest rate (and vice versa) for both countries in every year except 1977 for Japan and 1978 for the United States. Though the overall interaction of monetary and fiscal policy is beyond the scope of this chapter, it is essential to acknowledge the role of monetary policy in contributing to the observed patterns in real interest rates. In fact, the rise in real interest rates in both countries since 1978 is largely attributable to tight monetary policies.

One of the major differences between Japan and the United States in the supply of credit is the extremely high savings rate of Japanese households. Between 1970 and 1980 the average net savings rate was 20.7 percent for households in Japan and 7.7 percent for households in the United States, in comparison to the OECD average during that period of 13.2 percent.[47] A good indicator of the relative burden of the deficit is the ratio of the deficit to net private savings. Net private savings represent resources from households and business that are available to finance new business investment and the government deficit. An increase in the deficit will be at the expense of business investment when there is no change in the available savings. *Figure 9-6* shows

FIGURE 9-5
Growth of Money Supply

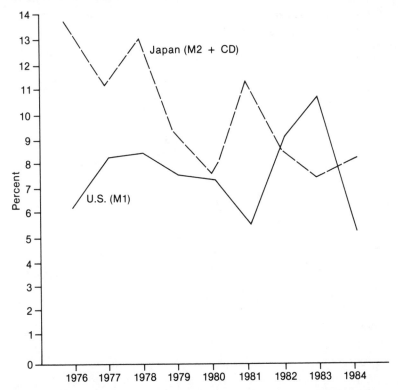

the trend in the deficit-to-savings ratio for Japan and the United States. Given the high savings rate in Japan, deficits are a smaller percentage of the available savings, even though they represent a larger percentage of GNP on average than those in the United States.

The final source of credit, in addition to that supplied by the central bank and the private sector, is foreign savings. Until ten years ago this was not a major source in either country—typically amounting to less than half a percent of GNP. In the early 1980s, however, the United States started borrowing over 2 percent of its GNP from overseas; and in 1984, the United States actually financed the equivalent of over half of its budget deficit from foreign capital flows. Japan, by contrast, has recently started to export capital overseas in quantities that exceed 2 percent of its GNP. One might well react to this situation by asking, "Since Japan wants to be banker to the world and the United States is able to borrow such large sums, why should business care?"

The reason is that large capital flows are not one-sided transactions. If more capital is flowing into the United States than is flowing out, it must mean that

FIGURE 9-6
Deficit-to-Savings Ratio for Japan and U.S.

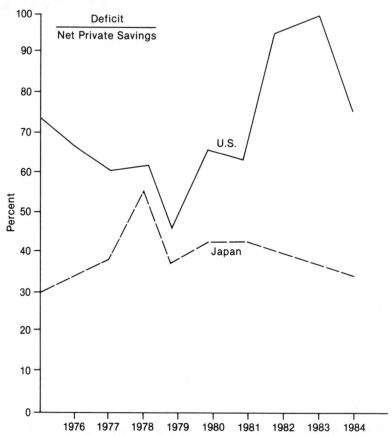

more goods and services are coming into the country than are flowing out—
that is, the United States must be running a trade deficit. The opposite case is
Japan, which is running sizable trade surpluses. For export-oriented or im-
port-competing American industries, these trade deficits have been threatening their very existence.

The problem of the dollar appreciation (and, for that matter, the appreciation of the yen relative to other major currencies) is also understandable as a
problem related to the fiscal deficits. As real interest rates rose higher in the
United States than comparable financial returns in other countries, foreign
investors demanded dollars to purchase American securities. The increased
demand for dollars then forced up the exchange rate of the dollar which, in
turn, hindered exports and encouraged imports, as noted above. Even the
depreciation of the dollar against the yen, which began late in 1985, did not
have any quick effect on this trend.

TABLE 9-9
Two Scenarios (Case A and Case B) of the Interaction of Savings, Deficits, Investment, and Trade Balances (as percentage of GNP)

	Net Private Savings	−	Budget Deficits	=	Net National Savings	=	Net Private Domestic Invest- ment	+	Net Foreign Invest- ment
	1		2		3		4		5
U.S.									
Case A									
Trade Deficits:	9	−	5	=	4	=	7	+	(3)
Case B									
Underinvestment:	9	−	5	=	4	=	4	+	0
Japan									
Case A									
Trade Surplus:	18	−	5	=	13	=	11	+	2
Case B									
Trade Balance:	18	−	5	=	13	=	13	+	0

SOURCES: *Economic Report of the President,* 1985, p. 250; OECD, *Japan, Economic Survey,* July 1984, pp. 84, 88.

It is necessary to work through a numerical example in order to grasp the magnitude of the deficit problem and its relationship to the issue of inadequate investment and trade competitiveness. If budget deficits remain at the same high levels that we have seen in the past few years, the United States inevitably will be confronted with the dilemma of inadequate investment or a persistent trade deficit. There is simply no possibility for policymakers to avoid this disagreeable choice, except by reducing the deficit. Japan, under the same assumption of continued fiscal deficits, will be forced to reduce investment from the high levels attained in the 1950s and 1960s; but nonetheless, it will still invest a proportion of national income at least twice that of the United States. Meanwhile, of course, Japan will not be immune to trade barriers imposed by other countries, particularly the United States. The worst outcome for Japan would be a trade war, not a reduced rate of investment. Most troublesome, though, is that these scenarios are likely to unfold even under the most optimistic assumptions about the performance of the U.S. economy, given the basic assumption that budget deficits of approximately 5 percent of GNP will continue in the future.

To understand these scenarios, consider the national income accounting identity, shown in *Table 9-9,* which presents the interrelationships of savings, budget deficits, investment, and trade imbalances. Essentially, this is a flow of funds relationship for the national economy, in which the sources (savings and foreign capital flows associated with a trade deficit or surplus) must by definition equal uses (the budget deficit and business investment).

The net private savings rate of 9 percent of GNP assumed for the U.S. in column 1 of *Table 9-9* is higher than for any period during the postwar years.[48]

On the other hand, the 18 percent figure for Japan is approximately equal to the average rate of savings over the past decade. For the sake of comparison, the budget deficits in the second column of *Table 9-9* are assumed to be fixed at 5 percent of GNP, a level that is approximately equal to those experienced in both countries over the past five years. These assumptions, it is important to understand, should make the outcome *as favorable as possible to the United States* and much less so for Japan. Yet the result is that U.S. net national savings in column 3 is in absolute terms only about a third of that available for Japan.

At this point the scenario hinges on whether the United States continues to run trade deficits while Japan accumulates trade surpluses (Case A) or trade returns to an approximate balance for both countries (Case B). For the United States neither scenario is attractive. In Case A, the U.S. will have an investment boom comparable to that of the 1960s (the 7 percent in column 4) but only if it borrows foreign savings of approximately 3 percent of its GNP from overseas. This would be equivalent to running a trade deficit that is even worse than that of 1984, when the United States borrowed savings of 2.6 percent of GNP from overseas. In the alternative Case B, the United States reduces its trade deficit and foreign borrowing to zero, but then it has only the domestically generated savings of 4 percent (column 3) that can be used to finance domestic investment (column 4). This would force up real interest rates and crowd out investment. The 4 percent level of investment would be the lowest rate of capital formation during the U.S. postwar period.[49]

For Japan, the prospects are less bleak. Choosing between Case A or Case B depends on whether it is more difficult for Japan to reduce its trade surplus or to forego an extra 2 percent of GNP in investment. The results of other chapters in this volume suggest that the former option is more difficult politically.[50] But even if investment is reduced, it still remains significantly higher than that of the United States.

As the previous scenarios illustrate, the story of how a deficit increases real interest rates and thereby harms capital formation and trade competitiveness has many chapters that must be read before one can ascertain the plot. Not until the end of the book does the reader start to recognize that the long-term loss is the decline in productivity owing to inadequate capital formation and the changes in industrial structure owing to decreased competitiveness. American politicians, recognizing that the story is complex and the potential damage is long-term, have every incentive to postpone the solution to this problem while they pursue other budgetary goals with more immediate rewards. Japanese bureaucrats, on the other hand, must face the short-term consequences of financing the deficits and therefore are more likely to avoid the long-term consequences of this problem.

THE EFFECTS OF RELATIVE TAX BURDENS ON BUSINESS

The relative tax burdens for corporations provide another measure of the costs imposed on business by government. The effective tax rate, which is the ratio of the taxes paid to the taxable income, is often used as an indicator of that burden.[51] By this measure it would appear that large corporations in both countries have essentially the same tax burden. In Japan the effective rate for the largest corporations is 53 percent and in the United States it is 51 percent if all federal, state, and local taxes are included.[52]

However, taxable income is an accounting entry subject to numerous deductions and exclusions that make cross-national comparisons extremely difficult. Alternatively, if one compares taxes to another measure that is less subjective than taxable income, such as corporate sales, one can get a sense of the relative magnitude of the tax burden by corporations in each country. This measure of taxes-to-sales has another characteristic that makes it useful in assessing the impact of taxes on price competitiveness. Since tax paid is a cost like any other cash expense, such as wage or interest expenses, it must be reflected in price.[53]

When the data are disaggregated into industries, the picture that emerges shows that U.S. taxes place a higher burden than Japanese taxes on companies in the same industry—even when two different measures of the tax burden are used. The data for selected industries are presented in *Table 9-10.*

The ratio of central government taxes to reported income is less variable across industries in Japan than in the United States. The range of rates for Japan is only 3 percent; for the United States it is 13 percent. Furthermore, the U.S. industries with the lowest tax rates are those not facing international competition, such as services, construction, and retailing. U.S. agriculture, with the lowest effective tax rate (32 percent), is an exception to this pattern. The four major export-competing industries of textiles, chemicals, metals, and machinery have an effective tax burden that averages about 6 percent higher for the U.S. firms compared to the Japanese firms in those same industries.

The Japanese aggregate tax-to-sales ratio has remained very stable at about 1.2 percent from 1969 to the present. The peak was 1.4 percent in 1973; the trough was 1 percent in 1976.[54] The American story was quite different. Tax-to-sales ratios were as high as 6 percent in the early 1950s, but have steadily declined to around 2 percent in the 1980s. It might be tempting to say that such small ratios as those currently existing in both countries imply that taxes are unimportant. However, the tax law covers not only the income that must be paid out in the form of taxes, but also the income that was exempted or deferred from taxation because of preferential treatment. It is that topic to which we now turn.

THE EFFECTS OF SELECTIVE TAX MEASURES ON BUSINESS

Selective tax measures are designed to promote some particular economic objective by granting special tax treatment for those engaging in that activity. Such measures are often (and quite aptly) called "tax expenditures" because they bestow through the tax system advantages which probably would not be

TABLE 9-10
Comparisons of Tax Burden Measures by Industry for Japan and the United States
(Selected Industries in 1981)

	Tax/Income		Tax/Sales	
	Japan	United States	Japan	United States
Agriculture	37	32	0.7%	1.4%
Mining	39	45	6.9	2.5
Construction	37	36	1.0	1.2
Textiles	37	44	1.0	1.9
Chemicals	38	45	1.5	3.5
Metals	38	42	1.2	2.4
Machinery	39	45	1.8	3.3
Food	38	45	1.3	2.0
Publishing	38	43	2.4	3.1
Wholesaling	37	39	0.5	0.8
Retailing	36	38	0.7	0.9
Finance	38	39	2.3	1.4
Transportation and Communication	37	44	1.8	2.2
Services	36	34	1.5	1.6
Total	38	43	1.1	1.9

NOTE: There are still unresolved issues with these data because differences in depreciation write-offs, tax-free reserves, loss carry-forwards, and tax credits are not incorporated. The evidence indicates that in both countries there is substantial room for hiding taxable income and therefore enlarging reported effective tax rates.

SOURCES: National Tax Administration Agency, *Hojin Kigyō no Jittai* (Sample Survey of Corporate Business), 1981, and Internal Revenue Service, *Corporate Income Tax Returns,* 1981.

politically feasible through more visible direct expenditures (even though direct expenditures could accomplish the same objective).

Japanese tax policy toward investment traditionally relied heavily on special depreciation allowances and tax-free reserves that could be set aside before calculating taxable income. During the late 1950s and 1960s, these were important tools of industrial policy.[55] At that time, for example, Japanese steel and automobile industries received between 25 and 50 percent of their total depreciation write-offs in the form of special depreciation in excess of standard depreciation. During that same period, the Japanese chemical industry received less than 10 percent in special depreciation. The amount of special depreciation claimed by various industries has declined significantly since the late 1950s, however, with fewer differences between industries. By the early 1980s the percentage of special depreciation for all industries was around 5 percent.

The magnitude of the selected tax expenditures for both countries is shown in *Figure 9-7* (A) and *9-7* (B) for Japan and the United States.[56] As indicated in *Figure 9-7* (A), the revenue losses to Japan's Ministry of Finance (i.e., the gains to the corporations) were grouped by MOF into five categories: savings promotion, environmental development, natural resource development, technology and investment promotion, and retained earnings protection. American tax expenditures as shown in *Figure 9-7* (B) can be grouped into the same categories, by excluding those categories from the more extensive list published by the Congressional Budget Office that were not comparable, such as agricultural promotion.

As an example, the technology and investment promotion measures in Japan include tax deductibility for R&D expenses, special deductions on technology income from overseas, a tax-free reserve for losses on computer repurchases, and special depreciation. The revenue losses to the Finance Ministry in 1984 from these measures (i.e., the gains to the corporations) amounted to 2.5 percent of all corporate taxes collected, or 0.1 percent of GNP. In other words, if all of these tax expenditures were eliminated, the Finance Ministry would increase corporate tax collections by 2.5 percent.

In the United States the tax expenditures that fall under this same category, such as the investment tax credit, accelerated depreciation beyond straight-line depreciation, etc., amounted to 59 percent of corporate taxes, and 0.9 percent of GNP. By these measures, the American use of special tax measures far exceeds the Japanese, and the American trend is rising while the Japanese have succeeded in maintaining or reducing these measures as a response to the growing deficits.

The total of American tax expenditures, including those not shown in *Figure 9-7* (B), have risen from 5.7 percent of GNP in 1976 to 7.7 percent in 1985.[57] The American legislative process seems to encourage interest groups to press for a tax expenditure in Congress, perhaps because Congress does not directly pay for the consequences of the eroding tax base in the way that MOF does. Congress specifies a budget and Treasury finances the deficit in the highly efficient American capital market. In Japan, additional deficits generated by the Tax Bureau create problems for the Financial Bureau, both of which lie within MOF. Furthermore, dissent among the members of the financing syndicate (primarily composed of the city banks and major securities firms) can mean additional conflicts for the Banking Bureau and the Securities Bureau. Fear of deficits may toughen MOF's resolve on some fronts, but the presence of alternative ways to finance an objective means that special incentives may not always show up as tax measures.

The principal alternative is to subsidize interest rate lending through FILP. The allocation of FILP funds has changed between 1953 and 1984 as shown in *Figure 9-8*. In 1953, 29 percent of FILP funds were used for assistance to key industries, compared to only 3 percent in 1984. The categories that include housing, welfare, education, small business, and agriculture have received the largest allocations.

FIGURE 9-7 (A)
Tax Expenditures in Japan (by objective)

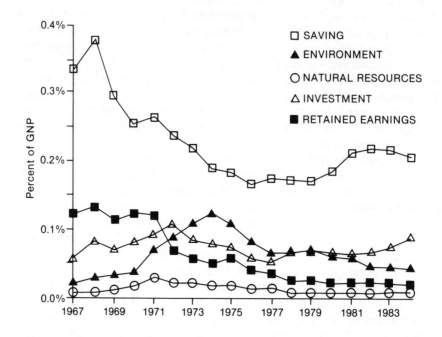

FIGURE 9-7 (B)
Tax Expenditures in the United States (by objective)

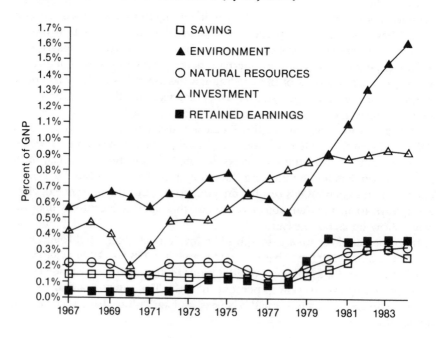

FIGURE 9-8
Changes in Utilization of Fiscal Investment and Loan Program (on the basis of initial plans) in Japan

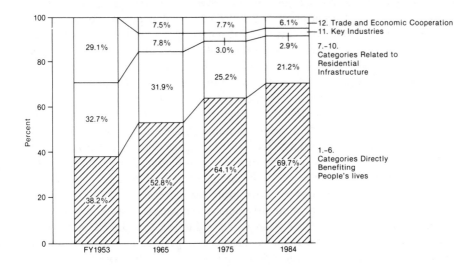

Categories Directly Benefiting People's Lives
1. Housing
2. Living Environment Improvement
3. Welfare
4. Education
5. Small Businesses
6. Agriculture, Forestry, and Fishing
Categories Related to Residential Infrastructure
7. National Land Conservation and Disaster Relief
8. Roads
9. Transportation and Communications
10. Regional Development
Other Categories
11. Key Industries
12. Trade and Economic Cooperation
SOURCE: The Japanese Bond Market (No. 5), Nomura Research Institute, April 1984, p. 147.

The recent benefits to Japanese businesses from interest rate subsidies have been larger than gains from special depreciation if the period from 1961–1973 is compared with 1974–1980.[58] The total gain from special depreciation measures and from interest rate reductions has increased, though only marginally, from 1.95 percent to 2.1 percent of the value of investments. But the *composition* has changed from a balanced reliance on taxes and subsidized credit in the period 1961–1973 to three times the reliance on subsidized credit in the period 1974–1980. The results for broad industry classes are roughly similar.

Budget deficits may have changed the method, but the objective of selectively targeting resources still remains.

Conclusion

In this chapter the economic objectives of fiscal policy were partitioned into the management of market demand and changes in business costs. Furthermore, the results of fiscal policy could be observed at either the national or industrial levels. For both countries, particularly since the first oil shock, fiscal policy has been directed at the national objectives of managing macroeconomic performance rather than implementing an industrial policy. Since the mid-seventies, when policymakers in Japan were faced with the choice of maintaining an overly stimulative fiscal policy or abandoning the fiscal incentives in their industrial policy, they have chosen the latter. The United States has never pursued an explicit industrial policy, but since the mid-sixties, it has used fiscal policy for national objectives of macroeconomic control.

These objectives are not always mutually compatible. For example, Japan's fiscal policy after 1976 was generally designed to reduce aggregate demand within the national economy by a corporate tax increase that added to the tax burden of business, and consequently, added to business costs. Likewise in the United States, the huge 1981 Reagan tax reduction that aimed primarily at stimulating economic growth by accelerating depreciation write-offs for corporations reduced the costs of capital-intensive businesses more than those of labor- or knowledge-intensive businesses. If policymakers have more than one objective for fiscal policy, they may be forced to trade off demand management for cost reduction and to trade off objectives at the national level in order to accomplish others at the industry level. In this sense, macroeconomic fiscal policy and microeconomic industrial policy will seldom be compatible if fiscal tools are the only instruments used.

Since World War II, the dominant objectives of fiscal policy for both Japan and the United States have changed. In Japan, fiscal policy started with the explicit pursuit of industrial objectives in the 1950s and early 1960s. From the mid-sixties until the first oil shock, Japan flirted with macroeconomic stabilization policies as a response to the recession of 1965. Since the mid-seventies, Japanese policymakers have had an implicit focus on the costs imposed on business—primarily costs from the national deficit. The United States, on the other hand, moved from fiscal objectives such as maintaining the prevailing ideology of "fiscal responsibility" in the 1950s and early 1960s to the national goal of stabilizing macroeconomic demand in the late sixties and 1970s. Under President Reagan's supply-side tax policies, the rhetoric of fiscal goals shifted to a national concern for business costs, but the reality has not yet followed, since the deficits threaten to impose costs that were eliminated by the corporate tax cuts.

Despite the potential of fiscal policy for influencing market demand, it is the use of fiscal policy to change business costs that has been relatively more important for explaining business-government relations in both countries. This is even more characteristic of postwar Japanese fiscal policy than that of the United States, because of the extensive fiscal apparatus to implement Japanese industrial policy established after the Occupation. Since the mid-seventies, the costs associated with the massive deficits are what has been most troublesome for policymakers in both Japan and the United States.

Business costs are the total burden on business of supporting government expenditures—a burden that will seldom be evenly distributed among all industries. Since increased government expenditures are paid for by either increased taxes or increased borrowing to finance the deficit, the burden on business will be the direct and indirect costs associated with these two options. First, the costs show up directly as increased corporate tax burdens. Postwar U.S. corporate tax burdens have been higher than the Japanese burdens. However, U.S. tax burdens have been declining, particularly after 1981, and have shown greater disparity between industries—in opposition to the trends in Japan, where corporate tax burdens have increased and have become more homogeneous across industries. Second, these costs show up indirectly as the increased interest expense associated with the higher real interest rates caused by a deficit, and the consequent effects on capital formation and trade competitiveness. Detailed empirical estimates of the contribution of deficits to each of these problems is difficult, but one can demonstrate that a continuation of deficits of the current magnitudes for the United States will necessarily lead either to decreased capital formation, or decreased trade competitiveness, or both. Japan will not suffer such dire consequences on account of its unusually high savings rate.

The broad movements in fiscal policy during the postwar years that have led to these consequences on business can be viewed as the outcome of a bureaucratic or political process which stamps each decision with its distinctive characteristics. In Japan, the primary fiscal actor, MOF, has attempted to maintain its relative power among the ministries and to minimize internal dissent, despite the shifting pressures for change. In the 1950s for example, MOF took advantage of the fiscal dividends of rapid economic growth by distributing selected fiscal incentives among industries. This move satisfied pressures from MITI, but it also established dependencies that increased MOF's own power. In the 1960s and early 1970s MOF yielded to domestic and foreign pressures for activist fiscal policies, but incrementally changed its rules so that its influence was not undermined.

By the mid-seventies in Japan, financing fiscal deficits in highly regulated financial markets had stirred deep-seated procedural problems within MOF that stiffened the will of bureaucrats to reduce future deficits. MOF has been willing to propose and implement drastic fiscal actions, even though the public has not perceived any immediate harm from the deficits. Moreover, individual bureaucrats anticipate that an unsolved problem now may create difficulties for them in their next assignment within MOF.

Although many of the problems of the deficit are borne within MOF, it also has the authority to solve them. MOF has chosen to eliminate selective fiscal measures and annual corporate tax reductions in an attempt to reduce the deficit; and it has yielded only reluctantly in allowing increased credit and regulatory incentives for the conduct of industrial policy. MOF has forced other ministries to be more focused and selective with their limited fiscal resources. This is not to say that MOF can be oblivious to the political pressure from outside its walls, but rather that it is an institutionalized budget problem-solver that can be expected to follow observable bureaucratic procedures. The progress is unlikely to be rapid, but the direction should be predictable and consistent.

This situation contrasts dramatically with that characteristic of the American government. During the entire postwar period, fiscal policy in the United States has followed the leadership and agenda not of bureaucrats but rather of the president. Until the early 1960s, most presidents were constrained by desire or ideology from pursuing activist fiscal policies. The persistent problem of slow growth, however, provided a catalyst for Presidents Kennedy and Johnson to transform fiscal policy into a tool for managing (or mismanaging) the economy. President Reagan succeeded in ushering in another fiscal revolution that promised supply-side growth and delivered unprecedented peacetime deficits.

Deficits did not present the same procedural problems for the U.S. Treasury that they did for MOF. Indeed, since the effects of deficits on business costs are difficult to document and explain to voters, it is hard for anyone involved in the fiscal policy process to take the initiative to oppose them effectively—especially if the agendas of interest groups or the president conflict with deficit reduction. Consequently, selective tax measures have become larger each year as U.S. interest groups manage to slip their proposals into the tax code, irrespective of any broader national economic strategy. Whether the "Packwood reforms" of the tax code initiated in 1986 will change this historic pattern remains to be seen.

Without leadership from some quarter, usually from the president, it is unlikely that the American institutional system will respond of its own accord to the deficit problem. There simply is no focal point for deficit criticism, except for the president, and the president may have other objectives with higher priority. It may be that action on the deficit will come only from mobilizing some other issue—tax reform, social security or Medicare bankruptcy—that will give the president the power and rationale to do something about the related problem of the deficit. Yet the possibility of a dramatic change in policy is at least conceivable in the United States, whereas discontinuities in policy remain very unlikely in Japan.

CHAPTER 10

Managing Retreat: Disinvestment Policy

DOUGLAS D. ANDERSON

Disinvestment—the process of removing resources from a business or an industry that no longer is competitive—may well be the most painful task any economy faces. The task is especially troublesome, moreover, when the overall rate of economic growth slows, as was the case in both the United States and Japan during the 1970s. Despite inherent problems, the disinvestment process remains central to continuing economic growth. No modern national economy can ignore its importance. From 1948 to 1966, for example, improvement in the allocation of labor and capital across industries and across sectors of the economy accounted for nearly 30 percent of the rise in U.S. total factor productivity.[1] While mobility of labor and capital alone does not guarantee economic growth, it is an important enabling factor. Growth facilitates mobility of resources and such mobility stimulates growth.

Used, as it is, in this way, the parlance of resource reallocation retains a rather antiseptic character. Human values seem remote when assets are "redeployed" and labor is "redistributed." Statistics represent, as someone has said, human beings without the tears. Broken promises, broken careers, and broken hopes are hidden in the numbers; yet they frequently become the most immediately visible by-products of the business decision to exit—to disinvest as a part of change.

But these human costs are not the only by-products of business disinvestment. Shifts in the competitive position of firms and industries are a natural part of the process of economic development. Policies designed to enhance the mobility of redundant factors of production—labor, capital, and technology—have been advocated by liberal economists since the Industrial Revolution. In their view, the ultimate test of an investment decision (whether it involves additional investment in a project or region, or taking resources away) is that of efficiency: are society's scarce resources being put to the most productive use? Because market forces are presumed to enforce this standard of allocative efficiency, good economics calls for reliance on the market to provide the signals which private entrepreneurs need to make their own decisions. Hence, the role of government, according to the economist, is limited to ensuring that markets function properly, and to intervening only when they do not.[2]

Of course, good economics often conflicts with good politics. A policy that may make everyone better off in an abstract sense can still create a class of losers. When those losers become sufficiently well organized and motivated, they can translate their wishes into public policy while the more numerous, but less directly affected winners stand by and watch. In fact, Americans have grown so accustomed to seeing politicians seek protection for special interests against all "winds of creative destruction" that we regard this political process as almost inevitable.

When, instead, government overrules the apparent losers and acts to facilitate the removal of excess resources from an industry that has become obsolete—it is news. We are interested. We want to know more.

Such is the case, apparently, with Japan. The news is that Japanese policy toward declining industries has managed to square the circle—to get good politics and good economics working in tandem. Consider this account:

> The most impressive thing about Japan's industrial policy is the way they manage the rational adjustment of their declining industries with a minimum of social pain and political obstruction.[3]
>
> Frank A. Weil,
> former Assistant Secretary,
> United States Department of Commerce

And this evaluation:

> The Japanese economy is pitted with many of the same troubles that beset other industrial nations. Foremost among those troubles is that of declining industries, primarily those that have lost their competitive edge because of high energy costs in Japan or cheaper labor in newly industrializing countries. . . .
>
> What makes Japan different from other industrial countries is that it has a comprehensive policy for helping those industries settle into gentle rather than convulsive decline. Government, business, and labor have worked together to shift resources out of the ailing sectors of the economy into the healthy ones with relatively little pain.
>
> *Fortune*
> January 10, 1983

And finally, this response by a Nobel Prize-winning economist who looked closely at Japan:

It is incredible. The government simply decides to reduce the capacity of an industry, and they reduce it.[4]

Wassily Leontief,
at a Berkeley symposium on
"The Japanese Challenge and the American Response," May, 1981.

Such impressive testimonies naturally raise our curiosity. Have the Japanese got it right? Are they really that much better than the United States at moving resources out of senescent industries? If so, how have they managed disinvestment? Have outcomes been principally (or exclusively) the result of government policy, as Leontief suggests, or has the Japanese experience with industrial retreat been largely conditioned by the structure of markets and of the firms which implement disinvestment decisions? All of these questions are important to Americans.

Yet finding answers remains a difficult task, one that imposes its own special limitations. Among other things, for example, any *complete* answer assumes some agreement as to the proper standard, or measure of performance; and that is, itself, controversial. In the remainder of this chapter, I will provide evidence that should help us to formulate a *partial* answer for these questions. The first task is to explain why the disinvestment process might not result in efficiency, if left to market forces. Next, I will look at the relative performances of the United States and Japan in adjusting to structural changes in the world economy at a macro, inter-industry level. Then, in the major part of the chapter, I will examine how the retrenchment process actually works in the United States and Japan, viewed in the special context of several "structurally depressed" industries.

Some practical boundaries on this inquiry must be laid down at the outset. When we talk of disinvestment, for example, we will be referring rather narrowly to the process of shrinking manufacturing industries which are no longer providing competitive rates of return. Much broader definitions are possible; they might encompass all resource shifts *among sectors* (e.g., from forestry, mining, or agriculture to manufacturing) and even product or process shifts *within a given industry or firm* (e.g., IBM's decision to kill the series 8000 and SCAMP computers in favor of the System 360). Here, our scope of reference intentionally remains narrow and specific. Similarly, when we use the term "disinvestment policy" we will *not* be referring to the myriad governmental actions that can affect resource allocation, but only to those measures which have a significant impact on the management of cutbacks.

Disinvestment: Why Do Markets Fail?

Measured against the standard of "efficiency," there are two broad reasons why the market might fail to disinvest as it should. One such reason emerges as a failure to generate the right amount of disinvestment; alternatively, market forces might stimulate disinvestment of the wrong type.

Elementary price theory holds that when markets are characterized by free mobility of resources, an unanticipated fall in demand will result (in the short run) in a drop in the price and volume of goods sold. Over the longer term, as firms begin to adjust to the decline in demand, resources will be shifted out of the industry, and this movement will cause the price to rise and output to fall further. When markets are functioning efficiently, this adjustment will take place with little or no friction; when there are barriers to exit, such adjustment might take place very slowly, or even lead to capacity withdrawals of the wrong kind.[5]

How might capacity of the wrong kind be retired first? Ideally, the process of capacity reduction requires managers to compare the future cash flows from operating a plant with the cash flows from closing it. If each firm is equally strong financially, managers will discount these flows at the same rate, with the effect that the least efficient capacity will be phased out first. A financially weaker firm, on the other hand, will discount the negative cash flows associated with closing capacity (severance payments and the like) at a higher rate than will a strong firm. Consequently, stronger firms might act first to shut down capacity, even though their plants may still be relatively more efficient.[6]

Organizational structure may also exert an important influence on the retirement of capacity. A multidivisional firm may be able to find uses for its redundant capital assets somewhere else within the same corporation. Moreover, managers and employees of a plant that is owned by (or associated with) a diversified company may be more willing to assist the process of capacity reduction if they believe in the possibility of reemployment elsewhere in the company. All of this suggests that a multidivisional firm may well face fewer substantial barriers to exit than does a single product firm, and may, therefore, act faster to curtail capacity.[7] If multidivisional companies also operate more efficient plants than do single product firms (which may not be the case) this could provide another reason why the wrong capacity would leave an industry first.

These are only a few of the many ways in which theory suggests the market might fail to generate the proper amount or quality of shrinkage in industries which have lost their competitive edge.[8] It is one thing to recognize that there are market failures which impede the achievement of economic efficiency; but quite another to design an administrative process to address such problems that does not result in "political failures" that are even worse.[9] Since this is a task at which Japan is said to excel, it is worth examining both the *outcome* as well as the *process* of disinvestment there, and in the United States.

Disinvestment Outcomes: Resource Reallocation Within Manufacturing

What evidence exists in either Japan or the United States concerning disinvestment and resource reallocation within manufacturing? Admittedly, we have only fragmentary data, but some conclusions still can be drawn. The

FIGURE 10-1
Convergence of U.S. and Japanese Manufacturing Productivity Levels

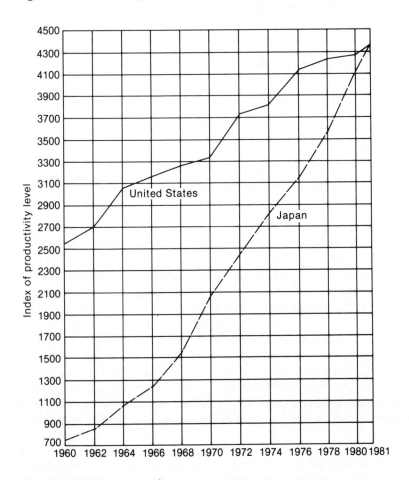

SOURCE: William J. Baumol and Kenneth McLennon, eds., *Productivity Growth and U.S. Competitiveness* (New York: Oxford University Press, 1985), p. 15.

superior performance of the Japanese economy in registering productivity gains is well established, as we see illustrated in *Figure 10-1*. The underlying statistics can be easily summarized: from 1973 to 1980, Japan's labor productivity in manufacturing grew by an average rate of 7.2 percent annually; the comparable figure for the United States was 1.7 percent. Given the contribution that resource reallocation can make to productivity growth, one possible explanation for Japan's superior growth performance is greater mobility of resources.[10]

TABLE 10-1
Estimated Reallocation of Employment in Covered Manufacturing Industries for the United States and Japan, 1973–1977

	United States	Japan
For 251 industries in United States and Japan:		
1. Reallocation of employment (thousands)	1,210	372
2. Total 1973 employment (thousands)	16,889	10,794
3. Reallocation of employment as a percent of total employment	7.2%	3.4%

SOURCE: Norman S. Fieleke, "Productivity and Labor Mobility in Japan, the United Kingdom, and the United States," *New England Economic Review,* November/December 1981.

With at least one such resource, however—labor mobility within manufacturing—this explanation does not seem relevant. A careful study based on Census of Manufactures data and reported by the Federal Reserve Bank of Boston concluded that while the United States may be troubled by "supply-side" difficulties of various sorts, "poor labor mobility between industries does not seem to be among them." The study covered 251 industries or industry groupings that could be defined in the same way in Japan and the United States. Together, these industries accounted for 85 percent of total 1977 manufacturing employment in the United States and 90 percent of total 1977 manufacturing employment in Japan. As reported in *Table 10-1,* the reallocation of employment between 1973 and 1977 amounted to 7.2 percent of total 1973 covered manufacturing employment in the United States, while the comparable figure for Japan was 3.4 percent. As the Federal Reserve study declares:

> This result suggests that the difference between recent productivity growth in Japan, on the one hand, and the United States . . . on the other hand must be explained by factors other than differences in the overall willingness and ability of labor to shift from one industry to another.[11]

A somewhat more nuanced finding is reported by Robert Lawrence of the Brookings Institution. Lawrence compared employment shifts among the high-growth and low-growth manufacturing sectors in the United States and other major economies in order to determine whether in fact U.S. industrial adaptation has been lagging. The results are summarized in *Table 10-2.* Interestingly, the share of employment in selected high-growth industries grew faster (8.9 percent) in the United States than in Japan (0.6 percent); whereas the shifts of employment out of low-growth industries were similar in magnitude in the two countries. While the United States moved out of labor-intensive industries

TABLE 10-2
Changes in Employment Share in Manufacturing,
High-Growth and Low-Growth Industries in the United
States and Japan, 1973 and 1979

Type of Industry and Year	United States	Japan
Selected high-growth industries[1]		
1973	30.4	31.0
1979	33.1	31.2
Percent change in share[2]	8.9	0.6
Low-growth industries[3,4]		
1973	34.0	37.5
1979	32.0	35.1
Percent change in share	− 5.9	− 6.4
Labor-intensive industries[3]		
1973	19.2	21.6
1979	17.3	20.4
Percent change in share	− 9.9	− 5.5
Capital-intensive industries[4]		
1973	14.8	15.9
1979	14.7	14.7
Percent change in share	− 0.7	− 7.5

[1] Industrial chemicals, other chemical products, plastic products, machinery, electrical machinery, and professional goods.
[2] Percent change in share is calculated as 100 [(1973 share−1979 share)/ 1973 share].
[3] Textiles, apparel, leather, footwear, wood products, and furniture.
[4] Iron and steel, nonferrous metals, metal products, and shipbuilding.
SOURCES: United Nations, *Yearbook of Industrial Statistics* (New York: UN 1979, 1980). From Robert Lawrence, *Can America Compete?* (Washington, D.C.: Brookings Institution, 1984).

faster than did Japan, the fall in total employment in slow-growth, capital-intensive industries was considerably faster in Japan than in the United States.[12]

These data give us valuable information on net changes in employment in various industries; but the data do not tell us how much employment would be optimal in any industry. Nor do they have anything to say about shifts of resources within industries. Yet, if we can accept the findings of the Brookings study as a first approximation, the United States seems to disinvest about as well as Japan. If we accept the conclusions of the Federal Reserve study, then the United States actually does a better job of reallocating labor than does Japan. Clearly, neither study provides support for the notion that the United States is doing worse than Japan at disinvesting.

This finding raises interesting possibilities. First, the overall similarity in labor reallocation rates within manufacturing in Japan and the United States could be taken to mean that companies in the United States and Japan face roughly equivalent exit barriers. A second possibility could be that Japan faces higher exit barriers (permanent employment, societal norms against layoffs, and so forth), but that it has developed compensating mechanisms (including government policy) which allow it to disinvest roughly as well as the United States. Yet another logical possibility is that U.S. corporations face less significant exit barriers than do the Japanese, but that the sign on the coefficient of government policy is negative.[13] To study these alternatives, let us look more closely at how Americans and the Japanese have gone about downsizing troubled industries.

Managing Retreat: American Style

Because the beneficial effects of disinvestment tend to be scattered widely throughout the economy, they can be easily overlooked. In the popular media, it is frequently the disruption caused by plant closings and massive layoffs—not the subtle moves designed to preserve and redeploy capital—which shows up in headlines.[14] During the last decade, conditions in America's "Frost Belt" generated a disproportionate share of such headlines. In late 1980, President Carter's Commission for a National Agenda for the Eighties issued a report concerned with that region's problems, *Urban America in the Eighties: Perspectives and Prospects.* In it, the Commission observed that an increasingly productive economy requires "simultaneous painful growth and shrinkage, disinvestment and reinvestment." The federal government could best discharge its responsibility to depressed industries and regions by "removing barriers to mobility that prevent people from migrating to locations of economic opportunity, and by providing migration assistance to those who wish and need it."[15] The endorsement of national mobility of the labor force was unmistakable.

As a statement of liberal economic thinking, the report garnered some support. But read as a political document, it provoked sensational opposition. A headline in the *New York Daily News* summarized its message in bold type: FEDS TO NORTHEAST: DROP DEAD.[16] Behind this banner stood an axiom of American political life: When it comes to preserving jobs, industries, or regions threatened by convulsive change, powerful economic interests can be expected to protect themselves with little or no reverence for the dictates of economic theory.

The record of the American policy response to these interests is mixed. Singly, and in coalitions, protectionist political forces have fought and won numerous battles against disinvestment, with the result that employment and capacity have frequently been retained in industries that should have been allowed to shrink more rapidly on efficiency grounds. U.S. shipbuilding, for example, has been described by the British House of Lords as "probably the most heavily protected industry in the world."[17] Footwear, autos, and textiles are only three of the many other industries which have succeeded in achieving short-term political relief to cushion long-term structural decline.[18] The recent history of carbon steel, developed more fully elsewhere in this volume, is one in which relief has been sought through nearly every policy device known to Washington, including tax incentives, loan guarantees, trade protection, and tripartite committees.[19]

These examples suggest that industry capture of the regulatory apparatus of government is a widespread, almost inevitable phenomenon in America. The subject has inspired a rich historical debate.[20] But is industry's influence over the policy process in the United States really any more extensive, or (to keep the question focused directly on the issue at hand) any more likely to result in measures that retard the flow of capital and labor out of declining industries than elsewhere? While it is true that the U.S. maritime industries have been heavily protected historically, we must ask whether this is evidence of a non-liberal economic policy, or evidence that the government has simply refused to allow the industry to shrink below a certain minimum size for strategic defense reasons. (Since the 1960s the U.S. share of the global shipbuilding market has consisted of about 1 percent, compared to a share of 12 to 25 percent for Western Europe and double that for Japan.) Moreover, despite the plethora of special relief measures adopted to deal with the "steel crisis" in the United States, these measures have not prevented massive outmigration of capital and labor from steel. From 1977 to 1984, 35 million tons (about 24 percent) of total integrated steel capacity was closed or decommissioned. This has led industry expert Robert Crandall, of the Brookings Institution, to con-clude that "restructuring and rationalization of the integrated sector has taken place more rapidly in the United States than in any other country except the United Kingdom."[21] U.S. Steel's David Roderick was correct when he remarked that American steel manufacturers have been self-liquidating with alacrity. Indeed, they have been doing so *despite* the best efforts of community activ-ists, labor unions, and political representatives to prevent it from happening.[22]

Some rather dramatic evidence that resource mobility does, in fact, charac-terize recent objectives as well as outcomes of American policy can be found in the deregulation of transportation, especially air travel. There, contrary to what might have been predicted by political economy theory, the general consumer interest seems to have prevailed over special interests, even though significant costs were imposed on the losers. Wage cuts, falling profits, and bankruptcy have been commonplace among airlines, as companies have been forced to disinvest in order to compete. But despite intense lobbying by pilots, other airline employees, and some airline managements and their suppliers, a broad coalition of conservatives and liberals was not prevented from dereg-ulating the industry in the 1970s. All attempts to reregulate fares and schedules in the industry since have failed.

Airline deregulation has been a highly visible confirmation of the power of liberal economic ideas to shape industry policy and industry structure in the United States. But it is not an isolated case. The experience of numerous less glamorous and less heavily reported industries suffering from declining demand or excess capacity supports the same broad conclusion that generally in America, the government manages decline by not managing at all. A detailed study of the "endgames" used by fifty-one firms in seven industries ranging from receiving tubes, to acetylene, to baby foods found that government policy had only an indirect influence on the exit rates of firms. In the soda ash and rayon industries, for example, government pollution standards encouraged some firms to leave the industry earlier than they otherwise might have.[23] Again, similar indirect effects showed up in the cigar industry, as an unintended result of the U.S. Surgeon General's 1964 announcement that cigarette smoking had carcinogenic effects. Paradoxically, his disclosure seems to have encouraged some ten million smokers to experiment with cigars (as a substitute for cigarettes), thereby creating a temporary surge in demand, at a time when long-term, negative factors were beginning to dictate a reduction in cigar manufacturing capacity. Despite this evidence of at least some government influence, firms in declining industries have typically developed their plans to sell out or shut down, relocate or reinvest without substantial reference to government policy objectives. Instead, structural conditions, particularly uncertainty surrounding the future of demand, interfirm rivalry, and the presence or absence of specific economic, strategic, or managerial exit barriers were the key determinants of exit.[24]

The contrast between the characteristic American policy of nonintervention in declining industries (or intervention by exception) and the more direct involvement by other governments is well illustrated by the case of petrochemicals. In recent years, as severe excess capacity has reduced the profit margins of petrochemical companies throughout the world, governments in Europe and Japan have taken a leading role (usually without much success) in devising schemes to revitalize and reinvigorate their domestic industries. In the United States, however, the government has not attempted to protect American petrochemicals through stopgap measures. Instead, as Joseph Bower has reported, the government has encouraged disinvestment in lower value-added materials through "informed benevolent neglect." Meanwhile, U.S. firms have taken the view that they, too, "must not seek to protect inefficiency."[25] Disinvestment in petrochemicals has been market-driven, a response to the government's refusal to intervene in the industry.

Ironically, some of the starkest evidence of the private sector's role in capital mobility in America has come not from liberal economists, but from two critics of corporate capitalism, Barry Bluestone and Benjamin Harrison. In a series of works (most notably, *The Deindustrialization of America*), they argue that America suffers not from insufficient disinvestment, but from *too much*. According to Bluestone and Harrison, between thirty-two and thirty-eight million jobs were lost during the 1970s as a direct result of private disinvestment in American business, while only two out of five smaller firms that existed in 1969 were still under the same owners in 1976.[26] In their view, this is evidence that corporations in America have mastered the ability to move capital from one venture to another with virtually no friction.[27]

Whether or not one accepts Bluestone and Harrison's argument that U.S. industry suffers from too much disinvestment, it is hard to quarrel with their depiction of America as a country in which political and financial exit barriers do not seriously hinder the flow of resources from one sector to another. Local politicians may rail at the "rape and betrayal" of their towns by corporations that shut down and move elsewhere. But while industrial relocation and capital redeployment generate strong human feelings of dismay, such moves are tolerated and even encouraged by American public policy.[28] During the last decade, legislation designed to control plant closings has been introduced in many legislatures; but as of the mid-1980s, only two states, Maine and Wisconsin, and one municipality, Philadelphia, had passed such laws. Even these days measures are weak (principally calling for thirty to sixty days' advance notice) and perhaps unenforceable. At the federal level, despite the fact that Congress has considered a plant closing bill every year since 1974, it still refuses to enact such legislation.[29] No change seems imminent.

Perhaps one reason why corporate managers in America have become so adept at capital redeployment is that Wall Street—quite independent of Washington—seems to reward such behavior. A newsletter from Merrill Lynch late in 1985, for example, alerted investors to an accelerating trend toward corporate restructuring. The trend was good news, according to the investment house, because "in numerous instances, poor performing operations are being sold or eliminated and assets redeployed to businesses that seem to offer the potential for higher returns. . . . We believe that the shares of firms that succeed in effecting such change could prove to be highly rewarding commitments over the long run. Not only would earnings prospects for those companies be enhanced, but the ability to manage their assets and capabilities so that they provide the greatest possible return could stand them in good stead for still different conditions in the years ahead."[30]

Merrill Lynch reviewed, among others, the recent experience of Brockway, Colgate-Palmolive, and Clark Equipment—three companies that the brokerage firm believed were making impressive headway in implementing corporate restructuring programs:

> *Brockway.* By early 1985, Brockway, Inc. . . . had begun to reap the benefits of a carefully planned program to reduce its dependence on the glass container business, which had suffered from excess capacity caused by the deep inroads of plastics. During 1984, the company reduced its glass operations by closing several plants and divesting itself of a glass tubing division; expanded its plastics operation by making two acquisitions; and continued to reduce costs and boost productivity by closing down unprofitable operations and consolidating others. Today, the company is still the nation's second largest

producer of glass containers, accounting for about 15 percent of the total market. But it also manufactures plastic and metal products; provides technical assistance to foreign producers of glass and plastic containers; and operates three commuter airlines. . . . The company has reduced the importance of its glass activities, from 90 percent of total sales five years ago to 65 percent currently, without losing its share of a shrinking market.

Colgate-Palmolive. As part of a major restructuring program, Colgate-Palmolive announced last August that it would divest itself of several subsidiaries, a move that, in effect, should take the company out of the food, athletic equipment, and textile businesses. At the same time, the company offered to buy back up to 12 million shares, or 15 percent, of its common stock. . . . The sale of the units, which the firm's management hopes will be completed by year end, should generate about $260 million after taxes, which along with borrowed funds, would be used to pay for the purchase of the company's stock. . . . Despite the net outlay of funds that those moves would entail, management believes that the company would still be in a strong financial position to make acquisitions . . . in health care.

Clark Equipment. The restructuring of Clark Equipment has been underway since 1982, when the company announced a major "revitalization" plan. . . . The comprehensive program undertaken has affected virtually all aspects of the firm's business. In a dramatic effort to cut costs, the company closed several high-cost, highly unionized plants in Michigan and replaced that capacity with highly efficient, non-union plants in North Carolina and Kentucky. The effect was to reduce Clark's worldwide capacity by 25 percent. . . . All things considered, our specialist sees earnings improving markedly as the benefits of [these and other] moves are felt.

The affection of Wall Street is not the only thing important to managers, of course. Yet, when the survival of their companies is at stake, it is probably more than just comforting to managers to know that Wall Street approves of their efforts to restructure and redeploy the assets of their corporations.[31]

These efforts have been facilitated by the recent upturn in the U.S. economy. In 1985, *The Wall Street Journal* reported that the country was experiencing an "unprecedented" amount of restructuring that was "profoundly altering much of U.S. industry." After studying the moves of 850 of the largest corporations in North America over eighteen months, the *Journal* found that 398 either had been, or shortly would be, in the midst of major restructuring, most of which involved shedding unwanted units or assets. During the eighteen-month period, some 825 business units valued at $40.2 billion were sold, and an untold number were shut down or liquidated. Fueling this disinvestment, the *Journal* concluded, were many forces: intensifying worldwide competition, disinflation, government deregulation, rapid technological development, and revived macroeconomic growth following the recession of 1981 and

1982. As one investment banker told the *Journal,* "Restructuring means, 'let's get rid of all the stuff we've done wrong in the past while we've got a window to do it.' "[32]

Federal Adjustment Assistance Programs

Washington has not ignored the issue of structural adjustment altogether. A variety of programs have been used over the years (not always successfully) as a way of "buying off" opposition to the effects of market-induced shifts in the allocation of corporate resources. The Economic Development Administration (EDA), the principal federal agency responsible for American regional policy, was created in 1965, in part to administer three specific programs that influence industrial relocation: business development finance, special economic development and adjustment, and trade adjustment assistance. Each of these programs merits a closer look.[33]

First, the Business Development Finance Assistance Program was established to provide direct loans and loan guarantees to private firms located in economically distressed places (where such help might not otherwise be available). In general, the amounts involved were small, as were the businesses served.[34]

Second, the Special Economic Development and Adjustment Assistance Program combined two elements: assistance to geographic areas experiencing long-term economic decline as manifested by reductions in jobs, income, and public infrastructure; and assistance to areas experiencing sudden and severe economic deterioration. Under the former, the federal government assisted states and other local governments in establishing revolving loan funds to help firms within their regions through direct loans, loan guarantees, grants, and interest subsidies. Under the latter part of the program, money was made available to provide extended unemployment compensation, rent and mortgage payments, training, and relocation expenses for individuals; and loans and loan guarantees for businesses to ameliorate the impact of sudden economic shocks and to develop new employment opportunities. Again, the combined costs of this two-part program remained modest. Under President Ronald Reagan, the Office of Management and Budget attempted to "zero out" the EDA's budget for these programs. Critics within the Reagan Administration charged that EDA programs had become essentially a pork barrel, with little or no purpose other than simple politics. Instead of facilitating structural change, these critics claimed, the net effect of EDA programs was to lock resources into unproductive use, despite explicit guidelines to the contrary.

While Congress has effectively prevented the OMB from eliminating all EDA programs, the third major federal attempt at active readjustment—the Trade Adjustment Assistance Program (TAA)—is, if not dead, then barely alive.[35] Trade adjustment assistance was first provided under authority of the Trade Expansion Act of 1962. Its rationale rested on the premise that unemployment and market disruptions resulting from a policy of liberalizing trade should not be borne by particular sectors of the economy alone. In addition to aiding firms and workers, the Act was intended to assist in the orderly transfer of resources. However, because of highly restrictive eligibility criteria and cumbersome administrative procedures, the TAA provided very little actual relief during the first twelve years of its existence. From 1962 to 1969, neither firms nor workers obtained benefits from the TAA program.

In response to general dissatisfaction with the program, and as a means of "buying off" opposition to trade liberalization, Congress amended the TAA program as part of the Trade Act of 1974. That law vested responsibility for assisting firms in the EDA, while assistance to workers became the responsibility of the Department of Labor. Firms and workers became eligible for assistance only after it was established that foreign imports could be identified as an important cause of either layoffs or production cutbacks, and that workers had been permanently laid off. Thus, assistance was rendered to discrete elements of an industry, and not under a comprehensive plan for solving problems on an industrywide basis.

Firms that qualified for help could get technical assistance from consultants paid by the government. These specialists would help businesses become revitalized through marketing, engineering, and management changes. Small firms could also obtain direct loans or loan guarantees for working capital, new machinery and equipment, and new or renovated buildings. No single firm could receive more than $1 million in loans and $3 million in loan guarantees.

In the first five-year period under this new authorization, TAA was extended to 655 firms in industries including footwear, textiles and apparel, electronics, steel, jewelry, and handbags. Total assistance granted amounted to $240 million, with less than 20 percent going to technical assistance. In 1977, 82 percent of the 112 certified firms were in footwear, apparel or handbag manufacture.[36] According to a 1978 study by the General Accounting Office (GAO), the few firms that received benefits "have not usually used them to become viable in their own or different industries." Consequently, the GAO observed, "the program is providing these firms with income maintenance, but is not providing for their long-term strength or competitiveness."[37]

The record for the worker assistance component of the plan did not differ greatly. Workers certified by the Labor Department became eligible to apply to state employment security agencies for weekly cash allowances; counseling, testing, training, and placement; job search allowances; and relocation allowances. Between April 1978 and May 1978, $463 million was paid to 335,000 workers, but little went for payments to encourage worker mobility or retraining. Of over 300,000 workers helped, only 1,075 applications for a job search allowance and 557 applications for a job reallocation allowance had been approved, and fewer than 10,000 workers had been referred for retraining.[38]

The program displayed a number of failings, but the record of TAA among auto workers now seems particularly dismal. According to the GAO, inasmuch as most laid-off auto workers received about 95 percent of their regular pay from state unemployment insurance and company/union supplemental funds, along with numerous fringe benefits, there were few incentives for workers to take advantage of adjustment assistance, training programs, or job search and relocation allowances.[39] Workers frequently received benefits only after they had returned to the job, with the result that such benefits merely repaid company and union supplemental unemployment benefit funds. Overall, because of its ineffectiveness, TAA lost credibility with organized labor, which began to refer to the program as "burial insurance."

Despite these inherent problems, the Carter Administration expanded the use of TAA, hoping to reduce the troubles in trade-impacted industries. In all, the number of approved applications more than doubled between 1977 and 1980, resulting in a "billion dollar overrun" program budget. To control this overrun (and to cut back a program that had become discredited), President Reagan tightened the rules on eligibility. Workers may now receive benefits only *after* their unemployment insurance payments have been exhausted, and benefits are restricted to fifty-two weeks. The result, according to some experts, has practically eliminated TAA as an effective alternative to protectionism.[40] Others continue to argue that an improved TAA or "displaced worker" program ought to be developed as an antidote for protectionism. But the Reagan Administration seems to have concluded that it could resist most political pressures to impede the structural evolution of the economy without beefing up the TAA program.[41]

Our review of the purpose and performance of federal adjustment assistance programs has filled in a few more lines in the picture of U.S. disinvestment policy. While still incomplete, that picture is now sufficiently clear to permit this generalization: With obvious exceptions and imperfections, U.S. microeconomic policy since World War II has typically sought to enhance (or at least not to disrupt) the mobility of national resources by allowing firms to invest or disinvest according to their own criteria. Whenever possible, American policymakers have striven to maintain a "hands-off" stance toward industry restructuring and the disinvestment that necessarily accompanies it. But what of Japan? That is the subject we turn to next.

Managing Retreat: The Japanese Way

In the introduction to the OECD's semiofficial description of industrial policy in Japan (1972), Yoshihisa Ojimi, MITI vice minister, wrote of "the necessity for a changeover in the structure of those industries characterized by low productivity, stagnation in technical know-how, and simplistic intensified use of labor." He went on to argue that Japan must learn to "give away" such industries to its lesser developed neighbors "much as big brother gives the suit he has outgrown to his young brother."[42]

As a description of governmental aspirations, Ojimi's family-oriented metaphor certainly is consistent with market-based shifts in comparative advantage; and a number of observers have found that Japanese policy is shaped along these lines.[43] Yet the evidence is not one-sided; especially in labor-intensive industries, Japanese disinvestment policy frequently seems to ignore the market, and to be sensitive instead to the same political constraints that are familiar in the West.[44] In a 1976 study, Trezise and Suzuki, for example, go so far as to suggest that "few things could be less accurate . . . than the proposition that Tokyo was ever prepared to have its older or weaker industries run down as a matter of deliberate planning."[45] More recently, in a 1981 survey, Ramseyer declares that "rather than use adjustment assistance programs to help phase out [labor-intensive] industries . . . the government succumbed in some cases to political pressure from the firms and workers and used economically inefficient means to keep the industries alive."[46] Again, we need to review more specific details.

Textile Restructuring

The experience of the Japanese government as it tried to restructure the domestic textile industry offers ample evidence of the inherent difficulties involved in any country's disinvestment policy. Efforts to control excess capacity in various branches of the Japanese textile industry began with laws passed in 1956 and 1964, designed to limit the number of spinning machines (spindles). Then in 1967, with passage of the Temporary Law for the Structural Reorganization of Specified Textile Industries, the government instituted a series of programs aimed directly at scrapping spindles. According to a study by Yoshie Yonezawa, the program was intended to reduce the number of spindles by 2.62 million; instead, during six years of existence, this measure proved ineffective, as the number of spindles actually increased by 204,000. In a parallel program during the same period, the Japanese government also sought to dispose of 116,000 weaving machines for cotton, spun rayon, and silk, but the result remained far less impressive, as only 26,000 machines went out of service.[47] In Japan, too, policy sometimes encountered pragmatic limitations.

One problem came from the difficulty in enforcing compliance with the government's capacity reduction program. With more than 100,000 firms in the textile industry, the Japanese could not monitor reductions closely, and some companies simply mothballed equipment for reuse later, as business conditions improved. Furthermore, despite an elaborate registration system, the government proved unable to prevent new firms from entering the textile industry, thus expanding (rather than reducing) overall capacity. In fact, according to MITI, by 1972 there were still some 162,000 illegal looms in existence—a number nearly equal to the 182,000 total of scrapped looms recorded under various government programs between 1956 and 1973.[48]

In Japan, the textile problem owed at least as much to the political strength of the industry as to its fragmented structure and low entry barriers. According to the U.S. General Accounting Office:

[Japanese] Government officials acknowledged that it is politically difficult to declare that an industry, or segments of an industry, should be phased out. Even though MITI may want to phase out the cotton spinning or textile mill products industries, it cannot present such a recommendation to the industry. MITI officials explained that this is why the government has instituted measures aimed at revitalizing the industry, while at the same time trying to lure these firms into other industries or into other more promising sectors within the same industry. MITI officials explained this is all part of the bargaining process—to get firms and workers to shift out of the industry, the government has to offer a comprehensive assistance plan that includes measures to encourage modernization as well as phaseout.[49]

The record of textile restructuring suggests that the best case for the effectiveness of Japan's disinvestment policy is *not* to be made on the basis of the government's role in shrinking highly fragmented, labor-intensive industries. Rather, as the data we reviewed from Robert Lawrence at the beginning of this chapter suggested, Japan seems to do better at shrinking such capital-intensive industries as aluminum and shipbuilding. We will turn to these industries next, after first considering the general policy framework of depressed industries laws that were adopted in the 1970s to facilitate structural adjustment.

The Policy Framework

More than any other historical event, the first oil shock in 1973 triggered the interest of MITI and other agencies of the Japanese government in cutting back the size of such industries as shipbuilding, which were once rising stars in the Japanese industrial complex. Prior to 1973, Japanese manufacturers took advantage of the lowest cost energy in the world, a surprising advantage since virtually all of Japan's oil had to be imported.[50] This advantage disappeared after 1973, as Japanese companies struggled with some of the highest energy costs in the world. Naturally, established Japanese industries which were either high energy users, or whose products depended on cheap energy, felt a severe impact.

Such was the case with shipbuilding and aluminum smelting—two of fourteen industries eventually designated by the government as "structurally depressed." (This designation derived from the 1978 Law on Temporary Measures for the Stabilization of Specified Depressed Industries.)[51] Eventually, the Japanese Depressed Industries Law (DIL) covered markets totaling some $80 billion; it was designed to facilitate an "orderly disposal of capacity" in industries that met the following criteria:

1. More than 50 percent of the industry's firms were experiencing financial difficulties;
2. The industry was characterized by severe overcapacity, with scant prospects for a turnaround;

3. Firms representing two-thirds of the industry's capacity were willing to sign a petition seeking designation as structurally depressed;

4. A broad agreement existed that some scrapping of facilities had become necessary.

When these conditions prevailed in a Japanese industry, MITI or some other designated agency was authorized to formulate a stabilization plan. The plan included a forecast of supply and demand, including imports and exports, designed to establish the extent to which capacity could be regarded as excess; and a determination as to the proper method of reducing excess capacity, including whether such capacity should be mothballed or scrapped. In formulating the stabilization plan, MITI was instructed to consult with relevant industry advisory committees, which operated under the umbrella of its Industrial Structure Council, a standing advisory body consisting of representatives of management, labor, consumers, and academics. The Depressed Industries Law also granted a right of review to the Japan Fair Trade Commission (JFTC). Once approved by the JFTC, the capacity reduction plans would be implemented by industrial cartels, formed under MITI's guidance and exempted from provisions of the Japanese Antimonopoly Law.

To facilitate such implementation, a special fund was created; it would guarantee the repayment of loans collateralized by equipment which was to be scrapped. The fund had a total guarantee limit of ¥100 billion, and it was capitalized with ¥8 billion from the Japan Development Bank and ¥2 billion from the private sector. Under provisions of the law, the responsible ministry could restrict new investment in plant and equipment in the designated industries, and use its administrative guidance to encourage a shift into different product lines. However, compliance with capacity reduction targets remained voluntary for private companies.

One reason for establishing the scrapping fund related to the financial situation of firms within the distressed industries. Typically, the net worth ratio of firms in Japan's manufacturing sector ranks among the lowest in the industrialized world. Consequently, a very high proportion of Japanese plant and equipment is collateral for long-term bank loans. Writing down or completely writing off this capacity therefore can be a significantly more complicated matter in Japan than in the United States. So the depressed industries' credit fund was designed specifically to address this problem.[52]

The overall origin of the Depressed Industries Law can be traced in part to a 1977 address by Toshio Komoto, head of the Liberal Democratic Party's Policy Affairs Research Council, who called for the implementation of countermeasures to assist industries suffering from structural recession. In general, these were industries whose profitability and long-term prospects would not significantly improve from the restoration of growth in aggregate demand. Acting on cue, MITI developed the idea into a legislative proposal, which MITI may well have expected to restore some of the authority and responsibility it had lost

TABLE 10-3
Reduction in Production Capacity 1978–81 in Specified Depressed Industries
(Unit: 1,000 tons/year)

	C/B (%)	Production Capacity (A) 1978	Targeted Reduction (B)	Actual Reduction (C)	Target Performance C/A (%)
(1)	Open hearth steel making & electric furnace	20,790	2,850	2,720	95.4%
(2)	Aluminum smelting	1,462	530	890	169.6
(3)	Nylon fiber (continuous)*	367	72	72.9	102.0
(4)	Polyacrylnitrate fiber (discontinuous)*	431	73	95.5	130.5
(5)	Polyester fiber (continuous)*	350	37	36.6	99.5
(6)	Polyester fiber (discontinuous)*	398	68	70.7	104.6
(7)	Urea*†	3,985	1,790	1,670	93.3
(8)	Ammonia*†	4,559	1,190	1,190	100.0
(9)	Phosphate (wet)	934	190	174	91.6
(10)	Cotton spinning†	1,204	67	52.1	77.9
(11)	Worsted yarn spinning*	182	18	17.6	96.2
(12)	Ferrosilicon	487	100	100	100.0
(13)	Corrugated paper board*	7,549	1,147	1,083	94.4
(14)	Shipbuilding	9,770	3,420	3,580	104.7

*Excess capacity cartels authorized under the Depressed Industries Law.

†Depression cartels authorized by the JFTC under the Antimonopoly Law.

NOTE: Some numbers have been rounded.

SOURCE: Frank K. Upham, in *Annual Review, Program on U.S.-Japan Relations* (Cambridge, Mass.: Harvard University, 1982–83), pp. 147–148.

since the mid-1960s. Whatever MITI's motivations, the law has since provided the basis for Japan's popular reputation for skillful management of industrial disinvestment.

Table 10-3 presents a summary of capacity reduction targets and recorded achievements for each of the fourteen industry stabilization plans authorized under the DIL. Targets ranged from less than 6 percent in cotton spinning to 45 percent in urea. In about half of the industries the targets were met or exceeded; only cotton spinning failed to achieve at least 90 percent of its reduction goal.

In his important book, *The Next American Frontier,* Robert B. Reich observed that the success of the DIL "lies in the explicit subsidies given to firms that agree to scrap excess capacity and in the firms' use of these subsidies to retrain and relocate their workers for more profitable endeavors." Reich concluded that the subsidies for scrapping accomplish two related objectives: "They induce the least competitive firms to exit from the industry, thereby improving the profitability of more competitive firms; and they provide workers with adjustment assistance that is geared to cushion and accelerate industrial change."[53]

Reich's observations support the use of economic efficiency as a measure of the effectiveness of disinvestment policy. Since opponents of the Depressed Industries Laws also accept this measure as the proper standard by which to judge the efficacy of government influence in declining industries, it would be useful to have available a definitive study of the economic effects of the DIL.[54] During the latter part of 1982 (when Reich's book was in press) the Japanese conducted a long debate about the advisability of extending the DIL until 1988. Eventually, the debate produced a beefed-up extension of the DIL, which was passed without significant opposition, under the title, "The Law on Temporary Measures for the Structural Improvement of Specified Industries" (Structurally Depressed Industries Law, or SDIL).[55] But before Japan's Fair Trade Commission lent its support to the new SDIL, its staff reviewed a report that sharply criticized MITI's proposal for extending the SDIL. That document argued that the adjustments which had occurred in declining industries were principally the result of market pressure, and *not* the outcome of careful planning by MITI and other Japanese ministries. Moreover, a number of Japanese academic economists, whose views also had been solicited by the JFTC, expressed skepticism that the DIL had always encouraged the least efficient producers to leave the market.[56]

Is there any basis for this argument? I think there is, but the evidence remains mixed. Assessing the net effect of the government's influence remains, in most cases, a difficult matter. However, the circumstances surrounding the restructuring of the aluminum smelting industry in Japan allow us to sort out some of these influences in more detail.

Aluminum Smelting in Japan

The history of Japan's aluminum industry since 1975, according to one recent study, is "one of the most dramatic examples of structural adjustment on record anywhere."[57] Assuming the truth of this observation, we still must ask: did this result derive principally from the influence of competitive forces and market structure, or was it owed to the success of a government-coordinated plan for the orderly reduction of capacity? The evidence seems to favor the former explanation.

Japanese aluminum refining was particularly hard hit by the increase in energy prices after 1973. Energy (specifically electricity) forms such a significant component of the total manufacturing cost of aluminum ingot that the metal is called "congealed electricity." Despite innovations in the use of energy that have made the Japanese the world's most efficient producers of ingots (as measured in kilowatt hours per ton), access to cheap hydroelectric sources in other parts of the world—notably Canada and the United States—provides some non-Japanese producers with an absolute cost advantage. By 1980, the power costs of ingot production in Japan were roughly nine times those in Canada and three times those in the United States. Subsequent estimates put the electricity costs per ton of aluminum produced in Japan in the range of ¥230,000 to ¥250,000, with comparable costs in the United States varying from ¥60,000 to ¥70,000. As of March 1982, the Aluminum Federation of Japan said that the domestic selling price of aluminum had reached ¥500,000 per ton. Meanwhile, at ¥300,000 per ton, landed aluminum imports from the United States were selling for only slightly more than what domestic producers were paying for their electricity bill alone.[58]

That domestic production should drop in the presence of such a severe cost disadvantage, then, was to be expected. Yet the suddenness of the decline remains striking. Domestic production fell from a high of 1,188,197 metric tons (mt) in 1977 to 255,900 mt in 1983. At the same time, employment in aluminum fell from 10,000 to 4,000; while imports rose as a share of domestic production from roughly 40 percent in 1977 to over 550 percent in 1983. Since 1980, domestic aluminum production in Japan has been in a state of free fall.

To understand business and government relations during the industry's decline, it is important to know something about its structure. A concentrated domestic industry with only six firms in the mid-1970s, aluminum smelting in Japan comprised about five percent of total world capacity. Each of the six firms was affiliated with one of the major *keiretsu.* Yet major end users of aluminum, such as auto companies, proved quick to switch to lower-cost imports once they became available, and apparently *keiretsu*-affiliated trading houses did little to prevent this type of buying behavior, preferring, instead, to promote the sales of imported ingots.

The aluminum industry seems to have been slow to recognize the full dimensions of the crisis it had entered. After expanding capacity throughout the first half of the 1970s, Japanese firms experienced significant excess capacity problems in the latter part of 1975—the year an Industrial Structure Council report forecast that total capacity in 1980 would equal 1,900,000 mt, and imports 600,000 mt (compared to actual current figures of 1,092,000 mt domestic and 736,000 mt imported). In 1978 the council, with MITI's approval, published revised but still overly optimistic forecasts of 1,141,000 mt domestic in 1985, with 1,250,000 mt of imports. Revisions were twice more repeated, and in late 1981, a council-endorsed stabilization plan used projections of domestic capacity of roughly 700,000 mt and expected imports of 1,500,000 mt in 1985. Within a few months MITI was using higher import penetration figures, but still retaining its estimate of domestic production. In reality, by the end of 1983, imports had already increased to over 1,415,000 mt; while domestic production was languishing at about 256,000 mt—less than 25 percent of its 1980 level.

In 1978, when the Industrial Structure Council was arguing that aluminum refining could recover its competitiveness within five years (provided that the industry scrapped excess capacity and undertook other reforms), MITI recommended that the entire Japanese industry be reorganized into two large groups, with the critical decisions on capacity reductions being made at the group level. This proposal was rejected by the firms, who pointed out that because of their small share of the world market, capacity reductions in Japan would have no appreciable effect on the world market price of aluminum. Instead, the industry argued for government protection in the form of tariff and quota barriers and lower (subsidized) electricity rates. One producer even argued for the establishment of a state trading company to market all aluminum inside Japan (presumably as a way of limiting imports to offshore Japanese smelters).[59]

While MITI eventually acceded to a request for special tariff measures that would require importers of primary ores to subsidize domestic smelters, it rejected other proposals. The aluminum industry, in turn, formed a capacity reduction cartel with a target of 32 percent for retirements by 1981. When 1981 arrived, however, 61.5 percent of the industry's capacity had actually been shut down—a much higher percentage than the amount targeted.

A second round of public/private negotiations over eliminating capacity began in April 1981, under the aegis of the Aluminum Industry Committee, a subcommittee of the Industrial Structure Council. The industry called for some additional protection to be used as "breathing space" while it pursued an "orderly withdrawal" from onshore aluminum smelting, in favor of offshore production. Now, the special tariff/quota system was extended, with a 9 percent duty placed on ingots imported on the spot market, with an exemption after April 1982 for imports brought in under long-term contracts or from overseas smelters owned by Japanese firms. Acting on an October 1981 advisory commission report, MITI called for a ban on plant expansion (excluding facilities for research and development), and a 424,000 ton reduction (37.3 percent) in capacity for the remaining five refiners. (One firm, Sumikei Aluminum, had already shut down altogether.) MITI tied its duty-free import policy to the 424,000-ton capacity reduction figure, while at the same time agreeing to share half of the funds collected from the special tariff (expected to amount to $45 million per year) with the industry.

Although MITI's proposal for capacity reductions in aluminum appeared to some foreign observers as merely one more mechanism for helping the industry settle into "gentle rather than convulsive decline," it did not strike all Japanese that way. For example, an editorial in the influential *Nihon Keizai Shimbun* (Japan's equivalent of *The Wall Street Journal*) took strong exception, blistering MITI's tariff program and arguing that "the government *only* imposes a 9 percent tariff on the importation of aluminum ingot and is not taking any special restriction measures. We cannot ignore the destruction of existing order caused by overly rapid imports. [The government's industrial restructuring effort] is about to be blown away before it is started."[60]

Such criticism seemed to reflect popular opinion, and in fact, within six months MITI's 700,000-ton capacity target became a nonbinding constraint. Imports continued to flow into Japan, unimpeded by the 9 percent tariff, causing firms to suddenly decide to withdraw from the business and close plants. The result was reductions "two or three times" what MITI and the advisory committee had anticipated in their stabilization plan.[61] By the end of 1982, the situation was so grave that MITI agreed to the industry's request for additional support—in the form of a ¥45 billion government-funded strategic aluminum stockpile, plus further interest payment guarantees.

Today, it seems intriguing to speculate about MITI's true motives throughout this period. Official forecasts and public pronouncements since 1976 suggest that MITI was surprised by the magnitude of the competitive disadvantage faced by Japanese domestic aluminum refiners. Time and again government stabilization plans were based on forecasts that quickly were overwhelmed by market forces. MITI seemed not so much to be leading an orderly retreat as following behind in the medic's van, bandaging the wounded and burying the dead.

Yet, there could be another interpretation: MITI recognized at an early date that the industry at anything close to its peak level of capacity was doomed. MITI also recognized that traditional capacity reduction schemes could be successful *only* in lowering fixed costs, since both pricing and variable costs were beyond its control (unless MITI was willing to implement a drastic program of protectionism, one equal to or exceeding the plan it had used for the textile industry). Instead, MITI made its decision to placate rather than to protect aluminum with a nonbinding tariff and quota policy, and that decision reflected the following considerations:

1. Drastic reduction in industry capacity did not pose a fundamental security threat;
2. Protectionism-induced higher prices would significantly impair other, export-oriented industries (such as autos) which were dependent upon aluminum as an input in their production process;
3. The six firms in the industry were all affiliated with *keiretsu*, which were sufficiently flexible and financially strong to be capable of sustaining the competition of imports;
4. Because the industry was capital intensive, a massive cut in employment base (in excess of 60 percent) would not result in exceptionally large job losses (only 6,000) and hence would not create insurmountable political problems.

It remains difficult to determine which of these interpretations stands closer to the full truth. If one accepts the first interpretation, MITI's strategy was mere patchwork, with little real impact on the timing, the magnitude, or the nature of the disinvestment process. If we accept another interpretation, MITI emerges as effective in inducing exit not by its intervention, but by its refusal to intervene.

Before attempting to reach a summary judgment on the Japanese approach to industrial disinvestment, we ought to look at one of the "success" stories of disinvestment management in Japan: the controlled reduction in capacity of the shipbuilding industry.[62]

Shrinking Shipbuilding

Among the many fascinating chapters in Japanese industrial history, the story of the shipbuilding industry ranks high. In fact, had the word not now been converted into a cliché by America's mass culture, "awesome" would be most appropriate as a description of the meteoric rise of shipbuilding in Japan, as statistics testify (see *Table 10-4*). In the first decade after World War II, Europe (led by Great Britain) dominated world shipbuilding. In 1949, British production was nearly ten times that of the Japanese. By 1956, however, Japan had passed Great Britain, to capture the number one position in the world. It has not relinquished that position since.

Worldwide, with the exception of the years between 1958 and 1961, the period 1947–1975 represented rapid growth in shipbuilding demand. With the reindustrialization of the West, world seaborne trade grew threefold, from 1.0 billion tons to 3.1 billion tons, and the demand for new ships grew apace. Ship completions increased from 8.3 million tons in 1960 to 34 million tons in 1974.[63] Crude oil, iron ore, coal, and grain became the four most heavily traded commodities during this period; in particular, the bulk carriers and crude tankers used to transport these cargoes supplied 70 percent of the total demand for shipping services. As buyers scrambled to place new orders, the backlog at major shipyards lengthened. In 1973, Japan captured one-half (48.6 percent) of the world's record level of new orders: 73.6 million tons. The Japanese share alone (35.7 million tons) was greater than the entire world output had been in any previous year! This was a golden era for Japanese shipbuilders. At its zenith, the industry was the country's number one or number two source of foreign exchange. (Eventually, 80 percent of Japan's

TABLE 10-4
The Development of the Japanese Shipbuilding Industry
(1959–1975)

Category	1975 Level	1975 Levels as Multiples of 1959 Levels
1. Ship Launchings (Japan)	18 million tons	10.5
2. New Ship Sales (Japan)	¥1.98 trillion	9.9
3. Shipbuilding Capital Investment (Japan)	¥73 billion	7.0
4. Ship Launchings (World)	35.9 million tons	4.1
5. Employees in Shipbuilding (Japan)	182,763	1.3

SOURCE: Japan Development Bank.

output was exported.) Employment rose steadily, peaking in 1974 at 274,000.[64]

During the 1970s, the Japanese shipbuilding industry consisted of well over 1,000 individual companies. Despite the large number of firms, output in the industry actually remained fairly concentrated, with the top twenty-three firms taking more than 90 percent of the market. About 70 percent of this total was shared among the so-called "Big Seven" firms: Mitsubishi Heavy Industries, Ishikawajima Harima Heavy Industries (IHI), Mitsui Engineering & Shipbuilding, Nippon Kokan, Kawasaki Heavy Industries, Hitachi Zosen, and Sumitomo Heavy Industries. All of the Big Seven were integrated heavy machinery companies that were also diversified into such lines of business as steel structures, "turn-key" plants, and aircraft engines and bodies.

Unlike these giants, the so-called "second-tier" Japanese companies (medium- and small-sized shipbuilders) focused more narrowly on shipbuilding, deriving over 80 percent of their sales from that industry. Second-tier builders relied heavily on first-tier firms for technology, marketing, financing and personnel. Bigger shipbuilders often maintained informal relations with smaller firms through this period, serving, for example, as purchasing agents for second-tier companies.[65]

The Japanese government maintained a pervasive influence on the industry. First, the Shipbuilding Act (1950) and later, the Law for Provisional Adjustment of Shipbuilding (1953) gave broad authority to the Ministry of Transport (MOT) to license construction of both building facilities and new ships, as well as responsibility for administrative guidance in all matters pertaining to "business improvement." By itself, the need to obtain construction permits meant that firms were required to report to the MOT the details of steel shipbuilding and repair as well as the manufacture of other marine equipment, including engines and boilers. MOT also had the power to restrict entry into the small-scale segment of the industry, in order limit overall capacity and to foster "healthy development."[66]

In return, the shipbuilding industry was made a beneficiary of other government programs designed to stimulate the sale of vessels and to modernize facilities and production processes. A "planned shipbuilding program" provided long-term, low-interest loans to domestic shippers through the Japan Development Bank (JDB). From 1963 until 1973, loans to the shipping industry represented the JDB's number one lending priority, comprising more than one-third of all JDB lending in six different years (and nearly 45 percent in 1965). Lending peaked in 1972, when ¥135 billion was committed to the industry. Prices for export were lowered through an unusual "sugar-link import program" that allowed shipbuilders to import raw sugar into Japan's protected market and then to use the proceeds as a subsidy for overseas sales of ships. Loans from the Export-Import Bank of Japan also played a role in stimulating exports; throughout the industry's golden era, shipbuilding received 48 percent of all Ex-Im Bank loans. During the 1950s, when the competitive foundations of the Japanese shipbuilding industry were being laid, this figure frequently exceeded 60 percent.

The golden age came to an abrupt end in 1974, when disaster struck in the aftermath of the 1973 oil shock. Demand quickly declined. In 1974, new orders fell by more than half. The same thing happened in 1975, and by 1976, new orders were under thirteen million tons—and still headed downward. In 1978, the world order book bottomed out at slightly more than eight million tons—the lowest level in thirteen years and scarcely more than one-tenth its 1973 level. Yet because of the lag between new orders and actual construction, the trough in the cycle did not come until two years later, in 1980, to be followed by a reverse mini-boom which lasted only two years and caused false hopes for the industry.

Of all ship types, the hardest hit during this depression were the massive, oil-carrying supertankers—the specialty of large Japanese shipbuilders. In 1975, tankers accounted for roughly two-thirds of total construction by tonnage, with 22.7 million tons. By 1978, tanker demand had shrunk to roughly one-quarter of the total, or 4.9 million tons. After this initial collapse, steady decline set in, until by 1983 tanker construction amounted to only 3.1 million tons, less than twenty percent of total tonnage. Throughout this period, the only major product categories to grow were ore carriers (which went from 4.6 million tons and 13 percent market share in 1975 to 7.7 million tons and 46 percent market share in 1982) and container ships (which started the period with 231,000 tons and 0.7 percent of the market, and reached 1.3 million tons and 8 percent in 1983).

Of course, the collapse in world shipbuilding forced not only Japan but all industrialized nations to consider the controversial issue of contraction—yet the depression in demand did not affect all countries in the same way. The United States, as mentioned earlier, produced only 1 percent of the world's share of commercial ships in 1975, and so was well insulated against the fall-off in demand.[67] Europe and Japan, which together accounted for roughly three-quarters of worldwide production when the crisis hit, had to bear the principal burden of adjustment. The shock to Japan was particularly severe. In 1975, Japan launched nearly 18 million tons; by 1979, launchings had fallen to approximately 4.3 million tons, scarcely more than the country had produced fifteen years earlier. At the same time, Japan's share of new ship orders dropped from roughly 35 million tons in 1973 to 3.65 million tons in 1978, a decrease of almost 90 percent. The virtual elimination of significant markets in the latter half of the 1970s naturally forced shipbuilders to contract employment. How quickly could Japan—with its celebrated "permanent" work force, adjust to new realities?

Table 10-5 presents data that relate the decline in employment to the decline in launchings. As can be seen from the table, employment dropped rapidly, falling from 274,000 in 1974 to 162,000 five years later, before registering a slight gain in 1980 and 1981. It is instructive to compare employment

TABLE 10-5
Production and Employment

| | New Launchings | | Employment | | | | Employment |
| | | | Total | | Regular | Subcontract | Elasticity |
	(1,000 GT)	% Change (A)	No. of Persons	% Change (B)	(No. of Persons)	(No. of Persons)	(B/A)
1972	12,866	7.3	247,276	0.3	169,236	78,040	0.41
1973	15,673	21.8	253,658	2.6	171,048	82,610	0.12
1974	17,609	12.4	273,904	8.0	184,198	89,706	0.65
1975	17,987	2.2	256,271	− 6.4	182,763	73,508	2.91
1976	14,310	− 20.4	244,161	− 4.7	174,971	69,190	0.23
1977	9,973	− 30.5	215,681	− 11.7	164,066	51,615	0.38
1978	4,921	− 50.5	176,350	− 18.2	137,063	39,287	0.36
1979	4,317	− 12.2	162,580	− 7.8	120,194	42,386	0.63
1980	7,288	68.8	164,210	1.0	112,602	51,608	0.02
1981	8,957	21.5	170,997	4.1	114,422	56,575	0.19

SOURCE: Lloyd's Register of Shipping and Ministry of Transport, *Handbook of Shipbuilding Statistics*.

statistics for the three years of rapid expansion leading up to the 1974 peak with the three years of contraction that followed. From 1972–1974, the average annual elasticity of employment—the ratio of the percentage change in employment occasioned by a given percentage change in new construction— was 0.39. During the early phase of contraction, employment elasticity was three times that, at 1.17, suggesting that the ability of shipyards to adjust to falling demand for labor was fairly substantial.[68] This flexibility owed much to the presence of subcontractors in the industry—workers who often perform the same jobs as regular, "permanent" employees, but who lack comparable job tenure. Large companies use subcontractors to meet sudden surges or fall-offs in demand. In 1975, two years after the first signs of oil shock, the subcontractor work force was cut by almost 20 percent, while the regular work force declined by less than 1 percent. On the other hand, this temporary work force was also the first to be expanded in the 1980–1981 "mini-boom."

Of course, companies used a variety of other methods, including pay cuts and lengthened work schedules, to increase labor flexibility. In November 1978, one firm, IHI, instituted a 5 percent wage cut, eliminated the increase in wages scheduled for 1979, cut the annual year-end bonus in half, and extended the work week.[69] Most of the other major companies made similar moves, while working conditions in small- and medium-sized firms showed an even more severe impact. At Sasebo Heavy Industries (SHI) workers were forced to accept a 15 percent cutback in basic wages, a three-year freeze in the annual base-up of wages, elimination of the annual bonus, and reinstitution of the six-day work week. As a result, the average wage of SHI workers fell to ¥641 per hour in 1979, about half of what it had been two years earlier. At ¥135,289 per month, the average wage for a thirty-five-year-old shipbuilder was barely above the unemployment compensation offered a worker with a family of four.[70]

Companies also instituted job transfers and "voluntary retirement" programs. In July 1980, 9,155 workers of Mitsubishi Heavy Industries (MHI) (roughly 11 percent of the company's 1974 work force) were working in other firms affiliated with the Mitsubishi Group, many of them in the group's auto company. MHI, like most of the other majors, also encouraged its older workers to take early retirement. MHI's special retirement bonus amounted to 160 percent of regular retirement benefits. During 1978–1979, some 2,048 workers signed up for MHI's program. In total, the industry spent nearly ¥90 billion in retirement money that year. At the other major firms, voluntary retirements from March 1978 to March 1979 were substantial:[71]

Ishikawajima-Harima Heavy Industries	4,600
Mitsui Shipbuilding and Engineering	2,200
Hitachi Shipbuilding	1,700
Kawasaki Heavy Industries	1,400
Sumitomo Shipbuilding and Machinery	950
Nippon Kokan	870

As has often been reported in America, the large, diversified companies did use their internal "group labor markets" as one means of adjustment. However, a recent study by Haruo Shimada of Keio University discounts the role of such job transfers in the labor adjustment process of companies in structurally depressed industries. Shimada found that, in general, the magnitude of transfers remained marginal; firms appeared to be able to avoid dismissals principally by shifting the burden of adjustment to their smaller, less flexible subcontractors.[72]

Another fact is also worth noting: most of the employment cuts occurred before the capacity reductions in shipbuilding were authorized under the Depressed Industries Law of 1979. Yet this does not mean that government programs failed to have any impact on the disinvestment of labor. Apparently, the government's actions did have an important signal effect; managers in the shipbuilding industry with whom I spoke, for example, suggested that government legislation "legitimized" the actions of those firms that began to take steps to cut employment.[73]

In contrast to their relatively rapid cutback of labor, Japanese shipyards proved slow to withdraw capacity from the industry. Here, much of the explanation must be found in the physical nature of the capital assets employed in shipbuilding. What else can one do with a giant building berth and a 450-ton crane—except to build massive marine structures? It may also be true that firms in the industry held off eliminating capacity until it became clear what their government was prepared to do to be helpful.[74] Whatever the reason, in Japan the number of very large building berths and docks remained virtually unchanged from 1975 to 1979.

Beginning in 1975, the Japanese government refused to authorize the expansion or construction of new facilities, acting under the Shipbuilding Act of 1950. In concert with banks, particularly the Industrial Bank of Japan and the Long-Term Credit Bank of Japan, both of which were heavily involved in lending to shipbuilding, the Ministry of Transport sought to organize an industrywide solution to the crisis, based on recommendations regarding both capacity reductions and operation curtailments received from the Shipping and Shipbuilding Rationalization Council (SSRC). At first, the industry experienced some difficulty in reaching consensus on the proper amount and formula for capacity reductions, but in November 1976, acting on the recommendation of the SSRC, the MOT introduced an administrative guidance system under which output was curtailed by 28 percent of peak year performance. In 1978, the operating rate of the forty largest shipbuilding firms was frozen at 67 percent, and in 1979, production was limited to 39 percent of peak. In August 1979, control over operating rates was vested in a formal antirecession cartel, established to avoid any complaint by the JFTC. Here, the operating ratios varied by company size, with the largest shipbuilders agreeing to limit production during 1979 and 1980 to 34 percent of peak. This agreement lasted until March 31, 1981 (the end of the 1981 fiscal year), at which time a second recession cartel was authorized. All firms entering the cartel were required to submit monthly output figures, in return for which they received authorization from MOT to build new ships. Spot checks would determine compliance, and violators could be fined.

By May 1978, when the Depressed Industries Law was enacted, the industry already had suffered from so much turmoil that initial disagreements about the magnitude of reductions necessary had disappeared. In July, the Shipbuilding Facilities Subcommittee of the SSRC published a forecast predicting that Japanese yards were likely to be producing around 6.4 million compensated gross register tons (cgrt) in 1985, compared with their actual installed capacity at that time of 9.8 million cgrt. The SSRC's study called for curtailment of 35 percent of the industry's current capacity. In August, shipbuilders using berths or docks capable of building vessels larger than 5,000 gross tons took on the designation of a depressed industry under the DIL, and in October, the SSRC at the MOT's request promulgated a stabilization plan. This program applied to sixty-one major shipbuilders, which represented over 95 percent of Japan's total shipbuilding capacity. The production target for each company was based on existing capacity and earlier production; the seven largest shipbuilders were scheduled to reduce their facilities by 40 percent; the next largest seventeen shipbuilders by 30 percent; sixteen other medium-sized firms by 27 percent, and smaller shipbuilders by 15 percent. These cuts were to be completed during fiscal 1979, which began on April 1. The rationale for higher capacity reduction targets for the majors was that they were more diversified and financially stronger, and that they would experience less difficulty in reducing capacity than would smaller firms that depended more heavily on shipbuilding.

As an additional measure, designed to speed the exit of smaller shipbuilding-dependent firms, the MOT established (in cooperation with the private sector) a joint purchasing agency with the unwieldy title of the Association for the Stable Operation of Specified Shipbuilding Industries. This new agency was given authority to purchase the assets of firms seeking to withdraw from shipbuilding and to dispose of these assets outside the industry. To qualify for a buy-out, firms needed to demonstrate that they had built vessels in the 5,000 ton class. They also were required to provide proof that their employees agreed to the sale, promise that they would cease to construct ships of 5,000 tons and above, and demonstrate that they would settle pending liabilities with subcontractors and creditors. Initially capitalized by ¥1 billion each from the government and the private sector, during fiscal 1979, the agency agreed to purchase properties valued at ¥36.8 billion. Outside funds were raised from the Japan Development Bank and from various commercial banks. These loans were to be redeemed by 1988 through sales of land and by an excise tax on new ship orders: 0.1 percent in 1979, 0.15 percent in 1980, and 0.2 percent in 1981. If these funds proved insufficient to keep agency financing charges at 3 percent, the government offered additional subsidies.

The Japanese Results

Overall, the shipbuilding industry proved successful in meeting its capacity reduction target. By the end of March 1980, 36.5 percent of all facilities had been cut back, exceeding the planned target by 1.5 percent. Some fifty docks with a capacity greater than 5,000 gross tons were closed or frozen; thirteen more reduced their production capacity to under the 5,000 ton limit. As a result, overall industry capacity fell from 9.8 million cgrt to 6.2 million cgrt. Roughly 20 percent of the 3.6 million cgrt of capacity that was retired came as a result of action by the joint purchasing agency, which bought the assets of nine shipbuilders. For those firms remaining in the industry, operating profit ratios, which had been dropping steadily, firmed up after 1978. In fact, at least two of the Big Seven reported that their shipbuilding divisions were their most profitable business units during 1981.[75]

During the process of overall reductions, each shipbuilder exercised the right to determine for itself which yards to close. Such factors as relation to company structure, future demand, and the local situation of the community played some role in these determinations. Smaller firms were allowed to seek joint production—capacity cutbacks with larger firms on a group basis. In general, shipyards in the provinces tended to be less vulnerable to closing, owing to their stronger ties to the local economy. Prefectural governors proved to be especially effective critics of plant closings, often pressing for specific government assistance that enabled certain yards to stay open. Such political pressures proved extremely important, as we can see from one example—the case of Sasebo Heavy Industries.

> In 1978, Sasebo, the country's eighth largest shipbuilder reached a state of crisis, and faced bankruptcy. Located in Sasebo City, a town of 250,000, the company was the single most significant employer in the region. Although its liabilities in early 1978 seemed considerable, they were not overwhelming by Japanese standards—only 120 billion yen. Much larger firms had gone bankrupt in the past, and it seemed that the banking community and major suppliers would allow the firm to fail. But this alternative appeared unacceptable to several parties: the mayor of Sasebo City; a group of individuals who counted on Sasebo to service a nuclear ship, the Mutsu; entrepreneurs interested in obtaining Sasebo's assets for use in shipbuilding; and finally to the U.S. government, which wished to maintain a ship repair facility in the city. With these pressures in mind, Prime Minister Fukuda stepped in, reversed the recommendation for the Ministry of Finance and the Bank of Japan, and ordered a rescue effort for Sasebo. The company was saved, its assets preserved within the industry, and its operations merged with the Kurushima Group, to form Japan's fourth largest shipbuilder.[76]

Given this account, how shall we evaluate Japanese disinvestment policy in shipbuilding? It is a complicated story, and there is much that could be said.

One major issue has to do with the definition of disinvestment and its economic meaning. From a statistical point of view, there is no denying that the program of cutbacks contributed to the elimination of capacity as officially measured in the industry. Berths and docks that had once counted as parts of the industry simply vanished from the record books. But what does this really mean? What happened to this "reduced capacity?"

In some cases, equipment was scrapped or sold, docks filled in, and land converted to other uses. All of this occurred at the Geibi dockyard, for example, which the Joint Purchasing Agency first bought and then sold to Kure City for residential construction. In many other cases, when the costs of filling in docks proved too high, or when equipment was either too specialized or too big and cumbersome to be broken down and transported elsewhere, literally nothing happened. Old building basins, such as the mammoth Dock #3 at Mitsui's Chiba dockyard, with its giant rotary crane rusting alongside it, sit idle today—frozen in time. Technically, this dock and crane are not a part of the industry. Neither is IHI's ultra-modern, one million gross ton facility at Chita. Because IHI agreed to dedicate its use to building offshore oil rigs and other non-ship marine structures, however, Chita qualifies as "shut down" under the terms of the capacity reduction program. Clearly this has contributed to the perception that the government's capacity reduction program was a success. Still, we must ask, is this outcome any different from that which would have occurred had there been no government program?

What, then, has fundamentally changed now that these assets are no longer *officially* counted as part of the shipbuilding industry? It would appear that the principal effect has been to change the assumptions used by Japanese planners. Now, when the planners estimate ship prices based on forecasts of supply and demand, they do so without any concern that either IHI's Chita, or Mitsui's Chiba #3 might be available for new building. This would not necessarily be the case in the absence of a government program. In effect, what the government did when it reduced capacity was to erect new barriers around part of the industry—by defining some 36.5 percent of its former capacity as "out-of-bounds."

This gives us some basis for assessing the *amount* of disinvestment that took place under the Japanese program. Now, what about the *kind* of disinvestment? Here, again, even though we do not have cost data that would allow us to estimate whether those facilities that were shut down represented high-cost yards, or relatively efficient yards, we can make some inferences from the decision rules that the Japanese government employed in reaching its overall target. In one interview, for example, I asked an official of the MOT to describe the process of decision making that his agency went through in introducing the capacity reduction scheme to shipbuilding. Here is his reply:

> In [the] Japanese system, the general procedure is as follows. The government will call on private experts and related industry personnel, and formulate an advisory council to get advice on the policy

before deciding the total plan and implementing it. But the govern-ment usually has the leading role in deciding the policy, because at the private sector level, each company would have [conflicting] inter-ests, and it would be hard [for them] to reach consensus. . . . Once [it] decides to formulate policy, the government would be very careful that *the policy would be a fair one in view of everyone involved.* [emphasis added][77]

Certainly, the concept of fairness is central. In this case, fairness was defined as requiring those firms which had the largest capacity and production (and which were also the most diversified) to take the biggest reductions, on the theory that they could adjust most easily. Fairness also meant that some smaller firms and their creditors were eligible for a government buy-out, with equipment valued at book minus depreciation, rather than at its (probably) lower liquidation value. In terms of the anti-recession cartel, fairness meant that the larger the firm, the greater its responsibility for cutting back on pro-duction.

Yet, if one assumes that there are significant economies of scale in shipbuild-ing, that the largest facilities can produce mid-sized (as well as large) ships efficiently, and that the major shipbuilders represent the most technically efficient producers in the industry—all of which are reasonable assump-tions—then applications of these decision rules must have resulted in an industrial structure that protected pockets of inefficiency. For example, be-cause of the production rules, the largest shipyards were prevented in princi-ple from utilizing so-called "parallel shipbuilding" techniques—the practice of building several ships at one time in the same drydock. This limitation pro-tected smaller shipbuilders whose traditional product niche of mid-sized ships became threatened when the majors looked to build smaller ships after super-tanker demand dropped off. In Korea, meanwhile, where no such rules prevent Hyundai from engaging in parallel shipbuilding, four different ships of various sizes are built at the same time in the same dock. So some economies have been lost to the Japanese rules of the game.

In other ways also, the capacity reduction and output curtailment schemes inhibited the industry's ability to compete internationally. Lloyds reported that in 1981 major Japanese yards put in bids for thirteen large, multiship contracts, involving a total of forty-three ships. Yet, not a single order was won out of this group, in part (according to Japanese sources) because of contract allocation required by the cartel. The United Arab Shipping Company, for example, was in the market for nine container ships. Because of the cartel's operating rate restrictions, no single Japanese yard could accommodate the buyer's wish to concentrate production in one yard. As a result, the bid went to Hyundai in Korea.[78]

Conclusions

Instructive as these specific cases are, we should focus on their larger impli-cations for the questions asked at the outset. We began the chapter by asking:

Are the Japanese much better at moving resources out of declining industries than Americans? Do politics and economics work together to achieve greater efficiency in Japan than in the United States? Have the outcomes of the Japanese depressed industries policy been principally (or exclusively) determined by government, or have other variables played important roles?

As the evidence reviewed in this chapter demonstrates, industrial restructuring—whether in Japan, the United States, or any other country—is easier to accomplish when the overall economy is rapidly growing than when it is not. Thus, those who argue that Japan's disinvestment record has proved superior to that of the United States may be ascribing to microeconomic institutions behavior that is more appropriately related to the country's macroeconomic performance. To put it another way, the story of Japanese success and American failure in enhancing productivity and competitiveness cannot be related primarily to the skill of Japanese companies or the ineptitude of American ones in divesting, shrinking, or shifting out of moribund enterprises. Nor did Japan's macroeconomic achievements—impressive though they were—derive chiefly from a unique national ability to restructure declining industries. Instead, the effectiveness with which the Japanese government was able to formulate and implement capacity reduction schemes varied, depending on structural characteristics of the individual industries.

For example, Japanese intervention in the highly fragmented, labor-intensive textile industry proved ineffective largely because government lacked certain abilities: to resist protectionist pressures, to police compliance with its policy, and to prevent reentry when improved profitability invited new resources. As the pool of capital in the Japanese economy has grown, and as entrepreneurs have become less dependent upon official or semiofficial sources of funds to overcome capital barriers, the government has experienced difficulty in blocking new entrants into fragmented industries. Here, the lesson of the textile restructuring efforts is clear: to facilitate and to sustain orderly exits, the Japanese government must be able to rely on some powerful economic barrier that will stop any reflow of capacity back into the industry as market conditions improve. Where such barriers are lacking, government fiat is *not* sufficiently strong to prevent reentry.

By contrast, aluminum and shipbuilding—the two capital-intensive industries that we examined—both met or exceeded the Japanese government's plan for capacity reduction. Aluminum was "destructured" because rivalry from imports proved especially keen, because user groups were powerful enough to demand access to low-cost sources of supply, and because the industry's relatively small size meant that Japan's production and capacity allocation schemes would have no appreciable effect on world market prices. Opposition among domestic producers was muted with the help of direct payments generated from an import surcharge; but otherwise, the government managed by allowing market forces to drive private disinvestment decisions.

Shipbuilding, the most highly touted example of Japanese disinvestment management, provided the Japanese government with a success story, but for a series of reasons specific to the structure of that industry. First, the sudden collapse of demand for supertankers generated strong consensus on the magnitude and certainty of the crisis. Second, because Japan was the world leader in shipbuilding and controlled more than half of the commercial market, Japanese shipbuilders had more to lose from chaos in the industry than did other producers. In fact, the biggest Japanese shipbuilders recognized that in the absence of a government-led and enforced agreement, a disastrous competition in price-cutting could break out; and that they, alone in the world, with their efficient manufacturing and large market share, held enough power to prevent chaotic competition. This view was shared by Japanese labor, which joined management in supporting the capacity reduction cartel. Buyers, meanwhile, were ineffective in preventing the formation of the cartel, since more than half of them were foreign, and many of those that were Japanese belonged to the same *keiretsu* that built the ships. Finally, barriers to entry, in the form of capital expenditures and government construction permits, proved effective in preventing new competition inside Japan, even after firms began to see some appreciable improvement in earnings.

At a very broad level, one can identify the role of government in both Japan and the United States as either "hands-on" or "hands-off," concerning the issue of industrial restructuring and disinvestment. If it is fair to make such a distinction, then the American choice is generally for "hands-off" management, just as the characteristic Japanese response favors a "hands-on" approach. Yet each country combines elements of both. In Japan, neither the government nor the *keiretsu* practice "hands-on" management with regard to every declining industry. For example, no capacity reduction program guided the decline of the Christmas tree light and plastic toy industries in Japan. Overall, the so-called temporary work force and many small supplier companies in Japan remain outside the advantaged circle whenever retreat is sounded. In the United States, the government has attempted at various times to decrease excess capacity in such sectors as agriculture and mining, and in such industries as steel, through a variety of means. Some of these have been direct, but most remain indirect. Such government actions in America invariably attract popular criticism and opposition, while in Japan people usually seem to welcome the government's direct involvement.

To suggest, as this chapter does, that Japan is better than the United States at "hands-on" disinvestment management is *not* to conclude that this should be the American response to decline, or even that this style of managing retreat invariably works well for Japan. The record that we have reviewed provides ample testimony for the observation that politics frequently triumphs over economics—even in Japan. For all its obvious shortcomings, "hands-off" management can be an effective antidote for economic distortion in both countries.

It is tempting to conclude on the basis of these examples that the political economy of disinvestment is not fundamentally different in Japan and the United States. Still, images of angry steelworkers occupying churches and factories in Pennsylvania, or copper miners throwing rocks in Arizona, suggest that there is a difference. To the extent that Japan has, in fact, signed an armistice between politics and economics, it may ultimately be because, relative to the United States, the pace and pattern of economic growth have lowered disinvestment costs and distributed these costs more widely.

CHAPTER 11

America versus Japan: Conclusions and Implications

THOMAS K. McCRAW

Conclusions

In the preface to this book, the authors expressed a wish to help explain the Japanese business-government relationship to American readers and the American one to Japanese readers. Later, a corollary goal became clear to us: that our research should also help explain each nation's business-government relationship to its own people. As the great historian Macaulay once wrote, "He knows not England who only England knows"; and our experience in writing the book has confirmed the wisdom of Macaulay's comment. Only by detachment from an ethnocentric perspective can anyone hope to understand his or her own society, let alone another. Thus, our reliance on the comparative method now appears even more valid to us than it did when we began.

Of course, the comparative approach proved to have disadvantages. Necessarily, it traded off depth in favor of breadth, sacrificing the narrow but fine detail of the microscope for the panorama of the wide-angle lens. Yet, we think that the *accumulated* evidence we have presented, taken from a variety of perspectives and discussed at great length with audiences in both America and Japan, leads to a number of clear conclusions. So we offer each of the following propositions with a good deal of confidence:

1. *The Two Countries Have Exhibited Different Conceptions of the Relationship Between Domestic and Global Markets.* From the Japanese viewpoint, the fundamental importance of a few basic areas of production such as steel ("the rice of industry") dictated that a modern economy must invest there. Within the export-oriented setting of Japan, the potential for scale economies in those same industries propelled them into competition for world markets. If Japanese business managers seriously intended to export any important industrial products—automobiles, heavy equipment—then they first

needed to bring the nation's steel industry up to world standards. Such momentum, once acquired, then drew the Japanese steel industry itself into an export strategy; and that commitment to export led to a deliberate national policy of building steel capacity well beyond domestic needs alone. By contrast, within the Japanese home market, public policies toward wholesaling, retailing, and agriculture could be rationalized in a more leisurely manner, if at all. Such measures as might apply to these sectors were not important to international economic competitiveness, so they could be allowed to respond instead to powerful domestic political pressures.

Within the United States, very different patterns emerged, for both production and distribution. In American public policy toward production, the idea of globalism dawned relatively late—not so much for individual companies, American multinationals having been pioneers in global markets even in the nineteenth century, as in formal national competition policy. Evidence of this native line of thinking could be seen in the endless debates within American antitrust circles over the notion of "relevant market." Such markets, in antitrust cases, were usually found to be regional or national. Only seldom were they defined as global. Thus, rather than construing the domestic American market as fundamentally integrated with a world economy, American policy often seemed to insist on a formal separation of the two, as illustrated in the chapter on energy and oil pricing.

2. *The Japanese Implicitly Tend to View Transactions as Continuous, the Americans as Ad Hoc.* In Japan, government bureaucrats and business executives have long regarded economic activity as occurring along an endless continuum. No single transaction, in either the economic or the regulatory sphere, can be considered autonomous and self-contained; instead, every transaction must be related to all others. If, for example, a company refuses to follow the guidance of the Ministry of Finance or the Ministry of International Trade and Industry, then both the ministry and the company assume that at some future time the ministry will exact appropriate recompense. Of course, this expectation does not prevent a company from rejecting the government's advice, but it does play an important role in every large firm's decision making. Similarly, in company-to-company dealings (as opposed to company-to-government ones), the same sense of historical continuity prevails. No transaction, however simple, can be separated from the continuum of inter-firm relationships. Whether the companies are members of the same *keiretsu,* or more loosely federated parts within the overall organization of Japanese group capitalism, or even if they are not related at all, every transaction still remains connected to every other occurring between the same parties. Thus, the entire Japanese business system, and Japanese business-government arrangements as well, are governed by complex webs of powerful long-term relationships.

The American system, in contrast, is characterized by thousands of separable ad hoc transactions. Americans generally view the buyer-seller relationship as impersonal. *Caveat emptor* remains the governing rule, in a way that would be unthinkable in Japan. In business-government relations, a firm's behavior in one regulatory episode generally cannot, by law, prejudice its treatment in some future case. Nearly all cases in the public sector, like most buyer-seller transactions in the private one, are regarded as self-contained and finite. In both business and government, the proper mode of management is thought to be arm's-length bargaining between autonomous entities.

In the future, conditions external to Japan will likely diminish the traditional emphasis on relationships. Earlier chapters in this book that deal with trade and foreign direct investment, for example, delineate ways in which host countries might force Japanese multinationals to depart from their natural impulses. Then, too, the powerful trends identified in the chapter on financial systems, with its description of moves from relationship to price banking, may spread from finance to other sectors of the Japanese economy. Meanwhile, however, the point seems incontestable that long-term business relationships remain more important in Japan than in the United States.

3. *The Number of Important Decision Makers Tends to Be Smaller in Japan than in the United States.* As the chapters on trade, agriculture, energy, the environment, fiscal policy, and disinvestment all make clear, important public policies in Japan usually are made by fewer persons than in America. It is true that Japan has achieved a democratic polity complete with free speech, a free press, and universal suffrage. In addition, the overall style of "consensual" decision making would seem in theory to imply a high rate of participation. Yet, in practice, the Japanese system of relationships and hierarchies tends to channel vital decisions into a few hands. In the United States, by contrast, the emphasis on arm's-length bargaining and individual autonomy promotes the opposite result. Every American citizen has not only the right, but often the inclination as well, to challenge authority and to carry disputes to ever higher levels of appeal.

These differences, of course, stretch far back into the histories of both countries: to the Tokugawa period in Japan, with its systematic stifling of dissent; and to the colonial and Revolutionary periods of the United States, with their glorification of individual freedom and their explicit rejection of European-style statism. Thus, the conspicuously litigious aspect of American society is deeply rooted in the nation's very founding, just as the relative acceptance of authority characteristic of Japan is embedded in that country's historical culture and ideology.

4. *Domestic Politics Profoundly Shapes Economic Policies in Both Countries.* In the case of Japan, a superficial analysis covering the last thirty years might come to a conclusion something like the following: Given MITI's extremely successful management of the production-for-export sector, it becomes difficult to believe that agriculture and internal distribution could not

also have been rationalized much more thoroughly, had the government been determined to do so. Had they been so rationalized, then the Japanese people might now enjoy much readier access to inexpensive food and other consumer goods. Cut-rate supermarkets might dot the Japanese landscape as densely as they do the American. Nor would the Japanese Ministry of Agriculture, Forestry and Fisheries find itself sponsoring heavy subsidies to rural families as a means of preserving income parity with urban dwellers, all at the expense of Japanese consumers and taxpayers.

Yet, had such rationalizations of agriculture and distribution actually occurred in Japan, the political cost to the Liberal Democratic Party would have been extraordinarily high. Rigorous rationalization of wholesale and retail trade would have played havoc with local Japanese customs. It might well have thrown several hundred thousand persons out of work. Similarly, a rapid and forced agricultural adjustment, whatever the economic benefits to Japanese consumers as a whole, would have disrupted the housing and income patterns of millions of Japanese families. And, had both agriculture and distribution simultaneously been subjected to government-mandated rationalization, then the coalition of interests that kept the LDP in office for an entire generation—and thereby preserved Japan's overall economic strategy for growth—would almost certainly have been endangered. Thus, the otherwise peculiar mixture of Japanese policies toward production, distribution, and agriculture represents, above all else, a delicate political settlement.

Ample illustrations of the power of politics to shape economic decisions are also easy to find in America. The chapter on energy, for example, demonstrated the ways in which domestic U.S. oil and gas producers were able to wheedle heavy subsidies from taxpayers. The same phenomenon could be found in agriculture as well, though not quite to the extent observable in Japan. Still another illustration appeared in the chapter on trade, which showed how the American textile industry succeeded in insulating itself from foreign competition through the oldest device of all: a high protective tariff.

By the middle 1980s, perhaps the most powerful evidence of political influence on American economic policy appeared in the prolonged failure of the United States to deal in a rational way with the federal deficit, and especially with the relationship of this deficit to the workings of the international economy. During the 1980s, the American people have simply been living far beyond their means. They have drifted into a pattern of financing high living with money borrowed from abroad, particularly from Japan. Because of the Americans' steadfast refusal to address the deficit problem realistically, much of the blame for the recent deterioration in American-Japanese relations, though by no means all of it, must lie at the door of the United States. The president, the Congress, and the electorate all share responsibility for this failure; and the long-term consequences of their paralysis during the middle 1980s will turn out to be far more severe than they seem to realize.

5. *In Its Public Policies, Japan Has Viewed Countries Primarily as Economic Competitors, While the United States Has Regarded Them Primarily as Geopolitical Entities.* Ever since the departure of the Occupation forces in 1952, the unambiguous objective of the Japanese government has been to strengthen its national economy in the world market. MITI, MOF, and other elite bureaucracies perceived their country as an economic competitor of the United States and other world powers. They thought of Japan's manufacturing industries as national representatives in a global contest for economic leadership. Consequently, their single-minded goal on the production side was to facilitate Japanese industries' ability to gain and hold world market share over the long run. Within this book, the Japanese view is best exemplified in the chapters on trade, foreign investment, steel production, and disinvestment. Focusing on world markets, Japanese policy assigned much less importance to the international competitiveness of its domestic distribution, agricultural, or energy sectors.

In contrast to Japan, the broader American perception of nations as geopolitical actors motivated public policy much more powerfully than did any thought of countries as economic competitors alone. Thus, in American foreign policy, the obvious rival appeared to be the Soviet Union, not Japan. In fact, Japan's success within the economic realm served the American national security interest extraordinarily well. This remained true although that same Japanese miracle displaced American supremacy in world markets, and even gained a substantial share of the American domestic market.

In historical terms, Japan's emphasis on economic nationalism called to mind mercantilist strategies of the eighteenth century, whereas the American focus on geopolitics more closely resembled the great-power diplomacy of nineteenth-century Europe. During the forty years after World War II, the United States behaved much like a traditional military power of the nineteenth century. The goal seemed to be the construction of a Pax Americana to replace the earlier Pax Britannica.

6. *Japan's Public Policies Have Emphasized Producer Values; Those of the United States, Consumer Values.* Almost innumerable examples of such differences appear throughout this book: the subsidization and consequent underpricing of energy in America during the oil crises of the 1970s; the exemption of consumer credit purchases from taxation in America, and the converse taxing of such purchases in Japan; the taxing of interest income from savings in America, and its exemption in Japan; the suppression of cut-rate chain stores in Japan, and the promotion of those same categories in America; the very different housing policies in each country; and so on. As a 1985 report from the Industrial Bank of Japan put it, "Being a trade-dependent nation, Japan is predisposed toward the 'logic of producers' that exports must be maintained as a prerequisite for sustaining a high standard of living. By contrast, the United

States, which embraces ample resources and a gigantic market, tends to revolve around the 'logic of consumers.' "[1]

Here it is important to underscore how deeply these contrasting values are
embedded in the ideologies and institutional structures of each country. Historically, the Japanese have taken their texts from the leading theorists of
production-oriented economic nationalism—writers such as Friedrich List,
the German apostle of nationalism. Considering the Japanese situation, it is not
difficult to understand the appeal of such ideas. Once the government determined that it must modernize its economy in order to avoid colonization—a
decision taken long ago, under the Meiji restoration of the mid-19th century—
then the die was cast: because Japan lacked abundant natural resources, it had
to have an explicit industrial policy, focused on exports and the production of
modern capital goods.

Viewed against this background, the Japanese experience since World War
II emerges as a clear historical continuity with earlier national imperatives—
and a remarkably sophisticated variety of twentieth-century mercantilism. In
recent years, the formula has differed from orthodox mercantilist assumptions
of the seventeenth and eighteenth centuries only in Japan's eschewing of
military power and in its abandonment of the mercantilist assumption of zero-
sum wealth in the world. In other respects, the parallel holds. Japan's transcendent commitment to economic nationalism has constituted a non-military
substitute for its earlier promotion of a Co-Prosperity Sphere embracing most
of East Asia.

In the United States, on the other hand, the reigning ideologies have been
mixed, but are best typified in the writings of three other theorists: Thomas
Jefferson, who argued that the best government governs least; Adam Smith,
whose invisible hand, unfettered by government regulation, moves automatically to promote the public interest; and, for international economics, David
Ricardo, who showed how free trade, based on each country's comparative
advantage in physical endowments, would maximize the world's wealth. All
three of these theorists attacked the idea of mercantilism, not only on economic grounds but on moral ones as well. To them, mercantilist policies were
so thoroughly grounded in economic nationalism that they would inevitably
encourage rivalries among nations that might eventuate in actual wars. Thus,
mercantilism came to be regarded as the economic equivalent of an arms race.
Since all countries could not win such a race, mercantilism violated those
Enlightenment premises about the brotherhood of man that so animated the
classical economists. (For all his emphasis on the utility of economic self-
interest, Adam Smith was at bottom a moralist—in fact, a professor of moral
philosophy.)

Thus, just as the statist texts of Friedrich List represented a good fit with the
fundamental Japanese situation of a large but resourceless population, so also
the anti-government arguments of Jefferson, Smith, and Ricardo seemed appropriate to the American setting. The United States represented a country in no

further danger of colonization, and blessed with boundless endowments which positively invited development by energetic individuals. Hence the American Dream—a dream rooted in the new values of egalitarian consumption; and hence also the very different Japanese Dream—a determined quest to preserve, within a modern setting, the ancient national character and culture. To be realized in Japan, such a dream must find its basis not in the values of individualistic consumption, but in those of collectivist production. And the implementation of any such strategy must require a rapidly adaptive system overseen by a powerful, meritocratic bureaucracy.

Implications

1. *Because of the Continuing Consumerist Orientation of the United States, the American Deficit Situation Will Become Worse Before It Becomes Better, and Japanese-American Relations Will Therefore Continue to Show Strain.* Here it becomes useful to place in historical perspective just a few numbers, in order to review the magnitude of the problem. Recall, as noted in an early chapter of this book, that for every single year between 1893 and 1971, the United States ran a trade surplus. Immediately afterward, during the period 1971–1978, it ran what now appear to be modest deficits. In 1979, the year of the second oil shock, the deficit suddenly ballooned to about $40 billion. And in every year since 1982, the United States has set a new world record for trade deficits by a single nation. During that same period, the trend in Japan has been just the opposite (see *Table 11-1*).[2] During this very same period, the American federal deficit climbed to previously unimaginable heights, as the national debt almost doubled (see *Table 11-2*).[3]

Overall, these trends within the American economy added up to an unsustainable situation. The numbers cited in the tables below simply could not continue to grow in the 1990s at the rate they had during the middle 1980s. Something would have to give, especially since so much of the American deficit was being financed from abroad. It is one thing for a country's national debt to be owed to its own citizens, but quite another for it to be in the hands of foreigners. The interest on foreign debts, as Latin American nations have discovered in recent years, usually must be paid through export earnings. Yet the United States continued to record huge deficits on the export side as well.

TABLE 11-1
American and Japanese Trade Balances

	With All Nations		U.S. Deficit with Japan	
	United States	Japan		
1982	$− 42.6 billion	$ 6.9 billion	1982	$− 17.0 billion
1983	− 69.4 billion	20.6 billion	1983	− 21.0 billion
1984	− 123.3 billion	33.5 billion	1984	− 37.0 billion
1985	− 143.8 billion	39.6 billion	1985	− 40.7 billion

TABLE 11-2

	U.S. Federal Deficit	Total Federal Debt
Fiscal Year 1982	$127.9b	$1,147.0
1983	207.8	1,381.9
1984	185.3	1,576.7
1985	212.3	1,827.5
1986*	175.5	2,076.9

*Estimate from Mid-Session Review of the 1986 Budget, OMB, August 30, 1985.

Overall, the United States, which had been a net creditor nation for every year since 1914, suddenly went into the red during 1985. As foreign money poured into the United States, some estimates projected that by 1990, net foreign claims on American debtors (principally the U.S. government) might exceed $700 billion, and by 1993 could actually pass the $1 trillion mark.[4] These figures dwarfed the estimated $500 billion owed by *all* Latin American governments as of the middle 1980s, and which caused so much hand-wringing over the international debt crisis.

To rectify this untenable situation, the American government would have to reduce the deficit, stop relying so heavily on foreign borrowing, and promote improved industrial productivity and exports. By the middle 1980s, these goals had become so obvious that practically no knowledgeable person in the United States could disagree with them. At the same time, as the chapters in this book on fiscal policy and financial systems illustrate, the means to the goals continued to provoke debate. Within the national government, neither the Democratic nor the Republican party wished the other to receive credit for effective remedies. So a political gridlock persisted throughout the middle 1980s. The president continued to insist on a combination of low taxes and immense military expenditures. Meanwhile, both he and Congress habitually shied away from cuts in other big items, such as social security entitlements. All of these actions confirmed the consumerist orientation that had long characterized the American political economy.

Yet, as the tables above make clear, unbridled American consumerism could not continue for much longer without doing irreparable damage to the economy. A vicious cycle had developed, which, carried to its logical conclusion, would lead to national insolvency. By the mid-1980s, the unusual way in which this cycle evolved had become all too familiar. The United States government's accelerated borrowing promoted high interest rates; these in turn attracted heavy loans from abroad, especially from Japan, which increasingly invested its trade surplus in American government bonds; next, the influx of foreign money elevated the value of the dollar against other currencies; and finally, foreign imports became more attractive to American consumers, while American exports were priced out of overseas markets.

Because the consumer remained king in the American way of looking at things, much of this appeared to be a great boon. A consumer spending spree took off in 1983, and continued for several years. Yet, a great deal of this spending obviously went for products made overseas—not only in Japan, but in many other Asian countries as well: Korea, Taiwan, Hong Kong, and Singapore, which together recorded a trade surplus with the United States rivalling that of the Japanese. Even American trade with the countries of the European Common Market, which traditionally had showed a comfortable surplus, now went into deficit. The U.S. economy, it seemed, had been turned into an extraordinarily efficient machine for sucking in imports. American manufacturers found it difficult to compete with high-quality and (now) much less expensive foreign imports. In addition, the American manufacturing sector continued to exhibit a relatively slow rate of productivity growth, and a steady decline in market share occurred both at home and abroad. Talk of the "deindustrialization of America" became common. Even the fall of the dollar's value against the yen, which began late in 1985, promised no quick cure for the overall problem of American competitiveness.

As a means of enhancing producer-oriented policies in America, and of tempering the nation's traditional consumerism, the obvious first step lay in reducing the federal deficit. This could only be accomplished through some combination of diminished public spending, higher taxes, and changes in the tax structure so as to promote saving and reduce borrowing, especially from abroad. Yet, as noted earlier, political gridlock over how to do these things persisted.

Meanwhile, a second controversy arose over the feasibility and wisdom of an explicit industrial policy for the United States. Such a policy would be designed to "target" particular growth industries. The strategy might even be modelled on the one that spearheaded the earlier Japanese economic miracle. For the authors of this book, little in their own research, nor in their reading of American history, suggests that such a policy would be likely to work well. In the first place, the entire structure of the American political system is conducive to the degeneration of industrial policies into pork-barrel giveaways. In addition, the government's own paralysis over the deficit issue would seem to raise grave doubts about its ability to administer an industrial policy wisely. For that matter, even the Japanese government is today less capable of directing an industrial policy of the 1950s and 1960s variety. In large part, this is because the very success of Japanese companies has made them wealthier and less dependent on government assistance. Thus, an American industrial policy alone does not seem to us a workable solution to the problems of the economy.

Whatever policy the American people do choose in the future, it is likely to be appropriate only if both the government and private citizens achieve a better understanding of the interdependent world economy, and especially the new role of Japan. One small example will underscore the woeful failure of the United States even to make a respectable effort. For every American student living in Japan, no fewer than fifteen Japanese are studying at American colleges and universities. Considering the disparity in the two countries' populations, this amounts to a 30-fold effort by the Japanese to understand the United States, compared with the American effort to understand Japan.[5]

2. *Significant Changes in Japanese Policies—as in American Ones—Will Be Essential to Preserve the Japanese-American Friendship and a Healthy World Economy.* Just as the consumer-driven American economy has become a machine for sucking in imports, so the producer-oriented Japanese system is one designed specifically to push out vast quantities of exports. These characteristics of both countries, as emphasized earlier, remain deeply embedded in their cultures. As every chapter of this book testifies, these same characteristics are built into the very structure of business-government relations. Thus, in Japan as in America, change will be difficult to accomplish. Inevitably it will be accompanied by pain for some segments of the Japanese population.

Paradoxically, however, for the Japanese people as a whole, change might also be accompanied by a good deal more *comfort* than that to which they are accustomed. Despite the nation's enormous wealth, many aspects of the quality of life in Japan remain low compared to the level enjoyed by citizens of other highly developed countries. The producer-oriented Japanese way of life, however admirable it may be from the standpoint of corporate performance and economic productivity, runs squarely up against contrary trends among Japan's trading partners in the rest of the industrialized world. So long as Japan remained a poor, struggling, underdeveloped nation, advanced industrial countries could tolerate, even admire, the characteristic Japanese devotion to work. But Japan is now indisputably one of the world's wealthiest nations. In this new setting, the overall issue of its domestic standard of living becomes relevant for the international economy precisely because of that interdependence and growth of trade that has benefited all countries, and particularly Japan, during the years since World War II.

Thus, just as it seems imperative that Americans bend their consumerist logic and pay more attention to the importance of productivity and living within their means, so also it appears essential that the Japanese become more consumption-minded. Many people in Japan argue that such a trend has long since begun, and a good deal of evidence supports their claim. Yet the pace of adjustment, as seen from abroad, remains relatively slow. In the rest of the world, the idea of a fundamentally ascetic Japanese way of life persists unabated. This kind of perception, whether correct or not, can become politically explosive, because many foreigners are convinced that Japan is engaged in the systematic export not only of goods, but also of unemployment. Because of these perceptions, it becomes doubly important that Japan accelerate its shift toward more consumerist policies.

Certainly it can hardly be denied that ample opportunities remain for doing so. Consider, for example, what might be accomplished within Japan to change some of the following conditions:

a. Japanese workers spend about 2,100 hours on the job each year, compared with about 1,800 for American workers and between 1,500 and 1,600 for Europeans. Whereas West German employees receive an average of just over 30 paid vacation days per year, French ones 25, and American ones nearly 20, Japanese workers receive only 14.6 days. Even more striking, private-sector Japanese employees actually take just over half the vacation days to which they are legally entitled—in 1984, a mere 8.2 of the allotted 14.6 days.[6]

b. Only 34 percent of Japanese cities and towns have modern sewer systems, compared with 97 percent in the United Kingdom and 85 percent in the United States. While the actual situation is not nearly so bad as these numbers imply, the percentages do suggest an opportunity for significant advancement in the domestic standard of living. The same point applies to Japan's system of roads, only about one-half of which are paved, compared with 85 percent of American roads.[7]

c. Many Japanese live in dwelling spaces that are tiny by international standards. Again, the situation has improved somewhat, but even today, the average size of new homes being built in the United States is still 50 percent larger than those being built in Japan.[8] From the perspective of outside observers, Japan's continued acceptance of small living quarters now seems unnecessary, and even perverse. Improved technology, these critics argue, makes possible in Japan the construction of the kinds of spacious high-rise dwellings common in all other advanced industrial countries, but long shunned by Japanese architects because of potential dangers from earthquakes. Overall, it is precisely here, in housing, that the greatest potential exists for simultaneously raising the Japanese standard of living and pacifying Japan's trading partners.

In suggesting that the Americans should move more rapidly toward producerist values and the Japanese toward consumerist ones, we do not mean to argue naively that the two countries must converge into some hybrid form and become indistinguishable from each other. But we do believe that if no significant changes are made, then serious consequences lie ahead: rising international protectionism, the gradual closing of markets for Japanese exports, and, in the end, a trade war directed specifically against Japan. Signs of such trends already have been apparent in Europe for several years. In the United States, they sprout up quickly whenever the national economy experiences a downturn. If they persist—if the numbers cited in the tables above do not change direction—then the outcome will be a situation of near-tragic proportions: for America and Japan individually, for their relationship with each other, and for the general health of the world economy. All of this would be a great pity, because in the last analysis the Japanese-American friendship represents a pearl beyond price—a hard-won achievement far too valuable to place in jeopardy merely because of short-term political inertia. The authors of this book acknowledge that change will be difficult; but it seems to us inescapable. Today, as in earlier times, the *choice* between change and drift lies with the leadership and people of both countries, and only with them.

CONTRIBUTORS

THOMAS K. McCRAW is a professor at the Harvard Business School, where he also serves as a Director of Research and chairs the Business, Government, and Competition Area. He received his B.A. at the University of Mississippi, then his M.A. (1968) and Ph.D. (1970) in history at the University of Wisconsin. He taught in the Department of History at the University of Texas before coming to the Harvard Business School in 1976. A widely published scholar, he has written several dozen articles, chapters, and reviews. In addition, he is author of *Morgan Versus Lilienthal* (William P. Lyons Award, 1970) and *TVA and the Power Fight* (1971), and editor of *Regulation in Perspective* (1981). His most recent book, *Prophets of Regulation,* won both the Pulitzer Prize in History for 1985, and the Thomas Newcomen Award for 1986, which is given for the best book on the history of business published during the preceding three years.

DOUGLAS D. ANDERSON is a lecturer at the Harvard Business School, where he teaches courses in competitive strategy, production and operations management, and business and government. In 1981, Mr. Anderson interrupted his academic career to serve as Deputy Counselor to the Secretary of the Treasury, and from 1982 to 1983 was Corporate Director/Special Projects at Bendix Corporation. He is the author of *Regulatory Politics and Electric Utilities* (1981) and numerous articles and case studies. Mr. Anderson received his B.A. and M.A. (economics, 1975) from Utah State University, then an M.P.A. (1976), and Ph.D. (political economy, 1979), from Harvard University. Prior to joining the Harvard Business School faculty, he taught economics at Harvard College.

JOSEPH L. BADARACCO, JR. is an associate professor at the Harvard Business School. A member of the Harvard faculty since 1981, Mr. Badaracco received a B.A. from St. Louis University, an M.A. (1973) from Oxford University, where he was a Rhodes Scholar, and an M.B.A. (1978) and D.B.A. (1981) from the Harvard Business School. His research interests are in the areas of business leadership and the external relations of firms. He is the author of *Loading the Dice* (1985), a study of business-government relations in Japan, the United States, and three European countries.

M. COLYER CRUM is the James R. Williston Professor of Investment Management at the Harvard Business School. He earned his undergraduate degree in chemical engineering from Cornell University, then received his M.B.A. (1960) and D.B.A. (1964), from the Harvard Business School. A widely recognized expert on domestic and international finance, Mr. Crum is noted as an outstanding teacher, and has served in a number of administrative posts as well. These include Associate Dean for Executive Education and External Affairs, Chair of the Faculty's Educational Policy Committee, and, currently, Chair of the Executive Education Policy Committee. Mr. Crum also serves on several corporate boards of directors. For the past six years, he has headed a faculty group working with the Nomura School of Advanced Management in Tokyo, where, each summer, he teaches and develops new course materials on Japanese business.

DENNIS J. ENCARNATION is an assistant professor at the Harvard Business School, where he specializes in the management of international business. He completed his B.A. at the College of Charleston, then his M.A. (1977) and Ph.D. (1981) at Duke

University in political science and public policy. He joined the Harvard faculty in 1982, after post-doctoral work at Stanford University. Mr. Encarnation has written several articles that examine bargaining relations among multinationals, national governments, and local enterprises in developing countries. Relations in one such country, India, is the subject of a book he is now completing. His next research project will expand on his chapter in this volume, examining the motivations and consequences of cross-investment between American and Japanese enterprises.

YASUO ENDO is an official in the Japanese Ministry of Agriculture, Forestry and Fisheries, which he entered in 1969 after graduating from Tohoku University. After joining the Ministry, he spent two years studying agricultural economics at the University of Illinois. In 1981–1982, Mr. Endo was an associate of the Program on U.S.-Japan Relations, Center for International Affairs, at Harvard University. He has served in many divisions of the Ministry, including those related to livestock, trade and tariffs, sugar, and fisheries, and has participated in agricultural trade negotiations with the United States. He is currently agricultural counselor at the Japanese Embassy in Washington.

DAVID M. MEERSCHWAM is an assistant professor at the Harvard Business School. He obtained his B.S. from the London School of Economics and Political Science, and his M.A. (1981) and Ph.D. (1983) in economics from Princeton University. His main interest is international finance, especially exchange rate theory. Currently his research is concerned with international capital markets and the effects of international financial integration. Mr. Meerschwam has taught in the General Management Area of the Harvard Business School since 1983.

PATRICIA A. O'BRIEN is an assistant professor at the Harvard Business School, where she teaches Business, Government, and the International Economy in the M.B.A. program. She received her B.A. from Boston College, M.B.A. from Simmons College (1977) and D.B.A. from the Harvard Business School (1986), specializing in Business Policy. She has taught at Brandeis University and the Harvard School of Public Health. Her current research interests are in the area of competition policies and their effects on the strategic decisions of firms, and she has written a number of case studies on this general topic.

SUSAN J. PHARR currently holds the Japan Chair at the Georgetown Center for Strategic and International Studies. She has recently joined the faculty of Harvard University, where she is professor of government and a member of the Reischauer Institute. A specialist on Japanese politics, she has focused her research on conflict management, policymaking, government-business relations, political and social change, and issues in Japan's foreign relations. Her forthcoming book, *Status Politics in Japan,* looks at how the Japanese deal with social conflict. She received her B.A. from Emory University, then her M.A. (1970) and Ph.D. (1975) in political science from Columbia University. She has been a Visiting Research Scholar at the University of Tokyo, a fellow at the Woodrow Wilson Center, and a Guest Scholar at the Brookings Institution. In 1983 she served as Senior Social Scientist with the Agency for International Development, where she was responsible for coordinating U.S. and Japanese foreign aid.

MICHAEL R. REICH is an associate professor and executive director of the Takemi Program in International Health, both at the Harvard School of Public Health. He received his B.A. in molecular biophysics and biochemistry, M.A. in East Asian Studies (1975), and Ph.D. in political science (1981), all from Yale University. Mr. Reich has done research on Japan for the past fifteen years and coauthored two books on Japan,

Island of Dreams: Environmental Crisis in Japan (1975) and *Six Lives/Six Deaths: Portraits of Modern Japan* (1979), as well as numerous articles. His research interests are in the area of comparative public policy and politics. In 1982–1983, he was a post-doctoral research fellow at the Harvard Business School.

MICHAEL G. RUKSTAD has been an assistant professor at the Harvard Business School since 1981. He received his B.A. degree from the University of South Dakota, then his M.S. (1978) and Ph.D. (1981) in economics from the University of California at Berkeley. He is the author of *Macroeconomic Decision Making in the World Economy: Text and Cases* (1986), and his general research interests concern the effects of macroeconomic policy on the business decisions of firms. Currently, he is investigating how changes in tax incentives may affect the investment decisions of U.S. and Japanese companies in the computer and semiconductor industries.

C. PETER TIMMER is the John D. Black Professor of Agriculture and Business at the Harvard Business School. He has written extensively on the economics of food and agriculture, with a focus on public policy issues relating to agricultural price policy, marketing, trade, and economic development, particularly in East and Southeast Asia. His book *Food Policy Analysis* (1983), coauthored with W. P. Falcon and S. R. Pearson, was awarded the Quality of Communication Award by the American Agricultural Economics Association. His most recent book is *Getting Prices Right: The Scope and Limits of Agricultural Price Policy* (1986). Mr. Timmer received his A.B., M.A. (1968), and Ph.D. (1969) degrees in economics from Harvard University. He taught at Stanford, Cornell, and the Harvard School of Public Health before coming to the Harvard Business School in 1980. He has been a trustee of the Agricultural Development Council and the Overseas Development Network and is a faculty fellow of the Harvard Institute for International Development.

RICHARD H. K. VIETOR is a professor at the Harvard Business School, where he teaches courses on the regulation of business and the international political economy. His research, which focuses on business-government relations, has been published in numerous journals, and he is the author of three books: *Environmental Politics and the Coal Coalition* (1980), *Energy Policy in America Since 1945* (1984), and *Telecommunications in Transition* (1986). Mr. Vietor earned his B.A. from Union College, M.A. in history from Hofstra (1971), and Ph.D. in history from the University of Pittsburgh (1975). He taught at the University of Missouri before coming to Harvard in 1978.

DAVID B. YOFFIE is an associate professor at the Harvard Business School. He received his B.A. from Brandeis University, and his M.A. (1978) and Ph.D. (1980) in political science from Stanford University. He taught for two years in Stanford's Department of Political Science before joining the Harvard faculty in 1981. Mr. Yoffie's research interests are in corporate strategy, and specifically in how firms manage international competition and business-government relations. He is the author of *Power and Protectionism: Strategies of the Newly Industrializing Countries* (1981) and several articles on international trade, political risk and corporate political strategies.

ACKNOWLEDGMENTS

Many hands went into the making of this book, and the book itself was put together in an unusual way:

First, because the majority of the fourteen authors know each other well. Most of us have worked and taught together at the Harvard Business School throughout the 1980s;

Second, because the book was conceived at the outset as a cooperative project that would place heavy demands on each author not only to compose his or her own chapter, but to criticize other chapters as well. Thus, we have benefited from continuous suggestions and criticisms from each other;

Third, because we received benefits of equal value from the insights of dozens of participants in numerous seminars held in America and Japan over a period of three years: students, colleagues, business executives, and government officials;

Fourth, because we were the beneficiaries of remarkable cooperation from librarians, archivists, and especially from the several hundred persons in the United States and Japan whom we interviewed, and from whom we obtained an extraordinarily broad spectrum of viewpoints: from private companies, government agencies, trade associations, and academic institutions. Without their cooperation, the book simply could not have been written, and their appearance in our footnotes (sometimes anonymously) constitutes only bare hints of the vast assistance they gave us;

Fifth, because access to many of these persons was enormously facilitated by some tireless interventions—in America, by the administration of the Harvard Business School, led by Dean John H. McArthur and the then Director of the Division of Research, E. Raymond Corey, both of whom encouraged us and provided generous financial support at every step; and also by Ezra Vogel and his colleagues at Harvard's Program on U.S.-Japan Relations. In Japan, we received truly indispensable assistance from the administration and staff of the Nomura School of Advanced Management, led by Dean Jiro Tokuyama and Messrs. Masasuke Ide and Ryōzō Ishihara;

Sixth, because our chapters have undergone rigorous and repeated revisions, supervised by the editor of the book in conjunction with Professor Kazuo Sato of Rutgers University—an authority on many aspects of Japanese political economy; and with Professor Earl N. Harbert of Northeastern University—a masterly critic of English prose;

Seventh, because approximately twenty-five research assistants and interpreters helped guide the authors through the maze of materials that underlie this study. In one sense, it is unfair to single out any individual from such a talented and dedicated group. Yet we feel compelled to acknowledge our immense debt to Mr. Takashi Hikino, who participated in the project from the beginning and lent his formidable learning and intelligence to every phase (and nearly every page) of the study;

Finally, because our predecessors in print—the scholars of business-government relations from many academic disciplines in both the United States and Japan—left us with a rich and exemplary legacy of work. Even a casual examination of our footnotes will reveal the extent of our debts to them.

NOTES

CHAPTER ONE

1. General works on the miracle include Kozo Yamamura, *Economic Policy in Postwar Japan: Growth Versus Economic Democracy* (Berkeley: University of California Press, 1967); Edward F. Denison and William K. Chung, *How Japan's Economy Grew So Fast: The Sources of Postwar Expansion* (Washington, D.C.: Brookings Institution, 1976); Chalmers Johnson, *MITI and the Japanese Miracle: The Growth of Industrial Policy, 1925–1975* (Stanford: Stanford University Press, 1982); Michio Morishima, *Why Has Japan "Succeeded"? Western Technology and the Japanese Ethos* (New York: Cambridge University Press, 1982); Miyohei Shinohara, *Industrial Growth, Trade, and Dynamic Patterns in the Japanese Economy* (Tokyo: Tokyo University Press, 1982); and Ezra F. Vogel, *Japan as Number One: Lessons for America* (Cambridge, Mass.: Harvard University Press, 1979).

2. Occupation-induced changes significantly affected the Japanese system of economic policymaking. See, in general, Jerome C. Cohen, *Japan's Economy in War and Reconstruction* (Minneapolis: University of Minnesota Press, 1949); T. A. Bisson, *Zaibatsu Dissolution in Japan* (Berkeley: University of California Press, 1954); and Eleanor M. Hadley, *Antitrust in Japan* (Princeton: Princeton University Press, 1970).

3. The numbers in Tables 1-1 and 1-2 are from the Organization for Economic Cooperation and Development, *National Accounts, 1953–1982* (Paris: OECD, 1984).

4. On long-term trends in Japan, see Takafusa Nakamura, *Economic Growth in Prewar Japan* (New Haven: Yale University Press, 1983); Takafusa Nakamura, *The Postwar Japanese Economy: Its Development and Structure* (Tokyo: Tokyo University Press, 1981); and Kazushi Ohkawa and Henry Rosovsky, *Japanese Economic Growth: Trend Acceleration in the Twentieth Century* (Stanford: Stanford University Press, 1973).

5. American economic growth since World War II is examined comparatively in Edward F. Denison, *Why Growth Rates Differ: Postwar Experience in Nine Western Countries* (Washington, D.C.: Brookings Institution, 1967); Angus Maddison, *Phases of Capitalist Development* (New York: Oxford University Press, 1982); and Martin Feldstein, ed., *The American Economy in Transition* (Chicago: University of Chicago Press, 1980).

6. The Japanese numbers in Table 1-3 are computed from Bank of Japan, *Economic Statistics Annual, 1969, 1971, and 1973*, as summarized in Bruce R. Scott, John W. Rosenblum, and Audrey T. Sproat, *Case Studies in Political Economy: Japan, 1854–1977* (Boston: Division of Research, Harvard Business School, 1980), p. 121 (hereafter cited as Scott et al., *Japan, 1854–1977*). The American numbers are computed from *Economic Report of the President 1985* (Washington, D.C.: Government Printing Office, 1985), pp. 234–235.

7. Based on data from the Bank of Japan, quoted in Toshio Matsuoka, ed., *Japan 1984: An International Comparison* (Tokyo: Japan Institute for Social and Economic Affairs, 1984), p. 10.

8. On Japanese industrial organization and economic policies since World War II, see Kozo Yamamura, *Economic Policy in Postwar Japan: Growth versus Economic Democracy;* Richard E. Caves and Masu Uekusa, *Industrial Organization in Japan* (Washington, D.C.: Brookings Institution, 1976); Isaiah Frank, ed., *The Japanese Economy in International Perspective* (Baltimore: Johns Hopkins University Press, 1975); Takafusa

Nakamura, *The Postwar Japanese Economy: Its Development and Structure*; Hugh Patrick and Henry Rosovsky, eds., *Asia's New Giant: How the Japanese Economy Works* (Washington, D.C.: Brookings Institution, 1976); and OECD, *The Industrial Policy of Japan* (Paris: Organization for Economic Cooperation and Development, 1972); Ira C. Magaziner and Thomas M. Hout, *Japanese Industrial Policy* (London: Policy Studies Institute, 1980); Ryutaro Komiya et al., eds., *Industrial Policy in Japan* (New York: Academic Press, forthcoming in 1987); Kazuo Sato, ed., *Industry and Business in Japan* (White Plains, N.Y.: M. E. Sharpe, 1980); Kazuo Sato and Yasuo Hoshino, eds., *The Anatomy of Japanese Business* (Armonk, N.Y.: M. E. Sharpe, 1984); Kozo Yamamura, ed., *Policy and Trade Issues in the Japanese Economy: American and Japanese Perspectives* (Seattle: University of Washington Press, 1983); Jimmy W. Wheeler et al., *Japanese Industrial Development Policies in the 1980s: Implications for U.S. Trade and Investment* (Croton-on-Hudson, N.Y.: Hudson Institute, 1982).

9. Peter G. Peterson, *The United States in the Changing World Economy* (Washington, D.C.: Government Printing Office, 1971), II, Chart 9. By the early 1980s, not only had Japan replaced the United States as the world's leading producer of motor vehicles, but Japan's exports of motor vehicles at one point exceeded the exports of all other countries combined. As barriers to Japanese imports rose in Europe, this last phenomenon proved short-lived.

10. The Dulles quotation is from *The New York Times*, June 7, 1985. On the American decision to build up Japan as a bulwark of democratic capitalism within the context of the Cold War, see Michael Schaller, *The American Occupation of Japan: The Origins of the Cold War in Asia* (New York: Oxford University Press, 1985).

One significant aspect of the continuing success of Japanese exports was the growth of general trading companies. See Yoshi Tsurumi, *Sogo Shosha: Engines of Export-led Growth* (Brookfield, Vt.: Renouf USA, 1980); Kunio Yoshihara, *The Sogo Shosha: The Vanguard of the Japanese Economy* (London: Oxford University Press, 1982); Alexander K. Young, *The Sogo Shosha: Japan's Multi-National Trading Companies* (Boulder: Westview Press, 1979). See also the chapters in the present book on trade, foreign direct investment, and production and distribution.

11. OECD, *The Industrial Policy of Japan*, p. 15, quoted in Scott et al., *Japan, 1854–1977*, p. 138.

12. The disinclination to borrow abroad heavily for industrialization goes back at least to the Meiji period. See Kamekichi Takahashi, *The Rise and Development of Japan's Modern Economy* (Tokyo: Jiji, 1969), pp. 185–186.

13. A case in point is automobiles. During the 1920s and early 1930s, both Ford and General Motors invested substantially in "knockdown" assembly plants within Japan, and thereby captured the major share of the Japanese market. When government authorities determined that Japan needed its own domestic production facilities for military requirements, the two American giants were encouraged to withdraw. The key measure was the Automobile Manufacturing Business Law of 1936, which mandated Japanese control of the industry and paved the way for the rise of Toyota and Nissan. See Masaru Udagawa, "The Prewar Japanese Automobile Industry and American Manufacturers," *Japanese Yearbook on Business History: 1985* (Tokyo: Japan Business History Institute, 1985); and Michael A. Cusumano, *The Japanese Automobile Industry: Technology and Management at Nissan and Toyota* (Cambridge, Mass.: Harvard University Press, 1985).

14. On Japanese policies concerning foreign firms, see Dan F. Henderson, *Foreign Enterprise in Japan: Laws and Policies* (Chapel Hill: University of North Carolina Press, 1973); and John O. Haley, ed., *Current Legal Aspects of Doing Business in Japan and the Far East* (Chicago: American Bar Association, 1978).

15. Johnson, *MITI and the Japanese Miracle,* pp. 246–247; Mira Wilkins, *The Maturing of Multinational Enterprise: American Business Abroad from 1914 to 1970* (Cambridge, Mass.: Harvard University Press, 1974), pp. 313–316, 349–350, 401, and 405; Michael Y. Yoshino, "Japan as Host to the International Corporation," in Charles P. Kindleberger, ed., *The International Corporation* (Cambridge, Mass.: MIT Press, 1970), pp. 345–369.

16. See the long article on state-owned enterprise in *The Economist* (London), December 30, 1978, from which the pie chart in the text has been adapted. On the Meiji government's activities in public enterprise—a complex subject in its own right—see the list in Yoshio Ando, ed., *Kindai Nippon Keizaishi Yōran* (Statistical Abstract of the Modern Japanese Economy) (Tokyo: Tokyo University Press, 1975), p. 57.

17. All of the following factors involved in the high savings rate have been examined in some detail by Japanese scholars, and several have been described as relatively unimportant. For a summary of this literature, in which the bonus system is emphasized, see Nakamura, *The Postwar Japanese Economy,* pp. 97–101. See also Miyohei Shinohara, "Japan's High Savings Ratio: Its Determinants and Behavior Patterns," pp. 153–181 of Shinohara, *Industrial Growth, Trade, and Dynamic Patterns in the Japanese Economy* (Tokyo: University of Tokyo Press, 1982). For an econometric analysis which concludes that the causes of Japan's high savings rate "yet remain an open question," see Tsuneo Ishikawa and Kazuo Ueda, "The Bonus Payment System and Japanese Personal Savings," in Masahiko Aoki, ed., *The Economic Analysis of the Japanese Firm* (Amsterdam: North-Holland, 1984), pp. 133–192.

18. The numbers in this table come from OECD, *National Accounts, 1964–1981* (Paris: OECD, 1983, Tables 6 and 7).

A slightly different set of numbers may be found in United Nations, *Yearbook of National Accounts Statistics* (New York: U.N., 1975), I, Tables 2 and 3, II, Table 10, cited in Scott et al., *Japan, 1854–1977.* All such numbers must be used with some caution, since definitions and reporting practices differ across nations. The overall point that Japanese savings rates easily surpass those of other industrial countries, however, is not in dispute.

19. On Japanese finance, see the chapters in the present book on financial systems and tax incentives; see also, in general, Raymond Goldsmith, *The Financial Development of Japan: 1868–1977* (New Haven: Yale University Press, 1983); Andreas R. Prindl, *Japanese Finance: A Guide to Banking in Japan* (New York: Wiley, 1981); and Yoshio Suzuki, *Money and Banking in Contemporary Japan* (New Haven: Yale University Press, 1980).

20. On the development of Japanese technology, see UNESCO, Japan National Commission, *Technological Development in Japan* (Paris: UNESCO, 1971); Masanori Moritani, *Japanese Technology* (Tokyo: SIMUL Press, 1982); Richard J. Schonberger, *Japanese Manufacturing Techniques* (New York: Free Press, 1983); and Yoshio Ohara, "Japanese Regulation of Technology Imports," *Journal of World Trade Law* 15 (January/February 1981), pp. 83–90. The guiding hand of MOF and MITI in screening technology and avoiding duplication is outlined in Terutomo Ozawa, *Japan's Technological Challenge to the West, 1950–1974* (Cambridge, Mass.: MIT Press, 1974).

21. Within the large literature on Japanese protectionism, the following works are representative: Robert S. Ozaki, *The Control of Imports and Foreign Capital in Japan* (New York: Praeger, 1972); James C. Abegglen, "Why Many Fail in Japan," *Far Eastern Economic Review* 98 (November 11, 1977), pp. 63–68; and Frank A. Weil and Norman D. Glick, "Japan—Is the Market Open?" *Law and Policy in International Business* 11 (1979), pp. 845–902. See also the chapter on foreign trade in the present book.

22. For overviews of the U.S. Congress, see Lawrence Dodd and Richard Schott, *Congress and the Administrative State* (New York: Wiley, 1979); Lawrence Dodd and Bruce Oppenheimer, eds., *Congress Reconsidered,* second ed. (New York: Praeger, 1980); Morris P. Fiorina, *Congress: Keystone of the Washington Establishment* (New Haven: Yale University Press, 1979); and David Mayhew, *Congress: The Electoral Connection* (New Haven: Yale University Press, 1974).

On the Japanese Diet, see Hans H. Baerwald, *Japan's Parliament: An Introduction* (New York: Cambridge University Press, 1974); T. J. Pempel, *Policy and Politics in Japan: Creative Conservatism* (Philadelphia: Temple University Press, 1982), especially Chapter 1; Ardath W. Burks, *The Government of Japan,* second ed. (New York: Crowell, 1963), Chapter 6; and Robert E. Ward, *Japan's Political System* (Englewood Cliffs, N.J.: Prentice-Hall, 1978), Chapter 3.

On the Liberal Democratic Party, see Haruhiro Fukui, *Party in Power: The Japanese Liberal-Democrats and Policy-Making* (Berkeley: University of California Press, 1970); Nathaniel B. Thayer, *How the Conservatives Rule Japan* (Princeton: Princeton University Press, 1969); and Gerald Curtis, *Election Campaigning, Japanese Style* (New York: Columbia University Press, 1971).

23. The role of the congressional committee system is discussed in Dodd and Schott, *Congress and the Administrative State,* Chapter 3, and in Richard Fenno, *Congressmen in Committees* (Boston: Little, Brown, 1973).

24. On the historical roots of the relationship between American liberalism and governmental fragmentation, see Louis Hartz, *The Liberal Tradition in America* (New York: Harcourt, Brace, 1955); Samuel P. Huntington, *Political Order in Changing Societies* (New Haven: Yale University Press, 1968); and Seymour Martin Lipset, *The First New Nation* (New York: Basic Books, 1963).

25. For a discussion of the policy-making relationship between the national executive and legislative branches, see Louis Fisher, *The President and Congress* (New York: Free Press, 1972).

26. On aspects of opposition politics in Japan, see Allen P. Cole et al., *Socialist Parties in Postwar Japan* (New Haven: Yale University Press, 1966); Margaret A. McKean, *Environmental Protest and Citizen Politics in Japan* (Berkeley: University of California Press, 1981); Kurt Steiner et al., eds., *Political Opposition and Local Politics in Japan* (Princeton: Princeton University Press, 1980); and James A. A. Stockwin, *Japan: Divided Politics in a Growth Economy* (New York: W. W. Norton, 1975).

27. The comparative weakness of the public bureaucracy in the U.S. is addressed in Thomas K. McCraw, "Business and Government: The Origins of the Adversary Relationship," *California Management Review* 26 (Winter 1984), pp. 33–52; Andrew Shonfield, *Modern Capitalism* (New York: Oxford University Press, 1965); and David Vogel, "Why Businessmen Distrust Their State: The Political Consciousness of Corporate Executives," *British Journal of Political Science* 8 (January 1978), pp. 55–65. On American "in-and-outers," see Carl Brauer, "Tenure, Turnover, and Post-Government Employment Trends of Presidential Appointees," Research in Progress Paper #4 (1985), John F. Kennedy School of Government, Harvard University.

28. On the recruitment of bureaucrats in Japan, see Akira Kubota, *Higher Civil Servants in Postwar Japan: Their Social Origins, Educational Backgrounds, and Career Patterns* (Princeton: Princeton University Press, 1969); on Japanese higher education, Ronald P. Dore, *The Diploma Disease: Education, Qualification and Development* (Berkeley: University of California Press, 1976); Michio Nagai, *Higher Education in Japan: Its Take-Off and Crash* (Tokyo: University of Tokyo Press, 1971); and Herbert Passin, *Society and Education in Japan* (New York: Columbia University Press, 1965).

29. On the Japanese bureaucratic system in general, see Burks, *The Government of Japan,* Chapter 7; Japan Culture Institute, *Politics and Economics in Contemporary Japan,* Chapter 4; and Ward, *Japan's Political System,* Chapter 5.

30. The most thorough analysis of MITI is Chalmers Johnson's landmark book, *MITI and the Japanese Miracle: The Growth of Industrial Policy, 1925–1975* (Stanford: Stanford University Press, 1982). For a critique of Johnson's views, see Kozo Yamamura's review in *Journal of Japanese Studies* 9 (Winter 1983).

31. On Japanese business-government relations, see ibid. (both sources); Eugene J. Kaplan, *Japan: The Government-Business Relationship* (Washington, D.C.: U.S. Department of Commerce, 1972); Chitoshi Yanaga, *Big Business in Japanese Politics* (New Haven: Yale University Press, 1968); William E. Bryant, *Japanese Economic Diplomacy: An Analysis of Business-Government Linkages* (New York: Praeger, 1975); and Hiroshi Itoh, *Japanese Politics—An Inside View: Readings from Japan* (Ithaca: Cornell University Press, 1973), Part 1.

32. The American bureaucracy is analyzed in Dodd and Schott, *Congress and the Administrative State,* Chapters 2, 6, and 7; Francis E. Rourke, *Bureaucracy, Politics, and Public Policy,* second ed. (Boston: Little, Brown, 1976); and Theodore Lowi, *The End of Liberalism* (New York: Norton, 1969), Chapters 4 and 5.

Occasionally, Japanese politics *has* become raucous, with actual fisticuffs occurring within the Diet during the 1960s. Even today, noisy loudspeakers in downtown Tokyo sometimes disturb the peace.

33. Standard works on the U.S. presidency include Richard Neustadt, *Presidential Power: The Politics of Leadership,* rev. ed. (New York: Wiley, 1976); Richard M. Pious, *The American Presidency* (New York: Basic Books, 1979); and Arthur M. Schlesinger, Jr., *The Imperial Presidency* (Boston: Houghton Mifflin, 1973).

34. On the Japanese political system, see the following general sources: Burks, *The Government of Japan,* second ed.; Itoh, ed., *Japanese Politics—An Inside View;* Japan Culture Institute, *Politics and Economics in Contemporary Japan;* and Ward, *Japan's Political System.*

35. Joel B. Grossman and Austin Sarat, "Litigation in Federal Courts: A Comparative Perspective," *Law and Society Review* 9 (Winter 1975), pp. 321–346; *International Directory of Bar Associations,* third ed. (Chicago: American Bar Foundation, 1973); *The New York Times,* May 17, 1977; James Willard Hurst, *The Growth of American Law: The Law Makers* (Boston: Little, Brown, 1950), pp. 249–375; Lawrence M. Friedman, *A History of American Law* (New York: Simon and Schuster, 1973), pp. 265–292.

36. On the Japanese legal system, see Arthur T. von Mehren, ed., *Law in Japan: The Legal Order in a Changing Society* (Cambridge, Mass.: Harvard University Press, 1963); and Dan F. Henderson and John O. Haley, *Law and the Legal Process in Japan: Material for an Introductory Course on Japanese Law* (Seattle: University of Washington Law School, 1978).

37. See Lowi, *The End of Liberalism,* Chapters 3 and 10; Karen Orren, "Standing to Sue: Interest Group Conflict in the Federal Courts," *American Political Science Review* 70 (1976), pp. 723–741; Richard Stewart, "The Reformation of Administrative Law," *Harvard Law Review* 88 (June 1975), pp. 1667–1813; J. S. Fuerst and Roy Petty, "Due Process—How Much Is Enough?" *The Public Interest* 79 (Spring 1985), pp. 96–110.

The overall fragmentation of American government and policymaking is described in a large body of literature that includes R. F. Fenno, *The Power of the Purse: Appropriations Politics in Congress* (Boston: Little, Brown, 1966); Ira Sharkansky, *The Politics of Taxing and Spending* (Indianapolis: Bobbs-Merrill, 1969); and Aaron Wildavsky, *The Politics of the Budgetary Process,* second ed. (Boston: Little, Brown, 1974).

The recent debate over the resulting weakness of American government and its relation to policymaking can be explored in Walter Dean Burnham, *The Current Crisis in American Politics* (New York: Oxford University Press, 1982); Lowi, *The End of Liberalism;* and Samuel P. Huntington, "The Democratic Distemper," in Michel Crozier, Huntington, and Joji Watanuki, *The Crisis of Democracy: Report on the Governability of Democracies to the Trilateral Commission* (New York: New York University Press, 1975).

38. Among many books on Japanese society and culture, the following are especially useful: Richard K. Beardsley et al., *Village Japan* (Chicago: University of Chicago Press, 1959); Ronald P. Dore, *City Life in Japan: A Study of a Tokyo Ward* (Berkeley: University of California Press, 1958); Tadashi Fukutake, *Japanese Society Today,* second ed. (Tokyo: Tokyo University Press, 1982); Chie Nakane, *Japanese Society* (Berkeley: University of California Press, 1972); Kazuko Tsurumi, *Social Change and the Individual: Japan Before and After Defeat in World War II* (Princeton: Princeton University Press, 1970); and Ezra F. Vogel, *Japan's New Middle Class: The Salary Man and His Family in a Tokyo Suburb* (Berkeley: University of California Press, 1971).

On the Japanese style of policymaking in general, see T. J. Pempel, *Policy and Politics in Japan;* Pempel, ed., *Policymaking in Contemporary Japan;* Ezra F. Vogel, ed., *Modern Japanese Organization and Decision-Making* (Berkeley: University of California Press, 1975). For specific case studies, see John C. Campbell, *Contemporary Japanese Budget Politics* (Berkeley: University of California Press, 1977); and Chikara Higashi, *Japanese Trade Policy Formation* (New York: Praeger, 1983).

Samples of influential American critiques of the Japanese system include Theodore H. White, "The Danger From Japan," *The New York Times Magazine,* July 28, 1985, pp. 19–22+; J. C. Abegglen, "America Will Really Get Angry," *The Oriental Economist* 52 (January 1984), pp. 34–40; Susan Chira, "Most Japanese Houses Still Lack Comforts of Those in the U.S.," *The New York Times,* October 30, 1985, and the *Times* editorial in the same issue, entitled, "Come On, Japan, Live Better!"

39. *Economic Report of the President 1986,* p. 378.

40. For the United States, data are from *Economic Report of the President 1986,* p. 339; for Japan, from the Ministry of Finance, as reproduced in Akira Nakayama, ed., *Japan 1985: An International Comparison* (Tokyo: Japan Institute for Social and Economic Affairs), p. 83.

41. *Economic Report of the President 1986,* p. 375. (For both Table 1-8 and Table 1-10, export numbers are reported f.o.b., imports c.i.f., so the trends and balances are somewhat distorted.)

42. *Japan 1985: An International Comparison,* p. 45.

43. *Economic Report of the President 1986,* p. 369.

44. I do not wish to be misleading here. Japan in fact runs heavy current-account deficits with many OPEC nations, but surpluses with most other countries. My overall point has as much to do with *perceptions* of Americans as with the facts of the case.

CHAPTER TWO

1. IMF, *Exchange Arrangements and Exchange Restrictions: Annual Report, 1984* (Washington, D.C.: IMF, 1984).

2. On a *constant* dollar basis, exports have grown from 7 percent of GNP in 1955 to 20.2 percent in 1981, and industrial production grew at an annual rate of 9 percent during the same period while exports grew at almost 19 percent. See *Statistical Survey of Japan's Economy, 1983* (Tokyo: Ministry of Foreign Affairs, 1983); and Jimmy Wheeler, Merit Janow, and Thomas Pepper, *Japanese Industrial Development Politics in the 1980s: Implications for U.S. Trade and Investment* (New York: Hudson Institute, 1982), p. 52.

3. Miyohei Shinohara, *Industrial Growth, Trade and Dynamic Patterns in the Japanese Economy* (Tokyo: University of Tokyo Press, 1982), p. 13.

4. Kent Calder, "Opening Japan," *Foreign Policy*, Summer 1982.

5. This argument suggests that governments, like firms, adopt strategies before they create their organizational structures. In Alfred Chandler's words: "Structure follows strategy. . . ." See Alfred D. Chandler, Jr., *Strategy and Structure: Chapters in the History of the American Industrial Enterprise* (Cambridge, Mass.: MIT Press, 1962), p. 14.

6. Some scholars trace the change in America's trade outlook to 1922 when, for the first time, the United States agreed to reduce tariffs on an unconditional most-favored nation basis. Raymond Vernon, "International Trade Policy in the 1980s," *International Studies Quarterly* 26 (December 1982).

7. Quoted from a 1942 Council on Foreign Relations document, in Charles Maier, "The Politics of Productivity," *International Organization* 31 (Autumn 1977), p. 617.

8. The only exception to these principles was in agriculture: from the outset, agricultural trade (which is discussed in a later chapter in this volume) had a high priority in American policy; free trade was not necessarily desirable, and farmers were not to be left to fend for themselves.

9. Robert Baldwin, Rachel McCulloch, J. David Richardson, and Andre Sapir, "U.S. Policies in Response to Growing International Competitiveness," Report on N.S.F. Grant, mimeo, April 15, 1982.

10. Joanne Gowa, "Subsidizing American Corporate Expansion Abroad: Pitfalls in the Analysis of Public and Private Power," *World Politics*, January 1985, pp. 180–204.

11. Raymond A. Bauer, Ithiel de Sola Pool, and Lewis Anthony Dexter, *American Business and Public Policy* (New York: Atherton Press, 1965).

12. U.S. Tariff Commission, *Reciprocity and Commercial Treaties* (Washington, D.C.: U.S. Government Printing Office, 1919), p. 42.

13. David B. Yoffie, *Power and Protectionism: Strategies of the Newly Industrializing Countries* (New York: Columbia University Press, 1983).

14. General Accounting Office, "Government Programs and Organization Affecting Exports," ID-79-41, August 17, 1979.

15. Robert Baldwin, "The Changing Nature of U.S. Trade Policy Since World War II," in Robert Baldwin and Anne Krueger, eds., *The Structure and Evolution of Recent U.S. Trade Policy* (Chicago: University of Chicago Press, 1984), pp. 5–33.

16. David B. Yoffie, "Zenith and the Color Television Fight," Harvard Business School Case, #9-383-070.

17. Judith Goldstein, "A Re-examination of American Trade Policy: An Inquiry into the Causes of Protection" (Ph.D. diss., University of California, Los Angeles, 1983).

18. Hugh Patrick and Henry Rosovsky, *Asia's New Giant: How the Japanese Economy Works* (Washington, D.C.: Brookings Institution, 1975), p. 11.

19. The principle of using public power to mobilize the private sector was used by Japan before World War II and is actually a common strategy among nations that are industrially weak and have a desire to catch up rapidly. See Alexander Gerschenkron, *Economic Backwardness in Historical Perspective* (Cambridge, Mass.: Harvard University Press, 1963).

20. One Japanese scholar explained this reliance through an analogy with Japan's traditional class hierarchy of the samurai, followed by the farmer, craftsman, and merchant. The United States, according to the analogy, had taken the role of samurai and farmer in international trade, while Japan was the craftsman and merchant. The United States could therefore be counted on to defend world capitalism, while Japan could work on its "craftsman-merchant abilities."

21. Yoffie, "Zenith and the Color Television Fight."

22. Gary Saxonhouse, "Foreign Sales to Japan," in William Cline, ed., *Trade Policy in the 1980s* (Washington, D.C.: Institute for International Economics, 1983).

23. Yoko Sazanami, "Japanese Trade After the Oil Crisis: A Structural Approach," *Journal of Japanese Trade and Industry,* (May–June 1983), pp. 46–49.

24. Chalmers Johnson, *MITI and the Japanese Miracle: The Growth of Industrial Policy, 1925–1975* (Stanford: Stanford University Press, 1982).

25. Yoshio Suzuki, *Money and Banking in Contemporary Japan* (New Haven: Yale University Press, 1980); Ann Gregory, *The Japanese Economy and Business System: Patterns and Influences upon Growth* (New York: New York University Press, 1982); Jimmy Wheeler, Merit Janow, and Thomas Pepper, *Japanese Industrial Development Policies in the 1980s* (Croton-on-Hudson, N.Y.: Hudson Institute, 1982); OECD, *The Export Credit Financing Systems in OECD Member Countries* (Paris: OECD, 1982); Ira Magaziner and Tom Hout, "Japanese Industrial Policy," Policy Papers in International Affairs, 1980, p. 97; and Bank of Japan, *Money and Banking in Japan* (Tokyo: Bank of Japan, 1973).

26. Wheeler, Janow and Pepper, *Japanese Industrial Development Policies in the 1980s,* p. 99.

27. Kunio Yoshihara, *Sogo Shosha: The Vanguard of the Japanese Economy* (Tokyo: Oxford University Press, 1982).

28. Chalmers Johnson, *MITI and the Japanese Miracle;* Rutaro Komiya, "Japan and the World Economy," in Fred Bergsten, ed., *Towards a New World Trade Policy: The Maidenhead Papers* (Lexington, Mass.: D. C. Heath, 1975), p. 191.

29. T. J. Pempel, "Japanese Foreign Economic Policy," *International Organization* 31 (Autumn 1977).

30. Haruhiro Fukui, "The GATT Tokyo Round: The Bureaucratic Politics of Multilateral Diplomacy," in Michael Blaker, ed., *The Politics of Trade: U.S. and Japanese Policymaking for the GATT Negotiations* (New York: East Asian Institute, 1978).

31. *Business Week,* April 8, 1985.

32. Ibid.

33. I. M. Destler, Hideo Sato, Priscilla Clapp, and Haruhiro Fukui, *Managing an Alliance: The Politics of U.S.-Japanese Relations,* (Washington, D.C.: Brookings Institution, 1976).

34. Yoko Sazanami, "Nihon no Bōeki Seisaku: Keizai Masatsu ni Shūshi shita Bōeki Seisaku," (Japan's Trade Policy: Trade Policy Which Is Consistent Toward Economic Conflict), *Gendai Keizai* 55 (Autumn 1983), pp. 110–127.

35. John Zysman and Laura Tyson et al., "U.S. and Japanese Trade and Industrial Policies," paper prepared for the U.S.-Japan Advisory Commission, mimeo, March 1984.

36. Interviews with MITI officials, 1985.

37. GATT, *International Trade, 1952,* p. 110.

38. U.S. Department of Commerce, *Historical Statistics of the United States: Colonial Times to 1970,* part 2 (Washington, D.C.: Bureau of the Census, 1975).

39. GATT, *International Trade,* various years.

40. Bruce Scott, "National Strategies: Key to International Competition," in Bruce Scott and George Lodge, eds., *U.S. Competitiveness in the World Economy* (Boston: Harvard Business School Press, 1984); see also, U.S. Department of Commerce, *An Assessment of U.S. Competitiveness in High Technology Industries* (Washington, D.C.:

Government Printing Office, 1983); and Otto Eckstein et al., *The DRI Report on U.S. Manufacturing Industries* (New York: McGraw-Hill, 1984).

41. This was also the conclusion of Alan Wolff, "International Competitiveness of American Industry: The Role of U.S. Trade Policy," in Scott and Lodge, eds., *U.S. Competitiveness in the World Economy.*

42. General Accounting Office, "Government Programs and Organizations Affecting Exports," ID-79-41, August 1979, p. 39.

43. Ibid.

44. David B. Yoffie, *Power and Protectionism;* and *Survey of Current Business* 65 (March 1985).

45. Interviews with six small and medium-sized Massachusetts exporters, 1983; Michael Blaker, "Export Myopia," *Quarterly Review of Marketing* 4 (Spring 1979); and H. Ralph Jones, "Clearing the Way for Exporters," *Business Horizons,* (October 1980).

46. Robert Gilpin, *U.S. Power and the Multinational Corporation* (New York: Basic Books, 1975).

47. IMF, *International Financial Statistics, Yearbook, 1983.*

48. John Roemer, *U.S.–Japanese Competition in International Markets: A Study of the Trade-Investment Cycle in Modern Capitalism* (Berkeley: Institute for International Studies, No. 22, 1975).

49. Kozo Yamamura, "General Trading Companies in Japan: Their Origins and Growth," in Hugh Patrick, ed., *Japanese Industrialization and its Social Consequences* (Berkeley: University of California Press, 1976).

50. This is the argument made by Gary Saxonhouse, "Foreign Sales to Japan," in William Cline, ed., *Trade Policy in the 1980s* (Cambridge, Mass.: MIT Press, 1983).

51. Minoru Tanaka, "Moving Beyond Merchandise—Japan's Trade in Services," *Journal of Japanese Trade & Industry* 4 (1984).

52. Only recently has Japan moved to use these facilities to expand the export of various services. The most prominent example of such expansion is the growth of third-country trading by Japanese trading firms in the early 1980s. Yet according to my interviews with the six largest Japanese traders, these types of services remain a tiny percentage of their business compared to traditional exporting and importing of goods.

53. Richard Cooper, *The Economics of Interdependence* (New York: McGraw-Hill, 1968), p. 66.

54. IMF, *World Economic Outlook* (Washington, D.C.: IMF, 1982, 1983, and 1984); and S. J. Anjaria, Z. Iqbal, N. Kirmani, and L. L. Perez, *Developments in International Trade Policy* (Washington, D.C.: IMF, November 1982).

55. W. M. Corden, *The Revival of Protectionism* (New York: Group of Thirty, 1984).

56. OECD, *Competition and Trade Policies: Their Interaction* (Paris: OECD, 1984).

57. IMF, *Report on Exchange Arrangements and Exchange Restrictions* (Washington, D.C.: IMF, 1984), p. 5.

58. David B. Yoffie, "Profiting from Countertrade," *Harvard Business Review* (May–June 1984); William R. Cline, *"Reciprocity": A New Approach to World Trade Policy?* (Washington, D.C.: Institute for International Economics, 1982); and Alex Scott, *EEC–Japan–U.S.: World Traders in Conflict* (Brussels: European News Agency, 1983).

59. S. B. Page, "The Revival of Protectionism and its Consequences for Europe," *Journal of Common Market Studies* 20 (September 1981), pp. 17–40.

60. William R. Cline, *Export of Manufactures from Developing Countries* (Washington, D.C.: Brookings Institution, December 1984).

61. My thanks to Mac Destler for suggesting this point.

62. CBS/NYT poll, *The New York Times,* June 9, 1985. It is interesting to note that only 41 percent of those polled continued to believe protectionism was a good idea if it meant retaliation against American exports. The poll also suggested that Americans viewed the Japanese government as the most important impediment to U.S. exports to Japan.

63. See, for example, Robert Z. Lawrence, *Can America Compete?* (Washington, D.C.: Brookings Institution, 1984); and C. Fred Bergsten, "The U.S.–Japan Economic Conflict," *Foreign Affairs* 60 (Summer 1982), pp. 1059–1075.

64. In the 1983 and 1984 *White Paper on International Trade,* written by MITI and published by JETRO, there are repeated claims that Japan has deemphasized exports, and is now encouraging imports and direct investment overseas.

65. *Asahi Shimbun* poll, quoted in *The New York Times,* June 9, 1985.

66. The account of Japanese policy toward Indonesian countertrade is based upon interviews conducted in 1983 and 1984 with the six largest Japanese trading companies, MITI and JETRO officials in Japan and Indonesia, and Indonesian countertrade officials.

67. *Asian Wall Street Journal,* August 6, 1982, and August 15, 1982.

68. Johnson, *MITI and the Japanese Miracle.*

69. Interviews with MITI officials and the leading producers of VCRs, 1985. An interesting twist on this theme is that there was a rumor in Japan that after Sony set up its manufacturing plant in Germany in 1982, the president of Sony asked MITI to impose export controls. If true, Sony probably hoped to restrict its competitors after it reduced its dependence on Japanese exports.

70. *Nihon Keizai Shimbun,* December 22, 1982.

71. Alex Scott, *EEC–Japan–U.S.: World Traders in Conflict,* p. 125.

72. A MITI official interviewed for this research disagreed with this interpretation. While one of his colleagues in a different bureau felt the agreement gave MITI "tremendous power," this official felt that MITI has less control than I have asserted.

73. F.o.b. prices for the export of basic VTRs to Europe before 1983 ranged from 45,000 yen to 60,000 yen. Since the floor price on exports to Europe was initially set at 70,000 yen, Japanese firms had a substantial cushion against a decline in volume. The major drawback to the agreement from the perspective of the manufacturers was that demand usually increased as prices dropped. Since European prices were being held artificially high as a result of the restrictions, the overall market demand may have been lower. In fact, in 1984 Japanese exporters were unable to meet their export quotas: it was difficult to sort out, however, how much of the decline in demand was due to slow economic growth in Europe versus high prices on VTRs.

74. See David B. Yoffie, "Interest Group Vs. Individual Action: An Analysis of Corporate Political Strategies," Harvard Business School Working Paper, No. 9-785-018, August 1985.

75. George C. Lodge and William Glass, "U.S. Trade Policy Needs One Voice," *Harvard Business Review* (May–June), 1983.

76. U.S. International Trade Commission, "A Baseline Study of the Telephone and Switching Equipment Industry," USITC Publication No. 946, Washington, D.C., 1979.

77. Stefanie Lenway, "The Politics of Protection, Expansion, and Escape: International Collaboration and Business Power in U.S. Trade Policy" (Ph.D. diss., University of California, Berkeley, 1982).

78. This account of Motorola is largely based on interviews with Motorola executives in Washington and Tokyo, and interviews with U.S. government officials in charge of telecommunications trade.

79. U.S. Department of Commerce, *The Telecommunications Industry* (Washington, D.C.: International Trade Administration, 1983).

80. According to data provided by the USTR, Japan consumes 8.8 percent of the world's telecommunications equipment compared with 16.1 percent for Europe and 38 percent for the U.S.

81. *The Economist,* March 30, 1985.

82. *Fortune,* January 7, 1985.

83. *Business Week,* January 28, 1985.

84. *Business America,* September 30, 1985, p. 3.

85. *The Wall Street Journal,* September 24, 1985.

86. Yoffie, *Power and Protectionism.*

CHAPTER THREE

1. For general comparisons of styles of business in the United States and Japan, see W. Mark Fruin, "Industrial Group Capitalism and the Japanese Enterprise System," unpublished paper presented at the Business History Seminar, Harvard University Graduate School of Business Administration, November 28, 1984; Thomas B. Lifson, "What Do Japanese Corporate Customers Want? A Guide for American Firms Selling to Japan," in *U.S.-Japan Relations: New Attitudes for a New Era,* Annual Review of the Program on U.S.-Japan Relations (Cambridge, Mass.: Harvard University Center for International Affairs, 1983–84); Rodney Clark, *The Japanese Company* (New Haven: Yale University Press, 1979), pp. 221–222; Hiroyuki Itami, "A Japanese American Comparison of Management Productivity," *Japanese Economic Studies* 7 (Fall 1978); Tadao Kagono et al., "Strategic Adaptation to Environment: Japanese and U.S. Firms Compared," *Japanese Economic Studies* 12 (Winter 1983–84); and Richard T. Pascale, "Communication and Decision Making Across Cultures: Japanese and American Comparisons," *Administrative Science Quarterly* 23 (March 1978).

2. The structure and functioning of Japanese group enterprise is examined in Yoshikazu Miyazaki, "Big Corporations and Business Groups in Postwar Japan," *Developing Economics* 14 (December 1976); and Hiroshi Okumura, "Interfirm Relations in an Enterprise Group: The Case of Mitsubishi," *Japanese Economic Studies* 10 (Summer 1982). These two articles summarize the well-known theories of these two Japanese authors. For their detailed arguments, see Miyazaki, *Sengo Nippon no Kigyō Shūdan: Kigyō Shūdanbyō ni yoru Bunseki* (Enterprise Groups in Postwar Japan) (Tokyo: Nihon Keizai Shimbunsha, 1976); Okumura, *Nippon no Rokudai Kigyō Shūdan* (The Six Major Enterprise Groups in Japan) (Tokyo: Daiyamondosha, 1976); and Okumura, *Hōjin Shihonshugi* (Corporate Capitalism) (Tokyo: Ochanomizu Shobō, 1984).

In the list of *keiretsu* mentioned in this paragraph, it should be noted that Fuyo was a descendant of the Yasuda *zaibatsu,* and in that sense had a significant pre–World War II history.

Recent articles on group enterprises may be found in Kazuo Sato, ed., *Industry and Business in Japan* (White Plains, N.Y.: M. E. Sharpe, 1980); Sato and Yasuo Hoshino, eds., *The Anatomy of Japanese Business* (Armonk, N.Y.: M. E. Sharpe, 1984). See also, Dodwell Marketing Consultants, *Industrial Groupings in Japan,* sixth edition (Tokyo: Dodwell, 1984–85).

3. For detailed historical examinations of U.S. diversified and conglomerate firms, see Alfred D. Chandler, Jr., *Strategy and Structure: Chapters in the History of the American*

Industrial Enterprise (Cambridge, Mass.: MIT Press, 1962); and Chandler, *The Visible Hand: The Managerial Revolution in American Business* (Cambridge, Mass.: Harvard University Press, 1977). See also Richard P. Rumelt, *Strategy, Structure, and Economic Performance* (Boston: Division of Research, Harvard Business School, 1974); and Paul R. Lawrence and Davis Dyer, *Renewing American Industry* (New York: Free Press, 1983).

4. Fruin, "Industrial Group Capitalism and the Japanese Enterprise System," p. 27; more generally, see also the sources cited in note 2 above.

5. Ken-ichi Imai, "Japan's Changing Industrial Structure and United States-Japan Relations," in Kozo Yamamura, ed., *Policy and Trade Issues of the Japanese Economy: American and Japanese Perspectives* (Seattle: University of Washington Press, 1982), p. 62; *Figure 3-1* is reproduced in Imai's essay, p. 61. For a detailed history of the evolution of Japanese automobile manufacturers, see Michael A. Cusumano, *The Japanese Automobile Industry: Technology and Management at Nissan and Toyota* (Cambridge, Mass.: Harvard University Press, 1985).

6. Imai, "Japan's Changing Industrial Structure and United States-Japan Relations," p. 61.

7. A critical description of practices of automobile subcontracting appears in Satoshi Kamata, *Japan in the Passing Lane* (New York: Pantheon, 1982); additional details about Japanese small business and subcontracting may be found in Tokutaro Yamanaka, ed., *Small Business in Japan's Economic Progress* (Tokyo: Asahi Evening News, 1971); Yamanaka, ed., *Small Business in Japan* (Tokyo: Japan Times, 1961); and Seymour Broadbridge, *Industrial Dualism in Japan: A Problem of Economic Growth and Structural Change* (Chicago: Aldine, 1966).

8. The historical evolution of Japanese guilds is examined in Charles D. Sheldon, *The Rise of the Merchant Class in Tokugawa Japan, 1600–1868* (New York: J. J. Augustin, 1958); and Johannes Hirschmeier and Tsunehiko Yui, *The Development of Japanese Business, 1600–1980,* second edition (London: Allen & Unwin, 1981), Chapter 1.

9. A huge literature exists on cartels, trusts, monopolies, oligopolies, mergers, and consolidations. A series of relevant articles and a thorough 29-page bibliography of recent work in the field may be found in Eleanor M. Fox and James T. Halverson, eds., *Industrial Concentration and the Market System: Legal, Economic, Social and Political Perspectives* (Chicago: American Bar Association Press, 1979). See also Harvey J. Goldschmid, *et al.,* eds., *Industrial Concentration: The New Learning* (Boston: Little, Brown, 1974); Robert H. Bork, *The Antitrust Paradox* (New York: Basic Books, 1978), Chapters 8, 10, and 13; Edwin Mansfield, ed., *Monopoly Power and Economic Performance: The Problem of Industrial Concentration,* fourth edition (New York: Norton, 1978); and Yale Brozen, *Concentration, Mergers, and Public Policy* (New York: Macmillan, 1982).

On the European experience, see the following essays, all in Norbert Horn and Jürgen Kocka, eds., *Law and the Formation of the Big Enterprises in the 19th and Early 20th Centuries* (Gottingen, West Germany: Vanednhoeck & Ruprecht, 1979): William R. Cornish, "Legal Control over Cartels and Monopolization 1880–1914. A Comparison," pp. 280–303; Leslie Hannah, "Mergers, Cartels, and Concentration: Legal Factors in the U.S. and European Experience," pp. 306–314; and Morton Keller, "Public Policy and Large Enterprise. Comparative Historical Perspectives," pp. 515–531.

10. Richard A. Posner, "A Statistical Study of Antitrust Enforcement," *Journal of Law and Economics* 13 (October 1970), p. 366; see also Walton Hamilton and Irene Till, *Antitrust in Action,* Temporary National Economic Committee Monograph No. 16 (Washington, D.C.: Government Printing Office, 1940), pp. 135–141.

For further details on the early years of enforcement, see Hans B. Thorelli, *The*

Federal Antitrust Policy: Origination of an American Tradition (Baltimore: Johns Hopkins Press, 1955); James Morison Russell, "Business and the Sherman Act, 1890–1914," (unpublished Ph.D. diss., History, University of Iowa, 1966); Peter Hamilton Crawford, "Business Proposals for Government Regulation of Monopoly, 1887–1914," (unpublished Ph.D. diss., Political Science, Columbia University, 1963); Richard Hofstadter, "What Happened to the Antitrust Movement? Notes on the Evolution of an American Creed," in Earl F. Cheit, ed., *The Business Establishment* (New York: Wiley, 1964), pp. 113–151; and Ellis Hawley, "Antitrust," in Glenn Porter, ed., *Encyclopedia of American Economic History* (New York: Scribner's, 1980), pp. 772–787.

11. This argument is made explicit in Thomas K. McCraw, "Rethinking the Trust Question," in McCraw, ed., *Regulation in Perspective: Historical Essays* (Boston: Harvard University Graduate School of Business Administration, 1981), pp. 2–17. An exceptionally vivid discussion of the legal difficulties involved in enforcing loose horizontal combinations may be found in Louis D. Brandeis's lecture notes for a course on business law at MIT in the 1890s: see the manuscript notes, pp. 320–321, Document 9 of *A Microfilm Edition of The Public Papers of Louis Dembitz Brandeis in the Jacob and Bertha Goldfarb Library of Brandeis University* (Cambridge, Mass.: General Microfilm Co., 1978).

12. The evolution of Japanese cartel policy is described throughout Chalmers Johnson, *MITI and the Japanese Miracle: The Growth of Industrial Policy, 1925–1975* (Stanford: Stanford University Press, 1982). On Japanese cartels in general, see Eleanor Hadley, *Antitrust in Japan* (Princeton: Princeton University Press, 1970), Chapter 15; and Masu Uekusa, *Sangyō Soshikiron* (Industrial Organization) (Tokyo: Chikuma Shobō, 1982), Chapter 6.

13. See, in particular, Johnson, *MITI and the Japanese Miracle*, pp. 98–99, 108–111, and 113–114.

14. Uekusa, *Sangyō Soshikiron* (Industrial Organization), pp. 206–207. Of the number of cartels listed for all three years, a large percentage applied to three categories: small- and medium-sized industries, export-related industries, and sanitation industries. The overall point, however, is that in the United States any such list of legalized cartels would be measured not in the hundreds but, at most, in the tens.

15. Japan's steel tonnages, which are usually measured in metric tons, were converted to net tons throughout this chapter to facilitate the U.S.-Japan comparison. (One metric ton equals 1.1 net ton.)

16. Most of *Table 3-1* is reproduced from Robert W. Crandall, "The Roots of the Current 'Crisis' in the U.S. Steel Industry: An International Perspective," in Harold R. Williams, ed., *Kent State Steel Seminar: Free Trade, Fair Trade, and Protection, The Case of Steel* (Ohio: Kent State University, 1978), p. 61. The data are from the following five well-known studies: Donald F. Barnett, "International Competitiveness in Steel and Dynamic Advantages," Working Paper, October 15, 1977; Charles Bradford, *The Japanese Steel Industry: A Comparison With Its United States Counterpart* (Merrill, Lynch, Pierce, Fenner and Smith, Inc., 1977); Council on Wage and Price Stability (CWPS), *Prices and Costs in the American Steel Industry* (Washington, D.C.: Government Printing Office, 1977); Federal Trade Commission, *Staff Report on the United States Steel Industry and Its International Rivals: Trends and Factors Determining International Competitiveness* (Washington, D.C.: Government Printing Office, 1977); and Hans Mueller and Kiyoshi Kawahito, *Steel Industry Economics: A Comparative Analysis of Structure, Conduct and Performance* (New York: Japan Steel Information Center, 1978).

17. Donald F. Barnett and Louis Schorsch, *Steel: Upheaval in a Basic Industry* (Cambridge, Mass.: Ballinger, 1983), p. 37.

18. Mueller and Kawahito, for example, assert that "The superior investment per-

formance of the Japanese steel industry is also evident from the scale economies in plant and equipment size and adoption of the 'best practice' with respect to several processes of steelmaking. We believe that these differences in new capacity, economies of scale, and modern technology are directly related to the divergent behavior of operating costs . . . ," *Steel Industry Economics,* p. 5. See also Robert W. Crandall, *The U.S. Steel Industry in Recurrent Crisis: Policy Options in a Competitive World* (Washington, D.C.: Brookings Institution, 1981), p. 72.

19. Mueller and Kawahito, *Steel Industry Economics,* p. 7. See also Institute for Iron and Steel Studies (IISS), Richard L. Deily ed., *Steel Industry in Brief: Japan 1977* (New Jersey: IISS, 1977), pp. 18–21 and p. 152; and IISS, *Steel Industry in Brief: Databook, U.S.A. 1960–1980.*

20. For example, in 1976, Japan had thirty-seven blast furnaces with an inner volume measuring in excess of 2,000 cubic meters compared to only five in the United States. At that time, 35 percent of Japan's crude steel was continually cast compared to 10 percent in the United States. In 1980, the average output of Japan's blast furnaces was 2.3 million tons a year while the average for U.S. blast furnaces was .84 million tons. By 1982, Japan had fifteen blast furnaces with inner volumes greater than 4,000 cubic meters. See, for example, *Japan's Iron and Steel Industry, 1981,* pp. 57–58; and Barnett and Schorsch, *Steel,* p. 59.

21. "Integrated" steel companies engage in all three stages of the steel-manufacturing process: ironmaking, steelmaking, and rolling. In ironmaking, the raw materials— iron ore, coke and limestone—are combined in a blast furnace and heated to reduce the iron ore to liquid pig iron. The pig iron is oxidized in a steel furnace to remove most of the carbon, silicon, and phosphorus, yielding "raw steel." The raw steel is then put through a series of additional steps, such as casting into ingots that can then be shaped into "blooms," "billets," or "slabs." These semifinished forms are cooled, and finally rolled and shaped into finished products. The typical American firm has actually integrated still further—backward into mining its own raw materials, forward into directly marketing its products.

All over the world, integrated companies dominate steelmaking. In the United States during the 1970s, integrated firms accounted for about 90 percent of all the carbon steel produced. Since that time, "minimills" have begun to cut into this high percentage.

22. Crandall, *The U.S. Steel Industry in Crisis,* p. 76. "Greenfield" refers to an entirely new plant rather than a renovated or "rounded out" plant.

23. Ibid., p. 11; Mueller and Kawahito, *Steel Industry Economics,* p. 6. Mueller and Kawahito contend that, for plants with deep-channel harbors, further economies can be obtained at twice or three times this size.

24. See, for example, Kenneth Warren, *World Steel: An Economic Geography* (New York: Crane, Russak and Co., Inc., 1975), pp. 90–93; and Steven B. Webb, "Tariffs, Cartels, Technology, and Growth in the German Steel Industry, 1879 to 1914," *The Journal of Economic History* 40 (June 1980), pp. 309–329.

25. The following description of the U.S. business-government relationship in steel owes a great deal to the work of Paul Argel Tiffany, in "The Roots of Decline: Business-Government Interaction in the American Steel Industry, 1945–1960" (Ph.D. diss., University of California, Berkeley, 1983).

26. Ibid., p. 94; "Shortage Inquiry Expected to Air Steel Capacity Controversy," *Iron Age,* July 31, 1947, p. 98; and "Steel Man Denies Output Curb," *The New York Times,* September 26, 1947, p. 37.

27. Quoted in Tiffany, "Roots of Decline," p. 84; Walter S. Tower, "Address of the President," in American Iron and Steel Institute *Yearbook 1947* (New York: AISI, 1947), pp. 635–636.

28. Tiffany, "Roots of Decline," p. 231.

29. For a discussion of declining U.S. steel consumption and substitute materials, see "Steel: It's a Brand-New Industry," *Fortune,* December 1960, pp. 123–127+.

30. In an interview with *Fortune* magazine in 1966, Bethlehem Steel's finance chief, William Johnstone, spoke for the industry in saying, "The way to face fair import competition is to get out ahead technically." "Steel Is Rebuilding for a New Era," *Fortune,* October 1966, p. 224. The industry took this position consistently throughout the 1960s. See, for example, Roger Blough's press conference statement, April 13, 1962, quoted in Roy Hoopes, *The Steel Crisis* (New York: The John Day Company, 1963), pp. 180–181.

31. The "Kennedy controversy" over steel prices is detailed in Hoopes, *The Steel Crisis.*

32. Crandall, *The Steel Industry in Crisis,* p. 45.

33. Quoted in Jack Robert Miller, "Steel Minimills," *Scientific American* 250 (May 1984), p. 33.

34. Ira C. Magaziner and Robert B. Reich, *Minding America's Business: The Decline and Rise of the American Economy* (New York: Harcourt Brace Jovanovich, 1982), pp. 162–163.

35. For a discussion of the Japanese government's philosophy on industrial rationalization, see Johnson, *MITI and the Japanese Miracle,* pp. 27, 81, 108–109; and Kozo Yamamura, *Economic Policy in Postwar Japan* (Berkeley: University of California Press, 1967), pp. 48–49.

36. In 1952, Japan produced 7.7 million (net) tons of steel. By 1953, steel output reached 8.5 million tons, equal to Japan's 1943 wartime high. (Output had fallen to below one million tons in 1946 and 1947.)

37. For discussions of MITI's view of excess competition, see: Hadley, *Antitrust in Japan,* pp. 396–398; Johnson, *MITI and the Japanese Miracle,* pp. 11, 204–207; and Yamamura, *Economic Policies in Postwar Japan,* pp. 78–79, 178–179.

38. For example, in April 1951, the domestic delivered price of steel plates in Japan was $137 per ton, compared to $82 per ton in the United States. See Nippon Tekkō Kyōkai, *Sengo Tekkō Shi* (Postwar History of Iron and Steel) (Tokyo: Nippon Tekkō Kyōkai, 1968), quoted in Kiyoshi Kawahito, *The Japanese Steel Industry: With an Analysis of the U.S. Steel Import Problem* (New York: Praeger, 1972), p. 23. Japanese steel became price-competitive with American-made products in about 1958.

39. Ministry of International Trade and Industry, *Industrial Rationalization White Paper* (Tokyo: MITI, 1957), p. 270, quoted in Yamamura, *Economic Policy in Postwar Japan,* p. 65. See also Hadley, *Antitrust in Japan,* p. 397.

40. From 1951–1956, MITI funded steel companies under the "First Modernization Program." As indicated in the table below, the government concentrated its funding in Japan's leading four firms:

	Percent of funds
Yawata Steel	25
Fuji Steel	19
NKK	14
Kawasaki Steel	14
Other:	
28 companies	28
11 companies	0

41. For a description of the notorious battle between MITI and Kawasaki Steel, see: Seiichiro Yonekura, "Entrepreneurship and Innovative Behavior of Kawasaki Steel: The

Post World War II Period" (Tokyo: Institute of Business Research, Hitotsubashi University, Discussion Paper No. 120, 1984).

42. *Japan's Iron and Steel Industry 1965,* p. 37; and Eugene J. Kaplan, *Japan: The Government-Business Relationship* (Washington, D.C.: U.S. Department of Commerce, Government Printing Office, 1972), pp. 146–147.

43. On more than one occasion, MITI suggested "that old type equipment be purchased and scrapped compulsorily." Economic Planning Agency, *Economic Survey of Japan 1957–1958,* p. 105.

44. Takafusa Nakamura, *The Postwar Japanese Economy: Its Development and Structure* (Tokyo: University of Tokyo Press, 1981), p. 74.

45. Ministry of International Trade and Industry, *Japan's Iron and Steel Industry 1960,* p. 86.

46. *Japan's Iron and Steel Industry 1981,* p. 57.

47. Nippon Kokan, *Annual Reports,* 1969–1980.

48. Japanese steel companies also rationalized relatively new blast furnaces. For example, the number of blast furnaces under 2,000 cu.m. in Japan changed as follows:

$$
\begin{array}{ll}
1969 & 44 \\
1970 & 38 \\
1976 & 35 \\
1979 & 26 \\
\end{array}
$$

See *Japan's Iron and Steel Industry,* 1970–1981.

49. Quoted in Kozo Yamamura, "Success That Soured: Administrative Guidance and Cartels in Japan," in Yamamura, ed., *Policy and Trade Issues of the Japanese Economy,* p. 83.

50. On the overseas distribution network, see Kunio Yoshihara, *Sogo Shosha: The Vanguard of the Japanese Economy* (Tokyo: Oxford University Press, 1983); Marubeni Corporation, *The Unique World of the Sogo Shosha* (Tokyo: Marubeni, 1978); Alexander K. Young, *The Sogo Shosha: Japanese Multinational Trading Companies* (Boulder, Col.: Westview Press, 1979); and Yoshi Tsurumi, *Sogo Shosha: Engine of Export-Led Growth* (Brookfield, Vt.: Renouf USA, 1980). In fiscal year 1984, Japan's nine *sōgō shōsha* accounted for 44.2 percent of exports from Japan, and 68.0 percent of imports into Japan; see Akira Nakayama, ed., *Japan 1985: An International Comparison* (Tokyo: Keizai Kōhō Center, 1985), p. 46.

51. Dodwell Marketing Consultants, *The Structure of the Japanese Retail and Distribution Industry* (Tokyo: Dodwell, 1981), p. 12. In the case of Japan, the numbers cited are for the year 1979; for Britain, 1974; for France, 1975; for West Germany, 1978; for the United States, 1977. In all cases, census data are reliable, but open to interpretation. For example, if one multiplies the figures in line 5 (number of retailers) by those in line 6 (employees per retailer), then Japan does not appear necessarily inefficient compared with the United States in number of retail employees per capita of population. However, the Japanese figures likely do not include large numbers of part-time employees—family members who live on the premises.

A related table from another source shows the following comparisons between the United States (1977) and Japan (1979): Ratio of wholesale to retail sales—5.2 in Japan, 1.7 in the United States; number of retail shops per thousand persons—13.6 in Japan, 5.9 in the United States; productivity in wholesale and retail trade (real GDP/capita, thousands of yen, 1980)—Japan 2,769, United States 4,014; one- or two-person shops as percentage of total shops—Japan 61 percent, United States 43 percent. Source: *OECD Economic Surveys 1984/85: Japan* (Paris: OECD, August 1985), p. 42.

52. Again, it should be noted that attempts at rigorous comparisons of productivity, particularly in distribution, remain far from conclusive. Among the most careful work is Hirotaka Takeuchi and Louis P. Bucklin, "Productivity in Retailing: Retail Structure and Public Policy," *Journal of Retailing* 53 (Spring 1977); and Bucklin, "Trade Productivity: Comparison Between Japan and the USA," in Dov Izraeli, Dafna N. Izraeli, and Frank Meissner, eds., *Marketing Systems for Developing Countries* (New York: Wiley, 1976).

A pair of old but insightful analyses are Paul W. Stewart and J. Frederic Dewhurst, with the assistance of Louise Field, *Does Distribution Cost Too Much?* (New York: Twentieth Century Fund, 1939); and Malcolm P. McNair, Stanley F. Teele, and Francis G. Mulhearn, *Distribution Costs: An International Digest* (Boston: Harvard University Graduate School of Business Administration, 1941). Subsequent studies include Margaret Hall, John Knapp, and Christopher Winsten, *Distribution in Great Britain and North America: A Study in Structure and Productivity* (London: Oxford University Press, 1961); Louis P. Bucklin, *Productivity in Marketing* (Chicago: American Marketing Association, 1978); Bucklin, ed., *Vertical Marketing Systems* (Glenview, Ill.: Scott, Foresman, 1970); K. A. Tucker, *Economies of Scale in Retailing* (Lexington, Mass.: D. C. Heath, 1975); and Tucker, *Concentration and Costs in Retailing* (Lexington, Mass.: D. C. Heath, 1978).

On more general issues of productivity, see Angus Maddison, *Phases of Capitalist Development* (Oxford: Oxford University Press, 1982); Kazukiyo Kurosawa, "International Comparison of Productivity," in Japan Productivity Center, *Measuring Productivity: Trends and Comparisons from the First International Productivity Symposium* (New York: Unipub, 1983); and John W. Kendrick, ed., *International Comparisons of Productivity and Causes of the Slowdown* (Cambridge, Mass.: Ballinger, 1984).

53. *Figure 3-2* is reproduced from McKinsey & Company, *Japan Business: Obstacles and Opportunities* (Tokyo: McKinsey, for the United States-Japan Study Group, 1983), p. 28. Similar charts may be found in Manufactured Imports Promotion Organization, *An Analysis of and Recommendations Regarding the Japanese Distribution System and Business Practices* (Tokyo: MIPRO, 1983), p. 9; Japan External Trade Organization, *Planning for Distribution in Japan* (Tokyo: JETRO, revised ed., 1982), pp. 21, 23, 29, 30, 32, 35, 37, 40, 42, 44, 46, 48, 50, 51, and 53; and Mark Zimmerman, *How to Do Business With the Japanese: A Strategy for Success* (New York: Random House, 1985), p. 135.

54. On Japanese distribution in general, see the following sources: Dodwell Marketing Consultants, *The Structure of the Japanese Retail and Distribution Industry;* Michael Y. Yoshino, *The Japanese Marketing System* (Cambridge, Mass.: MIT Press, 1971); Mitsuaki Shimaguchi, *Marketing Channels in Japan* (n.p.: UMI Research Press, 1978); Nomura Research Institute, *The Consumer in Japan* (London: Financial Times Business Information Ltd., 1980); Mitsuaki Shimaguchi and Larry J. Rosenberg, "Demystifying Japanese Distribution," *Columbia Journal of World Business* 14 (Spring 1979), pp. 32–41; Charles J. McMillan, *The Japanese Industrial System* (New York: Walter de Gruyter, 1984), Chapter 10; T. F. M. Adams and N. Kobayashi, *The World of Japanese Business* (Tokyo: Kodansha International Ltd., 1969), Chapter 10; C. Tait Ratcliffe, "Approaches to Distribution in Japan," Chapter 4 of Isaiah Frank, ed., *The Japanese Economy in International Perspective* (Baltimore: Johns Hopkins University Press, for the Committee for Economic Development, 1975); Yoshi Tsurumi, "Managing Consumer and Industrial Marketing Systems in Japan," *Sloan Management Review* 24 (Fall 1982), pp. 41–50; Philip Kotler and Liam Fahey, "The World's Champion Marketers: The Japanese," *Journal of Business Strategy* 3 (Summer 1982), pp. 3–13; and Jon Woronoff, *Japan's Wasted Workers* (Totowa, N.J.: Allanheld, Osmun, 1983), pp. 166–191.

Among Japanese scholars of marketing, Shūji Hayashi pioneered the widespread predictions of a "distribution revolution" in the early 1960s. While he was correct in arguing that mass retailers would soon emerge, his expectation that small operators would decline drastically turned out to be premature. See his *Ryūtsū Kakumei* (Distribution Revolution) (Tokyo: Chūō Kōronsha, 1962). See also Masao Uno et al., *Ryūtsū Gyōkai* (The Distribution Industry) (Tokyo: Kyōikusha, 1979); Masafusa Miyashita, *Nippon no Tonya* (Wholesalers of Japan) (Tokyo: Nikkei Shinsho, 1974); Hajime Sato, *Nippon no Ryūtsū Kikō* (The Structure of Japanese Distribution) (Kyoto: Yūhikaku, 1974); and Tadao Kiyonari, *Nippon no Ryūtsū Sangyō Kakushin* (Innovations in the Distribution Industry in Japan) (Tokyo: Shin Hyōronsha, 1975).

55. For the United States, the sources for *Table 3-4* are *Fortune*, June 11, 1984; *Moody's Industrial Manual 1983* (New York: Moody's, 1984); and *Chain Store Age Executive*, August 1984. For Japan, the figures are calculated from *Ryūtsū Tōkei Shiryōshū 1985 Nenban* (Materials on Distribution Statistics, 1985) (Tokyo: Ryūtsū Keizai Kenkyujo, 1985), p. 53.

56. Different practices of financial reporting also make exact cross-national comparisons impossible. For example, while U.S. figures are generally consolidated ones of parent companies and their subsidiaries, Japanese numbers are for parent companies only. The latest estimates of Japanese consolidated figures may be seen in Shin'ichi Kawasaki, *Sūpā Gyōkai* (The Supermarket Industry) (Tokyo: Kyōikusha, 1979), p. 17. Kawasaki's calculations confirm the argument made here about the significant size difference of U.S. and Japanese retailers.

57. For more details about Japanese distribution, see Shūji Ogawa, ed., *80 Nendai no Ryūtsū Vision: Shōgyō no Saihakken—High Tech Jidai ni okeru Ryūtsū Senryaku* (A Vision of Distribution in the '80s: Rediscovery of Commerce—Distribution Strategies in the High-Tech Age) (Tokyo: Ryūtsū System Kaihatsu Center, 1979), Chapters 2 and 4.

58. The Japan Real Estate Institute has calculated that the price index for land in six large Japanese cities increased from a base figure of 100 in 1955 to 7,817 in 1985. During this same period, the overall consumer price index grew to only 506—a figure approximately one-fifteenth the growth rate of land prices. See *Japan 1985: An International Comparison*, p. 88.

59. For general international comparisons of distribution and public policies, see George H. Wadinambiaratchi, "Channels of Distribution in Developing Economies," *The Business Quarterly* 30 (Winter 1965), pp. 74–82; Erdener Kaynak and Ronald Savitt, eds., *Comparative Marketing Systems* (New York: Praeger, 1984); J. Boddewyn and S. C. Hollander, *Public Policy Toward Retailing: An International Symposium* (Lexington, Mass.: Heath-Lexington Books, 1972); and Toshimasa Tsuruta, ed., *Sekai to Nippon no Ryūtsū Seisaku: Shōgyō Ricchi to Toshi Keisei* (Distribution Policies in the World and Japan: Commercial Location and Urban Organization) (Tokyo: Nippon Hyōronsha, 1980).

60. Representative of the large American literature on this subject are Carl Fulda, "Food Distribution in the United States: The Struggle Between the Independents and the Chains," *University of Pennsylvania Law Review* 99 (June 1951), p. 1051–1162; Joseph Cornwall Palamountain, Jr., *The Politics of Distribution* (Cambridge, Mass.: Harvard University Press, 1955); and Thomas K. McCraw, *Prophets of Regulation* (Cambridge, Mass.: Harvard University Press, 1984), pp. 101–107. For a useful survey of world trends, see Boddewyn and Hollander, *Public Policy Toward Retailing: An International Symposium*.

61. *Dr. Miles Medical Co. v. John D. Park & Sons Co.*, 220 U.S. 373 (1911).

62. General works on the Robinson-Patman Act include Earl W. Kintner, *A Robinson-Patman Primer* (New York: Macmillan, 1979); Richard A. Posner, *The Robinson-Patman Act: Federal Regulation of Price Differences* (Washington, D.C.:

American Enterprise Institute, 1976); and *The Robinson-Patman Act: 1936–1966* (American Bar Association Antitrust Section, 1966); An early symposium on the law may be found in Benjamin Werne, ed., *Business and the Robinson-Patman Law* (New York: Oxford University Press, 1938).

63. The Consumer Goods Pricing Act may be found in 15 U.S. Code, § 45, 89 Stat. 801 (1975).

On "fair trade," see Federal Trade Commission, *Resale Price Maintenance* (Washington, D.C.: Government Printing Office, 1945); Earl W. Kintner, ed., *The Legislative History of the Federal Antitrust Laws and Related Statutes* (New York: Chelsea House, 1978), pp. 457–982; Corwin D. Edwards, *The Price Discrimination Law* (Washington, D.C.: Brookings Institution, 1959); and B. S. Yamey, *Resale Price Maintenance* (Chicago: Aldine, 1966).

64. Palamountain, *The Politics of Distribution,* Chapter 6, especially pp. 173–187.

65. The Brandeis dissent may be found at 288 U.S. 568–569.

66. The leading case was *Dr. Miles Medical Co. v. John D. Park and Sons, Co.,* 220 U.S. 373 (1911). Other important cases included *Bobbs-Merrill Co. v. Straus,* 210 U.S. 339 (1908); and *Bauer & Cie v. O'Donnell,* 229 U.S. 1 (1913).

67. *Figure 3-3* was prepared by the Nomura Research Institute, Tokyo. It is reproduced, among other places, in Ito-Yokado, *Investors' Guide '85,* p. 28.

68. For a general history of distribution in the United States, see Glenn Porter and Harold C. Livesay, *Merchants and Manufacturers: Studies in the Changing Structure of Nineteenth-Century Marketing* (Baltimore: Johns Hopkins University Press, 1971); and Louis Bucklin, *Competition and Evolution in the Distributive Trade* (Englewood Cliffs, N.J.: Prentice-Hall, 1972).

69. On Japanese regulation of retailing before World War II, see, in general, Kin'ichiro Toba, *Nippon no Ryūtsū Kakushin: Kourigyō Hyakunen no Rekishi to Kigyōsha Katsudō* (Distribution Innovation in Japan: History and Entrepreneurship of 100 Years of Retailing) (Tokyo: Nihon Keizai Shimbunsha, 1979), Chapter 3; and Teiichirō Fujita et al., *Nippon Shōgyōshi* (Commercial History of Japan) (Kyoto: Yūhikaku, 1978), Chapter 8. For an evaluation of the changes in distribution policies in the 1930s, see Keiichi Yoshida and Eiji Oshima, *Nippon Shōgyō Kikōron* (The Examination of Japanese Distribution Structure) (Tokyo: Keiō Shuppansha, 1941).

70. See the sources cited in Note 54 above, especially Yoshino, *The Japanese Marketing System,* Chapters 7 and 8.

71. Yoshino, *The Japanese Marketing System,* Chapters 7 and 8; interview with Mr. Hirofumi Yamashita (Section Chief, Commercial Policy Section, Industrial Policy Bureau, MITI) and his associates, August 28 and December 5, 1985, hereafter cited as Yamashita Interviews, MITI.

72. Ibid. (both sources); see also Robert E. Weigand, "Aspects of Retail Pricing in Japan," *MSU Business Topics* 18 (Winter 1970), pp. 23–30. Mitsuo Matsushita and Eugene H. Lee, "Antimonopoly Regulation of Marketing," in Robert J. Ballon, ed., *Marketing in Japan* (Tokyo: Sophia University in cooperation with Kodansha International Ltd., 1973), pp. 47–71 provide a convenient summary of the role of legislation, administrative guidance, and the Fair Trade Commission.

The Japanese government has often taken the public position that the regulation of distribution is based on rational economic reasons rather than on political considerations. The following explanation by a MITI official typifies this position: "This [multilayered and complex structure of distribution] is mostly due to Japanese consumers' buying behavior in strongly demanding the wide range of choices, the quality, the functions, the safety in appearance, the immediate availability of goods, and so on. Such foreign criticism [of the distribution structure of Japan], therefore, seemingly misses the target. It is hereafter necessary that international understanding of our country's distribution channels and trade customs be promoted by providing relevant information." (Translated from Ogawa, ed., *80 Nendai no Ryūtsū Vision,* p. 224.)

73. Nikkei Ryūtsū Shimbun, ed., *Ōgataten Shin Kisei Jidai no Kourigyō* (Retailing Industries in the New Regulatory Age of Large-Scale Stores) (Tokyo: Nihon Keizai Shimbun, 1982), Chapter 4. See also the following sources: Ogawa, ed., *80 Nendai no Ryūtsū Vision;* and Tsuruta, ed., *Sekai to Nippon no Ryūtsū Seisaku.*

74. Seiyu and Ito-Yokado executive presentations at Nomura School of Advanced Management, Tokyo, August 1985; interview with Mr. Ohira of Ito-Yokado, December 5, 1985; Yamashita Interviews, MITI; Kawasaki, *Sūpā Gyōkai,* Chapter 10. The impression of a combination shopping center and country club is based on my own observation of Ito-Yokado complexes in Tokyo suburbs.

75. Internal MITI documents.

76. Ibid.; Yamashita Interviews, MITI.

77. For various viewpoints toward retailing policies in the 1980s, see Ogawa, ed., *80 Nendai no Ryūtsū Vision;* Nikkei Ryūtsū Shimbun, ed., *Ōgataten Shin Kisei Jidai no Kourigyō;* Uno et al., *Ryūtsū Gyōkai,* Part I, Chapter 5, Part 2, Chapter 5; and Shinya Nakada, *Ryūtsū Sangyō* (The Distribution Industry) (Tokyo: Tōyō Keizai, 1980), Chapter 4.

78. Yamashita Interviews, MITI; interviews with JETRO officials, Tokyo, August 28, 1985.

An episode that occurred in 1981 illustrates the ambiguous and somewhat vulnerable position of MITI in regulating retail operations. The LDP, under strong pressure from ten major national associations of small- and medium-scale retailers, tried to prohibit almost entirely the opening of new large stores by introducing a fundamental change in the Large Scale Retail Store Act of 1973. In response, MITI proposed instead a new administrative guidance, which would tighten control of large new stores. The LDP rejected MITI's plan as being too lenient, and the ensuing battle between the party and MITI became one of the salient political issues of 1981. Early in 1982, a compromise was reached, in which the LDP achieved its original goal of severely limiting new large stores, while MITI managed to save some face by avoiding a revision of the 1973 Act. Under the compromise, tighter administrative guidance by MITI would be directed at major retailing *corporations,* including department stores, which now came under the strong control of MITI. (The significant change here was that the companies themselves were now regulated, in addition to individual stores larger than a certain size.) Secondly, various kinds of cooperatives now came under administrative guidance for the first time.

79. *Figure 3-4* is from the Japanese Census of Commerce, as reproduced in Ito-Yokado, *Investors' Guide '85,* p. 23.

80. For Japan, in addition to the citations in earlier notes, useful overall views of competition policy may be found in the following books and articles: Eugene Rotwein, "Economic Concentration and Monopoly in Japan," *Journal of Political Economy* 72 (June 1964), pp. 262–277; Johannes Hirschmeier and Tsunehiko Yui, *The Development of Japanese Business 1600–1980;* J. Mark Ramseyer, "The Costs of the Consensual Myth: Antitrust Enforcement and Institutional Barriers to Litigation in Japan," *Yale Law Journal* 94 (1985), pp. 604–645; [Japan] Fair Trade Institute, *Antimonopoly Legislation of Japan* (Tokyo: Fair Trade Institute, 1984), especially pp. 301–331; and Elliott J. Hahn, *Japanese Business Law and the Legal System* (Westport, Conn.: Quorum Books, 1984). A source particularly relevant to the section on Japanese distribution policies is John O. Haley, "Anticompetitive Practices in the Distribution of Goods

and Services in Japan—Introduction," and Haley's accompanying translation of Ishida Hideto, "Anticompetitive Practices in the Distribution of Goods and Services in Japan: The Problem of Distribution *Keiretsu,*" *Journal of Japanese Studies* 9 (Summer 1983), pp. 318–334.

CHAPTER FOUR

1. Of Japan's net long-term outflow of $49.6 billion in 1984, $26 billion went into net purchases of foreign, principally government, bonds; less than $3 billion went into direct investments. See *The Economist,* September 21, 1985, pp. 79–80.

2. United States Department of Commerce, Bureau of Economic Analysis, *Survey of Current Business* 65 (October 1985), p. 27.

3. Reported in *The Economist,* July 6, 1985, p. 65.

4. *Survey of Current Business* 64 (August 1984), p. 31.

5. Japan, Ministry of Finance, "Japanese Data on Direct Investment Flows," mimeo, Tokyo, 1984. These data are also reproduced in Japan, Ministry of International Trade and Industry, *White Paper on International Trade, 1985* (Tokyo: MITI, 1985), p. 90.

6. For a discussion of the macroeconomics of U.S. foreign direct investment, see William H. Branson, "Trends in United States International Trade and Investment Since World War II," in Martin Feldstein, ed., *The American Economy in Transition* (Chicago: University of Chicago Press for the National Bureau of Economic Research, 1980), pp. 183–257. For an excellent survey of the macroeconomics of Japanese foreign direct investment, see Makoto Sakurai, "Japanese Direct Foreign Investment: Studies on Its Growth in the 1970s," Yale University, Economic Growth Center, Discussion Paper No. 397, February 1982.

7. Mira Wilkins, "American-Japanese Direct Foreign Investment, 1930–1952," *Business History Review* 56 (Winter 1982), pp. 498–518. U.S. direct investment in Japan probably peaked at $61.4 million in 1930; see Wilkins, Table 2, p. 506. Japanese investment in the United States probably peaked at $41 million in 1937 following a sharp increase that year; see Wilkins, Table 3, p. 507.

8. For prewar data, see Wilkins, "American-Japanese Direct Foreign Investment," p. 498. For postwar data, see United States, Department of Commerce, Bureau of Economic Analysis, *Selected Data on U.S. Direct Investment Abroad, 1950–76* (Washington, D.C.: Government Printing Office, 1982), pp. 1, 21.

9. See fn. 5 above, especially MITI, *White Paper on International Trade, 1985,* p. 88. For an excellent review and analysis of these trends, see Hideki Yoshihara, "Multinational Growth of Japanese Manufacturing Enterprises in the Postwar Period," in Akio Okochi and Tadakatsu Inoue, eds., *Overseas Business Activities: Proceedings of the Fuji Conference* (Tokyo: University of Tokyo Press for the Ninth International Conference on Business History, 1984), pp. 95–120.

10. Wilkins, "American-Japanese Direct Foreign Investment," p. 517.

11. Raymond Vernon, *Sovereignty at Bay: The Multinational Spread of U.S. Enterprises* (New York: Basic Books, 1971), especially pp. 60–112.

12. For an early review of and contribution to this literature, see Grant L. Reuber et al., *Foreign Private Investment in Development* (Oxford: Oxford University Press for the Organization of Economic Cooperation and Development, 1973), especially pp. 120–32; for a more recent analysis, see Stephen E. Guisinger et al., *Investment Incentives and Performance Requirements: Patterns of International Trade, Production and Investment* (New York: Praeger, 1985), especially pp. 48–54.

13. The discussion, in this paragraph and the next, of early investments in the Japanese auto industry is based on Wilkins, "American-Japanese Direct Foreign Investment,"

pp. 499–500; and William C. Duncan, *U.S.-Japan Automobile Diplomacy: A Study in Economic Confrontation* (Cambridge, Mass.: Ballinger, 1973), especially pp. 55–68; Ira C. Magaziner and Thomas M. Hout, *Japanese Industrial Policy* (Berkeley, Calif.: Institute of International Economics, University of California at Berkeley, 1980), pp. 67–79; Michael A. Cusumano, *The Japanese Automobile Industry: Technology and Management at Nissan and Toyota* (Cambridge, Mass.: Harvard University Press, 1985), pp. 27–72.

14. For a survey of postwar Japanese policies toward foreign investment, see M. Y. Yoshino, "Japan as Host to the International Corporation," in Charles P. Kindleberger, ed., *The International Corporation* (Cambridge, Mass.: MIT Press, 1970), pp. 345–369; Lawrence B. Krause, "Evolution of Foreign Direct Investment: The United States and Japan," in Jerome B. Cohen, ed., *Pacific Partnership: U.S.-Japan Trade* (Lexington, Mass.: Lexington Books for the Japan Society, 1972), especially pp. 162–166; Dan F. Henderson, *Foreign Enterprise in Japan: Laws and Policies* (Chapel Hill, N.C.: University of North Carolina Press, 1973), especially pp. 4–8, 195–290.

15. Chalmers Johnson, *MITI and the Japanese Miracle: The Growth of Industrial Policy, 1925–1975* (Stanford: Stanford University Press, 1982), especially pp. 172–173; Duncan, *Automobile Diplomacy,* especially pp. 31–52, 83–95.

16. For the history of Texas Instruments and other foreign companies in Japan, see Yasuzo Nakagawa, *Dokyumento: Nippon no Handōtai Kaihatsu* (Document: The Development of the Japanese Semiconductors) (Tokyo: Diayamondsha, 1981), pp. 154–166; Kikai Shinkō Kyōkai Keizai Kenkyujo (Economics Institute, Machinery Promotion Association), *Nichibei no Handōtai Sangyō ni Kansaru Chōsa Kenkyū* (Research Report on the Semiconductor Industry in Japan and the United States) (Tokyo: Kikai Shinkō Kyōkai, 1980), p. 115; Robert H. Silin, *The Japanese Semiconductor Industry, 1981–82* (Hong Kong: BA Asia Ltd., 1982), especially pp. 127–128.

17. Nippon Denshi Kikai Kōgyō Kai (Japan Electronics Industry Association), *Denshi Kōgyō Sanjūnen Shi* (A Thirty-Year History of the Electronics Industry) (Tokyo: Nippon Kikai Kōgyō Kai, 1979), pp. 102, 271. Japan's largest producer, then and now, was the country's first entrant, NEC, with 7 percent of the Japanese market in 1968.

18. For TI's negotiations with MITI, see Nakagawa, *Japanese Semiconductor Industry,* pp. 154–166.

19. Silin, *Japanese Semiconductor Industry,* pp. 127–128; Machinery Promotion Association, *Semiconductor Industry,* p. 162.

20. Silin, *Japanese Semiconductor Industry,* pp. 127–128.

21. Japan, Ministry of International Trade and Industry, Industrial Location Guidance Division, *Industrial Investment in Japan: 1984* (Tokyo: MITI, 1984), p. 10.

22. United States Department of Commerce, *Selected Data on U.S. Direct Investment Abroad, 1950–76,* pp. 24–25.

23. M. Y. Yoshino, *Japan's Multinational Enterprises* (Cambridge, Mass.: Harvard University Press, 1976).

24. Yoshi Tsurumi, *The Japanese Are Coming: A Multinational Interaction of Firms and Politics* (Cambridge, Mass.: Ballinger, 1976), pp. 71–100, 201–215; Terutomo Ozawa, *Multinationalism, Japanese Style: The Political Economy of Outward Dependency* (Princeton, N.J.: Princeton University Press, 1979), pp. 76–192; Hikoji Katano, *Japanese Enterprises in Asian Countries* (Kobe: Research Institute for Economics and Business Administration, Kobe University, 1981), pp. 33–119 and statistical appendices, pp. 127–223.

25. United States Department of Commerce, Bureau of Economic Analysis, *Foreign Direct Investment in the United States,* Volume 2, *Report of the Secretary of Commerce,*

Benchmark Survey, 1974 (Washington, D.C.: Government Printing Office, 1976), pp. 57–58, 60.

26. Johnson, *MITI and the Japanese Miracle*, pp. 275–304; *Far Eastern Economic Review*, June 13, 1985, p. 83. According to the *Review*, outstanding loans in this program grew fourfold in seven years, from ¥62.4 billion in 1977 to ¥258 billion in 1983.

27. See fn. 9 above; see also Export-Import Bank of Japan, Research Institute of Overseas Investment, *Exim Review* 5 (March 1985), pp. 37–68.

28. *Survey of Current Business* 64 (October 1984), p. 38.

29. For 1980 data, see United States Department of Commerce, Bureau of Economic Analysis, *Foreign Direct Investment in the United States, 1980* (Washington, D.C.: Government Printing Office, 1983), Table G-6, p. 146.

30. By comparison with Europe, intra-company sourcing from Japanese parents has exceeded comparable trade between European multinationals and their American subsidiaries. In 1980, for example, European parents exported $18.8 billion to their U.S. affiliates, compared to $21.9 billion shipped by Japanese parents to their U.S. subsidiaries. Moreover, European intra-company trade was spread across the wholesale (62 percent) and manufacturing (36 percent) sectors, while Japanese intra-company trade was concentrated (98 percent) in the U.S. wholesale sector. These figures reflect the greater concentration (relative to the Japanese) of European investments in U.S. manufacturing, and indicate that the very recent growth of Japanese-owned manufacturing plants in America should be expected to spur export growth in Japanese parts and subassemblies—thereby altering the future composition of Japanese exports to America. In fact, already between 1974 and 1980, exports by Japanese parents to their U.S. manufacturing subsidiaries grew more than 30 percent annually compared to nearly 20 percent for trade involving the much larger wholesale sector. See United States Department of Commerce, *Foreign Direct Investment in the United States, 1980*, Table G-9, p. 149 and Table G-10, p. 150.

31. United States Department of Commerce, *Benchmark Survey, 1974*, pp. 57–58, 60.

32. In 1983 exports (f.o.b.) by Japanese parents to their U.S. subsidiaries in U.S. wholesaling amounted to $26.9 billion according to Table 4-3 (77.1 percent of the $34.9 billion imported by these subsidiaries), while total Japanese exports (f.o.b.) to the United States equalled $42.8 billion, according to the Japan Economic Institute, *Yearbook of U.S.-Japan Economic Relations in 1983* (Washington, D.C.: JEI, 1984), p. 107.

33. For different reasons, Kiyoshi Kojima comes to the same conclusion in his "Direct Foreign Investment Between Advanced Industrial Countries," *Hitotsubashi Journal of Economics* 18 (June 1977), pp. 1–18. For a more recent test of his hypothesis, see Kiyoshi Kojima, "Japanese and American Direct Investment in Asia: A Comparative Analysis," *Hitotsubashi Journal of Economics* 26 (June 1985), pp. 1–35.

34. For a recent overview, see *The Economist*, December 8, 1984, pp. 75–76. For the Toyota-GM venture, also see *The New York Times*, January 30, 1985, p. D1; the special report in *Business Japan*, April 1983, pp. 18–20; and *The Wall Street Journal*, July 9, 1985, p. 2.

35. *The Wall Street Journal*, March 29, 1985, pp. 1, 10.

36. *The Economist*, December 8, 1984, pp. 75–76; *Fortune*, October 28, 1985, pp. 30–33.

37. Nippon Denshi Kikai Kōgyō Kai (Japan Electronics Industry Association), *Nichi Bei Ō no Denshi Sangyō no Genjō to Tenbō ni: Kansuru Chōsa Hōkokusho* (Report on the Current and Future Outlook of the Japanese, U.S. and European Electronics Industries) (Tokyo: Nippon Denshi Kikai Kōgyō Kai, 1983), p. 10.

38. Unless otherwise noted, data in this paragraph and the next three paragraphs were derived from interviews with industry analysts and company managers in Tokyo, June 1984.

39. *The Economist,* December 8, 1984, pp. 75–76; for an interview of the political economy of protectionism in semiconductors, see Daniel I. Okimoto, "Political Context," in Daniel I. Okimoto et al., eds., *Competitive Edge: The Semiconductor Industry in the U.S. and Japan* (Stanford: Stanford University Press, 1984), especially pp. 93–94, 100, 105–106, 122–129.

40. The production data in this paragraph are derived from the following sources (in order): Japan, Ministry of International Trade and Industry, *The Semiconductor Industry and Japanese Government Policies* (Tokyo, 1983), p. 3. United States Congress, Joint Economic Committee, *International Competition in Advanced Industrial Sectors: Trade and Development in the Semiconductor Industry* (Washington, D.C.: Government Printing Office, 1983), p. 105. United States Congress, Office of Technology Assessment, *International Competitiveness in Electronics* (Washington, D.C.: Government Printing Office, 1983), p. 141; Kikai Shinkō Kyōkai Keizai Kenkyūjo (Economics Institute, Machinery Promotion Association), *Handōtai Sangyō no Nichibei Kokusai Hikaku* (An International Comparison of the Semiconductor Industry in Japan and the U.S. (Tokyo: Kikai Shinkō Kyōkai, 1981), pp. 51, 106; Joint Economic Committee, *International Competition,* p. 106.

41. According to statistics provided by W. T. Grimm and Company, the Japanese were among the least likely to gain access to the U.S. market through acquisition:

Domicile of Foreign Parent	Number of Foreign Acquisitions of U.S. Companies	
	1979–1983	1984
United Kingdom	288	49
Canada	233	36
West Germany	77	4
France	71	7
Switzerland	43	7
Japan	39	6
Netherlands	37	5

42. James C. Abegglen, *The Strategy of Japanese Business* (Cambridge, Mass.: Ballinger, 1984), pp. 125–139; Sarkis J. Khoury, *Transnational Mergers and Acquisitions in the United States* (Lexington, Mass.: Lexington Books, 1980).

43. Economist Intelligence Unit, *Japanese Overseas Investment: The New Challenge,* Special Report No. 142 (London: Economist Intelligence Unit, 1983), pp. 109–114, 123–128.

44. The so-called follow-the-leader hypothesis is best tested in Frederick T. Knickerbocker, *Oligopolistic Reaction and Multinational Enterprises* (Boston: Graduate School of Business Administration, Harvard University, 1973). The so-called exchange-of-hostage hypothesis is best tested in E. M. Graham, "Transatlantic Investment by Multinational Firms: A Rivalistic Phenomenon?" *Journal of Post-Keynesian Economics* 1 (Fall 1978), pp. 82–99. For an excellent review of this logic and supporting empirical research, see Richard E. Caves, *Multinational Enterprise and Economic Analysis* (Cambridge, England: Cambridge University Press, 1982), pp. 97–100, 106–107. Tsurumi, *The Japanese Are Coming,* pp. 88–95, provides empirical support for this logic using data on Japanese foreign investments.

45. Kikai Shinkō Kyōkai Keizai Kenkyujo (Economics Institute, Machinery Promotion Association), *Nichibei no Handotai Sangyo ni Kansaru Chosa Kenkyū* (Research Report on the Semiconductor Industry in Japan and the United States) (Tokyo: Kikai Shinkō Kyōkai, 1980), p. 131.

46. The following estimates of market shares in the Japanese and American semiconductor industries were reported in: ibid., p. 96; and Semiconductor Industry Association, *International Microelectronic Challenge* (Menlo Park, Calif.: SIA, 1981), p. 35. See also Knickerbocker, *Oligopolistic Competition,* Chapter 6.

47. For the role of Japanese policies in promoting concentration generally, see Richard E. Caves and Masu Uekusa, *Industrial Organization in Japan* (Washington, D.C.: Brookings Institution, 1976), pp. 141–154; for the semiconductor industry, see the source cited in fn. 45 above, p. 122. The exception to this general statement was Kyōdō Electronics Technology Research Center, a joint venture formed by Pioneer, Alps Electric, Toyo, Japan Chemical Condenser, and Kōden Electric Works.

48. For the internal and external sales of Japanese semiconductor companies reported in this paragraph and the next, see: Joel Stern, "International Structural Differences in Financing," in Semiconductor Industry Association, eds., *An American Response to the Foreign Industrial Challenge in High Technology Industries* (Menlo Park, Calif.: SIA, 1980), pp. 133–134; Office of Technology Assessment, *International Competitiveness in Electronics,* p. 138; Joint Economic Committee, *International Competition,* p. 68.

49. This motive is explored in *The Wall Street Journal,* July 9, 1985, p. 2.

50. *The Wall Street Journal,* March 29, 1985, pp. 1, 20; *The New York Times,* July 6, 1984, p. D4.

51. According to Kiyoshi Kojima, such small-scale investment was long a hallmark of Japanese overseas operations, in marked contrast to American investments. See his *Direct Foreign Investment: A Japanese Model of Multinational Business Operations* (London: Croon Helm, 1978). With the notable exception of Japanese parts suppliers, his conclusion no longer seems applicable by the 1980s.

52. Kunio Yoshihara, *Japanese Investment in Southeast Asia* (Honolulu: University Press of Hawaii, 1978), pp. 133–178.

53. For a recent review of these policies and their effects on investment, see Guisinger, *Investment Incentives,* pp. 48–54.

54. For a survey of the strategies pursued by governments competing for investment, see Dennis J. Encarnation and Louis T. Wells, "Sovereignty En Garde: Negotiating with Foreign Investors," *International Organization* 39 (Winter 1985), pp. 47–48; Encarnation and Wells, "Competitive Strategies in Global Industries: A View from Host Governments," in Michael E. Porter, ed., *Competition in Global Industries* (Boston: Harvard Business School Press, 1986).

55. The competitive bids of Ohio and Tennessee are reviewed in Economist Intelligence Unit, *Japanese Overseas Investment,* pp. 109–114.

56. See John Rees, "Government Policy and Industrial Location in the United States," in U.S. Congress, Joint Economic Committee, *Special Study on Economic Change,* Vol. 7, *State and Local Finance: Adjustments in a Changing Economy* (Washington, D.C.: Government Printing Office, 1980), pp. 128–179.

57. This paragraph summarizes interviews with government officials, industry analysts, and company managers held in Tokyo, June 1984.

58. United States Department of Commerce, International Trade Administration, *International Direct Investment: Global Trends and the U.S. Role* (Washington, D.C.: Government Printing Office, 1984), Table 7, p. 48.

59. Ibid.; for the distribution by national origin of foreign direct investment in Japan, see citations in fn. 5 above.

60. See fn. 8 above.

61. MITI, *Industrial Investment in Japan,* p. 14.

62. *Survey of Current Business* 64 (October 1984), p. 38.

63. The American Chamber of Commerce in Japan, *United States Manufacturing Investment in Japan: Executive Summary* (Tokyo: The Chamber, 1980), pp. 17–32 and Exhibit 10.

64. MITI, *Industrial Investment in Japan,* p. 10.

65. See, Kazuhito Kondo, "The Japanese Pharmaceutical Industry: Its Present and Future," Nomura Research Institute, November 1983, p. 31; *Pharma Japan,* July 2, 1984, p. 13; Economist Intelligence Unit, *Japanese Overseas Investment,* p. 117.

66. Nippon Seiyaku Dantai Rengōkai, Hoken Yakka Kenkyūkai (Study Committee of the NHI Drug Price System, Federation of Pharmaceutical Manufacturers Association of Japan), *Seiyaku Sangyō to Yakka Kijun* (The Pharmaceutical Industry and Price Standards) (Tokyo: Nippon Seiyaku Dantai Rengōkai, 1984), p. 19; other information in this paragraph was gathered during interviews with industry analysts and company managers held in Tokyo, October 1984.

67. According to statistics provided by W. T. Grimm and Company, United States entry to the Japanese market through the acquisition of an existing company was virtually nonexistent, in marked contrast to U.S. corporate strategy in other markets:

Domicile of the Company Acquired	Number of U.S. Acquisitions	
	1979–1983	*1984*
United Kingdom	169	45
Canada	127	24
West Germany	53	13
France	53	3
Switzerland	25	3
Netherlands	24	3
Brazil	13	3
Mexico	11	0
Japan	8	7

68. *The Economist,* July 6, 1985, p. 65.

69. "Semiconductor Industry's Global Transition," *Semicon News* 6 (no date), pp. 21–24; Japan Economic Institute, "Semiconductor Equipment: An Example of Growing U.S. Investment in Japan," *JEI Report,* No. 44A (November 18, 1983), pp. 1–6.

70. *The Wall Street Journal,* July 18, 1985, p. 36.

71. American Chamber of Commerce in Japan, *Manufacturing Investment in Japan,* p. 22.

72. According to ibid., pp. 17–32, third-country suppliers played an important role in food products, pharmaceuticals, paper products, and electronics (including semiconductors). For comparisons of overseas sourcing patterns by U.S. and Japanese semiconductor companies, see the following: Franklin B. Weinstein et al., "Technological Resources," in Okimoto et al., eds., *Competitive Edge,* pp. 63–65; Joint Economic Committee, *International Competition,* p. 50; Silin, *Japanese Semiconductor Industry,* p. 165; Machinery Promotion Association, *Semiconductor Industry,* p. 160.

73. By comparison, in 1977, total U.S. exports to the Japanese affiliates of American companies were $1.2 billion; see United States Department of Commerce, Bureau of

Economic Analysis, *U.S. Direct Investment Abroad, 1977* (Washington, D.C.: Government Printing Office, 1981), Table II.I.3, p. 154 and Table II.I.7, p. 156. Data are for all nonbank affiliates of nonbank U.S. parents.

74. Merck's exports were reported in interviews held in Tokyo in October 1984; TI's exports in John L. Lazlo, *The Japanese Semiconductor Industry: Robust Industry Conditions to Persist Through 1984* (San Francisco: Hambercht and Quist, 1984), p. 17; IBM's exports in *Fortune*, April 8, 1985, p. 40.

75. American Chamber of Commerce in Japan, *Manufacturing Investments in Japan*, pp. 17–32.

76. The quotation is from *Fortune*, May 28, 1984, p. 16; for a survey of the incentives prescribed in "Act on Emergency Measures for Depopulated Areas," see MITI, *Industrial Investment in Japan*, p. 63.

77. The following is consistent with *Fortune*, May 28, 1984, pp. 14–19 and interviews conducted in Japan during June and October 1984.

78. Quotations are from *Fortune*, May 28, 1984, p. 16.

79. Of particular note here was the "one-village, one-product" campaign launched by Governor Hiramatsu (Oita Prefecture, Kyushu) and designed to target resources on activities for which a particular community had known expertise.

80. For an excellent survey of these policies, see MITI, *Industrial Investment in Japan*, pp. 62–69, 73–78.

81. The following is based on interviews in Tokyo, June 1984.

82. Governor Hiramatsu's success is detailed in an interview reprinted in *Japan Economic Survey* 8 (October 1984), pp. 6–11.

83. Reported in the *Journal of Japanese Trade and Industry* 1 (1983), p. 11.

84. For an account of this, see *Fortune*, May 28, 1984, pp. 17–18.

85. Quoted in *The Wall Street Journal*, March 29, 1985.

CHAPTER FIVE

1. Bruce F. Johnston and Peter Kilby, *Agriculture and Structural Transformation* (New York: Oxford University Press, 1975).

2. A provocative review of these issues is presented in Gregg Esterbrook, "Making Sense in Agriculture: A Revisionist Look at Farm Policy," *The Atlantic Monthly*, July 1985.

3. Ezra F. Vogel, *Comeback, Case by Case: Building the Resurgence of American Business* (New York: Simon and Schuster, 1985).

4. Donald Paarlberg, *Farm and Food Policy: Issues of the 1980s* (Lincoln: University of Nebraska Press, 1980).

5. Fumio Egaitsu, "Japanese Agricultural Policy, Present Problems and Their Historical Background," in Emery N. Castle and Kenzo Hemmi, eds., *U.S.-Japanese Agricultural Trade Relations* (Baltimore: Johns Hopkins University Press, for Resources for the Future, 1982), pp. 148–181.

6. Hiromatsu Kaneda, "Long-Term Changes in Food Consumption Patterns in Japan, 1878–1964," *Food Research Institute Studies in Agricultural Economics, Trade, and Development*, 8 (1968), pp. 3–32; *Nōgyō Hakusho Fuzoku Tōkeihyō* (Statistical Appendix for Agricultural White Paper) (Tokyo: Nōrin Tōkei Kyōkai, 1985), pp. 10–11.

7. I. M. Destler, "United States Food Policy 1972–1976: Reconciling Domestic and International Objectives," *International Organization* 32 (Summer 1978), pp. 617–653.

8. D. Gale Johnson, "World Commodity Market Situation and Outlook," in Bruce L. Gardener, ed., *U.S. Agriculture Policy: The 1985 Farm Legislation* (Washington, D.C.: American Enterprise Institute, 1985), pp. 19–50.

9. Johnston and Kilby, *Agriculture and Structural Transformation*, pp. 192–193.

10. Yujiro Hayami and Vernon W. Ruttan, *Agricultural Development: An International Perspective*, Second Edition (Baltimore: Johns Hopkins University Press, 1984).

11. Shunsaku Sekiya, *Nippon no Nōchi Seido* (Japan's Agricultural Land System) (Tokyo: Nōgyō Shinkō Chiiki Chōsakai, 1981).

12. Ronald P. Dore, *Land Reform in Japan* (London: Oxford University Press, 1959); and Haruhiro Fukui, "The Japanese Farmer and Politics," in Isaiah Frank, ed., *The Japanese Economy in International Perspective* (Baltimore: Johns Hopkins University Press, 1975), pp. 134–167.

13. This point is made especially clear in the discussion of structural change in Yujiro Hayami, "Adjustment Policies for Japanese Agriculture in a Changing World," in Emery N. Castle and Kenzo Hemmi, eds., *U.S.-Japanese Agricultural Trade Relations*, pp. 376–391.

14. Nōrinshō, *Nōgyō no Dōkō ni Kansuru Nenji Hōkoku, 1984* (Annual Report on Changes in Agriculture, 1984), p. 168.

15. Calculated from Yujiro Hayami and others, *A Century of Agricultural Growth in Japan: Its Relevance to Asian Development* (Tokyo: Tokyo University Press, 1975).

16. Statistical Appendix, note 6 above, p. 108.

17. In 1980, farms under 0.3 hectares required 88 hours to cultivate a hectare of rice and farms over 3.0 hectares required 48 hours per hectare. Statistical Appendix, note 6 above, pp. 58–59.

18. Nōrinshō, *Nōgyō no Dōkō ni Kansuru Nenji Hōkoku, 1984*, pp. 136–138.

19. Yujiro Hayami, "Japan's Rice Policy in Historical Perspective," *Food Research Institute Studies* 14 (1975), p. 363.

20. Ibid., p. 370.

21. Kym Anderson and Yujiro Hayamai et al., *Political Economy of Agricultural Protection: East Asia in International Perspective* (London: Allen & Unwin, forthcoming).

22. Hayami, "Japan's Rice Policy."

23. William T. Coyle, *Japan's Rice Policy*, Foreign Agricultural Economic Report No. 164, U.S. Department of Agriculture, 1981, p. 2.

24. *East Asia Outlook and Situation Report*, Economic Research Service, U.S. Department of Agriculture, May 1985.

25. Hayami, "Japan's Rice Policy," p. 375.

26. *Nihon Keizai Shimbun*, October 24, 1984.

27. Coyle, *Japan's Rice Policy*, p. 22.

28. Ibid., pp. 4, 12.

29. Keijiro Otsuka and Yujiro Hayami, "Goals and Consequences of Rice Policy in Japan, 1965–80," *American Journal of Agricultural Economics* 67 (August 1985), pp. 529–538.

30. Kenzo Hemmi, "Agriculture and Politics in Japan," in Emery N. Castle and Kenzo Hemmi, eds., *U.S.-Japanese Agricultural Trade Relations*, pp. 235–242.

31. This process is explained particularly well in Willard W. Cochrane, *The Development of American Agriculture: A Historical Analysis* (Minneapolis: University of Minnesota Press, 1979).

32. Hideo Sato and Timothy J. Curran, "Agricultural Trade: The Case of Beef and Citrus," in I. M. Destler and Hideo Sato, eds., *Coping with U.S.-Japanese Economic Conflicts* (Lexington, Mass.: D. C. Heath and Company, 1982), pp. 121–183.

33. Mike Tharp, "U.S. Can Export More Beef and Oranges to Japan Under New Farm-Trade Pact," *The Wall Street Journal,* December 6, 1978.

34. Interview by Michael R. Reich, February 4, 1983.

35. *Yomiuri Shimbun,* April 1, 1982.

36. Keizai Dantai Rengōkai (Federation of Economic Organizations) *Waga Kuni Nōgyō—Nōsei no Kongo no Arikata* (Future Course of Japan's Agricultural Policy) (Tokyo: Keidanren, 1982).

37. Office of the United States Trade Representative, "Implementation of the May 28 Package," memorandum, n.d.

38. Urban C. Lehner, "U.S. and Japan at an Impasse Over Trade Bars," *The Wall Street Journal,* November 3, 1982.

39. Hiroya Sano, "Nōsanbutsu no Shijō Kaihō Mondai ni Tsuite" (On the Problem of Opening the Market for Agricultural Products), *Konnichi no Wadai* (Today's Topics), MAFF, January 1983.

40. *Nihon Keizai Shimbun,* April 9, 1984.

41. For a brief description of Japan's system of agricultural cooperatives and political influence, see Fukui, "The Japanese Farmer and Politics," pp. 153–162; see also Takashi Tachibana, *Nōkyō: Kyodai na Chōsen* (Nokyo: A Colossal Challenge) (Tokyo: Asahi Shimbunsha, 1980); and Aurelia George, "The Strategies of Influence: Japan's Agricultural Cooperatives as a Pressure Group" (Ph.D. diss., Australian National University, 1980).

42. Yujiro Hayami, "Roots of Agricultural Protection," in Anderson and Hayami, *Political Economy of Agricultural Protection.*

43. Keizai Dantai Rengōkai, *Waga Kuni Nōgyō—Nōsei no Kongo no Arikata;* Keizai Dantai Rengōkai, "Kokusaiteki ni Hirakareta Keizai Shakai ni Okeru Shokuhin Kōgyō Seisaku no Arikata" (Policy Directions for the Food Industry in an Internationalized Economic Society) Tokyo, September 1983.

44. Seisaku Kōsō Fōramu (Forum of Policy Innovation), "Gyūniku Yunyū Jiyūka An" (Proposal for Liberalization of Beef Imports) Tokyo, April 1978; Seisaku Kōsō Fōramu (Forum of Policy Innovation), "Kokusai Hikaku Kara Mita Nippon Nōgyō no Hogo Suijun" (An International Comparative Perspective on the Level of Japanese Agricultural Protection) Tokyo, November 1983.

45. Kokumin Keizai Kenkyūkai (Research Institute of National Economy) *Nōgyō Jiritsu Senryaku no Kenkyū* (A Study on the Strategy for Independence of Japanese Agriculture) (Tokyo: National Institute for Research Advancement, 1981).

46. Nippon Shohisha Renmei (Consumers Union of Japan), "Nōsanbutsu no Yunyū Jiyūka ni Hantai Shi, Nippon Nōgyō no Saisei no Mezasu Tokubetsu Ketsugi" (Special Resolution to Oppose Agricultural Trade Liberalization and Rebuild Japanese Agriculture) Tokyo, June 5, 1982; and Nippon Seikatsu Kyōdō Kumiai Rengōkai (Japanese Consumers' Co-operative Union), "Nōsuisanbutsu no Jiyūka ni Kanren Suru Watakushi-tachi no Kenkai to Mōshiire" (Our Opinions and Recommendations on the Liberalization of Agricultural and Marine Products) Tokyo, May 14, 1982.

47. *Sankei Shimbun,* January 13, 1983.

48. Laurellen Porter, "Congress and Agricultural Policy, 1977," in Don F. Hadwiger and William P. Browne, eds., *The New Politics of Food* (Lexington, Mass.: Lexington Books, 1978), pp. 15–22.

49. Don Paarlberg, "The New U.S. Farm Policies," *Food Policy* 2 (1977), p. 180.

50. Ibid., p. 179.

51. Hemmi, "Agriculture and Politics in Japan." See also Michael W. Donnelly, "Setting the Price of Rice: A Study in Political Decisionmaking," in T. J. Pempel, ed., *Policymaking in Contemporary Japan* (Ithaca: Cornell University Press, 1977), pp. 143–200.

52. Walter Dean Burnham, "Party Systems and the Political Process," in William Nesbit Chambers and Walter Dean Burnham, eds., *The American Party System: Stages of Political Development* (New York: Oxford University Press, 1967), pp. 238–276.

53. James P. Houck, "Agricultural Trade: Protectionism, Policy, and the Tokyo/Geneva Negotiating Round," *American Journal of Agricultural Economics* 61 (December 1979), p. 863.

CHAPTER SIX

1. Energy statistics throughout this chapter, if not otherwise referenced, will be drawn from the following sources: OECD, *Energy Balances for OECD Countries, 1971–1981;* United Nations, *Energy Statistics Yearbook, 1982;* DeGolyer and MacNaughton, *Twentieth Century Petroleum Statistics, 1979;* The Japanese National Committee of the World Petroleum Congress, *The Petroleum Industry in Japan, 1972–1983;* American Petroleum Institute, *Basic Petroleum Databook;* Agency of Natural Resources and Energy, Ministry of International Trade and Industry, *Energy in Japan: Facts and Figures* (Tokyo: MITI, 1984).

2. Robert G. Burke, "Japanese Oil Policy, 1945–1974: The Influence of the Ministry of International Trade and Industry on the Structure and Development of the Japanese Oil Industry" (Ph.D. diss., Fletcher School of Law and Diplomacy, 1979), pp. 46, 203; Richard J. Samuels, "MITI and the Market: The Japanese Oil Industry in Transition" (MIT Energy Laboratory, working paper E1 84-016), p. 41.

3. Chalmers Johnson, *MITI and the Japanese Miracle: The Growth of Industrial Policy, 1925–1975* (Stanford: Stanford University Press, 1982), p. 126; Richard J. Samuels, "Public Energy Corporations and Public Policy in Japan," MIT Energy Laboratory, working paper MIT-E1 82-044WP.

4. Roger W. Gale, "Tokyo Electric Power Company: Its Role in Shaping Japan's Coal and LNG Policy," in Ronald A. Morse, ed., *The Politics of Japan's Energy Strategy* (Berkeley: Institute of East Asian Studies, 1981), pp. 85–105; Martha Caldwell, "Petroleum Politics in Japan: State and Industry in a Changing Policy Context" (Ph.D. diss., Political Science, University of Wisconsin, 1981).

5. Richard H. K. Vietor, *Energy Policy in America Since 1945* (New York: Cambridge University Press, 1984), chapters 5 and 12; U.S. Federal Trade Commission, *Concentration Levels and Trends in the Energy Sector of the U.S. Economy* (Staff Report, March 1974) p. 60; U.S. Department of Energy, *Statistics of Interstate Natural Gas Companies—1979* (Washington, October 1980).

6. Richard H. K. Vietor, *Environmental Politics and the Coal Coalition* (College Station: Texas A&M University Press, 1980).

7. Johnson, *MITI and Japanese Miracle,* pp. 120–122, 126, 168, 192, 296; for recent details of MITI's organization, see Tsūshō Sangyōshō, *Shigen Enerugī Seisaku no Jūten Jikō* (Important Items in Resource Energy Policies) (Tokyo: Tsūshō Sangyōshō, February 1983).

8. J. Cordell Moore, "Observations and Remarks on United States Energy Policy," presented to the Energy Committee of the Organization for Economic Cooperation and Development, January 26, 1967, in Office of Oil and Gas Files, 1967 (Department of the Interior, Washington, D.C.), p. 4.

9. *Public Law 95-91,* August 4, 1977. In 1980, Congress created the Synthetic Fuels Corporation, to finance and promote commercial development of oil shale, coal liquefaction and gasification, and biomass conversion.

10. There were exceptions, of course; Idemitsu Kosan usually took exception to MITI policies, and thus refused for one year to join the Petroleum Association. A few of the other companies, such as Toa Nenryo, also avoided participation in the Association's market-stabilization efforts.

11. Richard H. K. Vietor, *Energy Policy in America,* pp. 104, 155, 160, 308–309.

12. U.S. Congress, Senate, Committee on Government Operations, Subcommittee on Reports, Accounting, and Management, *To Amend the Federal Advisory Committee Act* (94th Cong., 2nd Sess.), March 1976, and *Energy Advisers: An Analysis of Federal Advisory Committees Dealing with Energy* (95th Cong., 1st Sess.), Committee Print, March 1977; Richard H. K. Vietor, "NIPCC: The Advisory Council Approach," *Journal of Contemporary Business,* 8 (1979), pp. 57–70.

13. Kanji Haitani, *Japanese Economic System* (Lexington, Mass.: D. C. Heath, 1976), pp. 68–75.

14. Kasei Oki, "Sekiyu Seisaku no 30 Nen o Kaiko Suru" (Reminiscences of 30 Years of Petroleum Policy), *Sekiyu Seisaku,* July, 1977, pp. 20–22; Martha Caldwell, "Petroleum Politics in Japan," pp. 94–96, 102–104; *Oil and Gas Journal,* May 31, 1965, pp. 61–62; and Japan Petroleum Consultants, *Japan Petroleum & Energy Yearbook, 1975,* II, p. J-3.

15. National Petroleum Council, "The NPC: A Unique Experience in Government-Industry Cooperation, The First Seven Years" (Washington, D.C.: NPC, 1961); Vietor, *Energy Policy in America,* pp. 37–42, 314–317.

16. Mark S. Brown, "The Emergence of Japanese Interests in the World Oil Market," USJP Occasional Paper, No. 83-01, pp. 17–32; Martha Caldwell, "Petroleum Politics in Japan," pp. 68–80. The outcome of this policy debate also led the oil refiners to organize the Petroleum Association of Japan, as a political counterforce to user groups.

17. Fred Shields, president, IPAA, "Remarks Before the Mid-Year Meeting of the West Central Texas Oil and Gas Association," Cisco, Texas, June 29, 1949, p. 3.

18. National Coal Association, *Coal Facts, 1978–79* (Washington, D.C.: National Coal Association, 1979).

19. Richard H. K. Vietor, *Energy Policy in America,* pp. 99–103.

20. Presidential Proclamation 3279, "Adjusting Imports of Petroleum and Petroleum Products into the United States," 24 *Federal Register* 1781–84, March 12, 1959.

21. "Testimony of Gulf Oil Corporation," Import Hearings, Department of the Interior, Washington, D.C., May 10–11, 1961 (Gulf Oil Corp., Pittsburgh, Pa.), p. 3.

22. Lawrence Olson, "Japan's Search for an Oil Policy," *East Asia Series,* 10 (1962), pp. 8–10. Also involved in this process was Yasuhiro Nakasone, then chairman of the Overall Energy Countermeasures Diet Members' Council, who had advocated establishment of an Energy Ministry; Martha Caldwell, "Petroleum Politics in Japan," pp. 96–97.

23. Japan Petroleum Consultants, *Japan Petroleum & Energy Yearbook, 1975,* pp. A-13–16.

24. Brown, "The Emergence of Japanese Interests in the World Oil Market," pp. 61–62.

25. Quoted in Caldwell, "Petroleum Politics in Japan," pp. 106, 122.

26. Fred Hartley, president of Union Oil, and DeVier Pierson, special assistant to the president, are both quoted in Richard H. K. Vietor, *Energy Policy in America,* Chapter 6.

27. Caldwell, "Petroleum Politics in Japan," pp. 288–294, 304–305.

28. Nomura Sōgō Kenkyūjo, *Enerugī Kiki Kanri no Taikeiteki Bunseki* (Systematic Analysis of Energy Crisis Management), commissioned by the National Institute for Research Advancement (Tokyo: NIRA, 1979), pp. 130–131.

29. Malcolm D. H. Smith, "Prices and Petroleum in Japan: 1973–1974—A Study of Administrative Guidance," *Law in Japan* 10 (1977), pp. 81–100. The term "cooperative action" (which meant cartels) was eventually stricken from the draft legislation. It was replaced by an inter-ministerial memorandum that designated certain cooperative actions, under MITI's guidance, as exempt from the Anti-Monopoly Act during an emergency.

30. Quoted in Japan Petroleum Consultants, *Japan Petroleum & Energy Yearbook, 1975,* II, pp. 1–45.

31. Law No. 122 of 1973, "Petroleum Supply and Demand Normalization Law," translated by Japan Petroleum Consultants, *Japan Petroleum & Energy Yearbook, 1975,* II, pp. A25–A30; Johnson, *MITI and the Japanese Miracle,* pp. 296–297.

32. Together, thirteen large oil companies recorded a loss of ¥52 billion for fiscal year 1974. See the Japanese National Committee of the World Petroleum Congress, *The Petroleum Industry in Japan, 1974,* pp. 15–16. The price of kerosene, for example, was increased by 56 percent, while gasoline went up 114 percent. Similarly, residential electric rates were raised 29 percent; industrial rates, 74 percent. See Japan Petroleum Consultants, "Chronology of the Japanese Oil Industry," in *Japan Petroleum & Energy Yearbook, 1975,* II, pp. K10–K12.

33. J. Mark Ramseyer, "The Oil Cartel Criminal Cases: Translations and Postscript," *Law in Japan* 15 (1982), pp. 57–78. The coordinating activities of the PAJ are remarkably reminiscent of the activities of the American Petroleum Institute's Planning and Coordination Committee, operating under the auspices of the National Recovery Administration during the 1930s. In both instances, antitrust authorities eventually prosecuted the private participants, despite their defense that they had operated with the government's approval; *United States vs. Standard Oil Company of Indiana et al.,* January 21, 1938, No. 11,365 in the Western District of Wisconsin, and *Kuni v. Sekiyu Renmei et al., Hanrei Jihō* (No. 983) 22, September 26, 1980.

34. Lawrence Repeta, "The Limits of Administrative Authority in Japan: The Oil Cartel Criminal Cases and the Reaction of MITI and the FTC," *Law in Japan* 15 (1982), pp. 37–38, 46–53; interviews with the author at various oil companies, Tokyo, 1984.

35. Charles R. Owens, "History of Petroleum Price Controls," in Office of Economic Stabilization, U.S. Department of the Treasury, *Historical Working Papers on Economic Stabilization Program, August 15, 1971 to April 30, 1974* (Washington, D.C.: Government Printing Office, 1975), pp. 1223–1340.

36. "Address to the Nation About Policies to Deal with the Energy Shortages, November 7, 1973," in *Public Papers of the Presidents: Richard Nixon, 1973,* pp. 916–922; *Public Law 93-159* (November 27, 1973) Sec. 4(b)(1); see also, Federal Trade Commission, Staff Report, "Evaluation of the Emergency Petroleum Allocation Program; Summary of Findings, Conclusions, and Issues," March 15, 1974.

37. H. Jackson to L. Engman, May 31, 1973, quoted in *Federal Trade Commission vs. Standard Oil Company of California,* U.S. Court of Appeals, Ninth Circuit, "Brief for the Respondents," October 1979, p. 4. The eight companies were Exxon, Mobil, Standard Oil of California, Texaco, Gulf, Shell, Standard Oil of Indiana, and Atlantic Richfield. See "Preliminary Federal Trade Commission Staff Report on Its Investigation of the Petroleum Industry," in U.S. Congress, House, Permanent Select Committee on Small Business, *Energy Crisis and Small Business* (93rd Cong., 1st Sess.), July 1973, Committee Print.

38. *In the Matter of Exxon Corporation et al.,* FTC Docket No. 8934, "Complaint Counsel's First Statement of Issues, Factual Contentions and Proof," October 31, 1980.

39. U.S. Congress, House, Permanent Select Committee on Small Business, Subcommittee on Activities of Regulatory Agencies, *Energy Data Requirements of the Federal Government* (93rd Cong., 2nd Sess.), January–May 1974, pt. 1, pp. 3–4.

40. U.S. Congress, Senate, Committee on Government Operations, Permanent Subcommittee on Investigations, *Current Energy Shortages Oversight Series: The Major Oil Companies* (93rd Cong., 2nd Sess.), January 1974, pt. 2, pp. 113–114.

41. William A. Johnson, "Why U.S. Energy Policy Has Failed," in Robert J. Kalter and William Vogely, *Energy Supply and Government Policy* (Ithaca: Cornell University Press, 1976), pp. 280–305.

42. "Recommendations of the Overall Energy Council," December 6, 1971, in Japan Petroleum Consultants, *Japan Petroleum & Energy Yearbook,* 1975, II, pp. C2, C4, C14–C15.

43. "Basic Direction of General Energy Policy," A Decision of the Ministerial Council on General Energy Policy, December 19, 1975, in Ministry of International Trade and Industry, *Japan's New Energy Policy* (Tokyo: MITI, 1976), p. 87.

44. "Recommendations of the Overall Energy Council," July 25, 1974, translated in Japan Petroleum Consultants, *Japan Petroleum & Energy Yearbook, 1975,* II, p. C-23.

45. Interviews with the author in Tokyo, 1984; MITI, "Special Account Budgets Relating to Energy, Fiscal 1984"; and the Japanese National Committee of the World Petroleum Congresses, *The Petroleum Industry in Japan, 1975* and *1983,* pp. 31 and 23–24 respectively.

46. Richard Nixon, "Presidential Energy Message to Congress, April 18, 1973," Commerce Clearing House, Inc., *Basic Energy Documents* (Washington, D.C.: CCH, 1973), pp. 504–517; in 1970, the Secretary of the Interior had asked the Council to forecast likely supply and demand balances for each fuel through 1985, with a continuation of present policies and likely scenarios given constructive changes in policy. See National Petroleum Council, *U.S. Energy Outlook: A Summary Report* (Washington, D.C.: NPC, 1972).

47. Gerald Ford, "The President's 1975 State of the Union Message Including Economy and Energy," January 15, 1975, in U.S. Congress, Senate, Committee on Interior and Insular Affairs, *Economic Impact of President Ford's Energy Program* (94th Cong., 1st Sess.), January–February 1975.

48. U.S. Congress, House, Committee on Interstate and Foreign Commerce, Subcommittee on Energy and Power, *Hearings on the Presidential Energy Program* (94th Cong., 1st Sess.), February 1975, pp. 578–582.

49. Executive Office of the President, *The National Energy Plan* (Washington, D.C.: Government Printing Office, 1977), and "Presidential Energy Address, April 18, 1977," Commerce Clearing House, Inc., *Energy Management, 1977,* pp. 739–743.

50. James Schlesinger, interviews with the author, January–February, 1982.

51. Ikuo Umebayashi, "Electric Power," *Industrial Review of Japan,* 1983, pp. 94–95; Neil W. Davis, "Nuclear Power Generation in Japan," *The Oriental Economist,* October 1983, pp. 30–35; James Cook, "Nuclear Follies," *Forbes,* February 11, 1985, pp. 82–100.

52. Hiroshi Anzai, *Toshi Gasu Jigyō ni okeru LNG Kōgyō Ron* (City Gas Business and the LNG Industry) (Tokyo: Tokyo Gas Company, 1982); also, Yasunobu Misato, *Dokyumento Mitsubishi Shōji Nenryō Honbu* (Document: Mitsubishi Trading Company Fuels Headquarters) (Tokyo: Nihon Keizai Shimbunsha, 1981), Chapter 4; also, Shigen Enerugīchō Sekiyubu, *Sekiyu Sangyō no Genjō* (Conditions in the Petroleum Industry)

(Tokyo: Sekiyu Tsūshinsha, 1980). This tax, then equivalent to ¥640 per barrel of oil, was reinstated by MITI in 1984 under pressure from petroleum refiners.

53. Anzai, *Toshi Gasu Jigyō ni okeru LNG Kōgyō Ron,* pp. 153–157.

54. Ministry of International Trade and Industry, *Energy Problems in Japan: A White Paper,* (in Japanese) translation in Japan Petroleum Consultants, *Petroleum and Energy Yearbook, 1975,* II, pp. B26–27.

55. Overall Energy Council, "Recommendations of the Coordination Committee, 1974," translation in Japan Petroleum Consultants, *Japan Petroleum & Energy Yearbook, 1975,* II, pp. C28–C43; Hiroshi Anzai, "LNG to Toshi Gasu Jigyō" (LNG and the City Gas Business), *Doryoku* 134 (1975), pp. 40–44; Ministry of International Trade and Industry, "Basic Direction of General Energy Policy," December 19, 1975, in MITI, *Japan's New Energy Policy* (Tokyo: MITI, 1976), p. 71.

56. Tetsuo Iizuka, executive director, Japan National Oil Corporation, "Financing of LNG Plants," World LNG Conference, Kyoto, April 1980. Also, the Japan Development Bank, *Annual Report, 1984,* pp. 6, 9; Shigen Enerugīcho Sekiyubu, *Sekiyu Sangyō no Genjō,* pp. 287–288; also, interviews with the author at Shell Sekiyu, Tokyo Electric, and Tokyo Gas, September 1984.

57. Just after the first oil shock, LNG had a significant price advantage over oil, because of fixed-price contracts for Alaska and Brunei. After 1975, the Brunei contract was renegotiated with an oil-base price escalator; all of the newer projects required similar terms. Thus, as the Alaskan LNG became a relatively small percent of total LNG imports, delivered price moved to parity with oil.

58. Richard H. K. Vietor, *Energy Policy in America,* chapter 7.

59. Christopher Gibbs and Richard H. K. Vietor, *El Paso LNG (A),* No. 1-382-043 (Boston: Harvard Business School, 1982); Federal Power Commission, *Opinion No. 786,* January 21, 1977; Energy Regulatory Administration, *Opinion and Order No. 11,* December 1979.

60. James Schlesinger, "Gas Prospects and Policy," remarks before the National Association of Petroleum Investment Analysts, New York, January 9, 1979; also, interview with the author, December 1979.

61. Christopher Gibbs and Richard H. K. Vietor, *El Paso LNG (B),* No. 1-382-050 (Boston: Harvard Business School, 1982).

62. The refining sector managed to earn net profits of $1.2 billion in 1980. Only in the summer of 1980, when exchange rate gains favored refiners, did MITI apply administrative guidance to stabilize prices. Fiscal 1981 saw losses of $1.2 billion; the ratio of net worth to total capital declined from 11 percent in 1973 to 3.3 percent in the first half of 1981. See the Japanese National Committee of the World Petroleum Congresses, *Petroleum Industry in Japan, 1980,* pp. 31, 35; Natural Resources and Energy Agency, Ministry of International Trade and Industry, *Energy in Japan—Facts and Figures;* also, Japanese National Committee of the World Petroleum Congresses, *Petroleum Industry in Japan, 1983,* p. 14.

63. The "Black Cartel" cases, initiated by the FTC in 1974, were finally decided by the Supreme Court in 1980. In the allocation case, officials of the trade association were found not guilty. In the price case, however, the oil company executives were convicted, fined, and given suspended prison sentences. See *Yomiuri Shimbun,* September 27, 1980.

64. Interviews with the author in Tokyo, 1984; also, Petroleum Department, Agency of Natural Resources and Energy, Ministry of International Trade and Industry, "The Petroleum Report—The Recent Petroleum Situation and Japan's Petroleum Policies," November 1982, pp. 12–13, 25–26.

65. "Gyōkai Kōzō Kaizen Rongi no Rekishiteki Keifu" (Historical Thoughts on the Debates for Improvement of the Structure of the Oil Industry), in *Sekiyu*, July 10, 1983.

66. Interviews with the author in Tokyo, 1984; also, Norio Tanaka, "Survival Strategy for Japanese Petroleum Industry," *Energy in Japan* 8 (March 1984), pp. 34–39, and Neil Davis, "Consolidation in Japan's Petroleum Industry?" *The Oriental Economist,* (February 1984), pp. 24–26.

67. For a good overview of LNG developments in Japan, see Tadahiko Ohashi (Tokyo Gas Co.), "New Orbit of LNG Demand in Japan," a paper presented at the World LNG Conference, Jakarta, May 1983; and Ohashi, "An Analysis of the Future of Natural Gas in Japan," February, 1985.

68. Ministry of International Trade and Industry, "Summary Report of Japan's Long-Term Energy Supply and Demand Outlook and Future Energy Policy," September 26, 1983, p. 3.

69. Chalmers Johnson makes this distinction in the conceptual framework of his book. Japan, as a developmental state, according to Johnson, is "plan rational," while the United States, as a regulatory state, is "market rational." Comparison of energy policies, however, would suggest an underlying "market rationality" to both systems of management, at least over the long run; see *MITI and the Japanese Miracle*, pp. 18–23.

CHAPTER SEVEN

1. The discussion of how the United States and Japan responded to the problem of vinyl chloride is derived from Joseph L. Badaracco, Jr., *Loading the Dice: A Five-Country Study of Vinyl Chloride Regulation* (Boston, Mass.: Harvard Business School Press, 1985). The figures cited in the account below are from that source.

2. See for example, Ezra F. Vogel, *Japan As Number One* (Cambridge, Mass.: Harvard University Press, 1979); Ezra F. Vogel, ed., *Modern Japanese Organization and Decision-Making* (Berkeley and Los Angeles: University of California Press, 1975); Haruhiro Fukui, "Studies in Policymaking: A Review of the Literature" in T. J. Pempel, ed., *Policymaking in Contemporary Japan* (Ithaca: Cornell University Press, 1977), pp. 22–59; John Creighton Campbell, "Japanese Budget *Baransu*" in Vogel, ed., *Modern Japanese Organization,* pp. 71–100.

3. Michio Hashimoto, "Development of Environmental Policy and Its Institutional Mechanisms of Administration and Finance." Paper presented at the International Workshop on Environmental Management for Local and Regional Development, Nagoya, Japan, June 9–13, 1985, p. 2.

4. Major sources on Minamata disease outbreaks in Japan upon which this account is based include Norie Huddle and Michael Reich with Nahum Stiskin, *Island of Dreams: Environmental Crisis in Japan* (New York: Autumn Press, 1975); Julian Gresser, Kōichirō Fujikura, and Akio Morishima, *Environmental Law in Japan* (Cambridge, Mass.: The MIT Press, 1981); Masazumi Harada, *Minamatabyō* (Minamata Disease) (Tokyo: Iwanami Shoten, 1972); Masazumi Harada, *Minamatabyō wa Owatte Inai* (The Minamata Disease Problem Has Not Been Solved Yet) (Tokyo: Iwanami Shoten, 1985); Asahi Jānaru Henshūbu, "Tokushū—Kiten to Shite no Minamatabyō" (Special Feature—The Minamata Disease as a Starting Point of Struggle), *Asahi Jānaru,* April 6, 1973, pp. 4–16; Bungei Shunjū Henshūbu, "Kōgai Gyōsei 15-nen o Kokuhatsu Suru" (Bringing an Indictment Against 15 Years of Government Policy for Pollution Control) *Bungei Shunjū,* Oct. 1970, pp. 94–108. A perspective from the vantage point of one of Japan's leading environmental activists is found in Jun Ui, *Kōgai no Seijigaku: Minamatabyō o Otte* (Politics of Pollution: A Study of the Minamata Disease Problem) (Tokyo: Sanseidō, 1968). The position of the company later held responsible for the outbreaks in Minamata is found in Chisso Kabushiki Kaisha Minamatabyō Mondai no 15-

nen Henshū Iinkai, ed., *Minamatabyō Mondai no 15-nen: Sono Jitsusō o Otte* (15 Years of the Minamata Disease Problem: In Pursuit of the Truth) (Tokyo: Chisso Kabushiki Kaisha, 1970).

5. Japan, Environment Agency, *Quality of the Environment in Japan 1984* (Tokyo: Environment Agency, 1985), p. 265.

6. Huddle and Reich, *Island of Dreams,* p. 107.

7. Chisso Kabushiki Kaisha Iinkai, ed., *Minamatabyō Mondai,* p. 111.

8. Kiotsu Shioguchi, " 'Kigyō wa Eizoku' no Ronri" (The Logic of "The Company Forever"), *Asahi Jānaru,* March 23, 1973, pp. 91–97; Ui, *Kōgai no Seijigaku,* pp. 86–88.

9. Harada, *Minamatabyō,* pp. 68–69.

10. *Yomiuri Shimbun,* September 27, 1968, p. 1.

11. Hashimoto, "Development of Environmental Policy," p. 10.

12. Chisso Kabushiki Kaisha Iinkai, *Minamatabyō Mondai,* pp. 320–330.

13. Interview with Michio Hashimoto, Tokyo, September 18, 1985.

14. Hashimoto, "Development of Environmental Policy," p. 10.

15. Ellis S. Krauss and Bradford L. Simcock, "Citizens' Movements: The Growth and Impact of Environmental Protest in Japan," in Kurt Steiner, Ellis S. Krauss, and Scott C. Flanagan, eds., *Political Opposition and Local Politics in Japan* (Princeton, N.J.: Princeton University Press, 1980), p. 187.

16. A number of scholars argue that the Japanese media play this role to the point that they have become the functional equivalent of a strong opposition, and thus fill a major void in Japan—a country where the opposition parties, singly or collectively, are quite weak. See Yukio Matsuyama, "Japanese Press and Japan's Foreign Policy," *Journal of International Affairs* 26 (1972).

17. In Minamata, for example, victims to this day are treated with relatively little sympathy by the community. The anger and shame community residents feel at having their town at the center of a controversy is reflected in their recent efforts, which have come to naught, to change the name of Minamata disease to remove the city's connection with it. Interviews with doctors and public officials in Minamata City, October 11, 1985.

18. *Asahi Nenkan, 1971,* p. 231.

19. See Michael Blaker, *Japanese International Negotiating Style* (New York: Columbia University Press, 1977).

20. Naoki Kuroda, "Japan's Auto Industry," *Journal of Japanese Trade and Industry* 4 (November/December 1985), p. 11.

21. Frank P. Grad et al., *The Automobile* (Norman, Oklahoma: University of Oklahoma Press, 1975), p. 334.

22. Interview with Buichi Oishi, Tokyo, October 4, 1985. His term as head of the Environment Agency is discussed in his book, *Oze Made no Michi: Midori to Gunshuku o Motomete* (A Road Toward Oze: In Pursuit of Green and Arms Reduction) (Tokyo: Sankei Shuppan, 1982).

23. Ibid.

24. *The New York Times,* November 10, 1973, p. 14.

25. Robert Cameron Mitchell, "Public Opinion and Environmental Politics in the 1970s and 1980s" in Norman J. Vig and Michael E. Kraft, eds., *Environmental Policy in the 1980s: Reagan's New Agenda* (Washington, D.C.: CQ Press, 1984), p. 55.

26. Enormous difficulties are involved in definitively designating victims of moderate forms of Minamata disease, especially in the case of older patients. The latter may have

infirmities from other causes that resemble those traceable to Minamata disease. Thus, recent court decisions in favor of those who came forward, long after Chisso had stopped discharging mercury, to claim victim status, have been the subject of much controversy. See, for example, Itsuo Saruta, "Sunao ni Yorokobenu Minamatabyō Niji Soshō no Genkoku Shōso" (Plaintiffs' Court Victory in the Second Minamata Disease Case Cannot Be Taken Simply), *Asahi Jānaru*, April 13, 1979, pp. 117–119.

27. Said one former MITI bureaucrat in an interview, "Japanese blame themselves at least 30 percent in such situations, but we can't help but feel a little tricked [by the United States]. It was a case of being naive. We assumed that the Muskie Law, coming out of such a technologically advanced country, would have much data and evidence to back it up. But we found that that was not so. Since then, we've been much more careful about blindly following the United States. We also see the irony, of course. Out of our naive mistake came the superiority of the Japanese auto industry."

28. *Asahi Nenkan, 1977*, pp. 549–550.

29. The debate over the NOx standard culminated in late 1974 and 1975. In that case, business was successful in winning a two-year extension on enforcement from the Environment Agency's advisory council. The larger makers hoped for a further relaxation of the NOx standard after the extension to 1978 was granted, but their position was undermined when four of the smaller companies—Mitsubishi, Tōyō Kogyō (Mazda), Honda, and Fuji Heavy Industries (Subaru)—announced that they could meet the NOx standard on schedule. The relationship between government and the auto industry thus moved into a more or less cooperative mode in the post-1974 period, in which government—led by a key advisory council—agreed to the extension, and then the auto industry, for its part, gradually lined up behind the goal of meeting the standard. In the stormy era, in contrast, such give-and-take was lacking; government, in the case of the HC and CO standards, forced the industry into compliance over the latter's objections. See Shigeru Hongō, *Dokyumento 0.25: Nipponban Masukīhō wa Seikō Shita ka* (Document 0.25 [NOx standard]: Has the "Japanese Muskie Law" Succeeded?) (Tokyo: Nippon Kankyō Kyōkai, 1978).

30. See Badaracco, *Loading the Dice.*

31. Environment Agency, *Quality of the Environment in Japan, 1984,* p. 7.

32. Environment Agency, *Quality of the Environment in Japan, 1984,* pp. 7–8 and 178–179. Air pollution from particulates is primarily due to the use of coal as a fuel. Smaller particles of ten microns or less in diameter suspended in the air have an especially deleterious effect on human health. Since the oil crises in the 1970s, use of coal has increased in Japan.

33. In 1973, the number of days for which alerts were issued reached an all-time high of 328, and thereafter diminished; but between 1982 and 1983, the number rose from 73 to 131. Ibid., p. 7.

34. Although there is no comprehensive legal requirement for assessment, numerous ministries and agencies and a number of local governments have incorporated assessment procedures into planning and implementing government projects. But proponents of the ill-fated bill continue to see the legal requirement as essential for protecting the public interest and securing the public's right to be heard. See Frank K. Upham, "Pollution Problems and Response," in Bradley M. Richardson and Taizo Ueda, eds., *Business and Society in Japan: Fundamentals for Businessmen* (New York: Praeger, 1981), p. 193; Hideo Ōtake et al., "Kankyō Gyōsei ni Miru Gendai Nippon Seiji no Kenkyū" (Modern Japanese Politics as Illuminated in the Politics of Environmental Pollution Control), *Chūō Kōron,* September 1982, pp. 82–112; and Michio Hashimoto, "Development of Environmental Policy."

35. Environment Agency, *Quality of the Environment in Japan,* 1984, pp. 14–15, for an assessment of current environmental issues and problems confronting Japan.

36. Interviews with experts in and outside government on this issue, Tokyo, October 1985. Numerous experts point out that much of the problem is due to cargo vehicle emissions, which have been regulated less stringently and expeditiously than passenger cars, due to industry opposition.

37. See for example, Upham, "Pollution Problems and Responses;" Gresser, Fumi-kura, and Morishima, *Environmental Law in Japan;* and Takahiko Furuta and Keiko Takahashi, "Wagakuni no Jōyōsha Haishutsugasu Kisei ni okeru Seisaku Kettei Katei no Bunseki" (An Analysis of the Decision-making Process over Automobile Emission Standards in Japan), unpublished paper, February 1982.

38. Walter A. Rosenbaum, *Environmental Politics and Policy* (Washington, D.C.: CQ Press, 1985), p. 36.

39. Weak controls at the state level also characterized early air pollution control. Before 1962, only eleven states had passed any laws to regulate air pollution. Cynthia H. Enloe, *The Politics of Pollution in a Comparative Perspective* (New York: David McKay Company, 1975), p. 147.

40. Rosenbaum, *The Politics of Environmental Concern,* 2nd ed. (New York: Praeger, 1977), p. 5.

41. Christopher D. Stone, "A Slap on the Wrist for the Kepone Mob," *Business and Society Review* (Summer 1977), p. 5.

42. Ibid.

43. Goldfarb, "Health Hazards in the Environment," pp. 647–648.

44. Ibid., p. 648.

45. Tolling agreements, which are common in the chemical industry, provide that another company performs processing work for a fee, or "toll," and then returns the final product to the original company. During the processing, legal title to the materials typically remains with the supplier. William Goldfarb, "Health Hazards in the Environment: The Interface of Science and Law—Kepone, A Case Study," *Environmental Law* 8 (Spring 1978), p. 649.

46. Brian Kelly, "Allied Chemical Kept That Kepone Flowing," *Business and Society Review* (Spring 1977), p. 19.

47. For accounts of conditions in and outside the plant, see ibid.; S. Prakash Sethi, "Allied Chemical and the Kepone Controversy" (Working Paper Series of the Center for Research in Business and Social Policy), Richardson, Texas: University of Texas at Dallas, School of Management and Administration, 1980; Stone, "A Slap on the Wrist"; and Michael R. Reich and Jacquelin K. Spong, "Kepone: A Chemical Disaster in Hopewell, Virginia," *International Journal of Health Services* 13 (1983), pp. 227–246.

48. Sethi, "Allied Chemical and the Kepone Controversy," p. 24.

49. Goldfarb, "Health Hazards in the Environment," pp. 650–651.

50. *Washington Post,* January 6, 1980, p. C7.

51. Though acknowledging that a do-nothing policy was "fraught with danger," and that the Kepone could be stirred up by a tropical storm or other natural disaster, state officials were reluctant to attempt a clean-up operation, partly because of the projected cost of $2 billion and partly because of fear that the dredging process would stir up the Kepone. *Washington Post,* June 29, 1985, p. C1; also February 8, 1978, pp. C1 and C4.

52. See, for example, Jun Ui, "A Citizens' Forum: 15 Years Against Pollution," *Japan Quarterly* (July–September 1985), pp. 271–276.

53. See Susan J. Pharr, *Status Politics in Japan: Social Conflict, Authority and the State,* forthcoming, for further discussion of this phenomenon.

CHAPTER EIGHT

1. For accounts of the prewar Japanese financial system, see Raymond W. Goldsmith, *The Financial Development of Japan, 1869–1977* (New Haven: Yale University Press, 1983), Chs. 2–5; G. C. Allen, *A Short Economic History of Modern Japan*, 4th ed. (New York: St. Martin's Press, 1981), Ch. 3, Part 1.

2. Federation of Bankers Associations, *Banking System in Japan*, 9th ed. (Tokyo: The Federation, 1984), p. 1.

3. Ibid., p. 2.

4. T. F. M. Adams and Iwao Hoshii, *A Financial History of the New Japan* (Palo Alto, Calif.: Kodansha International, 1972), pp. 104–108.

5. Federation of Bankers Associations of Japan, *Banking System in Japan*, 6th ed. (Tokyo: The Federation, 1976), p. 4. On the development of "special banks" and other financial organizations, see L. S. Pressnell, ed., *Money and Banking in Japan* (London: Macmillan Press, 1973), pp. 13–22, 29–35. For the prewar financial relationships within the *zaibatsu*, see Allen, *A Short Economic History of Modern Japan*, Ch. 8.

6. For accounts of the postwar, traditional-phase Japanese financial system, see Adams and Hoshii, *A Financial History of the New Japan*; Pressnell, ed., *Money and Banking in Japan*; Hugh T. Patrick, *Monetary Policy and Central Banking in Japan* (Bombay: University of Bombay, 1962); Bank of Japan, Economic Research Department, *The Japanese Financial System* (Tokyo: Bank of Japan, 1972); Henry C. Wallich and Mable I. Wallich, "Banking and Finance," and Gardner Ackley and Hiromitsu Ishi, "Fiscal, Monetary and Related Policies," in Hugh Patrick and Henry Rosovsky, eds., *Asia's New Giant: How the Japanese Economy Works* (Washington, D.C.: Brookings Institution, 1976); and Wilbur F. Monroe, *Japan: Financial Markets and the World Economy* (New York: Praeger, 1973).

7. For a review of the principal fields in which different types of Japanese financial institutions operated until the mid-1970s, see Wallich and Wallich, "Banking and Finance," pp. 278–284; and Pressnell, ed., *Money and Banking in Japan*, pp. 142–143 ff. On the flow of funds during the postwar, traditional phase, see ibid., Ch. 8.

8. See, for example, Eisuke Sakakibara et al., *The Japanese Financial System in Comparative Perspective* (Washington, D.C.: Government Printing Office, 1982), p. 24 ff.; and Yoshio Suzuki, *Money and Banking in Contemporary Japan* (New Haven: Yale University Press, 1980), p. 56.

9. On the control and structure of Japanese interest rates, see, for example, Adams and Hoshii, *A Financial History of the New Japan*, pp. 131–146; and Suzuki, *Money and Banking in Contemporary Japan*, Ch. 3. "For example, for many years the short-term prime rate was determined by a cartel of the city-banks. Since 1969, that rate was always pegged at ¼ percent over the Bank of Japan's official discount rate." Stephen Bronte, *Japanese Finance: Markets and Institutions* (London: Euromoney Publications, 1982), p. 16.

10. Explanations of the 1947 law, also translated as the Temporary Money Rates Adjustment Law, may be found in Adams and Hoshii, *A Financial History of the New Japan*, p. 131 ff.; and Pressnell, ed., *Money and Banking in Japan*, p. 116 ff. The official discount rate and bank interest rates were first linked directly in May 1957. However, the discount rate and the various bank rates were "coordinated" during the previous decade. See Adams and Hoshii, *A Financial History of the New Japan*, pp. 131–132.

11. The following sources outline Japan's official financial institutions during the period: Adams and Hoshii, *A Financial History of the New Japan*, pp. 116–122; Pressnell, ed., *Money and Banking in Japan*, Ch. 22; and Bronte, *Japanese Finance*, Ch. 14.

12. Personal Savings are defined to include accounts at city and regional banks, *sōgo* banks, *shinkin* banks, credit cooperatives, agricultural cooperatives, fishery cooperatives, post offices, and labor credit associations. See Bank of Japan, Research and Statistics Department, *Economic Statistics Annual, 1983,* pp. 161, 162.

13. The number of city banks has remained at thirteen since 1973, though the total fluctuated somewhat in earlier postwar years. See Bank of Japan, Research and Statistics Department, *Economic Statistics Annual, 1983,* p. 55. In 1976, the total number of city bank offices was 2,618. See Federation of Bankers Associations of Japan, *Banking System in Japan,* 6th ed., p. 19, Table I.

14. The restrictions on funding for banks were significant. Not only were deposit rates regulated but market segmentation plagued them. For example, city banks were not allowed to issue long-term debentures, since this would encroach on the territory of the long-term credit institutions. Adams and Hoshii, *A Financial History of the New Japan,* p. 108.

15. Wallich and Wallich, "Banking and Finance," p. 284 ff.; Suzuki, *Money and Banking in Contemporary Japan,* Part I; Akira Koizumi, "The 'Overloan' Problem," *Hitotsubashi Journal of Commerce and Management* 2 (November 1962), pp. 53–65.

16. Financial intermediaries are set forth in Adams and Hoshii, *A Financial History of the New Japan,* pp. 91–122; and A. Prindl, *Japanese Finance: A Guide to Banking in Japan* (New York: John Wiley & Sons, 1981), pp. 21–28.

17. On the Bank's overall organization, see Bank of Japan, Economic Research Department, *The Bank of Japan: Its Organization and Monetary Policies* (Tokyo: Bank of Japan, 1971).

18. "Moral suasion" is the term used to describe the effects on bank behavior of signals given by the money authority that indicate displeasure with the current behavior of the financial institutions. The signals used in moral suasion do not rely on actual policy actions, but instead on the "persuasive" abilities of the authorities. *Madoguchi kisei* (window guidance) is the practice whereby the Bank of Japan seeks to ration credit through the amounts individual banks may lend to customers. On the subject of "window guidance" and "moral suasion," see Bronte, *Japanese Finance,* pp. 145–146; Bank of Japan, Economic Research Department, *The Bank of Japan,* pp. 17–19; Suzuki, *Money and Banking in Contemporary Japan,* pp. 166–181; and Patrick, *Monetary Policy,* pp. 161–166.

19. Bronte, *Japanese Finance,* p. 141; Prindl, *Japanese Finance,* pp. 9–17.

20. On the relationship of the city banks and the Bank of Japan, see Presnell, ed., *Money and Banking in Japan,* pp. 197–198.

21. City banks have at times exceeded the level of loans "suggested" by the Bank of Japan through *fukumi kashidashikin* (off-balance-sheet loans). However, it is usually suggested that the quantity of such loans has been small. See Suzuki, *Money and Banking in Contemporary Japan,* p. 178.

22. See, for example, Suzuki, *Money and Banking in Contemporary Japan,* p. 42 ff.

23. For a more detailed discussion of Japanese monetary policy tools, see Suzuki, *Money and Banking in Contemporary Japan,* Part III; and Ackley and Ishi, "Fiscal, Monetary and Related Policies," pp. 196–206.

24. For accounts of financial stabilization policies during the Occupation, see Adams and Hoshii, *A Financial History of the New Japan,* pp. 53–56; G. C. Allen, *Japan's Economic Recovery* (New York: Oxford University Press, 1958), Ch. 2.

25. Nomura Research Institute, *Evolution of the Japanese Financial System* (Tokyo: Nomura Research Institute, 1974), p. 2.

26. For a discussion of the objectives of Japanese monetary policy, see Suzuki, *Money and Banking in Contemporary Japan,* Ch. 13; Ackley and Ishi, "Fiscal, Monetary and Related Policies;" and Adams and Hoshii, *A Financial History of the New Japan,* pp. 303–338.

27. Using an interest rate policy to stimulate (targeted) investments, a simple Keynesian multiplier model can be used to explain (part of) the spectacular Japanese growth performance for the postwar period. On the argument that the low interest rate policy was designed to encourage investment, see, for example, Suzuki, *Money and Banking in Contemporary Japan,* p. 37; Goldsmith, *The Financial Development of Japan,* p. 155; Charles Piggott, "Financial Reform in Japan;" and The Federal Reserve Bank of San Francisco, *Economic Review* (Winter 1983), p. 26 ff.

28. See Wallich and Wallich, "Banking and Finance," pp. 256–264; and Ackley and Ishi, "Fiscal, Monetary and Related Policies," p. 213 ff. Also, Edward F. Denison and William K. Chung, "Economic Growth and its Sources," in Patrick and Rosovsky, eds., *Asia's New Giant,* pp. 116–119.

29. The financial deficit of the public sector amounted to less than 2 percent of gross national product during the period 1956–1973. See Goldsmith, *The Financial Development of Japan,* p. 188.

30. For accounts of the development of the U.S. financial system, see Albert Bolles, *The Financial History of the United States, 1774–1885* (New York: Appleton, 1883–6), 3 vols.; Herman E. Krooss, *Documentary History of Banking and Currency in the United States* (New York: Chelsea House, 1969), 4 vols.; Fritz Redlich, *The Molding of American Banking: Men and Ideas* (New York: Hafner, 1940), 2 vols.; Herman E. Krooss and Martin R. Blyn, *A History of Financial Intermediaries* (New York: Random House, 1971); Margaret G. Myers, *A Financial History of the United States* (New York: Columbia University Press, 1970); William J. Shultz and M. R. Caine, *Financial Development of the United States* (New York: Prentice-Hall, 1937); Benjamin Klebaner, *Commercial Banking in the United States: A History* (Hinsdale, Ill.: Dryden Press, 1974); and Paul Studenski and Herman E. Krooss, *Financial History of the United States* (New York: McGraw-Hill, 1963).

31. Bray Hammond, *Banks and Politics in America from the Revolution to the Civil War* (Princeton, N.J.: Princeton University Press, 1957); Shultz and Caine, *Financial Development of the United States,* Chs. 1–10. For a discussion of the First and Second Banks of the United States, see Shultz and Caine, pp. 146–152 and pp. 169–180.

32. The twelve district banks do issue federal notes and operate in the open market. Membership in the system is required for all the nationally chartered banks, while the state chartered banks can elect to join. Membership brings the obligation to adhere to reserve requirements and gives access to the discount window of the reserve banks. On the traditional view that state banks safeguard the U.S. banking system from highly centralized federal government control, see, for example, Thomas W. Thompson, *Checks and Balances: A Study of the Dual Banking System in America* (Washington, D.C.: National Association of Supervisors of State Banks, 1962), Ch. 6, especially p. 71.

33. On challenges to the banking system brought about by the Depression and subsequent reform measures, see: Milton Friedman and Anna J. Schwartz, *A Monetary History of the United States, 1867–1960* (Princeton, N.J.: Princeton University Press, 1963), Chs. 7–8; William J. Shultz, *Financial Development of the United States,* Chs. 27–29; and Peter Temin, *Did Monetary Forces Cause the Great Depression?* (New York: W. W. Norton, 1976).

34. Dale C. Bregenzer, "The Federal Deposit Insurance Fund: Is It Adequate?" (Stonier Thesis, New Brunswick, N.J., 1981), Ch. 3.

35. Bank failures averaged 1,139 per year between 1921 and 1933 and only 14 per year between 1934 and 1970. See Friedman and Schwartz, *A Monetary History of the United States,* Table 16, pp. 438–439.

36. Harry D. Hutchinson, *Money, Banking and the U.S. Economy,* 5th ed. (Englewood Cliffs, N.J.: Prentice-Hall, 1984), pp. 47, 80; and David S. Kidwell, *Financial Institutions, Markets and Money,* 2nd ed. (New York: Dryden Press, 1984), pp. 332–333.

37. For descriptions and analyses of the modern U.S. financial system, see Charles N. Henning et al., *Financial Markets and the Economy,* 4th ed. (Englewood Cliffs, N.J.: Prentice-Hall, 1984); James B. Ludtke, *The American Financial System* (Boston: Allyn & Bacon, 1967); Tim S. Campbell, *Financial Institutions, Markets and Economic Activity* (New York: McGraw-Hill, 1982); Kidwell, *Financial Institutions;* Herbert E. Dougall and Jack E. Gaumnitz, *Capital Markets and Institutions,* 4th ed. (Englewood Cliffs, N.J.: Prentice-Hall, 1980); Donald P. Jacobs et al., *Financial Institutions* (Homewood, Ill.: Richard D. Irwin, 1972).

38. See Jacobs et al., *Financial Institutions,* Ch. 11; Dorris E. Harless, *Nonbank Financial Institutions* (Richmond, Va.: Federal Reserve Bank of Richmond, 1975). For recent events, see Michael J. Moran, "Thrift Institutions in Recent Years," in *Federal Reserve Bulletin* 68 (December 1982), pp. 725–738.

39. For accounts of the creation and development of the Federal Reserve System, see Roger T. Johnson, *Historical Beginnings: The Federal Reserve* (Boston: Federal Reserve Bank of Boston, 1979); Federal Reserve Bank of Philadelphia, *Fifty Years of the Federal Reserve Act* (Philadelphia: Federal Reserve Bank of Philadelphia, 1964); Friedman and Schwartz, *A Monetary History of the United States;* Board of Governors of the Federal Reserve System, *The Federal Reserve System: Purposes and Functions* (Washington, D.C.: Federal Reserve Board, 1974); Federal Reserve Bank of New York, *Open Market Operations* (New York: Federal Reserve Bank of New York, 1963).

40. Membership in the FOMC goes to the seven governors of the Board and five presidents of the Federal Reserve Banks, with the New York president serving automatically and four other presidents rotating.

41. For a discussion of postwar regulation of the U.S. financial system see Board of Governors of the Federal Reserve System, *Federal Reserve System;* Thomas F. Huertas, "The Regulation of Financial Institutions: A Historical Perspective on Current Issues," and George J. Bentson, "The Regulation of Financial Services," in The American Assembly, *Financial Services: The Changing Institutions and Government Policy* (Englewood Cliffs, N.J.: Prentice-Hall, 1983), Chs. 1–2.

42. See, Bregenzer, *The Federal Deposit Insurance Fund,* Chs. 3–4.

43. See Scott Winningham and Donald G. Hagen, "Regulation Q: An Historical Perspective," Federal Reserve Bank of Kansas City, *Economic Review* (April 1980), pp. 3–17; Charles F. Haywood, *Regulation Q and Monetary Policy* (Chicago: Association of Reserve City Bankers, 1971).

44. On U.S. monetary policy tools, see Federal Reserve Bank of Boston, *Controlling Monetary Aggregates* (Boston: Federal Reserve Bank of Boston, 1969), and Federal Reserve Bank of Boston, *Controlling Monetary Aggregates II: The Implementation* (Boston: Federal Reserve Bank of Boston, 1973); Warren Smith, "The Instruments of General Monetary Control," *National Banking Review* (September 1963), pp. 47–76; Paul Horvitz, *Monetary Policy and the Financial System* (Englewood Cliffs, N.J.: Prentice-Hall, 1979), Chs. 20–22. For a general description of the development of U.S. monetary policy, see Friedman and Schwartz, *A Monetary History of the United States.*

45. On the objectives of postwar U.S. monetary policy, see Horvitz, *Monetary Policy and the Financial System,* Chs. 28–30; George L. Bach, *Making Monetary and Fiscal*

Policy (Washington, D.C.: Brookings Institution, 1971); William G. Dewald and Harry G. Johnson, "An Objective Analysis of the Objectives of American Monetary Policy, 1952–1961" in Deane Carson, ed., *Banking and Monetary Studies* (Homewood, Ill.: Richard D. Irwin, 1963); and Friedman and Schwartz, *A Monetary History of the United States.*

46. See Leonall C. Anderson et al., "Monetary and Fiscal Actions: A Test of Their Relative Importance in Economic Stabilization," Federal Reserve Bank of St. Louis, *Review* 49 (November 1968), pp. 11–24; James R. Barth, "The Costs of Slowing Inflation: Four Views," Federal Reserve Bank of Atlanta, *Economic Review* 67 (January 1982); Friedman and Schwartz, *A Monetary History of the United States;* and The American Assembly, *United States Monetary Policy* (New York: Praeger, 1964).

47. On postwar U.S. fiscal policy, see Herbert Stein, *The Fiscal Revolution in America* (Chicago: University of Chicago Press, 1969); Lester C. Thurow, ed., *American Fiscal Policy* (Englewood Cliffs, N.J.: Prentice-Hall, 1967); Joseph A. Pechman, *Federal Tax Policy,* 4th ed. (Washington, D.C.: Brookings Institution, 1983). See also the discussion of fiscal policy in Chapter 9 of this volume.

48. On industrial policy, see Ira C. Magaziner and Thomas M. Hout, *Japanese Industrial Policy* (Berkeley: Institute of International Studies, 1981); Chalmers Johnson, ed., *The Industrial Policy Debate* (San Francisco: ICS Press, 1984); U.S. Congress, Congressional Budget Office, *The Industrial Policy Debate* (Washington, D.C.: Government Printing Office, 1983). On MITI, see Chalmers Johnson, *MITI and the Japanese Miracle: The Growth of Industrial Policy, 1925–1975* (Stanford: Stanford University Press, 1982).

49. For a discussion of the negotiable Certificates of Deposit, see Marcia Stigum, *The Money Market,* revised ed. (Homewood, Ill.: Dow Jones-Irwin, 1983), Ch. 15.

50. On the development of the Eurocurrency markets, see Stigum, *The Money Market,* Chs. 6, 15, 16; Kidwell, *Financial Institutions,* pp. 630–635.

51. On U.S. financial deregulation in the early 1980s, see Alan Gart, *The Insider's Guide to the Financial Services Revolution* (New York: McGraw-Hill, 1984); George J. Bentson, ed., *Financial Services: The Changing Institutions and Government Policy* (Englewood Cliffs, N.J.: Prentice-Hall, 1983); Harvard Business Review, ed., *The Transformation of Banking* (Boston: Harvard Business Review Reprint Department, 1984); Stigum, *The Money Market;* Andrew S. Carron, *Reforming the Bank Regulatory Structure* (Washington, D.C.: Brookings Institution, 1984); *Economic Report of the President 1984* (Washington, D.C.: Government Printing Office, 1984), Ch. 5.

52. Bank of Japan, Research and Statistics Department, *Economic Statistics Annual, 1983.*

53. The deficit averaged roughly ¥1 trillion between 1970 and 1974. Between 1975 and 1979, this number had risen to ¥9 trillion. Source: IMF, *International Financial Statistics, 1984.*

54. We do not wish to speculate here what it was that made the authorities decide to issue the large debt rather than curtail expenditure or raise revenues in alternative ways. These issues lie in the realm of fiscal policy, with which we are not concerned. On postwar Japanese fiscal policy, see Ackley and Ishi, "Fiscal, Monetary and Related Policies;" and Joseph A. Pechman and Keimei Kaizuka, "Taxation" in Patrick and Rosovsky, eds., *Asia's New Giant,* Ch. 5; Adams and Hoshii, *A Financial History of the New Japan,* pp. 285–302. For an account of more recent developments, see Chapter 9 in this volume.

55. On falling bank profitability, see Bronte, *Japanese Finance,* pp. 19–23. For further discussion of the effects of the bond issue, see Sena Eken, "Integration of Domestic and International Financial Markets: The Japanese Experience," International Monetary

Fund, *Staff Papers,* September 1984, p. 505 ff.; Charles Piggott, "Financial Reform in Japan," Federal Reserve Bank of San Francisco, *Economic Review,* Winter 1983, p. 29 ff.; Bank of England, "The Financing of Japanese Industry," *Quarterly Bulletin* (December 1981), p. 516 ff.; "As Borrowing Declines Japanese Banks Are Losing Their Corporate Leverage," *Asian Wall Street Journal,* January 18, 1982, p. 7.

56. On the internationalization of Japanese capital markets and the yen, see Bank of Japan, Economic Research Department, "Stepped-Up Capital Movements In and Out of Japan and Their Effect on the Japanese Financial Market," Special Paper No. 112, Tokyo, March 1984; Bank of Japan, Research and Statistics Department, *Annual Review of Monetary and Economic Developments;* Bank of Japan, Foreign Department, "Outline of Foreign Exchange Control in Japan," mimeo, Tokyo, March 1981; Eken, "Integration of Domestic and International Financial Markets;" Jeffrey A. Frankel, "The 1984 Campaign for Liberalization of Japanese Capital Markets," unpublished paper, n.d.; "Japanese International Finance," *Euromoney* (March 1984), pp. 159–192; Nomura Research Institute, "Evolution of the Japanese Financial System and Liberalization of the Japanese Financial Markets;" Daniel I. Okimoto, ed., *Japan's Economy: Coping With Change in the International Environment* (Boulder, Colo.: Westview Press, 1982); Charles Piggott, "Financial Reform in Japan;" Morgan Guaranty Trust Company of New York, "Japan's Financial Liberalization and Yen Internationalization," *World Financial Markets,* June 1984.

57. Accounts of the *gensaki* market may be found in Robert F. Emery, *The Japanese Money Market* (Lexington, Mass.: Lexington Books, 1984), Chs. 3 and 6.

58. Ibid., p. 17.

59. Ibid., Ch. 6. The Japanese government has, since the mid-1970s, started to deregulate the *gensaki* market. For example, in 1978 the total amount of *gensaki* transactions allowed for banks was increased from ¥5 billion to ¥20 billion, and again to ¥50 billion in 1979. Also, in 1979, nonresidents were allowed to enter into *gensaki* transactions. Further deregulation has occurred since then.

60. On the Japanese CD market, see Bronte, *Japanese Finance,* p. 207; Nomura Research Institute, *Evolution of the Japanese Financial System: The Path to Liberalization and Internationalization* (Tokyo: Nomura Research Institute, 1984), p. 3 ff.; Emery, *The Japanese Money Market,* pp. 81–86.

61. Surveys of recent changes in the Japanese financial system may be found in Emery, *The Japanese Money Market;* Nomura Research Institute, *Evolution of the Japanese Financial System;* Eken, "Integration of Domestic and International Financial Markets;" Piggott, "Financial Reform in Japan;" Bank of Japan, Research and Statistics Department, *Annual Review of Monetary and Economic Developments;* Dorothy B. Christelow, "Financial Innovation and Monetary Indicators in Japan," Federal Reserve Board of New York, *Quarterly Review* 42 (Spring, 1981), pp. 42–53.

CHAPTER NINE

1. Very few studies have attempted to explain differences in the relative size of the public sector among countries. This limited research has highlighted the role of cultural, social, and historical factors in supplementing the quantifiable political and economic determinants of government's size. For a brief review of this literature, see Peter Saunders and Friedrich Klau, "The Role of the Public Sector," *OECD Economic Studies* 4 (Spring 1985), pp. 114–118.

2. International Monetary Fund, *World Economic Outlook* (April 1985), p. 109.

3. A *Business Week* survey (April 18, 1983) found that 95 percent of the 600 American executives sampled disapproved of direct federal subsidies to "smokestack"

industries, but 61 percent favored tax incentives even though these have, in principle, the same effect on business.

4. This institutional section draws on the work of John C. Campbell, *Contemporary Japanese Budget Politics* (Berkeley: University of California Press, 1977), which discusses the political process up to the early 1970s; and on my interviews with MOF and LDP officials regarding current budget politics.

5. A countercyclical fiscal policy is a tax and spending program that is timed so that the policies stimulate the economy as it heads into the trough of a business cycle and restrains it as it approaches its peak, i.e., a program that "counters the cycle."

6. MOF has had a continual battle to prevent control over the budget from being moved to the Cabinet or a supraministerial coordinating agency. For a description, see Chalmers Johnson, *MITI and the Japanese Miracle: The Growth of Industrial Policy, 1925–1975* (Stanford: Stanford University Press, 1982), p. 75.

7. For support of the view that the role of the politician is becoming comparable to that of the bureaucrat in Japanese policymaking (this study is not specifically focused on fiscal policy), see Michio Muramatsu and Ellis Krauss, "Bureaucrats and Politicians in Policymaking: The Case of Japan," *American Political Science Review* 78 (March 1984), especially pp. 126, 142–144.

8. This applies to most legislation, not only budget bills. T. J. Pempel notes that "85 percent of the bills introduced in the Diet between 1945 and 1975 were drawn up and sponsored by government ministries, and over 90 percent of all the legislation passed in Japan was government sponsored. It is extremely rare for a nongovernment bill to pass; it is also rare for important government bills to fail." *Policy and Politics in Japan: Creative Conservatism* (Philadelphia: Temple University Press, 1982), p. 17. Similar support can be found in Edwin O. Reischauer, *The Japanese* (Cambridge, Mass.: Harvard University Press, 1977), p. 289.

9. Other rules besides a balanced budget rule include the "20 percent rule" (government tax revenues should not be more than 20 percent of national income), the "thirds" rule in taxation (tax revenue should come equally from personal income, corporate income, and indirect taxes), and the "bond dependency ratio" (bonds should be no larger than 15 percent and then 20 percent . . . and then 30 percent of expenditures).

10. In the United States, budget debates begin with an estimate of funds needed to maintain inflation-adjusted current services.

11. It is unusual among national budgetary systems (but important for MOF leverage) to have the appeals be directed to the agency responsible for the original cuts.

12. The control of information by MOF in the past decade has been eroding as more LDP politicians develop expertise in fiscal matters. See Muramatsu and Krauss, "Bureaucrats and Politicians in Policymaking," p. 143.

13. A related trend is the increasing number of ex-bureaucrats in the Diet and on the *shingikai* (deliberative councils), but this does not necessarily reduce bureaucratic power, according to some scholars. See Johnson, *MITI and the Japanese Miracle*, p. 47.

14. During the early 1960s, when the ceilings began and real economic growth was proceeding at double-digit rates, request ceilings were often set as high as 50 percent; but in the past decade, they have been set as low as zero percent nominal spending growth for most ministries.

15. The flagrant exceptions to the principle of balance are the three K's: *Kome* (price subsidies for rice), *Kokutetsu* (Japanese National Railroad), and *Kenho* (national health insurance). Interest payments have also complicated the strains between meeting

spending ceilings and achieving balance among ministries, since they now comprise 18 percent of general account expenditures compared to 4.9 percent in 1975.

16. For a more complete description, see Hugh Heclo, "Executive Budget Making," in Gregory B. Mills and John L. Palmer, eds., *Federal Budget Policy in the 1980s* (Washington, D.C.: The Urban Institute Press, 1984).

17. MOF tried this initiative in 1968 in its campaign to "break fiscal rigidification," but it failed. See Campbell, *Contemporary Japanese Budget Politics,* pp. 241–250.

18. Special Accounts are similar, in some ways, to trust funds in the United States. The Social Security Trust Fund, for example, has its own earmarked source of funds like Special Accounts. Also like many Special Accounts, social security is included in the unified budget, resulting in duplicate government budgets. Special Accounts are dissimilar to trust funds in that the source of funds need not be tax revenues but may be borrowings from some earmarked source.

19. The gross expenditure of these accounts is almost twice the size of the general account in recent years, but this is deceptive since there is substantial duplication among the accounts, as indicated in *Table 9-4.*

20. The GAE budget includes three public corporations (*kōsha*), ten financial corporations (*kōko*), and two banks (*ginkō*) that are tied to government policies and require Diet approval of their budgets. The three *kōsha* are the Japan Tobacco and Salt Public Corporation, the Japanese National Railway, and the Nippon Telegraph and Telephone, which is in the process of being broken up into several regional companies. The other eighty or so public corporations, such as the Japan National Oil Company or Japan Air Lines, are not subject to budgetary approval by the Diet. Some of the more important public financial corporations are the Housing Loan Corporation, the People's Finance Corporation, and the Small Business Finance Corporation. The two banks, which played a critical role in early postwar development, are the Japan Development Bank and the Export-Import Bank.

21. In all, there are four sources of FILP funds: (1) the Trust Fund Bureau, which includes the postal savings and public pensions (accounting for over 80 percent of FILP funds in recent years); (2) the Postal Life Insurance and Annuity funds (under 10 percent); (3) government-guaranteed bonds and borrowings (under 10 percent); and (4) the Industrial Investment Special Account (less than 1 percent now, but it accounted for more than a third during the 1950s). All of these funds are allocated to government-affiliated enterprises, local governments, and public financial institutions to pay for public works and loans for social or economic development. The interest rates charged are below market rates because of repressed deposit rates on Trust Fund deposits in the early years, and more recently because of interest rate subsidies from the general account. See Nomura Research Institute, *The Japanese Bond Market* 5 (April 1984), p. 121.

22. Since 1973, a small number of outlays, peaking at 0.7 percent of GNP in 1981, have been classified as off-budget, such as the Strategic Petroleum Reserve, the Postal Service deficit, and net lending by the Federal Financing Bank.

23. The major direct loan programs include the Commodity Credit Corporation, the Farmers Home Administration, the Rural Electrification Administration and the Export-Import Bank. The major guaranteed loan programs include the Federal Housing Administration, the Veterans Administration Housing, Guaranteed Student Loans, the Export-Import Bank, and the Commodity Credit Corporation. The net lending of the direct loan program, but not the guaranteed loans, is included in the unified budget. In addition, there are a number of government-sponsored enterprises (GSE) whose loans are not included in the unified budget or credit budget because they are privately owned. Some of the more significant GSEs are the Federal Home Loan Banks, Federal

Home Loan Mortgage Corporation, the Federal National Mortgage Association, the Farm Credit System, and the Student Loan Marketing Association.

24. For a complete description of the credit budget, see Office of Management and Budget, *Budget of the U.S. Government, Special Analysis F, Fiscal Year 1986.*

25. Johnson, *MITI and the Japanese Miracle,* p. 321.

26. See OECD, *Japan: Economic Survey* (July 1984), pp. 78–82, for a comprehensive list of international and domestic measures to liberalize financial markets.

27. In fact, recognition of a need to bring ministerial decisions in line with government policy has provided the motivation for establishing two Commissions on Administrative Reform within the past fifteen years. The background and politics of administrative reform are detailed in Pempel, *Policy and Politics in Japan,* pp. 255–271.

28. MOF usually reserves a small amount of funding (the amount was secret in early years; now it is disclosed) to be allocated among projects that were initially cut by budget examiners. Accompanied by much public fanfare, this reconsideration focuses once again on the ministries' top priorities.

29. Henry Rosovsky, *Capital Formation in Japan* (New York: Free Press, 1961), p. 138.

30. The major increases in military spending occurred during the Sino-Japanese War, 1894–95; the Boxer Rebellion, 1900; Russo-Japanese War, 1904–5; World War I and the Siberian Expedition, 1914–20; Shantung Expedition, 1927–8; Manchurian Incident, 1931–2; and the China Incident and Pacific War, 1937–45.

31. Ministry of Finance, *An Outline of Japanese Taxes, 1984,* p. 7.

32. Since personal tax reductions were usually achieved by raising exemptions, the income elasticity of the personal income tax remained high, allowing rapid income growth to provide room for future tax cuts. Elasticity is the ratio of the percentage change in tax revenues to a percentage change in personal income. With rapidly rising incomes only partially offset by increased exemptions, taxpayers were moving up into higher marginal tax brackets, which would increase the total tax collections. For the period 1955 to 1971, Joseph Pechman and Keimei Kaizuka estimated the average Japanese personal income tax elasticity to be 1.8 compared to 1.4 for the U.S. See their article in Hugh Patrick and Henry Rosovsky, eds., *Asia's New Giant: How the Japanese Economy Works* (Washington, D.C.: Brookings Institution, 1976), pp. 349–350.

33. Gardner Ackley and Hiromitsu Ishi, "Fiscal, Monetary, and Related Policies," in Patrick and Rosovsky, eds., *Asia's New Giant,* pp. 218–219 and 240.

34. Takafusa Nakamura, *The Postwar Japanese Economy* (Tokyo: Tokyo University Press, 1981), p. 132.

35. Ackley and Ishi, "Fiscal, Monetary, and Related Policies," p. 212. As the authors note, this "test" is of dubious value given the highly structured nature of the Japanese capital markets.

36. OECD, *Economic Outlook,* Occasional Studies (July 1978), pp. 11 and 31.

37. Johnson, *MITI and the Japanese Miracle,* p. 306.

38. Japan Development Bank, *Facts and Figures about the Japan Development Bank* (Tokyo: Japan Development Bank, 1981), p. 7; and *Japan Echo* 4, Special Issue (1979), p. 91.

39. Lawrence B. Krause and Sueo Sekiguchi, "Japan and the World Economy," in Patrick and Rosovsky, eds., *Asia's New Giant,* pp. 423, 433.

40. Professor Yukio Noguchi foresees a decline in the peaceful business-government relations as a result of these pressures. See "The Government-Business Relationship in Japan: The Changing Role of Fiscal Resources," in Kozo Yamamura, ed., *Policy and*

Trade Issues of the Japanese Economy: American and Japanese Perspectives (Seattle: University of Washington Press, 1982), pp. 123–142.

41. A more sophisticated version of this argument can be found in Yukio Noguchi, "A Dynamic Model of Incremental Budgeting," *Hitotsubashi Journal of Economics* 20 (February 1980), pp. 11–25.

42. These estimates are sometimes called "fiscal impulses." This measure weights the changes in expenditures and revenues by an estimate of their respective initial "multiplier" impact on GNP, and then standardizes by the GNP level of the previous period. Notice that this only estimates the direct contribution to GNP from the current year's fiscal policy and not the indirect effects on GNP induced by rising income. Averages of fiscal impulses from the OECD and IMF are estimated and calculated by the author. The period of the first oil shock for the United States extends to 1979, therefore the second oil shock begins with 1980 for the United States.

43. For detailed information on the beneficiaries of direct government purchases in the United States, see Irving Stern, "Industry Effects of Government Expenditures: An Input-Output Analysis," *Survey of Current Business* (May 1975), pp. 9–23.

44. For Japan, see the OECD, *Japan: Economic Survey* (July 1984), pp. 84, 92–93; for the United States, see *Economic Report of the President 1985* (Washington, D.C.: Government Printing Office, 1985), pp. 232–233, 352.

45. It should be noted that this and the preceding discussion assumes no changes or additional constraints from a nation's trade policy. In the case of Japanese voluntary export restraints, additional fiscal stimulus in the United States may not be readily transmitted to increased sales of Japanese autos.

46. Real interest rates, and not nominal interest rates, are the relevant variable in this story. If a firm borrows funds for one year at a 10 percent nominal interest rate and there is 10 percent inflation during that year, the firm can pay off the loan in cheaper (inflated) dollars, so there is no loss of purchasing power and thus no real cost to borrowing. Since real interest rates are unobservable, they can only be inferred by subtracting an estimate of expected inflation from the nominal interest rates, which are published in newspapers.

47. Derek Blades and Peter Stum, "The Concept and Measurement of Savings," in Federal Reserve Bank of Boston, *Savings and Government Policy* (Boston: Federal Reserve Bank of Boston, 1982), p. 6.

48. During the postwar years the sum of net private domestic savings and the state and local surplus (called "net private savings" here for simplicity) has averaged about 7.5 percent of GNP. The 9 percent estimate was obtained by combining the highest historical rate of net private domestic savings of 7.5 percent attained during the 1960s with the highest historical level of state and local surplus attained in the past few years.

49. The average level of net private domestic investment during the postwar years was approximately 6.5 percent. Between 1980 and 1984, it was 4.1 percent, largely because this period included the worst postwar recession in 1982–1983.

50. Notice that if the budget deficit in Japan could be reduced to 2 percent, Japanese policymakers could return to the approximately 14 percent investment of the past decade and still retain a trade surplus of 2 percent. Alternatively, foreign leaders would prefer some version of Case B in which Japan continues the economic stimulus of large deficits but increases its imports in order to reduce its trade surplus.

51. For a detailed discussion of the types of effective tax rates and their limitations, see Don Fullerton, "Which Effective Tax Rate," *National Tax Journal* (March 1984), p. 27.

52. Sangiin Zeisei Iinkai Chōsabu (Research Division, Tax Committee, House of Councillors of the National Diet), *Zaisei Dēta Bukku* (Databook on Public Finance) (Tokyo: Ōkurasho Insatsukyoku, 1984), p. 51.

53. The degree to which taxes are passed on in the form of higher prices—the incidence of the tax—will vary from industry to industry. If a firm in Japan and the United States are in global competition, they will face the same market conditions and will equally be able to pass on cost or tax increases. If, for example, all taxes were passed on to prices, then two firms residing in different countries with equal cost structures but different tax burdens will have different competitive positions. The country with the higher tax burden will be at a competitive disadvantage.

54. National Tax Administration Agency, *Hōjin Kigyō no Jittai* (Sample Survey of Corporate Business), various annual reports.

55. A recent study by Yukio Ikemoto, Eiji Tajima, and Yūji Yui indicates that tax savings owing to selective tax measures varied significantly among industries, indicating a systematic policy. For the period 1963 to 1980, the average tax savings for all industries was between 4.2 and 9.3 percent owing to tax-free reserves and 0.7 percent owing to special depreciation measures. See their article, "On the Fiscal Incentives to Investment: The Case of Postwar Japan," *Developing Economies* 12 (December 1984), pp. 372–395. This finding differs from earlier studies that found no significant differences among industries. See Sei Fujita, "Zaisei Seisaku to Kokumin Chochiku-ritsu" (Fiscal Policies and the National Saving Rate), in *Nihon Zaisei-ron* (Japan's Public Finance) (Tokyo: Keisō-shobō, 1972), and Ryūtanō Komiya, "Sengo Nippon no Zeisei to Shihon-Chikuseki" (Taxation and Capital Formation in Postwar Japan), *Tokyo Daigaku Keizaigaku Ronshū* 32 (July 1966).

56. These estimates only apply to "special tax measures" as defined in the text and not to "general tax measures." One very significant general tax measure is the exclusion of taxes on the interest income from postal savings, which is estimated to exceed ¥1 trillion annually. This is considerably larger than the total estimates for all special tax measures. Nonetheless, the sets of figures used in this chapter for tax expenditures in both countries are comparable, since only those U.S. tax expenditures that were in the same categories as those of MOF were included.

57. Stanley Surrey and Paul McDaniel, *Tax Expenditures* (Cambridge, Mass.: Harvard University Press, 1985), p. 51.

58. Ryūtanō Komiya, Masahiro Okuno, and Kōtarō Suzumura, eds., *Nippon no Sangyō Seisaku* (Japan's Industrial Policy) (Tokyo: Tokyo University Press, 1985).

CHAPTER TEN

1. Frank M. Gollop, "Analysis of the Productivity Slowdown: Evidence for a Sector-Based or Sector-Neutral Industrial Strategy," in William J. Baumol and Kenneth McLennan, eds., *Productivity Growth and U.S. Competitiveness* (New York: Oxford University Press, 1985), p. 181.

2. Any number of writings could be cited here. For a recent statement of this argument, see Ingo Walter and Kent A. Jones, "The Battle Over Protectionism: How Industry Adjusts to Competitive Shocks," *Journal of Business Strategy* 2 (Fall 1981), pp. 37–47.

3. Quoted in *The New York Times*, May 18, 1983, p. D-1.

4. Wassily Leontief, "Discussion," in *The Japanese Challenge and the American Response: A Symposium* (Berkeley: The Institute of East Asian Studies, University of California, 1982), p. 60.

5. Barriers to exit may be "economic" (durable capital assets or skilled workers whose value is highly specific to use in a particular function or business); "managerial/

strategic" (personal and corporate interrelationships which make it difficult to reach agreement about the necessity of disinvestment, or which, once agreement has been reached, deter the implementation of a cutback in one part of a business because of negative spillovers on other parts of the business), and "political" (governmental or community constraints). See Michael E. Porter, "Please Note the Nearest Exit," *California Management Review* 19 (Winter 1978), pp. 21–33.

6. See C. Baden Fuller and R. Hill, "Industry Strategies for Alleviating Excess Capacity: The Case of the Lazard Scheme for U.K. Steel Castings," London Business School, August 1984. For a theoretical argument that large firms will exit faster than small firms, see Pankaj Ghemawat and Barry Nalebuff, "Exit," *Rand Journal of Economics* 16 (Summer 1985), pp. 184–194; see also, D. Fudenberg and J. Tirole, "A Theory of Exit in Oligopoly," mimeo, Department of Economics, University of California at Berkeley, 1983.

7. See Porter, "Please Note the Nearest Exit," for an empirical evaluation of these issues in the United States.

8. For a wider examination of market failure as it relates to the general question of adjustment, see Robert B. Reich, *The Next American Frontier* (New York: New York Times Books, 1983).

9. On the concept of "political failures," see George Eads, "Picking Winners and Killing Dogs," *Wharton Magazine* (Fall 1981), pp. 33–41. See also William G. Watson, *A Primer on the Economics of Industrial Policy* (Ontario, Canada: Ontario Economic Council, 1983), pp. 18–36; and Charles Wolf, "A Theory of Nonmarket Failure: Framework for Implementation Analysis," *Journal of Law and Economics* 22 (April 1979), p. 107–140.

10. Gregory B. Christiansen and Jan S. Hogendorn, "Japanese Productivity: Adapting to Changing Comparative Advantage in the Face of Lifetime Employment Commitments," *Quarterly Review of Economics and Business* 23 (Summer 1983), p. 23.

11. See Norman S. Fieleke, "Productivity and Labor Mobility in Japan, the United Kingdom, and the United States," *New England Economic Review* (November/ December 1981), pp. 35–36.

12. Robert Z. Lawrence, *Can America Compete?* (Washington, D.C.: Brookings Institution, 1984), pp. 33–35.

13. A study of the Japanese labor market's adjustment to the oil shock found that "labor input elasticity" (percentage change in employment divided by percentage change in production) in Japan between November 1973 and September 1975 was 0.86 for Japan compared to 1.2 for the United States, while the "speed of adjustment coefficient" was virtually the same for both countries: 0.62 for Japan; 0.63 for the United States. (The speed of adjustment coefficient measures the time it takes for a firm to reach a state of complete adjustment of labor input in response to a change in output: i.e., $1/0.62 = 1.6$ months.) See H. Shimada, "The Japanese Labor Market After the Oil Crisis: A Factual Report" in OECD, *Structural Determinants of Employment and Unemployment* (Paris: OECD, 1979), pp. 337–338. See also K. Koike, "Employment in Japan, a 'Superdeveloped Country,'" *Japan Echo* 4 (1973), p. 43. Both studies cited in Derek T. Healey, "Structural Change and Structural Adjustment in Japan," Working Paper 81-5, University of Adelaide, Department of Economics.

14. On the nature and magnitude of the costs of disinvestment, see John Mutti and Howard F. Rosen, "U.S. Labor Market Adjustment: Trade-Impacted Industries and Adjustment Costs," mimeo, Institute for International Economics, November 20, 1984.

15. The report is cited in James Fallows, "America's Changing Economic Landscape," *Atlantic Monthly,* March 1985.

16. Cited in ibid.

17. House of Lords Select Committee on the European Communities, *Shipbuilding*, June 13, 1978, p. 24. Cited in Geoffrey Edwards, "Four Sectors: Textiles, Man-Made Fibers, Shipbuilding, Aircraft," in John Pinder, ed., *National Industrial Strategies and the World Economy* (London: Allanheld, Osmun, 1982), p. 103.

18. Each of these sectors has been carefully analyzed by academics. On footwear, see David B. Yoffie, "Adjustment in Footwear: The Consequences of Orderly Marketing Agreements," in John Zysman and Laura Tyson, eds., *American Industry in International Competition* (Ithaca: Cornell University Press, 1983). On autos, see James P. Womack, "Public Policy for a Mature Industrial Sector: The Auto Case" (Ph.D. diss., Political Science, Massachusetts Institute of Technology, 1982). For a history of efforts by the U.S. textile industry to develop political arrangements to ameliorate the effects of structural evolution, see Louis Galambos, *Competition and Cooperation: The Emergence of a National Trade Association* (Baltimore: Johns Hopkins University Press, 1966). A more recent history of textile politics is contained in Vinod K. Aggarwal, with Stephan Haggard, "The Politics of Protection in the U.S. Textile and Apparel Industries," in Zysman and Tyson, eds., *American Industry in International Competition.*

19. The steel industry has inspired a rich literature. See Donald F. Barnett and Louis Schorsch, *Steel: Upheaval in a Basic Industry* (Cambridge, Mass.: Ballinger, 1983); two books by William T. Hogan, S. J., *Steel in the United States: Restructuring to Compete* (Lexington, Mass.: D. C. Heath, 1984) and *World Steel in the 1980s: A Case of Survival* (Lexington, Mass.: D. C. Heath, 1983); United States International Trade Commission, "Carbon and Certain Alloy Steel," Report to the President on Investigation No. TA-201-51 Under Section 201 of the Trade Act of 1974, USITC Publication 1553, Vol. 1, July 1984; The Comptroller General, "New Strategy Required for Aiding Distressed Steel Industry," January 8, 1981; Michael Borrus, "The Politics of Competitive Erosion in the U.S. Steel Industry," in Zysman and Tyson, eds., *American Industry in International Competition;* Mary E. Deily, "Capacity Reduction in the Steel Industry" (Ph.D. diss., Department of Economics, Harvard University, 1985); Robert W. Crandall, "Rationalizing the U.S. Carbon Steel Industry: A Critical Perspective," paper prepared for the Institute for International Economics Project on Structural Adjustment, undated.

20. On the development of the "capture theory," see Marver H. Bernstein, *Regulating Business by Independent Commission* (Princeton: Princeton University Press, 1955); Gabriel Kolko, *The Triumph of Conservatism* (New York: Quadrangle, 1963); George Stigler, "The Theory of Economic Regulation," *Bell Journal of Economics and Management Science* 2 (Spring 1971), pp. 3–21; Thomas K. McCraw, "Regulation in America: A Review Article," *Business History Review* 49 (Summer 1975); James Q. Wilson, *The Politics of Regulation* (New York: Basic Books, 1980). Recent studies which examine the extent of capture on the state level include Douglas D. Anderson, *Regulatory Politics and Electric Utilities* (Boston: Auburn House, 1981); at the federal level, see Paul J. Quirk, *Industry Influence in Federal Regulatory Agencies* (Princeton: Princeton University Press, 1981).

21. Crandall, "Rationalizing the U.S. Carbon Steel Industry."

22. Roderick is quoted in Jack Robert Miller, "Steel Minimills," *Scientific American* 250 (May 1984), p. 33.

23. Kathryn Rudie Harrigan, *Strategies for Declining Businesses* (Lexington, Mass.: Lexington Books, 1980).

24. Ibid., pp. 372–374, 404–406. On the effects of taxes on exit, see Thomas Horst, "Income Tax Consequences for Corporations and Individuals Exiting from Declining Industries," mimeo, Taxecon Associates, November 16, 1984.

25. Joseph L. Bower, "Restructuring Petrochemicals: A Comparative Study of Business and Government to Deal with a Declining Sector of the Economy," in Bruce R. Scott and George C. Lodge, eds., *U.S. Competitiveness in the World Economy* (Boston: Harvard Business School Press, 1984), p. 299.

26. Barry Bluestone and Bennett Harrison, *The Deindustrialization of America: Plant Closings, Community Abandonment, and the Dismantling of Basic Industry* (New York: Basic Books, 1982), p. 9. For a criticism and rebuttal of the Bluestone and Harrison argument, see Richard B. McKenzie, *Fugitive Industry: The Economics and Politics of Deindustrialization* (Cambridge, Mass.: Ballinger, 1984) and Alfred E. Kahn, "Where Has All the Business Gone?" *New York Times Book Review,* December 12, 1982, pp. 11, 25.

27. Bluestone and Harrison, *The Deindustrialization of America,* pp. 104, 147–148. See also Bennett Harrison, "Rationalization, Restructuring, and Industrial Reorganization in Older Regions: The Economic Transformation of New England since World War II," Working Paper No. 72, Joint Center for Urban Studies, Harvard/MIT, February 1982, p. 33.

28. Mayor Angelo Martinelli of Yonkers, New York, for example, told *U.S. News and World Report* that he was furious about "the rape, the absolute betrayal" of Yonkers by United Technologies Corporation. In 1976, UTC acquired Otis Elevator, a company established in Yonkers by Elijah Otis in 1853. Despite public financial support for plant expansion, UTC phased out employment and eventually shut down the Yonkers operation in 1982. Ultimately, the headquarters of the division was moved to Farmington, Connecticut. *U.S. News and World Report,* July 22, 1985, p. 49. Although Mayor Martinelli claims that Yonkers was "devastated by pencil pushers," the devastation was not permanent, according to *U.S. News.* The old Otis site has since been acquired by the Port Authority of New York and New Jersey as an industrial park, and Kawasaki has announced plans to manufacture commuter-train cars there, providing some 2,600 manufacturing jobs.

29. James A. Craft, "Controlling Plant Closings: A Framework and Assessment," in Antone Aboud, ed., *Plant Closing Legislation* (Cornell: ILR Press, Key Issues Number 27, 1984), p. 47. See also Douglas D. Anderson and Judith Leff, "The Massachusetts Plant Closing Debate," Case No. 9-386-173, Boston: Harvard Business School.

30. "Update: The Reshaping of American Industry," Merrill Lynch Special Report, October 1985, pp. 2–4, 6.

31. For a discussion of the myth and reality of corporate strategic choice, see Gordon Donaldson and Jay W. Lorsch, *Decision Making at the Top: The Shaping of Strategic Direction* (New York: Basic Books, 1983), pp. 6–10.

32. *The Wall Street Journal,* August 12, 1985, p. 1.

33. This section has benefited from information provided to me by officials of the Economic Development Administration, and by Dr. Frederick T. Knickerbocker, Executive Director, Office of Economic Affairs, U.S. Department of Commerce. They do not bear responsibility for the views expressed here.

34. During the Carter Administration annual expenditures for the Business Development Finance Assistance Program averaged $170 million.

35. There are numerous evaluations of the Trade Adjustment Assistance programs. Several of the better studies include: three studies by the Comptroller General— "Worker Adjustment Assistance Under the Trade Act of 1974: Problems in Assisting Auto Workers," January 11, 1978; "Adjustment Assistance Under the Trade of 1974 to Pennsylvania Apparel Workers Often Has Been Untimely and Inaccurate," May 9, 1978; "Adjustment Assistance to Firms Under the Trade Act of 1974: Income Maintenance or

Successful Adjustment?" December 21, 1978; J. David Richardson, "Trade Adjustment Assistance Under the United States Trade Act of 1974: An Analytical Examination and Worker Survey," with comments by C. Michael Aho and Martin Wolf, in Jagdish N. Bhagwati, ed., *Import Competition and Response* (Chicago: University of Chicago Press, 1982); Gary Clyde Hufbauer and Howard Rosen, "Managing Comparative Disadvantage," mimeo, Institute for International Economics, January 6, 1984; J. Mark Ramseyer, "Letting Obsolete Firms Die: Trade Adjustment Assistance in the United States and Japan," *Harvard International Law Journal* 22 (Fall 1981); Martin Wolf, "Adjustment Policies and Problems in Developed Countries," World Bank Staff Working Paper No. 349, August 1979; and Malcolm D. Bale, "Adjustment Assistance: Dealing with Import-Displaced Workers," in *Tariffs, Quotas and Trade: The Politics of Protectionism* (San Francisco: Institute for Contemporary Studies, 1979).

36. Wolf, "Adjustment Policies," p. 162.

37. The Comptroller General, "Adjustment Assistance to Firms Under the Trade Act of 1974," p. ii.

38. Wolf, "Adjustment Policies."

39. The Comptroller General, "Worker Adjustment Assistance Under the Trade Act of 1974," p. ii.

40. Hufbauer and Rosen, "Managing Comparative Disadvantage," p. 61.

41. For an ambitious and interesting displaced worker proposal offered by Malcolm Lovell, who from 1981–1983 was U.S. Undersecretary of Labor, see Malcolm R. Lovell, Jr., "An Antidote for Protectionism," *Brookings Review* (Fall 1984), pp. 23–28.

42. OECD, *Industrial Policy of Japan* (Paris: OECD, 1972), pp. 22, 28.

43. See Thomas Hout, "Sources of Japanese Economic Performance Relative to the United States," in Allen Taylor, ed., *Perspectives on U.S.-Japan Economic Relations* (Cambridge, Mass.: Ballinger, 1973), p. 104; Gus Edgren, "Employment Adjustment to Trade Under Conditions of Stagnating Growth," *International Labour Review* 117 (May–June 1978), p. 297; Ira C. Magaziner and Thomas M. Hout, *Japanese Industrial Policy* (London: Policy Studies Institute, 1980), pp. 6–8.

44. See Miyohei Shinohara, "Japanese Experience in Managing Development," World Development Report 1983 Background Paper, The World Bank, October 1982; Kozo Yamamura, "Success that Soured: Administrative Guidance and Cartels in Japan," in Kozo Yamamura, ed., *Policy and Trade Issues of the Japanese Economy: American and Japanese Perspectives* (Seattle: University of Washington Press, 1982), pp. 104–106; W. W. Lockwood, "Japan's New Capitalism," in W. W. Lockwood, ed., *The State and Economic Enterprises in Japan* (Princeton: Princeton University Press, 1965), p. 501; Yoshie Yonezawa, *The System of Industrial Adjustment Policies for Trade in Japan*, mimeo, Economic Research Center, Tokyo, 1979, p. 66; and Kiyoshi Kojima, *Japanese Direct Foreign Investment: A Model of Multinational Business Operations* (Tokyo: Charles E. Tuttle, 1979), p. 167, cited in Healey, "Structural Change and Structural Adjustment in Japan," p. 14; Robert W. Crandall, "Remarks," in *Basic Industries in Trouble; Why . . . And Are There Solutions?—An LTV Forum* (Dallas, LTV Corporation, 1983), p. 87; Philip H. Trezise, "Industrial Policy Is Not the Major Reason for Japan's Success," *Brookings Review* 1 (Spring 1983).

45. Philip H. Trezise and Y. Suzuki, "Politics, Government, and Economic Growth in Japan," in H. Patrick and H. Rosovsky, *Asia's New Giant: How the Japanese Economy Works* (Washington, D.C.: Brookings Institution, 1976), p. 800.

46. J. Mark Ramseyer, "Letting Obsolete Firms Die: Trade Adjustment Assistance in the United States and Japan," *Harvard International Law Journal* 22 (Fall 1981), p. 614.

47. Cited in U.S. General Accounting Office, *Industrial Policy: Case Studies in the Japanese Experience,* Report to the Chairman, Joint Economic Committee, United States Congress, October 20, 1982, p. 50.

48. Brian Ike, "The Japanese Textile Industry: Structural Adjustment and Government Policy," *Asian Survey,* May 5, 1980, pp. 246–247.

49. GAO, *Industrial Policy,* pp. 56–57.

50. Gary R. Saxonhouse, "Industrial Restructuring in Japan," *Journal of Japanese Studies* 6 (Summer 1979), pp. 275–276.

51. This section has benefited from discussions with Frank Upham and from his articles: "Legal Framework of Structurally Depressed Industry Policy," in *U.S.-Japan Relations: Towards a New Equilibrium* (Cambridge, Mass.: The Program on U.S.-Japan Relations, Center for International Affairs, Harvard University, Annual Review, 1982–83), pp. 143–157; "Legal and Institutional Dynamics in Japan's Cartel Policy: One View of the Domestic Adjustment to External Economic Events," mimeo; "Law and the Prevention of Conflict: The Ideology of Informality and the Formulation and Implementation of Industrial Policy," mimeo. See also U.S. General Accounting Office, *Industrial Policy: Japan's Flexible Approach,* Report to the Chairman, Joint Economic Committee, United States Congress, June 23, 1982; Margaret A. McGregor and Katherine V. Schinasi, "Positive Adjustment Policies Toward Declining Industries in Japan," mimeo, submitted to the Congressional Research Service for publication by the U.S. Joint Economic Committee, undated; *Japan's Industrial Policies* (Washington, D.C.: The Japan Economic Institute of America, 1984); U.S.-Japan Trade Study Group, *Progress Report* (Tokyo: TSG, 1984); Jimmy W. Wheeler, Merit E. Janow, and Thomas Pepper, *Japanese Industrial Development Policies in the 1980s* (Croton-on-Hudson: Hudson Institute, 1982); Merit E. Janow and Thomas Pepper, "Industrial Adjustment in Japan," Hudson Institute Paper, HI-3715-D, November 1984.

52. Saxonhouse, "Industrial Restructuring in Japan," p. 318.

53. Reich, *The Next American Frontier,* p. 199.

54. Unfortunately, at this writing I am unaware of such a truly comprehensive study in either Japanese or English.

55. Upham, "Legal Framework of Structurally Depressed Industry Law."

56. See "Tei Seichō Keizai ka no Sangyōchōsei to Kyōsō Seisaku" (Industrial Coordination and Competitive Policy under the Low Growth Rate Economy), The Economic Research Council, November 1982.

57. Wheeler, Janow, and Pepper, *Japanese Industrial Development Policies in the 1980s,* p. 29.

58. Ibid.; see also Richard J. Samuels, "The Industrial Destructuring of the Japanese Aluminum Industry," *Pacific Affairs* 56 (Fall 1983).

59. Magaziner and Hout, *Japanese Industrial Policy,* p. 67.

60. *Nihon Keizai Shimbun,* March 8, 1982, cited in Samuels, "The Industrial Destructuring of the Japanese Aluminum Industry."

61. Ibid., p. 503.

62. The following section has benefited from interviews conducted in January 1984 with Japanese industry representatives and government officials. The interviews were arranged by individuals associated with the Nomura School of Advanced Management. The author is particularly indebted to Jiro Tokuyama, Masasuke Ide, Ryōzō Ishihara, and Mrs. Chikako Tsuruta, of Nomura, and to Mrs. Toshiko Calder, of Princeton, New Jersey, whose research assistance prepared him for the interviews. None of these individuals

bears responsibility for the views expressed here. For an excellent analysis of the growth and maturation of the Japanese shipbuilding industry, see Ezra F. Vogel, "Shipbuilding: High Priority Basic Industry," Working Paper, Harvard University, Spring 1984. See also Tuvia Blumenthal, "The Japanese Shipbuilding Industry," in Hugh Patrick, ed., *Japanese Industrialization and Its Social Consequences* (Berkeley: University of California Press, 1976), pp. 129–160.

63. Dong Sung Cho, "Global Competition and Global Strategy: A Case of the Shipbuilding Industry," Working Paper prepared for the Harvard Business School 75th Anniversary Colloquium on Competition in Global Industries, April 1984, pp. 32–34.

64. Yoshie Yonezawa, *Adjustment in Japanese Shipbuilding Industry and Government Shipbuilding Policy* (Tokyo: Japan Economic Research Center, 1980), pp. 66–67.

65. See Douglas D. Anderson, "Hyundai Heavy Industries and the Shipbuilding Industry," Case No. 9-385-212, Boston: Harvard Business School, pp. 17–21.

66. Yonezawa, *Adjustment in Japanese Shipbuilding Industry.*

67. Susan Strange, "The Management of Surplus Capacity: Or How Does Theory Stand Up to Protectionism 1970s Style?" *International Organization* 3 (Summer 1979), pp. 324–325.

68. For a similar analysis, see Yonezawa, *Adjustment in Japanese Shipbuilding Industry,* pp. 23–24, 71. We can only speculate about how many of the workers who were made redundant by the fall-off in demand remained employed by the shipbuilders. Magaziner and Hout estimated the figure to be roughly one-half of the regular work force in 1979. See Magaziner and Hout, *Japanese Industrial Policy,* p. 69.

69. Mainichi Shimbun Sha, *Ekonomisuto,* April 17, 1979, p. 16.

70. *Ekonomisuto,* February 26, 1980, p. 33.

71. *Ekonomisuto,* April 4, 1979, pp. 16–18, and September 12, 1980, p. 76.

72. Haruo Shimada, "Employment Adjustment and Employment Policies: Japanese Experience," Paper prepared for the workshop on Trade Policy for Troubled Industries, Institute for International Economics, October 1984, p. 43, in Gary C. Hufbauer and Howard F. Rosen, *Domestic Adjustment and International Trade* (Washington, D.C.: Institute for International Economics, forthcoming). In a survey of adjustment assistance in Japan, Gene Gregory concluded: "Effectiveness of measures to assist adjustment of small business have suffered by their proliferation. . . . There have been complaints that the system is too cumbersome, having grown like Topsy through successive piecemeal and ad hoc legislative measures, so that firms cannot make effective use of the assistance that is available. . . . *They have not been particularly effective in assisting conversions from declining to growth industries.*" Gene Gregory, "Adjustment Assistance in Japan: A Case Study," in ILO "Tripartite World Conference on Employment, Income Distribution and Social Progress and the International Division of Labor," Background Papers, Vol. 2, International Strategies for Employment, Geneva, June 1976, p. 111. Emphasis added.

73. Interviews in Tokyo, January 1984.

74. For a related observation having to do with MITI's control of *entry,* see Richard E. Caves and Masu Uekusa, *Industrial Organization in Japan* (Washington, D.C.: Brookings Institution, 1976), p. 56.

75. Interviews with officials of the Industrial Bank of Japan, January 1984.

76. For an excellent account of the Sasebo case, see Kent E. Calder, "Politics and the Market: The Dynamics of Japanese Credit Allocation, 1946–1978" (Ph.D. diss., Government, Harvard University, 1979), Appendix V.

77. Interview at the Ministry of Transport, January 1984.

78. *Lloyd's Shipping Economist,* "Japanese Shipbuilding: Shaping Up for Post-Cartel Challenges," May 1982, p. 12.

CHAPTER ELEVEN

1. "Coping with the Trade Friction Crisis," *Japanese Finance and Industry* (November 1985), p. 23. This informative and wide-ranging article is a translation from the July and August 1985 special issues of the Industrial Bank of Japan's Monthly Reports on Current Conditions of the Japanese Economy and Industry.

The concepts of "producer logic" and "consumer logic" as they applied to the oil industry were pioneered within Royal Dutch Shell during the 1960s and 1970s, by the scenario-planning group led by Pierre Wack.

2. *Economic Report of the President 1986* (Washington, D.C.: Government Printing Office, 1986), pp. 369, 375.

3. Ibid., p. 339.

4. "Coping with the Trade Friction Crisis," *Japanese Finance and Industry,* p. 25.

5. Ronald A. Morse, "Japan's New Popular Culture," *Wilson Quarterly* 9 (Summer 1985), p. 48. The actual numbers cited by Morse apply to 1982: 731 Americans studying in Japan, and just under 11,000 Japanese students in the United States.

6. *Boston Globe,* December 19, 1985, citing figures released shortly before by Japan's Ministry of Labor.

7. *The New York Times,* October 30, 1985. For other comparisons of Japanese and American roads, as well as automobile ownership, see the book compiled by the editors of *The Economist* and entitled *The World in Figures,* fourth edition (New York: Rand McNally, 1984), pp. 23 and 38.

8. *The New York Times,* October 30, 1985.

Index

and Japan compared, 78–79, 84–87, 93, 98, 371–372
Stern, Irving, 438n43
Stern, Joel, 415n48
Stewart, Paul W., 407n52
Stewart, Richard, 395n37
Stigler, George 441n20
Stiskin, Nahum, 425n4
Stockman, David A., 307
Stockman, James, 394n26
stocks: and Japanese corporate strategy, 262, 266–267, 292; and U.S. corporate strategy, 80, 276, 282–283
Stone, Christopher D., 428n41
Strange, Susan, 445n67
strikes, 90
structural adjustment, 337–372, 381; and Japan, 351–369; and labor mobility, 342–344, 346–347, 364; U.S. and Japan compared, 337–344, 369–372, 381
Studenski, Paul, 431n30
students, foreign: U.S. and Japan compared, 382
Stum, Peter, 438n47
subcontracting, 80–84, 371; and shipbuilding, 364–365
subsidies: in Japanese agriculture, 156, 161, 167–168, 170–172; and Japanese enterprises reduction of capacity, 355–356; and Japanese interest rates, 272, 331–333; and Japanese shipbuilding industry, 361, 366; and U.S. energy industry, 216, 376; and U.S. steel industry, 89–90
Sumikei Aluminum, 358
Sumitomo Bank, 268
Sumitomo group, 65, 79, 87, 100
Sumitomo Heavy Industries, 361
Sumitomo Shipbuilding and Machinery, 364
Sunkist, 182
Sun Oil, 199
supply side economics, 301, 334
Supreme Court (U.S.): and environmental control, 230–231; and retail industry, 104–106. *See also* antitrust law
Surgeon General (U.S.), 346
Surrey, Stanley, 439n57
Suzuki, Yoshio, 352, 393n19, 398n25
Suzuki, Zenko, 175
Suzumura, Kotaro, 439n58
Switzerland, 118

T

Taiwan, 99, 281
Takahashi, Kamekichi, 392n12
Takashimaya, 103

Takeuchi, Hirotaka, 407n52
Tanaka, Kakuei, 218
Tanaka, Minoru, 399n51
Tariff Commission (U.S.), 129
tariffs. *See* import restrictions; protectionism
Tax Bureau (of Ministry of Finance), 307
Tax Equity and Fiscal Responsibility Act (U.S.), 320
taxes: and credits, 299, 301, 309, 320, 328–332, 333–336; and finance industry, 265, 267, 274, 330; on income, 301–302, 314–315; on interest income, 11–12, 377–378; and Japanese export strategy, 45–47; Japanese reductions of, 313, 316; and local government, 133, 144; and retail industry, 105; and U.S. deficit, 380; and U.S. export strategy, 38, 41, 54–55; and U.S. inflation, 312, 318; U.S. reductions of, 333. *See also* corporate taxes; fiscal policy; *and names of specific industries*
tax-to-sales ratio, 328–329
technology: and agriculture, 161, 163; and aluminum industry, 358; Japanese aquisition of, 16–19, 123–124; and steel industry, 87, 98; and U.S. export licenses, 39–40
Technopolis Program (Japan), 144
Teele, Stanley F., 407n52
TEL (Tokyo Electron Laboratories), 139
telecommunications industry, 69–72, 124
Temin, Peter, 431n33
Temporary Interest Rate Adjustment Law (Japan), 265
Temporary Law for the Structural Improvement of Specified Industries (Japan), 356
Temporary Law for the Structural Reorganization of Specified Textiles Industries (Japan), 352
Temporary Measure for the Stabilization of Specified Depressed Industries (Japan), 353
Tenneco-Atlantic, 233
Tennessee Gas Pipeline, 223
Texas Instruments, 10, 123–124, 141, 144–145
textile industry: Japanese restructuring of, 352–353, 370; and taxes, 329–333; and U.S. protectionism, 53, 344, 350, 376
Thermco, 139
Thompson, Thomas W., 431n32
Thorelli, Hans B., 402n10
thrift institutions, 276, 278
Tidewater Associated Oil, 199
Tiffany, Paul Argel, 404n25, 404n27
Toa Nenryo, 197–198, 295
tobacco industry, 346
Toho Gas, 198, 221
Tokyo Electric Power Company (TEPCO), 198, 200, 218